Managing "Modernity"

Interests, Identities, and Institutions in Comparative Politics

———

The post–Cold War world faces a series of defining global challenges: virulent forms of conflict, the resurgence of the market as the basis for economic organization, and the construction of democratic institutions.

The books in this series take advantage of the rich development of different approaches to comparative politics in order to offer new perspectives on these problems. The books explore the emerging theoretical and methodological synergisms and controversies about social conflict, political economy, and institutional development.

———

Democracy without Associations: Transformation of the Party System and Social Cleavages in India, by Pradeep K. Chhibber

Gendering Politics: Women in Israel, by Hanna Herzog

Origins of Liberal Dominance: State, Church, and Party in Nineteenth-Century Europe, by Andrew C. Gould

The Deadlock of Democracy in Brazil, by Barry Ames

Political Science as Puzzle Solving, edited by Bernard Grofman

Institutions and Innovation: Voters, Parties, and Interest Groups in the Consolidation of Democracy—France and Germany, 1870–1939, by Marcus Kreuzer

Altering Party Systems: Strategic Behavior and the Emergence of New Political Parties in Western Democracies, by Simon Hug

Managing "Modernity": Work, Community, and Authority in Late-Industrializing Japan and Russia, by Rudra Sil

Managing "Modernity"

Work, Community, and Authority
in Late-Industrializing
Japan and Russia

RUDRA SIL

Ann Arbor
THE UNIVERSITY OF MICHIGAN PRESS

A CIP catalog record for this book is available from the British Library.

Library of Congress Cataloging-in-Publication Data

Sil, Rudra, 1967–
    Managing "modernity" : work, community, and authority in late-industrializing Japan and Russia / Rudra Sil.
        p.   cm. — (Interests, identities, and institutions in comparative politics)
    Includes bibliographical references and index.
    ISBN 0-472-11222-8 (cloth : alk. paper)
    1. Social change—Japan.   2. Japan—Economic conditions.
3. Social values—Japan.   4. Postmodernism—Social aspects—Japan.
5. Social change—Russia (Federation)   6. Russia (Federation)—Economic conditions.   7. Social values—Russia (Federation)
8. Postmodernism—Russia (Federation)   I. Title.   II. Series.
HN727 .S575   2002
303.4'0947—dc21   2001006443

To the memory of my mother

Contents

Figures

Preface

"Modernity" and Social Science— Beyond Universal History

The idea of progress is neither unique to the "modern" period, nor limited to those civilizations where "modernity" is commonly thought to have emerged. New techniques of crop rotation and irrigation incrementally altered people's work habits and the structure of daily life long before the Industrial Revolution. Breakthroughs in mathematics and science led to the invention of the decimal system and to numerous discoveries in astronomy, chemistry, and biology long before the elevation of secular rationalism and the scientific method during the Enlightenment. New feats in engineering and architecture, creative advances in city planning, and bureaucratic forms of administration appeared across such diverse civilizations as ancient Egypt, the Indic cities of Harappa and Mohenjo-Daro, the Chinese empire under the dynasties, and the native peoples of the Americas. Long-distance trade, overseas exploration, and multiethnic empires began to bring many communities in contact with new goods, values, languages, and life-styles long before the arrival of mercantilism, colonialism, or globalization.

What marks the advent of the "modern" era is the *amalgam* of a great many nearly *simultaneous* transformations that began with the Industrial Revolution in the West and proceeded to affect developments all over the world within a span of just two centuries. The shift from subsistence agriculture to the mechanized production of goods through progressively more efficient technologies; the dissolution of the joint household and the spread of urbanization, literacy, and social mobilization; the idea of an accountable, rational-legal nation-state that can mediate diverse interests and advance the human condition; the rise of the industrial proletariat and a new class of employers as rival economic and political forces; the rise and fall of colonialism and its impact on the consciousness and desires of new nations—all these changes, taken together, are simply unprecedented in terms of their magnitude, interconnectedness, and wide-ranging consequences. It is also via these very processes that "modernity" is thought to have emerged in the West, manifested in the concomitant elevation of such ideals as scientific and technological progress, secular rationalism, bureaucratic organization, industrial capitalism, political pluralism, and individualism—ideals often thought to *belong* together because they happened to *emerge* together in the course of the Industrial Revolution in the West.

This book, however, is not about the *emergence* of modernity in the West; rather, it is about the *engineering* of specific elements of "modernity" as variously conceived by elites and ordinary people across different *non-Western late industrializers* (NWLIs). The category of NWLI inherently suggests that the pressures of "catching up," the temptation to emulate the institutions and practices of "advanced" referent societies, the absence of the conditions present in the early stages of Western industrialization, and the varied legacies inherited from distinctive histories and cultural orientations all combine to produce a set of challenges and opportunities that earlier industrializers never had to contend with. Ever since their encounters with the West, usually in the form of colonialism, conquest, or military defeat, most elites in NWLIs have come to share the basic desire to emulate or construct *some* features of Western "modernity," even if they are frequently opposed to the wholesale replication of the West. In this process, they have also had to confront a fundamental challenge: how to define *modernity* in such a manner that its pursuit would bring international recognition and signify catching up to the West in material terms, while simultaneously representing a meaningful achievement in the eyes of ordinary people whose desires are shaped by distinctive historical memories and cultural sensibilities. The resulting discourses and policies in NWLIs point to quite varied conceptions of the essence of "modernity," most limited to common aspirations for technological progress, industrial production, the bureaucratic state, and military prowess, but only a few concomitantly embracing unfettered markets, liberal democracy, or an individualistic ethos. Even the most recent waves of democratic transition and economic liberalization do not decisively indicate that actors in NWLIs are engaged in anything more than necessary adaptations in their own particular quest for "modernity."

This basic observation is at the heart of some fundamental questions that will continue to be of relevance to social scientists in the new millennium: How exceptional was the appearance of those characteristics identified with "modernity" in Western societies? What ideas, practices, and institutions are transferrable to later industrializers elsewhere? How have individuals uprooted from preexisting communities responded to the sudden appearance of new ideas, institutions, and practices considered to be of foreign origin? More broadly, does the diversity of historical experiences around the world suggest alternative conceptions of "modernity" or merely alternative routes or strategies that will converge upon a single, global "end of history"?[1]

During the 1950s and 1960s, an earlier generation of social scientists had offered a sweeping answer to these questions: The general laws of societal evolution, they contended, suggested that the path traveled by earlier industrializers in the West could serve as a reasonable approximation of the developmental path of later industrializers elsewhere; as a result of new technologies and an increasingly complex division of labor, all societies were thought to be evolving and converging upon a "modern social system," the defining elements of which were assumed to be functionally interrelated.[2] This "modernization paradigm" later came under attack for its ahistorical conflation of change and evolutionary convergence, its treatment of societies as closed organic systems, and its lack of attention to external forces, varied historical inheritances, and the role of the state and individual actors.[3] Specific critiques also led to the formation of alternative research programs ranging from world-systems analysis and studies of state-led development to rational choice theory and new variants of structural, institutional, and cultural analysis. While these newer research traditions are quite sophisticated and may represent scholarly "progress" for their respective adherents, they have also tended to shy away from the "big questions" once addressed by modernization theorists in favor of more narrowly defined projects that bear elective affinities to the methodologies favored by a given research tradition.

There are, however, several reasons why we need to continue exploring problematiques that can match those constructed by modernization theorists in scope while discarding the latter's metatheoretical foundations and universalist assumptions about the origins, nature, and consequences of "modernity." First and foremost, the teleological characterization of history in modernization theory and its expectation of convergence are portable and, in fact, are frequently reconstructed as claims or assumptions in much contemporary scholarship. Openly "neomodernist" perspectives, for example, insist on the validity of the universal history ideal and even suggest that the collapse of communism and worldwide trends toward economic liberalization and democratization vindicate this ideal in the terms suggested by modernization theory.[4] Others characterize the present era as a brand new "postmodern" or "global" age, but contend that particular thresholds of material and technological progress are likely to bring about an increasingly convergent gestalt of institutions, technologies, worldviews and life-styles across regions and locales.[5] More focused explorations, while rooted in quite sophisticated theoretical frameworks derived from quite different research traditions, often reveal a common interest in the uniform logics and dynamics that can facilitate the proliferation of free-market economies, democratic polities, liberal international regimes, and secular worldviews—all assumed to be universally viable and desirable components of "modernity."[6] These varied projects, although suggesting different loci for analyzing change in the contemporary era, still imply the unfolding of a universal history and, as such, their assumptions need to be subjected to the same critical scrutiny to which modernization theory has been subjected.

In fact, as many studies of ethnonationalism, religious fundamentalism, and grassroots social movements suggest, distinctive sets of interests, identities, and institutions remain very much a part of this global age, challenging homogenizing processes and their agents. These competing tendencies—what one scholar has polemically characterized as the "old world of Jihad" attempting to survive in "the new world of McWorld"—may not be unrelated although they tend to be analyzed as distinct phenomena within separate problematiques.[7] This coexistence of the universal and the particular, and the relationship between them, remain fundamental to the comparative study of political, economic, and social change worldwide. Thus, even as this book forcefully rejects the universalist assumptions and methods of modernization theorists and their successors, it articulates a problematique that matches theirs in scope by examining the mechanisms and processes through which elites and masses in the non-Western world encounter, and respond to, those values, institutions, practices, and technologies identified with the "modern" or the "global" in the West.

There is another reason for reconsidering the broad questions and interconnections of the sort examined by modernization theory. Area specialists and native scholars in different parts of the world have been producing rich empirical analyses of social change, often pointing to the persistence and functionality of traditional elements in modernization processes.[8] For modernization theorists and their successors, these mixtures have been viewed as evidence of incomplete transitions toward "modernity" rather than as evidence that social change frequently involves the reproduction or reconfiguration of traditional elements. Now, in the midst of new debates over the nature and consequences of globalization, it is worth reassessing the contributions of area specialists over the years within the context of an alternative problematique that acknowledges the complexity and indeterminacy of change and considers how diverse historical legacies, external influences, and competing actors can facilitate, hinder, or redefine the quest for "modernity" worldwide.

Still another, quite different, reason for posing the kinds of broad, sweeping questions driving this book is to employ them in better integrating research conducted within the boundaries of disciplines, subfields, or contending research traditions in the social sciences. Modernization theory itself had transcended such boundaries, driving theoretical discourse and empirical research in fields as diverse as comparative politics, sociology, economic history, anthropology, organization theory, and even psychology. In moving away from all-encompassing grand theory, contemporary theorizing in the social sciences has tended to be characterized by increasingly narrow subfields and increasingly competitive research traditions, each favoring questions that it is particularly suited to address. Such trends, while certainly conducive to new insights and lively exchanges, can only contribute to whatever progress is possible in the social sciences if they are also accompanied by complementary mechanisms designed to integrate research across disciplines and research traditions. This does not require that we seek to build a new unifying paradigm, nor does it require that we dismantle or reject existing disciplinary structures or research traditions. It simply requires that we make some room for problematiques that are essentially interdisciplinary in character, incorporating relevant concepts, hypotheses, interpretations, and methods in an eclectic manner regardless of which disciplines or research traditions these may have originated in.[9]

Finally, I want to emphasize that while this book is primarily aimed at important theoretical issues in the social sciences, it is also the product of a humanistic concern for the millions of people worldwide who are still embroiled in the drama of political and economic development. The tension between, and interplay of, the "traditional" and the "modern," the local and the global, remain an inherent part of their lifeworld, as individuals and communities continue to seek—and find—ways to protect their identities and interests in the face of unfamiliar institutions, practices, technologies, and goods that will supposedly bring them prosperity and prestige. For these people, it is still necessary to ask questions, at whatever level of generality, concerning the kinds of creative strategies and institutional designs that can bring material well-being to those who seek it while reducing the levels of physical suffering, social turmoil, and psychological alienation, experienced individually and collectively in the course of large-scale processes of change. This requires keeping an open mind as to whether the quest for "modernity" can better the lives of ordinary people where the modern institutions and technologies eagerly sought by elites prove incongruous with long-standing norms and practices embedded in local communities. Even though the social sciences are fraught with uncertainty, scholars sharing some basic concern for human betterment must continue to address such big questions in a self-reflective manner regardless of whether they can be analyzed in terms of whatever concepts, approaches, and methods are currently fashionable.

I am indebted to several individuals whose advice, help, and support have made this project what it is, although I alone must bear the responsibility for remaining errors. First and foremost, I am grateful to Ken Jowitt, Ernie Haas, and Franz Schurmann for nurturing this project with constructive criticism and unwavering support. I also owe a huge debt of gratitude to the late Reinhard Bendix, whose final seminar I was fortunate to take and whose classic study *Work and Authority in Industry* served as an important source of inspiration for this book. Special thanks are due to Tadashi Anno, Stephen Hanson, Andrew Janos, and Mark Lichbach for the impact they have had on my thinking and this book.

I also gratefully acknowledge the comments and assistance I have received at various points from Robert Bellah, Tom Callaghy, Calvin Chen, Robert Cole, Eileen Doherty, Peter Evans, Marissa Golden, Gaven Helf, Kiyoko Inoue, Peter Katzenstein, Oleg Kharkhordin, Atul Kohli, David Laitin, Gail Lapidus, Xiaobo Lu, Ian Lustick, Susan Martin, Mari Miura, Gregory Noble, Eileen Otis, Elizabeth Perry, Joao Resende-Santos, Gilbert Rozman, Robert Scalapino, Kenneth Shadlen, Valerie Sperling, Sven Steinmo, Arun Swamy, Carrie Timko, Ezra Vogel, Veljko Vujacic, Andrew Walder, Chuck Weathers, and Victor Zaslavsky. I am particularly indebted to Chuck for his detailed remarks and suggestions in relation to the chapter on Japan. I am also grateful for the research assistance and valuable feedback provided by students at the University of Pennsylvania, notably Cheng Chen, Todor Enev, Joanne Lee, Eric Lomazoff, and Dani Miodownik. In addition, numerous individuals in Japan and Russia were kind enough to share their thoughts on my project and help me gain a more intimate sense of their respective countries' histories.

My debt to these individuals is too substantial and too diffuse to be properly acknowledged here.

The research and publication of this book were also supported by the Institute of International Studies at Berkeley and the Janice and Julian Bers Chair at the University of Pennsylvania. The excellent staff of the University of Michigan Press, especially Jeremy Shine, Kevin Rennells, and Janice Brill, helped make this book more readable, and offered timely assistance during the production process.

Finally, a special thanks to my wife, Marina, whose understanding and encouragement proved indispensable to the completion of this book. My father, Bijan, and my sister, Chandani Flinn, also provided nurturing support in their own ways. My daughter, Analyn, came along just in time to make the final months of writing a most enjoyable challenge!

Rudy Sil
Philadelphia

Chapter 1

The Problem, the Argument, and the Study

Beyond what commands can effect and supervision can control, beyond what incentives can induce and penalties prevent, there exists an exercise of discretion important even in relatively menial jobs, which managers of economic enterprises seek to enlist for the achievement of managerial ends.

—Reinhard Bendix[1]

Incongruence in authority patterns must induce a degree of 'cognitive dissonance,' . . . and such dissonance is always discomfiting and may be seriously damaging. It must be uncomfortable to live with norms in one context of one's life that are contradicted in another but binding in both.

—Harry Eckstein[2]

This book is about efforts to construct and manage new institutions in non-Western late industrializers (NWLIs). It seeks to define and explore a problematique that captures a common and important dilemma in NWLIs arising from the relationship between two stylized groups of actors: institution-builders, who are generally more likely to be exposed to knowledge about the performance and practices of institutions in advanced referent societies, and the subordinates they recruit, who are seeking to preserve some familiar understandings and templates for making sense of their new institutional environments and potentially disorienting social transformations. The broad question addressed in this book is, How do institution-builders in NWLIs devise and legitimate organizational structures and routines they consider to be in the service of important "modern" objectives while enlisting the cooperation of subordinates whose expectations and behaviors are conditioned by the more familiar "traditional" norms and practices inherited from past communities?[3]

To explore this problem in concrete settings and historical contexts, the book focuses on *institutions of work*—large-scale industrial enterprises—where the vast majority of socially mobilized individuals in NWLIs encounter the tasks, roles, and authority relations associated with modern production in their everyday lives. Thus, the substantive concerns of the book have to do with the sources and implications of tensions between, on the one hand, *formal* managerial ideologies and management practices influenced by Western models and, on the other hand, the *informal* norms and social relations on the shopfloor that reflect the legacies of past communities of work. In this concrete context, this book seeks to address the question, What strategies have best served managerial elites in NWLIs attempting to balance the competing influences of existing management models and inherited legacies in the course of designing institutions of work that will be viewed as authoritative by workers?

The argument to be offered has emerged out of a comparative-historical study of typical large-scale bureaucratic firms in late-industrializing Japan and Russia. This study addresses a specific empirical question: Why was managerial authority, as evident in the generalized cooperation and commitment of workers in large-scale enterprises, significantly higher in postwar Japan (1950–80) than in either prewar Japan (1868–1940) or Soviet Russia (1917–90)? The diachronic country studies are designed to engage competing perspectives in Japanese and Russian studies while reinterpreting key historical facts and trends in light of the theoretical concerns of this book. The interpretations in each case hinge on identifying the salient work-related norms and practices that constitute the distinctive legacies inherited by different generations of Japanese and Russian modernizers, and relating the ideologies and routines devised by managerial elites in each case to one of four ideal-typical *institution-building strategies*—modernist, traditionalist, revolutionary, and syncretist.

These four approaches (defined in section 1.1) are distinguished in terms of the extent to which institution-builders deviate from borrowed institutional models and the manner in which they define the significance of preexisting norms and social relations insofar as these are reflected in the behavior of subordinates. Within the context of industrial enterprises, the four strategies correspond respectively to whether managerial elites opt to ignore, preserve, destroy, or selectively redeploy those familiar norms and forms of social organization inherited from past communities of work as they determine which aspects of Western management doctrines and techniques to emulate, reject, or modify. In fact, the cases examined in this book are not countries but rather periods corresponding to distinct institution-building strategies identifiable within the framework of national industrial relations.

The diachronic comparison of prewar and postwar Japan and the synchronic comparison across Japan and Russia inform, and provide initial support for, the emergent hypothesis that the path of least resistance for managerial elites (and other institution-builders) requires neither the dismissal or destruction of historical legacies, nor the principled preservation of preexisting ideals in new institutions, but rather a *syncretic* process of related, mutual adjustments between selected aspects of the inherited legacy and flexible aspects of work organization. A syncretist strategy as approximated by the managerial approach adopted across postwar Japanese firms, may not always be the product of deliberate sequences of choices; but, where attempts are made to adapt preexisting norms and practices of cooperation and coordination in past communities of work, and where there is some effort to modify management ideologies and practices found in existing institutional models to suit local conditions, managerial authority is likely to be greater over the long run.

While the hypothesis has emerged from the case studies and comparisons, it does have a logic of its own that is discussed in detail below. *Congruence,* between the formal and informal organization of work and authority, as well as between the technical (material) and normative (ideal) aspects of management, is viewed as functional for the coherence and legitimacy of managerial commands and work routines. Such a congruence is likely to enable individuals to better cope with the anxiety they encounter in a new, potentially disorienting, institutional environment by rendering the formal tasks, roles, and authority structures they encounter recognizable in terms of the more familiar norms and practices embedded in past communities of work.

The remainder of this chapter is divided into four sections that collectively provide an overview of the book. Section 1.1 defines the problem of institution-building in NWLIs in relation to borrowed models and inherited legacies; in the process, it offers a flexible ontology for locating categories of actors within institutions and wider social environments, and it provides an analytic foundation for distinguishing and comparing institution-building strategies in relation to the problem of maintaining authority. Section 1.2 focuses on large-scale industrial enterprises as a particularly illuminating case of a modern institution, translating the theoretical framework into a substantive investigation into managerial approaches in

NWLIs and summarizing the book's central argument about the benefits of a syncretist approach for the maintenance of managerial authority. Section 1.3 briefly previews the comparative-historical analysis of managerial strategies and authority relations in large-scale enterprises in late-industrializing Japan and Russia, concluding with a discussion of the assumptions informing the cross-national and diachronic comparisons. The last section highlights some distinguishing features of the middle-range comparative-historical method and theoretical framework employed in this book.

Chapter 2 elaborates upon the problematique and argument in this book in light of the wide-ranging debates in political economy, economic sociology, organization theory, and comparative industrial relations over the sources of uniformity and variation across institutions in diverse historical settings. Universalist perspectives on institutions and social change are opposed to arguments about the historical specificity of Western organizational models, the implications of late-industrializer effects and historical legacies for industrial management, and the significance of elites' own choices in regard to the design of their institutions. Relating these arguments to the concerns of this book, chapter 2 identifies some indicators of managerial authority and elaborates on the defining characteristics of the four ideal-typical institution-building strategies within the context of enterprise management. The chapter concludes with a more detailed examination of the logic behind the hypothesis constructed in this book.

Chapter 3 examines the evolution of work and authority in Japan, laying out the contrast between a relatively ineffective traditionalist managerial approach in prewar Japanese industry and a markedly more successful syncretist approach in postwar Japan. Chapter 4 examines the changes and continuities in industrial management in Stalinist and post-Stalin Russia, emphasizing how a "revolutionary" approach that initially resonated with key segments of the work force became progressively less coherent as routines and practices influenced by Western scientific management increasingly diverged from both original Bolshevik proclamations and informal norms and practices on the shopfloor. These chapters consider competing perspectives in Japanese and Soviet/Russian studies in the process of laying out distinctive historical interpretations that partially account for large differences in the levels of managerial authority; at the same time, the interpretations of the cases are sufficiently stylized so as to permit theoretically salient comparisons and inferences.

Chapter 5 concludes with a review of the essential points of comparison in the experiences of managers and factory workers in prewar Japan,

The Problem, the Argument, and the Study

postwar Japan, Stalinist Russia and post-Stalin Russia. The comparisons and contrasts allow for a brief and tentative evaluation of the hypothesis in light of its potential contributions to contemporary debates over development strategies and institutional design in late industrializers.

Finally, appendixes A and B discuss further issues in relation to, respectively, the theoretical approach and comparative study. Appendix A outlines ontological and epistemological assumptions that speak to the intended contribution of this book, emphasizing the need for eclectic, pragmatic foundational perspectives that can resuscitate fruitful communication across research traditions, disciplinary structures, methodological orientations, and area-specific discourses. Appendix B discusses competing strands in Japanese and Russian studies in order to demonstrate how the similarly balanced consideration of sources in each case informs the interpretations offered in chapters 3 and 4.

1.1. The Problem: Building Modern Institutions in NWLIs

The problematique explored in this book pulls together several conceptual elements and theoretical assumptions that need to be made explicit before the substantive argument can be introduced. These include: (a) the category of non-Western late industrializer (NWLI); (b) the concept of legacies as a means to capture the varied significance of past norms and social relations in new institutional settings; (c) an integrated framework for the study of institutions in relation to the roles, identities, and material and ideal dispositions of different categories of actors; (d) a set of four ideal-typical strategies for comparing the construction of modern institutions in NWLIs; and (e) a conceptualization of authority in institutional contexts that provides the basis for the outcome of interest in the substantive argument.

The Context of Comparison: Non-Western Late Industrializers

The category of non-Western late industrializer, while rarely invoked explicitly, reflects familiar assumptions that implicitly inform many comparative inquiries into patterns of political, economic, and social change.[4] The "late industrializer" component of "NWLI" is simply intended to capture the common imperatives, challenges, and opportunities that face elites who see their economic position as relatively backward in relation to some set of "advanced" referent societies.[5] That is, the very fact of late industrialization is assumed to lead to departures from the patterns of economic, social, and political change found among the first industrializers. For example, the pressures of catching up frequently prompt late industrializers to seek institutional mechanisms to coordinate the accumulation of capital and development of industry so as to leapfrog earlier stages of industrialization.[6] Moreover, elites in late industrializers are in a position to emulate, for better or for worse, the institutions and technologies that contributed to material progress in early industrializers; they are also in a position to be seduced by the life-styles and consumption patterns of elites in referent societies.[7] At the same time, the social and psychological dislocation accompanying forced attempts to catch up, together with the desire to avoid the social unrest evident in the history of earlier industrializers, tend to make stability and order at least as important an imperative as efficiency from the perspective of elites in late industrializers.[8]

The non-Western component of the category NWLI is intended to highlight the assumption that the emergence of modernity among the first industrializers of the West was a product of an exceptional set of historical processes and sociocultural transformations that are not likely to be automatically replicated elsewhere. The original Western vision of modernity is generally thought to be "rooted in the ideas of the Enlightenment, of progress, of the unfolding of the great historical vision of reason and self-realization of individuals, of social and individual emancipation."[9] Outside of the West, however, the meanings of *modernity,* as well as the institutional features, political processes, and cultural projects associated with it, have varied widely both within and across societies. While the Western/non-Western distinction does not do justice to the rich and distinctive histories of societies identified with either category, it is reasonable to assume that the United States and most West European countries, through various routes, eventually came to share enough similarities in technology, economic organization, social structure, and political culture so that whatever differences remain may be assumed to be *relatively* insignificant when compared to the larger differences that distinguish the West from other regions of the world. The category of non-western is even more heterogeneous, but for the questions addressed in this book, it does serve to capture an essential similarity: the potential influence of Western ideas and institutions in areas where many of the distinguishing features of the West are largely absent.[10]

Of particular significance for the argument to follow is the association of *individualism* with the understanding of modernity in the West. *Individualism* is understood here not as a personality trait (egoism) or the absence of a sense of solidarity, but as a normative value attached to social actions within a particular group, society, or institution; it is a set of social norms that allows a person to be regarded in favorable terms for publicly justifying his/her action in terms of the pursuit of self-expression, self-interest, or the achievement of personal goals. *Collectivism* is understood not as the submergence of individual interests or identities within a tight-knit group but rather a set of shared normative orientations that enable the members of some organization, community, or society to positively value social action that is publicly justified in terms of its contribution to the collective goals or interests of some group.[11] Although the distinction is ideal-typical and masks important differences in specific norms and values, in laying out the problem of institution-building in a comparative-historical context it is plausible to assume that the features identified with Western institutional models evolved at a time when a distinctive cultural transformation was already in progress, one that was weakening the appeal of collectivist ideals while elevating an individualistic ethos as a common foundation for social, political, and economic organization.[12] By the same token, it is also plausible to suggest that to the extent individualism remains a marginal social value outside the West, this is a theoretically significant condition in view of the possible consequences for the transferability of certain institutional practices beyond the West.

As will be evident in chapter 2, distinctive historical circumstances and the gradual spread of an ethos of individualism paved the way for the emergence and acceptance of key managerial precepts, administrative practices, and even technologies of production in the large-scale bureaucratic firms that emerged in the course of industrialization in the United States, Britain, and elsewhere.[13] This does not suggest that all characteristics of Western institutions are historically specific and unlikely to be successfully transplanted in NWLIs; it does, however, suggest that the particular cultural transformations that enabled the construction, justification, and acceptance of key institutional features in the West cannot be assumed to have functional equivalents everywhere.

Historical Legacies in the Quest for "Modernity"

In the absence of the kind of large-scale cultural transformation that accompanied early industrialization, it is necessary to consider the implications of surviving norms and social practices for the nature of social change and the design of ostensibly modern institutions in NWLIs. Modernization theorists—as well as many contemporary studies of political and economic development—have tended to assume that preexisting values, beliefs, attitudes, and habits, if they have not already dissipated, must give way to values, attitudes, identities, and habits of the sort already evident across modern industrialized societies in the West. The mechanism through which this transformation would take place has been assumed to be some variant of "social mobilization": in the course of industrialization, individual actors are uprooted from their traditional communities and thrust into new roles in modern environments where new encounters and experiences allow them to embrace new worldviews, attitudes, roles, and identities.[14] This thesis may be consistent with the experiences of Britain and the United States where the gradual acceptance of a similar set of values and work practices among the working masses of the two countries may have accompanied the institutionalization of new tasks and production processes in progressively bureaucratized structures.[15] However, it is impossible to draw any general inferences from these experiences in the absence of systematic comparisons of the actual impact of industrialization processes on social values and psychological orientations elsewhere.

In the particular case of NWLIs, while social mobilization and exposure to new institutional environments may serve to uproot individuals from preexisting communities, this does not automatically sever these individuals' ties to the normative understandings and social relations previously embedded in these communities. It cannot be assumed that the simple act of taking on a role in a new institutional environment in and of itself weakens the strength of preexisting norms and leads to the elevation of values and orientations similar to those that crystallized in industrialized societies across the West. This book proceeds from the assumption that, in the absence of a cultural revolution approximating the Protestant Reformation in character and scope, preexisting, frequently *collectivist,* orientations are likely to prove resilient and consequential in NWLIs at least while they are engaged in the process of catching up.[16] While such an assumption cannot be decisively proven or disproven, it is significant that a range of cross-cultural studies (including some studies by modernization theorists) point to the resilience of collectivist social values in NWLIs, particularly when contrasted with the prevalence of individualistic values in most Western societies.[17]

This does *not* mean that there exists an identifiable package of traditional features that survives unchanged and uniformly shapes the character of political and economic institutions in NWLIs. The concept of *legacy* is used here as a more nuanced and less restrictive alternative to the concept of *tradition* to capture both the diversity of, and varying influence of, preexisting norms and social practices in changing institutional contexts. The term has at least four connotations as used here. First, *legacy* connotes that while industrialization and its concomitant social changes may lead to the dissolution or transformation of preindustrial communities, *some* core norms and forms of social organization frequently survive in NWLIs in the absence of a prior cultural transformation on the scale of the Protestant Reformation. Although no longer embedded in past social structures, these inherited elements are *portable* in the sense that they can be consciously or reflexively reconstructed in the form of *informal* understandings and expectations by actors seeking to maintain some sense of familiarity even in *formally* modern settings.

Second, the concept of *legacy* also suggests that while preexisting norms and social relations in NWLIs may be broadly collectivist, the *specific* norms and practices characteristic of particular regions and societies must also be considered significant in tracing the construction of new institutions. That is, in contrast to the notion of tradition, which emphasized the uniform characteristics of preindustrial communities and downplayed their specific features, legacies are assumed to be heterogeneous, having in common only the absence of individualism as a core social value.

Third, the actual *implications* of the legacies of preexisting norms and social ties for the construction of modernity is regarded as an open question, and the answer to this question depends in part upon the particular project that modernizing elites in NWLIs embark upon and the particular strategies they employ. Moreover, to understand whether or how preexisting collective orientations may facilitate or hinder the prospects of efforts to construct a given aspect of modernity in NWLIs, it is necessary to focus on specific contexts of analysis, emphasizing only those norms and practices that are likely to be of any relevance given the outcome of interest.[18]

Finally, the survival of preexisting norms and social patterns is not inherently assumed to present an obstacle to modernizing elites' objectives in NWLIs. In fact, as Geertz noted as early as the 1960s, aspects of preexisting communities ties can, in principle, aid in the establishment and expansion of modern economic activities and institutions in NWLIs.[19] Similarly, more recent studies have emphasized the role of social capital and soft technologies in institutional change, pointing to the possibility that preexisting norms and social networks can serve to make people collectively more productive in the pursuit of development ends in ways that incentive structures and the flexibility of markets cannot.[20]

Whether or not this happens, however, depends on how modernizing elites themselves interpret the significance of the legacies they recognize as they cope with a common trade-off: on the one hand, elites are understandably tempted to emulate features found in advanced referent societies in the process of envisioning the future of their own societies and conceptualizing the processes that will lead to this future; on the other hand, many of these features, even if transferable, may not prove to be normatively desirable or politically viable in view of the distinctive legacies inherited from past communities. How modernizing elites respond to this trade-off is the subject of this book, but the character and consequences of their varied responses can best be appreciated within the context of concrete *institutions*.

An Integrated Framework for the Study of Institutional Life

Institutions are formally defined as any set of routinized practices and social relationships among a group of individuals that reflect an internal differentiation of roles and tasks that are, in turn, horizontally and vertically structured according to some set of organizing principles, and coordinated for the purpose of achieving some set of common goals identified by institutional elites.[21] The differentiation need not be complex, the organizing principles need not be rational-legal (in the Weberian sense), and the goals need not be highly specific. Thus, a firm, a government bureaucracy, a caste-based agrarian community, and even a Bedouin tribe may all constitute institutions to the extent that there is some purposeful and systematic role differentiation. Understood in these terms, institutions represent unitary actors, insofar as their objectives are defined and shared by the more powerful members of institutions, but they are also social arenas within which there exist conflictual relationships between categories of actors, each with different resources and objectives, and each in a dialectical relationship with material and ideal structures that shape their preferences, dispositions, and common understandings.

The integrated view of institutions in this book proceeds from several important assumptions about the actors in institutions and about the particular mechanisms through which their material and ideal dispositions are influenced and acted upon within institutional settings. The assumptions

are primarily cast at the level of ontology and, significantly, do not incorporate any epistemological first principles. These assumptions can be summarized in terms of several related dichotomous concepts intended to capture the duality of the material and ideal dimensions of social life and the
dialectical relationships between agency and structure along both dimensions.[22] These include the interests or dispositions of actors as influenced by
varied material and ideal structures, the *roles* and *identities* they are
expected to take on as participants within an institution, the formal *organization* and *ideology* that superordinates articulate to ensure that these roles
and identities are taken on by relevant individuals, and the conflictual relationship between *superordinates* and *subordinates* as it is played out in *formal* and *informal* institutional settings. These distinctions are ideal-typical,
often blurred, and sometimes not even observable, but they are analytically
significant insofar as they provide a foundation for eclectic efforts to understand the complexity of institutional life in NWLIs (see fig. 1).

All individuals, whatever their position within an institutional hierarchy, possess a wide range of preferences. These reflect not only the conscious material and ideal interests of individual actors but also reflexively
formed consumption habits and psychological dispositions. However conscious or reflexive the process through which individuals arrive at preferences, their actions are assumed to be in a dialectical relationship with
broadly structural forces—that is, with the (material) social structures that
constrain opportunities for action and with the (ideal) cultural orientations and templates through which individuals assign meanings to their
experiences. As members of an institution, however, individuals are
assumed to take on a particular *role* and *identity* associated with a particular task and a particular set of relationships vis-à-vis their peers, superordinates, and subordinates. The concept of role suggests a separation of
what Mead called the "I" from the "Me," with the former representing the
individual "self" and the latter representing a projected "generalized
other" that enables one to adopt a socially recognized set of tasks and
interests within a wider social context.[23] Opposed to *role, identity* corresponds to the ideal dimensions of social life, emphasizing the meaningful
and emotional content of one's orientation toward the role, enabling a
person to recognize a certain continuity in his/her role within a collectivity,
as well as a sense of purpose shared with other persons in that institution.
The inner coherence and very existence of an institution depend upon each
individual fulfilling a role within the institution, but this, in turn, requires
a belief—a sense of identity—that can provide some sense of continuity

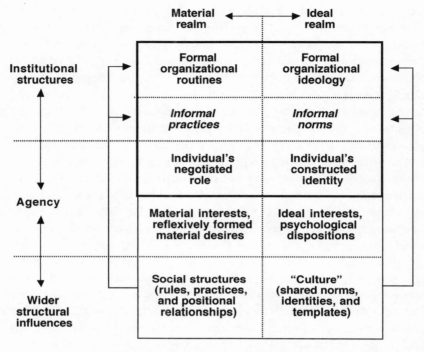

Wider structural influences may include influences of communities from which subordinates are recruited as well as demonstration effects and influences of model institutions in relevant organizational fields.

Fig. 1.   An integrated view of institutional life

and emotional satisfaction to the individual through the performance of that role.[24]

In practice, neither roles nor identities are merely passively taken on by individuals; both are products of a creative and negotiated process that is frequently conflictual as actors with different sets of objectives and resources, often influenced by different extrainstitutional forces, struggle to define or redefine roles and identities.[25] The view of institutions articulated here incorporates this conflictual dynamic by positing two distinct sets of assumptions about the varied motivations of two distinct categories of stylized actors. Institution-builders, or *superordinates,* are the actors who are in a position to define the collective goals supposedly shared by the members of institutions; *subordinates* are the actors who are recruited to implement the former's commands according to stipulated routines but are not necessarily trusted to do so promptly and willingly in the absence of supervision. While a large minority of individuals in most concrete institutions probably experience both sides of this conflict in different contexts (lower-level supervisors or foremen, for example), the superordinate-subordinate distinction is intended to provide a basis for characterizing the tensions and conflicts among actors with different objectives, resources, and levels of identification with the institution.[26]

In the face of these challenges, to achieve the objectives they define on behalf of institutions, superordinates establish *organizational routines* consisting of rules and principles through which roles may be differentiated and through which tasks can be regularly coordinated. To justify the resulting distribution of responsibilities and authority, superordinates typically offer an *ideology,* an "organizational ideal" that provides a sense of higher purpose to organizational routines by emphasizing continuity between past achievements and present goals of the institution.[27] This ideology is invoked by superordinates in an attempt to shape the identities of subordinates in such a way that the latter will offer their willing compliance and carry out assigned tasks even in realms where supervision is minimal or difficult. Subordinates are generally assumed to enter an institution with less of an interest in, and less identification with, the institution as a unitary purposive actor; though they may eventually come to identify many of their interests with the interests of the institution, subordinates generally face a greater level of anxiety not only in consideration of the power wielded by their superordinates but also in light of fears that their institutional roles might not make sense in terms of their past forms of participation in collective endeavors.[28] Thus, at least initially, they seek to defend their material and ideal interests and reproduce more familiar norms and forms of social organization, all of which can be expected to have been conditioned by material and ideal structures *outside* the specified institution, and all of which can undermine organizational routines established by superordinates.[29] Superordinates, too, are subject to extrainstitutional influences, but these are assumed to be less embedded in the local communities and more conditioned by ideals and practices evident in a wider "organizational field" that encompasses "successful" institutions in other societies.[30] The differential impact of external influences and past communities on superordinates and subordinates is assumed to intensify the tensions normally present in relationships between the two sets of actors.

The ideal-typical struggle between superordinates and subordinates over the former's right to define the latter's roles and identities is not necessarily manifested in overt confrontations or explicit negotiations. In fact, for the argument to follow, it is highly significant that the conceptualization of *institution* emphasizes a frequently blurred distinction between *formal* and *informal* dimensions of institutional life, a distinction intended to capture the different sets of structural forces simultaneously at work within institutional contexts as these forces affect the worldviews and interests of superordinates and subordinates.[31] While the formal is generally evident in the official ideologies and organizational routines embraced by institutional elites who have been exposed to the influence of external models, the informal is evident in norms, expectations, and social relations that subordinates come to share in their everyday interactions. It is precisely in this informal realm that subordinates, barring a very strong sense of identification with the institution and its objectives, can develop understandings and practices that enable them to preserve some discretion of their own and even to covertly subvert formal organizational routines.[32] The extent to which this does or does not happen is a crucial aspect of institutional dynamics everywhere, but it is all the more crucial in the process of adapting institutional models in NWLIs.

Building Modern Institutions in NWLIs:
Four Ideal-Typical Strategies

Modern institutions are defined here simply as institutions in which there exist a recognizable division of labor and a functional administrative hierarchy, both based on some relationship between the competences of individuals or groups and the organizational tasks they perform for advancing objectives typically defined by elites.[33] This definition leaves ample room for variation in the design of institutions, particularly in organizational ideologies and routines. While there are constraints posed by the technologies, resources, and goals associated with particular types of institutions, these do not weaken the significance of a range of factors over which superordinates can and do make consequential choices.[34] The resulting variations can be identified and compared in terms of such features as the organization of tasks and the extent of specialization, the steepness of administrative hierarchies, the mechanisms for motivating subordinates, and the opportunities for the latter to exercise discretion, whether to facilitate or undermine the goals identified by superordinates. These possibilities for variation are significant in that therein lie opportunties for managing or reconciling tensions between the goals, worldviews, and expectations of superordinates and subordinates.

Within the particular context of NWLIs, the influence of external models on superordinates and the familiarity of preexisting norms and social relations among subordinates combine to provide a distinctive set of challenges for the former. Superordinates, with their own role to play as their nations catch up and with their own particular interests in matching the performance of institutions in referent societies, are tempted to borrow organizational features and ideological elements that appear to have worked in the referent societies.[35] Subordinates may have a diffuse sense of commitment to their institution's performance and their nation's advancement, but their material and ideal interests are more likely to be conditioned by their past experiences within more familiar communities. Thus, the norms, expectations, and patterns of social relations they exhibit within a new institutional setting may very well come into conflict with the roles and identities that superordinates attempt to thrust upon them. The resulting tension is reflected in the potential discrepancies that develop between formal organizational practices and ideologies that superordinates articulate, on the one hand, and the informal norms and social relations that subordinates are able to reproduce to advance material and ideal interests that reflect familiar understandings inherited from the past.

The problem is not, however, an intractable one. There are alternatives available to institution-builders for interpreting and adapting the models they encounter and the legacies they inherit as they design new ideologies and organizational frameworks. Which alternatives they opt for can be systematically compared in terms of four ideal-typical *institution-building strategies,* all defined within the context of the quest for an industrialized national economy in NWLIs. The strategies are distinguished in terms of institution-builders' own sense of how problematic preexisting legacies are, what they expect to happen to these legacies in the future, and how these constrain the emulation of institutional models in advanced referent societies (see fig. 2).

1. Modernist institution-builders dismiss the preindustrial legacies they inherit as irrelevant given the expectation that institutional models borrowed from modern industrialized powers will provide the necessary foundations for the performance of their institutions. This strategy—to the extent that it is a strategy at all—is based on assumptions that preindustrial norms and social relations of individuals would be reshaped and

Institution-Building Strategies	Orientation toward Institutional Models in Referent Societies	Orientation toward Legacies Inherited from Past Communities
Modernist	Emulate freely both the ideals and practices on assumption that these are universal	Ignore, expect to disappear eventually as institutions take hold and shape new habits
Revolutionary	Emulate some practices in short run, but interpret as compatible with new order	Eliminate, forcibly or through socialization, while promoting new normative order
Traditionalist	Emulate practices and organizational features, but not ideology	Retain and co-opt as part of official ideology, even if ideals embedded in specific social contexts
Syncretist	Emulate practices selectively and introduce adaptations to adjust for differences in historical situation and objectives	Identify portable aspects that can be separated from original contexts and reinterpret to justify organizational routines

Fig. 2.   Ideal-typical institution-building strategies

standardized by new institutional roles and contexts. Hence, the wholesale replication of borrowed institutional models is viewed as feasible and desirable.

2. *Revolutionary* institution-builders believe they are making a radical departure from the past and seek to destroy the legacies inherited from preindustrial communities in order to build a new social and economic order on a *tabula rasa.* From the perspective of revolutionary institution-builders, all remnants of the past—including traditional institutions, and the norms and practices embedded in them—must be totally and irreversibly eradicated so that new roles and identities can be molded by the revolutionary vanguards in new institutions. Institutional practices may be borrowed from elsewhere in this process, but these would be viewed as essentially novel as they would now be supported by new revolutionary norms and ideals.

3.   Traditionalist institution-builders also leave open the possibility of borrowing the practices and organizational routines from referent societies given the imperatives of catching up, but they simultaneously articulate ideological formulas based on preexisting cultural ideals to justify the status of superordinates. Like the modernists, they do not view these preexisting values as problematic for the achievement of their objectives, but whereas the modernists expect preexisting attributes to fade away, the traditionalists seek to reproduce them, dismissing the possibility of any tension between the preserved ideals and the organizational requirements of complex institutions.[36] And, while they join the revolutionaries in linking borrowed practices to a different set of norms and ideals, the latter are viewed as extensions of the past rather than as original constructions of a new order.

4.   Finally, somewhere between the traditionalist on the one hand, and the modernist or revolutionary on the other, there is the *syncretist* approach to institution-building. The term *syncretism* has traditionally been used in the study of religious, linguistic, or artistic conventions to trace how existing beliefs, languages, or rituals have been synthesized with new or imported ones in everyday practice in diverse cultural contexts.[37] Syncretism has also been invoked by political scientists to identify political processes or nationalist ideologies in which competing norms and ideologies in a given society are blended to generate political support or stability.[38] Within the context of the problematique explored here, syncretism represents the *adaptation* of certain norms, practices, and patterns of social organization embedded in functionally similar communities of the past, alongside the *modification* of roles, responsibilities, and authority structures within complex institutions created, or borrowed, for the purpose of achieving developmental goals. Thus, syncretist institution-building is neither simply the "invention of tradition"[39] nor the preservation of existing traditional ideals in new institutional environments. Rather, it involves an active process of mutual adaptation as borrowed doctrines and practices are adjusted while aspects of preexisting models of community are selectively incorporated into formal ideological tenets and organizational routines. The features of new or borrowed modern institutions can only be modified within the limits permitted by the technological or organizational requirements of the primary tasks of the institutions; however, within these limits, syncretist institution-building engages in the selective reconfiguration of preexisting norms, practices, and forms of social organization for the purpose of rendering the ideological and organizational features of the new institutions recognizable from the point of view of the members of the institution.

It must be remembered that these strategies are ideal-types (in the Weberian sense) and as such cannot be confused with the broader objectives elites may pursue in a given society or in a given institutional context.[40] In particular, the traditionalist and syncretist variants of institution-building cannot be defined without reference to a particular historical and social context since the defining aspects of these strategies include the identification and reconstruction of *distinctive* elements of an inherited legacy. It is even more important not to confuse the labels of strategies with characterizations of the wider political context: for example, even within a broader context of a large-scale social revolution, it is possible to identify competing *strategies* of institution-building although the specific content of a given type of strategy may differ from the corresponding strategy in the context of postcommunist transition or postcolonial nation-building.[41] At the same time, for all of these ideal-typical strategies to be invoked to compare actual institution-building efforts, it is necessary to pay attention to the constraints resulting from technological or organizational requirements for particular types of institutions and objectives. Thus, while the logic invoked to conceptually distinguish the four ideal-types of institution-building strategies is universal (in fig. 2), the *implications* of strategies that approximate one of these types depend upon the particular social contexts and institutional settings being investigated.

Comparing and Evaluating Institution-Building: The Problem of Authority

The implications that are of particular concern to this book relate to one of the classic concepts in social science: authority. *Authority* refers to what Weber meant by "domination by virtue of authority": "the situation in which the manifested will (command) of the ruler or rulers is meant to influence the conduct of one or more others (the ruled) and actually does influence it in such a way that their conduct to a socially relevant degree occurs as if the ruler had made the content of the command the maxim of their conduct for its very own sake."[42] While the motives for obeying commands can vary depending upon the material and ideal interests of actors and the degree of affectual relations among them, it is the legitimacy of claims—or more precisely, the validity of claims to legitimacy—that Weber viewed as the key to whether commands routinely elicited *disciplined* obedience, the "prompt and automatic obedience in stereotyped forms" by virtue of habituation.[43]

Brute power is relatively simple to understand: it requires only an unequal distribution of capacities to inflict suffering; once achieved, it will elicit compliance but that compliance may prove difficult to monitor and costly to sustain in the long run. Authority is a more subtle matter: it is more difficult to acquire in practice; but once acquired, it is much more likely to elicit willing and prompt cooperation with much less supervision. Moreover, whereas the sources of power may be universally understood, the sources of authority are much more varied across particular contexts because the conditions under which the commands of powerful agents are regarded by subordinates as legitimately deserving "prompt and automatic obedience" can vary widely. This book is about the sources of authority in a particular scenario: new, modern institutions in NWLIs where millions of people find themselves confronting new roles, tasks, and institutional environments devised by ambitious superordinates eager to match at least the material components of modernity as evident in the referent societies of the West.

The problematique articulated here thus pulls together several aspects of the drama of institution-building in NWLIs: the impact of institutional *models* originating in referent societies on the *formal* administrative structures and organizational routines adopted by institution-builders, the likely influence of distinctive *legacies* inherited from preexisting communities as these are reproduced in the *informal* norms, expectations, and practices of subordinates, the alternative *strategies* available to institution-builders in terms of how freely they choose to emulate the modern practices of existing institutional models and in what manner they respond to norms and social relations they consider to be traditional, and the implications of these choices for the *authority* of superordinates and the commands they issue in the eyes of subordinates (see fig. 3).

1.2.   The Argument: Managerial Authority and the Logic of Syncretism

The substantive argument previewed in this section has emerged largely from a comparative-historical study of a particular type of modern institution, the large-scale industrial enterprise, in which two stylized categories of industrial relations actors—managerial elites and workers—approach each other with distinct material and ideal considerations framed under the influences of different sets of material and ideal structures. This section discusses why the large-scale enterprise represents a

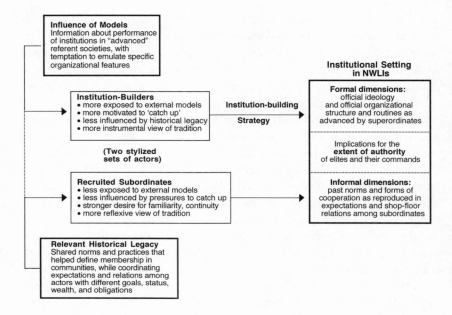

Fig. 3.   Models, legacies, and institution-building in NWLIs

particularly illuminating case of a modern institution, translates aspects of the problematique into substantive categories of comparison, previews the central hypothesis to have emerged from this study, and briefly lays out a logic that renders this hypothesis plausible. Chapter 2 elaborates on these points as part of a broader discussion about firms and organizations in historical and theoretical contexts.

The Large-Scale Industrial Enterprise as a Modern Institution

An *industrial enterprise* is defined as any institution, however large or small, that is designed to process raw materials through the means of machinery and timed labor in order to manufacture a list of products for sale to a consumer (whether an individual, a group, a government, or another firm). By contrast to traditional communities of work, the industrial enterprise represents a novel form of production, one that is organized around the performance of distinct, interdependent tasks none of which independently or directly provides for the subsistence of individuals or their families and communities.[44] Moreover, the everyday activities and interactions of managers and workers in individual factories have a great deal to do with the political stability and economic performance of regions and nations. And, in the course of industrialization, the factory is perhaps the most pervasive and most relevant new institution to enter the day-to-day lives of millions of people who are uprooted from typically agrarian, subsistence-oriented communities and who are faced with new patterns of work and authority in unfamiliar institutional environments. In all these respects, arguments about economic and political development in NWLIs are inherently about the construction of industrial enterprises and the experiences of the people that work in them.

This book focuses specifically on the *large-scale* industrial enterprise, defined as any industrial enterprise administered by salaried managers charged with overseeing and coordinating production, distribution, and accounting in relation to distinct products or phases of production.[45] Large-scale enterprises may be distinguished from small firms or family businesses in several specific ways that are of consequence for the theoretical problematique and the comparative study to follow. They employ a larger number of people (often in the hundreds or even thousands) usually recruited from more diverse social settings;[46] they require multiple layers of administration and supervision; and their organization reflects a much higher degree of differentiation in which each individual or workgroup is consciously performing tasks that are of no value in isolation from those performed by other units. Thus, the size, complexity, structure, and scale of production in the large enterprise distinguish it as a "new institutional and cultural form of world-historical significance."[47]

This definition points to two related reasons for limiting the analysis to large enterprises. First, it is the management of the large-scale enterprise that most closely approximates the challenges identified above with respect to the problem of institution-building in NWLIs. In contrast to smaller enterprises in earlier periods of industrialization, where employers and their family members directly administered production and expected to form "diffuse, high-trust" relations with workers, owners of large-scale bureaucratic enterprises necessarily have had to rely on a new class of managers for the day-to-day administration of production. In this setting, managers have confronted new problems of authority and new dilemmas in enlisting the support and cooperation of a newly recruited work force; and workers have found themselves having to perform increasingly mechanized, specialized tasks involving relatively less discretion in the formal organization of production.[48] In addition, it is the managerial corps in large-scale enterprises that are most likely to be informed about, and influenced by, the performance and practices of their counterparts in more advanced referent societies. This also means that the potential gap between the formal and informal dimensions of workplace social relations, and the conflicts between overt managerial control and covert worker resistance, are likely to be greater and more consequential than in the case of smaller businesses involving fewer, more familiar, individuals.

Second, in view of the design of the comparative-historical study (which includes cross-national comparisons of large firms), it is significant that large-scale enterprises are more intimately connected to *national* programs for development than are small family businesses. While small-scale businesses have played a crucial role in supporting the takeoff of industrialization, it is the large-scale bureaucratized enterprise that represents what Schumpeter called "the most powerful engine of progress."[49] The scope for the introduction of new technologies and the scale of production and extraction make large enterprises more significant from the point of view of national elites in the process of establishing the economic infrastructure, acquiring greater international prestige, and satisfying the rising expectations of consumers. This is especially true for NWLIs, where the pressures to catch up to earlier industrializers spurs national elites to promote the borrowing of technology and to coordinate the accumulation and deployment of human and material capital. In addition, given the latent threat of social unrest accompanying the growing concentration of workers in industrial regions, labor relations and management practices in large-scale enterprises are more likely to attract the state's attention than those in smaller firms. Where the state does not by itself administer industrial production, it is likely to exert a strong influence on managerial elites in large firms, especially given the shared interest in boosting production and maintaining social peace in the course of industrialization. These factors not only justify the focus on large-scale enterprises in this book, but also suggest that there are good reasons to compare certain features of industrial management across nations.[50]

Firms and Organizations in NWLIs:
The Possibilities for Variation

With the ascendence of Taylorist "scientific management" and Fordist assembly-line production in the United States and elsewhere in the West,[51] it was frequently assumed that the technical requirements of production in the large-scale industrial firm dictate a more or less standardized system for the organization of work and authority.[52] Even with the arrival of the "human relations" perspective following World War II, theories of firms and organizations continued to be predicated on the assumption that the design of production processes, incentive structures, work environments, and factory administration are invariably constrained by the technologies of production and by standard dilemmas arising from the bureaucratization of firms.[53] In more recent years, while Fordist mass production is thought to have fallen by the wayside with the crossing of a new "industrial divide," "lean" or "flexible" production is being viewed as a new model of work organization assumed to be driven by new technologies and new challenges in a global economy.[54] Such approaches, although conceived of in quite different eras, share a tendency to assume a singular correspondence between a given technology of production and a particular system for organizing production, and they view this correspondence as a basis for positing universal models and convergent trends across firms and nations.

These studies, however, often discount the role of particular historical processes, political conflicts, and sociocultural contexts that accompanied the initial creation of supposedly standard models of management. They also ignore the wide range of important variations in the distribution of power, status, rewards, and responsibilities within similarly efficient administrative structures employing similar types of technology.[55] The approach taken in this book assumes that technology-driven analyses of firms and organizations miss an important and interesting part of the story of industrialization, particularly in the case of NWLIs. As will be argued in chapter 2, the influence of external referents for defining success, the tendency to rely on mechanisms of coordination to force the pace of industrial production, the imperative of preempting social unrest and industrial conflict in the midst of belated industrialization, and the legacies of preexisting, typically collectivist, norms and identities—all combine to produce distinctive opportunities and challenges for managerial elites in NWLIs as they seek to generate authority in large-scale institutions of work. Under such conditions, it cannot be taken for granted that the managerial ideologies, production systems, and employment practices originally developed in the advanced industrial West will suffice to generate managerial authority.

The problem of institution-building in NWLIs can be translated into a historically grounded comparative study of industrial enterprises precisely by focusing on whether and how managerial elites are able to reconcile the influence of Western models of management with the legacies inherited from preexisting communities of work. As institution-builders, industrial managers in NWLIs must deal not only with the standard demands for better pay and improved working conditions, but also with the issues of authority relations, work motivation, and social peace among a newly recruited work force with its own understandings about what constitutes legitimate hierarchical authority, legitimate differences in roles and tasks, and legitimate differences in rewards or employment terms. The workers must not only concern themselves with their wages and benefits, but they must also adapt to new roles, tasks, routines, and administrative hierarchies within a new environment, while facing an alliance of managers and state actors who share a common interest in boosting production and preserving social order in the belated process of industrialization.

Moreover, in the absence of a prior large-scale cultural transformation, institution-builders in NWLIs must take into account the possible implications of distinctive historical legacies inherited from functionally similar institutions of the past. In examining the creation of modern institutions of work, the legacies of consequence are those inherited from *preindustrial communities of work*.[56] Certainly, the nature of work in preindustrial communities is different from that in bureaucratic enterprises in view of the latter's reliance on machinery and timed labor, complex production processes consisting of specialized tasks, and elaborate systems of recruitment, supervision, and promotion. Nevertheless, while the specific practices and organizational devices that structured work in simple, agrarian communities may not be directly applicable to more complex, bureaucratic firms, there are certain generalizable norms and "everyday forms of cooperation"[57] that can continue to shape the understandings and expectations of subordinates within modern institutions of work. These include the ideals and mechanisms employed in the justification and coordination of collective tasks and resources; the extent of stratification considered "fair" and the ideals invoked to justify and reproduce social hierarchies; and the norms and practices related to the distribution of responsibilities, rewards, and status along those hierarchies. In the industrial enterprise, these are the kinds of norms and practices that are portable and that are likely to be manifested in the informal expectations and social relations that crystallize on the shopfloor.

At the same time, the resilience of preexisting norms and social relations need not be inherently problematic; in fact, some norms or social relations may well be compatible with, or even conducive to, the creation of stable and productive industrial enterprises. To explore this possibility further, it is necessary to consider how managerial elites themselves interpret, and respond to, evidence of inherited social legacies while ensuring that their own objectives and production routines are not undermined by their subordinates. In this context, the ideal-typical institution-building strategies outlined above can be translated into *managerial strategies,* particular sets of choices that managerial elites are in a position to make by virtue of their superordinate positions in institutions of work. These choices reflect the managers' own interests, imperatives, and worldviews, and they include the particular manner in which managerial elites opt to respond to the conflicting modes of organization suggested by imported management models and past communities of work. Managerial strategy is thus evident in company ideology, employment terms, wage practices and incentive systems, and the organization of work and authority. Chapter 2 considers in greater detail what each of the four ideal-typical managerial strategies (modernist, traditionalist, revolutionary, and syncretist) might look like in NWLIs, and chapters 3 and 4 will provide empirical referents for these strategies within the historical contexts of Japanese and Russian industrialization.

Comparing Managerial Strategies:
The Significance of Managerial Authority

The comparative study that follows focuses on the implications of different managerial strategies for *managerial authority.* As noted above, the concept of authority is essentially a relational term, a quality that is possessed by superiors only insofar as it is acknowledged in the view of the subordinates; thus, managerial authority is generally understood here as the ability of managers to generate *worker commitment*—that is, to elicit prompt, automatic, and disciplined obedience among workers in relation to their assigned tasks, to their workplaces, and to the overall production goals of management. This does not require a total identification with any one firm or with any particular task or skill-set, but it does require something beyond mere obedience or the casual execution of assigned tasks in response to instructions. This something has to do with the willingness of workers to use whatever discretion they find (for example, in the promptness and attentiveness with which they execute tasks) in the service of formal production goals because they generally accept as legitimate the right of managers to determine these goals and the methods for realizing them.

Worker commitment may be invoked to demonstrate the level of authority possessed by individual managers in particular firms, but here it is
invoked more broadly to include orientations of workers toward *systems*
of production as reflected in standardized management ideals and practices across firms and sectors in a given society.

The problem examined in this book can now be reframed for the comparative study to follow: in what ways did foreign management models,
legacies inherited from past communities of work, and, especially, managerial strategies for coping with these two influences contribute to differences in levels of managerial authority in late-industrializing Japan and
Russia? The outcome of interest here—the fact that managerial authority
was significantly greater in postwar Japan than in prewar Japan or Soviet
Russia—is not considered to be controversial. The variance is fairly large
and can be established by reference to a range of factors: the frequency
and intensity of industrial conflicts (or, the measures applied to deter labor
unrest); sharp differences in levels of productivity (as measured by gross
output per worker); the extent of labor turnover, absenteeism, or tardiness; as well as less obvious factors such as violations of labor discipline,
pilferage, time theft, and collusion on the shopfloor to pursue goals that
are at odds with the achievement of managerial objectives. While a standardized scale can offer more precise measurements of variances in worker
commitment,[58] this would only enable meaningful comparison across
roughly similar systems of industrial relations in comparable political
environments; this is not the case in NWLIs where there exist sharp differences in labor market characteristics and state structures. Thus, for the
limited purpose of establishing the relatively large variance in the outcome
explored here, it is necessary and reasonable to rely on the above indicators, as long as adjustments are made in light of labor market conditions
and other factors, and as long as these indicators collectively and consistently point to rising or declining levels of worker commitment.[59] Chapter
2 (section 2.4) discusses further the viability and significance of the aforementioned factors in capturing the variations in managerial authority in
NWLIs.

The related notions of managerial authority and worker commitment
are not intended to obscure the essentially adversarial and hierarchical
character of the relationship between workers and managers, whether in
capitalist or socialist economies. Managerial authority does not suggest
the absence of exploitation and domination, and worker commitment
does not suggest that the interests of workers become identical with those

of managers. Workers will everywhere seek higher wages, better working conditions, greater respect, and more autonomy; and managers will everywhere seek to maximize control over the labor process and extract as much of the workers' energies as possible in achieving their own ends. However, within the context of the problematique being explored here—the building of complex, bureaucratic institutions in NWLIs—it is assumed that both managers and workers stand to gain something where they are able to reach some reciprocal understandings and accommodations that make managerial hierarchies more bearable—perhaps even more "fair"—from the point of view of workers. Managers stand to benefit when workers willingly offer more than the minimum of effort in fulfilling tasks; yet, workers would only do so when they expect to derive *some* material and/or emotional benefit in return. The significance attached to managerial authority and worker commitment is predicated on the assumption that such an outcome reflects the emergence of *some* reciprocal understandings and arrangements that are highly valued by both managers and workers in spite of the essentially adversarial and hierarchical character of labor-management relations.[60]

The Logic of Syncretism: The Emergent Hypothesis

The study, previewed in section 1.3, provides a partial explanation for increases and decreases in levels of managerial authority across prewar Japan, postwar Japan, Stalinist Russia, and post-Stalin Russia. In doing so, it also points to a broader hypothesis concerning the relative merits of different managerial strategies. This emergent hypothesis may be summarized as follows:

> All other things being equal, a syncretist institution-building strategy is more likely to generate a higher level of institutional authority in the eyes of subordinates encountering new institutional settings in NWLIs.

While each of the four ideal-typical institution-building approaches may produce high levels of authority under specific conditions, the hypothesis suggests that, all other things being equal, a syncretist strategy will prove to be the path of least resistance in NWLIs. Within the context of institutions of work, the hypothesis suggests that, even taking into account the constraints posed by a given technology of production, *managerial syn-*

cretism is likely to produce a higher level of managerial authority than would a modernist, traditionalist, or revolutionary approach to industrial management in NWLIs.

Managerial syncretism is essentially the application of a syncretist institution-building approach within the framework of the industrial enterprise. It may be defined as a set of managerial ideologies and organizational practices in a firm that simultaneously does three things: (a) selectively incorporates and institutionalizes *some* of the portable norms and social practices previously embedded in past communities of work, particularly those that engendered cooperation and established the principles for membership in communities and the distribution of tasks and resources; (b) modifies the management practices and labor processes adopted from firms in advanced industrial countries so that the resulting organization of work and authority are at least partially recognizable in terms of these familiar norms and practices; and (c) still manages to fulfill all of the technical requirements of production over the long term. Preindustrial communities of work and complex industrial enterprises obviously vary in the degree of specialization in the division of labor; however, they do have one thing in common: the need to preserve order and coordinate collective endeavors among people with different resources and status performing separate tasks that have consequences for a larger entity. Norms and practices that speak to these imperatives are portable across production processes and technologies. Managerial syncretism represents a creative approach that selectively invokes such norms and practices while simultaneously modifying models of management to make them less incongruous with the historical inheritance. The content of a syncretist managerial approach may vary across time and space, but, as the comparative study will demonstrate, its outlines can be identified by way of comparison to hypothetical approximations of what modernist, traditionalist, or revolutionary strategies might look like in any given context.

Leaving aside the historical comparisons that inform this hypothesis, its plausibility also rests on a distinctive logic that has been anticipated in past and recent examinations of the developmental experiences of NWLIs. This logic has to do with differentiating the functional and dysfunctional dynamics that might result when two seemingly contradictory sets of principles and institutions come into close contact with each other. Even during the heyday of modernization theory, some scholars had anticipated that the confrontation between tradition and modernity might lead not to evolutionary trends toward the latter but to unprecedented and unanticipated outcomes, either in the form of recurrent conflicts between competing visions of the past and the future or in the form of new, hybrid institutional structures and behavioral patterns.[61] In more recent discourses of political economy, one finds more refined treatments of the opportunities and calamities that result from the clash between the outward-looking ambitions of state elites and the social norms and practices embedded in different regions and locales. Evans, for example, has emphasized the positive consequences of engineering a synergy between state institutions and objectives and preexisting "norms of cooperation and networks of civic engagement among ordinary citizens," suggesting that the reciprocity and trust fostered by the latter can serve as a source of valuable "social capital" in pursuit of developmental ends.[62] In the context of democratization, Schaeffer has compellingly shown how "local communities assimilate imported ideas selectively and transform them to fit their own life conditions."[63] From a more skeptical standpoint, Scott has noted how the blind pursuit of "high modernist" objectives by ambitious state elites has produced formal schemes of development that ubiquitously failed because they ignored or rejected preexisting forms of *metis,* the practical experience and knowledge embedded in local communities.[64] And, Badie has argued that the imposition of universal rules that originated in the West "enunciates a unification of worlds without unifying meaning."[65] Despite their quite different attitudes toward the state, these views converge on the point that the less severe the tension between existing sensibilities embedded in communities and the new initiatives launched in the quest for modernity, the more stable and effective the results will be from the perspective of both modernizing elites and society at large.

Ironically, this logic has been most explicitly articulated in an argument that originally developed out of a study of an industrialized Western democracy, Norway, by the late Harry Eckstein. This argument emphasized the gains to political stability resulting from the *congruence* or fit in patterns of authority across various levels of governmental and nongovernmental segments of institutional life. According to Eckstein, where there is a greater congruence in authority patterns across adjacent segments—that is, where disparities in authority patterns are successfully reduced and managed—polities are likely to be more stable.[66] In this book, a similar, but not identical, logic is suggested in the hypothesis about the benefits of syncretist institution-building in NWLIs: Syncretism is expected to produce a higher degree of legitimacy for superordinates and their commands because it is more likely to produce a higher degree of congruence along two distinct dimensions *within* an institution or a type of institution: the mutual intelligibility between the formal and informal realms of institutional life and the compatibility between the normative (ideal) and technical (material) aspects governing everyday tasks and interactions.[67] Where congruence is high, subordinates are more likely to view the informal norms and social relations they share as cohering with formal hierarchies and routines, and are thus more likely to willingly carry out their tasks in accordance with the directives and objectives defined by their superordinates. Where congruence is absent along these two dimensions, this is likely to negatively affect the perceptions of subordinates toward their institutional environments and, consequently, the legitimacy of the commands issued by superordinates.

The relevance of congruence for institutional stability rests not only on the fit between distinct sets of norms and practices, but also on a set of individual-level assumptions that provide the motivational basis for the argument. One assumption has to do with the likelihood that incongruities will produce "strain" among individuals by forcing them to confront conflicting normative prescriptions and role expectations, for example, where formal and informal norms diverge within a given institution or across similar institutional settings.[68] A second assumption emphasizes the psychological benefits of *familiarity* in coping with anxiety accompanying organization life under conditions of rapid social change. Certainly, individuals with different personalities will respond differently to particular sources of anxiety in institutional environments; to the extent that any kind of generalization about individual motivations and tendencies can be made, however, the assumption that individuals will typically prefer some sense of familiarity and continuity in coping with anxiety-inducing aspects of institutional life is a plausible one, rooted in research conducted by students of organizational psychology. This research indicates that while rewards and sanctions may affect the disposition of individuals toward the institution in which they participate, there is also a powerful, less consciously articulated, sense of anxiety that subordinates share in organizational life that predisposes them toward a predictable, familiar, and reassuring social environment within which to carry out routine tasks.[69] Where such an environment is not available, subordinates—far from becoming committed to organizational goals—will tend to withdraw from institutional life, refraining from offering their cooperation and commitment wherever they have some room for discretion and even joining together informally to develop "social defenses" to cope with anxieties in firms or organizations.[70]

In the case of NWLIs, these dynamics are likely to be more pronounced for the simple reason that the rapid social mobilization accompanying belated industrialization is likely to produce more sudden and more dramatic encounters with new institutional settings, with more profound consequences for anxiety.[71] Under these conditions, incongruities between formal managerial ideologies and practices, on the one hand, and informal norms and social relations among workers, on the other, not only give rise to conflicting normative prescriptions and role expectations at the workplace, but also to the desire to preserve the more familiar norms and social relations wherever possible even if this compromises formally prescribed roles, identities, and organizational routines. This does not in any way suggest that material incentives and sanctions will be irrelevant; it only suggests that subordinates' calculations will be affected by the extent to which the formal system of incentives and sanctions is understandable in terms of the more familiar norms and practices that governed the distribution of tasks, rewards, and obligations in past communities.

It is important to bear in mind that all of the institution-building strategies, including syncretist ones, are defined not in terms of their consequences for congruence or authority, but in terms of orientations toward competing influences of inherited legacies and existing institutional models. In the case of the large-scale enterprise, while congruence is viewed as directly and proportionately related to managerial authority, this congruence can, in principle, be produced by various combinations of circumstances and strategies.[72] However, the fact that syncretism partially draws upon familiar norms and practices embedded in past communities of work does serve to reduce the likelihood of incongruities between the formal and informal dimensions of the industrial enterprise and between the normative and technical aspects of the production process. This is why it is plausible to suggest that syncretist managerial formulas, all other things being equal, are more likely to engender higher levels of managerial authority (see fig. 4). Chapter 2 offers a more elaborate discussion of managerial syncretism in relation to contending perspectives on firms and organizations.

1.3. The Study: Work, Community, and Authority in Late-Industrializing Japan and Russia

The argument in this book has emerged from a comparative-historical study of industrial management and labor relations in typical large enterprises in Japan and Russia. These two countries are particularly appropri-

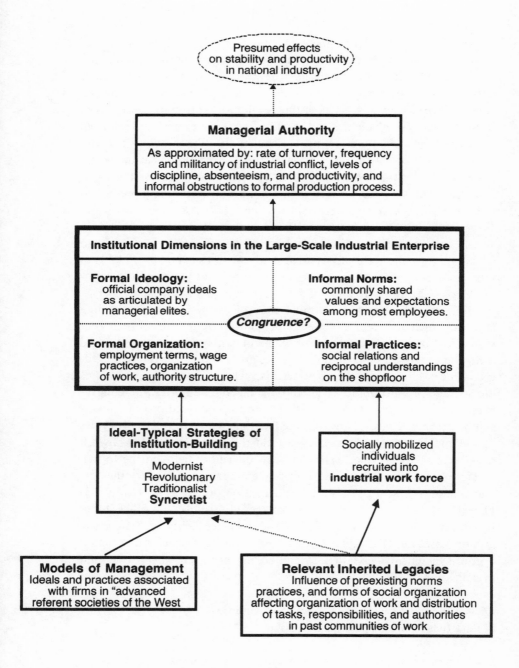

Fig. 4. Schematic representation of the hypothesis

ate for such an analysis not only because of their general world-historical importance as two NWLIs that have long sought to compete with the West, but also because their sharply divergent experiences over the past century provide an empirical basis for a hypothesis-generating comparison. Important shifts over time are evident in management ideologies and practices in both countries (particularly in Japan), enabling diachronic comparisons of managerial strategy in light of changing management models. At the same time, it is possible to identify discrete periods during which patterns of industrial management in large-scale firms are sufficiently uniform across sectors and regions to permit some reasonable cross-national comparisons. This section briefly discusses the framework of comparison, previews the salient points of the case studies, and considers some features of the design of the comparative study.

The Framework of Comparison: Two Countries, Four Cases,
Varied Outcomes

Japan and Russia both represent non-Western countries that were once on the periphery of the drama of industrialization and that may be legitimately classified as late industrializers for the better part of the past two centuries.[73] Both had significant encounters with the West that led to generalized commitments among new modernizing elites to build up industrial and military power in order to catch up to the West. These elites also faced the common dilemma of distinguishing between industrialization and Westernization in the course of defining their development strategies and designing new institutions. In fact, in both Japan and Russia, national elites at one time or another proclaimed lofty goals aimed at challenging and transforming the liberal world order created by Western powers.[74] Nevertheless, elites in both countries viewed their ambitious transformative agendas as long-range projects that were predicated on first matching or surpassing the material and technological achievements of the West; as a result, they invested enormous resources in rapid industrialization and found themselves relying frequently on foreign inputs as they sought to compete with the West and become recognized as a worthy adversary.[75] But, in spite of these similarities, for the purpose of generating broader hypotheses it is significant that institutions of work in late-industrializing Japan and Russia exhibit marked differences in eventual outcomes as well as in inherited legacies and institution-building strategies.[76]

Given the variations over time, the cases being compared are not

actually the countries but discrete managerial approaches that are recognizable across sectors in the typical management ideals and practices that
emerged in large-scale firms in each country under the auspices of a clearly
identifiable leadership over a given time period. In effect, there are not two
but *four* cases considered here, identifiable with typical managerial approaches found in prewar Japan (1868–1930s), postwar Japan (1950–70s),
Stalinist Russia (1917–53), and post-Stalin Russia (1960s–80s).[77] The varia-
tion-finding comparison relates the stylized managerial approaches evident
in each of these cases to one of the institution-building strategies noted
above and considers its consequences for managerial authority.

It is important to emphasize that the outcome of interest in this book
is the variation in levels of managerial authority, not in levels of economic
growth or technological innovation. This variation is evident in the fact
that postwar Japanese managerial elites—in the wake of military defeat,
foreign occupation, economic chaos, and social dislocation—managed to
succeed in doing what elites in prewar Japan had tried in vain to do and
what Soviet elites had expected to do automatically: generate and maintain a high level of commitment among the industrial proletariat. Coercion and hierarchical control over workers in Stalinist Russia did serve to
prevent strikes, but even with all the restrictions over labor mobility and
all the benefits associated with employment in large enterprises, high
turnover and collusive shop-floor behavior consistently posed a problem.
In the post-Stalin era, as the use of coercive measures declined, work slowdowns, absenteeism, corruption, and apathy came to pose increasingly
serious problems for industrial production while turnover remained a serious problem. Despite the ideological emphasis placed on the traditionally
"warm" social customs and the "family firm" in prewar Japan, industrial
disputes and turnover, to the extent these were kept in check at all, were
only brought under control through coercive measures. In the postwar era,
Japanese workers may not have been the uniquely "diligent" or "docile"
employees frequently portrayed in some studies, but they did offer a
significantly higher level of cooperation and commitment than did workers in either prewar Japan or Soviet Russia.[78]

Chapters 3 and 4 of this book trace the evolution of the industrial
enterprise in the two countries in order to generate a partial explanation
for these variations in levels of managerial authority. This explanation
involves a complex historical process that can be analytically separated
into (a) the character of a particular legacy, consisting of values and social
relations embedded in preindustrial communities and later borne by indi-

viduals entering the industrial work force, (b) the character of management ideologies invoked on a nationwide basis during a given period in order to legitimate managerial authority and motivate employees, and (c) the extent of congruence of these formal managerial ideologies, on the one hand, with concrete management practices and, on the other hand, with the more informal norms and practices shared by a majority of employees within the enterprise. Where the congruence was greater, there also proved to be higher levels of managerial authority. This was not the case in prewar Japan or Soviet Russia, but it did prove to be the case for three decades in postwar Japan where a syncretist managerial strategy had gradually crystallized around the mid-1950s.

Preindustrial Communities of Work: The Japanese Mura and the Russian Mir

The explanations in both cases begin with the relevant historical legacies inherited by modernizing elites. In neither country did the dissipation of preindustrial communities of work pave the way for the rise of individualistic social values; in fact, in both countries collectivist norms and social relations proved to be quite resilient, influencing the informal expectations, understandings, and practices among groups or networks within the enterprise.[79] At the same time, there were marked variations in the specific norms and practices that guided the coordination of collective endeavors and the distribution of obligations and rewards within typical preindustrial communities of work—the Tokugawa village (the *mura*) and the Russian peasant commune (the *mir*). The similarities and differences between the two institutions do not directly point to any particular managerial solution, but they do shape the environment within which workers and managerial elites had to negotiate new understandings about work and authority.

Like agrarian communities anywhere, both the Tokugawa *mura* and the Russian *mir* were corporate entities that distinguished between insiders and outsiders and had a strong sense of collective identity rooted in the concrete contexts of everyday social interaction. In both communities, there were clear signifiers of community membership; for example, all of the households participated in an annual cycle of rituals, all were eligible to make claims on collectively owned resources, and all had the right to expect mutual assistance from neighbors.

The Tokugawa-era *mura,* however, may be distinguished from other village communities by the stronger emphasis placed on duty, harmony, and conditional hierarchy as positive attributes of orderly group life. The network of mutual obligations was evident in practices designed to ensure the reciprocal exchange of labor during harvest, while the value placed on harmony was evident in extralegal mechanisms to resolve disputes. The notion of conditional hierarchy is reflected in the fact that the high concentration of wealth, status, and decision-making authority in the hands of a narrow stratum of landlords was accompanied by expectations that they were required to be benevolent and attentive to specific needs of less fortunate households. And, while the value placed on harmony was evident in elaborate mechanisms to resolve or mediate social conflicts, protest and rebellion remained available as responses where the obligations of landlords were not met.

The Russian *mir,* even if it was not the blissful, harmonious communal entity that the *mura* aspired to be, was the primary source of identity for its members and the primary framework within which collective rights and obligations were defined. What distinguishes the *mir* is that it was markedly more egalitarian, not only in comparison to the Tokugawa *mura,* but also in comparison to many other agrarian communities. This egalitarianism was reflected both in the shared norms of commune members, as well as in such practices as the periodic redistribution of common resources and arable land. The latter practice suggested that every household had a right to have an opportunity to meet its subsistence needs, and that changes in the needs and resources of households warranted changes in the allocation of landstrips within the commune. The egalitarian ethos also had implications for patterns of collective decision making: the commune assembly, for example, included the heads of all member households, not just the wealthiest or highest-ranked ones (as in the case of the Tokugawa *mura*), and all members of a household were allowed to participate at meetings even if the heads were the only ones to vote.

The Russian *mir* and Japanese *mura* survived the first attempts to transform agriculture engineered by Japanese and Russian modernizers, but were ultimately dissolved as a result of, respectively, Stalinist collectivization and Occupation-era land reforms. Many of the core norms and organizational features underpinning these institutions, however, were reconstructed by socially mobilized actors in new institutional settings. The available evidence on attitudinal change in Japan and Russia, while it does not decisively confirm continuities in cultural values, does render plausible an important assumption behind the interpretations offered in chapters 3 and 4: that legacies of past social institutions did not inevitably give way to individualistic norms in Japan and Russia. In the particular case of industrial relations, while workers and managers in both countries undoubtedly had to make numerous individual decisions in the course of everyday factory life, most workers' shared expectations and responses to particular management practices, as well as informal aspects of workplace social relations continued to reflect norms and practices that had shaped collective endeavors and social relations in past communities of work. Indications of the influence of these resilient legacies are considered in chapters 3 and 4.

Prewar and Postwar Japan: A Diachronic Comparison

The discussion of prewar Japan, where the crystallization of a coherent strategy is identifiable for only a brief period of time (the end of World War I through the early 1930s), provides the necessary background against which the character and merits of managerial syncretism in postwar Japan may be better appreciated. Immediately following the Meiji Restoration in 1868, Japanese modernizers followed an approach that more closely resembled a modernist institution-building strategy than any of the other three ideal-typical approaches. They eagerly borrowed Western organizational models in the hope of breaking down preexisting habits and social structures that they believed were holding Japan back. By the end of the 1880s, however, political and economic elites became increasingly aware of the possibility of widespread social unrest among the newly mobilized work force and, to preempt this possibility, began to pay more attention to the potential uses of tradition. Business elites frequently invoked references to traditional "warm customs" not only to obviate legislation pertaining to workers' rights and working conditions, but also to preserve order and justify managerial hierarchy within the large-scale firm.

By the end of World War I, price distortions and increasingly independent union activities sparked new fears of labor unrest. In response, managerial elites, with the support of state officials, adopted a more active traditionalist strategy centered on the ideal of the "family firm." This ideal rested on the analogy between authority relations in the factory and those within the traditional patriarchal household, or *ie*. This analogy, however, neither extended to other aspects of traditional collective organization (e.g., the right to expect benevolence from superiors) nor captured the diversity, the size, or the complexity of the large enterprises that spearheaded industrialization. More importantly, from the vantage point of most workers, the behavior of managerial elites in regard to employment terms, wage practices, and work organization did not in the least bit correspond to the kind of treatment workers expected to receive even within the confines of the large-scale bureaucratic firm; the few categories of workers that received employment security and seniority-based wage increases only served to remind the rest of the kinds of rewards they were being denied. Through the 1910s and 1920s, workers regularly challenged managerial authority in overt and covert ways, occasionally invoking the language of individual rights or class conflict, but more commonly framing the issues in terms of the same norms of fairness, reciprocity, and conditional obedience that had shaped social relations in past communities of work. The "family firm" ideal was further undermined during the late 1920s and 1930s by the enthusiastic emulation of Taylorist management techniques that prompted managers to rely more heavily on output-based wages and more narrowly defined individual tasks. The result was a lack of congruence between official management practices, on the one hand, and managerial ideology and workers' own sensibilities, on the other. Thus, not surprisingly, worker commitment remained low in prewar Japan as evident in small-scale industrial strikes, frequent petitions to employers, and labor turnover, all of which were checked by the late 1930s not by new managerial initiatives but by the creation of a state-led labor front and strict labor codes to enforce labor discipline and check turnover.

Japan's defeat in World War II is viewed here as an important break in history, not because it provided a tabula rasa for the construction of new institutions, but because it provided an opportunity for a new labor movement and postwar managerial elites to reassess the strategies of their predecessors in light of the constraints generated by Occupation-era reforms. During the Occupation, in response to the rapid growth of legalized trade unions, widespread labor unrest, and the restraints placed on managerial elites, the new employers and managers were forced to revise their approach to industrial management. In the process, they were aided by a new managerial doctrine emerging in the West, one that broadly emphasized "human relations" but (unlike scientific management) did not offer any specific dicta about how to organize work and authority in the factory. Thus, the idea of human relations was reinterpreted to incorporate elements of the newly emergent cultural discourse of "Japanese national character" (*Nihonjinron*), providing the basis for a distinctive conception of the company community. Japanese-style human relations continued to suggest collective identification with the firm's goals; but, unlike the one-sided relationship of obedience and dependency suggested by the "family firm," the emphasis shifted to interdependence, reciprocal obligations, cooperation, and, above all, common signifiers of community membership.

This new formula also seemed more meaningful in light of the new standardized practices adopted by large firms in postwar Japan. After a period of intense conflict between 1948 and 1953, organizations such as the Japan Productivity Center, along with moderate business associations and trade unions, eventually were able to negotiate a common pact linking rising productivity to new terms of employment that strongly resembled what workers had been aspiring to in prewar Japan. The new employment system that crystallized across large firms became evident in the offer of lifetime employment to regular workers and in the relatively greater weight placed on the seniority-based component of wage increases (as opposed to purely output- or merit-based calculations). Moreover, since the 1950s, patterns of work organization moved away from the Taylorist model of maximal specialization and individually defined tasks and rewards; instead, job boundaries became blurred while managers emphasized "job enlargement" and the use of "small-groupism" to create greater involvement and more diversified skill-sets across categories of employees. Managerial hierarchies remained in place, more radical unions were marginalized, and there were still complaints related to the quality of working life; but the postwar approach did contribute to a relatively high level of managerial authority during the 1960s and 1970s, as evident in the low frequency and intensity of industrial conflict, reduced turnover and absenteeism, increased productivity, and reduced violations of company rules.

Thus, ideology and organization in postwar Japan enabled companies to meet the technical requirements of industrial production while maintaining a familiar, group-oriented social atmosphere that bore a strong resemblance to the organization of cooperation and authority relations in the preindustrial *mura*. These shifts point to the emergence of a syncretist managerial approach, reflecting the innovative adaptation of borrowed managerial principles and of related adjustments in inherited norms and patterns of social relations. It is this syncretist strategy and not the specific features of Japanese industrial management that are being treated as fruitfully replicable by institution-builders across NWLIs.[80]

Soviet Russia: The Failure of "Revolutionary Modernity"

In Soviet Russia, many segments of the urban work force initially did identify with key aspects of the Bolshevik ideology of labor, particularly with such ideals as "workers' control," "collective labor," and "equality of labor and wages." While these terms were intended to suggest a revolutionary transformation guided by a vanguard party and were interpreted as such in the theoretical writings of leading Bolsheviks,[81] the casual manner in which the Bolsheviks employed the language of "workers' control" and "equality" in public speeches led many segments of the urban work force to legitimately believe that the "workers' revolution" would overthrow capitalist factory owners and management techniques while allowing workers to realize their own familiar norms of autonomous collective labor and distributive justice. Many policies and resolutions adopted immediately after the 1917 revolution even suggested some movement in the direction of these ideals. Several months into the Russian civil war (1918–21), however, the Bolsheviks began to retreat from their initial pronouncements and introduced "pragmatic" management practices in order to promote labor discipline and boost industrial production. Key elements of Taylorism and Fordism, including piece rate wages and centralized managerial control, were enthusiastically introduced into the "socialist" factory in order to realize the ideal combination of "Russian Revolutionary sweep and American efficiency."[82] Although the "New Economic Policy" initiated after the civil war signaled a partial retreat from nationalized industry, the party-state apparatus retained control of large-scale enterprises in heavy industry and steadfastly expanded the use of piece rates and intensified labor discipline, crushing opposition groups that had urged a return to greater collective self-management and a more egalitarian wage structure. In addition, a new movement for the "scientific organization of labor" sought to inculcate a new industrial work culture among millions of workers while vigorously promoting Taylorist-Fordist methods of work organization.

Following Lenin's death, many respected Bolsheviks called for a reconsideration of many policies initiated during the civil war, with many proposing a syncretist approach to institution-building (within the overall context of pursuing revolutionary transformation). Such programs not only suggested a more gradual process of change, involving a lengthy process of education and socialization, but also sought to draw attention to the affinities between the Bolsheviks' own ideals and selected preexisting social norms. Upon his rise to power in 1928, Stalin decisively put an end to any such alternatives in favor of a dramatic revolution from above consisting of agricultural collectivization, renationalization of all industry, rapid industrialization in keeping with the high targets of his Five-Year Plans, and the promotion of individuals from working-class backgrounds. Within the context of industrial management, however, the revolutionary campaigns and slogans belied a continuing preoccupation with the core elements of scientific management. This was evident in the fact that leading Russian Taylorists, although criticized by Stalin for not pushing the boundaries of rationalized production, were retained to design a complex system of job classification, with a sharply differentiated piece-rate wage system tied to individual production norms for thousands of elemental individual tasks. In addition, a steeply hierarchical system of control and supervision was consolidated under "one-man management," with managerial power concentrated in the hands of a new cohort of "Red Directors." "Socialist competition," initially introduced as a friendly challenge between factories or work brigades, was turned into an instrument for spurring more intensified competition among *individual* workers, with the most productive "labor heroes" rewarded through disproportionate material rewards and rapid promotion. Stalin and the new enterprise directors may have assumed that the destruction of preexisting social institutions and the abolition of tsarist state capitalism were sufficient to produce a new socialist industrial work culture, but what specifically was "socialist" about labor in Soviet factories never became clear to the vast majority of workers although a narrow stratum of newcomers did take advantage of new rules and campaigns to improve their own positions.

In effect, like the Japanese "family firm," the Stalinist enterprise came to be characterized by a marked lack of congruence between Bolshevik ideology and management practices and between the formal and informal aspects of the workplace. And, as in prewar Japan, these incongruities set the stage for a decline in managerial authority that, given the reduced scope for overt protest, was largely evident in the informal aspects of workplace social relations: workers found ways to bypass official regulations and reconstruct their own networks on the shopfloor, while collective labor essentially came to mean collusion among brigade members on ensuring norm-fulfillment and adequate earnings even if this meant subverting official work organization and wage practices. Thus, while Stalin's cultural revolution did wipe out traditional social institutions, it failed to create the "new Soviet man" committed to the official production goals of the Soviet factory.

The post-Stalin era did not witness a fundamental shift in institution-building strategy, but the changes that did appear may be viewed as a "neo-traditional" variant of the original approach: the revolutionary rhetoric and the modernist impulse to borrow the latest management techniques remained in evidence, but were muted by a pervasive sense that existing production processes only had to be marginally adjusted to provide workers with a greater sense of stability and security. The decline of terror and the new discourse of human relations did result in important shifts in Soviet industrial relations. Khrushchev's rejection of terror and harsh labor codes was accompanied by an emerging consensus on guaranteeing workers full employment, steady improvements in living standards, reductions in base wage differentials across job categories, and cheap access to basic necessities. This shift in employment terms, evident in official programs and statements, appeared to be remarkably similar to the offer of lifetime employment, steady wage increases linked to seniority, and a reduction in overt forms of control in postwar Japan. These similarities proved to be quite superficial, however. Although Soviet management specialists did begin to make increasing reference to human aspects of production, this was typically understood to mean that productivity and commitment could be improved *within* the existing system of production simply by better meeting workers' needs for job security and material satisfaction. The managerial ideals touted by the past regime were considered to be sacrosanct and entirely consistent with this "humanized" variant of NOT. Thus, in contrast to the restructuring of ideology and work organization in postwar Japan, Soviet management science continued to rely on the existing system of work organization while allowing informal adjustments to wage practices and labor processes so as to preserve labor quiescence.

Khrushchev's campaign to formally restore wage egalitarianism, combined with the Brezhnev-era promotion of brigade *khozraschet* (joint responsibility for tasks and collective remuneration), might have made a difference had these reforms been systematically implemented. Instead, the Brezhnev regime chose to focus on preempting social unrest by turning a blind eye to informal management practices and quasi-legal exchange relations that not only contradicted official ideology but undermined the formal system of production. This only served to further underscore the size and permanence of the gap between ideology and reality. These factors account for a pattern of labor relations that may not have become openly adversarial, but did contribute to increasing problems with work slowdowns and stoppages along with continuing turnover, declining productivity, absenteeism, alcoholism, and the proliferation of informal networks tht diverted workers' energies to a shadow economy. By the time Gorbachev set out to stimulate productivity by implementing sharper performance-related wage differentials, workers only took advantage of glasnost to voice their criticisms of the regime while engaging in more regular and more protracted strikes and work stoppages. Thus, although both postwar Japan and post-Stalin Russia witnessed improvements in workers' conditions and an increase in worker *quiescence,* postwar Japanese enterprises enjoyed a high level of worker *commitment,* while workers in post-Stalin Russia became even more cynical about the value of official production goals and management ideals and practices.

Comparing Firms, Managers, and Workers across Nations:
Clarifications and Caveats

Most "big-case comparisons," as Tilly has argued, assume the a priori coherence and concreteness of national-level units of comparison simply on the basis of the existence of states.[83] Although the cases here are defined in terms of strategies rather than countries, there is still the question of how to justify cross-*national* comparisons of attributes that are defined at the level of the industrial enterprise. Certainly, each firm is to some extent unique, each with its own product mixes and production processes, together with distinctive ideological formulations and operational rules and procedures; and, certainly, differences across regions and sectors account for some of the variation in organizational culture across different enterprises within nations. At the same time, as North has shown, firms are also subjected to certain standardizing pressures as a result of common "institutional environments" that provide uniform rules of the game shaped by the interaction of customs, laws, and politics.[84] This institutional environment does not have to be defined at the national level, but in the case of large enterprises in NWLIs, there are several specific mechanisms and processes that make national-level typifications of labor relations in large-scale firms plausible for the purposes of this comparative study.[85]

First, the very fact that state elites in NWLIs are committed to late industrialization means that they will take an active role in establishing the infrastructure for industrial production and providing the resources needed to support large firms in the process of expanding production. This is true of firms in both the public sector, where the state directly owns the means of production, and the private sector, where the developmental state intervenes in the economy to provide "administrative guidance," mitigate competition, and ensure stability in industrial production.[86] Moreover, although they have separate interests, managers and national elites do share a common commitment to boosting industrial production and preserving industrial peace, while business-elites depend heavily on state support when establishing large enterprises (for example, for licenses, subsidies, protection, and the enforcement of contracts). The state also provides the legal and institutional framework for industrial relations, particularly in the case of large firms where conflicts between labor and management can have especially important political ramifications from the point of view of both managers and state elites. In addition, the fact that state elites in NWLIs also engage in nation-building means that the enterprises operating within the national environment will be subject to some standardizing pressures in terms of their ideologies and organizational forms. For example, national systems of education and training represent channels through which managerial elites may be able to develop a common managerial ethos and a common understanding of the dilemmas they face in building authority; this is especially likely where certain universities or institutes have played a disproportionate role in the training of bureaucrats and managerial elites, as they have in Japan, Russia, and most other NWLIs.[87] Last but not least, national patterns of industrial relations, at least in NWLIs, can be viewed as a particularly compelling "organizational field" for mimicry, producing a degree of "institutional isomorphism" as the managerial ideals and practices in one firm in a given NWLI influence those of other firms across sectors.[88] All these mechanisms, taken collectively, represent a basis for assuming that there are typical features that render large-scale enterprises recognizable within nations and, thus, comparable over time and across nations. These mechanisms may not always be present everywhere, but they are likely to be present in the case of most NWLIs, and they most certainly are evident among large-scale industrial enterprises in Japan and Russia as the extensive literature on *"the* Japanese firm" and *"the* Soviet firm" suggests.[89]

It is also necessary to qualify the designation of the two sets of stylized actors involved in the the drama of institution-building: *workers* and *managers.* This dichotomous classification of enterprise personnel is certainly not unprecedented in comparative political economy or industrial sociology,[90] but, more importantly, the level of generality at which the comparison is cast requires dispensing with separate analyses of principal-agent dilemmas in enterprise administration or of specific kinds of employee behavior corresponding to particular skills and skill levels (although these issues are addressed in the case studies where they impact the broader argument). Within the specific contexts of Japanese and Russian industry, *managerial elites* and *workers* may not refer to identical sets of actors, but the *relationships* between the two groups are assumed to be generally comparable.

Among the managerial elite in Japanese enterprises are included employers, enterprise directors, division managers, and section heads, but not foremen or other supervisory personnel on the shopfloor whose relationship to superordinates and workers can vary across contexts. In the case of Soviet Russia, given the structure of the command economy, managerial elites include the enterprise directors, the economic bureaucrats in the ministry that has responsibility for a given enterprise, as well as key party leaders and apparatchiki who are in a position to issue directives or shape official managerial doctrine. Lower-level managers, section heads, and shop-floor chiefs, while often cooperating with higher-level personnel, are considered the functional equivalent of the foreman in Japanese industrial enterprises since their relationship with regard to workers below them and managerial personnel above them is ambiguous within the broader system of planning and enterprise administration. In both cases, however, the managerial elites are presumed to constitute a unitary actor for the purposes of comparative analysis, with the proviso that the study is *not* intended to be a detailed empirical study or a critique of specific choices made by individual managers. At the same time, in both cases, the extent to which lower-level supervisory personnel act as agents of higher-level superordinates or form collusive relations with subordinates—that is, the extent to which principal-agent problems have been manifested within enterprises—may be regarded as one indicator of the level of managerial authority in a given context.

When dealing with the category of workers or employees, some additional caveats are in order. First of all, within any modern large-scale enterprise, there are obviously significant differences in skill-types and skill-grades that undoubtedly affect attitudes toward work and authority. Important distinctions are frequently drawn between white-collar employees, skilled blue-collar workers, and semiskilled or unskilled workers, as well as across particular skills and responsibilities associated with groups within each of these categories. These distinctions are considered in chapters 3 and 4 only where they are relevant to distinguishing the content and consequences of particular managerial approaches, but the level of generality of the comparative analysis requires limiting systematic analyses of the specific experiences of each category of worker or employee.[91] The relationship among categories of workers within large enterprises, however, does feature prominently in the interpretations of each of the cases insofar as these indicate the content or consequences of management practices in Japan or Russia (for example, the steepness of workplace hierarchies, wage and status differentials across categories of workers, the specificity of job descriptions for categories of workers, and the ability of employees of varied skill-types and grades to coordinate their formal and informal activities).

It should also be noted that gendered aspects of workplace social relations are not given the systematic consideration they deserve. This does not mean that the role and experiences of women in NWLIs do not deserve to be closely scrutinized; however, given the purpose and design of this study, a separate analysis of the experience of women workers and managers in Japan and Russia is neither feasible, nor warranted. In the case of Japan, girls and young women constituted the majority of the work force in the early stages of industrialization, particularly in textile factories; however, the proportion of women in the industrial work force dropped significantly with the expansion of industrial manufacturing in the 1910s through the 1930s, and the postwar increase in the number of female employees was accompanied by unusually low glass ceilings that limited the careers of women largely to support positions, often without the kinds of benefits associated with the employment of "regular" workers. In the Soviet Union, women came to constitute over 40 percent of the work force, but their opportunities for upward mobility were circumscribed by the double burden of managing their work lives while attending to most of the needs and chores associated with their family lives. While both observations merit attention in comprehensive portraits of Japanese and Russian workplaces, they also point to reasons why the gendered aspects of the workplace are not systematically addressed in the case studies. The level of generality at which this comparative study is cast requires focusing on the activities of, and relations between, two sets of stylized actors: managers seeking to build authority in modern work institutions and workers in large-scale industrial enterprises in those sectors deemed important by economic elites. To the extent that women are in a position to challenge managers or attain managerial status, they are assumed to be incorporated into the analysis as workers or managers, but the distinctive experiences and constraints they face in either capacity are necessarily left unexamined.[92]

1.4.   Characterizing the Book: Method and Approach

This book represents an effort to develop a flexible, integrative theoretical framework for exploring the challenges and dynamics of institution-building in NWLIs. In the process, it also hopes to make useful contributions toward relating the strikingly similar debates in Japanese and Russian studies to each other and to general arguments about authority relations, institutional design, political economy, organizational sociology, and socioeconomic change in the course of industrialization (see appendix B). The resulting product is not clearly identifiable with any of the currently popular methodological or metatheoretical perspectives in the social sciences although their proponents are likely to find aspects of this book to be recognizable within their respective systems of concepts, theories, and methods. In fact, this entire endeavor has been predicated on the assumption that there are important communicative and intellectual benefits to be had from scholarship based on approaches that are self-consciously eclectic, systematically combining the relevant concepts and contributions of diverse subfields, contending research traditions, and studies cast at various levels of abstraction. As this book is intended to be such an eclectic offering, this last section of the chapter seeks to briefly characterize the sort of comparative method and theoretical approach adopted here, while appendix A summarizes their underlying foundational assumptions.

The Aims and Challenges of Middle-Range
Comparative History

While most historically grounded comparative studies generally follow an inductive strategy, this is true of the approach in this book only insofar as it rejects the quintessentially deductivist claim that "formal, explicit theorizing takes intellectual, if not temporal, precedence over empiricism."[93] For the most part, induction and deduction are ideal-typical logics that must be simultaneously invoked in the ongoing process of seeking and revising generalizable propositions in light of empirical analysis and novel historical interpretations. To the extent that prior theoretical *ideas* have shaped the study, it is significant that these ideas are not in the form of

axioms or "laws" that suggest any a priori explanatory principles; at the
same time, the problematique could not be meaningfully explored without
the construction of a set of concepts and ideal-typical constructs that
could be used in heuristic fashion to help formulate a stylized interpretation of complex historical processes. The actual process that has led to the
final hypothesis in this book may be characterized generally as iterations
of a sequence proceeding from initial efforts to relate theoretical constructs (based largely on intuitive responses to existing theoretical discourses) to an examination of historical materials (a first cut at the country studies), to a quasi-inductive effort to formulate a general proposition
(through the comparison of prewar and postwar Japan), to a quasi-deduc-
tive effort to reexamine this proposition (through the extension of the
proposition to Soviet Russia), followed by a largely inductive inference of
a falsifiable hypothesis.

The substantive analysis is best described as a hypothesis-generating
middle-range comparative-historical study. Its main intention is to produce stylized interpretations of the historical experiences of particular
actors and regions, and to simultaneously invoke synchronic and
diachronic comparison so as to infer modest hypotheses concerning the
consequences of varying combinations of actions and contexts.[94] This
approach is "middle-range" in that it is neither so ambitious as to apply
Mill's canons of induction for the purpose of offering full-blown macrocausal explanation, nor content to merely juxtapose narratives to highlight
the distinctiveness of historical patterns, nor designed to test or apply
hypotheses deduced from existing theoretical models.[95] What it *is* designed
to do is to generate partial explanations of divergent trends in a limited
number of comparable cases, provide compelling interpretations of the
stylized historical sequences in those cases, and offer modest hypotheses
that can have meaningful historical referents in other contexts that fit the
framework of comparison (in this case, other NWLIs). Moreover, because
middle-range comparative history is not wedded to the discourses
identified with a given area or research tradition, it is especially well-suited
for exploring "big" questions and engaging multiple area-specific and
subfield-specific discourses while paving the way for more meaningful
communication across disciplines and research traditions. Moreover, this
approach also has the advantage of building on a pragmatic foundational
perspective that enables the eclectic scholar to steer between, but also to
engage, dogmatic adherents of competing methodological and epistemological perspectives. The third section of appendix A discusses how this

type of comparative-historical approach represents a valuable alternative to recent attempts to extend the logic of statistical methods or formal models in linking idiographic studies to nomothetic projects.[96]

The particular tenor, and challenge, of middle-range comparative history is evident in the interpretations developed in chapters 3 and 4. These interpretations are sufficiently stylized so as to be comparable in view of the theoretical questions posed, but they also endeavor to be attentive to country-specific discourses although they necessarily rely heavily on secondary sources. Certainly, multiple historical records and rival interpretations present serious dangers for historically minded comparativists relying on secondary sources; but, just as area specialists and historians must be careful about how they interpret primary material, comparativists can, in principle, avoid gross theoretical and evidentiary errors through more self-conscious and systematic attention to the diversity of historical accounts.[97] In this regard, it is significant that the middle-range comparative-historical approach in this book may be distinguished from more ambitious macrocomparative analyses that sometimes ignore important controversies over historical "facts," relying solely on those interpretations they find most convenient in generating explanatory propositions.[98] The comparative study in this book may be distinguished from such approaches in three respects.

First, and most significant, the interpretations in chapters 3 and 4 are a product of a careful consideration of the competing intellectual traditions and wide-ranging scholarly debates found in the studies of particular areas or countries than is typical in many macrocausal approaches. This consideration has extended beyond the subject matter of industrial relations to encompass diverse perspectives in the study of Japanese and Russian history, which are briefly reviewed in appendix B for the purpose of distinguishing stark oppositions on recurrent issues from the interpretation offered in chapters 3 and 4.[99] Second, where possible, the narratives draw upon historical facts that appear in rival interpretations in area-specific discourses; in many cases, even if interpretations of particular historical events or processes diverge significantly, many specific observational statements are not themselves contested.[100] Third, where the facts themselves are disputed, plausible accounts of historical processes have been projected that can either subsume or reconcile the relevant aspects of rival interpretations; alternatively, where this is not possible, it has been necessary to rely on selected interpretations by reputable scholars whose work is widely regarded as authoritative even by those who embrace competing interpretations. These measures do not definitively exclude selection bias in the use of secondary sources, but they do reflect an effort to be self-conscious and consistent in the manner in which existing facts and accounts are invoked in constructing the interpretations of Japanese and Russian industry offered in chapters 3 and 4.

Characterizing the Theoretical Approach: "Synthetic Institutionalism"

The overall theoretical approach, if it must be given a label, may be referred to as "synthetic institutionalism" and needs to be distinguished from the various "new institutionalisms" that have recently appeared in political science, sociology, and economic history.[101] These other new institutionalisms—usually nested in either structuralist, culturalist, or rational-choice research programs—differ from one another in their prior assumptions about several foundational issues regarding social reality and the practice of social science. For example, they differ over the ontological primacy of individual actors and their preferences as opposed to the range of factors that shape the available alternatives and produce variations in preference orderings (i.e., the agent/structure divide). They also differ over the importance of "hard" rules and material dimensions of structures as opposed to the role of normative and symbolic aspects in structuring individual cognition. In addition, they embrace competing methodological approaches, differing over the relative merits of adopting a formal, deductive approach to the analysis of institutions as opposed to a more historically grounded inductive approach. Finally, they differ over the extent to which institutions, their designs, and their internal dynamics are conceived of in terms of their causal significance as opposed to the fit between their components.

Even if one were to treat all of these issues as strictly dichotomous choices and adopt an absolute position on each, it is theoretically possible for these various permutations to produce not three, not four, but at least ten distinct kinds of institutionalism! The synthetic institutionalist framework adopted here is based on a particular combination of entirely plausible intermediate assumptions on the aforementioned ontological, epistemological, and methodological issues (outlined in appendix A), and it is this *combination* that distinguishes it from the other new institutionalisms and from the research programs of rational choice, cultural, and structural analysis.

First, the view of institutions outlined above neither reduces institutions to rules and procedures that cut transaction costs for gain-maximizing actors nor reifies institutions by treating them as unitary actors capable of constraining and directing the actions and thoughts of individual actors over time. Institutions are seen here as comprised of real individuals with different resources, identities, roles, and interests; and the distinction between formal and informal institutional structures suggests the possibility of internal tensions and external influences. Thus, the unity, coherence, endurance, and effectiveness of institutions are viewed as contingent and variable, depending on the management and reconciliation of diverse identities and interests of individuals located in different positions within an institution. These understandings point to a type of institutionalism that rejects both the methodological individualism of rational choice institutionalism and the unambiguously structuralist approach of most historical institutionalists.

In addition, without reifying *culture,* the synthetic institutionalist approach adopted here takes seriously the contention of the new sociological institutionalism concerning the importance of incorporating some understanding of cultural frameworks and the symbolic meanings shared by actors in organizational environments, both at the level of collective experience and at the level of individual cognition. But, while this new sociological institutionalism deserves credit for bringing culture back into institutional analysis, there is no reason to a priori assign the cognitive or cultural aspects of organizational life the epistemological center stage. Nor is there any reason to diminish the importance of the facts that the dynamics within institutions are often a product of rational actors pursuing material interests, and that the more powerful actors are in a position to enforce hard constraints on the behavior of less powerful actors through an enduring system of rules and procedures (with or without the support of organizational myths and rituals). Nevertheless, the insights provided by proponents of the new sociological institutionalism can be useful if they are regarded as less of a new paradigm for research and as more of a corrective to the tendency to emphasize rational behavior or formal rules and procedures.[102]

Furthermore, the institutionalist framework adopted here emphasizes the empirical analysis of the extent to which different agents are in a position to identify and pursue distinct interests as well as the extent to which various structural forces are regularly reproduced through the behavior of more powerful agents or through a combination of material and ideational processes. That is, as evident in figure 1 and the accompanying discussion, the view of institutions offered here proceeds from a foundational perspective that embraces a fruitful agnosticism with respect to the debates over agency, culture, and structure. Such a position may be loosely identified with Weber's interpretive sociology as well as with more recently articulated structurationist perspectives, both of which treat the relationships between agency and structure, as well as between material and ideal dimensions of social life, as dialectical and mutually constitutive.[103]

Finally, it is worth noting that the synthetic institutionalist approach followed here is designed not to yield parsimonious or comprehensive causal explanations of outcomes, but to trace how the "fit" between different dimensions of institutional life—as affected by external influences— produces comparable but distinctive historical configurations and processes. This understanding is not at all dissimilar from some recent treatments of institutions in which actors are assumed to construct shared "mental maps" to simplify complex environmental conditions, and in which the self-reinforcing properties of original institutional constructs can increase the costs or returns of adopting particular practices.[104] This does not suggest that less effective strategies or institutional designs will be naturally "selected out" under certain environmental conditions, nor does it suggest that there exists a singular functional one-to-one correspondence between goals, practices, social structures, and cultural values in response to a priori universal "needs." But, it does suggest that certain combinations of ideas, resources, norms, and practices do work better than others in certain environments for the purpose of achieving institutional objectives, sustaining formal institutional structures, and enabling certain categories of institutional actors to pursue their material and ideal interests. Such an approach may be regarded as loosely "functionalist" to the extent that the effectiveness of institutions and the dispositions of individual actors within them are ultimately explained not in terms of causal sequences, but rather in terms of the extent to which the constitutive elements of institutional life share "elective affinities" that favor certain trajectories in certain environments.[105] At the same time, this sort of analytic logic should not be confused with traditional functionalist explanations in which agency all but disappears and in which social phenomena are explained primarily in terms of the higher needs these may serve for some entity.[106]

This particular combination of assumptions and objectives—together with the middle-range comparative approach outlined above—is what distinguishes the institutionalist perspective articulated here from those of rational-choice theorists, culturalists, and structuralists. As such, the chief contributions of this book lie not in new empirical observations or hard tests of existing theories, but in its eclectic attempt to selectively employ useful concepts and insightful interpretations that bear on the problem on hand, regardless of whether these are "new" or whether they are cogently embedded in an established subfield or research tradition. Such an eclecticism is not intended to pave the way for a unified alternative approach to all social inquiry; it can, however, provide a reasonable and pragmatic foundation for the problematique, argument, and comparative study offered in this book.

Chapter 2

Institutions of Work in Theoretical and Historical Context

Sources of Variation in the Course of Industrialization

Deviations from allegedly ideal use of the new ideas, previously regarded as temporary shortfalls, unavoidable failures wed to the poverty of the country and the backwardness of its people, are reinterpreted as signs of national inventiveness; and once the unavoidable deviations are understood as virtues, the hunt for variations of the technology most suited to local circumstances begins in earnest.

—Charles Sabel[1]

'Copied' and transplanted institutions that lack the moral and cultural infrastructure on which the 'original' can rely are likely to yield very different and often counter-intentional results.

—Claus Offe[2]

This chapter elaborates upon core aspects of the argument against the background of the wide-ranging debates on the sources of uniformity and variation in firms and organizations across historical and cultural settings.[3] The chapter is divided into four sections. Section 2.1 surveys different strands of the literature where one can find explicit universalist logics in the analysis of modern institutions of work.[4] It begins with a brief discussion of views of complex production and rational administration in classical political economy (from Adam Smith to Max Weber) and proceeds to an examination of the universalist assumptions behind the first models of the firm in organization theory and modernization theory; it then turns to arguments that challenge these earlier models but substitute alternative sets of universal assumptions or classificatory principles, while continuing to discount the relevance of historical sources of variation.

Section 2.2 represents the first step in the conceptualization of a more historically grounded approach to the comparative study of firms and organizations, emphasizing the contingent manner in which many core features of Western firms first emerged. In this regard, the ideals and practices associated with "scientific management" in the United States and its later incarnations elsewhere in the West are represented as products of distinctive historical processes and cultural assumptions that one would be hard pressed to find elsewhere. And, defining features of large-scale bureaucratic firms in the West—despite variations across societies, sectors, and firms—are interpreted as sufficiently uniform insofar as these constitute essentially similar points of reference for managerial elites in NWLIs.

Section 2.3 considers some well-known studies about sources of variation across firms and organizations, with a particular focus on those arguments that represent a point of departure for the analysis offered in this book. These arguments concern the potential significance of late-industrializer effects for firms and organizations in non-Western societies, the impact of diverse historical inheritances on patterns of industrial relations, and the significance of alternative choices in accounting for variations in patterns of management. The first of these issues relates to the category of NWLI and the problem of institution-building; the latter two issues provide a basis for a more elaborate exposition of two core components of the argument outlined in chapter 1: the relevance of *legacies* inherited from past communities of work, and the availability of diverse *managerial strategies* insofar as these reflect approximations of the ideal-typical institution-building strategies.

Section 2.4 revisits the argument constructed in this book while relating the broader themes discussed in this chapter to the historical referents invoked in chapters 3 and 4. This section includes a more elaborate discussion of how large differences in levels of managerial authority may be approximated through attitudes and behaviors that speak to different levels of worker commitment. It also elaborates on the logic of congruence that is invoked to render plausible the main contention in this book concerning the relative merits of syncretist institution-building.

2.1. Universalist Images of Modern Firms and Organizations

Although the term *modernity* was never employed by the founders of political economy and sociology in eighteenth- and nineteenth-century Europe, their writings anticipated many of the features that later scholars would associate with the term. Well-known arguments about the sources of individual motivation, the benefits and pitfalls of rationalization and specialization, and the relationships between technology, ideas, interests, and institutions all have their roots in the writings of these earlier European writers. This section traces the logic of such arguments across different eras and branches of scholarship, identifying the features that reveal universalist assumptions about social and organizational change.

The Ambivalent European Heritage

The most unequivocally positive interpretations of the inevitability and functionality of specialization in economy and society are perhaps those found in the writings of Adam Smith and Herbert Spencer. In *The Wealth of Nations,* Smith was among the first to draw attention to the productivity gains from increased specialization through his famous example of how "dexterity" (the efficient deployment of skills) in pin-making could be improved by breaking the process into eighteen distinct operations, thereby permitting the application of simpler skills and enabling savings of time.[5] Although Smith did have concerns about what the costs of dexterity would be for the worker's mental state, he had already anticipated a core idea in nineteenth-century social theory: that progress depended upon "differentiation," the evolution of an increasingly complex division of labor driven by increasing numbers of distinct units performing increasingly specialized roles.[6]

For Spencer, whose view of change reflected the impact of Darwin's writings on evolution, differentiation was the engine for transforming primitive "militant" societies into more complex "industrial" societies (in much the same manner that single-celled organisms evolved into progressively larger and more complex life forms). Differentiation, for Spencer, was also functionally linked to the decentralization of political structures, the emergence of multiple layers of bureaucracies to coordinate and integrate activities in society, the protection of individual and local rights, an accompanying increase in individual creativity and diversity of thought, and the shift from status to class, with the middle class thought to play a particular dynamic role. Thus emerged an elaborate theory of unidirectional social evolution in which the shift to industrialism was inevitably accompanied by the simultaneous and interrelated processes of differentiation, bureaucratization, decentralization, and individuation.[7]

Theorists whose formative intellectual experiences were on the European continent (rather than in Britain), however, were more sanguine about the implications of differentiation for the human condition.[8] Marx's theory of history focused on progressively more efficient modes of production punctuated by revolutionary class struggle. While offering an elaborate critique of capitalism in the process, Marx also shared Smith's faith in the benefits of maximal differentiation in production processes: In *Capital,* he contended that the same machines that enabled the bourgeoisie to enslave workers under capitalism could, following the abolition of private property, also serve to simplify production to such an extent that individuals would be able to increase the time spent on leisure or self-enrichment as they speedily accomplished a variety of equally simple tasks without the discipline of material inducements and sanctions.[9] At the same time, Marx's analysis of the labor process under industrial capitalism also anticipated a central theme in twentieth-century critiques of scientific management: that the breakdown of the production process into specialized tasks under industrial capitalism was devised in part to enable employers to better monitor and control workers while more uniformly subjecting them to the stern "discipline of the barracks."[10]

Durkheim's view of differentiation built on Spencer's social evolutionism, but where Spencer was more concerned with the implications of industrialism for individuation and the dispersal of power, Durkheim paid closer attention to the psychological needs of individuals and the role of shared meanings in enabling "solidarity" in social life. Thus, for Durkheim, the emergence of complex, highly differentiated societies suggested neither the arrival of the confident, self-reliant individual glorified by Spencer nor the painful loss of community feared by Ferdinand Tönnies;[11] instead, Durkheim treated solidarity as a *universal* prerequisite for social coherence and psychological stability, while differentiating the "mechanical solidarity" based on the likeness of roles among members of communities from the "organic solidarity" arising from the functional interdependence among self-aware individuals, each adopting a specialized role in an increasingly complex division of labor.[12] At the same time, writing on continental Europe at a time when the social tensions accompanying industrialization were in full view, Durkheim questioned the ease with which organic solidarity would be reconstructed in the course of differentiation, fearing that "society's insufficient presence in the individual" could lead to the spread of *anomie,* manifested in such disturbed individual behaviors as suicide.[13] In the end, however, Durkheim feared that an increasingly complex and specialized division of labor was inevitable and necessary in view of the needs of an increasingly dense population, and he put his faith in the occupational group in which individuals could discharge their particular responsibilities while learning to view their interdependence as a meaningful and moral one rather than an isolating and anomic one.[14]

Weber's treatment of social change reflected neither the economic determinism of Smith and Marx nor the evolutionary functionalism of Spencer or Durkheim, but his view of rationalization suggested a general world-historical trend involving increasing complexity and bureaucratization in various spheres of society—political (the growth of rational-legal forms of authority), economic (the emergence of rationalized cost-accounting), and sociocultural (the secularization of religious beliefs). Weber's ideal-typical articulation of "rational-legal" authority and "rational" types of social action also provided the foundations for much of the subsequent literature on firms and organizations.[15] In regard to the process of differentiation, Weber specifically noted that "the specialization of functions . . . is crucial to the modern development of the organization of labor."[16] While he never asserted that differentiation inevitably paved the way for uniform material and ideal structures, his discussion of the role of ideas suggested certain constraints in terms of what kinds of values could coexist with what modes of economic activity.[17] Thus, Weber's thesis in *The Protestant Ethic,* despite his own qualifications about its generalizability, paved the way for the assumption in later social theory that the evolution of bureaucratic rationalism and industrial capitalism went hand in hand with secularization and individuation.[18]

Although Weber once proclaimed that "the future belongs to bureaucratization,"[19] like Durkheim, he had his own concerns about the consequences of rationally administered societies for the individual. He not only feared that bureaucratization could lead to administrative secrecy and the subversion of democracy, he also worried that individuals entering a rationalized, demystified, bureaucratic organization could be trapped in an "iron cage," becoming little more than "a single cog in an ever-moving mechanism which prescribes to him an essentially fixed route."[20] Within the context of industrial labor, Weber feared that as production became more rationalized, subordinates would come to perform more minutely specialized tasks, subsequently becoming powerless in the labor market, increasingly unable to maintain their formally equal status in contracts entered into with superiors.[21] Thus, Weber was acutely aware that the gains to efficiency from mechanization and rationalization in production could come at a high price. As he himself put it:

> An inanimate machine is mind objectified. Only this provides it with the power to force men into its service and to dominate their everyday working life as completely as is actually the case in the factory. Objectified intelligence is also that animated machine, the bureaucratic organization with its specialization of trained skills, its division of jurisdiction, its rules and hierarchical relations of authority. Together with the inanimate machine it is busy fabricating the shell of bondage which men will perhaps be forced to inhabit some day.[22]

Several decades later, the ambivalent treatment of industrial capitalism seen in Marx, Durkheim and Weber would give way to an unequivocal narrative about the promise of modernity and the triumph of technology and rationality in the United States. The conflation of history and progress in Smith and Marx, the evolutionary functionalism of Spencer and Durkheim, and Weber's conceptualization of rational administration all provided the foundations for a new model of the modern organization as a complex, bureaucratic entity that was a uniform, inevitable, and universal concomitant of new technologies and new social structures. However, the anxieties about modern forms of organization evident in the writings of Marx, Durkheim, and Weber also provided the point of departure for new perspectives that were more attentive to the implications of the boundedness of rationality for the psychology and behavior of subordinates, and that subsequently promoted new techniques for eliciting the cooperation of subordinates in a complex organizational environment. More critical perspectives viewed bounded rationality as the basis upon which the owners of the means of production sought to refine their methods for controlling and monitoring subordinates in the production process. Other approaches, building largely upon Durkheim's notion of anomie and Weber's fear of an "iron cage," focused on the universal social or psychological needs of individuals in organizational environments. Still others developed standard classificatory schemes for capturing limited variations in administrative structures each of which had specific consequences for organizational efficiency across diverse social settings. Despite their differences, all of these approaches interpreted the experiences of large-scale bureaucratic firms in the West as indicative of standard, uniform processes and dilemmas related to the evolution of technology and differentiation everywhere. The remainder of this section reviews these different universalist treatments of modern firms and organizations as captured in the four stylized propositions presented in figure 5.

Technology, Efficiency, and Convergence: Industrialization and "Industrial Man"

In addition to the influence of Weber's ideal-type of the rational-legal bureaucracy, the first models of firms and organizations in the United States were heavily influenced by the writings of Frederick Taylor and Thorstein Veblen, and by the consolidation of "scientific management" in large-scale firms during the early twentieth century (discussed in a historical context in section 2.2). This influence came to be evident in a conception of social and organizational change that took for granted the inevitability and irreversibility of bureaucratization and differentiation, while relating these to industrialization, the advancement of technology, and the image of a uniformly rational "industrial man," operating in complex social and organizational "systems."

Although the spread of scientific management was a result of specific historical processes, Taylor himself conceived of it as a model of management that was primarily informed not by empirical investigation but by abstract universal principles about the nature of individual behavior and bureaucratic systems.[23] With a background in mechanical engineering in an era when engineers were becoming increasingly important in the administration of industrial production, Taylor set out to challenge traditional schemes of collective remuneration and group responsibility in work organization which he held to be the reasons for free-riding, soldiering, and poor performance on the shopfloor. In a paper delivered in 1895, Taylor insisted on the need to "scientifically" measure and standardize time and output norms in relation to individual tasks, while invoking sharply differentiated piece rates to reward optimal performance and punish sub-par work. Thus, in contrast to traditional wage schemes (such as those introduced by Henry Towne and Frederick Halsey in the metalworking industry) which relied on past experiences to establish output norms, Taylor called for precise time-and-motion studies to determine absolute standards of productivity as a basis for wage differentials.[24]

Taylor subsequently went on to articulate an all-encompassing model of factory administration and shopfloor organization. This model called

1. *Universalism and convergence:* The division of labor is marked by increasing differentiation and bureaucratization (Smith, Spencer, Durkheim, Weber): higher levels of technology and differentiation are correlated with higher efficiency gains through individualized tasks and incentives (Taylor, Veblen, Woodward, Thompson, etc.) and with greater individuation and adaptability (Parsons, Inkeles and Smith), leading to convergence across industrialized societies (Kerr et al., Zweig, Blauner, Bell) and, more recently, across post-Fordist systems of flexible specialization and lean production (Piore and Sabel, Womack et al., Adler, Kenney and Florida).

2. *Broader technologies of organization and control:* Positive interpretation emphasizes strategies to cope with cognitive uncertainties, bounded rationality and organizational slack by invoking sanctions and inducements to elicit greater support for organizational goals from otherwise indifferent subordinates (Simon, Cyert and March); Negative interpretation of this same process, inspired by Marx, views key aspects of labor process as means of controlling and monitoring subordinates (Braverman, Edwards) or more subtly manufacturing consent (Burawoy); also extended to critique system of lean production (Parker and Slaughter; J. Price; Rinehart et al.).

3. *Human side of organizations:* These approaches, partly influenced by Durkheim and Weber, emphasize standard social and psychological needs of subordinates for purpose of enhancing productivity and sense of satisfaction among employees. Includes Mayo and human relations school, as well as Tavistock Institute approach (Bion, Miller, Trist et al.) and later discussions of quality of working life based on attending to higher needs of employees (Maslow, Argyris, Likert, McGregor); most recent incarnation is the literature touting universal *social* benefits of Japanese style of management and lean production (Drucker, Ouchi, Kenney and Florida, Adler).

4. *Constrained universalism:* Critiques of universal assumptions about organizational rationality and individual motivations, but possibilities of variation sharply circumscribed by focus on standard classifications. Examples include classifications of complex organizations in terms of the extent of hierarchical control, forms of employee involvement, and the balance of material and moral inducements (Gouldner, Etzioni, Blau); more recent organizational models based on East Asian firms (Ouchi, Hamilton and Biggart); discrete structural alternatives for minimizing transaction costs in view of existing technologies, asset types, and market conditions (Williamson).

Fig. 5.   Universalist logics in the analysis of "modern" institutions

for separating mental and manual labor, distinguishing between direct production tasks and support or maintenance tasks, expanding the number of personnel in charge of coordination and monitoring, and breaking down production into the most elemental tasks and operations (each linked to a single individual), so that managers would be able to minimize the skill requirements for any task, reduce job-learning times, and more precisely monitor and reward individual performance. Within the Taylor system, the principle of piece-rate wages was incorporated into an elaborate incentive system, based on supposedly objective norms of production for discrete individualized tasks. This system would enable managers to more objectively identify the "first-class" worker and match individual skills to production tasks; thus, positive evaluations and correspondingly higher earnings indicated a suitable correspondence of skills and tasks, while negative evaluations resulted in sharp reductions in wages that would force workers with the "wrong" abilities to "voluntarily" quit.[25] Though he realized that workers would initially resist the implementation of these principles, Taylor conceived of his system of scientific management as the "one best way" for factory administration, precluding the arbitrary judgments and petty politics that he thought to be the basis for industrial conflict.[26]

Veblen, a great admirer of Taylor, viewed the principles of scientific management through a wider lens, as a basis for the most efficient possible appropriation of personnel and technology in society at large. His numerous publications and his attempts to mobilize the American Society of Mechanical Engineers for social and political action helped draw attention to the broader implications of scientific management for the perfection of industrial administration. Although Veblen also flirted with racial and cultural categories in evaluating the efficacy of scientific management in different contexts, his primary contribution to organization theory was to cast in theoretical terms the functionality of linking particular technologies to particular forms of bureaucratic administration so as to maximize the efficiency with which these technologies were appropriated by disciplined, trained individuals. In this regard, just as Taylor saw middle-class professionals as the most industrious segment of society, Veblen condemned the undisciplined life-styles and wasteful "conspicuous consumption" of the leisure class while praising the natural "instinct of workmanship" that was only evident among industrious workers and only appreciated by engineers.[27]

The core assumptions of Taylor and Veblen became incorporated into a more grand, all-encompassing sociological project as a result of the efforts of Talcott Parsons. Parsons not only viewed himself as the leading American authority on Weber's work, but was also, like Veblen, an admirer of Taylor.[28] Most important for the purposes of understanding Parsons's influence on social science disciplines in the United States were two noteworthy conceptual schemes that were to be uncritically accepted as the foundations of what became known as the "modernization paradigm."[29] First, there was the notion of *functional equilibrium:* societies were treated as whole, coherent *systems* that could only remain stable as long as there was an equilibrium among their constituent subsystems (behavioral, social, cultural, and personality), each of which structured individual actions and dispositions in particular ways that fulfilled crucial *functions* (adaptation, goal orientation, integration, and latency) for the social system as a whole.[30]

Second, Parsons introduced a set of five dichotomous "pattern-variables" that supposedly constituted two, and only two, mutually exclusive systems of action and coordination in equilibriated social systems: particularism, self-orientation, affectivity, ascriptive evaluation, and functional diffuseness would define traditional systems of social action, while universalism, collectivity-orientation, affective neutrality, achievement-based evaluation, and functional specificity would define modern systems.[31] The latter set of pattern-variables represented Parsons's formalization of what was left implicit in Spencer and Durkheim: that differentiation (the rise of functional specificity), individuation (the emergence of a self-orientation) and the rise of a universal type of rationally administered, bureaucratic pattern of organization (the emergence of achievement-based evaluation and affective neutrality) were all functionally interrelated.[32] Thus, Parsons's theoretical edifice effectively transformed Weber's traditional and rational-legal *ideal-types* of authority into *real* endpoints of a universal process of evolutionary change.[33] Not altogether surprisingly, at the end of this process lay a uniform model of a modern industrial society the defining features of which were thought to have emerged already in the United States and Britain.

For nearly a quarter century following World War II, social scientists in a variety of disciplines invoked Parsons's system of concepts and his evolutionary epistemology in interpreting the processes of modernization as they were unfolding in different parts of the world. Scholars differed in terms of the causal sequences they analyzed, the particular pattern-variables they emphasized, and the extent to which they anticipated problems, delays, or tensions in the processes of modernization. But they accepted as

a common assumption that modernization consisted of several functionally interrelated transformations that would produce a convergence across
all stable social systems, with the processes of industrialization and differentiation accompanied by social mobilization, the expansion of literacy
and mass communication, the secularization of traditional cultural beliefs,
the emergence of a more pluralistic political culture, and the appearance of
a new, achievement-oriented individual capable of taking on modern attitudes, roles, and identities. The various economic, political, social, and
cultural transformations experienced by earlier industrializers were viewed
not as products of historical circumstances but as the manifestations of a
universal process of evolutionary change that later industrializers, too,
would eventually follow. The survival of preexisting social or cultural features, or mixtures of traditional and modern elements from both sets of
pattern-variables, were automatically interpreted as indications of incomplete transitions.[34]

In analyses of firms and industrial relations, these assumptions about
the nature of modernization combined with the rationalism underlying the
managerial revolution in the United States to inspire a number of theories
predicting convergence across industrial societies and worker attitudes.
Clark Kerr and his colleagues, for example, contended that industrialization processes spurred the emergence of "industrial man," a modern type
of individual who was well adjusted to the requirements and expectations
of life in industrial factories and industrial society; moreover, the common
experience of industrial labor and the growing number of increasingly specialized jobs would enable individual workers to climb higher along separate job ladders, thereby reducing their propensity to strike and gradually
producing increasingly uniform social structures characterized by industrial peace and individual job satisfaction.[35] Others built on this thesis and
argued that increasing levels of wealth and the introduction of more
efficient technologies would enable the "embourgeoisement" of workers
across societies, reducing the material and social distance between the
middle class and the working class as the latter increasingly accepted the
former's image of the good life and sought to improve their lot through
individual efforts.[36] Applying a somewhat different logic, sociologists such
as Blauner fended off the challenges posed by Marx's alienation and
Durkheim's anomie, suggesting that the changing nature of work and
increasing level of technology enabled workers to supervise their machines
rather than be enslaved by them, giving them the satisfying experience of
exercising discretion much like their supervisors.[37]

Many comparative studies of industrial organization in late-industrializing societies also reflected an expectation of convergence across firms and organizational structures. Arthur Stinchcombe, although acknowledging that the persistence of traditional social relations would initially require adjustments to work processes, incentive systems, and role structures, ultimately viewed these adjustments as temporary measures to increase efficiency under suboptimal conditions until the crystallization of new values made possible the application of methods and inducements typical of firms and organizations in industrialized societies.[38] Others simply took for granted Veblen's view that the exposure of people to new technologies or institutional environments would serve to break down old habits and create the attitudes appropriate for disciplined, efficient industrial production. Inkeles and Smith, for example, assumed that standard methods of factory administration and the experience of timed, specialized industrial labor would turn the factory into a "school in modernity," as millions of uprooted workers gradually evolved into educated, self-oriented, individuals capable of meeting the demands of modern production in a disciplined and efficient manner.[39]

Among many organization theorists, too, it came to be frequently assumed that the progress of technology and increasing differentiation were irreversible and that these processes were inextricably linked to an eventual convergence in the size, structure, and practices of organizations.[40] The specific advantages of differentiated organizational structures were thought to everywhere include the rearrangement of roles and tasks for the maximally efficient pursuit of goals, economies in recruitment and training, better assessment of performance and promotions, more effective decision making in relation to fewer goals and tasks, and the improved capacity for adapting to changing circumstances.[41] In effect, Taylor's principles of scientific management, Veblen's technological determinism, and Parsons's evolutionary functionalism paved the way for the tendency to view characteristics of firms and industrial relations in the West as universal, uniform components of modernity everywhere.

Beyond Rationality: Broader Technologies of
Organization and Control

During the 1940s and 1950s, however, some organization theorists had come to be troubled by the unqualified assumptions of rationality and uniformity in the images of organizations offered by Taylor, Veblen, and modernization theory. This marked the beginning of various alternative strands of analysis rooted in a different set of assumptions about the social and psychological aspects of organizational life. One strand is evident in the formulation of broader, more nuanced perspectives on firms and organizations inspired in part by Chester Barnard's *The Functions of the Executive,* which had been published just before World War II and which emphasized the importance of combining material inducements with indoctrination so that informal groups formed by subordinates could be enlisted to direct their energies toward the achievement of common goals.[42] This view essentially called into question the assumption, evident in the writings of Taylor and Veblen, that formal administrative hierarchies, maximally differentiated production processes, and material inducements would suffice to elicit disciplined and efficient contributions on the part of subordinates. At the same time, however, efficiency continued to be viewed as the paramount goal, attainable through universally applicable strategies for improving the productivity of individuals and the effectiveness of organizations.

In this context, the contributions of Herbert Simon, James March, and Richard Cyert are particularly noteworthy. Simon famously argued that managers generally tended not to optimize but, rather, to "satisfice" in an environment of "bounded rationality" characterized by imperfect information and unclear lines of communication.[43] Similarly, in their classic study of industrial firms, Cyert and March introduced the concept of "organizational slack" to capture the inefficiencies, irrationalities, and competing interest coalitions that regularly contributed to suboptimal outcomes in typical firms.[44] Significantly, although both of these approaches questioned the image of the perfectly rational organization capable of delivering optimal efficiency, they did so in a manner that emphasized essentially similar kinds of limitations on rationality, implying that there existed similar kinds of solutions for optimizing organizational efficacy under these limitations. Simon, for example, continued to view higher levels of differentiation as crucial to all modern organizations since it served to define specific roles, standardize goals and practices, restrict choices and tasks, simplify information and communication, and better socialize and evaluate individuals. While paying greater attention to cognitive aspects of decision making than Taylor had done, Simon, March, and their colleagues continued to search for a more comprehensive "technology of organization" that would yield standardized decision-rules through which to engineer support for organizational goals from the "zones of indifference" inhabited by uncommitted subordinates.[45]

This perspective on technologies of organization, however, also gave rise to new concerns about the autonomy and status of subordinates in organizations. For some organization theorists, most notably William H. Whyte, while the broader technologies of organization envisioned by Simon and March may have improved control from above, they also served to ensure rigid conformity and the disciplined execution of narrow tasks while suppressing individual creativity and initiative.[46] Similarly, Marxist critics of capitalist labor relations argued that the level of specialization in work organization and the narrowing of job descriptions were partly a result of the search for mechanisms for achieving more effective managerial control over the activities of employees, sharply circumscribing the latter's autonomy and reducing the value of their preexisting skills.[47] Other critical treatments were more nuanced, some acknowledging the opportunities workers may find to informally exercise greater autonomy by taking advantage of ambiguities in instructions or negotiating understandings with lower-echelon supervisors, and others focusing on how governmental regulation of labor-capital relations affects the organization of labor processes across production regimes.[48] But, important variations notwithstanding, these various critiques shared a similar concern that the broader "technologies of organization" through which superordinates might seek to get the most out of subordinates would result in a different sort of convergence: the disappearance of whatever skills, autonomy, and creativity the latter had left.

More interestingly, at a more abstract level, these critical naratives also happen to share with Simon and March a universalist template through which to identify and interpret the most significant dynamics within firms and organizations: in this template, variations across historical contexts are deemed to be epistemologically less significant than the fundamental tensions in the relationship between superordinates and subordinates as the former seek to motivate the latter to achieve organizational goals. For Simon and March, this was a matter of devising strategies for coping with indifference or organizational slack from above; for their various critics, it was a matter of the uniform effects of these strategies on the autonomy and involvement of subordinates in firms and organizations.[49]

The Human Side of Organizations: Sociological and Psychoanalytic Perspectives

A different, but still universalist, approach to the social dynamics in firms and organizations can be traced back to the fears expressed by Durkheim about the negative implications of differentiation in the absence of sufficient organic solidarity. These fears were not unfamiliar to Parsons and the modernization theorists, but social disturbances and anomie were typically understood to be temporary difficulties to be encountered in the course of industrialization until new mechanisms of integration emerged.[50] Parsons himself dealt with the question of how to preserve integration amid progressive differentiation virtually by fiat, contending that the emergence of free-market competition would serve to simultaneously enhance organizational adaptability and enable greater cooperation among members of firms in the pursuit of organizational goals.[51] These putative solutions to the problem of integration, however, did not require a fundamental shift in the theoretical assumptions of modernization theory since they interpreted social tensions and anomie as indicative of the *process* of modernization rather than as an ongoing dilemma to be solved in modern institutional settings.

It is precisely this dilemma that Elton Mayo and several of his contemporaries set out to empirically examine largely outside of the framework of modernization theory, with the Hawthorne studies representing the most well-known of the resulting investigations. The subsequent crystallization of the "human relations" school reflected a different kind of reaction to Durkheim's concerns about anomie and to Barnard's insights into the behavior of subordinates in bureaucratic organizations. In contrast to Simon, who inferred from Barnard's analysis the importance of combining positive and negative sanctions with normative appeals to motivate subordinates, Mayo and proponents of the human relations approach focused on the role of the work environment in generating a meaningful and integrated community, relegating the question of inducements or sanctions to the background.

Mayo himself was explicitly preoccupied with Durkheim's problem of anomie, hoping to find a substitute for the sense of "lost community" that he felt pervaded the American work force ever since the crafts tradition went into decline. In marked contrast to Simon, Mayo did not fear the indifference of subordinates, believing that "the eager human desire for cooperative activity still persists in the ordinary person and can be utilized by intelligent and straightforward management." In fact, he argued that it was precisely by drawing upon the "spontaneity of cooperation, that is teamwork" that alienative indifference could be mitigated while making subordinates more emotionally satisfied and productive.[52] Other members of the human relations school were less concerned about anomie and much more concerned about employee productivity; nevertheless, they shared the general view that the appearance of increasingly large, complex institutions brought with it a distinctive set of social problems and managerial challenges that Taylor had not anticipated; achieving productivity under these conditions required more energetic efforts to provide a greater sense of participation and emotional satisfaction for subordinates.[53] As one advocate of human relations put it: "To increase productivity, heighten job satisfaction, and raise the level of employee morale, it is necessary to arouse the intelligent interest of the employee. It is urgent to enlist his feelings as well as his ability in his work."[54]

Extending beyond the human relations school, other strands of organization theory proceeded on the basis of psychological investigations into the emotional needs and unconscious dispositions of individuals in firms and organizations. In Britain, members of the Tavistock Institute of Human Relations adopted a distinctive psychoanalytic approach emphasizing the manner in which the psychodynamics of organizations detracted from the functionality of individuals and the effectiveness of organizations; their objective was to explore not only the relationship between the worker and the work environment (as Mayo had sought to do) but also the manner in which "people internalized the feel or character of the groups in which they worked, while projecting their unconscious hopes and anxieties into the group."[55] Around the same time, in the United States, a great deal of attention was generated by Abraham Maslow's behavioral analysis of a "hierarchy of needs" which suggested the importance of satisfying not only the needs of physical security but the higher social needs for self-esteem and "self-actualization" in the workplace.[56]

These psychoanalytic approaches to organizations, whatever their differences, collectively paved the way for a new generation of studies during the 1960s and 1970s that took Mayo's concerns one step further, emphasizing not only improvements in the work environment but the "humanization" of work itself through the delegation of more varied tasks and greater responsibilities to subordinates. It was thought that this would make employees a more integrated part of the organization, improve their sense of satisfaction with their working lives, and enable them to satisfy their needs as members of organizations.[57] More recent efforts to cope with the problem of meaning in the workplace are evident in recent treatments of "lean production" that attempt to combine attention to the technological and organizational imperatives of a postindustrial era with a recognition of the emotional benefits of job redesign, team-oriented work organization, and increased participation.[58]

These various efforts to characterize and help resolve the social and psychological dilemmas faced by individuals in modern organizations are considered further in the historical discussion of Western firms and management practices (section 2.2). Here, the significance of these different kinds of organizational analysis lies in the manner in which they collectively serve as an important corrective to the image of modern firms, whether as unitary actors in which individuals play specific roles in a rationalized system of administration, or as boundedly rational organizations in which material and moral inducements are needed to secure the cooperation of subordinates. At the same time, however, the human relations school in the United States, the Tavistock Institute in Britain, and the later proponents of the "humanization of work" all remained concerned with universal characteristics of industrial work, all interpreted the particular conditions present in American or British industry following World War II as indicative of standard social problems in all industrial societies, and all presumed that the solutions to these problems lay in essentially similar transformations of the work environment across societies.

Constrained Universalism: Classifying
Organizational Structures

A fourth universalist approach to the analysis of firms and organizations recognized the possibility of diverse organizational structures under similar economic and technological conditions, but limited the diversity to a fairly restricted set of alternatives based on uniform principles of classification. Many organizational sociologists who were contemporaries of Parsons, Mayo, and Simon were not content to simply note the limits of rationality or the need for meaning; they preferred to examine the implications of particular kinds of variations in organizational structures related to the extent of hierarchical coordination or the kinds of incentives and sanctions in similarly differentiated environments. This was a significant shift in the analysis of complex firms and organizations, one that remains in evidence today in important strands of organizational economics and economic sociology. Yet, it is important to note that the primary goal was to identify standard schemes for classifying and comparing the dynamics of modern institutions without reference to historical processes or wider social contexts. Hence, this perspective is categorized here as "constrained universalism."

Two early examples of this approach were evident in Alvin Gouldner's distinction between "punishment-centered" and "representative" bureaucracy and Amitai Etzioni's contrasts between organizations invoking varying combinations of "moral," "calculative," and "alienative" involvement among members.[59] In a somewhat different vein, Peter Blau devised a typology of organizations based on different levels of autonomy and control, while Hage and Aiken examined the implications of different distributions of power for other aspects of organizational structure, both suggesting the possibilities for important structural variations within equally complex organizations.[60] These treatments did not assume that a particular organizational structure was universally determined by technology or by the requirements of large organizations, but at the same time they downplayed historical or cultural contexts in favor of universally applicable categories for comparing organizations. While "constrained universalism" represents a significant departure from the other three perspectives outlined above, it is still significant that the sources of variation were confined to ahistorical, idealized contrasts in such standard variables as the degree of hierarchy, the mode of involvement, or the balance of material and moral inducements.[61]

More recently, organization economists such as Williamson have challenged uniform models of the market-coordinated firm and have instead focused on variations across organizational forms. The emphasis is on distinguishing firms and organizations in terms of the extent to which they rely on hierarchical governance structures in attempting to minimize asset-specific transaction costs and to reduce "cognitive uncertainty" in market environments.[62] Such approaches take their cue from Coase and Schumpeter, who long ago stressed the necessity of higher levels of coordination and cooperation within firms for innovation and economic growth,[63] and from business historians such as Chandler who traced the increasing importance of hierarchical coordination within American multidivisional firms in response to new technologies, new systems of cost and control, and the rapid expansion of mass production and distribution at the turn of the century.[64] In a similar vein, economic sociologists have recently offered new models of organizations that generalize from the features of successful industrial or bureaucratic organizations in East Asia; these features are viewed not as responses to particular historical or social contexts but as elements of more widely replicable organizational structures that can enable more effective coordination and greater efficiency in the achievement of organizational goals.[65] All of these approaches, too, reflect cases of "constrained universalism" in that they reflect possibilities for limited variation across modern firms and organizations employing similar technologies, but the variation is limited to alternative models whose effectiveness may be gauged by relating specific differences in organizational form to specific benefits in an environment marked by uncertainty.

Beyond Universalism: Historical Context and
Organizational Variation

The various strands of social and organizational analysis reviewed in this section, despite their differences, have all taken for granted the fact that for any given technology or environment, there exist certain standard administrative imperatives that point to specific organizational responses, even if one takes into account the constraints posed by bounded rationality, cognitive uncertainty, or the emotional needs of individuals. Moreover, all of these approaches have tended to treat the social dynamics manifested in Western firms and organizations as universal features of modern organizational life, discounting variation resulting from historical processes or diverse cultural contexts. Given the objectives and contexts in which students of firms and organizations were writing, this was not necessarily a problem. For most, the unit of analysis was the firm or the organization, and so it was only reasonable to emphasize the general at the expense of the particular. Indeed, to some extent, the technologies of industrial production *do* require a more complex division of labor and a more elaborate system of supervision than was possible in simple agrarian communities; uncertainty and bounded rationality *do* require more proactive efforts to overcome indifference among subordinates; there *are* important social and psychological benefits to be derived from the "humanization of work"; and the extent of autonomy or the balance of material and moral inducements *do* have some standard implications for the nature of employee involvement.

There are, however, significant intellectual gains to be had from widening the scope of comparison and searching for further sources of variation in firms and organizations across different societies, particularly where some of the assumptions informing studies of Western firms and organizations cannot be automatically assumed to hold. This is very much the case in the study of industrial enterprises in NWLIs, where the overall rise in production and the preservation of social stability tend to be regarded by political and economic elites as no less significant than the maximization of efficiency or productivity at the individual level. To examine more carefully the potential sources of organizational variation in NWLIs, it is worth considering four other stylized sets of propositions found in the literature on industrialization, firms, and organizations (see fig. 6). These perspectives collectively represent the point of departure for the argument in this book.

The four stylized propositions are treated here as benchmarks in the study of organizational variation, each identifying a distinctive source of variation, and each accounting for progressively greater levels of heterogeneity across firms characterized by similar technological and organizational imperatives. The first, elaborated upon in section 2.2, sets the stage for the others by emphasizing the historical specificity of the processes that led to the emergence of modern models of management in the West, particularly in the United States. The other three propositions, considered in section 2.3, emphasize respectively the imperatives associated with late-industrializer effects, the role of distinctive historical and cultural influences on organizational styles or patterns of management, and the importance of leadership strategies in the building of organizations infused with meaning and purpose. These latter two dynamics also provide the basis for a more elaborate examination of the core components of the theoretical argument in this book.

2.2.   Western Management Models in Historical Context: The Case for Exceptionalism

The image of modern institutions as complex, differentiated, rationally administered organizations was largely informed by the emergence of large-scale enterprises in the West, especially in the United States, where, indeed, the widespread establishment of Taylorist scientific management and Fordist assembly-line manufacturing appeared to represent an ideal system of mass production. It is an open question, however, as to whether the specific assumptions, ideals, and practices identified with large industrial firms in the United States represent portable features of a universal model of industrial production. The point of departure for the comparative study in this book is a set of arguments advanced by several noted students of industrial relations: that technological determinism cannot in and of itself account for all of the particular features identified with Taylorism

1. *Exceptionalism of Western experience:* The particular experiences of industrialization and scientific management in the U.S., and later, Europe— including the ideal of rational administration, the high degree of specialization, assembly-line mass production, and the focus on individual productivity and material inducements—are a result of the convergence of historical processes, political struggles, and the emergence of individualism (Bendix, W. Moore, Maier, Sabel, Rueschemeyer, Guillen); later appeal of human relations, quality of working life approach, and lean production models represent historically contingent adjustments to change (Guillen, Turner and Auer, Thomas).

2. *Systematic variation from late-developer effects:* Emphasizes that imperatives of development in late industrializers are distinctive, requiring proactive strategy that protects domestic industry and enables accumulation of capital (Fichte, List, Hirschman, Gerschenkron); catching up involves a higher level of coordination or administrative guidance on the part of a developmental state (Johnson, Wade, Evans); at the level of the firm, these logics, together with the premium placed on stability and the absence of individualism, necessitate organizational features and management practices that are appreciably distinct from the market-oriented firm in Britain or U.S. (Dore 1973).

3. *Historical sources of variation:* A more total rejection of universalist propositions in figure 5; emphasizes further variations across regions and societies as evident in influence of preexisting historical or cultural inheritances on distinctive content of organizational ideologies and routines, and on distinctive worldviews and behaviors of superordinates and subordinates in similarly complex, bureaucratic institutions (Bendix, Aiken and Bacharach; Crozier, Cole, Dore, Thomas, Tilly and Tilly).

4. *Variations linked to leadership strategies:* Institution-level or firm-level analysis that generally emphasizes the possibilities for variations as a result of choices and strategies adopted by superordinates within particular environments and organizational contexts (Child, Selznick); one strand emphasizes whether and how administrative strategies address organizational gestalts imported into formal organization from the wider social environment (partly anticipated in Barnard, most explicit in Selznick).

Fig. 6. Sources of variation across firms and organizations

and Fordism; that many of these features were shaped by specific historical processes as well as particular worldviews and cultural assumptions;
that even the selection of particular technologies was a contested process
affected by distinctive historical contexts; and that, as a result, the experiences of firms and managers in the West, particularly in the United States,
need to be considered exceptional in many respects.[66]

Historical Contingency in the Emergence of Scientific Management

During much of the nineteenth century, industrial manufacturing reflected
the persistence of preindustrial norms among workers and employers, as
well as periods of often violent social unrest triggered by efforts to impose
new patterns of work and authority. In the case of Britain, well into the
nineteenth century, industrial manufacturing was accompanied by a
reliance on traditional apprenticeship-based and kinship-based authority
systems, along with an emphasis on group cohesion and group-based
piecework.[67] Moreover, neither the patterns of work nor the systems for
enforcing labor discipline were "differentiated entirely from the more diffuse community ties of the pre-industrial social structure."[68] In the United
States as well, industrialization until the late nineteenth century consisted
of varied forms of production—ranging from the single-industry city and
large-scale textile mills to plantation production—in which a strong crafts
tradition dominated manufacturing, and age-old methods of accounting
obviated more centralized structures of control.[69]

With the appearance of *large-scale* enterprises toward the end of the
nineteenth century, however, the traditional solutions to problems of
recruitment and labor discipline become progressively more dysfunctional
from the point of view of a new class of professional engineers and managers hired by owners of the enterprises. Under these conditions, aspects
of workplace social relations that may have sufficed to maintain order in
early industrialization eventually turned into a barrier to the bureaucratization of enterprises. The initial reliance on kinship ties, the apprentice-
ship model, and the authority of the shop owner proved to be increasingly
incompatible with the larger, more specialized firms in which accuracy,
standardization, and a regular and steady pace of mechanized work came
to be valued more than individual initiative and pride in one's own tools.[70]
Thus, the process of rationalizing production and centralizing management structures brought with it new waves of social protest as artisans and

craftsmen were anxious about what the shift to mechanized work implied for the skills and tools of their trade.[71] Other, less skilled, categories of workers were frustrated by the gap between their own expectations and the authority claimed by a new class of professional managers who simply did not enjoy the kind of legitimacy previously enjoyed by paternalistic owner-managers. Not surprisingly, key segments of the working class in Britain and the United States resisted the introduction of new machinery and new authority structures, frequently engaging in community-based collective protest and violating labor discipline in the factories.[72] These conflicts and tensions suggest that the emergence of new managerial ideologies and practices in large-scale industrial enterprises was hardly a smooth or inevitable transformation as some accounts suggest.

Moreover, at the outset, neither the difficulties posed by preexisting norms and social ties nor the conflicts accompanying the introduction of new technologies and managerial hierarchies pointed to any single managerial solution as self-evident. In fact, while American managerial elites increasingly looked to Taylorist scientific management to restore order in the industrial enterprise, British managers opted for ad hoc ideological appeals and administrative measures to cope with specific problems, showing little interest in, and sometimes even resisting, standard models of scientific factory administration.[73] This suggests that the emergence of scientific management as a novel system of work organization and factory administration was not the inevitable product of a continuous, uncontested, uniform process of increasing rationalization. It was a product of specific historical factors *in the United States;* elsewhere in the West, the eventual adoption of similar management principles was a result of a variety of other historical factors, not the least of which were the pressures brought to bear by World War I as will be evident shortly.

As previously noted, Taylorism refers to the set of principles and techniques outlined by Frederick Taylor as a means for realizing progressively greater efficiency gains through specialized management structures, scientifically determined time and output norms, the division of production processes into elemental tasks, and differentiated wage structures designed to reward optimal individual productivity and sharply penalize subpar performance. Within the context of U.S. industry at the turn of the century, this meant a new role for a growing class of mechanical engineers and professional managers who would perform time-and-motion studies in basic work actions to define work organization, establish productivity standards, minimize training costs, and more precisely evaluate and reward individual productivity. Under the influence of the Taylor system, large enterprises throughout the United States proceeded to established new planning departments that would provide programmed instruction cards for each task, define standard time and output norms for thousands of distinct tasks, and employ competitive individual evaluations to determine material rewards and sanctions for each worker.[74]

Some of Taylor's contemporaries—most notably, railroad manager Harrington Emerson, mechanical engineer Frank Gilbreth, industrialist Henry Gantt, and consultant Charles Bedaux—raised questions about, and introduced variations on, specific aspects of the Taylor system. Emerson, for example, questioned whether the functional specialization of foremen was as effective as the introduction of a staff of specialists who could assist works managers or superintendents on the line. The Bedaux system attempted to achieve many of the same objectives Taylor sought to introduce through more gradual and subtle transformations of the labor process.[75] In the end, however, none of these alternatives challenged Taylor's basic assumptions about the efficiency gains from the scientific analysis of time and motion, the benefits of maximal specialization based on elemental tasks, the matching of individual abilities to the tasks, and the use of performance evaluations and material inducements to optimize individual productivity. Most of the proposed variants implemented by plants—most notably, the rejection of Taylor's insistence on several functionally distinct foremen to oversee separate aspects of coordination, control, and performance—reflected adaptations designed to ensure coordination and maintain a centralized line of authority between the shopfloor and upper management.[76] In fact, Gantt and Bedaux, in their own separate ways, ended up contributing to the widespread acceptance of scientific management principles among engineers and industrialists after Taylor's death in 1915, with Bedaux's consulting firm advising hundreds of U.S. businesses during the 1920s and 1930s.[77] These variants of scientific management, whatever their differences, collectively contributed to the internalization of what Bell has called "the cult of efficiency" in American industry, marked by a commonly held managerial belief in a single ideal system of rational administration for maximizing efficiency in production.[78]

Beyond the narrowly technical discussions among engineers, the wider popularity of the scientific management model was largely a result of the concomitant emergence of Fordist assembly-line mass production which essentially extended the logic behind Taylorism. Between 1908 and 1914, Henry Ford's Model T plant evolved into a model of modern mass production consisting of the standardization of parts and products, a mechanized assembly line, workers trained to perform specific individual tasks on that line, and a sharply differentiated wage structure related to higher levels of efficiency and productivity. Of particular significance here is the five-dollar day that Ford introduced in order to more than double the daily minimum wage for workers. This move did blunt the effects of the "sticks" that Taylor had viewed as essential in prompting inefficient workers to quit. However, the five-dollar day neither contradicted the basic principles of Taylorism nor reflected concerns for social justice; rather it enabled Ford and other employers to break down the resistance of workers and circumvent signing a contract with unions (until 1937), while expanding managerial control over production and dramatically economizing on the cost of labor per unit of production.[79] Thus, for most employers and managerial elites, scientific management became inextricably linked to the mass production technologies associated with Fordism; even in sectors and regions where the assembly-line system of production was not feasible, Fordism helped to turn the principles and techniques of scientific management into a powerful *ideal* of work organization throughout large firms in the United States and, later, across most of Europe as well.[80]

It is important to recognize here that the rationale and popularization of scientific management were only possible as a result of the confluence of a number of unanticipated historical processes. For one, Taylorism and Fordism gained widespread attention only as the wider economy was in the process of being dramatically transformed, with the appearance of increasingly diversified product lines, the completion of the construction of railroads, the expansion of a unified market, and the possibility of adopting economies of scale in the ensuing era of mass distribution and consumption.[81] Also, the adoption of Taylorism in the United States was initially accompanied by a high level of resistance from both crafts workers and union leaders for whom what was "scientific" happened to correspond all too frequently to the preferences of managers rather than to those of workers.[82] Hence, the implementation of scientific management practices became feasible only after the popularization of Fordism had helped to weaken the resistance of workers through the five-dollar day and only after new social pacts had been negotiated with the unions with the aid of an increasingly active U.S. government in the aftermath of World War I.[83] The convergence of interests among government and business elites, as well as the new package of welfare benefits they devised to cope with the growing trade union movement, were crucial for the widespread implementation of scientific management techniques during the 1920s. A significant role in this process was also played by union leaders, many of whom helped promote scientific management, believing that the growing number of ranks and job classifications would provide separate job ladders and reduce competition among workers for promotion.[84] Thus, the emergence of unified markets, the specific initiatives taken by Ford and other industrialists, the social pacts negotiated in the interwar period, and the strange role played by the unions during this period all combined to spur the acceptance of the ideals and practices associated with scientific management in the United States.

Elsewhere in the West, the adoption of scientific management was tied to quite different historical processes with World War I being a particularly important catalyst. To begin with, it was the images of mass production associated with Fordism, rather than the narrowly technical discourse of Taylorism, that drew the attention of European political elites and spurred the eventual acceptance of scientific management practices.[85] In the case of Britain, the initial resistance to Taylorism had been especially strong, and it came not only from workers, but *managers* as well! After all, the Industrial Revolution had first taken off in Britain, and British managers believed they had a competitive edge given their experience in pioneering new solutions to problems of administration long before Taylorism or Fordism appeared in the United States. It was only when World War I raised the stakes of economic competition in Europe that the technological and material promise identified with Taylorist-Fordist production began to make inroads into British industrial management; interestingly, the Fabian socialists (of all people) played a role in this process by joining with the Tories to encourage scientific management techniques to counter the growth of industrial power in Germany.[86]

By contrast, the competition with Britain actually pushed elites on the European continent to more quickly take notice of the latest managerial techniques being developed across the ocean. In Germany, the government, business conglomerates, industrial engineers, and even labor leaders collaborated to energetically promote the scientific management movement almost as soon as it had become established in the United States. In addition, during World War I, other U.S. allies (and after the war, Germany and Austria as well) began sending experts to the United States to study scientific management methods; Georges Clemenceau, then the French minister of war, even instructed military units to adopt Taylorist techniques.[87] After the war, the shortage of labor and the concomitant need to develop mass production and employ unskilled workers contributed to the further weakening of resistance to these methods. The subsequent mobilization for war production during the 1930s essentially resulted in a "radical Americanism" in managerial practice, including variants on the five-dollar day, although these practices were interpreted in terms of the particular ideological visions of the various national elites.[88] Finally, whatever resistance remained to scientific management virtually disappeared after World War II, when councils established by Marshall Plan agencies during postwar reconstruction actively promoted American management techniques along with social pacts to preempt opposition to these by the labor unions.[89]

The manner in which scientific management came to be established in Europe suggests two reasons for challenging the view of industrialization as an evolutionary, uniform process characterized by similar administrative prerequisites. First, the interest in scientific management in Europe was influenced by *external* factors, including the rising stakes of economic and military competition as well as the perception that the tremendous economic achievements of the United States were a result of the unyielding adherence to principles of technological rationality. Second, the selective adoption of Taylorism and Fordism within different national systems of production was mediated by particular political dynamics in the midst of new nationalist discourses and emerging systems of national planning.

At the same time, however, the assumptions behind scientific management were not entirely alien to most Europeans. While Taylor and Ford may have been Americans, the desire for efficiency, the faith in rational bureaucracy, the promise of technology, and the justification of the individual's desire for advancement through hard work and material gain were all part of an emergent Western worldview, a view that was largely anticipated in the writings of Smith, Spencer, Durkheim, Weber, and other Europeans. Moreover, in the United States and in Europe, the initial labor unrest spurred by the introduction of scientific management gave way to the presumption on the part of unions that aspects of scientific management enabled new possibilities for individual advancement without competition among workers. The presumption may have overlooked some of the costs of relying on competitive performance evaluations in determining rewards and promotion, but at the same time it demonstrated that many of the ideas and practices associated with Taylorism and Fordism cohered with aspects of quite familiar discourses about modernity, rationality, and the modern individual self. Hence the need to consider further the *cultural*

assumptions that may have influenced the character and eventual acceptance of these ideas and practices in much of the West.

*The Cultural Context: Individualism and Industrial Relations
in the West*

Any examination of the portability of Western management practices
requires considering the role played by a broadly individualistic cultural
ethos in influencing key assumptions in scientific management and in
enabling its eventual acceptance among the unions and the work force at
large. As noted in chapter 1, the distinction between individualism and
collectivism is an ideal-typical opposition of social values shared by the
members of some society, region, or institution: *individualism* refers
broadly to commonly held values and norms in a given society, region, or
institution that enable a person to be regarded in favorable terms for publicly justifying his/her action in terms of self-interest and self-expression,
whether material or ideal. While the category of individualism masks
important variations in specific norms and in the level to which these are
internalized by members of groups or institutions, it generally suggests a
higher valuation of the ontological primacy and sacredness of the individual person and, in more practical terms, a belief in the right of that person
to independently define, express, and advance his/her interests and personal goals.[90] In this sense, individualism does not necessarily suggest
intrinsically asocial or egoistic behavior; rather, it represents a recognizable shared template for identifying and rewarding social action justified
in terms of self-advancement. As such, it also provides a basis for a shared
civic identity in those Western institutions or societies where the core components of modernity were first articulated.[91]

The origins of individualism and its role in the emergence of industrial
capitalism have been the subjects of heated debate since the nineteenth
century. While these debates do not directly concern this book, the argument here is predicated on a qualified version of Weber's *Protestant Ethic*
thesis that incorporates points made by Weber's critics and defenders.
Weber's argument is understood here in the following terms: It may well
be that the Judeo-Christian religious tradition had always been more
favorable to this-worldly material pursuits than other world religions (e.g.,
Buddhism). It may also be that the recognition of the individual as a juridi-
cal entity in Roman law, the subsequent focus on the sacredness of the
individual in early Christianity, as well as the ideals of the Renaissance and

the Enlightenment all paved the way for a strong sense of self in Western civilization before the effects of the Protestant Reformation or Counter-Reformation were felt.[92] But, in the specific context of tracing the ideas that the first capitalist entrepreneurs invoked to justify their activities, it is the Calvinist doctrine of individual salvation as articulated in Britain and Holland that is most directly relevant. Smith's *Wealth of Nations* and the utilitarianism of Bentham and Mill had already provided tentative justifications for the pursuit of individual gain in terms of its contribution to the public good. However, among a nascent middle class that was seeking to define and justify a new way of life in a society still dominated by the vestiges of the old aristocratic order, it was still necessary for the individual pursuit of profit to be regarded as a virtuous, *moral* activity in its own right. Calvinism (and, later, Puritanism) suggested that religious duty mandated the greatest possible gain from work; material success was a sign that the chosen profession was the right one, and profit and its reinvestment represented a further contribution to the glory of God. This association of moral self-worth and this-worldly individual gain-seeking provided a way for entrepreneurs to buttress their authority as the owners and managers of factories while justifying their activities as captains of industry before the wider society. Thus, Calvin's conception of the "calling," while it did not "cause" capitalism, provided the new entrepreneurial class with a spiritual foundation for its material activities, helping to justify differences in wealth and status in terms of individual work for God and subsequently enabling the legitimation and spread of the institutions of industrial capitalism in the wider society.[93]

Within the particular context of industrial relations, the individualist ethic invoked by entrepreneurs into the mid–nineteenth century, because it was primarily designed to justify the role and authority of the first owner-employers in the eyes of both the work force and society at large, generally tended to focus not so much on the motivation of workers as on the achievements, independence, and initiative of the entrepreneurs themselves.[94] The wide popularity of Samuel Smiles's slogan of "self-help" and of Spencer's social Darwinism among the middle classes in Britain reflected the latter's own efforts to justify their wealth, social status, and superordinate role before a growing but still impoverished working class in a changing society. Similarly, in the United States, as Weber was fond of noting, Benjamin Franklin came to personify for the middle classes the systematic and rational pursuit of individual gain by the pious, sober, and creative entrepreneur. In both societies, these ideals and symbols were parts of an *entrepreneurial* ideology rather than a *managerial* one, focused not on inspiring efficiency on the shopfloor but on glorifying the individual achievement, creativity, personal character, and self-reliance of a new class of owner-employers.[95]

By the turn of the century, however, the emergence of the large-scale bureaucratized firm and the separation of ownership from professional management led to new problems and challenges as the new managerial class sought to justify their own authority as the overseers of industrial production among an increasingly large and specialized work force. This transformation did not necessitate a radical break with the earlier entrepreneurial ideologies, but it did require the adaptation of a Calvinist ethic in a manner that could provide industrial workers with their own template for understanding the very different forms of work they were beginning to encounter in the large-scale factory. The attention shifted away from the justification of disparities in wealth and status in terms of self-reliance and individual ingenuity, and toward the inherent sense of self-worth that came with fulfilling assigned tasks in a prompt and disciplined manner: in effect, to please God, work could not be casual or intermittent; it now had to be "methodical, disciplined, rational, uniform, and hence specialized work."[96]

In both Britain and the United States, this shift became evident in new conceptualizations of factory discipline even before Taylor or Ford appeared on the scene. With the expansion of industrial production and the growth of firms in the late nineteenth century, the liberal individualism of the middle class was transformed into an individualist work ethic designed to provide a substitute for the paternalistic forms of factory authority previously claimed by the owner-managers in smaller firms. The ideals associated with Smiles's self-help and Spencer's social Darwinism became transformed into new ideals emphasizing individual efficiency and achievement in any category of work, no matter how simple or how narrowly specialized. In the United States, this shift became most explicit with the appearance of the New Thought movement (between 1890 and 1914), which marked an explicit attempt to adapt the earlier ethos of individualism so as to emphasize the notion that success came to any who had a mental desire to be more productive in any type of endeavor, however great or small.[97] Similarly, in Britain, the individualistic ideology of a nascent middle class was now invoked not to justify the material and social distance between the employer and the subsistence wage–earning worker, but to make the attitudes of the latter correspond to those of the former while relentlessly attacking traces of "Idleness, Extravagance, Waste, and Immorality" (as one slogan put it).[98]

This trend was accelerated with the emergence of scientific management and the definitive separation of management from ownership, making it even more important for managers to develop new justifications for the increasingly complex system of work organization they were required to administer. For this purpose, the individual-centered definition of tasks, competitive performance evaluations, and productivity-related material inducements were all promoted by a new corps of engineer-managers as rational mechanisms to enable workers to realize their individual goals and personal ambitions.[99] Although Taylor did not concern himself with ideology given his faith in the universal benefits of scientific management, he shared the assumption that individuals could be motivated to perform assigned tasks in the most efficient manner possible so as to maximize material gain. As long as managers and engineers designed differentiated wage-scales and production processes on the basis of the "exact scientific knowledge," individual workers would have to look no further than their own abilities, desires, and performance in accounting for their rewards or lack thereof.[100] Thus, many of the defining aspects of the Taylor system— especially the extent of specialization, the one-to-one correspondence between narrowly specialized tasks and individual workers, and the use of sharply differentiated piece rate wages to optimize individual performance of a specific task—reflected an unquestioning faith in the idea that workers were universally responsive to opportunities to realize their personal ambitions and higher material rewards, regardless of their past experiences or cultural differences.[101]

At least as important is the fact that the ethos of individualism, although viewed with suspicion by workers during the nineteenth century, eventually came to be internalized at some level among the growing industrial work force across Western societies. In the United States, it has been suggested that Puritanism, together with the unique experiences of frontier-building among European settlers, produced a distinctive, rugged type of individualism.[102] While some have questioned whether the particularly radical strand of individualism in the United States still serves as a viable source of moral order and civic consciousness,[103] a host of empirical evidence generally corroborates the acceptance of an individualist work ethic among the American work force until well after World War II.[104] Despite their initial resistance to scientific management, most workers were found to be more or less amenable to the linkages drawn by American managers between material rewards and individual ambitions and abilities. Even among the poor, unemployed, and less skilled, paternalistic solutions and the downward redistribution of wealth were generally viewed less favorably than the principle of equal opportunities to direct individual skills, ambitions, and energies toward the realization of higher material rewards.[105]

The significance of an individualistic work ethic in the stabilization of industrial relations in Europe is less clear. Nevertheless, there is reason to assume that a broadly individualistic cultural ethos did eventually come to be shared widely, whether through the dynamics of international diffusion and competition or through the influence of the United States during the periods of postwar reconstruction following each of the two world wars. In the case of Britain, the spread of Puritanism beyond the middle class to the lower classes was already evident by the latter half of the nineteenth century when the lower classes, faced with increasingly difficult economic and social conditions in a rapidly changing economy, seized upon the same ideology that the middle class had employed in justifying their economic and political power to demand "their rightful place in society" as socially recognized individuals and equal members of the political community.[106] In Germany, despite the rapid spread of Protestantism since the sixteenth century, the focus was on the writings of Luther, not Calvin, and was limited to the religious sphere until the late nineteenth century; nevertheless, this strand of individualism was sufficiently strong that it could be redirected toward the justification of economic activities in the wake of World War II and the American Occupation.[107] Individualism arrived in Catholic France much earlier, but by a completely different route, with the main role being played not by Protestantism but by the intellectual and political inheritance from the era of the Enlightenment and the French Revolution.[108] Although this brand of individualism was not initially tied to the justification of economic activities in France, the incorporation of scientific management after World War I and the influence of U.S. management specialists during post–World War II reconstruction appear to have paved the way for at least a tentative acceptance of individualistic values among the industrial work force in France.[109] And, more generally, comparative studies of work-related values bear out the overall predominance of individualistic values in the West as a whole, at least when compared to attitudes toward work and inequality in non-Western regions.[110]

These observations suggest that even if the particular sources and character of individualism varied across particular regions in the West, it is plausible to assume that a broadly defined ethos of individualism did permeate Western societies, eventually enabling at least a qualified acceptance among workers of the legitimacy of core features of scientific management. A similar cultural transformation elsewhere is not implausible; it would, however, require a dramatic social upheaval or revolutionary transformation that was not only comparable in scope to the cultural transformation in Europe since the Protestant Reformation but was also accompanied by active efforts on the part of political or cultural elites to elevate individualism at the expense of preexisting norms. This has generally not been the case across NWLIs, which is one of the compelling reasons why efforts to adapt Western institutional models in these societies bears close examination.

Beyond Taylorism: Continuity and Change in Western Managerial Discourse

If one is to characterize the core features of Western management models as largely exceptional, it is also necessary to consider the significance of changes in managerial discourse since the consolidation of scientific management. The shifts evident in the human relations movement, the "quality of working life" movement, and "lean" production models have been touched upon in the preceding section on universalist perspectives on firms and organizations; here, the question is one of the extent to which each of these perspectives might have contributed to *actual* transformations in managerial ideology and practice in Western industry, particularly in the United States.

Although Mayo himself vigorously criticized Taylor's narrowly technical view of workers' motivations and production tasks,[111] it is important to note that much of the research informing the human relations perspective has its origins in efforts to implement the Taylor system. Most noteworthy in this regard is the work of Hugo Muensterberg, a contemporary of Taylor, who played a major role in promoting psychological testing as a basis for matching workers to particular tasks. Taylor had viewed this as a strictly managerial problem that could only be solved by closely monitoring the efficiency of workers and manipulating incentives to select out those that were ill-suited for certain tasks. Muensterberg attempted to bypass this process by using psychological testing to determine the extent to which individual dispositions could be immediately matched with scientifically designed tasks, thereby reducing variations in the performance of tasks as well as the fatigue or monotony that might result from workers having to continually perform tasks they were ill-suited for.[112] The psychological testing departments set up by Muensterberg eventually set the stage for the empirical investigations that would inform the human rela-tions approach. In any case, from the point of view of managers, the aim of both psychological testing and human relations was essentially the same as that of Taylorist factory administration: to ensure that the individual was able to perform a task as well as it could be performed. To the extent that managers believed "a sense of participation" would help increase the cooperation and productivity of workers, they only created realms for employee participation at lower levels of decision making, usually on questions pertaining to the physical work environment.

That is not to say that the human relations movement was inconse-quential. Indeed, it did produce some concrete changes in management practices—for example, the establishment of personnel departments, sug-gestions systems, morale surveys, and company magazines.[113] Moreover, the basic concept of human relations had a profound effect on managerial discourses elsewhere, including in Japan and Soviet Russia, where man-agerial elites attached their own understandings to the term as they sought strategies to adapt their workplaces and work forces to a new era of pro-duction in the 1960s and 1970s.[114] Within the particular context of West-ern management models, however, the basic premises of Taylorism con-tinued to inform the organization of work and authority as well as the systems for allocating tasks and rewards for individual employees. In fact, most of the initiatives launched by management under the banner of human relations were generally not a response to considerations about the nature of industrial work or the psychology of the industrial worker; rather, they constituted one component of a strategy for coping with the rising level of industrial conflict following World War II.[115] Such initia-tives simply enabled managers to demonstrate some concern for employee morale while strengthening their ability to pursue their primary objectives: to stimulate individual productivity, reassert managerial control over the shopfloor, and check the influence of unions.[116] While this effort pointed to assumptions that extended beyond Taylor's unemotional rationalism, it essentially came to represent what Mills referred to as the creation of "pseudo-gemeinschaft islands," designed to artificially induce worker cooperation without actually transforming the production process or altering the structure of managerial hierarchies.[117]

During the 1960s and 1970s, drawing upon the psychological research produced by Maslow and others, a new generation of management spe-cialists in the United States attacked both Taylorism and the human rela-tions school for assuming that the worker in his/her original condition could only be motivated and disciplined through the satisfaction of his/her *basic* needs, whether material or social; instead, they urged managers to proceed on the assumption that workers had *higher* needs that could be satisfied through greater identification with, and integration into, their workplaces.[118] This perspective gained more salience during the 1970s following the publication of the report "Work in America" by a special government task force commissioned under President Nixon. The report and the plethora of studies it spurred took as their point of departure the observation that the human relations movement had not succeeded in reducing the growing dissatisfaction of the work force, that this dissatisfaction was reducing the productivity of workers, and that the problem had to do in part with the extent to which employees found their jobs meaningful and felt integrated into the *production process* itself (not just into the work environment).[119] These studies collectively drew attention to the importance of "job enrichment," suggesting for the first time that the tedious, repetitive performance of elemental tasks or assembly-line work diminished the "quality of working life" (QWL) of workers.

Like the human relations revolution, however, the resulting QWL movement drew a great deal of attention to the *possibility* of redesigning work organization to enrich work lives, but it did not contribute to any concrete shifts in management practice during the 1970s. The assumptions on which the arguments of the QWL movement were predicated—most notably, the view that workers were experiencing malaise because their "higher needs" were not being satisfied—were considered to be exaggerated or flawed in light of newer empirical research into workers' attitudes and newer psychological research challenging Maslow's "hierarchy of needs." Even labor leaders questioned the motives of those attempting to promote such ideals as "job enrichment" and "integration" in the workplace, viewing them as ivory-tower academics or "cultural imperialists" who used their own experiences as templates for interpreting labor relations and thus failed to grasp the essentially adversarial character of labor-management relations.[120] Moreover, to the extent that some managers took the idea of job enrichment seriously, the result was often inconsequential from the point of view of blue-collar workers who simply found themselves having to perform two or three dreary, narrow tasks instead of just one.[121] Thus, in marked contrast to Japan, where significant changes in the organization of work were in evidence even before the 1970s (most famously, at Toyota), shifts in management practices in the United States by and large corresponded to available technologies and political currents rather than to any systematic reevaluation of the organizational requirements of production in the bureaucratized enterprise.

Ironically, it is precisely the increasing competitiveness of Japanese firms that finally prompted managerial elites in the United States to seriously consider alternative modes of work organization. Thus emerged widespread discussions of a new post-Fordist model of lean production that supposedly represented a fundamental challenge to core assumptions of scientific management and existing production processes. Instead of the high-volume assembly-line mass production of Fordism, lean production was thought to yield small batches with higher per-unit profits, enable a fast turnover in inventories, keep suppliers close and updated, promote job diversity and teamwork, and enable employees and managers to work simultaneously on manufacturing and continuous design improvements.[122] Theoretically, for proponents of lean production, this meant that the scope of jobs would be expanded to include all tasks necessary to complete a process, that workers would be given greater discretion over the pace of work and the sequence of tasks, that outside agents would play a reduced role in the control and monitoring of quality, and that, as result of all these trends, there would be greater employee voice and solidarity within the firm albeit at the expense of sectorwide or nationwide union bodies.[123]

The significance of these shifts is presently the subject of much debate among specialists in comparative industrial relations, many of whom challenge the idea of a single post-Fordist model of lean production.[124] The relative merits of competing perspectives on the question of post-Fordism, however, are largely inconsequential for the purposes of this book if only because the focus here is on the forces affecting managers and firms in NWLIs. While the argument being advanced here does take for granted that there is such a thing as a recognizably Western style of management that affects the choices of managers in NWLIs, this does not require a definitive position on whether the core features of that style of management are *now* in the process of being challenged in postindustrial Western societies. For the purposes of the problematique analyzed here, what is significant is that the ideals and practices associated with scientific management—as evident in Taylorist-Fordist production processes in the United States and Europe—may be regarded as sufficiently uniform insofar as these constitute a point of reference for managerial discourses in NWLIs.

2.3.   Sources of Variation: Late Industrialization, Historical Legacies, and Strategies

Upon taking into account the distinctive historical circumstances and normative assumptions accompanying the emergence of Western manage-

ment models, it becomes possible to identify three distinct dynamics, corresponding to the latter three propositions in figure 6, that contribute to
substantial variations in institutions of work across NWLIs. The first of
these dynamics is a defining element of the problematique of institution-
building in NWLIs, while the latter two constitute components of the substantive argument. First, there are the common dynamics related to the
fact of late industrialization: the need for greater coordination to expedite
belated industrialization, the conscious efforts to avoid the kind of social
unrest evident in the course of early industrialization in the West, and the
marginal significance of individualism. Second, the distinctive historical
and social legacies inherited by particular late-industrializing regions or
societies will exert some influence on the worldviews, goals, expectations,
and behaviors of actors in new institutions of work; this influence will be
more readily apparent among subordinates than superordinates, but the
specific implications of this for the coherence and performance of institutions will depend partly upon the latter's choices. Thus, the third dynamic
of consequence here consists of the specific strategies adopted by institutional elites, including the efforts of managers to deal with the wider social
environment within which their firms must recruit and manage workers.

Late-Industrializer Effects and the Organization
of Work in NWLIs

The general observation that the dynamics of late industrialization involve
higher levels of coordination than in referent societies may be traced back
to nineteenth-century Germany where leading intellectuals such as Johann
Fichte and Friedrich List first articulated the case for a high degree of
administrative intervention for the purpose of protecting the economy
from the destabilizing effects of foreign influences and enabling Germany
to catch up to Britain, the referent society.[125] During the early twentieth
century, Veblen also pointed to Germany's apparent success in catching
up to highlight a related dimension of late industrialization: the advantages of "situational backwardness" for societies that aggressively borrowed new technologies from referent societies without incurring the
wasted energies and social costs that accompanied the initial development
of those technologies.[126] During the 1950s and 1960s, Gerschenkron's thesis on the necessity of "historical substitutes" to overcome relative economic backwardness, the emergence of a new strand of development economics emphasizing the importance of development strategies, and a
number of other studies that pointed to the potential economic achieve-

ments of "mobilization regimes" all attempted to trace how the dynamics of catching up required a more proactive strategy for mobilizing and coordinating material and human resources in the course of late industrialization.[127] Later arguments about the developmental state, partly anticipated in the analysis of Latin American "bureaucratic-authoritarianism" but more systematically articulated in the context of East Asian political economy, proceeded further, highlighting the necessity and advantages of particular forms of state intervention and particular kinds of coalitions between the state and social forces in efforts to simultaneously achieve industrialization and social stability.[128] Still others also pointed to a negative side effect of late development, namely, the consequences of "international demonstration effects" (IDE) for patterns of savings and consumption among elite groups influenced by the ideas and life-styles of their counterparts in more advanced societies.[129] In the context of analyzing institutions of work in NWLIs, these various implications of delayed industrialization are reflected in the widespread tendency among managerial and state elites to rely on mechanisms of hierarchical coordination to force the pace of industrialization and to look to the material and technological achievements of particular referent societies in defining key indicators for the success of their own modernizing projects.

A second set of assumptions concerning late industrialization is equally pertinent for the argument in this book: that elites in NWLIs will be extremely concerned about the implications of social mobilization for social stability and political order, which are far more indeterminate (and potentially far more problematic) than assumed in universalist treatments of social and organizational change.[130] While modernizing elites in late industrializers are impressed by the economic achievements of earlier industrializers, they are also acutely conscious of the problems of social unrest that plagued Western societies well into the twentieth century.[131] At the same time, the urgency with which industrialization is pursued, and the resulting *compression* of the pace of social mobilization, means that the potential intensity of social disturbances accompanying industrialization may be significantly greater, necessitating more proactive strategies for preempting or resolving these disturbances than was the case with the referent societies. In light of these considerations, managerial elites and state elites in late industrializers share a common interest in the prevention of industrial conflict, particularly in the case of large enterprises that have a larger number and greater concentration of workers. What this suggests is that managers facing the pressures of late industrialization and social mobilization will understandably consider more active measures for maintaining cohesion and discipline among the work force in an effort to maintain the capacity for steady, sustained industrial production even if achieving these objectives comes at the expense of optimizing productivity at each stage of the production process. This does not suggest that efficiency will be consciously sacrificed or that industrial firms cannot be efficient institutions in late industrializers; but it does suggest that efficiency itself may well be understood in broader terms, related not only to the productivity of the worker but to the overall ability of the firm and the economy to achieve *sustained* increases in output while avoiding large-scale social unrest.[132]

These dynamics are evident across late-industrializing societies, including many European societies through the early 1900s. In the particular case of non-Western late industrializers, however, there is a third point to consider in relation to the possibilities for departing from original institutional models. In the previous section, it was noted that individualism has played a significant role in the ideologies and incentive structures invoked by entrepreneurs and managers in the large, bureaucratic firms in the West; and it is because the wider society had also come to internalize this individualism that these managerial ideologies came to resonate to some extent among key segments of the work force. Such a transformation elsewhere would require a dramatic social upheaval or cultural revolution that was similar in scope and character to that which followed from the confluence of industrialization and the Protestant Reformation in the West. That is, the emergence of individualism in NWLIs, while not impossible, cannot be assumed to be a concomitant of industrialization; such a transformation would not only require that preexisting norms, identities, and social relations be dissolved, but that individualism be viewed by political and cultural elites, and by the citizenry as a whole, as a positive good on the basis of which to construct a new economic, political, and social order.[133] In the absence of such a transformation, preexisting, typically *collectivist,* ideals and symbols are likely to be invoked in managerial and nationalist discourse even as preindustrial communities are themselves dispersed or dissolved. While the effectiveness of collectivist appeals depends on a number of other factors, the very fact that workers recruited from a certain cultural milieu may be more responsive to norms and symbols typical of that milieu does produce certain distinctive challenges and opportunities for managers in NWLIs as they seek to emulate the material and technological achievements of firms in advanced societies.[134]

All of these observations about the implications of late-industrialization were anticipated in a famous argument made in the early 1970s by Ronald Dore in *British Factory, Japanese Factory,* a comparative study of

British and Japanese industry that was pathbreaking for its time. Dore acknowledged that technological progress and the increase in complexity and differentiation had certain common consequences that all industrializers shared, but he pointed to a variety of factors that produced a very different pattern of industrialization in Japanese firms, a pattern that he viewed as typical for all late industrializers. Dore pointed out that firms in late-industrializing societies not only placed a greater premium on social cohesion, but they also required long-term stability in employment patterns. In addition, the absence of market individualism allowed for the construction of alternative systems of work and authority in which hierarchical coordination from above was combined with a strong sense of common membership in the enterprise community. He even suggested in Veblenian fashion that late industrializers had the advantage of looking back and avoiding the social turmoil and conflicts that had plagued earlier industrializers in Europe. Thus, Dore concluded that firms in late industrializers would gravitate toward a distinct "organization-oriented" model of management that placed a significantly greater premium on hierarchical coordination, long-term stability, and a sense of community than was the case in the "market-oriented" firms that had emerged in the more individualistic West.[135]

While these observations effectively challenged universalist theories of technological determinism and convergence, however, Dore initially discounted the possibility of diverse patterns of management and diverse collectivist legacies across late industrializers. As he himself later came to recognize, the organization-oriented model was driven solely by the contrast between British and Japanese firms; thus, the analysis neglected to weigh the possible contributions of distinctive historical patterns and cultural characteristics to the evolution of the typical Japanese firm.[136] The pressures of catch-up industrialization under the influence of external referents of success, the premium placed on preserving stable employment patterns and social order, and the absence of individualism certainly combine to produce organizational dynamics that are not reflected in Western scientific management; but these challenges and opportunities still leave considerable room for variation, shaped in part by the influence of distinctive historical inheritances and in part by the choices of actors in new institutions.

Historical Sources of Variation: Conceptualizing Legacies

As noted in chapter 1, during the 1950s and 1960s, modernization theorists generally interpreted preexisting norms and practices as remnants of *tradi-*

tion that would give way to a more *modern* set of values and interests in the course of industrialization. During the 1970s, however, some critics of modernization theory noted that supposedly traditional norms and behaviors were simply rational responses of actors pursuing their own independent interests within the context of the material conditions and social constraints of a subsistence economy.[137] As other critics argued, *tradition* was largely a residual category, defined in opposition to *modernity* and, as a result, obscuring important differences across preindustrial communities in diverse historical contexts.[138] The approach taken in this book shares with the first critique the general assumption that much social action in any society is indeed "rational" within a particular context; but it also shares with the second critique the assumption that there are meaningful and consequential differences in the specific cultural frameworks and social structures of different communities that affect the distinctive preferences and responses of actors as these communities undergo change.

In the particular case of industrial management, Bendix's classic study *Work and Authority in Industry* (1956) had already argued that variations across similarly bureaucratized enterprises were likely to persist in the course of industrialization, and that these variations could be traced in part to diverse historical *legacies* inherited by managerial elites in different societies.[139] Bendix relied on synchronic and diachronic comparisons (between early British and Russian factories, on the one hand, and between later American and East German enterprises, on the other) to demonstrate how the bureaucratization of enterprises created similar dilemmas for managers across societies in the East and West, requiring the use of managerial ideology to ensure that subordinates would use the discretion available to them to support, not hinder, managerial objectives. At the same time, the comparisons demonstrated how the responses of managerial elites to this problem in different times and places reflected the continuing influence of diverse historical legacies even in bureaucratic settings. This observation not only challenged universalist treatments of firms and organizations, but also anticipated the limitations of models intended for firms in late industrializers (for example, Dore's organization-oriented model). While the case studies and the comparative framework in *Work and Authority* may now be outdated in many respects, Bendix's fundamental insight about historically conditioned variations across similarly complex firms and organizations has continued to be echoed in later studies of firms, organizations, and industrial relations systems (the present study included).[140]

Without minimizing the intellectual debt this book owes to Bendix, however, it is necessary to address a number of issues left unresolved in his treatment of *how* past norms and structures relate to diverse patterns of industrial management. In his characterization of historical legacies, Bendix did not offer a clear specification of *which* preexisting norms and structures were relevant in analyzing the attitudes and behavior of different industrial relations actors; instead, he relied primarily on sweeping studies of national political culture, ignoring the more pertinent norms and social relations embedded in everyday communities of work. Moreover, Bendix made no systematic effort to theorize the differential impact of preexisting norms and practices on workers and managers given their respective positions, experiences, and interests within the institutional hierarchy; as a result, while the case studies included rich discussions of managerial ideologies and practices, there was no effort to examine the significance of tensions and contradictions *between* ideology and practice, or between the formal and informal aspects of the workplace. Finally, Bendix viewed preexisting authority patterns as the main source of influence on the organization of work and authority, without considering how managers might choose to consciously reject, ignore, or modify the legacies they inherited.[141]

In offering a partial corrective for these problems, the approach in this book refines Bendix's approach in three ways: First, greater pains are taken to identify the relevant legacies in view of the institutional context; thus, the focus here is specifically on norms and practices embedded in preindustrial communities of work, and not those that supposedly constitute attributes of national culture. Second, the problematique is predicated on recognizing the differential impacts of legacies on institution-builders (managers) and subordinates (workers) and, consequently, on formal and informal dimensions of work-related ideals and practices. Third, managerial elites are viewed as being in a position to make important choices about how they interpret and address their inherited legacies. The first two points are elaborated upon here, while the third is addressed further below in the discussion of *managerial strategies.*

The theoretical framework in this book adopts a more nuanced treatment of the units to which legacies might be attached. It is assumed here that the appropriate frame of reference for the analysis of a particular modern institution must necessarily be a *functionally equivalent* past institution; in the case of institutions of work, historical sources of variation need to be traced specifically to norms and practices embedded in past communities of work. In the case of the approach adopted in this book, such communities are thought to be constructed at the level of the village rather than the household or a larger social entity. Empires, nations, or prefectures, through their control over taxation and militaries, may have affected the character of local socioeconomic structures, and they may even have contributed partially to the social identities of some villagers by upholding the quasi-religious authority of kings, emperors, or their representatives. But whatever larger-scale political entity or social structure may have bound together more immediate face-to-face communities within the territory of a would-be nation-state, it is in the communities themselves, not the broader political or social system of which they were a part, where everyday dilemmas of cooperation and coordination among distinct units had to be systematically addressed through the institutionalization of stable norms and practices. Similarly, while the beliefs, values, and practices at the level of the household are not irrelevant for the purposes of drawing a comprehensive picture of community life in preindustrial contexts, these are not consistently or proportionately reflected in the norms and practices related to cooperative work. Not only was power highly concentrated in the hands of a household head, but separate individual identities and interests were neither acknowledged nor routinely or systematically negotiated within the household. Thus, for the most part, it is at the level of the village that members of different households—each acknowledged to have separate identities and interests—had to regularly negotiate their mutual obligations, identify collective endeavors, coordinate their everyday tasks, jointly manage collective resources, resolve disputes among households, and justify hierarchies of wealth and status.

For this reason, it is village-level communities of work that are assumed to exert the most significant influence over the conscious and reflexive orientations of individuals toward their tasks, interactions, and expectations in new institutions of work. Several aspects of preindustrial communities of work are deemed to be sufficiently diffuse to be portable across institutional contexts and comparable in terms of their effects on workers' expectations and responses in changing conditions. Even with a shared ethos of collectivism, it is still necessary to specify who is and who is not a member of the group whose common purposes need to be achieved through the coordination of individual activities. In this regard, it is possible to ask, for example, what kinds of rights and responsibilities are associated with membership, and to what extent membership depends on common attributes as opposed to interdependence. It is also possible to systematically compare the norms invoked to facilitate mutual aid (for example, during harvest time) and coordinate the management of common resources and endeavors. In particular, it is worth noting the steepness of hierarchies and the extent to which this affects the distribution of resources and obligations in coordinated endeavors. That is, what constitutes a legitimate basis and extent of stratification in the distribution of status and rewards, and how does this stratification affect the rights of members to participate in discussions and decisions that collectively affect the working lives of community members (such as the joint payment of taxes to higher authorities or the distribution of new meadows)? Do the norms and mechanisms governing the redistribution of resources emphasize the rights of members to expect a minimal level of resources with which to provide for themselves, or do they emphasize direct, paternalistic assistance for those closer to the subsistence level from those more fortunate? The manner in which preindustrial communities of work responded to such questions point to significant differences in the legacies they might leave behind in different NWLIs, affecting how individuals respond to their roles and tasks in institutions of work, what kinds of expectations workers have of their superiors, and what norms and principles can be meaningfully invoked to determine the distribution of responsibilities, resources, and authority.

Certainly, the industrial firm is not an agrarian village, and manufacturing technologies and the institutional environment within complex firms do create problems that may be incomprehensible from the point of view of peasants engaged in subsistence agriculture. Industrial work suggests that there will be a dramatically greater number of highly differentiated tasks, that certain work routines and schedules must be adhered to, and that tasks must be completed with some minimum level of efficiency and productivity. At some point, poor performance will have to be punished, possibly by the loss of membership in the enterprise community. Moreover, in all cases, once individuals move from subsistence communities to wage labor, incentive structures and working conditions will undoubtedly have a profound impact on their calculations, since all workers in all societies presumably prefer higher wages, better working conditions, and greater respect. Nevertheless, the *manner* in which individual material interests, market forces, and productivity requirements shape the behavior and expectations of workers and managers is *variable,* and part of this variation is a result of how preexisting norms and practices that are related to cooperative work, community membership, and social hierarchies mediate perceptions of work and authority in the industrial enterprise. As Malinowski noted long ago, preindustrial communities of work, like modern bureaucratic enterprises, are part of a wider network of social exchange norms and practices that make normative orientations to structures of work and authority relations comparable across agrarian communities and industrial enterprises.[142] It is these norms and practices that are regarded as portable insofar as they can serve as idioms on the shopfloor, providing some sense of familiarity and continuity to workers as they adapt to industrial labor.[143]

Several specific examples can be cited in this regard. Preexisting norms and practices governing the distribution of wealth, status, and power may be extremely relevant to workers' diffuse attitudes toward highly differentiated reward systems and their expectations about what constitutes appropriate behavior on the part of superiors or white-collar employees. Workers may also have their own understandings about what constitutes a serious violation of work rules or an unacceptable level of performance, and about what punishment ought to be meted out and by whom. Similarly, preexisting norms may influence what obligations are associated with the power of superordinates to issue commands, and what conditions are viewed as fair grounds for the termination of employment or for promotions and bonuses. Moreover, within the range of variation in the distribution of responsibilities and tasks that is permitted by the technologies of production (which is assumed here to be much wider here than in the case of Taylorism), workers valuing participation within common endeavors may respond poorly to an individual-centered system for the assignment of tasks and evaluation of performance. It is precisely in these regards that legacies inherited from typical preindustrial communities of work in a given NWLI are considered a possible source of national distinctiveness in patterns of industrial relations.[144]

There remains the question of whether legacies inherited from past communities of work can be presumed to affect the behavior of managers in the same way that they shape the norms and expectations of workers. Bendix did not take a clear position on this issue. This study assumes explicitly that workers are more directly influenced by—and more active in reproducing—those resilient norms, practices, and organizational patterns embedded in more familiar past communities. While some managers may consciously or unconsciously participate in the reconstruction of preexisting ideals and practices, managerial elites in NWLIs generally represent a distinct class, one that is directly enlisted in the pursuit of national developmental objectives. They are not only under pressure from state elites to engineer catch-up industrialization while maintaining social order, but they are far more likely than workers to be attentive to the ideals, practices, and achievements of their counterparts in advanced referent societies. Thus, whatever hold preexisting norms and social relations may exert on managers can be expected to be diluted or mediated by other external influences and political pressures that they regularly encounter in the course of industrialization. This suggests that evidence of preexisting legacies is likely to be found in official management ideologies and practices most commonly when managerial elites consciously choose to draw upon them.

Workers are in a quite different situation with respect to the factory hierarchy as well as with respect to extra-institutional influences. Given their subordinate position, they have far less power and resources at their disposal to ensure that their preferences are regularly acceded to; as a result, it is not surprising that they will draw upon preexisting understandings and social ties to find ways to ensure some degree of employment and wage security, and to preserve some degree of autonomy on the shopfloor. Moreover, because they are less directly involved in the modernizing projects of state elites and less exposed to ideas and practices in the referent societies, preexisting norms and practices can be expected to be more meaningful and resilient among members of the work force than among managerial elites. With the move from long-standing tightly knit communities into large-scale, bureaucratized systems of work and authority, past norms and symbols—far from steadily and irreversibly disappearing—are likely to influence the construction of templates for making sense of the tasks, roles, and authority structures workers encounter in the industrial factory.

For the purposes of the argument in this book, these observations also suggest that the influence of legacies may vary along different dimensions of factory life. For example, while formal management *practices* may be more influenced by external management models, it is quite possible that official managerial *ideologies* may conform to traditional ideals in the interest of preserving social order. Similarly, while *formal* production processes may be geared toward the emulation of production processes in firms in referent societies, these may not succeed in displacing or coopting *informal* aspects of work organization among workers that reflect norms and social relations different from those promoted by managers. In fact, the extent to which these possible discrepancies pose problems for orderly industrial production depends in part on how managerial elites themselves choose to invoke, or respond to, evidence of preexisting ideals and norms.

Managerial Behavior as a Source of Variation:
Conceptualizing Strategy

This brings us to the third problem in relation to Bendix's approach: his failure to address the scope for superordinates to make important choices that might affect the significance of inherited legacies. On the one hand, role conflicts, social tensions, or corrupt practices may proliferate as old norms and identities come into conflict with new normative structures established in modern institutions.[145] On the other hand, it is also possible that a synergy may evolve between preexisting norms and social relations and new developmental institutions, thus providing a more spontaneous (and less costly) means to elicit cooperation in the pursuit of developmental objectives.[146] Which scenario is more likely, however, depends in good measure on how institution-builders themselves understand and address the significance of legacies in formulating their organizational ideologies and practices. In the case of the industrial enterprise, whatever influence preexisting norms and social relations may exert on workers' attitudes and behaviors on the shopfloor, managerial elites have the power and resources to put into action their own normative perspectives and pragmatic solutions, and the particular manner in which they do so needs to be taken into account in analyzing the characteristics and dynamics of firms and organizations. This component of the argument thus speaks to the strand of organization theory that recognizes the significance of leadership and *strategy* in accounting for organizational variation.[147]

Much organization theory has tended to embrace a top-down view of strategy that views the survival of informal realms and distinct worldviews among subordinates as a problem that needs to be decisively solved by clever superordinates. Chester Barnard's *The Functions of the Executive* had already laid the groundwork for this view of managerial strategy. Barnard rejected the mechanistic image of modern firms in Taylorism and viewed enterprises as inherently moral organizations, but he also believed that executives constantly had to work on "indoctrinating those at the lower levels with general purposes" in order to ensure cooperation between superiors and subordinates and enlist the support of the informal groups formed by the latter in the service of the objectives defined by the former.[148] Thus, Barnard treated the competing expectations of managers and workers as well as the existence of informal groups not as inherent constraints on management but as solvable problems that simply required executives to engineer a uniform set of goals and values.

This top-down understanding of strategy was also incorporated into many universalist perspectives on organizations. Simon, for example, was acutely conscious of the danger that insufficiently indoctrinated subordinates might become indifferent to organizational goals and might therefore withhold some of their energies in the performance of essential tasks. He thus noted the importance of managerial cadres who would regularly have to engineer consent among their subordinates by simultaneously invoking the "authority of ideas" (to indoctrinate subordinates) and the "authority of sanctions" (to monitor and control subordinates) in order to gain not only the compliance of subordinates but their unquestioning support for organizational goals.[149] More recent treatments of organizational strategy, although viewing the existence of covert realms of noncompliance and diverse worldviews as more complex issues than Simon appeared to suggest, have continued to focus on the intentional decision making of superordinates in coping with these problems and improving organizational efficiency, leaving aside the implications of profound differences in the objectives, interests, norms, and expectations embraced by managers and subordinates.[150] In all of these top-down perspectives, *strategy* has been understood in relation to standard organizational techniques for getting subordinates to accept official goals and values, and for checking the latter's ability to exercise discretion in ways that do not consistently support these goals and values. Little attention has been paid to the perspective of subordinates themselves and how they might also manipulate aspects of organizational life to retain some autonomy and control of their own.

The notion of *strategy* employed here is based on an understanding of the term that is more fluid and dialectical, accepting the different worldviews and goals of superordinates and subordinates as an inherent feature of institutional life. Thus, strategy is treated as a category that encompasses varied approaches for managing these differences, including the possibility of accommodating them, in the course of realizing organizational goals. This perspective is influenced not by Barnard or Simon, but by Selznick's view of administrative leadership and Burawoy's treatment of manufactured consent in the workplace. Selznick may have been influenced by Barnard as well, but in contrast to Simon and Child, he developed a theory of leadership that allowed for the continuation of distinct worldviews and informal social relations within the formal structure of an organization. Selznick emphasized the value of administrative strategies that could channel or accommodate—rather than break down or transform—the informal norms and patterns of behavior evident among subordinates.[151] Burawoy, while working in a Marxist tradition and emphasizing the politics of class conflict, emphasized how managers, rather than seeking to overtly control and exploit workers, sought to channel their energies toward the achievement of managerial objectives; they did so by framing the labor process as a game in which workers could regularly engage with lower-level managers as they sought to preserve zones of autonomy without directly challenging managerial authority. The extent to which these subtle forms of eliciting worker cooperation succeeded, however, was contingent on whether workers themselves were able to perceive some positive benefits from participating in the game (e.g., a greater sense of workplace solidarity and less tedium in daily work routines).[152]

In Burawoy's treatment, superordinates' motivations are certainly not viewed in the benign terms suggested in Selznick's treatment of administrative leadership; but, significantly, both approaches consciously accommodate the perspective of subordinates as part of their quite different projects. In neither case do the informal dimensions of the firm or organization disappear as a result of the ingenuity of superordinates; rather, subordinates retain their distinctive norms and expectations, and superordinates focus on negotiating an accommodation that will prove functional given the goals of their organization. Building on this convergence between Selznick and Burawoy, the understanding of *strategy* adopted here takes a more fluid and dialectical view of hierarchical relations in firms and organizations, emphasizing the nontechnical process of mutual adjustment between superiors and subordinates, punctuated by opportunities for *both* groups to revise the cognitive maps they employ to interpret a situation at the workplace.[153]

Thus, rather than assume that standard techniques exist for indoctrinating and coopting workers everywhere, the understanding of *managerial strategy* here allows for a variety of outcomes depending on the specific content of ideologies *and* practices defined by managers. For the purposes of this book, the discussion of managerial strategies is limited to the comparisons of specific ideological claims and workplace practices that suggest a particular stance toward the features of existing management models and toward the legacies inherited from preexisting communities of work. Managerial ideologies are "*attempts* by leaders to justify the privilege of voluntary action and association for themselves, while imposing upon all subordinates the duty of obedience and the obligation to serve their employers to the best of their ability."[154] But, to be meaningful and effective, these attempts must also bear some correspondence to concrete management *practices* in such areas as the terms of employment, the distribution of rewards and status, the organization of production, and the structure of authority in the workplace. It is in this context that the ideal-typical institution-building strategies outlined in chapter 1 (see fig. 2) provide a basis for distinguishing diverse approaches taken by managerial elites in NWLIs. In anticipation of the comparative analysis to follow, the remainder of this section outlines what the four institution-building strategies—modernist, revolutionary, traditional, and syncretist—might look like within the particular context of industrial management in NWLIs.

A *modernist* managerial approach is one in which the legacies inherited from past communities are dismissed as unproblematic given the expectation that the experience of industrial work will break down old habits and enable workers to grow progressively accustomed to new, more differentiated roles and new, more bureaucratic authority structures. This strategy—to the extent that it is a strategy at all—would allow managerial elites to freely emulate the ideologies and practices of scientific management borrowed from the West and, in the process, adopt some version of an individualist work ethic while promoting an individual-centered system for assigning specialized tasks, employing competitive individual performance evaluations, and differentially rewarding individual productivity. In the view of managers opting for such an approach, collective ideal interests would be irrelevant, and sanctions and rewards related to individual performance would be adequate in the process of gaining obedience.

A *revolutionary* managerial strategy not only anticipates that preindustrial legacies will be problematic in the construction of a new system of production, but views any evidence of such legacies within the new enterprises as a threat to both the production goals of the enterprise and the construction of a new social order. As a result, the revolutionary manager seeks to find ways to more thoroughly indoctrinate workers and to completely eradicate preexisting values and social relations whether in the formal or informal realms of newly established industrial enterprises. As long as the process of indoctrination is deemed to be successful, it does not really matter if some technologies and work routines are similar to those found in "scientifically managed" Western firms, but these are reconstituted as elements within a system of work and authority thought to be qualitatively different and normatively superior. Thus, from the point of view of revolutionary elites, the terms of employment, the system of work-related evaluations and rewards, and the distribution of non–work-related resources would collectively represent extensions of a normative frame-work quite different from that underpinning management practices in Western firms. In addition, because the enterprise would be not only an institution of work but also an arena in which to evaluate the extent to which new ideals have been internalized by society at large, it is likely that workers would be rewarded or penalized not only on the basis of how well they perform their tasks but also on the basis of whether they demonstrate the "correct" moral qualities.[155]

A *traditionalist* managerial strategy in NWLIs points to efforts to preserve familiar work-related ideals and symbols as defining components of the managerial ideology in order to convince workers that their workplaces are essentially the same kinds of moral communities that they and their predecessors had been accustomed to. Such a strategy does not acknowledge or consider any tension between these traditional ideals and the formal organizational requirements of large-scale industrial production since traditionalist managers assume that preindustrial collectivism can be deployed solely at the level of ideology, and that this will suffice to preserve order at the workplace while the production process itself is based on borrowed technologies and work practices. These appeals to tradition do suggest an awareness of the potential for social tensions and conflicts in the course of importing scientific management, but the problem of coherence between familiar collectivist ideals and novel workplace practices is dismissed since the former are simply assumed to provide adequate justification for whatever managers choose to do.

Finally, somewhere between the traditionalist strategy on the one hand, and the modernist or revolutionary strategy on the other, there is *managerial syncretism.* Following the general definition offered in chapter 1, managerial syncretism in NWLIs suggests the modification of Western scientific management as well as more selective consideration of the portability of past norms while still fulfilling the technical requirements of production. In such an approach, managerial ideology is not an extension of past cultural ideals, but rather a creative adaptation of those generalizable norms, symbols, and practices that supported past communities of work in the hope that these will now support the organization of work and authority in the industrial enterprise. In contrast to a traditionalist approach, close attention is paid to the concomitant adaptation of concrete management practices—employment terms, work organization, the distribution of authority and responsibilities, and the system of rewards and promotions. Departures from Western management models will be constrained by the need to fulfill the technical requirements of production, but they are also expected to yield tangible benefits in the particular cultural milieu in which managerial elites are seeking to generate a stable understanding that workers will share without necessarily identifying with all of the methods and objectives of the company. The merits and logic of syncretism have been briefly noted in chapter 1 and are explored further in the following section.

It is important to note that none of the four managerial strategies reflects a greater or lesser difference in the value attached to industrial production; given the problematique and substantive concerns of this book, all four strategies, including the revolutionary one, are predicated on the assumption that orderly industrial production and the prevention of industrial conflict are extremely high priorities that managerial and state elites converge upon. The variations among the four types are thus based solely on managerial elites' *own* common considerations of the benefits of emulating or modifying specific features associated with management models in referent societies, and of the nature and implications of inherited legacies in production processes. In the latter context, managerial strategies reflect expectations of what will happen to preexisting norms and practices in the course of industrialization as well as assumptions about just how much attention needs to be paid to these norms and practices in devising managerial strategies. Thus, while revolutionaries and modernists both view the remnants of the past as something temporary, traditionalists and syncretists expect at least some of the preexisting norms and social relations to survive over the long run; and while revolutionaries and syncretists adopt a more proactive stance in addressing legacies inherited from the past, modernists and traditionalists view the evidence of past norms and social relations as generally unproblematic—the former expecting them to fade away gradually, and the latter expecting to invoke them indefinitely (see fig. 7).

These ideal-typical strategies are intended to serve primarily as heuristic devices for classifying and comparing patterns of management in NWLIs; the specific content of a managerial approach may include elements of different ideal-types and must be understood within particular historical contexts. For example, in a wider environment of revolutionary upheaval, the distinction between a revolutionary or syncretist managerial strategy still holds, although neither approach will look much like its respective analogue in a nonrevolutionary context. That is, even among revolutionaries, there are choices to be made in terms of how quickly and through what means revolutionary objectives are to be pursued while

Inherited Legacy

		Unproblematic	Problematic
Future of Legacy	**Disappears**	Modernist	Revolutionary
	Contributes to distinctiveness	Traditionalist	Syncretist

Fig. 7.   Inherited legacies and managerial strategies

industrial enterprises are being established and an industrial work force is being trained; a syncretist approach in this context would not require abandoning revolutionary aims so much as adopting a more gradual process of social transformation where the legitimacy of the new elites is predicated on demonstrating certain compatibilities between preexisting cultural characteristics and the qualities identified with revolutionary behavior.[156] By the same token, a modernizing elite that has no intention of remaking the world may very well draw upon revolutionary strategies to more emphatically force a break with the past and enable the adoption of technologies, behaviors, *and* attitudes typical of existing referent societies.[157] Thus, while the strategies themselves should not be confused with the ultimate ends of elites in NWLIs, the basis for distinguishing the ideal-typical strategies is adaptable across political contexts and lends itself to meaningful comparisons in terms of their implications.

2.4. Authority, Syncretism, and Congruence: The Argument Revisited

In light of the aforementioned discussions of potential sources of variation in firms and organizations in NWLIs, this chapter concludes with a closer look at the outcome of interest in this book, managerial authority, as well as the logic behind the argument offered. The first part of this section offers a more elaborate discussion of ways to establish large differences in managerial authority in NWLIs, focusing on the collective significance of various indicators of worker *commitment*. The second part revisits the substantive hypothesis about the merits of syncretism, focusing on the notion of *congruence* in order to suggest a plausible mechanism through which syncretist strategies can contribute to higher levels of authority in newly introduced institutions.

Gauging Managerial Authority: Indicators of Worker Commitment in NWLIs

In chapter 1, it was noted that *authority* in a Weberian sense is a relational term: one does not possess it unless others actually acknowledge it; that is, the commands issued by superordinates are authoritative only insofar as subordinates view these commands as legitimate and choose to respond in a prompt, automatic, and disciplined manner.[158] In the context of the industrial enterprise, managerial authority points to the ability of managers to elicit prompt and disciplined obedience on the part of workers, particularly in those areas where workers are in a position to exercise considerable discretion in the absence of formal supervision. By the same token, the *lack* of managerial authority is evident in any range of behaviors on the part of the worker that reflect the withholding of prompt and automatic attention to managerial commands, ranging from direct disobedience or work slowdowns to more passive acts that subvert managerial objectives (for example, through inattention, tardiness, or apathy). In other words, the extent of managerial authority is directly and proportionately related to, and must be necessarily gauged by, the behavior of workers themselves.

This does not suggest that such standard concerns as material rewards and working conditions are irrelevant for the purpose of understanding the actions of workers. Undoubtedly, labor turnover and adherence to workplace rules are everywhere in part a function of a worker's search for higher wages or better working conditions, just as a low level of productivity may be an indication of the absence of incentives or necessary tools. However, such obvious considerations do not negate the independent effects of managerial ideology and practice *within* a given material context; nor do they say anything about the norms and templates workers rely on in comparing options, ordering preferences, and interpreting their relationships to one another and to the enterprise as a whole. For example, while higher wages are everywhere preferable to lower wages, there can still be differences across contexts on the question of how high a wage would have to be in a particular social context in order for an employee to switch jobs and forfeit familiar ties with coworkers or superiors. Similarly, while working conditions may be poor, workers can still choose to be more or less disciplined and conscientious in the performance of their tasks depending on the extent to which they view the distribution of rewards and responsibilities as fair and reasonable. This is why the choices made by workers, while "rational" in the sense that they reflect a calculated response to a given choice situation, are more broadly indicative of a *normative* assessment of the legitimacy of managerial ideologies and practices.[159]

The specific workers' attitudes and behaviors that are invoked to gauge managerial authority may be collectively understood as employee *commitment*. The notion of commitment effectively represents the flip side of authority. It suggests that the prompt and disciplined performance of tasks is stimulated not only by rewards and sanctions but by a positive view of managerial values and goals. According to one widely used definition, *commitment* refers to

> the relative strength of an individual's identification with and involvement in a particular organization. Conceptually, it can be characterized by at least three factors: (a) a strong belief in and acceptance of the organization's goals and values; (b) a willingness to exert considerable effort on behalf of the organization; and (c) a strong desire to maintain membership in the organization.[160]

The vagueness of such terms as "relative strength," "strong belief," and "considerable effort," however, suggest that the concept of commitment is not without its problems. In fact, there is considerable debate among scholars in organization theory, industrial relations, and occupational psychology on the questions of just what counts as commitment, how important commitment is for organizations, and whether individuals in subordinate positions can genuinely learn to identify with an organization.[161] The most significant variation is evident in the manner in which scholars have related commitment to the interests of employees and managers.

One approach, evident in the human relations school and among some advocates of lean production, has been to interpret employee commitment as evidence that employees' social and psychological needs were being satisfied as a result of their participation in the activities of a firm, paving the way for a near-total convergence in the goals of employees and employers, reducing the scope for conflicting interests, and enabling the worker to be cooperative, loyal, trusting of management.[162] A somewhat different interpretation, most clearly evident in the assumptions of the "quality of working life" movement and other versions of lean production, suggests that commitment stems not from some general sense of identification with organizations but from the particular satisfaction employees derive from the *kinds* of tasks they are able to perform in view of their skills or professional competence.[163] Some occupational psychologists have also downplayed the significance of positive identification with an organization, highlighting instead the more generalized "normative commitment" that reflects wider social norms concerning employee-organization relationships and that emerges from familial, cultural, and organizational socialization.[164] Despite their differences, all of these views proceed from the assumption that commitment is a highly significant and positive aspect of organizational life, simultaneously fulfilling important needs for the individual and the organization.

In contrast to such views, many treatments of commitment view it as an indication of deliberate calculations made by employees to offer something more than mere obedience in exchange for receiving something more than what employers are normally expected to offer; in effect, commitment is viewed as a product of side bets made by employees in a peculiar social-exchange relationship whereby employers offer above-market wages and workers reciprocate by exceeding productivity expectations and remaining "loyal" to an organization.[165] Those approaching the problem from a Marxian tradition are even more skeptical about the possibilities of genuine commitment given their assumptions about the essential character of capitalist wage labor; to the extent that certain behaviors are considered supportive of managerial goals, these are understood in instrumental terms, as efforts to negotiate for some degree of shopfloor autonomy.[166] Some occupational psychologists, too, find expressions of commitment to be artificial at best given the more fundamental problem of powerlessness, confusion, and insecurity that overwhelms subordinates in complex organizational hierarchies.[167]

In between these positive and critical perspectives on the significance of commitment, it is possible to identify a modest understanding of the term that makes it a reasonable proxy for gauging sharp differences in levels of managerial authority. Such an understanding would require a degree of skepticism toward those who view commitment as an essential quality of "good" organizations, while also recognizing that, even in the most hierarchical organization, there are meaningful variations in the *extent* to which workers positively or skeptically respond to managerial ideology and practice. In other words, if commitment is seen as a side bet by employees, then the *level* of commitment may be viewed as directly related to the *kind* and *size* of the side bets employees place when deciding how much energy to expend on behalf of managerial goals; and, while wage labor and managerial hierarchies in an industrial firm will everywhere involve exploitation and domination, the extent of autonomy, the mechanisms of control, and the steepness of hierarchies can be a source of greater or lesser social conflict and emotional strain. Proceeding from these assumptions, it becomes possible to identify a flexible understanding of *worker commitment,* defined here as

> the willingness of workers to accept the right of managers to define the goals of a firm and the methods through which to realize these goals; to tolerate (not share) official ideologies invoked to justify management practices; to accept these practices as sufficiently legitimate so as to warrant regular adherence to managerial commands and workplace rules; and to cooperate with each other and with supervisors in carrying out assigned tasks so as to achieve managerial goals, even in areas where discretion can be exercised without supervision.

This definition of worker commitment neither assumes an idealized harmony of workers' and managers' goals nor serves as a synonym for mere compliance or obedience; rather, it extends to the wide-ranging possibilities in between these two scenarios, emphasizing the *variability* of commitment. Moroever, this definition allows for the possibility that managers can, in principle, do something about increasing worker commitment while recognizing that their success in doing so depends on whether the employee ultimately accepts the manager's definition of the firm's goals and the stipulation of employees' identities and roles. That is, even assuming the essentially adversarial and hierarchical character of industrial relations, the conceptualization of commitment here is predicated on the assumption that some managerial hierarchies are perceived to be more fair and reasonable than others, and that the difference matters to both workers and managers, albeit for different reasons. Used in this way, worker commitment and managerial authority become essentially interchangeable concepts for capturing the outcome of interest in this book.

The next question concerns how aspects of worker commitment might be invoked to gauge meaningful variations in managerial authority across different systems of industrial relations. A number of organization theorists and occupational psychologists have attempted to construct elaborate scales of organizational commitment based on statistical analyses of employee surveys. The problem with such scales is that they rely entirely on the stated responses of individuals without attending to aspects of workplace behavior. More importantly, they assume conditions that are typical of labor markets and industrial relations in the industrialized West.[168] While formal scales based on statistical analysis may be valuable for comparing levels of commitment across societies with comparable systems of industrial relations, such scales are not easy to translate in the context of enterprises in NWLIs, not only due to a paucity of comparable survey data, but also due to the sharply different institutional environments and labor market conditions that affect the motivations and behavior of workers and managers.[169] Thus, for the purposes of the comparative-historical analysis of industrial enterprises in NWLIs, a much more context-sensitive approach is needed that simultaneously examines trends across several distinct indicators of employee attitude and behavior while giving due consideration to the particular institutional environment corresponding to a given system of industrial relations. Such an approach will not yield a precise or uniform scale for comparing levels of worker commitment everywhere; it is, however, replicable in principle for the purpose of gauging sharp changes over time or large variations across space. Following are the factors collectively invoked to establish the largely uncontroversial observation that managerial authority in postwar Japan was significantly higher than in prewar Japan and Soviet Russia:

   1. The frequency and intensity of industrial conflict. Industrial conflict may be one readily apparent reason to suspect poor worker commitment in certain kinds of environments. Of course, strikes are a pervasive feature of industrial relations wherever coercive measures are not employed to preempt them and may occur even among committed employees in the most productive firms within the most harmonious systems of industrial relations. In fact, under many conditions, strikes may very well represent what Hirschman has called the "activation of voice," reflecting the efforts of loyal workers to improve their organizations before they would consider the "exit" option.[170] Thus, it is important to focus not simply on the number of strikes, but also on the frequency and intensity of industrial conflict, while also paying attention to the actual issues involved and the aftermath of strikes. Recurrent or prolongued disruptions of the production process, where they are the result of collective protest motivated by a widespread belief that managers or employers are violating prior agreements, provide good reason to suspect a low level of worker commitment and the failure to construct authoritative institutions of work in NWLIs.[171] The *lack* of industrial conflict, however, cannot be regularly equated with a high level of commitment; in certain environments, the decline of strikes may reflect the coercive pressures brought to bear by the state or the success of managerial efforts to undermine organized labor.[172] It is thus necessary to consider industrial conflict alongside such factors as productivity, discipline, and less overt challenges to managerial power in order to identify significant differences in commitment.

2. *Levels of productivity.* The concern with commitment has often been a product of the assumption that higher levels of commitment will yield higher levels of productivity. To the extent that this is true, it is also possible in some contexts to reverse this assumption and employ shifts in productivity as indicators of shifts in commitment. Thus, even though the emphasis in this book is on stability and legitimacy rather than productivity, productivity (as approximated by the gross output per worker) can be taken as a possible indication of worker commitment as long as the impact of changes in technology or available inputs are also taken into consideration. In the context of late industrialization, the massive influx of labor and initial investments in new technologies can rapidly multiply gross output in a given enterprise or industry, thereby distorting the relationship between worker commitment and productivity. Conversely, low productivity is not always a reflection of low levels of commitment in many late industrializers where scarce resources and difficult working conditions may prohibit the worker from maximizing the use of his/her energies. Nevertheless, steadily increasing or declining productivity within similar settings can be used in conjunction with evidence of industrial conflict or other indicators of worker behavior in providing an overall assessment of sharp increases or decreases in managerial authority.

3. *Turnover, tardiness, and absenteeism.* From the point of view of managerial elites, employees who frequently change jobs or fail to show up at work on time can pose serious problems for the maintenance of shopfloor routines and the meeting of production targets. Of course, where any kind of labor market exists, some level of turnover is to be expected and may even have positive benefits in allowing firms to recruit those skilled in the most advanced techniques and in allowing workers to exert some pressure on firms that are slow to adapt to changing environments. Moreover, extremely low levels of turnover might point either to restrictions on labor mobility or, as Hirschman has noted, to an "excessive" form of loyalty

that reflects stubbornness and inertia rather than genuine commitment to an organization's goals.[173] Similarly, some minimum level of tardiness and absenteeism may be expected even among committed employees, and this can actually have some positive consequences for the organization in the long run (for example, by reducing job-related stress and enabling the diffusion of skills among other members of a workgroup).[174] But these observations do not change the fact that there are thresholds beyond which the levels of absenteeism and turnover *do* increase the costs of production and *are* acknowledged to be serious problems by managers themselves.[175] Where, for example, the incidence of unexpected departures or absences is high in the estimation of managerial elites themselves, high turnover rates and absenteeism do create problems by requiring managers to revise work routines, delay production, and invest in training and supervision for new arrivals. In such situations, high turnover, absenteeism, and tardiness may very well suggest that workers are skeptical of management appeals and promises, or do not derive adequate material or emotional benefits from their involvement in the firm.

4.   *Everyday forms of noncooperation.*   The most telling indicators of levels of managerial authority in NWLIs, however, are the hundreds of choices workers consciously or reflexively make every day in the execution of their tasks. Inattentiveness and delays in the completion of assignments, demonstrated apathy or cynicism toward managerial pronouncements, recurrent violations of work rules or labor discipline (notably, alcoholism), the theft of time and resources in ways that benefit particular workers at the expense of the production processes, and collusion among informal groups to preempt punishment for such behaviors—these are all aspects of working life in large-scale enterprises that are not easy to systematically document or quantify. They are, however, observable in principle and do pose real problems for managers in NWLIs. Even though these aspects are much more difficult to compare across contexts, they may be the most reliable indicators of low worker commitment. Certainly, such problems as indiscipline, production slack, alcoholism, and informal collusion have been present at the early stages of industrialization in all countries, particularly among unskilled new arrivals with little experience in industrial factories. But, at some point, these problems do have to be overcome before large-scale industrial firms can establish a predictable, orderly process for regularly achieving production goals. Thus, where similar categories of workers have been exposed to industrial labor for similar amounts of time, large differences in worker commitment can be estab-

lished by examining qualitative evidence of workplace discipline, time theft, pilferage, apathy, or collusion in the workplace.[176]

Each of these presumed indicators of worker commitment is undoubtedly affected by a range of factors, and the significance of each must be understood within the broader system of industrial relations. Within any given context, however, such factors as industrial conflict, productivity, turnover, absenteeism, and the overt or covert subversion of formal production processes can *collectively* provide a reasonable approximation of sharp changes or large differences in worker commitment. As long as one makes commonsense adjustments for the effects of national industrial relations systems and the wider political economy (for example, particular labor laws, labor market conditions, or the extent of political repression), these indicators can provide some sense of significant differences in levels of managerial authority across societies. Certainly for the purpose of examining labor relations in Japan and Russia, this sort of "contextualized comparison" can provide an empirical basis for the outcome examined: that managerial authority in postwar Japan was significantly higher than in prewar Japan, and that this increase stands in sharp contrast to the decline in managerial authority in Soviet industry despite the initial commitment of some segments of the work force to the idea of "socialist labor."[177]

Managerial Syncretism and the Logic of Congruence

The hypothesis in this book may now be restated in light of the above discussion of sources of variation in firms and organizations: to the extent that managerial elites in NWLIs are able to choose particular combinations of ideology and practice under the constraints related to a given technology of production and the dynamics of late industrialization, a syncretist approach is more likely than the three other ideal-typical strategies (traditionalist, modernist, and revolutionary) to enhance managerial authority across large-scale industrial firms. This hypothesis does not suggest that a syncretist strategy is optimal for the attainment of all managerial ends; in fact, it is quite possible that a modernist strategy or a revolutionary strategy may yield more efficacious institutions in the short run by emphasizing, respectively, material incentives or an extraordinary sense of higher purpose. However, short-term efficiency gains or revolutionary breakthroughs, if engineered through institutions that appear alien or illegitimate in the eyes of the working masses, can prove costly to maintain over the longer term. Hence the value of evaluating managerial approaches in terms of their implications of managerial authority, and hence the significance of the syncretism hypothesis where managerial authority is viewed as necessary or desirable for the achievement of other managerial ends.

As noted in chapter 1, the idea of syncretism is related to arguments that either warn against the dangers of ignoring local structures and practices in the pursuit of ambitious modern objectives, or emphasize the benefits of engineering a synergy between modernizing initiatives and existing constellations of norms and social relations in the wider society.[178] The logic informing such arguments is essentially similar to that informing the hypothesis offered here about the benefits of managerial syncretism. Despite increasing levels of technology and complexity in modern institutions of work, certain portable norms and social practices evident among past communities of work continue to be part of the templates through which workers attempt to make sense of the organization of work and authority in industry; thus, within the range of organizational variation permitted by a given techology of production, managerial elites can develop ideologies and work routines that are understandable in terms of those templates, thereby avoiding conflicts, tensions, and ambiguities that can lead to a decline in worker commitment.

What remains to be considered is the mechanism through which syncretist approaches might lead to higher payoffs for managerial authority. As noted in chapter 1, the plausibility of this hypothesis rests on the logic of *congruence* along two dimensions of institutional life, between the material (technical) and the ideal (normative) aspects, and between the formal and informal realms. The relevance of congruence along the first dimension—between the material and ideal realms—echoes Geertz's observation that social integration everywhere depends on avoiding "incongruity between the cultural framework of meaning and the patterning of social interaction."[179] In the context of institutions of work, this points to the relevance of the tensions or complementarities between the normative aspects in a factory (the official company ideology or the informal values shared by workers) and the more observable aspects structuring workplace relations (the formal organizational routines set up by managerial elites or the less formal practices reproduced by other members). It is possible, for example, that a managerial ideology emphasizing collectivist themes will resonate with the sensibilities of workers, but will bear little resemblance to a system of work organization based on individual contracts, individual responsibilities, and competitive performance evaluations.

At the same time, although a complete convergence of interests between managers and workers is neither likely nor necessary, it *is* necessary to ensure that competing systems of work and authority—one *formally* articulated by superiors, the others *informally* created by subordinates—do not create contradictory, mutually exclusive, expectations for the behavior of workers in the same workplace. For example, managers may announce certain official wage practices related to individual output, but may leave the distribution of earnings to workgroup leaders who invoke their own criteria for determining what constitutes a fair wage; in such a case, the possibility looms large that the expectations of managers will be routinely contradicted by what actually happens on the shopfloor.

Thus, the idea of congruence at the workplace suggests two sets of relationships worth examining: (a) the compatibility of work-related normative structures (whether in the form of official managerial ideology or informal worker norms) and the concrete work routines and practices on the shopfloor (whether officially sanctioned or not); and (b) the relationship between the formal and informal systems of work and authority in the workplace—the formal articulated in official ideologies, hierarchies, and work routines established by managers, and the informal reflected in the more spontaneous understandings and interactions among workers on the shopfloor (see fig. 8).[180]

But why specifically should congruence, or the lack thereof, along either of these axes make a difference in tracing the impact of managerial strategies on managerial authority? As noted in chapter 1, the logic invoked here has been partly influenced by Eckstein's famous argument about the benefits of congruent patterns of authority across governmental institutions and various nongovernmental segments of social life. For Eckstein, *congruence* did not necessarily mean "isomorphic authority patterns," but it did suggest some sort of fit or essential compatibility between patterns of authority found at the governmental level and those found in municipal organizations and various nongovernmental communities; where such a fit does not exist and incongruities are too pronounced, official patterns of authority are likely to be unstable.[181] But Eckstein's argument was not driven by the "higher needs" of political systems; in fact, Eckstein made quite explicit the motivational basis for his argument, pointing to the psychological dilemmas individuals face—in the form of strain or anomie—as a result of conflicting normative prescriptions and role expectations created by incongruent patterns of authority.[182] Although Eckstein did not specifically address industrial relations, the

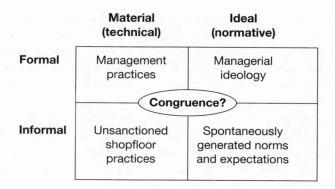

Fig. 8.   Dimensions of congruence in the industrial enterprise

implications of his theory for the firm and other forms of "private govern-ment" are readily apparent.[183]

The conceptualization of *congruence* here respectfully extends or chal-lenges Eckstein's theoretical constructions in several respects. In conclud-ing this chapter it is worth elaborating on how Eckstein's treatment resem-bles, but differs somewhat from, the use of the concept here. First of all, Eckstein's approach, because it was an investigation into an existing stable democracy, did not explicitly address the relevance of historical legacies or external influences. The idea that congruence in authority patterns enables stability implicitly suggested some continuity over time, particularly in norms and structures at the community level; but the logic of congruence is not systematically articulated in relation to the resilience of *past* norms or the impact of referent societies. In this book, the question of congruence is explicitly related to the question of how the past relates to the present and how indigenous templates relate to borrowed or "alien" practices. As previously noted, it is assumed that two stylized categories of actors—managerial elites and workers—respond differentially to external stimuli and past influences: the former, reflected in the influences of management models in referent societies, are presumed to leave a more profound impression on managerial elites; the latter, reflected in the resilient norms and cooperative practices in preexisting communities of work, are pre-sumed to more reflexively affect the attitudes and expectations of workers.

Second, rather than assume that incongruent authority patterns in quite different social contexts will lead to instability, the relevance of con-gruence here is limited to a single institutional context or *functionally sim-*

ilar institutional contexts. That is, the relevant legacies in examining institutions of work are assumed to be those specific norms and practices inherited from past communities of work, and the problem of congruence is limited to the question of how these legacies relate to newly established managerial ideals and practices. Moreover, although the conceptualization of *congruence* here is loosely related to the idea of a fit across patterns of authority in Eckstein's work, here the fit is along two distinct aspects *within* the same institution (as suggested in fig. 8). The influences of other social or normative structures do remain relevant, as evident in the influence of a wider cultural ethos on past communities of work, or of foreign management models on the design of firms in NWLIs, but these influences are relevant only insofar as they are actually manifested in actual choices and behaviors in the workplace. By limiting the question of congruence to specific institutional contexts, the result is a much more focused analysis of normative and social structures that are competing but functionally comparable, and the burden of justifying such an analysis is significantly less than that taken on by Eckstein.

Third, the microfoundational assumptions underpinning the concept of congruence here extend and refine the motivational basis for Eckstein's argument. Eckstein simply assumed that incongruent patterns of authority in different social contexts will inevitably create conflicting expectations and produce strain in individuals, failing to take into account the possibility that individuals may be able to compartmentalize the roles and identities they take on in different institutional settings. At the same time, there is no reason why Eckstein's assumptions cannot be reframed in the context of different dimensions inside a single institutional context, within which conflicting normative prescriptions and role expectations *could* very well produce social tensions and psychological strain. Thus, in this analysis, it is assumed that workers will find themselves in such a situation where they encounter competing sets of norms and practices identified with the formal and informal systems of work and authority on the shopfloor. In fact, because competing authority patterns are thought to coexist within a single institutional setting here, it is possible to anticipate even more intense role conflicts and more powerful strain than is suggested by Eckstein's analysis. Thus, the effectiveness of managerial syncretism is related in part to the individual-level benefits of reducing the incongruence between formal and informal systems of work and authority and thereby providing some scope for the worker to satisfy the expectations and role requirements of both systems.

Fourth, the motivational basis underpinning the concept of congruence is extended further in this book by drawing attention to the psychological benefits of *familiarity* in coping with the anxiety and uncertainty that subordinates face by virtue of their position within new organizational hierarchies. As research in the field of occupational psychology suggests, while rewards and sanctions may affect the disposition of individuals toward the institution in which they participate, there is also a powerful, less consciously articulated, sense of anxiety that subordinates share in organizational life. Thus, where a predictable, familiar, and reassuring social environment is not provided by formal organizational ideologies and routines, subordinates will tend to covertly withdraw, refraining from offering their cooperation and commitment, and even joining together informally to develop "social defenses" to cope with anxieties.[184] This dynamic is assumed to have even more profound consequences for the psychology of workers in NWLIs: the formal system of management in NWLIs, because it is likely to have been influenced by management models established in "alien" contexts, is not likely to provide a very reassuring and secure environment; at the same time, the compression of economic and social change faced by workers in NWLIs paves the way for even more sudden and more dramatic transformations in the environment.[185] Under such conditions, sharp incongruities between formal and informal systems of work and authority will make it all the more likely that the worker will tend to withdraw from the former and seek the security of the latter even if this compromises formally prescribed roles, identities, and work routines. These aspects do not point to an intractable problem, but they do suggest the need for concerted action to shift the balance back so that formal management ideologies and practices can offer something in lieu of the "traditional sources of security" workers were previously accustomed to relying on.[186]

Finally, the possibility for concerted action to address the problem of incongruence represents another marked departure from Eckstein's approach. Although Eckstein was careful to identify the individual-level assumptions underpinning his argument, he did not systematically incorporate categories of agency that could speak to the choices and strategies adopted by elites. Eckstein's empirical analysis of Norway's stable democracy, for example, applied the notion of congruence in a highly deterministic manner, suggesting that cohesion and stability at the national level were a result of the fact that the styles and patterns of authority in government were congruent with those at the community level. In his last essays, Eckstein did attempt to spin out the implications of his research for approaches to democratization and postcommunist transitions, suggesting that "democratization should proceed gradually, incrementally, and by the use of syncretic devices."[187] But, even here, Eckstein did not concern himself with the problem of systematically distinguishing and evaluating strategies in terms of their varied implications for institution-building; and, in the latest incarnation of his general argument, he continued to treat congruence as a "normal" state that incongruent authority patterns will inevitably gravitate toward through "adaptive" changes.[188] In contrast, this book places a great deal of emphasis on the identification and evaluation of distinct institution-building *strategies,* suggesting that elites are in a position to make critical decisions about which combinations of ideology and practice to invoke in view of the competing influences of inherited legacies and institutional models. Thus, for the purposes of this book, congruence essentially represents an intervening mechanism through which the effects of particular managerial strategies—construed as a response to inherited legacies, external influences, and historical circumstances—have an impact on the responsiveness of the work force to commands issued by managerial elites.

Returning once more to the hypothesis, it must be remembered that although a syncretist strategy is expected to produce greater congruence, the engineering of congruence is not a defining feature or objective of syncretism or of any of the institution-building strategies; in fact, all of the ideal-typical strategies are defined and distinguished solely in terms of the orientation of institution-builders toward the past and toward external models (see figs. 2 and 7). Moreover, under certain combinations of historical circumstances, it may be possible for modernist or revolutionary approaches to produce congruence as well. Where, for example, a catastrophic event results in large numbers of people abandoning preexisting norms and practices, the emulation of existing models or the construction of revolutionary orders may succeed in producing congruence because the informal norms and practices within new institutional contexts will be more malleable, unable to offer the emotional benefits of familiarity or reassurance to subordinates. At the same time, under particular technological or organizational constraints, while some institution-builders may stumble upon a syncretist formula, others consciously attempting to devise one may fail to do so because it may be difficult to identify any elements in existing repertoires of cooperative work that support the desired organization of work and authority.

These scenarios notwithstanding, the discussion in this chapter has suggested that there are some good reasons to believe why, all other things being equal, syncretist formulas are more likely to lead to higher levels of managerial authority in NWLIs by comparison to the approaches approximating the other three ideal-typical strategies. Modernist managerial elites are likely to have underestimated the strength and significance of preexisting norms and social relations; while the official managerial ideals and practices they introduce may be congruent with one another, these are likely to contradict at least some of the more familiar norms and practices reconstructed informally by workers on the shopfloor. Traditionalist managers, for their part, are likely to have underestimated the implications of the tensions created by the incompatibility of borrowed management practices and a traditional ideology that resonates with—and maybe even reinforces—workers' preexisting norms; here the most likely incongruity will be between the normative and material aspects of the workplace. And revolutionary managerial approaches, unless they *happen* to promote ideals that turn out to be resonant with preexisting norms, will run into the problematic trade-offs between the promotion of novel ideals and practices and the maintenance of a stable system of production; the former will undoubtedly require a great deal of time and patience as new norms and ideals are internalized by the work force, but in the meantime, it may be difficult to articulate a system of work and authority that meaningfully reflects management ideals as understood from the vantage point of the workers supposedly being socialized.

By contrast, the fact that managerial syncretism selectively draws upon existing norms and forms of cooperation in defining management ideologies and framing management practices can help to reduce, though not eliminate, the incongruities between the normative and technical aspects of management and between the formal and informal systems of work and authority; this, in turn, points to several benefits at the individual level, namely, the reduction of conflicting role expectations for the worker, and the reduced distance between formal aspects of management and the more familiar informal shopfloor norms and practices. In light of the motivational component of the argument noted above, it is expected that these benefits will ultimately redound to the collective attitudes of the work force toward the formal system of production, presumably enhancing managerial authority in NWLIs. The following two chapters examine the dilemmas and strategies of institution-building as evident in the evolution of large-scale industrial enterprises in late-industrializing Japan and Russia.

Chapter 3

Work, Community, and Authority in Late-Industrializing Japan

Prewar "Traditionalism" to Postwar "Syncretism"

The advantage of being one of those who follow is that it gives one the opportunity to take note of the history of those who have gone before, and to avoid taking the same path.

—Kaneko Kentaro, 1896[1]

The company is neither made up simply of capital, nor should be responsible solely to the interest of capital . . . The company is a place of production . . . it is also a place of employment and a provider of welfare. The scientific promotion of productivity is not only a necessary condition for its own survival, but also a way to lighten employees' hardship at work, to improve their standard of living, and to provide good, cheap products to society.

—Japan Committee of Economic Development, 1955[2]

During the 1880s, when the modernizing elites of Meiji Japan were sending mission after mission to Western countries in search of institutional models to emulate, British sociologist Herbert Spencer reportedly told Japanese envoy Lord Kido that the cohesiveness of Japan's traditional social institutions, the sense of obligation toward superiors, and the shared identification with national welfare presented Meiji Japan with an opportunity to industrialize without the social turmoil experienced by the more individualistic early modernizers.[3] After the turn of the century, however, as the industrial enterprise became progressively larger and more complex, the accompanying growth of unionism and industrial conflict made it clear to business and government elites that a more proactive effort would be necessary. This effort, which most closely approximates a *traditionalist* institution-building strategy, resulted in the 1910s through 1930s in the

123

juxtaposition of a "family firm" ideal alongside management practices largely borrowed from Taylorism. The strategy ultimately failed to generate managerial authority, however; while coercion and steep managerial hierarchies kept overt conflict and turnover in check as Japan mobilized for war, the incongruities between a familiar ideal and the stark realities on the shopfloor provided little basis for worker cooperation or commitment. It is only after defeat in war, followed by a period of intense labor militancy and social unrest, that managers and workers in large-scale industrial firms finally managed to negotiate some of the key components of what is interpreted here as an approximation of a *syncretist* managerial approach. This strategy involved a more nuanced and selective use of familiar normative constructs alongside management practices that represented a partial retreat from Taylorism as well as an innovative adaptation of newer trends in management models abroad.

This chapter examines and compares how effectively managerial elites in prewar and postwar Japan coped with the legacies they inherited and the models they encountered in organizing work and authority in typical large-scale industrial enterprises. The comparison of Japanese enterprises in the prewar and postwar period also presents an opportunity to develop a distinctive interpretation that takes into account, and partially reconciles, contending perspectives on Japanese industrial relations and management practices in the prewar and postwar periods. Section 3.1 briefly considers those features of communities of work in Tokugawa Japan that are thought to constitute a distinguishable and portable legacy for institutions of work developed in Japan after 1868. Sections 3.2 and 3.3 examine the characteristics of Japanese enterprises and firms in the prewar and postwar periods respectively, focusing on the evolution of managerial ideologies, as well as the emergence of such aspects of Japanese management as the employment system, the wage- and bonus-system, and the organization of production. Section 3.4 interprets the contrast between prewar and postwar managerial approaches as indicative of the differences between traditionalist and syncretist institution-building strategies, providing a basis for the central hypothesis of this book. In addition, since the treatment of Japan here is based on careful consideration of multiple, sometimes conflicting, narratives on central issues in Japanese studies, appendix B presents a discussion of diverse perspectives on Japanese history, society, and industry, while identifying the more nuanced treatments that provide the points of departure for the interpretation developed in this chapter.[4]

3.1. The Legacy: Communities of Work in Tokugawa Japan

As noted in chapter 1, the salience and portability of preexisting norms and practices in the course of industrialization is assumed to be limited to those features that were invoked to define and regulate the preindustrial communities of work. In the case of late-industrializing Japan, it is the typical village hamlet of the Tokugawa era, the *mura,* that represents the relevant unit of analysis for the purpose of identifying and tracing the influence of preexisting norms and practices that defined and regulated communities of everyday work. The *mura* is the first non–kinship-based bounded social unit within which expectations about cooperation, mutual assistance, and the obligations of those with wealth and status had to be routinized and institutionalized; the *mura* is also the primary arena where the distinct identities and interests of different households *(ie)* were acknowledged and had to be systematically reconciled, and where signs of peasant unrest first came into evidence. Thus, it is the *mura* where norms related to reciprocal cooperation, the management and distribution of resources, and the obligations associated with wealth and status were institutionalized in the context of everyday life and work.

There were certainly important variations across village communities throughout Japan, but for the purposes of the broader comparative study, these variations are assumed to be less significant than the more generalized norms and practices that make it possible to recognize and compare typical village communities in Japan and Russia. This assumption is neither unusual nor without some basis in the social processes through which similar kinds of common normative and social structures have historically emerged in other regions of the world. Some level of homogenization may be presumed to have occurred even before the sixteenth century with the gradual emergence of recognizable Japanese dialects, along with the spread and fusion of Shinto, Confucian, and Buddhist beliefs and practices over a period of centuries. Subsequently, the gradual process of state formation in Tokugawa Japan between the seventeenth and nineteenth centuries, the increasing exposure to common beliefs and myths identified with the code of the samurai *(bushido),* the increasing levels of social contact across villages and prefectures, the spread of village schools in the late Tokugawa era, and the similar kinds of institutional and economic pressures faced by villages administered by the same prefectural *(han)* administration all may be presumed to have further contributed to the emergence of some recognizable norms and practices across village communities. While it is unlikely

that these processes eroded long-standing differences across many locali-
ties, they may be reasonably assumed to have narrowed the extent of variation across Tokugawa village communities, at least relative to the
significantly more wide-ranging variations found in cross-national comparisons.[5]

   This section provides a stylized account of the typical shared norms
and social practices that enabled members of the Tokugawa *mura* to maintain social order, legitimate hierarchy, and regulate the distribution of
rewards and obligations in the course of everyday life and work. In addition to a strong sense of collective identity related to participation in
everyday work-related activities, these norms and practices included an
unusually high value placed on a dense network of mutual obligations as a
basis for cooperation and harmony, as well as a tolerance of steep hierarchies of wealth and power provided these were accompanied by expectations of benevolence toward the less fortunate. These features of Tokugawa village life certainly did not prevent instances of peasant conflict and
rebellion against village or prefectural authorities; but, in keeping with a
well-established interpretation of peasant rebellion in Japan, these instances are viewed as indicative of strong responses provoked by perceived
violations of norms and expectations associated with membership in the
mura. Thus, without exaggerating the sense of order and harmony in
Tokugawa Japan, it is possible to recognize certain norms and practices
that make the Tokugawa *mura* a distinctive type of preindustrial community, especially when contrasted with the Russian peasant commune.[6]

Community Membership, Norms of Reciprocity,
and Collective Harmony

Like traditional peasant communities elsewhere, the Tokugawa *mura*
formed the most important basis of collective identity and cooperation
beyond the household unit. Every villager was in constant contact with fellow villagers, interacting with them over a vast range of shared social
activities and drawing sharp distinctions between insiders and outsiders.
Each *mura* had its own shrine and had clear boundaries within which there
was a high level of village consciousness cultivated over a long period of
time. A person's social identity and reputation continued to rest not upon
his/her individual personality *(hitogara)* but upon the standing of the family *(iegara)* within the village community; the bearer of moral and legal
responsibility (e.g., for criminal acts or nonpayment of taxes) was always

a family group or the community as a whole.[7] While individuals undoubtedly made rational calculations in their everyday lives, in terms of *moral* action, the open pursuit of individual interests and individual self-expression were regarded as legitimate only within certain narrowly defined realms and only if they were subordinated to group loyalty and harmony in the wider social realm; in fact, personal gratification was to some extent predicated on the fulfillment of one's roles and obligations within the family and community.[8] In all these respects, the Tokugawa *mura* was more or less similar to agrarian communities throughout the preindustrial world.

In contrast to the Russian peasant commune and village communities elsewhere, however, membership in the *mura* was defined not in terms of extended kinship principles, primordial ties, or other pre-given attributes but rather in terms of actual interactions and cooperation in the course of everyday life and work.[9] Thus, the ties binding the members of the village community were intertwined with concrete practices for coordinating everyday mutual assistance, the exchange of labor among households during harvest time, the management of common resources (irrigation, firewood, fertilizer, etc.), and the payment of rice taxes to prefectural authorities. The strong sense of community identity and the bases for continued membership in that community were intrinsically connected to the actual management of communally owned resources and to "the investment of huge amounts of human labor in the cooperative preparation and upkeep of rice paddies."[10] The very language employed in referring to agricultural work in social contexts incorporated connotations of reciprocal obligations: cooperation among different families was referred to as *yui,* the system of exchanging labor during key periods such as the period for planting rice; similarly, *suke* referred to labor, but only the labor given by a dependent to a benefactor in exchange and gratitude for benefits such as a loan of lands, animals, or a house.[11] Thus, participation in the collective affairs of the *mura* was not simply a matter of institutionalizing cooperation to cope with practical difficulties of agrarian life. The village was considered a single *moral* sphere, within which "exchange of labor between neighbors and kin was the rule [and] compromise and accommodation were highly valued."[12]

The moral basis for cooperation in the *mura* is further distinguishable in terms of the high value members generally placed on the notions of duty and reciprocal obligations shared by members of the community. While the Russian peasant commune was also characterized by the joint management of resources and traditions of mutual aid, the normative foundation for these practices derived from a sense that all households had a right to adequate shares of resources so that they may satisfy their needs; this is a different kind of value than one that emphasizes mutual indebtedness and the preservation of community harmony as the primary basis for cooperation. Even by comparison to other East Asian societies shaped by Confucian moral precepts, the sense of duty linked to reciprocal obligations in everyday social relations stands out as an unusually strong feature in defining and regulating the *mura* as a community.[13] The familiar ideal of *on* (mutual indebtedness) provided the normative foundation for defining membership in the *mura* in terms of both duties and expectations as expressed in an ongoing process of diffuse reciprocal exchange and mutual aid in concrete contexts of life and work.[14]

In addition, the ideal of harmony *(wa)* was frequently invoked to justify mechanisms designed to preserve cooperative arrangements and pre-empt social conflict. While social order and cooperation are undoubtedly valued in all communities, the ideal of harmony took on a special concrete significance in the *mura* since the absence of social conflicts signified whether members of the community understood their duties and properly discharged their obligations to one another. Moreover, ideas about collective advancement or group achievement were assumed to be predicated on first achieving harmony within the group.[15]

This does not, of course, mean that intravillage conflicts were absent or that individual households did not adopt separate identities and pursue separate interests; in fact, conflicts, jealousies, and petty squabbles were no less evident in the *mura* than in other preindustrial communities.[16] But the fact remains that members of the *mura* placed a higher *moral value* on the maintenance of social harmony than did many other communities, and this accounts for the speed and urgency with which mediators informally attempted to resolve legal disputes and reestablish harmony among feuding groups or individuals.[17] Thus, while the value placed on harmony did not necessarily make the *mura* a harmonious community in reality, it did serve to promote a variety of extralegal mechanisms to rapidly restore order and project an image of conformity and harmony in order to preserve the village's reputation as a functioning moral community. These included the practice of *jidan,* the arrangement of an informal discussion among conflicting parties, often mediated by a third party (usually a village elder), with the possibility of taking the matter to higher authorities if no agreement was reached.[18] If a settlement deemed fair by the elder and by nondisputants was not accepted by a party thought to have violated village rules, *muraharai* (cleansing or ostracization) could be invoked to expel the recalcitrant household from the village if it persisted in ignoring the terms of a settlement or violating village codes.[19] Typically, however, before any one party was expelled or before outside authorities had to intervene, villages generally managed to resolve internal conflicts through the intervention of leaders and elders in the village, persons with higher status and greater age, who were usually able to engineer consensus or forge a compromise.[20] These practices attest to the particularly high value placed on the mechanisms for informally resolving disputes and preventing overt displays of adversarial behavior.[21]

Hierarchy as a Conditional Virtue: Stratification and Mutual Obligations in the Mura

It is important to recognize that the value placed on collective harmony and group identity was intrinsically linked to the acceptance of steep patterns of social stratification and submission to those with greater status and authority within the village hierarchy. Hierarchical authority and social stratification are surely found in any society; but in the Tokugawa village, hierarchy was considered to be an important aspect of orderly group life, and the steepness of hierarchical social structures was more readily apparent, particularly when considered alongside the more egalitarian norms and practices of the Russian peasant commune. Anthropologists and sociologists have frequently emphasized the steepness of hierarchy as a distinctive characteristic of group life in preindustrial Japan, with those in positions of authority—from family heads and village elders to the master in a master-apprentice *(oyabun-kobun)* relationship—viewed as more experienced and more deserving of respect and obedience.[22] The respect shown toward authority figures in Tokugawa society is interpreted in many of these studies as positive or functional, because it not only allowed for the diffusion of conflict through the mediation provided by elders, but also brought benefits for less prosperous or lower-status members of the community. Thus, just as the apprentice *(kobun)* benefited from the protection and tutelage of the more experienced master *(oyabun)*, the less fortunate peasant who had fallen on hard times benefited from the material assistance offered by prosperous village leaders.[23]

Although a revisionist strand of analysis has critiqued this interpretation for its overly benign view of authority and hierarchy in Tokugawa Japan,[24] the emphasis in these works on conflict and oppressiveness in

Tokugawa Japan does not fundamentally contradict the observation that conditional hierarchy was a defining and valued feature of collective life and work in the *mura*. In fact, revisionist historians themselves recognize that the steep hierarchies in wealth and status were accompanied by a set of reciprocal expectations, evident in a pattern of demonstrated deference to prosperous village elders and officials in exchange for the expectation of benevolent treatment. Indeed, much peasant protest was spurred by the shared sense of less fortunate *mura* members that village elders and officials were not, in fact, tending to the welfare of the community; most petitions and protests also evinced a remarkably similar form of expression, emphasizing humility on the part of "honorable" petitioners who only sought to ensure that "the moral duties of the just and benevolent lord" would be carried out.[25] That tenants could and did demand specific actions from higher-status figures (such as reductions in tax burdens or assistance in times of crisis) was thus consistent with the tolerance of hierarchical authority, and differentials in status and wealth were generally regarded as legitimate as long as landlords and other village authorities acted upon their moral obligations to attend to the special needs of poorer households facing dire predicaments. In fact, the growth and strength of successful peasant protest was a result not of growing class consciousness but of the cohesiveness of peasant communities and their ability to mobilize members by appealing to the duties and obligations associated with authority.[26] Furthermore, when considered alongside peasant rebellions in the Russian countryside, it is highly significant that rural unrest in Tokugawa Japan was usually propelled not by participants' commitment to egalitarian ideals but by their frustrations over unmet expectations of benevolence and protection from prosperous elders in times of difficulty. Thus, as in the case of the value of harmony, the significance of steeply hierarchical authority relations in Tokugawa Japan is not that they effectively suppressed dissent or conflict, but that the normative basis for these relations was tied to a sense of reciprocal obligations that made obedience and respect for authority figures conditional upon benevolent protection and assistance.

In the concrete context of social practices, hierarchy in the *mura* was generally manifested in a series of ranks and status distinctions related to property ownership as well as in the procedures for reaching collective decisions and dividing up collective responsibilities. The typical social hierarchy was headed by one or two landlord families, with the rest of the village population divided equally among owner farmers, tenant farmers, and farmers who owned part of their land and leased the rest. A village register *(kotohyo)* ranked all of the families from top to bottom according to the levels of wealth and income, and their records in handling money. The primary function of this system of ranking was not to bind members to particular duties associated with any ascribed role but to define and legitimate the steeply hierarchical socioeconomic stratification within the village and, in the process, to identify the different kinds of obligations expected of members of households of a given status and rank.[27] In terms of dyadic relations within the *mura,* hierarchically defined reciprocal obligations were manifested in landlord-tenant relations with the landlord *oyabun* helping the tenant *kobun* in times of trouble, the tenant showing great respect and deference to the landlord, and the landlord sometimes even standing as a guarantor for the tenant farmer when the latter joined a cooperative credit organization. Even if a systematic stratification within the peasantry never evolved across the villages and *han*s, landlord-tenant relations within a village were an important case of crystallized status differentials and hierarchical personal ties passed down through succeeding generations of the respective families.[28]

Decision-making authority corresponded to the sharply stratified social structure of the *mura* and was thus extremely centralized. The village headman *(shoya* or *nanushi),* usually a powerful landlord, was responsible to the provincial *(han)* administrators for law-abiding behavior throughout the village and the collective payment of taxes. The headman was usually the patriarch of the most powerful family in the village, usually the largest landholder or the landlord with the most tenants. It was he who mediated between the village community and all outsiders, including other village headmen and feudal authorities.[29] There existed a village assembly consisting of farmers' representatives *(mura yoriai)* and a council of high-ranking leaders, each representing groups of five neighboring households *(gumi).*[30] These bodies were supposed to approve all the collective decisions of the hamlet; they even determined the tax burden for each household in the course of collecting the land tax assessed collectively for every village by *han* authorities. In everyday practice, however, most representatives in the assembly usually deferred to the headman's decisions; their main function was thus limited to ensuring that the households or five-family groups abided by the laws and met their collective obligations.[31] Thus, village leadership became virtually hereditary, suggesting continuity of status relations over generations and the concentration of leadership functions in the hands of the heads of the highest ranking families within each village.[32]

It is important to note that these aspects of hierarchy, and whatever value was attached to them, did not preclude the diffuse sense of equality that emerges from the mere fact of shared identity and common membership in the *mura*. While this diffuse equality is nothing like the more explicit egalitarianism of the Russian *mir,* it does point to some important limits to the exercise of hierarchical authority in group contexts. Unlike the household, which was ultimately based on some notion of common ancestry and patrilineal descent, the *mura* was a large community defined not through ascriptive or kinship ties but through a concretely bounded framework of social and economic interaction. Within this framework, despite the deference to authority and the steepness of social stratification, the definition of a common identity had to incorporate some standard notion of rights and responsibilities associated with membership in the village community. Thus, all member households in the *mura* participated in the traditions of mutual assistance in harvest time, expected special assistance in times of need, regularly made claims on collectively managed resources, and defined goals in pursuit of higher economic and social status within the community.[33]

The Household (Ie) *as a Corporate Group: A Comment*

Because many discussions of the cultural inheritance in Japan have focused on the structure of the traditional Japanese household *(ie),* and because the *ie* was specifically invoked by managerial elites to support the ideology of the "family firm" in prewar Japan, it is worth briefly comparing the nature of membership and participation in the *ie* and the *mura*. Some Japanese scholars have suggested that the *ie* and the *mura* were traditionally organized in terms of the same essential characteristics: each pursued collective goals that included the perpetuation and expansion of the group, symbolized by hereditary group leadership; each emphasized long-term attachment and loyalty to the same group once a member joined that group whether or not kinship ties were invoked to define group boundaries; each sought to balance vertical organization and complementary measures emphasizing group homogeneity; and each emphasized the autonomy of the group by having its members collectively discharge all the tasks necessary for its perpetuation.[34] In this view, the *ie* and the *mura* were not fundamentally different kinds of groups; the latter was simply a larger, less tightly knit, less homogeneous, and less hierarchical version of the former.

Underneath these formal similarities, however, there are at least three important *qualitative* distinctions worth considering that bear directly on the kinds of ideologies and norms found in prewar and postwar Japanese enterprises. First, while membership in the *ie* was less restrictive than in households elsewhere that were based solely on kinship ties (that is, servants could gain entry into the *ie,* and an adopted son could theoretically become its head), the household in Tokugawa Japan still represented a "continuing entity, perpetuated in principle by patrilineal descent, from ancestors to descendants, an entity of which the family group at any one time is only the current manifestation."[35] This was not the case for the *mura,* in which membership had more to do with the fulfillment of obligations and participation in everyday village activities than with common primordial attributes or generational continuity.

It is also worth noting that the basis for hierarchy within the household was invariable: according to the system of patrilineal descent, the eldest son always inherited the position of household head and control over the family possessions, and the stem family *(honke)* set up by the eldest son always retained greater property and greater authority than the branch families *(bunke)* set up by younger sons.[36] This system of primogeniture, buttressed by a Tokugawa ban on the division of family holdings, had the effect of further strengthening the status and power of the elder son as the future head of the household who would be in a position to determine the distribution of collective possessions owned jointly by the *ie.*[37] The status hierarchy of the village community, by contrast, while largely reproduced over generations, generally reflected the distribution of wealth, which is, in principle, variable; and there remained widespread expectations about the obligations that those in wealth and power were expected to take on. Thus, unlike the virtually unassailable authority of the household head (even one perceived as failing in his obligations), the authority of the village head and assembly leaders could, and frequently was, challenged by members of lower-ranking and less fortunate households.

Finally, the idea of interdependence was more elaborately institutionalized in the *mura* precisely because everyday cooperation within the *mura* was potentially more problematic than was the case within the *ie.* Although the division of labor in both cases was relatively simple, it is significant that within the household, the notion of separate individual identities, interests, and contributions was not given much legitimacy. Certainly, individuals may have pursued personal goals and may have refused to cooperate with other members of their households, but the ideas of self-sufficiency and separate goals among the constituent elements of the *ie* had no social meaning.[38] As a result, apart from the commands of the household head, standard mechanisms were not deemed necessary to ensure cooperation or reconcile separate identities and interests among household members. In contrast, the members of the *mura* could legitimately claim to belong to subunits of the community with separate household identities, interests, and property; indeed, the households themselves were expected to demonstrate some level of self-sufficiency if they were to partake of the common resources or make claims on the benevolence of village leaders. Thus, while notions of cooperation and interdependence among constituent units within the household were almost superfluous, the separate identities, interests, and property of the constituent members of the *mura* made it necessary to develop explicit norms and institutionalized mechanisms to diffuse conflict, manage commonly shared resources, and coordinate mutual assistance among neighboring households in a village.

Certainly, cooperation and hierarchy within villages has everywhere been a more complicated matter than within households; what makes the above three distinctions between the *ie* and the *mura* particularly relevant is the fact that scholarly discussions of "groupism" in Japan treat both social units as manifestations of the same organizational principles. More to the point, Japanese institution-builders themselves have often regarded this groupism as a continuing foundation for social order, without considering whether the model of the *ie* or the *mura* might be more functional for the purpose of generating organizational commitment within complex bureaucratized institutions. The distinction, however, is significant for understanding why managerial ideologies promoting the "family firm" in prewar Japan were inherently operating at a disadvantage when compared to the more generalized ideals of cooperation, interdependence, and community membership embraced by postwar managerial elites.

Social Change and the Survival of Community Norms:
Justifying an Assumption

As previously noted, this book is predicated on the assumption that in NWLIs individualism generally remains on the margins, and portable features of preexisting communities of work continue to influence the norms and expectations shared by workers entering the industrial enterprise. In the case of Japan, such an assumption is not likely to be definitively validated given the fundamental and unresolvable differences in the foundational assumptions with which scholars working in different intellectual traditions attempt to characterize social change.[39] Nevertheless, many well-regarded studies offer similar kinds of observations that may be plausibly interpreted as evidence that the attitudes and expectations of prewar and postwar Japanese workers have not gone through a fundamental transformation when compared with norms and ideals underpinning everyday life and work in the *mura*.

In relation to workers in the prewar period, it is significant that competing perspectives in early-twentieth-century historiography do not differ over what it is that workers most wanted from their superiors: dignity, respect, and, above all, greater attention from superiors to the welfare of subordinates in exchange for the latter's obedience. Some studies inevitably overemphasize the distinctiveness of Japanese work culture, frequently suggesting a rather benign view of managerial behavior and interpreting managerial paternalism—and the workers' preference for it—as an extension of the basic principles underlying status relations in the Tokugawa era.[40] Yet, more critical treatments of prewar industrial relations, although placing greater emphasis on the history of conflict and distrust in labor-management relations, generally accept the notion that workers were neither concerned about the "natural rights" of the working class nor inherently opposed to notions of benevolent authority within the factory, but were primarily concerned with greater social respect and more fair treatment as members of the factory community.[41] These competing interpretations thus partially converge on the characterization of worker protest in Thomas Smith's famous essay:

> The idea of rights did not call forth the expressions of moral feeling that status did. The employment relation was seen as one between status unequals, similar to the relations between lord and vassal, master and servant, parent and child, calling for benevolence on one side and loyalty and obedience on the other. For ignoring the ethical code governing such relations, employers were denounced as unrighteous, cruel, barbarous, selfish, inhumane, and ignorant of the way of heaven and man. Such injustice was to be overcome by employer reformation,

bringing workers 'improved treatment' *(taigu no kairyo)* and 'higher status' *(chii no kojo),* the two overarching demands of workers from the 1890s into the 1920s.[42]

That is, workers' demands in much of the prewar era tended to be couched not as claims based on universal conceptions of rights but as appeals to employers for just and benevolent treatment, not unlike the appeals of less prosperous villagers for assistance and consideration from village leaders or landlords. Even union activists in prewar Japan emphasized that employers had an opportunity to create a more harmonious community at the workplace if only their behavior had reflected genuine respect and benevolent treatment of the workers; what they decried was not the ideal of benevolent paternalism, but the fact that it was being trumpeted solely as an ideology to manipulate workers, with no tangible benefits or payoffs for the latter.[43] Thus, although workers may very well have been skeptical of the ideology of paternalism invoked by managerial elites, it is also significant that they did not reject the basic principles behind that ideology and that they frequently appropriated the language of paternalism themselves to demand better treatment and greater job and wage security.

Studies of worker attitudes in postwar Japanese firms—again conducted on the basis of quite different foundational assumptions and intellectual agendas—also suggest that workers continued to adhere to the expectation that the authority of superiors rests on their willingness and ability to offer concrete expressions of "benevolence" in exchange for obedience to commands. This expectation does not necessarily suggest that Japanese workers have been culturally predisposed toward being uniquely loyal or diligent, as some naive treatments of Japanese factories have suggested.[44] At the same time, it is significant that even evidence gathered by studies attempting to dispel such treatments indicates that Japanese workers have been more comfortable with the notion of benevolent authority and diffuse personal relations in the firm than workers elsewhere. One such study, intended to emphasize the convergence between Japanese and Western industrial relations, acknowledged the difficulty of explaining why 80 percent of Japanese workers in a random sample indicated a preference for paternalistic managers who might demand extra work in exchange for taking a greater interest in the welfare and personal affairs of employees even if this meant deviating from formal workplace rules.[45] Similarly, a comparative study of Japanese and American work attitudes—again, aimed at downplaying exaggerated views of Japanese workers' loyalty to their firms—found that "the Japanese generally favor close, diffuse relations with supervisors and reciprocal obligations linking the employee and the company."[46] Such observations suggest that postwar Japanese workers' attitudes, while neither unique nor unchanging, at least partly reflect an adaptation of familiar norms that guided past forms of cooperative work.

Patterns of conflict resolution in the postwar era also point to certain portable characteristics of the *mura*. For example, labor conflict was frequently characterized by demands not unlike those made by prewar workers on the basis of ideals about reciprocal obligations and rights signifying community membership. Thus, even at the height of labor militancy in the late 1940s, most workers and unions pressed primarily for the kinds of employment terms that would signify a common basis for full membership in the community, notably, the expansion of job security and seniority-based wages to all categories of regular workers.[47] During the 1970s, workers' strikes became largely institutionalized and predictable "rituals of rebellion," signaling the initiation of a routine pattern of annual wage-bargaining *(shunto)* that would not significantly disrupt the production process.[48] Also reminiscent of the Tokugawa *mura* is the tendency of industrial disputes to be resolved through informal mediation and compromise rather than through a final verdict in court.[49] This tendency does not suggest that Japanese society is inherently more harmonious and less litigious; it does, however, point to the continuing relevance of the idea that social relations within the community *should* be harmonious, and that extended conflicts reflect evidence of one party's failure to fulfill its obligations to another.[50]

Also worth noting is the evidence from surveys of postwar Japanese workers. This evidence generally suggests that Japanese employees continued to downplay the significance of individual performance and emphasize the meaningfulness of the factory as an enduring community. The surveys indicate that Japanese employees during the 1960s and 1970s, in marked contrast to U.S. employees around the same time, were particularly fearful of personnel policies that emphasized the performance of individual employees or publicized comparisons of individual achievement.[51] Similarly, in terms of their orientations toward the distribution of material rewards, postwar Japanese workers continued to be skeptical of wage systems tied to individual performance and skill-types; instead, they consistently favored standard, predictable seniority-based wages and collective rewards (that is, "equal pay for equal age" rather than "equal pay for equal work").[52] In addition, a number of studies of Japanese attitudes, including some conducted by Japanese scholars who are generally critical of Japanese society, point to the resilience of collectivist norms and the relative weakness of individualistic values.[53] This is supported by qualitative studies indicating that preferences for collectivism, order, and hierarchy continue to be more valued in the Japanese workplace and society than individualism.[54] Such findings are reinforced by evidence from cross-national attitude surveys that indicates that Japanese workers, even at the end of the 1970s, continued to more strongly embrace collectivist values compared to Western industrialized societies (although individualistic psychological attributes may have made more inroads in Japan than in less industrialized non-Western societies).[55] Finally, it is worth noting that studies emphasizing the persistence and distinctiveness of Japanese national character (*Nihonjinron*) did strike a chord throughout postwar Japanese society;[56] while such studies have been criticized as unsystematic efforts to propagate a conservative nationalist ideology, it is significant that they were enormously popular during the 1960s and 1970s.[57]

These observations do not point to an unchanging, distinctively Japanese collectivist ethos, but they do suggest that the relative decline of traditional social structures in the course of Japanese industrialization, while accompanied by increasing opportunities for independent choice, did not produce the individuation that accompanied early industrialization in the West.[58] Thus, while both the *ie* and the *mura* became marginalized as social institutions, widely respected interpretations of prewar workers' expectations and demands, as well as studies of postwar workers' preferences and attitudes, suggest that core norms and ideals found in past communities of work may be plausibly assumed to be portable and to exert a strong influence on the sensibilities and expectations of industrial workers at least during the periods under consideration. What effects these legacies may have had on labor relations and managerial authority, however, depend on the choices of managerial elites over time. These are examined in the two sections that follow.

3.2.   Western Learning, Japanese Spirit, and the "Family Firm" in Prewar Japan

The fact that modernizing elites often make appeals to aspects of tradition to legitimate new institutions does not mean that these appeals will enhance their authority or resonate with subordinates. The process of institution-building in prewar Japan (1868–1940) is worth examining precisely because it offers an excellent glimpse into how elites consciously sought to invoke or invent traditional ideals and symbols while attempting to emulate the practices and designs of Western institutional models. Within large-scale industrial enterprises, the fact that managerial elites, supported by business associations and government bureaucrats, increasingly trumpeted the virtues of "beautiful customs" of paternalism and Japanese familialism suggests that these elites were aware of the potential for labor unrest in the course of industrialization. At the same time, the system of enterprise administration and work organization came to be heavily influenced by principles directly borrowed from Western models of scientific management. Although prewar managers did sow some of the seeds for postwar industrial relations, the incongruities between management ideologies and practices did not provide them with much of an opportunity to generate managerial authority in the eyes of the majority of the industrial work force. This section first considers the interplay of traditional themes and Western influences in the entrepreneurial discourses in Meiji Japan (1868–1912), then proceeds to trace the subsequent emergence and failure of a traditionalist managerial approach centered on the "scientifically" managed "family firm."

The Meiji Inheritance: "Western Learning" and "Warm-Hearted" Customs

Although the Meiji Restoration of 1868 brought to power a group of samurai committed to "expelling the barbarians," the first generation of Meiji leaders was also united by a more pragmatic philosophy of "civilization and enlightenment" *(bummei kaika),* which suggested that "Western learning" was a prerequisite for unifying Japan and catching up to the West.[59] Meiji elites did not assume that economic development or the introduction of new institutions would be unproblematic; they did, however, assume (in Veblenian fashion) that Western learning was necessary to transform old habits and attitudes. Thus, the rampant borrowing of Western institutions during the 1870s was initially accompanied by a revolutionary effort to transform old attitudes and social structures through new programs of "national learning"—the propagation of new (mostly Western) ideas and forms of knowledge—in order to provide a modern cultural foundation to support the establishment of modern institutions.[60]

In the realm of industry, the effort to adopt new technologies and spur industrial production was accompanied by new laws and programs initiated by the Meiji state to encourage both the samurai class and the old mercantile houses to adopt new entrepreneurial attitudes and participate in new forms of commerce.[61] The "company-foundation" program, established in the early 1870s, set the stage for the incorporation of the old merchant stores *(ya)* and provided mechanisms for the former samurai to invest their savings and assets in modern "companies" *(kaisha)*. Other laws were subsequently enacted to establish joint-stock companies and banks as well as the Bank of Japan.[62] In addition, in the late Meiji period (1880s–1912), the government arranged for hundreds of overseas fellowships for top managers and economic bureaucrats so that they could study Western commerce, industrial technology, and personnel training.

It is in the context of developing an ideological foundation for new forms of commercial activities that the interplay of modern and traditional ideals first became evident in the discourses of the Meiji business elite. The entrepreneurial ideologies in the 1870s and 1880s, best typified by the exhortations of Meiji businessman Shibusawa Eiichi, interpreted modern business neither as an extension of traditional mercantile activities nor solely as a new means to realize individual gain, but rather as a bold, forward-looking activity that would simultaneously benefit the entrepreneur and the nation. "The claim of the Meiji business leader was that he had demonstrated his sincere concern for the defense of the nation by undertaking the arduous task of developing an economic base for national greatness, thereby proving himself as worthy a successor to the mantle of leadership of the Tokugawa samurai as those who served in the military or government."[63] Even though Meiji business elites may have eschewed the economic individualism openly invoked by business elites in Britain or the United States, however, their ideology was predicated on an adaptation of Samuel Smiles's notion of "self-help" that associated national progress with "individual industry, energy, and uprightness" rather than with the ideals associated with the traditional samurai and merchant classes. Thus, while Shibusawa spurned monopolistic aggrandizement, he also scorned the attitudes of old-fashioned merchants trying to hold on to the guild system; instead, he urged businessmen to expose themselves to new forms of knowledge so that they could create and lead new joint-stock enterprises "for profit and for Japan."[64]

In their relations with workers, however, government and business elites expected the experience of industrial labor itself would be sufficient to pave the way for the emergence of the right attitudes and work habits.

Problems with absenteeism, discipline, or low productivity on the shopfloor were initially interpreted by employers as evidence that individual workers were either irresponsible or still unaccustomed to factory time and factory work. And while Shibusawa and others were beginning to make ideological appeals to gain social respect for business activities, managers on the shopfloor simply relied on technical supervisors to monitor the performance of workgroups and remained unconcerned with working conditions or worker motivation in the factory.[65] Complaints about poor working conditions or low wages were viewed as an unavoidable part of the early stages of industrialization as people left their agrarian communities and flooded into the urban industrial centers in search of new work. Workers' ties to families or rural communities were regarded neither as an analogy for social relations in the factory nor as an impediment to acquiring the right skills and attitudes; rather they were viewed as providing a safety net for impoverished or unemployed workers, with neither the firm nor the government having to shoulder any responsibility.[66] Thus, through the 1870s, while Western learning provided the basis for new forms of knowledge and new attitudes among political and economic elites, a laissez-faire approach was followed in relation to workers on the shopfloor, with the expectation that whatever problems were in evidence would work themselves out as industrialization took off.

By the 1880s, however, increasing evidence of absenteeism, alcoholism, and poor discipline on the shopfloor, as well as the growing problems of pauperization in urban centers such as Tokyo, began to spur more serious fears of the kind of widespread social unrest that had accompanied industrialization in the West. The Ministry of Agriculture and Commerce, in a pamphlet published in 1884, expressed the fear that the "natural friendship and intimacy" of master and apprentice was beginning to break down in the new factories.[67] At the end of the 1880s, more than 80 percent of all industrial workers had been on the job less than three years. Most worked long hours, remained extremely poor, and, when the hardship got unbearable, simply left their employers and returned to their ancestral homes or village communities. Though workers in smaller-scale firms faced the greatest hardships, in larger firms as well, low wages, poor working conditions, and little job security sparked scattered instances of angry protest as well as high levels of worker turnover, particularly among the more capable apprentices and employees.[68]

Not surprisingly, from the late 1880s onward, Meiji political and economic elites began to pay more careful attention to the possible uses of tradition in coping with problems of turnover and worker protest.[69] In the wider society, in anticipation of the kinds of conflicts and tensions that had accompanied industrialization in the West, Meiji leaders were already reducing the emphasis on Western learning in favor of more explicit appeals to feudal or traditional ideals, which, they asserted, provided Japan with a distinctive opportunity to construct its own unique brand of industrial capitalism.[70] In this context, they embraced the doctrine of *kokutai* (literally, "the body of the state"), which popularized the idea of Japan as a "one-family nation" and explicitly defined membership in the Japanese nation in terms of shared ancestry.[71] They also highlighted Japan's native Shinto traditions and called for "moral education" that would promote the traditional ideals of benevolence, loyalty, and filial piety, thereby fostering a sense of cultural distinctiveness and national unity.[72]

In this environment of nationalist fervor, managerial elites shifted their attention from the justification of profit-oriented entrepreneurial activity to the search for new ideological formulas for stable and harmonious relations between workers and managers. In contrast to the laissez-faire approach seen earlier, the 1880s and 1890s witnessed a much more proactive effort as managerial elites, hoping to fend off restrictive labor legislation, increasingly pointed to past traditions of superior-subordinate relations to reassure state elites that Japanese industrial relations would remain harmonious. Thus, just as the political elites trumpeted the virtues of filial piety and benevolent authority, Shibusawa Eiichi began to stress the importance of Confucian ethics in redefining the industrial workplace as a moral community, exhorting businessmen to fulfill their paternalistic obligations to protect and nurture workers so that they could maintain a moral basis for their authority in the workplace. Through a new organization designed to bolster workplace harmony and check labor turnover *(Ryumonsha),* Shibusawa encouraged managers and workers to view themselves as part of a collective entity dedicated to a common goal: national strength and respect.[73] At the same time, oft-repeated references to the unique "warm-heartedness-ism" *(onjo-shugi)* of benevolent employers and to the "beautiful custom of master-servant relations" were intended to suggest that managerial elites could attend to the needs and welfare of employees in a way that managers in Europe had failed to do.[74] As the director of Mitsubishi Shipyards put it:

> Since ancient times, Japan has possessed the beautiful custom of master-servant relations based firmly on the spirit of sacrifice and com-

passion, a custom not seen in many other countries of the world. Even with . . . the growing scale of industrial society, this master-servant relationship persists securely. It is not weak like that of the Western nations. . . . Because of this relationship, the employer loves the employee and the employee respects his master. Interdependent and helping each other, the two preserve industrial peace.[75]

It is significant that these attempts to invoke tradition were aimed at government bureaucrats and not at the typical factory worker. This suggests that managerial elites in the 1880s and 1890s were primarily interested in asserting their moral qualities and preempting bureaucratic intervention; they still did not view workers' attitudes or labor relations *within* the factory as relevant to managerial authority on the shopfloor.

For their part, Meiji government officials, although they embraced the basic idea of paternalistic welfare, became progressively more concerned with the implications of growing urban poverty, high turnover, and an increasingly restless industrial work force. Acutely conscious of the experience of earlier industrializers, they worried that "if we leave things as they are today, we will soon witness the onset of a virulent social disease of the type which befell England at the beginning of this century."[76] Beginning in the 1890s, the government, calling into question the adequacy of relying on the natural "warm-heartedness" of employers, organized a series of national conferences to examine workplace conditions with the objective of preserving industrial harmony in the course of rapid economic development. In 1903, the Ministry of Agriculture and Commerce published its first authoritative labor survey, *Shokko jijo* [Conditions of factory workers], documenting the problems created by unrestrained industrialization as seen in the miserable conditions faced by most industrial workers and the exploitation of women and children in textile factories. Armed with this evidence, government officials, particularly in the Home Ministry, set out to push more firmly for factory legislation to regulate health and safety standards and restrict child and female labor.[77]

Managerial elites and their political allies resisted these efforts, continuing to insist that the unique norms of friendship and harmony among employers and workers in Japan obviated factory legislation or government regulation. For example, the Tokyo Chamber of Commerce and other business associations, concerned that the Ministry of Finance might step in to control turnover, insisted that stricter enforcement of contracts by managers, along with the natural benevolence of employers, would eventually resolve the problem of employees leaving their masters.[78] A watered-down Factory Bill was eventually passed in the Diet in 1911, but only after the Home Ministry, acknowledging that Japanese labor relations were uniquely harmonious, convinced the business elite that basic welfare issues such as health and safety could be subject to government legislation as they were directly connected to harmonious labor relations and increased productivity.[79] As Shibusawa himself framed the issue, although conditions in Japanese factories were inherently better than in Western factories, some laws were still necessary to preserve the trust and harmonious relations between employers and employees, thereby preemptively guarding against the social unrest that had plagued industrialization in the West.[80]

The initial resistance to legislative protection for workers, the logic employed to finally pass labor legislation, and the repeated references to the preservation of warm-hearted benevolence and the "beautiful custom of master-servant relations" all demonstrate that managerial elites at the end of the Meiji period still felt it desirable and possible to maintain social order in the factory without any standard policies or concrete measures. Even in acceding to a weak version of the Factory Bill, they were still unprepared to view labor management in Japan as a problem requiring proactive efforts to address workers' attitudes and expectations. Evidence of worker dissatisfaction and social unrest were still not apparent on a large scale, and so they were seen as temporary problems that could be resolved as workers were increasingly exposed to the experience of industrial labor in conjunction with those "beautiful customs" of benevolent paternalism. However, if workplace disturbances in the late Meiji period were already prompting government officials to question these assumptions, the intensification of political conflict, trade unionism, and industrial disputes during the Taisho period (1912–26) would finally prompt managerial elites in large-scale firms to seek a more proactive and concerted strategy for addressing labor-management relations.

Taking Labor Relations Seriously? The Diffusion of the
"Family Firm" Ideal

With the disappearance of the Meiji oligarchy and the coronation of a weak, inexperienced emperor, the period of Taisho democracy (1912–26) ushered in a new era of party politics, bureaucratic infighting, class conflicts, and social movements.[81] Although Japan's GNP and trade surplus grew dramatically during World War I, spurred primarily by the demand for Japanese exports, after the war distortions in the price structure and the decline in exports led to a sharp economic downturn.[82] Under the pressures of declining real wages, rice riots broke out in 1918 and spread quickly to the nation's major cities and several prefectures, lasting two months before being quelled by the army. Industrial unrest and an independent labor movement began to exert increasing pressure on managerial and political elites. Between 1914 and 1919, as the number of workers in privately owned factories rose from 950,000 to 1.6 million, the number of industrial strikes went up almost tenfold (from 50 to 497), and the number of participants in those strikes rose from 7,900 to 63,100. In addition, the number of independent unions quadrupled, while the largest prewar labor federation, the Yuaikai (Friendship Association) retreated from its initial position of promoting "harmony and cooperation between labor and capital" and now set out to "rid the world of the evils of capitalism" and "destroy the zaibatsu."[83]

It is important to recognize, however, that labor unrest during the first two decades of the twentieth century did not reflect the same kind of working-class mobilization one finds in the United States or Western Europe at the turn of the century. Part of the reason for this is that, as late as 1910, over half of the work force labored in small-scale factories, with the vast majority of these being girls or young women doing piecework in the textiles sector. But it is also significant that for those (mostly male) skilled or semiskilled workers flooding into the large-scale industrial enterprises during the 1900s and 1910s, the main concerns were framed quite differently than was the case with organized labor in the West.[84] As noted in section 3.1, most prewar workers were neither making claims on the basis of the natural rights of the working class nor rejecting the ideal of paternalism; they were primarily concerned about their basic welfare, their social standing, and their treatment as members of the enterprise community.[85] Thus, the growing labor unrest of the Taisho period and the leftist rhetoric invoked by trade union activists should not be mistaken for a revolution in most workers' basic attitudes and expectations; at the same time, the growth of the labor movement does suggest that workers were eager to see some concrete evidence of the benevolence that managerial elites had been promising in their fight to stave off restrictive labor legislation.

Thus, the growing threat posed by independent unionism finally prompted the increasingly better educated and experienced managers of the Taisho era to recognize labor-management relations as a serious problem that had to be addressed through concrete, systematically coordinated measures.[86] Government bureaucrats such as Home Minister Tokonami Takejiro and the business community led by Shibusawa Eiichi agreed to several measures to restore "harmony" and improve labor-management cooperation. They attempted to appease the trade unions by publicly urging restraint in police action against "agitators" as mandated by the infamous Article 17 of the 1900 Public Order Police Law, although the article was not formally rescinded until 1926, and trade unions themselves were not legalized. For their part, managerial elites proceeded to call for the establishment of a national organ designed to promote industrial peace and obviate independent unionism within the framework of "labor-capital verticalism." This organ was the Cooperation and Harmony Society (Kyochokai), established in 1919 at a ceremony attended by key government and business leaders (but not by union leaders).[87] Implicitly acknowledging that workers may have separate interests, the Cooperation and Harmony Society recognized that there was a need for mechanisms or bodies that could address problems and conflicts that arose at the level of the enterprise on a day-to-day basis. But, at the same time, the Society viewed as its main objective the *prevention* of industrial conflict in the first place and to this end devoted significant resources to "social education" designed to persuade workers of the common interests of workers and managers and teach them the "true meaning of social cooperation."[88]

The Cooperation and Harmony Society embraced the now familiar argument that the traditions of reciprocity, mutual sacrifice, and the spirit of community would enable Japanese labor relations to evolve along a path different from that followed by the West where the emphasis on individual competition and profits made labor-management relations inherently more conflictual. But this argument was no longer aimed at government officials to preempt labor legislation as in the late Meiji era; it was now aimed at workers in the hope that cooperative labor relations at the workplace would divert attention from the independent trade union federations. Managerial elites themselves participated in this effort by expending more energy *within* their factories on a more coherent ideology of collectivism and harmony, this time framed in terms of "managerial familialism" *(keiei kazoku shugi)* rather than in terms of master-apprentice relations. Some managerial elites had implicitly used the household as the model in defining the factory as a moral community during the 1880s and 1890s, but toward the end of the 1910s and in the 1920s, the notion of the "family firm" (or the "one-family company") became a much more fre-quently used concept, embraced by factory managers as well as bureau-crats to promote internal harmony and cooperation.

The idea of a family firm may have made some sense among many of the smaller firms or merchant houses that literally employed family mem-bers; even the owners and directors of the zaibatsu and independent large-scale industrial enterprises were frequently members of related fami-lies subscribing to the ancient code of the original *ie*.[89] However, with respect to labor-management relations on the shopfloor of large-scale enterprises, the managerial ideal of the "family firm" was supposed to have a quite different meaning rooted not in actual family ties but in an *analogy* between the factory and the family, interpreting "the class rela-tionship between the capitalist-manager and the worker in terms of the status relationship between parent and child within an *ie*."[90] In other words, workers from different villages and different social backgrounds were to relate to each other as the members of a single household that would be perpetuated over generations. While the *dyadic* relationship between the individual worker and manager could still be idealized as an extension of traditional master-apprentice relations, the emphasis on the family allowed for a more explicit emphasis on the common identities and interests of all of the factory workers and managers as a whole. Within the one-family nation led by the divine emperor, there was now the one-fam-ily company—a tightly knit moral community headed by a paternalistic and benevolent manager who was dedicated to the company and its employees just as the benevolent head of an *ie* was dedicated to his family and children.

While some have interpreted this managerial familism as a direct extension of feudal status relations found in Tokugawa-era merchant houses or prefecture-run shops, revisionist historians generally view the "family firm" as an *invented* tradition intended to cope with the chaos and conflicts typical of early industrialization everywhere.[91] Whatever the case may be, both perspectives converge on the essential point that managerial elites were now explicitly attempting to battle for the loyalty and coopera-tion of workers and, in the process, were consciously relying on familiar models of authority relations within collective entities. Although the model of the *ie* may have made the analogy difficult to swallow for work-ers coping with the unfamiliar environments they encountered in large enterprises, managerial elites invested a great deal of time and effort in organizing "morality lessons" designed to promulgate the ideal of the family firm and convince workers that "everyone is a member of the same family and they should live together harmoniously as a result."[92]

Goto Shimpei, a former bureaucrat and one of the first ardent advocates of managerial familism, made frequent speeches to railroad workers to make the analogy explicit: "I preach that all railroad workers should help and encourage one another as though they were members of one family. A family should follow the orders of the family head and, in doing what he expects of them, always act for the honor and benefit of the family."[93] Similarly, the founder of a cotton-spinning company, stressed the distinctiveness of Japanese familism and its applicability to industry:

> The difference between Western and Japanese family systems is that in Japanese families, each one works according to his own ability, and that the whole family is based on a warm, loving feeling, and is permeated with the spirit of respect and self-sacrifice. Nobody, not even those with the most radical ideas, would reject the warm loving feeling within the family. . . . The paternalism that I argue is necessary in labor questions is nothing more than the application of the warm relationship that exists in the family to the relationship between employer and employee which is necessary for their mutual benefit.[94]

This approach was picked up and echoed throughout private industry in the early Taisho period. The fact that the top managerial elites were drawn from very similar social and educational backgrounds probably contributed to the rapid diffusion of the family firm ideal across firms and sectors during the 1920s.[95] Thus, in addition to the "National Railways family," there quickly emerged the "Nihon Steel Pipe family," the "large familism" of Kanegafuchi Spinning, and "one mine, one family" throughout the mining industries.[96]

From the point of view of workers, however, the question was whether this analogy bore any resemblance to what they were witnessing and experiencing in the large-scale firms of prewar Japan. Preindustrial communities in Japan—whether families or villages—had emphasized *mutual* indebtedness and *reciprocal* obligations; the authority of both family head and village head was conditional on the fulfillment of certain obligations to protect group members against unexpected hardships. In most "family firms," however, managerial hierarchies only served to reaffirm the status, authority, and rewards of superiors without specifying the paternalistic obligations of these superiors. That is, the parallel between managerial authority on the shopfloor and one's dutiful obedience to the household head ended up being the only aspect of the family analogy that actually bore some resemblance to actual practices in large-scale firms; in every other respect, the large-scale factory hardly resembled the concrete household. Instead, the "family firm" came to be characterized by a highly restrictive definition of membership in the enterprise community (usually limited to white-collar staff), strict controls over blue-collar workers' rights, bureaucratic organization with separate tasks in separate work-shops, and a new generation of well-educated autocratic managers who were seldom visible on the shopfloor.[97]

Workers' Councils, Employment Terms, and Membership in the "Family Firm"

Whatever the inherent limitations of the family analogy in the large-scale enterprise, it is the actual choices made by the managerial elite that threw into sharp relief the gap between rhetoric and reality. This was evident in the response to industrial conflict, the differential terms of employment offered to different categories of employees, and the virtually wholesale adoption of scientific management practices during the drive for rational-ization and efficiency. In all these respects, managerial elites generally failed to address the incongruities between their ideological pronounce-ments and the practices they adopted. In the end, it is this failure that con-tributed to the bankruptcy of the "family firm" as a moral community in the eyes of most industrial workers.

In relation to the representation of workers' interests and the resolu-tion of industrial disputes, the government and business associations relied on the Cooperation and Harmony Society to set up "deliberative workers' councils," enterprise-level councils designed to settle disputes before they could turn into widespread labor unrest involving the union federations. As part of its campaign to promote the family firm ideal, the Cooperation and Harmony Society was willing to acknowledge those "sound" unions that could work together with the new factory councils to serve as channels of communication between managers and workers to address shopfloor prob-lems and speed reconciliation.[98] In principle, the idea of preventing or quickly resolving disputes before they became widespread was a familiar one, rooted in traditional notions of conflict-management and community harmony. In reality, however, these "sound" unions and workers' councils essentially acted as management-backed surrogates for more independent trade unions such as those connected to Sodomei or other, more militant, labor unions. In the wider political context, although new laws were passed in 1926 to call for reduced maximum work hours and repeal Article 17 of the Public Order Police Law (which had been regularly invoked to crush strikes and limit union activities), the Diet scuttled attempts to legalize independent trade unions, relying instead on the Labor Disputes Conciliation Law that essentially strengthened the enterprise-level councils that the Cooperation and Harmony Society was promoting.[99]

Interestingly, both the push for cooperative unions and workers' councils, and the legislative response to industrial conflict—while being packaged as creative measures suited to distinctive aspects of Japanese labor relations—were very much influenced by similar approaches to labor relations in many Western countries.[100] That is, while trumpeting the distinctive virtues of the "family firm," managerial and government elites attempted to emulate those aspects of labor relations in the West that strengthened their hand and prevented the independent expression of the goals and interests of workers. The results, however, proved to be less than encouraging. Although the Cooperation and Harmony Society's role in strike mediation did draw an increasing number of workers into the factory councils, the number of workers joining the councils was much smaller than the number joining the trade union federations during the 1920s.[101] The number of trade union participants in industrial disputes, after dipping down in 1922, nearly doubled by 1930, while the number of industrial disputes nearly quadrupled in the same time.[102] And many of the labor federations now adopted a more unified militant posture, banding together to form the Japan Council of Labor Unions (Nihon Rodo Kumiai Hyogikai) in 1925 which proceeded to condemn the "reactionary and deceptive thought" being propagated among factory workers while they were "trampled upon under the influence of capitalists' venom."[103] All these trends signified that "cooperation and harmony" made little sense to workers in the absence of a more realistic and comprehensive articulation of the "family firm" ideal on the shopfloor.

By the mid-1920s, business elites did begin to institutionalize some concrete changes in employment practices to retain the services of their most prized employees. In the face of economic uncertainties in the 1920s, workers of all categories and qualifications—including white-collar employees and college graduates—had been repeatedly calling for greater job and wage security.[104] It was in this context that permanent employment *(shushin koyo)* and seniority-based wages *(nenko joretsu)*—two of the key features of the postwar firm—first began to make their appearance. In addition, employers and managers began to selectively offer generous benefits in the form of retirement pay, aid for sick or injured employees, and benefits for survivors of deceased employees. Gradually, these policies came to be applied in a more standardized fashion across increasing numbers of large-scale firms, thanks in part to such organizations as the Japan Industrial Club and the Industrial Training Association that were committed to checking unionization among the most prized employees whom managerial elites were fearful of losing.[105] That is, these policies were not so much a response to worker protest as an effort to retain key staff members and familiar supervisory personnel whose white-collar skills, trustworthiness, and managerial potential were precious commodities in an uncertain labor market.

Thus, while permanent employment and seniority-based wages were widely sought, their beneficiaries ended up being only a narrow stratum of employees comprised mainly of university-educated employees or trusted individuals hired through family-based networks or personal ties. For these employees, the notion of company paternalism was not merely an abstract expression of personalized family sentiments but a predictable, *institutionalized* set of practices for rewarding seniority and loyalty among a select group of staff and employees through employment security and predictable material rewards and welfare benefits.[106] At the same time, from the point of view of government and managerial elites, the new employment terms were implicitly contingent on a retreat from union activities and an acceptance of the factory councils, along with a greater workplace cooperation and commitment; in fact, white-collar employees in prewar Japan were expected to—and generally did—trade their involvement in trade unions for the privileges they alone were designated to receive.[107]

By restricting these benefits to a narrow stratum of employees, however, managers only ended up undermining or distorting the family firm ideal. They effectively increased the steepness of the hierarchical relations and the status differences between most blue-collar workers, on the one end, and white-collar *saraarimen* and highly skilled supervisory employees, on the other.[108] With their new benefits and the greater degree of job and wage security, white-collar employees and supervisors became a distinct, privileged class, marked off from blue-collar workers not only in their overall material well-being, but also in their life-styles, attitudes, and, significantly, their lack of interest in trade unions designed to improve the common lot of all workers.[109] But for every employee who received employment guarantees, seniority-based wages, and welfare benefits, there were dozens of other workers who were considered regular employees of the company but denied these same benefits.[110] Moreover, most managers and staff had little or no personal contact with the vast majority of employees in large-scale bureaucratic firms. As one government official lamented: "a majority of the managers do not even know the names of their employees, not to speak of where they are from. Among the employees, there are many who do not recognize the manager by sight."[111] The increase in stratification and the lack of direct social contact across different social strata might have been anticipated in large-scale firms, and to some extent, workers may have learned to tolerate hierarchy and stratification in view of the nature and structure of past communities of work. But the new terms of employment ended up *intensifying* existing hierarchies without providing any countervailing mechanisms to signify common membership, reciprocal obligations or collective purpose.

From most workers' point of view, it was not simply a matter of lower wages and fewer benefits, but rather a question of why one narrow stratum of employees within the company should be offered different *kinds* of benefits that the rest of the regular workers were denied.[112] Most blue-collar workers were not only denied employment security, but received little by way of profit-related or seniority bonuses or compensatory benefits in the event of injury or illness.[113] As a result, the long-standing frustrations of much of the industrial work force over their low status were only magnified by the "benevolent" welfare benefits and job security being offered to higher-status employees. By offering permanent employment, seniority-based wages, and welfare benefits to a select group of employees, the managerial elites had concretely institutionalized an *ideal* of paternalistic employment that all workers aspired to but that only a few could attain. Thus, the net effect of the new practices was to signify exclusion, not membership, for most workers in the "family firm."

Scientific Management and Work Organization in the Japanese Factory

The gap between the rhetoric of managerial familism and the reality of the shopfloor was also increased by changes in the organization of work from the 1910s through the 1930s, largely in response to the growing influence of Taylorism among Japanese managers. As early as 1913, just two years after the publication of Taylor's treatise *Shop Management,* a pamphlet entitled *The Secrets of Eliminating Wasted Work* was published in Japanese that would sell nearly 1.5 million copies, with many employers giving free copies to their employees.[114] By 1915, the writings of both Taylor and his contemporary Frank Gilbreth had been translated into Japanese. With the production boom accompanying the rising demand for Japanese goods during World War I, more and more Japanese firms—from spinning factories to Tokyo Electric and Mitsubishi—began to incorporate Taylorist methods in work organization. By the end of World War I, Japan National Railways, at the same time that it was adopting the family firm ideal, became one of the first companies to incorporate scientific management principles in a comprehensive manner, with the full-blown rationalization of planning and production based on standardized parts, task-specific production schedules, and detailed record keeping.[115] By the early 1920s, scientific management was sufficiently entrenched in Japanese managerial discourse that lectures on the Taylor system were being given at Tokyo and Keio Universities, while Ueno Yoichi, "the Taylor of Japan," led the way for a growing movement of efficiency engineers committed to the propagation of scientific management.[116]

Certainly, there were debates about which aspects of Taylorism to emphasize and how narrowly to interpret principles of scientific management. Ueno himself sought to promote a more comprehensive "mental revolution" aimed at creating a greater awareness of the possibilities for increasing efficiency in production as well as other aspects of public life. A second group, led by Kanda Koichi, emphasized the more narrowly technical emulation of specific scientific management techniques in organizing production and handling machinery on the shopfloor. While Ueno and his efficiency experts played a major role during the 1910s and early 1920s in increasing consciousness among managers and politicians of the possible applications and returns of scientific management, it is the group of "technicians" who took the lead in the movement for industrial rationalization *(sangyo gorika)* from the late 1920s through the mid-1930s. This corresponds to the period during which American scientific management techniques were most widely and directly emulated throughout Japanese industry with the active encouragement of government officials.[117] Japanese delegates returning from the 1925 International Management Congress in Brussels and the 1927 International Economic Conference in Geneva viewed themselves as part of an international network of Taylorists, destined to engineer in Japan the same leaps in productivity that had already been engineered in the United States and in some European countries.[118] They were particularly impressed by the manner in which scientific management techniques had been incorporated into Fordist assembly-line production with its high volume output and low unit costs. New government agencies such as the Production Management Committee and the Rationalization Bureau coordinated the dissemination of scientific management techniques across various sectors—from textiles and railroads to the shipyards and the naval arsenal—for the purpose of lowering production costs and improving international competitiveness.[119] Even the Cooperation and Harmony Society, while relying mainly on German models in promoting cooperative workers' councils, also established a special section—the Industrial Efficiency Institute—devoted to the propagation of American scientific management techniques. The Japan Industrial Association also contributed actively to the dissemination of information concerning scientific management practices and techniques as many large companies—and even some smaller ones—performed time-and-motion studies and developed detailed work schedules tailored to individual skills and production tasks.[120]

Critics of scientific management invoked some of these observations to question the motives and efficacy of the Japanese Taylorists. Leftist intellectuals not only echoed the standard socialist critiques of how Taylorism degraded work and extended capitalist exploitation, but invoked a new "labor science" that supposedly demonstrated the counterproductive aspects of Taylorism once its long-term physical and psychological consequences among workers were taken into account.[121] Other critics were skeptical of whether any features of American scientific management could be successfully transplanted in Japanese industry; the noted labor consultant Uno Reimon, for example, specifically disparaged managerial elites for adopting "American-style" management techniques without accounting for the "spiritual" factors motivating Japanese workers.[122] However, such critics were largely silenced or marginalized in the drive for industrial rationalization, as most managers formed an informal consensus that the basic thrust of scientific management—with its implications for reducing cost and waste and improving efficiency and productivity—was more or less compatible with the "well-being" of workers and the spirit of "cooperation" and "mutual sacrifice" associated with the family firm ideal.[123]

The latter position was not *inherently* an untenable one: indeed, both

Taylorism and the family firm ideal were designed to produce a disciplined, cooperative work force, and, in principle, many features of scientific management could have been selectively adapted to suit some of the ideals being trumpeted by Japanese managers.[124] As it turns out, however, prewar managers—without an organized labor movement to check their power to determine the organization of work—were content to simply imitate existing scientific management models without considering whether Taylorist incentive schemes, job classification systems, or performance evaluation procedures might be congruent with the kinds of norms and expectations evoked by images of the harmonious "family firm."

Now that occupational specialization and work schedules were taken to the level of the individual employee, responsibilities and production tasks became individualized; workgroups, which had been the fundamental unit within the hierarchically organized enterprise, simply became an aggregate of individual employees each with specific tasks to perform. The dualistic employment structure that had emerged during the Taisho period remained in place as a small minority of salaried employees were granted job and wage security, but even skilled workers and white-collar employees, despite their senior standing in companies and seniority-based wages, found themselves being evaluated on the basis of their individual performance of particular tasks, tasks that were defined according to a high degree of specialization.[125] While the larger firms tended to rely less on individual piece rates than did smaller factories, the earnings and promotion prospects of most workers remained tied to their skill-types and individual output.[126]

Thus, at the same time that managers and business leaders continued to exhort their employees to be productive through traditional ideological appeals to loyalty and collectivism within the "family firm," these same elites also encouraged a system of work organization that was based on individuals independently performing narrowly defined, separately measured tasks within the overall production process. The introduction of Taylorism in work organization, in conjunction with the sharp differences in status and in the employment terms offered to white-collar and blue-collar workers, only further weakened the prospects for a genuine reconciliation of interests within the "family firm." Thus, for most of the work force, "so long as far greater power lay in management hands, jobs would be insecure, wages would depend greatly on diligence, skill, and output, sullen resentment would pervade the workplace and an uneasy stalemate would continue."[127]

*"Industrial Service to the Nation": The Widening Gap between
Ideology and Practice*

The transformation of the political landscape by the mid-1930s brought
with it talk of a "new order" throughout Japan and East Asia, but the
basic incongruities between management ideology and practice would
continue through the period of wartime mobilization. During this time, a
new generation of bureaucrats, working in close quarters with the military
establishment, took over the reins of government and went about pressur-
ing the business elites to join in a more coordinated program of economic
and military expansion.[128] While the political leadership engaged in a
more concerted effort to employ an ethic of collectivist nationalism, the
managerial elites engaged in a reinvigorated effort to trumpet the distinctiveness and effectiveness of their system of industrial management. As
part of this effort, workers' councils were now attached and subordinated
to the state-run movement for "industrial service to the nation" (Sanpo,
short for *sangyo hokokukai*), the "imperial work ethic" replaced and subsumed the "family firm" ideal, and management practices were reframed
as part of the "imperial way of efficiency."[129]

Because of the Sanpo movement's renewed emphasis on the distinctiveness of Japanese traditions of work, the "imperial work ethic" not only
called for attendance, discipline, and efficiency, but also reaffirmed the traditional obligation of Japanese managers to trust, respect, and care for all
of their employees. Some key leaders in the Sanpo movement even suggested concrete changes in employment terms so that all employees would
be subject to the same kinds of treatment, for example, through the expansion of permanent employment and the blurring of status distinctions
between workers and white-collar salarymen. Others specifically suggested
revised wage scales that would be framed in terms of the life-cycle needs of
workers (not unlike the seniority-based wages of white-collar employees),
so as to differentiate the Japanese "family firm" from the more selfish and
impersonal behavior prompted by the individualized wage scales in Western factories.[130] These ideas, however, would not be seriously considered
or widely implemented until the 1950s as a result of the pressures generated by wartime mobilization.

In the meantime, Japanese managerial elites continued to tout the distinctiveness and effectiveness of Japan's existing labor institutions and
management practices, while consciously downplaying the foreign origins
of these institutions and practices. For example, Yoshida Shigeru, the

head of the Home Ministry's Social Bureau, praised the factory workers' councils as a "distinctively Japanese" means to achieve harmony in labor-management relations although these councils were actually modeled after Germany's 1934 Law for the Organization of National Labor. Similarly, right-wing labor organizations were coopted and unified under the supposedly unique national Sanpo movement although, again, the inspiration had actually come from the unified labor organization established by the German National Socialists.[131] And the "imperial way of efficiency" was proclaimed to be an extension of distinctively Japanese production practices that were superior to the "translated mimicry" of the 1910s and 1920s, although these practices were basically borrowed from scientific management.[132]

Despite the widespread rhetoric about the unique character and distinctive origins of Japanese labor-management relations, however, the general approach adopted by managerial elites was essentially a more elaborate and more coordinated effort to promote the same things that organizations like the Cooperation and Harmony Society and the Japan Industrial Association had been promoting during the 1920s. For example, the Sanpo movement merely extended the basic agenda of the Cooperation and Harmony Society by continuing to press for the widespread establishment of factory councils to preempt industrial conflict.[133] The treatment of unions also echoed the earlier strategy of supporting "sound" cooperative unions and undermining more independent ones: thus, the new unions associated with Sanpo generally opposed strikes, promoted the efficiency objectives of management, and were quick to accept compromises negotiated by the government—even to the point of forcing workers to accept across-the-board wage cuts; the more independent older unions were ignored and eventually forced out of the most important industrial sectors by 1938.[134] Similarly, Taylorist methods continued to be studied and promoted in new campaigns, led by organizations such as the Japan Industrial Association and the Efficiency Institute, to boost efficiency, promote rationalization, and eliminate waste. And despite talk of linking wages to livelihood needs in some circles, the early years of the war saw a more widespread and systematic application of piece rates and steep wage differentials related to individual output and skills.[135]

Perhaps the main change brought about during the late 1930s and early 1940s was in the more overt application of coercive measures to achieve production objectives. New labor codes, such as the national mobilization law of 1938 and the anti-turnover law in 1941, criminalized frequent turnover and established strict controls over wage increases.[136] The new laws, together with the proliferation of state-controlled labor association and the marginalization of independent unionism, did bring about a decline in overt instances of industrial conflict and labor turnover. At the same time, that such draconian measures were required to check industrial conflict and labor turnover, however, suggests that government and managerial elites had essentially failed in their earlier efforts to generate managerial authority. If anything, the widening gap between the Sanpo's rhetoric and the reality of factory employment became even more visibly evident to industrial workers, who responded by unofficially switching jobs or frequent absenteeism whenever they could get away with it, or failing that, by slowing down production, producing goods with greater defects, and showing indifference or even contempt for workers' councils.[137]

Worker Commitment and Managerial Strategy
in the Prewar Era

Throughout the prewar era, large-scale firms in Japan faced enormous difficulties in generating managerial authority as evident in the low level of worker commitment. From the turn of the century until 1930, there was a steady growth in the number of industrial disputes, the number of participants in strikes and lockouts, and the number of working days lost per striking worker. Between 1930 and 1940, the number and intensity of overt industrial conflicts declined sharply, but this trend primarily reflected the increasing pressure brought to bear on workers after the defeat of the trade union bill in 1931 and the increasing restrictions on union activities.[138] Even so, up until the time that harsher labor codes were introduced in the late 1930s, the substantial growth of trade unions and high labor turnover pointed to continuing frustrations among workers over the terms of their membership in the "family firm." Although unions remained weak and fragmented, and although managers and government organs actively sought to head off unionization and offer alternative mechanisms for dispute-resolution, the number of trade unions grew from only 107 in 1918 to 973 in 1936, while the total trade union membership grew rapidly from 100,000 in 1923 to 420,000 by 1936.[139] Moreover, given the limited bargaining power of employees in a period of fluctuating labor markets and a rising labor supply, workers frequently expressed their dissatisfaction by continuously searching for new employment opportunities that would bring increased job security and more systematic rewards for their loyalty and service.[140] That elites grew increasingly concerned with the high turnover and growth of unions became evident in the increasingly coercive measures and harsh labor laws that managerial and political elites would have had to invoke to control labor mobility and improve productivity and labor discipline. Even so, as noted above, the low level of worker commitment continued to be evident in hidden forms of resistance, ranging from unofficial job switching and production slowdowns to inattentiveness to product quality and indifference to workers' councils.[141] These trends may not be exceptional among industrializing societies, but they do stand in stark contrast to the significantly higher level of worker commitment evident across large Japanese firms between the 1950s and 1970s.

This section has suggested that one reason prewar managerial elites failed to do as well as their postwar counterparts in bolstering their authority is that their ideological appeals overemphasized the analogy to traditional Japanese familism, with little attention paid to whether management practices would sustain that analogy. Managerial elites in prewar Japan did learn to take labor relations seriously and, in the process, did come to appreciate the potential value of making appeals to familial traditional ideals in eliciting worker commitment. But they were ultimately unsuccessful in achieving a high level of managerial authority, in part because they relied on an ideology that simply bore little resemblance to the reality most workers had to contend with on the shopfloor of large-scale enterprises. In effect, they adopted a traditionalist institution-building strategy that sought to invoke preexisting norms and ideals while simultaneously adopting practices modeled largely upon bureaucratic firms in the advanced industrial West.

Even though such general themes as paternalistic benevolence and group membership might have resonated with workers, the terms of employment and the organization of work that evolved in Japanese factories did very little to support the notion of a family firm. Independent unions were ignored or harassed, while workers' councils were clearly intended to serve as instruments to socialize workers and preempt conflict rather than as forums where members of a community could collectively address common grievances. Although a narrow stratum of employees did get to enjoy job and wage security in exchange for their administrative skills and loyal service, the vast majority of regular workers were simply excluded from the kinds of rewards and benefits that might even remotely signify some sort of long-term membership in the company. In the meantime, the organization of work, increasingly influenced by scientific management principles borrowed from the West, emphasized narrowly defined individualized job assignments, output-based wages, and performance evaluations emphasizing individual skills rather than the collective endeavors of a workgroup. These practices served to make managerial hierarchies and workplace stratification all the more steep, with no countervailing measures to substantiate the rhetoric of familism or benevolent paternalism. Despite some talk of reforming wage practices during the Sanpo movement, no fundamental changes would take place until new legal and political institutions, as well as a newly empowered labor movement, forced managerial elites in postwar Japan to consider alternative management ideals and practices in their quest for authority.

3.3. Ideology and Organization in Postwar Firms: The Emergence of Syncretism

Managerial and state elites in postwar Japan had to confront anew the questions of past legacies while attempting to recover from the physical destruction and social dislocation left behind by World War II. New restrictions on the use of nationalist symbols and rhetoric, the banning of the old zaibatsus and their top directors, stricter limits on government intervention in the labor market, the legalization of trade unions, and the expansion of workers' rights all provided unprecedented opportunities for workers to organize, demand better conditions, and freely switch jobs. Indeed, in the first decade after the war, the rapid growth and militancy of the labor movement appeared to suggest that industrial conflict would be the norm in the postwar era as it had been in earlier periods of Western industrialization. Yet, from the mid-1950s through the 1970s, as Japan's economy caught up with those of the advanced industrial powers, large-scale firms came to be characterized by very little industrial conflict, a low rate of turnover, reduced violations of work rules, higher levels of discipline and productivity, and greater worker involvement. The interpretation in this section points to one important reason for this trend: in contrast to prewar elites who persistently tried to juxtapose traditional ideological constructs and managerial practices borrowed from Western firms, postwar managerial elites, under pressure from a much larger and more independent labor movement, agreed to a new social pact while adopting a number of management ideals and practices that may be regarded as elements of a *syncretist* institution-building formula. This formula became evident in the systematic cultivation of the borrowed notion of human relations to capture a sense of community membership, reciprocity, and interdependence that prewar familism had failed to provide.

Not only was the notion of community suggested by human relations diffuse enough to capture the complexity and size of the large-scale enterprise, but membership in the firm was given concrete significance through new employment practices along with a more innovative approach to work organization.[142]

From Conflict to Commitment in Postwar Japan

Although historians remain divided over what counts as the postwar era in Japanese history, this section focuses on the period from about 1955 through the late 1970s, corresponding roughly to the last twenty-five years of Japan's experience as a late industrializer. While Japan's industrial output may have already surpassed that of many Western nations by 1970, Japan's per capita annual national income in 1971 was still less than half that of the United States, and most Japanese still thought of themselves as being relatively backward in relation to the advanced industrialized countries of the West; it was only by the end of the 1970s that this gap narrowed and Japanese political and economic elites ceased to think of themselves as being in the process of catching up to the West.[143] Thus, the economic recession since the late 1980s and any subsequent shifts in employment practices or labor relations are not accounted for in this analysis since these trends are thought to reflect new challenges that Japan has faced as an advanced industrial power rather than as a NWLI.

In addition, the focus in this section is limited to the period after the mid-1950s; in the turbulent conditions prior to that time it is difficult to identify anything resembling a coherent managerial strategy. Even among those who view the political economy of postwar Japan as having its roots in prewar or wartime practices,[144] the first decade following the war is generally thought of as a "radical interlude"[145] during which parties of the left and right engaged in vicious political battles while economic elites sought to stake their claims in a new institutional environment. In industrial relations, new labor laws passed in 1946 and a rapidly rising unionization rate were accompanied by an unprecedented level of industrial conflict as the newly legalized trade unions, with the backing of the communist and socialist parties, engaged in dramatic confrontations with a restructured business elite.[146] The "reverse course" after 1947, reflecting the Occupation authorities' growing concern over social unrest and the increasing strength of the Left, only served to further embolden organized labor. MacArthur's ban on a nationwide strike in 1947, the mass dismissals accompanying the introduction of the Dodge Line the following year, the revision of labor laws to ban public sector strikes, and the Red purge orchestrated by the Yoshida cabinet after the outbreak of the Korean War all led to the hardening of battle lines and the intensification of labor unrest between 1949 and 1953.[147]

Moreover, during this time, both business and labor were divided. On the labor side, the more militant "first unions," mostly associated with Sohyo, demanded employment security and greater influence in wage practices, promotions, work organization, and shopfloor management; the Sodomei (General Federation of Labor) and the newly created Zenro (Japan Labor Union Congress) consisted of relatively moderate "second unions" that sought to link productivity to improved working conditions and livelihood-based wages. The business elites were similarly divided between the reform capitalists (Keizai Doyukai, or Economic Friends' Association), which consisted of new businesses that acknowledged the legitimacy of some of the unions' demands, and the more aggressive Nikkeiren (Japan Federation of Employers' Association), which sought to roll back union gains and supported the crackdown on strikes and leftist agitation.[148]

These conflicts within and between labor and business, the intensifying pressures collectively exerted by the former on the latter, as well as the unusual political circumstances under the Allied Occupation, all contributed to subsequent developments in postwar labor relations, but it was not until the mid-1950s that a relatively stable political environment and a distinctive type of capitalist development allowed for the crystallization of a coherent institution-building strategy across large-scale Japanese firms. With the formation of what has been called the 1955 system *(55 nen taisei)*, a relatively stable pattern of political contestation and accommodation emerged under the leadership of the newly unified Liberal Democratic Party (LDP) and its bureaucratic allies.[149] The subsequent marginalization of leftist and liberal critics provided the new political leadership with an opportunity to forge a social compact focused primarily on the demands of the moderate second unions, supported by the newly created Japan Productivity Center, other economic bureaucrats, and a business community that now adopted a more conciliatory posture.[150] This compact was based primarily on several key principles that officials of the Japan Productivity Center touted as key to gaining the cooperation of the moderate unions: a commitment from employers to preserve employment levels even during rationalization, livelihood-based wages tied to increases in productivity, and some level of consultation with enterprise unions in the introduction of new methods for promoting productivity.[151] It is on the basis of this emergent consensus that a recognizable set of management ideals and practices emerged across the large firms of postwar Japan.

Students of postwar industrial relations still differ over the distinctiveness of the Japanese firm and over the extent to which genuine labor incorporation took place. However, most nuanced treatments of postwar industrial relations converge on the observation that whatever compromise was reached in the mid-1950s eventually paved the way for a long period of industrial stability and a steady rise in managerial authority during the 1960s and 1970s.[152] This shift is evident in several noteworthy trends that collectively suggest a marked increase in worker commitment compared to any time in the prewar period; these include declining industrial conflict, rising productivity, reduced turnover and absenteeism rates, as well as changing employee attitudes toward their workplaces and labor discipline.

The decline in industrial conflict since the mid-1950s is most clearly evident in the decline in the duration and intensity of labor disputes since 1955 as evident in the sharply reduced number of working days lost for each participating worker in a labor dispute.[153] By 1980, despite the growth in the size of the work force and the number of firms, even the total number of industrial disputes (strikes, lockouts, and slowdowns) had declined sharply, with nearly three-quarters of the strikes lasting less than four hours.[154] Moreover, where major industrial disputes did break out from time to time, they were consistently followed by the election of labor leaders who adopted more conciliatory postures.[155] The famous strikes at Mitsui's Miike mines in 1959–60 indicate that the post-1955 social compact was not consistently adhered to and did not pay immediate dividends; but it must also be noted that the mines were among the few employers to actually initiate mass layoffs and reduce welfare benefits, while insisting on piece rate wages and strengthening line authority. In fact, the eventual resolution of the strike only strengthened the postwar social compact: Mitsui made wage concessions and rehired workers who had been dismissed for striking; the government agreed to assist in the reemployment of other dismissed workers; and more moderate unions gained the upper hand over the more militant Sohyo-backed first unions.[156] The biggest strikes of the 1970s and 1980s were those organized by unions in the public sector, most notably the national railways: in the 1970s, these unions primarily sought—and eventually won—the right to strike (which had been taken away in the late 1940s); but, the 1980s strikes were largely unsuccessful attempts to block plans for privatization in some sectors (as in the case of the railway strikes).[157]

Meanwhile, in the private sector, where workers retained the right to strike, unions took the lead in abandoning strikes as a weapon.[158] The majority of the strikes in the 1970s and 1980s were thus limited to those conducted during the annual spring wage offensive *(shunto)*, which had been initiated by Sohyo in 1955 but evolved into an institutionalized ritual accompanying the process of wage bargaining during which negotiations in certain key industries (e.g., steel) set the pattern for wage revisions in other sectors.[159] The decline in disruptive industrial conflict does not by itself point to rising worker commitment, but it is one indicator that, alongside trends in productivity and worker behavior, can be highly suggestive.

The trend toward increased labor productivity became evident as early as the 1950s as the hourly productivity rate per employee nearly doubled between 1953 and 1961 (while rising only 22 percent in the United Kingdom and 24 percent in the United States during the same time). This growth of labor productivity continued to rise between 1960 and 1973, reflecting not only the introduction of more efficient technologies and production processes but continued increases in worker productivity; comparisons of total factor productivity, for example, noted that the average annual rate of growth for labor inputs was higher in Japan than in the advanced industrial economies of the West, with most of this growth coming from the increase in man-hour productivity.[160] More recent studies designed to compare productivity based on similar types of production technologies also indicate that the level of production value per worker in Japan grew rapidly, surpassing productivity levels in other advanced industrial countries employing similar technologies (though not necessarily similar production processes).[161] The rise in worker productivity may have many causes, but it can be considered one of the indicators of rising commitment when considered in tandem with other trends in the postwar enterprise.

In contrast to prewar Japan and Stalinist Russia where draconian measures had to be introduced to check labor mobility between 1938 and 1945, the Japanese work force since the mid-1950s has been characterized by a significant decline in turnover rates. While some culturally driven analyses of Japanese factories have overemphasized the degree of attachment of Japanese workers to their firms,[162] more sophisticated studies generally confirm that separation rates in Japanese firms proved to be consistently lower than in U.S. firms.[163] Moreover, one systematic study of labor mobility in comparable industrial regions of Japan and the

United States (Yokohama and Detroit) suggests that labor turnover in postwar Japan was not only significantly lower than in the United States, but declined sharply in comparison to the prewar era; while less than 10 percent of the employees surveyed in Yokohama never switched employers in the prewar years, by 1970, more than three-quarters of the employees had never switched jobs.[164] Even scholars who discount the distinctiveness of employment patterns in Japan have reported that the vast majority of workers, even in the sectors with comparatively higher turnover rates, ideally preferred to remain at their workplaces indefinitely rather than seek out alternative opportunities for new employment or further advancement.[165]

A comparatively high level of worker commitment is also evident in the attitudes of Japanese employees toward absenteeism, workplace discipline, and the significance of the company. Absenteeism rates in postwar Japanese firms, for example, have been found to be extraordinarily low. One study of four representative large-scale Japanese factories notes that more than 90 percent of the blue-collar workers at these factories had perfect attendance records in 1976, while estimating real rates of real absenteeism (taking into account paid or sickness-related leaves) to be under 2 percent.[166] Another study indicates just 20 percent of the work force took all of the paid leave available to them, with the majority citing "unavoidable" problems such as illness, fatigue, or familial obligations as the reason for taking their leaves.[167] Also suggestive is a comparative study of workers' attitudes, which notes that, while both American and Japanese workers were found to be generally willing to accept rules and penalties set by their superiors to enforce labor discipline, Japanese workers were more likely to support the *enforcement* of workplace rules and penalties and to regard violators of company rules as "undesirable coworkers" even if the rules were thought to be unfair. By contrast, twice as many American employees were willing to evade rules and penalties and tolerate colleagues who violated the rules as a means of keeping managerial power in check.[168] In addition, Japanese employees in the 1960s and 1970s were much more likely than American employees to positively value their involvement in the enterprise in relation to their personal lives; in surveys conducted in 1967 and 1980 more than two-thirds of the Japanese workers consistently stated that they viewed their companies as "at least as important" as their personal lives, while less than one-quarter of the U.S. sample offered the same response.[169]

While each of these trends might be the result of a number of factors, taken collectively, they point to a significant rise in worker commitment among employees in large firms. This does not suggest that workers became completely satisfied with their work lives or that their interests coincided entirely with those of their employers. Indeed, critical treatments of Japanese management suggest that such trends as the rise in productivity and the decline in absenteeism actually reflect excessively long working hours and a high pace of work accompanied by increased mental stress and insufficient leisure time.[170] It is significant, however, that such studies tend to explicitly or implicitly use working conditions in advanced industrial economies of the West as the comparative referent. When the frame of reference is limited to working conditions in late-industrializing societies (including many Western societies before World War II), the social costs of postwar industrialization appear much less significant in light of the major gains made by workers in postwar Japan, as evident in the improvements in wages and working conditions, better employment security, and the gradual reduction in total working hours.[171] In addition, the decline in industrial conflict, the rise in productivity, the reduced rates of turnover and absenteeism, and the positive attitudes toward the company and its work rules cannot *all* be explained away in terms of coercion or lack of labor autonomy, especially when one considers that these trends unfolded under conditions where new labor laws and even the moderate unions placed greater constraints on managers than was the case in prewar Japan or Stalinist Russia where managerial power was virtually unchecked. This may be why even labor historians who are skeptical of exaggerated claims of postwar industrial harmony concede that the period from the mid-1950s through the 1970s was one during which a "cultural consensus" engineered by managers and moderate unions contributed to increased worker commitment.[172]

The remainder of this chapter attempts to provide a partial explanation for this phenomenon in terms that are both consistent with the theoretical concerns of this book and attentive to the competing interpretations of key features of postwar Japanese industrial relations. In contrast to arguments that explain these features as products of cultural characteristics, economic rationality, or managerial hegemony, the nuanced interpretation in this chapter attributes the rise in managerial authority in the postwar era to a syncretist managerial approach marked by a distinctive understanding of human relations that was concretely signified through a standard set of management practices across large firms.

*The Ideological Context: National Character and Japanese-
Style Human Relations*

Immediately following World War II, the Allied Occupation authorities
set out to dismantle the ideological and institutional foundations of the
prewar Japanese state in the hope of orchestrating a democratic revolution
in Japan. In this environment, a number of "progressive" intellectuals
were cautiously hopeful that the remnants of prewar collectivism would
give way to a cultural transformation that would provide a social foundation for a liberal democratic order much like the Protestant Reformation
had done in the West.[173] By 1948, however, the "reverse course" spurred
by rising labor militancy and fears of the spread of communism brought
about a shift in priorities as the Occupation authorities retreated from the
goal of transforming the Japanese polity and focused on the more immediate objectives of preserving social order and promoting economic
growth.[174] This shift proved to be an extremely significant one as it presented Japanese elites and intellectuals with an opportunity to reconsider
the question of the past in defining the postwar polity. As a result, the liberal project of the progressives was put on hold, and a new establishment
historiography began to engage in the "recovery of a positive past."[175]
This emergent historiography—embraced by conservative intellectuals,
future leaders of the Liberal Democratic Party, and much of the business
elite—downplayed the familism of the prewar ideology and the excesses of
the 1930s and wartime period, but nonetheless adopted a new discourse of
national distinctiveness that emphasized cultural continuities dating back
beyond the Meiji period.

This discourse focused on the defining features of *Nihonjinron* (Japanese national character), offering matter-of-fact statements emphasizing
the resilience and functionality of unique Japanese cultural and psychological characteristics. Thus, such values as group loyalty, deference to
(and dependency on) elders, status hierarchy, and social harmony were not
only thought to persist alongside the formal institutions of postwar Japan
but were viewed as the basis for Japan's distinctive route to economic
prosperity and social harmony.[176] Although the empirical validity of many
of the claims made in the *Nihonjinron* literature has since been challenged,[177] what is significant for the purposes of this chapter is that the
very notion of a distinctive cultural heritage actually struck a chord in
postwar Japan. Thus, compared to the early 1950s, when many of the
popular books had tended to be highly critical of Japanese traditional val-

ues in the immediate aftermath of defeat, the 1960s and 1970s witnessed an extraordinarily high volume of scholarly and popular publications echoing *Nihonjinron* themes and providing a positive "affirmation of Japan" *(Nihon koteiron)*.[178] Even critical discourses began to embrace notions of national distinctiveness, some emphasizing the necessity of recapturing the virtues of ordinary Japanese peasants and others viewing aspects of Japanese tradition as compatible with the construction of socialism.[179]

One of the most receptive audiences for the new cultural nationalism turned out to be the postwar managerial elites who were themselves in the process of finding a substitute for prewar managerial familism while attempting to incorporate the latest management ideas found abroad, particularly the notion of human relations.[180] The arrival of human relations in Japan was indicative of the continuing influence of American management models on Japanese managerial discourse. Although the human relations "revolution" did not initially point to a definitive shift in employment practices or work organization in the United States, it was enthusiastically embraced in Japan as the latest idea in effective management, regarded as a new means for simultaneously improving productivity and addressing the motivational basis of rationally organized work. Just as scientific management had a tremendous impact on the imagination of Japanese managers in the 1910s through the 1930s, so did human relations come to heavily influence managerial discourse in the 1950s through the 1970s. Just as the works of Taylor and Gilbreth had been translated into Japanese shortly after their publication in the United States, so was Elton Mayo's new work on human relations translated and published by the Japan Efficiency Institute in the early 1950s.[181]

There are, however, important differences in the manner in which scientific management and human relations were imported into prewar and postwar managerial discourse respectively. Scientific management had been touted as a necessary basis for rationalizing production and organizing work, but it had not been incorporated into the part of the ideological apparatus aimed at securing the cooperation of the industrial work force; the latter purpose had been served primarily by the rhetoric of the family firm that, by itself, suggested obedience, harmony, and paternalistic benevolence but had little to do with individual skills, productivity or efficiency. Even during the time of the Sanpo movement, while managers attempted to portray scientific management as an indigenous element of the "imperial way of efficiency," workers were simply exhorted to work harder and be more productive for the sake of the nation and the emperor, but there was no coherent conceptual apparatus for linking productivity-maximizing techniques to managerial familism.

The appropriation of human relations in postwar Japan, by contrast, involved a significantly greater degree of adaptation and refinement. To some extent, this is because the idea of human relations itself was vague and had not been identified with any specific injunctions or principles of management in the United States.[182] But the vagueness of human relations is precisely what enabled managerial elites in Japan to appropriate the idea in a distinctive manner, deviating from the unitary conception of the family firm, but explicitly linking the postwar drive for productivity to the national discourse of *Nihonjinron*. Specifically, human relations in Japan suggested that productivity depended on a distinctively Japanese ethos of community and on the ability of managers to imbue employees with a sense of membership and participation in this community.

This linkage between productivity and Japanese distinctiveness initially began to take shape in the early 1950s. While the Japan-U.S. Council for Promoting Productivity (established in 1954), U.S. foreign aid advisers, and the Ministry of International Trade and Industry (MITI) joined forces to introduce the latest management methods to promote rationalization and exports, "reform capitalist" business organizations such as the Keizai Doyukai began to simultaneously embrace the promotion of productivity and the stabilization of labor relations based on "respect for the human being."[183] The Japan Productivity Center, founded in February 1955, became the focal point for the crafting of a managerial ideology emphasizing productivity in conjunction with "social responsibility" on the part of managers toward workers. Even the hard-line business organization (Nikkeiren), which had previously attacked the "evil egalitarianism" of the unions for eroding managerial authority and undermining productivity, and the first-union labor federation (Sohyo), which had wanted to be an equal partner in shopfloor management, acceded to the outlines of this basic formula, acknowledging that increased productivity was tied to cooperative relations in the workplace, and that both were preconditions for improvements in working conditions.[184]

By the end of the 1950s, the concept of "warm human relations" was already being invoked in full swing to provide a coherent ethical basis for the new consensus. Just as *kokutai* (the doctrine of the one-family nation under a divine emperor) had provided a foundation for the family firm ideal in prewar Japan, the discourse of *Nihonjinron* provided the basic intellectual environment for defining *human relations* in a distinctive manner. In contrast to U.S. workplaces, where the human relations revolution did not fundamentally alter the basic individualist thrust of managerial ideology, Japanese-style human relations came to suggest a diffuse sense of community, along with some understanding of the benefits and reciprocal obligations associated with membership in that community. Although the concept did not suggest any one particular way of managing workplace social relations, it quickly became a widespread assumption among managers that "warm human relations" suggested a strong sense of identification with the "company community," and that "poor human relations" was one important reason why companies failed to improve their productivity.[185]

The general importance attached to the ideal of human relations is most evident in the time and resources managerial elites devoted to "capturing" employees through extensive socialization, training, and recreational activities.[186] In most postwar companies, entering employees were frequently housed in company houses and hostels, often in regions where they had no preexisting local ties, and were expected to become very familiar with their cohorts. Older cohorts took the lead in organizing joint tasks, seminars, training sessions, and recreational activities that all trainees would be required to participate in. Even in casual conversation, the oft-repeated phrase "good human relations" was regularly invoked to characterize the importance of ethical behavior, cooperation with peers, orderly execution of collective tasks, and identification with the achievements and future fate of the company.[187] At Toyota, for example, managers created common living and training facilities for the purpose of creating the "Toyota Man" who would not only work productively for the enterprise but would exhibit "Toyota Spirit" and contribute to "warm human relations."[188] And as the president of a bank put it in his welcoming speech to new employees:

> When we get into a branch, your biggest problem will not be using the abacus; it will be human relations. You will have to be able to deal with our customers in the proper spirit. You will have to be able to work well with others. The president feels the ideas in our bank code and in his teachings are absolutely necessary in order to assure correct behavior on our part.[189]

Undoubtedly, such language was less likely to be heard in casual discussions among workers than in speeches by managers or company presidents, but the notion of human relations was trumpeted throughout Japanese industry with sufficient vigor that it became an integral part of the communication between workers and managers.[190]

Despite the common themes of harmony, cooperation, and ethical conduct, there are several respects in which the connotations attached to the prewar "family firm" and to postwar human relations differed. In contrast to managerial familism, which invoked the analogy between firm and household to suggest the value of shared identity and deference to paternalistic managers, the postwar human relations formula suggested a broader notion of community, one that still emphasized the fulfillment of reciprocal obligations and the mutual benefits of cooperation but now allowed for the existence of diverse interests and backgrounds within the "company community." Whereas the family firm ideal relied on an analogy to the *ie,* within which membership was most often not a matter of choice, the postwar ideal of human relations interpreted the company as a *voluntary* community, within which continuing membership was a matter of choice, reflecting a partial convergence of interests and values:

> The Japanese company is *a community of volunteers,* a body of people who have willingly come together to share common aims, activities and values. When a man joins or leaves a company his action implies a moral choice of agreeing or disagreeing with those values, and indirectly expresses an opinion about what he is or wants to become. . . . Recruitment, resignation and dismissal do not merely provide an inverse definition of who is currently associated with a company; they are important indications of the aims and values of the company community.[191]

Moreover, while prewar and postwar managers both appealed to the employee for cooperation in the interest of the collective good, the postwar rhetoric of human relations emphasized the necessity and functionality of cooperation among discretely defined units rather than the value of unwavering loyalty to the unitary family. The common refrain was that "as long as each constituent element fulfills its tasks, the entire scheme can be expected to operate smoothly."[192] Throughout Japanese companies and society at large, human relations was framed not as employee dependence on a paternalistic employer but in terms of *interdependence*—among employees on the same workgroup, among workgroups and sectors within a firm, and even between a firm and other components in society at large.

In effect, the postwar discourse "shifted away from possible discussion of the costs of dependency to the exercise of cooperation, teamwork, and mutual support to achieve mutual goals."[193]

Of course, "warm human relations" and "teamwork" did not mean the absence of ranks or the reduction of managerial control, but they did characterize hierarchy in functional terms, emphasizing the roles that managers and workers of different ranks needed to fill in the wider division of labor. That is, while managerial hierarchies remained steep, the postwar ideal of human relations suggested an abstract sense of equality linked to common membership and common purpose in the company community. Hence, in contrast to prewar Japan, where marked differences in rank and privilege existed between managers, staff, white-collar employees, and blue-collar workers, in postwar Japanese firms a greater effort was made to create concrete, visible representations of a diffuse sense of equality among workers and managers of all grades. Thus managers and workers in the postwar firm—whatever their ranks and skills—viewed themselves as "middle class," reporting to work in the same uniform, dining in the same canteen, working in the same open workplaces, and participating in many of the same social and recreational activities.[194]

In sum, at the level of ideology, "the prewar analogy of genealogical and ideological equivalence of family and firm [was] transformed into a postwar simile of organizational culture."[195] This simile evoked familiar notions of community, reciprocity, and interdependence, but did so in a flexible manner that could more effectively capture the complexity and diversity of the bureaucratic enterprise. In contrast to the prewar demand for obedience and loyalty to the unitary "family firm," the postwar rhetoric of human relations appealed for cooperation in view of the functional interdependence among dissimilar units engaged in a common endeavor in spite of their dissimilar interests and roles.[196] The language of familism continued to be occasionally heard, but now it was simply an alternative means for capturing the same ideals suggested by human relations.

The problem with the prewar managerial strategy, however, was not simply the content of the family firm ideology but also the lack of correspondence between managerial rhetoric and the reality that workers faced on the shopfloor. It is therefore necessary to examine whether the connotations of community membership attached to human relations resonated with postwar workers in view of the new terms of employment and new forms of work organization they encountered.

The New Terms of Membership:
The Three "Sacred Treasures"

As a result of the new terms of membership that evolved on the basis of the post-1955 social compact, workers gained job and wage security and a measure of representation in consultative bodies in exchange for commitment to cooperation and productivity. Even though this trade-off reflected primarily a compromise worked out between business, government, and the more moderate unions, it was in part a response to the pressure exerted by the trade union movement as a whole; it is only because the demands of the more militant first unions extended to greater involvement in management procedures and shopfloor control that the position of the second unions could be defined as moderate. Thus, although employers and economic elites in the bureaucracy were ultimately able to spell out and implement the new conditions of labor-management relations on their own terms, the actual measures were fairly consistent with what most workers had been demanding all along since the 1920s.[197] With the Japan Productivity Center and MITI's Industrial Rationalization Council leading the way, the Nikkeiren and other business associations such as the Keidanren (Federation of Economic Associations) contributed to the rapid spread and standardization of a new set of employment practices across large-scale firms.[198] The resulting system of industrial relations has been variously referred to as the "three sacred treasures" or "three pillars" of the Japanese employment system, consisting of (a) cooperative unions active primarily at the enterprise level, (b) the system of "lifetime" employment, and (c) a seniority-based system of wages *(nenko joretsu)* linked to predictable promotion tracks.

The establishment of cooperative enterprise unionism on the basis of the second union movement proceeded more easily after the Miike strikes of 1959–60. Although it is the militant first unions that were responsible for extracting important concessions for Miike employees, in the aftermath of the strikes, it is the moderate second union representatives that concluded the new collective agreements and subsequently agreed to focus on enterprise-level labor relations. In some respects, this outcome may be viewed as the "greatest in a series of defeats for a union-dominated workplace culture,"[199] as the first union movement subsequently went into decline. Indeed, the standard system of cooperative enterprise unionism that dominated labor relations between the 1950s and 1970s was far from the ideal vehicle for fostering genuine worker participation as some have made it out to be.[200] Enterprise unions were not in a position to give voice to the independent interests of workers on such issues as the evaluation of merit or the assignment of tasks.[201] In many firms, they were even bypassed by the management-sponsored "joint-consultation machinery" when it came to the resolution of day-to-day disputes that arose on the shopfloor.[202] Moreover, relying on cooperative enterprise unionism, the national trade union federations became progressively more restrained: while the public sector federations did struggle for the right to strike into the 1980s, industry-wide and nationwide strikes coordinated by private sector federations were largely limited to the ritualized annual spring offensive *(shunto)* which primarily served to reflect labor solidarity during the process of patterned wage-bargaining across sectors.[203]

At the same time, it is necessary to recognize that cooperative enterprise unions were not simply reduced to consultative status or coopted by management as had been the case with the prewar factory councils promoted by the Cooperation and Harmony Society. Enterprise unions became permanent fixtures within firms, a body within which workers of all ranks could collectively unite to consider whether their expectations were being met. They held managers responsible for eliminating the arbitrary treatment of workers and for ensuring predictability in the system of wages and promotions in relation to length of service. They continued to exert some pressure on management to increase the rate of wage adjustments during the annual wage-bargaining sessions.[204] Moreover, enterprise unions and trade union federations continued to exist as legal, institutionalized bodies that could, in principle, coordinate large-scale strikes if conditions warranted. And to the extent that private-sector unions refrained from using the strike as a weapon, it is significant that they did so voluntarily and in exchange for the satisfaction of their long-standing demands in relation to greater social recognition and job and wage security.[205] Thus, even if the deal struck between moderate unions and management may be characterized as a "coercive consensus," it is significant that postwar enterprise unionism still involved a greater degree of independent organization and participation when compared to the prewar factory councils or the Sanpo-led labor front of the late 1930s; that enterprise unions tended to be cooperative should not mask the fact that they did have some choice in the matter.[206]

It is also significant that enterprise unionism helped to cultivate a sense of shared membership in the company community, blurring—but not erasing—the differences between different categories of employees and managers. That is, enterprise unionism provided a means through which workers could simultaneously satisfy two imperatives: to have an organization that could at least nominally protect their separate interests, and to be treated as essentially equal members of the company community whatever the differences in rank or salary. Unlike the 1920s and 1930s, when privileged white-collar personnel generally stayed out of unions, white-collar employees in postwar Japan, although recruited out of universities and put on a management track, actively participated in enterprise unions alongside blue-collar workers, providing leadership in collective bargaining and attempting to protect job and wage security on behalf of all grades of employees.[207] As a result, rather than viewing themselves as members of a "working-class 'us' opposed to a managerial 'them,'" workers in large firms came to accept the company community as the primary source of identity, forming "a society in which cleavages did not run between social classes but between particular corporate groups which embraced white- and blue-collar workers alike."[208] Thus, while enterprise unionism may not have provided the basis for meaningful workplace participation or genuine labor incorporation in the economy as a whole, it did serve the purpose of making the company the focus of labor-management relations while bringing concrete gains to most workers in exchange for their cooperation.[209]

The most significant of these gains were represented in the other two pillars of the Japanese employment system: the extension of lifetime employment and seniority-based wage scales to all regular employees of large firms. As noted in section 3.2, the idea of lifetime or permanent employment originated in prewar Japan when some large firms began to offer employment guarantees to retain key staff members and select employees; at the time, however, for most workers permanent employment remained an ideal that they could only aspire to. Under the new labor laws introduced in the Occupation era, courts could theoretically intervene to reverse the dismissal of regular employees if no "reasonable" cause could be found for the dismissal, but companies were not required either by law or by stipulations in employment contracts to offer lifetime employment. Yet from the 1950s onward, the offer of permanent employment quickly became a widespread and standard *voluntary* practice that remained in place for at least a quarter century in most large firms and many medium-sized firms.

The extension of lifetime employment to blue-collar workers and some categories of support workers undoubtedly have to do with the intense labor conflicts of the 1949 through 1953 period. As the Dodge Line encouraged Japanese companies to streamline their work force in order to increase productivity and international competitiveness, organized labor—both first and second unions—fiercely resisted plans for dismissals. In fact, the confrontations at the Miike mines largely focused on Mitsui's plans for cutting the work force by 15 percent as part of its blueprint for rationalizing production. Precisely because this plan deviated from the emerging post-1955 social compact, the strike and its aftermath actually helped to strengthen the consensus around the provision of employment security in exchange for workers' commitment to productivity. The fact that the government stepped in to assist in the retraining and reemployment of dismissed workers provided even more credence to the emergent consensus.[210] In fact, at the time of the strike, Mitsui's Miiki mines were already the exception rather than the rule, as the norm of employment security had already become evident in the majority of large firms; by the end of the 1950s, nearly three-quarters of the large firms that introduced technological innovations and reorganized production managed to avoid layoffs through job transfers.[211]

To some extent, the practice of permanent employment was not a major burden on management in view of the shortage of skilled labor during the productivity drive of the 1950s and 1960s. At the same time, the legitimacy and resilience of permanent employment practices across different sectors and over three decades suggest that it cannot be dismissed as merely a temporary response to labor market conditions as some have contended.[212] The longevity and legitimacy of the permanent employment system may be traced to its functionality in both the material and normative dimensions of industrial work: on the one hand, it permitted managers to allocate labor skills to meet minimum efficiency norms of output, maintain the services of key personnel on whom the enterprises' operations are dependent, create devices to penalize movement out of the system to control the sunk costs of training, and provide some sense of security and some system of incentives to motivate workers; on the other hand, permanent employment was consistent with familiar, long-standing norms not unlike those that had previously guided the terms of membership and participation in past communities of work.[213]

The normative significance of permanent employment is evident in the fact that it not only lasted for several decades but also endured through changing economic circumstances. Between 1964 and 1990, Japan's unemployment rate consistently remained below 3 percent. Even during times of economic turmoil, the rate of employment reduction in Japanese companies was significantly lower than the reduction in the rate of production, especially by comparison to the labor force reductions in Western societies experiencing similar economic difficulties.[214] During the recession of the mid-1970s, when some companies were forced into cutting their payrolls, employers attempted to resolve their difficulties through a wide range of other cost-cutting measures before attempting to lay off any of the regular employees; even then, many of the layoffs in the most affected companies were either targeted senior employees nearing retirement or part-time workers (often hired on a temporary basis to begin with). In any case, as soon as the recession ended, the practice of permanent employment was immediately reinstated and, in some cases, even extended to cover new categories of employees.[215] For their part, the vast majority of workers had long sought greater employment security, and they responded to the practice of lifetime employment by electing continued service within the same company in lieu of potentially higher earnings with another company.[216] Thus, whether or not permanent employment can be said to have run its course in the 1990s, it is still noteworthy that for over three decades of catching up during the postwar era, despite the rapid expansion of the economy followed by sharp fluctuations in economic growth, the Japanese system of permanent employment continued to provide workers in large firms with the job security they had long sought, while concretely symbolizing the ideal of common membership in the company community.

The third pillar of the postwar employment system came to consist of a distinctive set of wage practices that, like the practice of lifetime employment, had been introduced selectively in the prewar era but was now extended to regular employees of all ranks. Again, initially, the impetus for this shift came largely from organized labor rather than from management. After wartime controls on wages were abolished in 1945, managers had attempted to institutionalize the idea of pay linked to worker output, an idea to which they had become even more deeply attached in the process of expanding the use of piece rates during the war. But while managers called for "equal pay for equal work," unions demanded seniority-based, automatic annual pay raises, that is, "equal pay for equal age." The latter position was given a boost as early as 1946 when the electric power unions won concessions on the wage system, with the majority of their wages subsequently calculated on the basis of age, seniority, and family size.[217] During the late 1940s and early 1950s, the increasingly militant labor unions in other sectors continued to struggle for nonoutput wage bills linked to the livelihood of workers, leading to a new compromise whereby a more diffuse linkage was established between increased productivity and seniority-based wages. Even though the total company wage bill was to correspond to the total output of the firm, the wage increases for individuals consisted mainly of automatic rewards for seniority with only a small percentage of the increase reserved for merit considerations. Workers were accustomed to the idea that different degrees of responsibility, experience, and skill level could and should be rewarded differently; what they had challenged in the prewar era was the fact that certain grades of employees were compensated in terms of wages and benefits that were entirely different in *kind,* signifying a separate category of membership. The standardization of seniority-based wages, calculated in the form of annual salaries, provided postwar employees in large firms with another indication that they were now full-fledged members of the company community and that this community took into account the changing needs of workers as they aged and gained in seniority.[218]

By the early 1960s, most large companies had put all regular employees on the same monthly salary with a uniform incremental salary system, with the base salary varying only with the category of work, education level, and the related promotion-track. The standard annual wage for workers was calculated not in terms of individual output, but in terms of a combination of age, length of service, skill levels, and general performance evaluations. The first two factors represented standard, predictable salary increases, reflecting the norm of automatic rewards for seniority and length of service. The latter two factors theoretically reflected differences in skill and merit between employees with the same level of seniority and in the same category, but typically represented a much smaller percentage of the wage increases granted to individual employees. In addition, the annual income of each employee included a supplementary wage in the form of paid holidays, injury disability guarantees, and a housing allowance, as well as generous compensation for overtime, extra shifts, and holiday work.[219]

Moreover, the linkage between productivity and improved working conditions was signified by the widespread practice of paying standard annual or biannual bonuses—tied to the firm's profits—to both managers and workers (in marked contrast to both the U.S. and Soviet firm where bonuses for managers far exceeded those awarded to employees). The practice of paying bonuses was initiated in the prewar era by some of the larger zaibatsu such as Mitsubishi, but it is only in the postwar period that the distribution of profit-sharing bonuses became a permanent provisional salary paid to all regular employees.[220] As in the case of permanent employment, most large firms made no reference to profit sharing in the formal contract, but 97 percent of firms with thirty or more employees paid standard annual bonuses to all of their employees as long as company targets were met and profits generated.[221]

Tied to the shift in wage practices, the system of promotion similarly became less arbitrary and more predictable, with much greater consideration given to seniority and length of service than was the case in the prewar era. For college-educated employees, promotion tracks were standardized and uniform, with every employee automatically rising to the position of deputy section chief (after reaching the age of thirty-three and ten years of service), with 90 percent attaining the rank of section chief. Beyond that point, promotion tracks narrowed significantly, and merit-related criteria were necessarily invoked more frequently to determine advancement to the highest echelons of management, but seniority and length of tenure essentially guaranteed steady promotion to higher ranks through the first half of one's career.[222] While blue-collar workers remained on separate career tracks that were not likely to lead to a management position, they too were guaranteed a series of promotions, accompanied by increasing base wages, as they gained seniority and experience within the same company. The fact that blue-collar workers were not on management tracks was not viewed as an arbitrary or discriminatory practice since the basis on which white-collar employees and blue-collar workers were originally recruited varied considerably, with the latter regarding the former as having earned their status by surviving the intensely competitive university entrance exams followed by several years of education at top universities.[223] Thus, in marked contrast to the prewar period, when most workers were on day wages and only office staff and managerial personnel were granted automatic wage increases and promotions, the systematic introduction of seniority-based wages and promotions suggested predictable, fair rewards that all full-time regular employees could experience throughout their careers simply by remaining loyal and expanding their experience and range of skills for the sake of their companies.[224]

The emergent seniority-based system of wage increases and promotions represented one of the principles employees had long sought as a substitute for wages tied to job categories or on-the-job individual performance.[225] From the point of view of most workers, the wage and promotion system brought the industrial world into line with a social world in which age was generally correlated with experience and wisdom; it brought order and predictability into the distribution of rewards, preventing arbitrariness in the treatment of different workers and maintaining a high degree of worker solidarity; and, as long as blue-collar employees also received salary increases and promotions, the system appeared more objective than skill- or output-based wage systems given that differentials in age and length of service are less disputable than differentials in individual contributions to the success of a company. At the same time, for managerial elites, rewarding seniority and length of service, rather than strictly individual performance, did not involve significantly greater costs: seniority also suggested increased experience, a wider range of skills, greater evidence of commitment to the employer, and a greater investment on the part of the firm.[226] Even if merit continued to be factored into the overall wage increase, this was a far cry from management practices in the 1910s through the 1930s when, under the influence of scientific management, output-based criteria and job categories were the primary, if not sole, determinants for whatever wage increases and promotions the average worker received.[227] Thus, for workers and managers alike, the standard wage practices of the postwar firm came to represent a deeply embedded norm in industry as well as a pragmatic solution to what had been one of the most contested issues in prewar labor relations.

There is no reason to believe that any of the three "sacred treasures" of the Japanese employment system was a product of managerial benevolence or led to uniquely harmonious workplaces; indeed, as critics note, enterprise unionism may not provide the extent or kind of voice that most employees sought, and job and wage security may have come at the cost of control over the pace and intensity of work.[228] At the same time, it is important not to lose sight of the sharp contrast between prewar and postwar employment practices. Even if militant unions had been systematically marginalized and the labor movement partly coopted, enterprise unions were in a fundamentally different position in light of their legal status; to the extent they were cooperative, it is significant that the cooperation did involve a degree of choice and was only extended in exchange for unprecedented benefits corresponding to what most workers had been demanding since the prewar years. Even if managers had only grudgingly acceded to union demands for job and wage security, the longevity of permanent employment and seniority-based wages through changing economic circumstances points to the crystallization of "normative assumptions mutually shared by management and workers."[229] Unions may not have been satisfied with the degree of managerial control over the shopfloor, but the most consistent demands articulated by workers—employment security, social recognition, and fair compensation for their loyalty and effort—were not insignificant gains.[230] The combination of enterprise unionism, lifetime employment, and seniority-based wage and promotion systems thus represented a fundamental shift in light of the more severe constraints and more dismal working conditions most workers had faced in the prewar years. In contrast to the gap between the rhetoric of the family firm and the reality of prewar employment practices, the postwar firm provided full-time employees with concrete benefits to elicit their commitment, and for the first time, these benefits were sufficiently similar to suggest that these employees were being treated as members of the company community. Further signifiers of this community would become apparent in the course of important transformations in the organization of production.

Work Organization in the Postwar Enterprise: Job Redesign,
Skill-Sets, and QC Circles

It was noted in chapter 2 that the ethos of individualism provided an ethical foundation for the Taylorist emphasis on a one-to-one correspondence between individual skills and maximally specialized tasks. During the rationalization movement of the 1920s and 1930s, this system of individual-level task-specialization was enthusiastically implemented on the shopfloor by managerial elites as a key feature of scientific management, although individualism was neither a common social value nor a component of elite ideology. Since the end of the 1950s, however, work organization in large Japanese firms came to be marked by a retreat from the principles of maximal specialization and individualized performance evaluation, and by the emergence of a different pattern of organization that revolved around such concepts as job redesign, small-groupism, and, of course, the quality-control circle. The interpretation offered here suggests that the emergent system of work organization in postwar large firms constituted neither a natural extension of culturally unique tendencies, nor the calculated anticipation of a post-Fordist era of lean production, nor simply a refinement or adjustment of Taylorist-Fordist production practices; rather, it represented a qualitatively different approach that replaced the prewar emulation of scientific management with a more innovative linkage between productivity, job diversity, small-group participation, and the signification of common membership in the company.

It is true that the concepts of job redesign, small-group activities, and quality control (QC) originally appeared in American management discourse during the 1940s and 1950s, particularly in the new research on productivity by such individuals as Edward Deming and Peter Drucker (who were themselves influenced by Mayo and the human relations movement). Significantly, these ideas had a much more powerful impact in concrete aspects of Japanese work organization than they had in American workplaces, thanks largely to the enthusiasm with which they were propagated by such organizations as the Japan Productivity Center and the Japan Union of Scientists and Engineers. These organizations not only took the new programs introduced by American industrial engineers very seriously, but they vigorously and systematically engineered the implementation of small-groupism, all-employee management participation, and total quality control—organizational precepts that were viewed as inherently connected to the distinctive understanding of human relations being promoted by Japanese managers.[231] The concrete impact of these new organizational doctrines was evident in less complex schemes of job classification, greater reliance on group-based task responsibilities, and the systematic implementation of statistical quality-control schemes and other small-group activities.

As in virtually all complex large-scale firms, the production process remained systematically divided into groups of related tasks, each connected to different shops or sections. Significantly, however, the division of labor was no longer extended all the way down to precisely defined and sharply distinguished individualized tasks and roles. Whereas Taylorism emphasized detailed job classification schemes and precise, narrowly defined individual skills and tasks, the production process in the postwar Japanese company was broken down only to the level of the shop or workgroup, with individual responsibilities left undefined and job boundaries left fluid.[232] The performance of the individual could, in principle, be commented upon by coworkers, but it was no longer systematically and discretely measured in the individual execution of minutely specified, highly specialized tasks. While certain individuals in the company hierarchy (e.g., section heads or foremen) did have distinct responsibilities in ensuring that their subordinates collectively discharged their tasks, most employees shared responsibility for the completion of related tasks within a specified period as part of production teams or workgroups as a whole. Thus, in marked contrast to U.S. factories, where a separate relief-man or utility-man role had to be defined to provide substitutes for absent employees, Japanese factories simply mandated that members of a work team cover for the absence of a workmate, relying on group norms to deter absenteeism, encourage the timely completion of tasks, and share the rewards for their productivity.[233]

This reliance on group-level task responsibility went hand in hand with the diffusion of skills and greater job diversity through a system of off-the-job training and periodic job-rotation in most postwar enterprises. Most firms provided in-house training every five years or so in order to expand the range of skills any one employee could possess and the variety of tasks any one employee could perform, making the concept of job enlargement a reality for most workers. The training also supported a regular process of systematic job-rotation, designed to improve the exchange of relevant information and good communication across departments, while enabling blue-collar workers to acquire some technical problem-solving skills normally within the domain of white-collar employees. This process not only helped to diversify skill-sets and bring some variety to employees' work lives, but also provided a greater understanding of the interdependence between different levels and sections within the organization. Moreover, the pattern of substituting a firm-specific set of skills for a task-oriented skill specialization dovetailed nicely with the permanent employment system: managers and employers were less likely to lay off someone in whom they had invested several years of training organized around production tasks that are specific to their firm; and employees themselves were better off remaining within the firm in which their sets of skills were more valued and more likely to yield a higher degree of job variety.[234] Thus, long before the concepts of post-Fordism or lean production had become defined in the United States, the majority of Japanese employees in large firms were already in the process of acquiring a wider range of skills, experiencing a wider range of tasks, gaining a better sense of the production process as a whole, and even confronting some of the intellectual aspects of problem solving previously usually reserved for employees in white-collar positions.[235]

The systematic movement away from individualized tasks toward job enlargement and small-group organization is nowhere more evident than in the establishment of quality-control circles throughout Japanese industry. Although the idea of quality control was originally introduced by

Deming, it was in Japan that the idea was most enthusiastically embraced and rapidly incorporated into standard management practices across sectors. In 1948, the Japan Union of Scientists and Engineers (JUSE) enthusiastically endorsed the idea of statistical quality control within the context of Fordist production, proceeding in 1951 to establish the Deming Prize for the best quality-control program in Japan. By the early 1960s programs of total quality control and the quality-control (QC) circle were not only being touted by business associations but were actually being integrated into the work process at several large firms.[236] The following two decades witnessed the rapid proliferation of QC groups across firms, rising rates of employee participation, and the organization of company-wide, sectorwide, and nationwide conferences for recognizing the achievements of particular QC programs. Several high-profile firms such as Nissan and Suzuki led the way, prompting others (such as Toyota) to establish QC circles of their own. In 1964, there were already 1,000 QC circles in existence, and by 1978, there were more than 87,000 QC circles throughout Japanese industry, involving nearly 80 percent of all workers throughout firms with more than 5,000 employees and nearly 60 percent of workers throughout all firms with 1,000 to 5,000 employees.[237] Thus, in contrast to the limited conceptualization of QC in the United States, the QC movement in Japan turned into a much more widespread phenomenon, representing a significant workplace innovation with its own original identity and its own set of distinctive practices.[238]

The typical quality-control circle consisted of groups of five to ten people who voluntarily planned to meet regularly, usually under the leadership of a foreman or a section chief. The main objective of these groups was to get more employees familiar with timetables and problem-solving statistical methods with the intention that these groups would be able to suggest techniques for improving upon product quality, the production process, and task schedules. QC circle meetings stressed the importance of spontaneous participation in "self-improvement" activities, ideally through involvement in study-groups or other small-group activities involving new and varied tasks. The efforts of QC circles were recognized and rewarded through public ceremonies at company meetings and even at regional and national conventions where awards and trophies were handed out (but where the financial rewards were downplayed). Moreover, employee participation rates in QC groups, despite variations across individual companies and sectors, were reported to be generally high among workers of large firms.[239] Not surprisingly, most managerial personnel came to regard the QC-circle in highly favorable terms, viewing it as an effective mechanism for stimulating production, innovation, and worker participation.[240]

While workers probably did not share the enthusiasm of their managers, their widespread involvement in QC activities cannot be explained away solely as a response to managerial pressure or manipulation, especially when one considers the past history of labor protest against practices considered unfair. Moreover, in light of the fact that workers in the postwar era came to enjoy a much higher degree of legal protection, job and wage security, and opportunities for labor mobility, it is plausible to assume that the high level of participation in QC activities was at least partly a result of choices made by workers and that these choices reflected the acceptability of the premises underlying the idea of the QC. Also, while it is the case that much of the work done in QC circles represented uncompensated after-hours work, the overall decrease in hours worked annually since the 1950s, the sense of involvement and camraderie associated with QC activities, and the opportunity to use QC circles to expand skill-sets and devise alternatives to staffing cuts and work speed-ups all contributed to making involvement in QC circles much less onerous than critics of Japanese production practices have made it out to be.[241]

Cultural arguments tend to interpret these features of postwar work organization as natural extensions of culturally ingrained habits and tendencies that had supposedly made scientific management untenable in prewar Japan.[242] Proponents of the "lean production" thesis also praise the innovative work organization of Japanese firms, but in more universalist terms, viewing teamwork and job redesign as indicative of a worldwide transformation of production processes in response to the spread of new technologies and post-Fordist production processes.[243] Critical perspectives of Japanese management reject both of these views, contending that the basic features of Japanese management remained essentially Taylorist, and that the supposedly innovative aspects of postwar work organization only provided new tools with which managers could pressure employees into offering uncompensated time and effort at the workplace.[244] While all of these interpretations may be partly correct, each inherently exaggerates or discounts the significance of particular aspects of Japanese management.

While preexisting norms of work did play a role in conferring a degree of legitimacy upon small-group activities and job enlargement in Japanese firms, a cultural account neglects to consider the complex historical processes, political conflicts, and social pacts that paved the way for key features of postwar work organization; such an approach also downplays the influence of foreign management doctrines and practices, as well as the enthusiasm with which Japanese managers sought to adapt them. The lean production thesis discounts the particular circumstances that permitted the rapid proliferation of QC circles and job redesign in postwar Japan; it also ignores the fact that key features of postwar Japanese work organization *preceded* the arrival of the debates over post-Fordism in the West, with many of the innovations in production occurring at a time when the United States was still viewed as holding a substantial advantage in technology, industrial output, and per capita national income. The starkly critical perspective, while offering a much needed corrective to overly effusive treatments of Japanese-style management, overemphasizes the exhaustion and exploitation produced by uncompensated after-hours work, neglecting to consider important changes over time (such as the decline in total working hours per year) as well as the value workers themselves may have attached to the improved job variety and greater sense of involvement that came with participation in small-group activities.

As in the case of permanent employment and seniority-based wages, if the shifts in work organization are viewed in a comparative-historical context, then the features of postwar work organization must be regarded as successful at least insofar as these produced a relatively high degree of worker commitment (especially in comparison to prewar Japan and Soviet Russia). The emergent movements for job redesign, skill expansion, and quality control may have left much control over the labor process in the hands of management and may have paved the way for greater flexibility in adjusting to new economic conditions; but these shifts also helped to partially diffuse one of the tensions in the prewar era (that between individual-level task specialization and the ideology of familism) while making it easier for the day-to-day experience of industrial labor to cohere with long-standing familiar norms emphasizing social recognition, interdependence, and mutually beneficial cooperation within communities.[245] The new emphasis on collective responsibility for the fulfillment of tasks, the blurring of boundaries between white-collar and blue-collar skill-sets, and the interdependence among workgroups through participation in small-group activities all continued to fulfill the technological requirements of industrial production, but in contrast to the atomizing experience of work in prewar firms, these organizational changes also furnished further evidence that Japanese workers had a real opportunity to become members of the company community as the postwar credo of human relations suggested.[246]

3.4. Conclusion: Prewar Traditionalism
versus Postwar Syncretism

The reflexive reconstruction of certain elements of tradition among the industrial work force has a great deal to do with whether managerial elites actually succeeded in building and sustaining their authority within large-scale enterprises. Consistent with the theoretical argument offered in the previous chapters, this chapter has employed the distinction between prewar and postwar enterprises to demonstrate that sharp variations in managerial authority in Japan were in part a result of the degree to which managerial ideologies and practices appeared both reasonable and recognizable to employees (i.e., the degree of congruence).

Section 3.2 traced the emergence of the family firm ideology and followed the evolution of employment practices and work organization from the Meiji period through the beginning of World War II. The goals were to provide some historical context for the analysis of postwar Japanese enterprises and to offer a distinctive interpretation for why the prewar years did not witness a higher level of worker commitment despite the deployment of familiar ideals and symbols in the workplace. The argument on the prewar era may be summarized as follows.

First, the family firm ideal, rooted in an analogy between labor-management relations and relations within the traditional corporate household *(ie)*, was not a syncretic ideological construction in light of its inability to capture the increasing size and diversity of firms, the progressive differentiation of tasks, the complexity of workplace hierarchies, and the economic hardships and uncertainties encountered by most workers. Moreover, the terms of employment and the organization of work did not provide any institutional backbone to the notion of the family firm. It was hard for most workers to interpret factory employment in terms of common membership in a single household when different grades of employees were offered qualitatively different terms of employment and starkly different levels of social recognition. Although managers and employers did come to recognize that the ideal of the family firm had to be accompanied by higher wages and better terms of employment, only a narrow stratum of the work force received guarantees of lifetime employment and seniority-based wages, while the rest were left to fend for themselves in times of uncertainty. Moreover, the incorporation of Taylorist practices disaggregated workgroups into individual workers who performed narrowly defined and sharply demarcated tasks; thus, despite the collectivist rhetoric of familism, workers found their *individual* skills and contributions increasingly becoming the focus of the campaigns for efficiency and rationalization.

Workers, for their part, surely wanted higher wages and job security as would low-paid workers anywhere; indeed, to some extent the indications of labor unrest, low discipline, and high turnover can be interpreted as evidence that they were unsatisfied with their material conditions. However, as noted in section 3.2, it is significant that in their struggles and petitions, prewar workers rarely insisted on their natural rights and rarely challenged the principle behind "paternalistic benevolence" touted by managers; for the most part, workers viewed higher wages and job security as indicators of their membership within the company, bringing both increased social recognition as well as increased protection in times of difficulty. That is, workers in prewar Japan were prepared to view factory work in terms of duties and obligations to be performed within the context of the collective achievement of a corporate group, but only if the exercise of managerial authority, the terms of employment, and the organization of work and authority within the factory were more consistent with the experience of membership in more familiar past communities (see fig. 9).

Section 3.3 took up the experiences of managerial elites and workers in the postwar era. A new institutional environment and a growing labor movement eventually gave way to a social pact on the basis of which a new, more syncretist, managerial approach eventually crystallized during the mid-1950s. While employers were ultimately able to subdue the labor movement and coopt organized labor into the system of enterprise unionism, managers also adopted a new formula for labor relations that related productivity to a more inclusive and concrete definition of membership in the company community.

In terms of ideology, the shift was evident in the particular understanding attached to the concept of human relations in postwar Japan. Although borrowed from the United States, the concept was appropriated in a peculiar fashion that drew upon a wider discourse of cultural distinctiveness (most notably, the discourse of *Nihonjinron*), linking productivity to mutually beneficial gains to be had from interdependence and teamwork within the company community. Unlike the family-based model of community based on the steeply hierarchical superior-subordinate relationship within households, human relations suggested a more flexible, less unitary model of community with more clear signifiers of membership and more concrete stipulations concerning the rights and obligations of

Indications of Problems with Worker Commitment
Increase in number of strikes, number of workers participating, and working days lost (through 1930), with subsequent decline related to state role in suppressing labor movement; trade union membership quadruples between 1923 and 1936 despite efforts to suppress unions and provide management-controlled surrogates; labor turnover in Meiji era high as in all industrializers at early stages, but high turnover rates persist, necessitating government enforcement of contracts and strict controls to deter labor unrest and labor mobility (and even then, illegal switching of jobs continues); petitions emphasizing insecurity, lack of welfare, and desire for respect and status.

Partial Explanation
Growing absence of congruence between (A) traditionalist ideology of "beautiful customs" and "family firm" invoked to justify obedience and loyalty within the framework of "benevolent paternalism," although meaningful only to small stratum of mostly white-collar employees, (B) management practices, though presented as extension of traditional Japanese work culture, shaped by Western scientific management and organized around centralized factory administration, progressive task specialization, and output-based piece-wages, and (C) informal norms and expectations on shopfloor influenced by preexisting forms of collective labor.

A. Managerial Ideology
Initially, emphasis on the "natural intimacy" and "beautiful customs" of the traditional master-apprentice relationship; however, by 1890s, increasing evidence of social turmoil and labor-management tensions gives way to more active search for a managerial ideology. Result is evident in mid-1910s in the emergence of the "one-family firm" ideal, nested within broader ideology of kokutai ("one-family nation" under divine emperor). Family firm suggests obedience and loyalty from all workers as members of a single family in return for benevolent treatment from managers whose authority was akin to that of the household head; by late 1930s, "family firm" linked even more strongly to ideals of "industrial service to the nation" (Sanpo) and Imperial Work Ethic.

B. Management Practices
Initially, predominance of piecework; managers in large-scale firms rely mainly on technical supervisors exercising shopfloor control and labor discipline. By mid-1920s, new employment practices emerge with new lifetime employment offered to a select category of employees who are given generous benefits but through a seniority-based wage system; however, result is a dualistic wage structure with vast majority of workers still paid on basis of output. Growing excitement over Taylorism leads to reorganization of production with maximal specialization and detailed work schedules turning workgroups into aggregates of individuals with distinct tasks; although most work groups paid collectively, total earnings reflect accumulated piece-wages; stark distinctions in status across skill-types.

C. Norms and Expectations of Workers As Conditioned by Legacies of Past
Despite education, urbanization, and dissolution of ie system, worker behavior continues to reflect some of the core work-related norms and practices of preindustrial village communities (mura). Most petitions and protests reflect preexisting understanding of fairness: workers not as interested in standard rights or class struggle as in "benevolent" treatment from superiors as members of a community of work (even left-wing trade unions recognize that "paternalistic benevolence" might have resonated with workers were it reflected in management practices).

Fig. 9. Ideology, practice, and managerial authority in prewar Japan, 1868–1940

workers as well as managers and employers. The ideology itself placed less emphasis on obedience and dependence within the unitary household and greater emphasis on voluntary identification with, and interdependence within, a community of work. Given that some degree of choice was built into the commitment one made to a company, what counted was not myths of fictive ancestry but manifestations of mutual reciprocity, cooperation, and a shared sense of community within a concrete social and occupational context. Thus, Japanese-style human relations continued to emphasize reciprocal obligations and cooperation in collective pursuits, but the new formula better captured the logic of cooperation among distinct units as well as the diffuse sense of equality through common membership and participation in the company community.

The postwar settlement that emerged in the mid-1950s was one that reflected not only the managerial elites' desire to coopt the labor movement through enterprise unionism but also their acceptance of some of the very employment practices that workers had been petitioning for prior to World War II. This settlement reflected a commitment to productivity on the part of workers in exchange for increased employment security and more predictable patterns of wage increases and promotions. But the specific employment practices and new forms of work organization that emerged by the end of the 1950s also served the purpose of concretely signifying the sense of common membership in the community suggested by the managerial ideal of human relations. The vast majority of employees in a large firm came to be considered regular workers, and all regular workers were offered permanent employment, a full complement of company-sponsored welfare benefits, and a standardized set of wage and promotion practices that primarily reflected age and length of service. At the same time, the movements for job redesign and quality control brought new opportunities to participate in the production process, albeit in a controlled fashion, while allowing workers to gain new technical skills, experience more varied tasks, and, in the process, improve their value to the company. Although specialization and merit-related rewards were still evident, the importance placed on the group-based organization of work limited the degree of individual specialization and placed less emphasis on the evaluation of individual merit (which, in any case, included personal qualities such as loyalty and attentiveness to social relations). The net effect of all these changes in management practice was to lend substance to the rhetoric of mutually beneficial cooperation associated with the idea of human relations and to provide concrete signification to the notion of membership and interdependence within the company community.

These shifts coincided with a significant increase in the level of worker commitment among employees in postwar firms, as evident in declining levels of industrial conflict and labor turnover as well as increasing productivity, discipline, and attachment to companies. This does not suggest that the postwar management ideals and practices were *inherently* superior to the prewar formulas. It does suggest that postwar ideological constructs, while incorporating preexisting understandings linked to past communities, were reformulated so as to better represent the size, complexity, and diversity of the large-scale bureaucratic enterprise, and that these constructs were given some concrete, institutionalized expressions in the form of standardized employment practices and innovative features of work organization. Thus, the differences in levels of managerial authority in postwar and prewar firms can be at least partially traced to the level of congruence between features of management ideology and organization on the one hand, and the portable aspects of the more familiar norms and practices associated with past communities of work on the other (see fig. 10).

Although the interpretation in this chapter is primarily framed in terms of the theoretical problematique outlined in previous chapters, it is also consciously designed to address central issues over which competing perspectives in Japanese studies markedly differ. Appendix B provides an overview of these perspectives for purposes of framing some recurrent points of contention and identifying points along which nuanced versions of these narratives might converge. While this chapter has drawn upon a wide range of sources to support relevant points, it is these nuanced treatments of Japanese political economy and industrial history that represent the point of departure for the interpretation of prewar and postwar industrial relations offered here.

Finally, it should be noted that there is one respect in which even the more nuanced treatments are limited: the scope of the comparative context. Almost every well-known argument about Japanese industry implicitly or explicitly invokes the West as a comparative referent. This is obviously true of arguments that emphasize the similarity or convergence between Japan and other Western industrialized societies, but it is also implicit in arguments about the uniqueness of Japanese industrial relations, models of political economy or work organization based on postwar Japan, as well as critical treatments that compare the quality of working

Indications of High Worker Commitment
High labor productivity and high figure for average number of man-hours worked, with remarkably low absenteeism rates; few protracted strikes with minimal loss of production days, despite legalized trade unions and restrictions on managerial power; labor turnover rates were significantly lower in postwar Japan, and the rates declined despite expansion of new employment opportunities and desirability of fluid labor market in era of high-speed growth and industrial restructuring; attitude surveys do not attest to "diligent Japanese worker" myth, but do show high level of organizational attachment and high degree of identification with goals of firm.

Partial Explanation
Shifts in, and congruence between, (A) new managerial ideology that relates human relations to more generalized conception of community membership, (B) management practices that provide concrete signification to "company community" through expansion of lifetime employment, seniority-based wages, cooperative unionism, and through the modification of standard Taylorist practices to emphasize collective responsibility, job enlargement, and small-group activities, and (V) informal norms and expectations still influenced by familiar, portable understandings of cooperation, group identity, and benevolent authority.

A. Managerial Ideology
In national discourse, shift from one-family nation to matter-of-fact characterization of Japanese national character *(nihonjinron);* accompanied by shift in management ideals from family firm to human relations. Though adapted from U.S. managerial, discourse, distinctiveness of Japanese-style human relations evident in collectivist themes such as teamwork and interdependence in performance of collective tasks. Importance assigned to the concept evident in attention given to it in employee socialization, company training, and daily meetings in large firms. Shift from paternalism and familism to more diffuse sense of group membership linked to shared goals, responsibilities, and rewards in "company community."

B. Management Practices
New social compact negotiated with cooperative unions leads to concrete changes in management practices providing concrete significance to idea of common membership in company community, although managerial hierarchies retained. Permanent employment and wage-and-bonus system tied to seniority and profit-sharing now extended to all regular employees regardless of rank and status. Work organization reduces focus on job boundaries and individual performance of tasks, and emphasizes collective workgroup responsibility, job rotation, job enlargement, and small-group activities cutting across skill-grades and ranks. Also, reduced stratification within large-scale firms with common participation in enterprise unions and common access to company facilities.

C. Norms and Expectations of Workers As Conditioned by Legacies of Past
Traditional *ie* (invoked as part of prewar ideology) on genealogical continuity and common ancestry, with nearly complete unity in household goals and no separation of roles or tasks. By contrast, membership in *mura* is more closely associated with cooperation among distinct units of production in concrete context of everyday work. Basic principles of community membership and expectations of reciprocity and benevolent authority represent norms sufficiently diffuse to be portable across institutional settings. Resilience of such norms in postwar Japan seen in relatively positive orientations of postwar Japanese work force to new combination of ideology and practice in postwar firm, with continuing preferences for close, diffuse social relations with peers and superiors extending to concerns beyond the workplace.

Fig. 10. Sources of managerial authority in postwar Japan, 1950–80

life in Japan to that in other Western societies. Once the comparative referent is explicitly shifted to emphasize NWLIs, the stark oppositions over the distinctiveness, historical continuity, and social costs evident in Japanese industrial history become somewhat muted. Whether or not postwar Japanese workers now enjoy the same kinds of material benefits and working conditions their counterparts in Britain or Sweden have been enjoying, the high productivity, declining industrial conflict, rising managerial authority, and improving working conditions of the 1950s through 1970s era are noteworthy by comparison to trends in industrial relations in other NWLIs. This does not suggest an alternative model of development or industrial management for NWLIs, but it does suggest that there are *lessons* to be learned from the quite different outcomes produced by the approaches that prewar and postwar managerial elites adopted to cope with historical legacies and borrowed models. The significance of these lessons might be more fully appreciated upon consideration of the following chapter, which addresses the case of larger scale enterprises in late-industrializing Russia.

Chapter 4

Work, Community, and Authority in Late-Industrializing Russia

Socialist Revolution and the "Scientific Organization of Labor"

American efficiency is that indomitable force which neither knows nor recognizes obstacles, which continues at a task once started until it is finished, even if it is a minor task. . . . The combination of Russian revolutionary sweep and American efficiency is the essence of Leninism in party and state work.

—Josef Stalin (1924)[1]

The present state of production is still far from guaranteeing all necessities to everybody. But it is already adequate to give significant privileges to a minority, and convert inequality into a whip for the spurring on of the majority. That is the first reason why the growth of production has so far strengthened not the socialist, but the bourgeois features of the state.

—Leon Trotsky (1937)[2]

Although the first labor codes in Russia appeared as early as 1741, it was only under Tsar Nicholas I (1825–55) that the "labor question" began to receive serious attention. The tsar, eager to avoid the social unrest plaguing European cities during his reign, planned to locate newer factories at a distance from the big cities in order to limit the number and concentration of factory workers. Many of the tsar's advisers, however, viewed the Russian industrial work force as quite different from the oppressed "landless proletariat" in the urban industrial centers of Europe; they steadfastly maintained "that Russia had no working class, and that the people employed in urban factories remained *peasants,* as both their mentality and their ties to the village attested."[3] Ironically, these same ties, and the shared norms and networks formed by "semiproletarian" workers in urban Russia, may well have contributed to the political upheavals of 1905 and 1917.[4]

Lenin and the Bolsheviks identified Russia's urban workers as a genuine industrial proletariat that required guidance from a "vanguard" party with advanced revolutionary consciousness; and they viewed the survival of rural identities and social institutions as a serious obstacle to the orderly construction of a socialist industrial state. At the same time, Lenin's institution-building efforts had been focused on the Bolshevik party and did not extend to a coherent program for managing the everyday aspects of production in the course of socialist industrialization. Thus, his death was followed by meaningful debates over alternative strategies of institution-building, all inspired by a vision of "revolutionary modernity,"[5] but with real differences over how extensively to borrow from Western institutional models and how much to stress any affinities between socialist ideals and traditional understandings of collective labor and egalitarianism. Stalin's victory in 1928, however, marked the beginning of a cultural revolution consisting of the destruction of preexisting rural institutions, a relentless attack on "class enemies," and rapid, militarized industrialization. Significantly, however, within the context of the industrial enterprise, Stalin's campaigns to elevate revolutionary heroism were accompanied by the official endorsement of managerial techniques influenced directly by Western scientific management. This juxtaposition, as in the case of prewar Japanese "family firms," never evolved into a coherent synthesis, leaving marked incongruities between management ideology and practice, and between formal and informal aspects of shopfloor production relations. The result was not the "new Soviet man," but a bifurcated work force in which a disillusioned majority proceeded to rely on informal understandings and networks on the shopfloor that reflected the legacy of past communities of work rather than the internalization of official management doctrines.

Stalin's successors, attempting to maintain industrial order without resorting to overt coercion, would initiate their own version of human relations, offering guarantees of physical safety, full employment, steady improvements in living standards, and reduced wage differentials across job categories. In contrast to postwar Japanese firms, however, these new commitments were not accompanied by a restructuring of work and authority within the Soviet firm. Instead, the regime merely turned a blind eye to informal understandings and practices that managers had to rely on to retain workers and to stave off labor unrest. In the absence of a systematic transformation of the formal system of production, these measures only made the gap between ideology and reality wider and more apparent, contributing to a further decline in worker commitment. This set the stage for the more overt challenges to the regime when Gorbachev set out to promote glasnost and boost discipline and productivity.

This chapter examines the Soviet effort to implement a standard set of managerial ideals and practices that would simultaneously promote a revolutionary vision and establish a complex, orderly system of production. The interpretation developed below explicitly or implicitly addresses—and seeks to partially reconcile—contending perspectives on the question of the extent to which the transformation of Russian economy and society reflected an "ordinary" and continuous process of change comparable to that in other modernizing societies (see appendix B). The analysis also identifies certain crucial features of the Soviet experience that are to be fruitfully contrasted with the experience of firms in prewar and postwar Japan in the concluding chapter (see fig. 13). Section 4.1 begins by considering the typical norms and practices of the prerevolutionary Russian peasant commune *(mir)* insofar as these reflected resilient understandings about mutual cooperation and the distribution of responsibilities and rewards. Section 4.2 notes that, although these inherited norms were not entirely at odds with the original ideals of Lenin and the Bolsheviks, methods to boost labor discipline and productivity in Soviet enterprises increasingly deviated from these ideals and came to more closely resemble the core features of Western scientific management, even in the heyday of Stalin's cultural revolution. This section also considers the conditions and responses of different categories of workers in the Stalin era. Section 4.3 considers the post-Stalin period, noting that the regime's version of human relations, while effective in staving off labor unrest, only made the gap between ideology and practice more transparent and permanent, leading to persistent dilemmas that Gorbachev's reforms only exacerbated. Finally, section 4.4 captures the stylized interpretation of Soviet labor relations in terms of the theoretical argument laid out in chapters 1 and 2, noting that despite the public skepticism toward official communist ideology, long-standing norms emphasizing collective labor and distributive justice were unintentionally reinforced during the Soviet era and continue to shape aspects of post-Soviet industrial relations.

4.1. The Legacy of the Peasant Commune: Community and Egalitarianism

In approaching the question of the prerevolutionary inheritance, some historians and anthropologists have emphasized the legacy of steeply hierarchical patriarchal authority, pointing either to the centuries-old authority relationships between a divine tsar, the landed nobility, and the ostensibly deferential rural masses[6] or to the typical peasant household *(dvor)* in which severe paternal discipline was enforced by a nearly omnipotent patriarch *(bol'shak)*.[7] Others have emphasized the legacy of an enduring set of distinctly Russian cultural ideals that include a commitment to unitary and absolute values, linked to a strong sense of equality in material conditions among members of a moral community.[8] Still others have pointed to the lasting effects of such factors as the distinctive characteristics of agrarian life under Russia's harsh climatic conditions, the religious psychology associated with Russian Orthodoxy, or the traditions of local self-governance predating Muscovite Russia.[9]

All of these observations undoubtedly constitute a part of the varied, complex, multilayered inheritance from prerevolutionary Russia. However, when it comes to understanding the experiences and responses of the millions of individuals who left the countryside and joined the Russian work force from the mid–nineteenth century onward, the most relevant inheritance consists of those norms and practices formed within the concrete context of everyday life and work in village communities throughout rural Russia. While manorial authority and the figure of the tsar did factor into the worldview of the average peasant, and while the welfare of the household was very likely more important to most peasants than the collective welfare of the village, it is the village that represented the most relevant social arena for the day-to-day coordination of work-related activities among distinct households, and it is the village within which one finds specific norms and organizational features related to the definition of group boundaries, the mediation of conflicts, the management of common land and other resources, and the distribution of tasks and responsibilities. Thus, the following discussion on prerevolutionary inheritance is confined to the norms and social relations that shaped everyday life and work at the level of the village community.

Village Life in Prerevolutionary Russia: The Mir *as a Community of Work*

As in most preindustrial communities, agrarian life in prerevolutionary Russia was generally characterized by a dense network of intensely personal relations shared among members of households who worked daily in close proximity on several small strips of land scattered around the village.

While the term for village *(derevnya)* generally refers to the territory on which a group of peasants lived and farmed, it is the peasant commune (the *obshchina* or, as the peasants themselves referred to it, the *mir*) that represented the single most important social institution in regulating life and work on this territory. The commune may not have corresponded exactly to a single village, but each commune represented a distinct, local community, sometimes incorporating as many as a hundred households from two or three neighboring settlements.[10] Up until several years after the Bolshevik Revolution, the vast majority of the rural population participated in agricultural activities regulated by the *mir*.

There is some disagreement among historians on how and when the *mir* first emerged as a functioning community of work. One famous view holds that the *mir* was originally formed out of the ancient Slavs' tribal groups—some fifty or sixty persons related by blood and working their fields as a single corporate unit; over time, these units gave way to a more generalized pattern of communal organization consisting of the joint regulation of agricultural activities and redistribution of jointly held lands.[11] Others have argued that the commune was established, and subsequently manipulated, by the Muscovite state beginning in the sixteenth century in order to preserve social order and facilitate the collection of taxes in the countryside.[12] For Russian revolutionary populists such as Herzen and Chernyshevskii, the origins and functions of the *mir* were similar to those of typical agrarian communities in precapitalist Europe, but the fortuitous backwardness of Russia could enable the *mir* to provide a moral basis for a new social order.[13] None of these contending views, however, disputes the fact that, between the sixteenth century and the period of Stalinist collectivization, the *mir* was the most significant social institution in the countryside, with remarkably similar generalized norms guiding the regulation of land use, the collective payment of taxes, the distribution of tasks and resources, the mediation of disputes, the organization of mutual assistance, and even the building of local facilities (such as schools and bridges).

As in the case of Japan, there were certainly important variations in specific local practices and social structures across the Russian empire, but for the purposes of distinguishing the typical *mir* from the Japanese *mura,* these variations are less significant than the relatively high degree of homogeneity in work-related norms and practices across the countryside.[14] The emergent similarities of commune structure and function are partially related to the spread of common cultural, linguistic, and religious traditions dating back well before the Muscovite period. The Orthodox Church and its calender probably played a particularly important role in propagating a recognizable set of beliefs and an annual cycle of rituals that produced a high degree of solidarity in communal life, although preexisting local traditions were frequently blended with Orthodox rituals, and parish priests were sometimes regarded as outsiders.[15] The homogenization of more concrete work-related norms and practices was even more closely related to the gradual process of state formation and bureaucratic centralization in Muscovite Russia between the sixteenth and eighteenth centuries. Although the tsarist state was primarily interested in using the *mir* to strengthen its hold on the peasantry, its efforts contributed to the strengthening of communal authority and the crystallization of a distinct "village political culture" that survived during the period of serfdom and proceeded to shape rural life in post-Emancipation Russia.[16]

For the purposes of the argument to follow, two points emerge as especially significant when the Russian peasant commune is compared to communities of work elsewhere. First, the *mir*, like the *mura* and most other agrarian communities, was thought to be a tightly knit moral community that served as a basis for collective identity and solidarity, transcending both the interests of individuals and the formal administrative apparatus of the state. But, second, in marked contrast to the *mura* and many village communities elsewhere, the *mir* was significantly more egalitarian in terms of both the actual degree of stratification, as well as generalized norms guiding distributive practices and collective decision making.[17]

The Mir *As a Source of Collective Identity and Solidarity*

Membership in the *mir* depended primarily on being part of the dense network of social relations and interactions that shaped everyday life and work, especially as neighbors frequently had to traverse each other's plots to tend to the widely scattered strips of land allotted to them by the commune. As in other village communities, the separate interests and identities of individual households did not disappear, but these were regularly subordinated whenever in conflict with the goals of regulating collective labor, managing collective resources, or maintaining community solidarity. But the *mir* was more than an institution that fostered cooperation among individuals interested primarily in the welfare of their families; it was also regarded as a deeply moral community of individuals whose common faith reinforced their shared identity as Orthodox believers *(pravoslavnyi)* and gave special meaning to their cooperative endeavors and social relations.[18] That is, the *mir* represented a tightly knit "living and unitary community of all believers in whose association love, truth and freedom were all located."[19]

The salience of communal identity was evident in a relatively high level of mutual trust not extended to outsiders and in the common disinterest of peasants in the affairs of outsiders. When peasants did have to deal directly with outside authorities, they viewed these dealings strictly in instrumental and impersonal terms even if they publicly displayed deep reverence toward tsarist officials.[20] In any case, in the course of everyday life and work, one was unlikely to regularly encounter individuals who were not members of the commune, and the occasional outsider simply was not accorded the same degree of trust, intimacy, or cooperation reserved for members of the commune. Although this did not preclude conflicts or drunken brawls among commune members, most peasants found it difficult to think of life or work in terms that did not involve participation in activities regulated by the commune, and most recognized that there were practical and moral benefits to acting *po vole mira,* in accordance with the will of the commune.[21]

The specific regulatory functions of the *mir* varied over time, especially with the markedly different constraints it faced before, during, and after the period of serfdom. Immediately prior to the consolidation of serfdom in seventeenth-century Russia, the peasant *mir* was the key institution in maintaining and coordinating the three-field system of farming that had become prevalent throughout the Russian countryside over the centuries. According to this system, common and individual meadows were divided by collective decisions taken by the *mir* into three sections so that one would be sown in spring for summer crops, one at the end of summer for winter crops, and one left fallow. It was left to the council of the *mir* to coordinate the division of the meadows so as to enable all households to coordinate their work across, and maintain access to, the widely scattered strips of land they had to tend at any given time of year.[22] The *mir* also introduced and enforced concrete measures to resolve internal conflicts, redistribute resources to match the changing needs of households, and coordinate assistance to help out households in difficulty. Moreover, even if the *mir* may well have been regarded by the tsarist state as an instrument for the purpose of effectively controlling and taxing the countryside, it is significant that the peasants themselves embraced the idea of commune members collectively taking responsibility for the payment of taxes (however unjust) and determining the tax burden of individual households.

As serfdom became entrenched in the eighteenth century, especially under the reigns of Peter I (1682–1725) and Catherine (1762–96), the *mir* continued to regulate collective village life. Distributive practices that had emerged during the sixteenth century continued in the form of reassessing the responsibilities for cultivating lands among different households, with special consideration extended to reduce the burden of less fortunate households facing difficult circumstances (such as the death of able-bodied peasants or some natural catastrophe). Moreover, despite the tsarist state's efforts to intensify its hold on the countryside through manorial administration, the *mir* continued to perform several key functions: it maintained a reserve of grain for use in crises, continued to settle minor disputes among peasants to limit outside intervention, and regulated the selection of recruits from the villages who would serve in the army.[23] Thus, throughout the period of serfdom, the *mir* remained an extremely significant institution in regulating collective life and preserving collective solidarity despite the formal authority claimed by tsarist officials and the manorial administration.

Following Alexander II's Emancipation Edict (1861), the *mir,* rather than dissolving or becoming irrelevant, became the official holder of the lands allotted to the peasantry on behalf of households that were formally free and independent.[24] The commune remained the primary basis for ensuring cooperation and regulating land use in everyday agricultural work, especially as peasants still had to organize and coordinate the timing of activities on open strips of land scattered across wide distances around the village. In addition, the *mir* took responsibility for the collective payment of state taxes as well as the newly levied redemption dues (intended to compensate former gentry members for the loss of land and serf labor).[25] The principle of the circle of mutual responsibility *(krugovaia poruka)* was invoked to ensure that all households met their obligations and that assistance or credit was made available to households facing catastrophic situations (such as a fire or the death of a household head).[26] Similarly, the *mir* revived the tradition of *pomoch,* a centuries-old system of mutual aid used to cement ties among neighbors: nearby commune members offered joint tilling, harvesting, or barn-raising to help out a household in need during religious holidays; the beneficiary's only obligation was to return the favor in due course and to offer food, drink, and entertainment to those who had donated the free labor. While participation in this practice did vary with changing circumstances—for example, poorer households could not afford the rising costs of food and entertainment in lean years—the tradition of *pomoch* remained an important part of the collective life of the *mir* into the early twentieth century.[27] The *mir* even began to take over the functions of maintaining local roads, providing new educational facilities, creating a local court resembling a jury system, and organizing welfare services to orphans, the aged, and the handicapped—all functions that the tsarist state had hoped to regulate through its own rural and municipal administrative units.[28] Thus, despite variations accompanying the establishment and abolition of serfdom, by the end of the nineteenth century, the collectivist features of the *mir* were comparable to those of the Japanese *mura* in terms of their significance in regulating cooperative labor.

The one area in which the *mir* may be contrasted to the Tokugawa *mura* is on the extent to which harmonious relations were valued in everyday life and work. In contrast to the *mura,* in which harmony was generally regarded as an indication that responsibilities and obligations were being fulfilled in an appropriate manner, the commune's ideal of collective solidarity was not so tightly bound with the preservation of harmony in day-to-day life. In addition to the evidence of rural rebellions and peasant uprisings, historians point to incidences of theft, lying, petty squabbles, and generational tensions, as well as *buntarstvo,* the spontaneous brawls and riots that disrupted village life from time to time. There was also factionalism among members of the commune assembly, and peasants were always ready to denounce as heretics or even physically assault those who attempted to permanently leave the commune or to close off meadows and access routes normally regulated by the commune.[29] Problems were also evident in the Japanese countryside, but there was a much greater sense of urgency in restoring harmony through the intervention of mediators. That this was not the case with the *mir,* however, does not indicate that the *mir* was ineffective or irrelevant in the maintenance of social order in the countryside; it merely suggests that there was less of a preoccupation with maintaining the appearance of harmony at all times.

In fact, the most serious confrontations in the Russian countryside were those instigated by the *mir* to defend established norms and community interests from external threats such as unjust officials or households acting in defiance of commune decisions.[30] While peasant uprisings in the Russian countryside may have been more frequent than in the case of Tokugawa Japan, the purpose in both cases was essentially the same: not to achieve sweeping transformations but to attack specific targets in order to achieve specific objectives consistent with the norms and interests of the commune.[31] In the case of attacks against households attempting to set up independent farmsteads *(khutor),* the violence was often viewed by commune elders as necessary for the preservation of established norms and practices. As for petty squabbles or brawls that arose in the course of everyday life, these were tolerated so long as they did not escalate; the function of the *mir* was not to preserve harmony at all times but to ensure that these minor conflicts or individual actions did not threaten community interests. Thus, tensions and conflicts in the Russian countryside should not detract attention from the fact that the *mir* was the most significant embodiment of collective norms and interests in the regulation of everyday life and work.

Egalitarian Norms in Action: Land Redistribution and
Collective Decision Making

What distinguishes the Russian peasant commune most starkly from the Japanese village and many other agrarian communities are its strongly egalitarian norms and practices. This egalitarianism not only suggested a diffuse equality of opportunity, but was related to specific distributive practices that had implications for actual material conditions among the Russian peasantry.[32] Certainly, some households were wealthier than others, prompting early Soviet historians to portray the *mir* as an exploitative institution dominated by a narrow class of rich capitalist peasants *(kulaks);* but such an interpretation fails to recognize that the level of stratification in other rural communities was significantly higher and that challenges to the *mir*'s distributive practices often came from the marginally wealthier peasants.[33] This may be why many Russian socialists—including members of the agrarian Socialist Revolutionary party as well as the first agricultural commissars in the new Soviet regime—found the commune to be a distinctive entity that lacked the sharp class differentiation of agrarian communities in the West, with the Socialist Revolutionary Chernov even characterizing the *mir* as a "wild plant" that socialists could fruitfully cultivate, rather than destroy, in the process of building a new order.[34]

The egalitarian ethos of the commune is captured most explicitly in norms governing agricultural work, specifically the principles of the "right *of* labor" and the "right *to* labor." The former held that land should be in the hands of those who till it; the latter suggested that every family in the village, no matter how poor, had the right to a sufficiently large land allotment so as to be able to work the fields as a means of subsistence. While the right *of* labor implicitly challenged serfdom and tenant farming, the right *to* labor was an explicit indication of the value placed on distributive justice; it meant that peasant households not only would be guaranteed access to common resources regardless of their wealth and status, but would also be granted special considerations (by way of credit, mutual assistance, or additional land allotments) were their needs or difficulties to increase relative to those of other households—even if this meant that resources accumulated by wealthier peasants would have to be reallocated.[35]

The egalitarian norms of the *mir* were most concretely institutionalized in specific procedures for the management and redistribution of land, by far the most precious commodity in an agrarian economy. In the case of the repartitional commune, the type of commune found across most of European Russia, the council of the *mir* engaged in a periodic redistribution of land that effectively limited the extent of stratification. In the post-Emancipation period, major repartitions sometimes took place around the time of the government census, but for the most part, the redistribution of lands was timed to coincide with the beginning of the three-field rotation system. According to the system of land repartition, each peasant household could keep a small plot around the house on a hereditary basis *(usadba)*, but the bulk of arable land was distributed by the commune as allotments of strips *(nadel)*, with the needs of households, available labor, the quality of soil, and tax burdens taken into account to ensure that all households could meet their subsistence needs. In addition, between successive projects to repartition all commonly held land, there were often partial redistributions, sometimes voluntary, involving specific households that had encountered particularly difficult circumstances. In the process, "even lands that had been held for generations . . . could [be] (and were) taken away and reallocated by the commune assembly."[36] Moreover, in the case of the division of household property following the death or incapacitation of a household head, the commune intervened either to ensure that the common property would be administered by a new head, or, alternatively, it would make adjustments in land allotments in the event that any of the sons decided to set up their own separate households (as was their right).[37]

Certainly, there were occasions when the wealthiest households attempted to block repartitions or tried to leave the commune and establish their own farmsteads *(khutora)*. There were also squabbles among brothers over the partitioning of strips under the control of their household. But these were exceptions to the rule; for the most part, households voluntarily acceded to the periodic repartition process as well as the inheritance system.[38] Even in parts of Russia (especially lands previously under Polish or Baltic-German rule) where communes generally did not engage in systematic repartitioning of lands owned by households, the commune assembly still redistributed common meadows, adjusted tax burdens, coordinated mutual aid, and introduced specific rules in order to prevent excessive stratification and ensure collective subsistence and communal solidarity.[39] As a result of the widespread concern for an equality in the distribution of material resources, the level of socioeconomic differentiation among the Russian peasantry was markedly lower in comparison to most other agrarian social structures, with the material possessions and life-styles of rich and poor peasants largely indistinguishable during years when the harvest was good.[40] Simply put, such practices as mutual assistance, the periodic redistribution of lands, and the adjustment of tax obligations all "reinforced a system that did not tolerate glaring inequities in economic standing among peasants."[41]

As in the case of landownership, the process of collective decision making in the Russian countryside was also less hierarchical and more inclusive than in the case of the *mura*. While decision-making authority in the latter tended to be concentrated in the hands of the most wealthy, highest-ranked households, leadership in the commune never became hereditary and was subject to some expression of the will of *all* households in the commune. The head of the assembly was usually a single elderly village leader *(starosta)* who was periodically subject to reelection; other village elders, also subject to reelection, acted as officers charged with overseeing land-use management, tax collection, and mutual assistance. The *mir* typically reached collective decisions through regular meetings of an assembly consisting of the heads of *all* the member households, whatever their wealth, status, or reputation. Although the decisions of the *mir* consistently emphasized unanimity, risk-avoidance, and social stability, the deliberations had an informal democratic quality; they were open to all individuals in member households and allowed for "considerable freedom of action and expression."[42] While only the household heads could actually vote on joint decisions, no household was excluded and nonrepresentatives regularly participated in discussions of a range of issues. It is true that proceedings sometimes degenerated into raucous arguments and drinking bouts, and wealthier peasants did have somewhat greater leverage over the decision-making process, sometimes resorting to bribery or seeking to get elected by buying the most drinks for others. Nevertheless, by comparison to other rural institutions, the *mir* represented "an institution of an extremely democratic character, its periodic meetings providing an informal forum at which any villager could speak . . . with the entire commune participating in the making of most decisions."[43]

Thus, while the hierarchical character of tsarist autocracy and the patriarchal household led some to suggest that the prerevolutionary inheritance consisted primarily of a deeply entrenched authoritarian political culture,[44] the actual regulation of agricultural activities and everyday village life suggests that "concern for equality of burdens and obligations lay at the heart of the Russian repartitional commune."[45] This did not necessarily suggest the absence of petty jealousies or self-interest; however, self-interest or envy toward better-off households did not stand in the way of the widespread adherence to shared norms emphasizing collective subsistence, communal solidarity, and an equality of material conditions among members of the *mir*.[46] The question that arises now is just how resilient and portable the norms and practices of the commune would prove to be in the course of Russian industrialization.

The Resilience of the Mir, *1861–1920s*

Following Alexander II's Emancipation Edict of 1861, the *mir* was to encounter several new challenges and pressures that would threaten its survival. Population growth in the latter part of the nineteenth century, together with the burden of state taxes and redemption dues owed to the gentry, brought down the threshold of peasant subsistence, prompting increasing numbers of peasants to seek supplemental incomes through factory work.[47] At the same time, the tsarist state continued to seek ways to weaken the authority of the peasant commune, eventually initiating a campaign to consolidate land strips and promote individual landholding (the Stolypin reforms). Similarly, the new Soviet state proceeded to introduce new policies and institutions in the hope of weakening and supplanting the *mir*. Until Stalin's forced collectivization, however, the commune actually became progressively *more* important in the eyes of most peasants, providing security, familiarity, and a much needed safety net during a turbulent and uncertain time.

Under the burden of taxes and redemption dues, peasant out-migration did increase steadily, but rather than become overwhelmed by the contact with the rapidly expanding commercial economy of the late nineteenth century, "the Russian peasant commune proved itself to be quite resilient as an institutionalized scheme for the collective defense of peasant interests and the collective fulfillment of peasant obligations."[48] In fact, the commune became a key institution in regulating the departures from the countryside and in preserving or reorganizing the distribution of resources and tax obligations to account for the changing situations of households. For the most part, peasants who departed for the city did so with the blessing of the commune so long as they returned regularly to their farmsteads and so long as they contributed to their respective households' tax burdens. Once in the city, the exposure to factory work and urban life-styles did result in new tensions among commune members, but most peasant-workers *(otkhodniki)* "selectively incorporated a few urban ways into their culture, without abandoning their traditional worldview."[49] Common village ties *(zemliachestvo)* frequently served as the basis for networks to help newcomers find jobs and dwellings, with most *otkhodniki* remitting wages regularly and retaining close ties to their villages, partly out of a sense of nostalgia for the "familiarity and intimacy of the village" and partly to help their households meet tax obligations and thereby retain access to the commune's resources and mutual aid schemes.[50]

A potentially more significant threat to the commune came in the form of the tsarist state's efforts to gain control over the countryside and transform agricultural practices in the course of industrialization. Both Alexander II (1855–81) and his successor, Alexander III (1881–94), were eager to undermine the commune, but at the same time, they were wary of directly challenging the institution of the *mir* for fear of triggering rural unrest. Alexander II's Emancipation Edict officially recognized the right of individual peasants to leave the commune, but, fearing instability in the countryside, the tsar also included a clause that acknowledged the commune's right to take over the lands allotted to departing households. As part of a more indirect strategy to undermine the commune, Alexander II chose not to formally recognize the local authority of the commune, while promoting alternative administrative bodies and assemblies in the hope that these would eventually obviate the *mir.* These included the *volost,* the official unit of administration encompassing several village clusters, as well as provincial and district-level *zemstvo* assemblies, which consisted of educated professionals, many of them former aristocrats, ostensibly committed to building schools, hospitals, roads, and rest homes for the rural masses. Alexander III continued this strategy, even appointing a land chief *(zemskii nachal'nik)* from the ranks of the nobility to oversee the administration of rural districts. Yet these efforts never achieved the desired objective, as the new administrative bodies were generally regarded by most peasants as alien, representing the interests of outsiders rather than those of the village community; across most of the countryside, the commune remained the most important regulative body and continued to fulfill its long-standing functions. The resilience of the commune finally convinced Alexander III in 1893 to abrogate the right of individual households to leave the *mir,* basically extending formal recognition to the commune's authority in local affairs and acknowledging its significance in mediating the relationship between the government and its rural subjects.[51]

Shortly after the upheaval of 1905, during the reign of Nicholas II (1894–1917), the tsarist administration went back on the offensive, launching its most direct and concerted attack on the *mir* to date. The Stolypin plan, set in motion in 1906, was designed to dissolve communal agriculture altogether in order to promote full-scale capitalist agriculture based on independently owned individual farmsteads. Various laws were passed in 1906 and 1910–11 in order to break up the commune, consolidate the strips of land into larger plots, and make all householders legal proprietors whether or not they chose to withdraw from the commune. Implementing these policies, however, proved to be a very different matter. Throughout the Russian countryside as a whole, even the most optimistic estimates—based on official figures of the tsarist government—indicate that less than a quarter of the communal households had withdrawn from the commune as of 1916. Less optimistic estimates, focusing on landholding patterns in European Russia (where the repartitional commune prevailed, suggest that no more than 10 percent of the households had established individual farmsteads as of January 1917. And some estimates note that less than 5 percent of arable land was farmed without some sort of communal regulation.[52]

Following the 1917 revolution, there was a veritable flood of return migration as large numbers of peasant-workers returned to their villages in the hope of resuming farming without the burden of any further state taxes or redemption payments.[53] In the countryside, the Bolsheviks attempted to establish Committees on Poor Peasants *(kombedy)* in order to reduce the influence of the commune and take control of the land redistribution process. But once the remaining possessions of the old gentry had been handed over to them, most peasants lost interest in the *kombedy* and reverted to the commune, relying on the original system of mutual aid and land redistribution. Similarly, the Bolsheviks got nowhere when they attempted to declare commune decisions illegal and sought to establish a new system of local administration; most peasants ignored the Soviet-established rural councils *(selsoviet)* and the communal assembly continued to make key decisions in its usual manner, ignoring the Official Agrarian Code that required that assembly representatives be elected by all who were eighteen years of age.[54] To the extent that peasants paid any attention to Bolshevik ideology, such ideals as collectivism and egalitarianism, while conceived of as part of a revolutionary project, only ended up unintentionally signaling the regime's acceptance of the peasants' traditional norms and practices.[55] Thus, during the period of the New Economic Policy (from 1921 to about 1926), with the reestablishment of a private sector, even the most experienced industrial workers continued to own a share of communal property through their ties to family in the countryside, and the commune itself went through a period of revival and expansion, rolling back whatever progress had been achieved by the Stolypin reforms.[56]

However, this state of affairs could not be maintained indefinitely given the basic contradictions between the objectives and understandings of the regime and those of the peasantry:

> With the political leadership committed to a misleading conception of rural society, with its local representatives out of touch with the peasantry . . . , with the power of the communes decisive in local affairs, yet unable to dictate national policy and bound to be defeated in a full-scale confrontation with a modern state, the stage was set . . . for the drama of collectivization.[57]

With Stalin's rise to power, those partial to a more gradual approach to building socialist agriculture were forced out, and a brutal attack commenced on the traditional commune in order to establish large-scale, state-managed collective farms that could be squeezed to support industrialization. The resilience of the *mir* was evident one last time in the manner in which peasants vigorously defended the commune and resisted collectivization, frequently resorting to violent attacks on party officials and hiding or destroying property to prevent party officials from seizing it. In the end, however, such acts did not amount to a coordinated resistance to the regime's policies, and, by the early 1930s, the commune finally succumbed to the collectivization campaign.[58] The remainder of this chapter addresses whether and how the legacy of the *mir* influenced the growing industrial work force and conditioned its response to management practices adopted in the course of Soviet industrialization. The conclusion addresses the portability and current relevance of elements of this legacy in the context of considering some of the peculiarities of post-Soviet industrial relations.

4.2. Revolution, Scientific Management, and Socialist Competition from 1917 to the 1940s

Shortly after their ascendance, the Bolsheviks found themselves juggling several imperatives: serving as a vanguard for the workers' revolution, protecting their hold on power from internal and foreign enemies, building a social base for the party, and industrializing rapidly so as to catch up to and surpass *(dognat i peregnat)* the West. While a number of strategies were available for reconciling or prioritizing these imperatives, formulas that advocated gradual programs of transformation or stressed the affinities between revolutionary goals and preexisting ideals were rejected during the 1920s in favor of a relentless "revolution from above"[59] consisting of purges of class enemies, the destruction of traditional social institutions, and the creation of new political and economic institutions designed to ensure both loyalty to the regime and rapid industrialization. This approach *did* produce a social revolution in that a new industrial work force emerged, at least a portion of which supported the regime's broad goals; and this work force eventually became accustomed to the tasks and routines of factory production, learning to speak and act in terms acceptable to the regime.[60] At the same time, however, the utopian campaigns and revolutionary rhetoric belied an ongoing fixation with American managerial efficiency that dated back to Lenin's own fixation with Taylorism. The Soviet enterprise thus came to be characterized by steep managerial hierarchies, more complex schemes for job classification, "objective" production norms for thousands of elemental tasks, and a sharply differentiated wage structure within and across job categories. These practices led not to a committed, unified proletariat with increasing revolutionary consciousness but rather to a fragmented work force in which a narrow stratum made rapid gains at the expense of a majority progressively disillusioned with the growing gap between officially sanctioned management practices and "socialist" ideals that had once resonated with preexisting sensibilities.[61] In order to appreciate the sources of this disillusionment, it is instructive to consider briefly how an earlier generation of workers in tsarist Russia coped with urban life and working conditions between 1861 and 1917 (a period roughly corresponding to the Meiji era in Japan).

*Factories in Prerevolutionary Russia: Workers' Artels and
Village-Based Networks*

Prior to the abolition of serfdom in 1861, most workers had been serfs con-
tracted out temporarily to factory owners by manorial lords. After the
abolition of serfdom, increasing numbers of peasants migrated to the cities
and became free laborers, mostly as seasonal workers *(otkhodniki)* who
returned to their villages at harvest time, or as full-time workers who
worked regularly in factories but remained "noncitizens," lacking the
rights or facilities accorded to permanent urban dwellers. Most of these
peasant-workers, unlike the few established workers whose scarce skills
were in high demand, worked long hours, lived in cramped dormitories,
and stubbornly resisted socialization into the system of disciplined labor
and factory time, viewing industrial labor as temporary drudgery and
expecting to return to their villages if or when circumstances permitted.[62]

Factory owners and managers, for their part, relied on steeply hierarchical authority to supervise workers, enforce labor discipline, and even
regulate workers' daily lives. These managerial elites were not inattentive
to the potential uses of familiar symbols and ideals; but, like their counterparts in Meiji Japan who invoked the "beautiful custom" of master-servant relations to reinforce their authority, tsarist managers invoked familial patriarchal authority *(popechitelstvo)* rather than the norms and social
organization of such institutions as the commune. For most workers,
however, the norms and expectations associated with patriarchal authority were meaningful only within the context of the household; as far as the
coordination of labor was concerned, the relevant traditions consisted of
egalitarian norms and collective participation in the management of
resources and obligations. But this tension was neither recognized nor relevant from the point of view of managers in view of the extremely severe
enforcement of labor discipline, regularly supported by heavy-handed
police methods.[63]

It is true that, in contrast to prewar Japan (where the first Factory Bill
was not adopted until 1911), the tsarist government, eager to preempt
labor unrest, had introduced a number of labor laws and regulatory measures ostensibly to reform industrial relations and oblige factory owners to
maintain some minimum standards for working conditions. In the 1860s,
the Shtakel'berg Commission provided a detailed account of working and
living conditions and offered several proposals designed to reform labor
practices and improve working conditions.[64] A Factory Inspectorate set

up in the 1880s was extremely active, sending officials to hundreds of factories where arbitrary penalties and violations of labor laws were documented in great detail. As one inspector noted: "Extreme regulations and regimentation are very common in our factories—regulations entangle the workers at every step and burden them with more or less severe fines which are subtracted from their often already inadequate wages."[65] But such reports by a few dozen inspectors proved to be inadequate for prompting reform, and very rarely were actions taken to punish repeated violations of labor laws even where they had been independently verified.[66] Moreover, unions remained illegal through 1905, and even after they were legalized in 1906, meaningful challenges to the regime remained virtually impossible in view of a statute forbidding "political" strikes.[67] Thus, the longer history of labor codes in Russia did not contribute to a fundamental difference in the oppressive working conditions faced by most of the Japanese and Russian work force at the turn of the century.

Eager to retain access to a safety net under such conditions, most peasant-workers retained a share of communal property and helped their households meet their financial obligations to the commune. In the absence of class solidarity, when working conditions got unbearable, many workers expressed their dissatisfaction not through collective action but by simply quitting their jobs and returning to their villages.[68] Among those who began to settle down in the city, a sharply bifurcated work force emerged, consisting of a narrow stratum of established skilled workers alongside a mass of less skilled peasant-workers.[69] The latter operated primarily through tightly knit networks formed by workers originally from the same communities *(zemliaki)*, frequently living in the same neighborhoods and relying on familiar patterns of cooperation and mutual assistance to cope with difficult conditions and guard against exploitation and cheating by untrusted foremen and managers. The result was not unified working-class consciousness, but balkanized enterprises in which "diversity led to clannishness rather than assimilation."[70]

In this environment, the continuing influence of the communal norms and practices was most clearly revealed in the formation of collective workgroups *(artels)*, especially among workers who came from the same region. Members of *artels* lived and traveled as a group, contracting with shopfloor bosses and managers to jointly offer their labor in exchange for collective remuneration that would be equally divided up. They employed their own sanctions to maintain group discipline, took care of the welfare of newer members, and elected an elder *(starosta)* to negotiate their collective contracts and manage the distribution of tasks and earnings. Certainly, the elder wielded greater power than other *artel* members, but, as in the case of the village community, abuse of this power could result in the election of a new elder. While more established members were more influential and sometimes domineering, the resulting hierarchy was based on the common acknowledgment that recent arrivals would eventually acquire the experience, skills, and knowledge of the labor market that accompanied the status and influence of the more established members of the workgroup.[71] In short, whatever hierarchy existed *within artels* did not constitute a basis for permanent stratification (as in the case of the work force at large), but rather a pragmatic response to flux and uncertainty based on quite familiar principles; older, more experienced workers necessarily played a greater leadership role, but the group as a whole performed collective tasks and distributed obligations and earnings among themselves in a relatively egalitarian manner. In the turbulent and uncertain environment of the post-Emancipation period, for most workers, the *artel* seemed to be "the only institution capable of mitigating the isolation of the peasant *otkhodnik* in a strange city and allowing him to share the burden of his employment and subsistence problems with fellow villagers."[72]

By the turn of the century, workers were gradually becoming a more permanent urban class, now less concerned with conditions in the countryside and more concerned with wages, shopfloor activities, and working and living conditions. In this environment, while *artels* did decline in importance among skilled workers, the village still continued to serve as a form of social security in the event of unemployment, injury, illness, or old age; and village-based identities continued to form the primary basis for networks of recruitment and socialization as well as distinct neighborhood communities and groupings of workers.[73] These social ties and networks may not have constituted a basis for widespread collective protest, but they diluted the commitment of workers to their formal units of work organization and contributed to sporadic outbursts against specific individuals who bore the brunt of workers' resentment toward management.[74] Even during the tumultuous events of 1917, despite the support the Bolsheviks began to enjoy among urban workers, the behavior of most workers was only revolutionary in the sense that there was a growing frustration with the status quo; while some workers were genuinely class conscious and eager to be in the forefront of a proletarian revolution, most retained ties to the countryside and acted on the basis of normative commitments similar to those invoked in defense of the *mir*.[75]

After 1917, not only did many workers return to their villages to claim a share of the new lands acquired by their communes, but even among those workers who remained in the cities, the continuous exposure to urban life and a nascent sense of class solidarity never supplanted the intensely particularistic neighborhood loyalties that had originally crystallized around village-based identities and networks.[76] In fact, during the 1920s and into the 1930s, it was these networks of *zemliaki,* rather than Soviet bureaucrats, that would play the most active role in the regulation of peasant out-migration and the recruitment and socialization of new workers.[77] Similarly, the norms and practices of *artels* survived in the guise of production collectives and production communes that, for a time, were interpreted by the Bolsheviks as an indication of the advanced consciousness of workers, although the latter simply sought to reproduce familiar modes of organization.[78] Stalin's cultural revolution would destroy old social institutions and produce a large, permanent urban working class, but the disjuncture between the tight sense of community within *artels* or among *zemliaki,* and the absence of such a sense at the factory level, would not disappear; it would evolve into new incongruities between the formal system of Soviet industrial management and the informal norms, networks, and practices among workers on the shopfloor.

Revolutionary Rhetoric to Shopfloor Realities:
The "New Exploitation of the Proletariat"

Following the abdication of the tsar in March 1917, although the Bolsheviks made no secret of their commitment to a far-flung revolutionary transformation, their efforts to gain the support of urban workers—through repeated reference to such phrases as "workers' control" and "equality of labor and pay"—*unintentionally* reinforced norms embedded in past communities of work, leaving most with an impression that these norms would be put into practice in the place of the steep hierarchies, sharp inequalities, and severe disciplinary measures of tsarist factories. Whatever specific meanings Lenin and his followers themselves may have attributed to "workers' control" and "equality," casual references to these terms resonated with the large segment of the urban work force that still retained ties to the countryside and still valued the familiar ideals associated with the *mir* and *artel.* This resonance would prove short-lived, but it may well have accounted for some of the support the Bolsheviks came to enjoy among urban workers in 1917.[79]

Of course, Lenin's theoretical treatises, particularly those aimed at fellow Bolsheviks or other Russian Social Democrats, might have provided a hint that the requirements for "building socialism" did not coincide with the workers' own aspirations for greater shopfloor autonomy and a more egalitarian wage structure. As early as 1902 (in *What Is To Be Done?*), Lenin had attacked other Russian Social Democrats for failing to grasp the importance of centralization, discipline, and secrecy, and he had argued against mass membership in the party in favor of a "committee of professional revolutionaries" that had to direct the working masses' attention away from petty "trade-unionism" toward the attainment of proletarian consciousness.[80] In his famous treatise *The State and Revolution*, Lenin explicitly noted that the lower stage of communism (that is, "socialism") would require not mass spontaneity but a "dictatorship of the proletariat," a workers' state administered not by bureaucrats but by "armed workers"; this proletarian state was needed to destroy the remnants of the old bourgeois state and establish "strict, iron discipline" until all citizens acquired the consciousness to voluntarily work in keeping with the principle of "from each according to his ability, to each according to his needs" (thus creating the conditions for communism and the "withering away" of the state).[81] Moreover, when Lenin referred to "workers' control," he specifically defined the term to mean control over the capitalists and over the workers' state and not direct control over factory production (as Russian syndicalists defined the term).[82] Lenin also emphasized that equality under socialism meant only that all members of society were formally equal in relation to the means of production, and that wages would be distributed according to the principle of "equal wages for equal work"; under the higher stage of communism, this "formal equality" would give way to "actual equality," with all individuals working voluntarily according to their (different) abilities for the benefit of society while partaking freely from available products according to their (different) needs.[83] Significantly, in neither stage did Lenin envision absolute equality in material conditions given inherent differences in individual abilities and needs.

However, most workers could not have been expected to grasp all the nuances of Lenin's theoretical writings; for the most part, what they paid attention to were public speeches or short pamphlets that promised the empowerment of workers, wage egalitarianism, and the end of capitalist speedups. For example, before changing his mind about the potential benefits of Taylorism just before the revolution, Lenin publicly condemned the reliance on piece rate wages in Western scientific management as a brutal system for "squeezing sweat" out of workers and rewarding the young and strong at the expense of the old and weak.[84] As part of his famous "April Theses," aimed at an audience of politically active workers in April 1917, Lenin also seemed to indicate that workers' own organizations were more important than any revolutionary party. He declared that the "Soviets [councils] of Workers' Deputies are the *only possible* form of revolutionary government," adding that the Bolsheviks intended "only to bring social production and the distribution of products at once under the control of the Soviets of Workers' Deputies" so as to destroy monopoly capitalism and pave the way for a "commune state."[85] Shortly afterward, even though the Bolsheviks had not previously adopted an official position on "workers' control," Lenin proceeded to endorse a resolution at a joint conference of the Petrograd factory committees specifically noting the importance of factory committees and trade unions in establishing *direct* control over production at the shopfloor level.[86] Moreover, while Lenin may have stressed discipline and unity of action for party members, in matters of day-to-day administration and decision making, the Bolsheviks publicly endorsed the principle of *kollegial'nost'*, that is, leadership through collegial decision making and consensus-building rather than through administrative diktat.[87] Finally, Lenin's careful definitions of socialist and communist equality notwithstanding, some trend toward income-leveling could reasonably be inferred from frequent references to the more simplified formula of "equality of labor and wages" and to Lenin's famous declaration that "technicians, foremen, accountants, as well as all officials, shall receive salaries no higher than 'a workman's wages'."[88]

In the first few months following the 1917 revolution as well, official statements and policies adopted by the Bolsheviks further strengthened the impression that "socialist" factories would be characterized by trends toward collective forms of labor and wage egalitarianism. In November 1917, in an exchange with leaders of other socialist parties, Lenin declared in nearly anarchist fashion: "Socialism is not created by order from above . . . it is the creation of the mass of the people themselves."[89] Taking the idea of workers' control seriously, the newly formed People's Commissariat of Labor helped to establish factory committees that would make binding decisions concerning day-to-day production and factory administration in enterprises throughout Russian industry. An All-Russian Council of Workers' Control was established to coordinate the activities of the factory committees, monitor the costs of production, and even settle budgetary accounts directly. At many factories, workers took the factory committees very seriously and went about setting up conferences, drawing up detailed procedures for making joint production decisions, and setting up "comrades' disciplinary courts" to collectively enforce labor discipline.[90] Moreover, Lenin publicly continued to insist that every "conscious worker" would become a "master of his enterprise"[91] and later proceeded to praise the spontaneity of the workers who had initiated the *Subbotnik* movement to contribute a day of uncompensated labor on Saturdays.[92]

Similarly, *some* movement in the direction of reduced wage differentials could be perceived in the April 1918 Labor Code which, while establishing productivity norms as the basis for material rewards, appeared to heed the trade union's concerns about worker exhaustion and excessive wage-differentiation by establishing upward limits on output-related wages and bonuses.[93] In addition, in 1919, the All-Russian Trade Union Council introduced a proposal that would have established a unified national wage-scale for each industry, featuring sharp reductions in wage differentials across four categories of employees and instituting an eight-hour workday and benefits related to unemployment and illness.[94] While this proposal never became official policy, the attention it received at least gave cause to think that the trade union bodies could be counted upon to promote the workers' objectives of income-leveling at the highest levels (even as the factory workers' control committees and their national council were already becoming less important).

Thus, whatever the *real* Lenin's understanding of workers' control and socialist equality, given the revolutionary rhetoric most workers read or heard about during 1917, it was not unreasonable for them to expect that, as the privileged revolutionary class, "their own values should command respect, that they should have a role to play in deciding what behaviors were or were not appropriate to life in a proletarian state."[95] Nor was it unreasonable for them to assume that "socialist labor," at a minimum, would increase workers' participation in factory administration, reduce the steep wage differentials in tsarist industry, and put an end to capitalist speedups. It is also significant that such measures, while revolutionary in that they suggested an end to standard practices in capitalist factories, would not have been particularly novel when understood as expressions of long-standing norms of collective self-management and distributive justice. As a result of this superficial, but potentially fortuitous, convergence between most workers' expectations and the Bolsheviks' initial espousal of workers' control and equality of labor and wages, "for a short period, it appeared that this organic relationship between the Soviet state and the 'toiling masses' might be able to sustain itself and serve as the basis for building the new socialist order."[96] This meant that the door was open to institution-building strategies that would build on, rather than deny, whatever affinities existed between the Bolsheviks' vision of socialist factories and preexisting ideals about collective labor and wage egalitarianism.

Such strategies never materialized, however, as the Bolsheviks soon became engaged in a protracted civil war and were faced with the task of boosting sagging industrial production if only to support their war effort. In this period of "War Communism" (1918–21), Lenin now began to explicitly treat workers' control as nothing more than a temporary means to restrain private industrialists, until such time as factories could be brought under direct state control. In the meantime, he stressed the importance of raising "the working people's discipline, their skill, the effectiveness, the intensity of labour and its better organization," even if this meant learning about management from bourgeois specialists.[97] With the civil war in full swing, Lenin even blamed initial attempts at workers' control on the shopfloor for the "chaotic, disorganized, primitive and incomplete" state of production, and he sought to reverse this trend through a "workers' industrial administration on a national scale" that would draw upon the expertise of those specialists who had the knowledge and experience to restore production.[98] Trotsky, concerned about the provision of supplies to his Red Army, echoed Lenin's calls for discipline and centralization, declaring the need for the "militarization of labor" with strict discipline and complete subordination of the unions to centralized authority.[99]

Lenin also declared that *kollegial'nost'* was a leadership style only suited for a later stage, when socialism was already in the process of evolving into communism, and by 1919, the Party Congress officially approved the shift from *kollegial'nost'* to "one-man management" *(odinonachalie)* with production decisions in the hands of a single administrative leader— the enterprise director. Despite protests from newly trained directors and workers in Moscow and Petrograd managers, engineers, and technocrats who had once worked in tsarist industry were now given the authority to make day-to-day technical decisions in factory management; workers, while being schooled in certain administrative tasks, were systematically prevented from being involved in direct management functions. By 1920, the All-Russian Council of Trade Unions, which had previously vied with the All-Russian Council for Workers' Control for influence among rank-and-file workers, formally approved the shift from *kollegial'nost'* and workers' control to managerial centralization under the "bourgeois specialists." Some Bolsheviks reasoned that since *all* workers collectively owned *all* factories under the dictatorship of the proletariat, workers' control did not require self-management in the factory and could be effected through trade union committees and newly created centralized bodies such as the People's Commissariat for Workers' and Peasants' Inspections that could monitor the activities of managers and specialists.[100]

The policies of War Communism have been regarded by many as constituting a temporary response to the exigencies of the time in light of the fact that Lenin initiated a New Economic Policy (NEP) after the civil war in 1921. NEP limited the state's direct control over industry to strategically important and heavy industrial sectors (the "commanding heights") and reinstated private ownership and market exchange in light industry and agriculture.[101] But, whether NEP itself represented an evolution toward a more normal course of socialist industrialization or merely a tactical retreat to stave off economic disaster, it is significant that there was no fundamental change in the large-scale factories that remained nationalized. If anything, those hoping to resurrect workers' control or wage egalitarianism found their hopes dashed by the expansion of piece rate wages, managerial control, and centralized industrial administration.

Both within the party and among the workers, there was plenty of opposition to this process, especially near the end of the civil war. A "Workers' Opposition" faction within the party was formed at the Ninth Party Congress of March 1920 by prominent Bolsheviks and many trade union officials who sought to defend autonomous unions and workers' control in the original spirit of the revolution. As Alexandra Kollontai, an outspoken leader in the group, put it: "Who, after all, shall be called upon to create new forms of economy; shall it be the technicians, businessmen who . . . are bound up with the past, . . . or the working class collectives which are represented by the unions?"[102] Beyond the ranks of the party elite, there were sporadic outbursts of labor unrest, a host of public demonstrations (some orchestrated by the Workers' Opposition), and the armed rebellion of sailors at Kronstadt naval base—all of which featured consistent demands for an end to the party's dominance over workers' organizations, greater autonomy on the shopfloor, and a more egalitarian wage structure.[103]

Although too fragmented to constitute a coherent threat, the combination of intraparty opposition and labor unrest was regarded by Lenin as a serious enough challenge to warrant decisive measures. In addition to swift action to quell labor unrest, Lenin and his allies proceeded to attack the "syndicalist and anarchist deviation" of the Workers' Opposition and declared a ban on intraparty factionalism at the Tenth Party Congress (1921), the very meeting where the New Economic Policy was introduced.[104] This set the stage for the further intensification of labor discipline and the further consolidation of managerial control in the hands of the bourgeois specialists, at least in large-scale state enterprises. Factory-level trade union committees and workers' control councils were subject to more strict control by their respective national federations, and the latter were increasingly subjected to the influence of the Bolshevik party leadership. In fact, leading Bolsheviks vigorously supported "governmentalizing" the trade union apparatus, suggesting central coordination of union activities in conjunction with governmental units dealing with industrial administration and national social policy.[105] Moreover, a new wage policy was formally established as part of the 1922 Labor Code of the USSR (supposedly drafted by the All-Russian Trade Union Council and the People's Commissariat of Labor); it not only expanded the use of piece rate remuneration, but established penalties for failure to meet quotas and removed upward limits on output-based earnings.[106]

While expectations about greater participation in management and trends toward more egalitarian wage practices might have been deferred in the course of the civil war, most workers certainly did not envision the socialist factory to be one in which they had no independent voice, in which piece rate wages were accepted as the norm, and in which production decisions and labor discipline came to be enforced by the same managers and specialists who had engineered capitalist speedups in tsarist factories. But this is precisely what happened during and after the civil war, prompting increasingly frustrated workers to give a new meaning to the acronym NEP: New Exploitation of the Proletariat.[107]

The "Scientific Organization of Labor":
Revolution or Replication?

The Bolsheviks were not simply concerned with raising production; even more than the social engineers of Meiji Japan, they were eager to bring about a radical transformation of habits and attitudes across every segment of society. By far the most concerted effort to achieve this goal was led by the movement for the "scientific organization of labor" (*nauchnaia organi-*

zatsiia truda, or NOT).[108] More than any other institute or movement, NOT was promoted at the highest levels of the party-state apparatus, received serious attention from managers, and took the lead in training workers and organizing production in Soviet factories. The origins and character of this movement deserve a closer look in light of the fact that, despite its intended role in the creation of a new industrial culture, NOT set the stage for the incorporation of Western scientific management techniques within the Soviet factory, exposing a growing fascination among the leading Bolsheviks with Taylorism, Fordism, and "Amerikanizm" in general.[109]

After the turn of the century, leading tsarist officials and management specialists had already begun to promote the incorporation of technology and management techniques found in American and Germany industry, with foreign specialists engaged to directly manage some of the factories.[110] Most Russian socialists had steadfastly opposed the emulation of Western capitalist management methods on the grounds that these were designed more for exploitation than efficiency, but by the time Russia was embroiled in World War I, Lenin, for one, was already beginning to move away from this position: "The war taught us . . . that those who have the best technology, organization, discipline, and the best machines emerge on top. . . . It is necessary to master the highest technology or be crushed."[111] On the eve of the 1917 revolution, Lenin not only tempered his criticism of American scientific management but emphasized that the core principles of Taylorism, once extricated from the capitalist system in which it was embedded, could be productively redeployed by workers' commissions who would ensure the proper distribution and regulation of all social labor while finding "thousands of opportunities to cut the work time of the organized workers by a quarter, providing them with four times as much well-being as now."[112] Moreover, before workers could be "masters of the factory," Lenin emphasized the need to learn the correct methods of work, specifically through the study of Taylorism:

> The task that the Soviet government must set the people in all its scope is—learn to work. The Taylor system, the last word of capitalism in this respect, like all capitalist progress, is a combination of the refined brutality of bourgeois exploitation and a number of the greatest scientific achievements in . . . the elimination of superfluous and awkward motion, the elaboration of correct methods of work, the introduction of the best system of accounting and control, etc. . . . We must organize in Russia the study and teaching of the Taylor system.[113]

In the course of the civil war, Lenin and other Bolsheviks proceeded to heap further praise on Taylorism and Fordism, exhorting citizens to act as "Russian Americans" who would harness the power of American technology and efficiency within socialist factories.[114] Lenin was backed by Trotsky, who actively promoted Taylorist methods in defense plants in 1920 and attempted to explicitly link the benefits of Taylorism to his own vision of the "militarization of labor": "If you take militarism, then you'll see that in some ways it has always been close to Taylorism. Compare the movements of a crowd and of a military unit, one marching in ranks, the other in a disorderly way, and you'll see the advantage of an organized military formation . . . And so the positive, creative forces of Taylorism should be used and applied."[115]

Of course, key Bolsheviks continued to insist that Taylorism was inconsistent with Marx's own denunciation of piece rate wages as "the most fruitful source of reductions of wages and capitalist cheating."[116] Although he generally supported Lenin in promoting party-union coordination, Mikhail Tomsky, the head of the All-Russian Trade Union Council, pointed out that "piece wages are exactly the kind of wage norm to which we always objected" and insisted on limits on above-quota piece wages.[117] Philosopher Alexander Bogdanov, who had previously split with Lenin over the question of party unity and had encouraged a radical group known as the "Workers' Truth" in 1920 and 1921, claimed that new Soviet bureaucracy was using Taylorism to exploit workers and dull their senses through mechanical repetitive work, thus preventing them from developing the collective consciousness and intellect necessary to manage production and administration in socialist factories.[118] Lenin, however, forcefully rejected such arguments as petty bourgeois anarchism and signaled his support for the expansion of Taylorist methods in Soviet factories by endorsing the First All-Russian Conference for the "Scientific Organization of Labor" held shortly after the Tenth Party Congress in 1921.

The central figure at the conference was Alexei Gastev, the "Russian Taylor," on whom Lenin and Trotsky counted to give institutional and practical significance to their assertions about the benefits of Taylorism. Gastev viewed Taylorism as an unparalleled system of social engineering capable of completely mechanizing and minutely controlling every human activity through the scientific analysis of time and motion. Already in 1920, Gastev had set up the Central Institute of Labor to promote new training methods based on the "biomechanics of the stroke" so as to enhance muscle control, reflex conditioning, and economy of motion. At the first NOT conference, Gastev introduced his famous tract "How Work Should Be Performed" *(Kak Nado Rabotat'),* with its set of sixteen detailed rules for designing the labor process, training workers, and carrying out elemental tasks with a minimum waste of time and motion. This tract was widely circulated, and the various rules of work later became slogans posted everywhere, including outside Lenin's office.[119] At the second NOT conference (March 1924), Gastev and his Central Institute of Labor became even more dominant, acquiring the central role in determining the organization of labor, the correct methods of work, and individual productivity norms. Following the lead of Gastev's institute in Moscow, hundreds of local labor institutes were established to facilitate the training of a half million workers and to support the research of hundreds of specialists. The specialists focused on applying Taylorist techniques to improve the rationalization of the production process and the workers periodically engaged in rhythmic drills paced by metronomes so that they might perform every type of task at the correct pace with economical, regular motions. The NOT movement's momentum continued through the 1920s, culminating in the creation in 1927 of the Council on Technical Norm Determination to bring the latest time-and-motion studies to bear on the precise chronometric determination of norms for thousands of individualized tasks in every branch of industry.[120]

With NOT's ascendance, Taylorism was no longer attacked as incompatible with socialism, but a new challenge emerged in the form of the Time League, created in 1923 under the leadership of Pavel Kerzhentsev with the support of Trotsky for the purpose of bringing about a revolutionary consciousness of time throughout Soviet factories. Although Gastev was among its founding members, the Time League increasingly began to criticize the NOT movement for focusing exclusively on the limits posed by rationalized production and the biomechanics of work at the expense of the hidden energies of the revolutionary working masses.[121] Gastev and the NOT movement would survive the challenge, but the tensions between the NOT movement and the Time League during the 1923–26 period speak directly to the core problem of institution-building in Soviet Russia: whether and how methods borrowed from the capitalist West could be used to advance the socialist revolution.

Lenin himself supported both NOT and the Time League on the grounds that each had a critical role to play in transforming the peasant into a disciplined yet enthusiastic socialist worker; indeed, his own conception of Bolshevik party organization suggested a synthesis between revolutionary dynamism and impersonal procedural rationalism.[122] In fact, in contrast to the earlier opponents of Taylorism who viewed it as inseparable from capitalist exploitation, the Time League had no objection to incorporating scientific management in Soviet factories and even helped further Gastev's own objectives by vigorously promoting a new "industrial time sense based on abstract hours and minutes measured by mechanical devices."[123] Campaigns and slogans were drawn up to emphasize the importance of time in factory work, and all workers were prompted to acquire watches and taught to diligently apportion time for particular tasks while recording the time spent on these tasks on a "chronocard" to be checked regularly by supervisors.[124] In light of the Time League's commitment to transforming attitudes toward work and time, something NOT also sought to achieve, it is hardly surprising that Gastev initially supported the League's creation and became a founding member.

What Gastev did not realize at the time, however, was that surpassing the techniques and achievements of Taylorism and Fordism was, for the Time League, at least as important an objective as successfully creating a "modern" industrial culture. Kerzhentsev and other members thus frequently criticized the NOT movement for paying excessive attention to the ordinary analysis of time and motion in work, and for thereby ignoring the prospects for tapping into the energies of a work force animated by the spirit of revolution. Thus, while Gastev openly sought to emulate American management methods and even dared to compare Henry Ford to Karl Marx on their views on productivity,[125] Kerzhentsev chastised Gastev for wanting "to conduct work on NOT in Saratov and Perm as if it were taking place in Massachusetts or Pennsylvania."[126] Eventually, Gastev was expelled from the Time League; but the League itself was disbanded in 1926 by Trotsky's opponents (mainly Bukharin and Stalin) during the struggle to succeed Levin. Thus, Gastev and the NOT movement continued to extend their influence over Soviet industry, although whether this influence would survive under Lenin's eventual successor still remained to be seen.

Revolutionary Transformation and Planned Industrialization:
Toward a Synthesis?

At the time of Lenin's death in 1924, the Bolsheviks had been in power for less than seven years, and for most of those years, Lenin was either coping with the exigencies of civil war (1918–21) or was incapacitated (1922–24).

Thus, there had not been much of an opportunity to produce a viable synthesis of revolutionary dynamism and modern scientific rationalism at least in terms of specific measures or concrete practices within the factory.[127] This meant that there were real opportunities to reconsider aspects of Soviet industrial relations and, in the process, to bring official management practices in line with norms of fairness implied by both socialist ideology and preexisting forms of collective labor. In the mid-1920s, for example, renewed opposition to the growth in wage differentials led to lower ceilings for specialists' wages, and a lingering desire for some form of workers' control led to renewed calls for new measures to ensure "public control" over management decisions and the labor process.[128] These proposals did not lead to a restructuring of Soviet industrial relations, but they do suggest that the ideals of collective labor, workers' control, and egalitarianism were still very much part of both official and casual discourses about the meaning of socialist labor. That is, it was still legitimate for committed Bolsheviks to raise questions about what level of managerial centralization was permissible in a workers' state, what level of wage differentiation was consistent with the broad ideal of equality of labor and wages, and what features of Western scientific management could be justifiably incorporated under revolutionary socialism.

In the course of the struggle to succeed Lenin, these questions acquired a new significance as part of the debates among key contenders over alternative strategies for constructing a socialist industrial state.[129] Prior to Stalin's decisive victory in 1929 (and even after), leading figures in the party as well as the Soviet government, whose loyalty to the party and commitment to socialism were unquestionable, offered well-received arguments and critiques that pointed to the outlines of an institution-building approach quite different from the one the regime would pursue. The head of the unions, Mikhail Tomsky, though previously supportive of the Bolshevik party leadership, now resisted governmental efforts to turn unions into organs to promote maximum labor productivity, calling instead for plant production conferences where workers could exert some influence over the organization and pace of production and defend their interests against the burgeoning economic apparatus of the state (just as they might have against capitalists).[130] The unions also renewed their opposition to piece rate wages as inconsistent with Bolshevik ideology and called for new wage scales featuring collective bonuses to be distributed evenly among members of production collectives. They were also supported by noted Bolshevik economist Evgenii Preobrazhensky, who specifically suggested a scheme for collective payments and bonuses to work brigades and enterprises so as to stimulate a more advanced collective consciousness and reduce the increasing significance of individualized incentives.[131] In relation to work organization, the head of the Rationalization Bureau—a unit of the Supreme Council of the People's Economy (VSNKh), the governmental body charged with overall economic policy—questioned whether Fordist mass production methods were appropriate for Soviet plants, specifically noting that the breakdown of the production process into too many single-task operations would not be as efficient for the Soviet economy as a more flexible style of production coordinated through previously established industrial networks.[132] Bukharin, who was to emerge as leader of the Right Opposition, advocated a more gradual mode of economic and social transformation and shifted toward a more syndicalist posture, arguing that only the stimulation of "mass participation" among "progressive" workers could halt the growth of bureaucratism in industrial administration and enable progress toward Lenin's "commune state." In specific reference to work organization, Bukharin also called into question a key principle of scientific management by suggesting that workers may profit by reducing the number of hours workers spent on the same repetitive task so that they may more speedily learn about other related tasks in the production process (thereby being able to participate more fully in shopfloor management).[133]

While such proposals did not question the *goal* of simultaneously advancing industrialization and socialist revolution, they are suggestive of a *strategy* that may be considered more syncretist than the one Stalin would pursue in a number of respects. There is, for example, evidence of caution toward the borrowing of institutional models and organizational technologies from Western capitalist countries, accompanied by specific fears that these might not only be inconsistent with socialism but also inappropriate for Russia's conditions. In addition, ideas or suggestions for reforming industrial management—a less differentiated wage structure, work organization based on a more diverse set of tasks jointly assigned to production collectives, collective remuneration and collective responsibility rather than individual piece rates, and conferences to expand the opportunities for workers to join in discussions of production goals and processes—are all consistent with quite familiar norms and practices embedded in past communities of work. Even if these notions were conceived of by their proponents as novel features of socialist factories, there was a potentially fortuitous convergence between these socialist features and preexisting organizational forms that could provide the foundation for a more continuous, and perhaps more sustainable, process of revolutionary transformation that would challenge international capitalism while also resonating with existing collectivist orientations of the working masses. In this regard, it is worth noting that many of the leading figures who are being identified with a syncretist posture founded their positions on a "mechanist" interpretation of Marxist philosophy that—in contrast to the "dialecticians" Stalin would favor—posited a continuous teleology underlying historical processes while emphasizing the interrelatedness of different kinds of phenomena (physical, cultural, psychological, and so forth).[134]

With Stalin's consolidation of power in 1929, however, such perspectives were condemned as "anti-revolutionary" or "opportunist" conceptions that failed to "distinguish between bourgeois and proletarian elements of culture."[135] The next several years revealed the outlines of Stalin's own strategy for combining a "cultural revolution," intended to decisively obliterate past habits and "class enemies" and create a new "proletarian" culture, with a frenzied pace of industrialization, which would be engineered through a series of Five-Year Plans and production campaigns. With the 1928 Shakhty trials and the 1930 Industrial Party trials, thousands of engineers, most of them either former "bourgeois specialists" or industrial managers who had been critical of high plan targets, were accused of being "wreckers" or "saboteurs"; they were replaced en masse by a new cohort of "Red Directors" trained in the Soviet era, often recruited from working-class backgrounds, and ostensibly committed to the fast pace and grand projects of the Five-Year Plans.[136] At the same time, other political opponents and hidden "class enemies" were viewed as ongoing threats to the regime, justifying a violent assault on all institutions that were potential loci for the preservation of alternative identities and loyalties.

In this process the Russian peasant commune was effectively destroyed during Stalin's campaign for agricultural collectivization. Relatively rich and influential peasants were labeled as members of a kulak class that had to be eliminated so as to end the exploitation of the impoverished rural masses. Gigantic collective farms and state farms were established to provide a more structured, factory-like environment that would turn peasants into rural workers, while creating avenues for young, able-bodied individuals to migrate to the cities and join the industrial labor force.[137] In addition, factories and shops that had been denationalized under the New Economic Policy once again became state-owned enterprises, and production methods and targets for all factories were now stipulated within a series of Five-Year Plans drawn up by central planners. As Stanislav Strumilin, chief architect of the first Five-Year Plan, contended, the objective of the plans was to engineer "an optimal balance under which the maximal revolutionary intensification of labor time would take place within rational limits."[138] In effect, the plan was to be a concrete manifestation of the possibilities of "planned heroism," the very synthesis that Lenin had envisioned between modern scientific rationalism and revolutionary heroism and that Stalin believed to be the logical extension of the dialectical strands of Marxist philosophy.[139]

On the surface, this project represented a far more revolutionary approach than the institution-building strategies advocated by Stalin's rightist opponents. Preexisting institutions were viewed as a threat that had to be proactively dealt with; the ideals and institutions propagated by the regime were conceived of as means to completely remake Russian society; and the objective was to create a distinctive "socialist" entity and a distinctive "new Soviet man" that had no precursors in Russia or anywhere else. However, a closer look at some of the assumptions behind the collectivization and industrialization campaigns suggests that Stalinist institution-building also had a significant modernist component inasmuch as it relied heavily on the standardizing effects of urbanization and factory work: once collectivization uprooted the peasantry, norms and habits associated with traditional rural institutions were expected to disappear and, with exposure to factory work, individuals were expected to automatically gravitate toward a uniform proletarian consciousness.[140]

It is true that, in contrast to those who believed it possible to gradually engineer socialist institutions without completely annihilating preexisting social institutions,[141] Stalin considered the destruction of these institutions to be a precondition for advancing the socialist revolution. The commune, in particular, represented a particularly obstinate and dangerous obstacle to the building of socialism. Even if some of the norms and practices of the *mir* might have borne at least a superficial resemblance to the socialist ideals espoused by the regime, what mattered for Stalin was that the *mir* represented a holdover from the past and remained an alternative locus of loyalty that would undermine the legitimacy of new socialist institutions. Yet, when it comes to the deeper norms and patterns of social relations around which the *mir* had been organized, Stalin adopted a much less proactive stance, expecting that these would naturally evolve into proper socialist attitudes and habits once preexisting institutions were replaced by new ones. Stalin appears to have assumed that as long as factory work took place within a command economy under the guidance of politically reliable Red Directors, the scientific organization of labor would suffice to create the consciousness appropriate for a revolutionary proletariat.[142] In doing so, however, Stalin may have underestimated the resilience of the long-standing norms and social relations that survived the physical destruction of the commune; as will be evident below, the ensuing urban migration led not to a malleable unified proletariat but to the influx of millions of peasants who either had fled collectivization and were resentful toward the regime or else understood the ideals of the revolution as extensions of their own sense of fairness.[143]

The Stalinist Factory: Scientific Management in the Guise of Socialist Competition

While the high targets of the Five-Year Plans and the frenzied campaigns to "overfulfill" them reflected a faith in a revolutionary heroism that could transcend rational limits of production, what is significant for the argument in this book is that officially sanctioned practices *within* the institution of the Soviet factory were frequently at odds with the *substantive* revolutionary commitments once proclaimed by the Bolsheviks.[144] In fact, from the point of view of both established workers and new arrivals, the methods used to stimulate productivity on the shopfloor came to bear more than a superficial resemblance to the efficiency-oriented methods and speedup techniques thought to characterize Western capitalist firms. Despite a slew of revolutionary slogans and campaigns, and despite declining official enthusiasm for the emulation of foreign production methods, the basic methods of factory administration essentially expanded upon the same Taylorist and Fordist principles that the NOT movement had promoted throughout the 1920s.[145] Thus, as in prewar Japan, management practices influenced by Western management models—whether this influence was publicly acknowledged or not—were simply *juxtaposed* alongside the ideology propagated by the state and managerial elite, with the tensions between ideology and practice becoming increasingly transparent in the course of industrialization.

Three features of the Soviet enterprise progressively undermined the original ideals propagated by the old Bolsheviks at the time of the revolution. First, the consolidation of steep managerial hierarchies brought an end to any lingering thoughts of "workers' control." Second, the permanent establishment of complex schemes of job classification, with standardized methods of norm determination for thousands of individualized tasks, contributed to the waning of the ideal of "collective labor." Finally, a sharply differentiated system of wages and bonuses, along with "socialist competition" campaigns, intensified the focus on *individual* performance and evaluation, leading not to wage leveling of any kind but to vastly disproportionate material rewards for more productive individuals in more valued job categories.

Under Lenin, although enterprise directors were granted the formal authority to make technical decisions, they were still viewed as potentially unreliable in view of their former bourgeois training; the party-cell secretary and trade union committee chairman kept an eye on the director within the factory, while the trade union federation and the People's Commissariat of Labor remained in place to check systematic abuses of managerial power.[146] Although Stalin himself retained these institutions and even temporarily revived the workers' control movement during 1928 and 1929, this was primarily to aid in identifying and purging his critics and the old bourgeois specialists. Once these class enemies had been replaced by a new cohort of politically reliable Red Directors, it was no longer deemed necessary to check their power and authority except through the relevant ministries (which were also staffed by personnel handpicked by Stalin).[147] Most of the new directors possessed neither the managerial expertise of their predecessors nor a familiarity with general issues of economic theory; but this quality also meant that they were more open to being influenced by the new political environment and the experience of planned industrialization and, thus, were more likely to be reliable allies in helping reestablish full control over production within the context of the Five-Year Plan.[148]

With the elevation of the Red Directors, the factory now became completely subjected to "one-man management" *(odinonachalie),* officially defined as the "complete subordination of all the employees in the productive process to the will of one person—the leader—and his personal responsibility for the assigned work." In practice, this meant that routine managerial decisions no longer required the approval of party or trade union officials; that unusual or important decisions required only the consent of superiors in the ministries and the approval of party cells; and that workers were fully subordinated to managers and could no longer appeal to trade union committees or workers' inspection bodies when an order required immediate execution.[149] In effect, one-man management was intended to create a new class of autocratic enterprise directors who were expected to reassert complete managerial control over the shopfloor while exuding "tough leadership" *(zhestkoe rukovodstovo)* of the sort Stalin himself demonstrated. As Stalin's lieutenant, Lazar Kaganovich, put it, "the earth should tremble when the director is entering the factory." This sort of approach made a virtue out of the crude and harsh treatment of subordinates in formal authority relations, blatantly contradicting the diffuse sense of equal status implied by the idea of comradeship touted by the regime.[150]

Trade union committees and other workers' bodies remained in place but effectively became "transmission belts" for party policy, concerned more with the coordination of cultural activities and political training of workers than with the independent representation of workers' ideas or interests. Echoing Lenin's critical remarks about workers' control in factories, Stalin now dismissed any independent suggestions by workers as "destructive criticism" that was interfering with rational factory administration.[151] In the meantime, new decrees were issued to penalize violations of workplace discipline, with one decree even obliging managers to sack workers for a single day of unauthorized absence or tardiness. Moreover, the continuing campaigns against "wreckers" and "saboteurs" meant that repeated problems with absenteeism or labor discipline could be written up in the industrial-campaign press as cases of class enemies exposing themselves. By the time of World War II, even harsher labor codes were instituted to restrict labor mobility and severely penalize the slightest violations of increasingly detailed factory rules. Under these conditions, the movement for workers' control was now decisively defeated while the power of factory managers became virtually unassailable from below.[152]

In terms of work organization and the production process, the Taylorist principles propagated by Gastev and the NOT movement became even more deeply entrenched on the shopfloor. Even the People's Commissariat of Workers' and Peasants' Inspection, originally created to serve as a check on the behavior of managers and specialists, enthusiastically supported the NOT movement and called for the expanded use of Taylorist principles in the organization of production. Lazar Kaganovich, who regularly spoke for Stalin on industrial matters, specifically called for greater emulation of American mass production methods to speed up industrialization.[153] Even more telling is the fact that Gastev, although attacked at first for his "narrowly managerial" understanding of work and his excessive reliance on a "capitalist, Fordist approach,"[154] was retained to chair the committee for standardization that dealt with job classifications and work norms. During the 1930s, the Taylorist principle of maximal segmentation of tasks and skills remained the basis for the increasingly complex schemes of job classification within each sector and even each factory, with the number of narrowly defined tasks increasing exponentially; one factory reported 35,000 productivity norms for distinct tasks as part of its plan to meet production targets! Moreover, the same chronometric techniques of norm-determination that Gastev had advocated during the 1920s were invoked to establish standardized norms for each individualized task and to eliminate any opportunity for production slack on the shopfloor (although in practice many foremen still made norming decisions in a more casual manner).[155] Thus, "even while NOT all but disappeared from the Soviet lexicon in the 1930s, the principles which had animated the movement were by no means abandoned."[156]

The intensification of rationalization schemes inspired by Taylorism was necessarily accompanied by new wage scales that decisively ended any hope of movement toward wage egalitarianism. Lenin himself had supported piece rate wages from 1918 onward, noting that equality of labor and wages meant not absolute equality in material conditions but a proportional relationship between contributions and earnings. Still, there had been limits on how much the most productive workers could earn through piecework, and, through much of the 1920s, many managers still paid workgroups for collectively performed labor, leaving the brigade leader to distribute earnings. As a result, wage-differential levels had remained more or less where they had been in tsarist industry. Under the new wage scales and competitive productivity campaigns promoted by Stalin, however, wage differentials would dramatically *increase,* surpassing the differentials found in tsarist factories for the first time.

The new wage agreements formulated in 1928 increased the differentials in wages within and across categories of workers, but not very sharply, as there was still opposition to dramatic differences in earnings at the time. By 1931, however, Stalin was more fully in control and decisively ended any debate over the issue, condemning "petty bourgeois egalitarianism" and insisting on "new methods of management" that would put an end to "the 'Leftist' practice of wage equalization."[157] In the early 1930s, none other than Gastev was invited to chair a committee to devise new, more elaborate wage scales to correspond to the new system of job classification and technical norm determination he had helped put in place. These scales sharply increased officially sanctioned wage differentials, while introducing more substantial bonuses and privileges for the most competent specialists and the most productive workers. Even the new trade union leader,

N. M. Shvernik, defended the new wage system, arguing that it "not only does not betray socialism but turns wages into a powerful lever for the organization of labor and for the improvement of the material conditions of working-class life."[158] By the mid-1930s, wage differentials had already increased dramatically, with the highest-paid 10 percent of industrial workers earning nearly four times as much as the lowest-paid 10 percent.[159]

The sharply differentiated wage scales were also accompanied by a series of "socialist competition" campaigns intended to spur workers to break production records. The shock work *(udarnichestvo)* movement, for example, originally conceived of by Trotsky in the mid-1920s, was turned into a new movement in the early part of Stalin's first Five-Year Plan (1929–31) that would reward workers for overfulfillment of output norms and for devising new methods to improve quality and reduce costs. Similarly, the beginning of the second Five-Year Plan in the mid-1930s was marked by the Stakhanovite movement, named for Alexei Stakhanov, a Donbass coal miner who supposedly cut 102 tons of coal in a single shift through intense work and creative alterations in the production process.[160] Stakhanovites were not only diligent in performing assigned tasks, but could also engineer revolutionary breakthroughs in production by revising their assignments and ignoring the boundaries set by rationalized plans. Both movements, in theory, suggested an effort to promote revolutionary efforts to transcend ordinary limits suggested by rational planning. Stakhanovism in particular appeared to represent "a protest against time-and-motion techniques, which were charged with placing artificial, 'scientific' limits on production."[161]

In practice, however, shock work and Stakhanovism, far from representing novel forms of production, helped to institutionalize the same kind of incentive schemes and competitive performance evaluations used to speed up production under Western scientific management. The idea of "socialist competition" had been originally introduced in Lenin's time to encourage friendly competition among factories and work brigades to boost productivity, but under Stalin, the concept was reframed within the context of the intensification of rationalization. As a consequence, the competition was now extended to *individuals* to overfulfill their specific task norms, and the most productive individuals were now rewarded not by marginally greater rewards, but by substantially higher packages of wages, bonuses, and access to a range of special resources (medical services, paid vacations in rest homes, opportunities for education, etc.).[162] It is true that the achievements of the best workers were expected to have the effect of lifting up all other workers, but by disproportionately rewarding the most productive individual workers without regard to the collective achievements of their brigades or shops, Stalin's version of socialist competition resembled Western scientific management in that "workers were individualized and their performance measured on a percentage basis, which permitted ready comparisons."[163]

As further evidence that shock work and Stakhanovite labor were extensions of principles originally promoted by NOT, Gastev himself was called upon to help organize and coordinate the Stakhanovite movement (after briefly acknowledging his tendency to overemphasize the technical aspects of production). When managers and planners caught up in the frenzy sought a radical upward revision of norms corresponding to the output of Stakhanovites, Stalin himself came to the defense of principles and techniques behind the existing system of norm determination, stressing the importance of rational planning and reasonable targets.[164] Even idealistic American workers who had come to help "build socialism" in the 1930s complained about the striking parallels between capitalist speedups and socialist competition, while foreign engineers found the methods of organization so familiar that they even used their own corresponding terms to refer to these.[165]

In the end Stalin's socialist competitions, for all their revolutionary fervor, failed to contribute significantly to either the creation of a distinctive ethic of socialist labor or the construction of a stable, sustainable system of production. Most of the gains in industrial production in the 1930s came more from the massive influx of labor than from any leap in productivity stimulated by socialist competition.[166] From the point of view of the managerial elite, the highly skewed system of rewards and the emphasis on individual heroism tended to interfere with efforts to increase the efficiency of the production process as a whole.[167] Shock workers and Stakhanovites were frequently seen not as gifted workers but as fortunate individuals who had managed to draw easily "overfulfilled" tasks or receive special assistance from supervisors because of their class backgrounds or party affiliations while other workers were being dismissed as breakdown-prone without consideration of mitigating circumstances or the nature of the task.[168] In fact, the main consequence of these movements was the declining position and status of more established workers, many of whom had supported the Bolsheviks in 1917, relative to newly arrived unskilled workers who took advantage of Taylorist deskilling and socialist competitions to gain an important place in the new order.[169] These latter groups did sometimes achieve extraordinary feats, but, far from lifting up their peers, they became a narrow stratum of privileged workers who, in exchange for their outward loyalty to the regime, were given status and privilege, as well as substantial material rewards.[170] By the late 1930s, more and more shops and factories were reporting Stakhanovite feats, but this was primarily an indication of the growing collusion among supervisors and workers to "fix" production figures and reports so as to effectively bypass or subvert official modes of evaluation.[171] But for the most part, the few thousand workers who jumped ahead when the socialist campaigns first started maneuvered themselves into positions of authority, while the vast majority of workers struggled to meet rising norms and tried to defend preexisting practices and arrangements against what they considered to be norm-busting and production speedups.[172]

Stalin had briefly revived the "workers' control" movement to push out old managerial elites, but he had then handed enormous power to the new Red Directors. He had criticized the narrowly technical approach of the Russian Taylorists, but the emergent system of job classifications, piece rate wages, and individuated tasks and norms replicated the fundamental principles of Western scientific management. He had condemned "petty bourgeois" efforts to achieve material equality, but his new wage schemes and campaigns for productivity produced higher differentials in earnings and living standards than had been the case in tsarist industry. Thus, by the end of World War II, the original Bolshevik ideals of collective labor, workers' control, and equality of labor and pay—ideals that had once resonated with much of the urban work force—were being openly contradicted by officially sanctioned management practices. This proved to be one powerful reason for the decline in managerial authority in the course of Soviet industrialization.

The Erosion of Managerial Authority in Stalinist Industry

Between 1920 and 1940, increasing numbers of workers were systematically incorporated into the rank and file of the CPSU, quotas were instituted to recruit and promote engineers and managers from working-class origins, and more than a half million workers were able to move into white-collar occupations in the early 1930s.[173] The experience of work in industrial factories and training programs instituted by the NOT movement incrementally altered the work habits of millions of established workers and enabled new arrivals to become more familiar with machine operations, factory time, and specialized production. Many workers were swept up in the frenzied campaign for "building socialism" and learned to speak and act in terms consistent with official ideology and language,[174] while some developed a stronger acquisitive impulse and sense of selfhood in striving for security, rewards, and recognition.[175] For the most part, however, these various trends did not lead to "the new Soviet man" or a uniformly committed work force; rather they reflect the different ways in which some individuals responded to a system that most workers considered to be inconsistent with both their own understandings of fairness and officially stipulated standards of "proletarian" culture.

Opposition to the policies of the regime from rank-and-file workers, particularly in response to the retention of "bourgeois specialists" and the imposition of piece rates and centralized industrial administration, was evident from 1920 onward. There was, for example, a sharp rise in industrial unrest in various forms, ranging from angry attacks on "bourgeois" technicians and managers to public demonstrations and large-scale strikes, with one strike at a munitions plant culminating in a state of siege and mass arrests.[176] Although the absence of a unified opposition enabled the regime to quickly bring these events under control, once NEP got under way, there was once again a rise in strike activity through the mid-1920s.[177] Also indicative of low worker commitment was the fact that, despite efforts to prosecute "deserters," labor turnover *(tekuchest)* also skyrocketed in the 1920s as the resurgence of the peasant commune prompted thousands of workers to return to their villages if they did not find the terms of employment satisfactory.[178] In addition, widespread alcohol consumption, while to some extent an inherent feature of working-class male culture, evolved into a form of "sustained daily resistance" as workers regularly and openly contested the regime's efforts to curb drinking and rejected the "officially sanctioned culture of sobriety" as nothing more than a tactic to expand control over the work force from above.[179]

By the early 1930s, Stalinist methods for stimulating productivity and intensifying labor discipline, from the point of view of most workers, had become "uncomfortably reminiscent of the picture of exploitation associated with capitalism—even if no one dared say so."[180] Although overt protests and criticisms had become dangerous in the face of increasingly harsh punitive measures and the purges of "wreckers" and "saboteurs," frustrated workers still found ways to signal their opposition to Stalinist management practices, often linking their own sense of fairness to elements of official ideology in the process of challenging specific practices without appearing to be "class enemies."[181] The most overt challenges were in the form of sporadic incidents of strikes and protests, usually aimed at specific individuals or factories rather than at the regime or its leaders. As the 1932 strike by cotton workers at Teikovo suggests, workers were never fully suppressed by the intense pressures and disciplinary sanctions brought to bear during Stalinist industrialization; rather, they creatively appropriated official ideology to simultaneously signify loyalty to the regime and provide justification for strike activities aimed at particular shops or factories.[182] In addition to strikes, there were sharp, often violent confrontations between workers and foremen, on the one hand, and technicians in charge of determining production norms, on the other; the latter effectively personified efforts to further Taylorist deskilling and speed up shopfloor production, and the persecution they faced at the hands of workers actually led to a decline in the number of people seeking jobs as norm-setters.[183]

By the late 1930s, with severe punitive measures in place to deter overt challenges to managers, labor turnover increasingly became a popular form of worker protest.[184] In the early 1920s, turnover had been largely the result of workers leaving their jobs to return to their communes, suggesting a general lack of commitment to industrial labor rather than opposition to management practices. Following Stalinist collectivization, most workers had little choice but to remain in the cities where they had been assigned jobs and residence permits. Even so, the level of turnover steadily climbed during the early 1930s as dissatisfied workers frequently switched jobs in search of new places of employment that would provide greater security and more control over their pace of work.[185] Older workers, in particular, coped with the intensification of socialist competition campaigns by leaving factories that vigorously promoted the competitions and seeking out employment where managers either openly or covertly arranged for groups of workers to undertake collective responsibility for the distribution of tasks and earnings (thereby diffusing the pressures of high productivity norms for individuals).[186] The growth in turnover is all the more telling given that workers who changed jobs more than once risked being labeled "disorganizers of production" in their labor books and, consequently, losing the work and residence permits necessary to guarantee access to housing, food rations, and other basic necessities.[187] While some level of turnover was to be expected given the rapid influx of new peasant-workers and the need to break down the resistance of established workers, the rate of what Soviet planners considered "unplanned" turnover rose to the point where it was acknowledged as a serious economic problem, prompting harsh measures in 1938 to punish the selfish actions of these "floating" workers.[188]

Perhaps even more indicative of the failure of the Stalinist enterprise to "capture" its work force is the significance of unsanctioned but familiar norms and practices in the form of informal social relations at the workplace. One telling fact in this regard is the survival of the *artel,* either in the guise of formal units of work in Soviet factories, or, less directly, in the manner in which collective responsibilities and earnings were actually managed by members of shops and brigades.[189] Although *artels* were officially disbanded as traditional units that interfered with the scientific organization of labor, "production communes" formed in the late 1920s and early 1930s functioned almost exactly like *artels,* with groups of workers living together, taking collective responsibility for a set of tasks, and relying on a leader to divide up the collective earnings giving more consideration to family needs than skill levels. Unlike officially sanctioned production *collectives,* production *communes* were not recognized as part of the formal organization of work, but they were preferred by managers because they made the administration of tasks and wages simpler, and they were touted by their members as higher forms of work organization that were closer to the ideal of communist labor than shock brigades.[190] With the intensification of socialist competitions during the 1930s, production communes, too, came to be denounced as obstacles to socialist labor that prevented worker consciousness and spawned a "parasitical psychology."[191] But, even as managers felt the pressure to eliminate production communes, in the day-to-day administration of tasks and earnings, many shop chiefs and work brigade leaders continued to resist sharp demarcations in individual responsibilities and treat their subordinates' wages as collective earnings to be divided up as the members saw fit; more often than not, this meant that the job assignments and wage schemes mandated by the formal system of production were consciously being bypassed in favor of more egalitarian distributive practices, sometimes with provisions to ensure that all members could meet their families' subsistence needs.[192]

The erosion of official factory authority is also evident in the proliferation of *blat,* the use of personal connections to obtain favors or scarce commodities, and the *krugovaia poruka,* "circles of protection" formed to circumvent factory regulations and evade penalties for low productivity or violations of factory rules.[193] In Soviet industry at large, these informal aspects of social relations became evident in the collusion between enterprise directors, trade union officials, and shopfloor supervisors who sought to cover up problems in plan fulfillment and keep production targets from being ratcheted up too much.[194] Workers, foremen, and managers similarly made use of personal connections and informal networks within the factory to help bypass official methods for raising productivity norms and imposing labor discipline, for example, by misreporting which tasks were completed by whom or concealing evidence of absenteeism and slack. In fact, the rising number of registered shock workers (in the early 1930s) and Stakhanovites (in the late 1930s) reflected not the increasing appeal of Stalin's socialist competitions but the fact that workers, managers, and norm-setters frequently struck deals to enable workers to overfulfill quotas and reap substantial material rewards without actually speeding up production or altering work routines.[195] Thus, rather than supporting official production goals and methods, the informal aspects of the Stalinist workplace evinced the reconstruction of familiar norms and understandings on the basis of which workers sought to limit the extent of wage differentials and the segmentation and pace of work at the expense of adherence to officially sanctioned management practices.

Western studies of Soviet industrial relations through the 1940s offer conflicting interpretations of the relationship between workers and the Stalinist enterprise, each exaggerating certain aspects at the expense of others. More extreme versions of revisionist labor history overemphasize the inclusiveness and egalitarianism of the workplace, suggesting that the factory became a "social melting pot" and that the socialist competitions enabled the regime to create a homogeneous, unified workplace characterized by "a striking degree of working-class quiescence."[196] In marked contrast, critical treatments, some inspired by Marxist analyses of Soviet production relations, contend that the regime essentially created a labor aristocracy as a base of support while exploiting and fragmenting the majority although the latter was still capable of hidden acts of resistance on the shopfloor.[197] The interpretation of workers' responses to the Stalinist factory outlined above effectively combines the most persuasive aspects of both accounts. The symbols and language endorsed by the regime did increasingly become part of everyday discourse at the workplace; but these were frequently "invested . . . with meanings quite foreign to those intended by the regime."[198] New arrivals without ties to existing urban networks did take advantage of socialist competitions to bypass older, more established workers; but, rather than producing a unified, homogeneous work force, this process led to new hierarchies in which the majority of workers offered hidden resistance in the form of sporadic outbursts against norm-setters, high rates of unplanned turnover, and collusion to protect existing, more familiar, work rhythms. Thus, to the extent that the Stalinist factory *did* evince cooperation and inclusiveness among workers, this was largely confined to *informal* social relations in the workplace that enabled workers to subtly resist officially mandated methods for stimulating productivity.[199] What remains to be seen is whether worker commitment could be recaptured in the post-Stalin era through the creation of a new "social contract" and the arrival of the discourse of human relations.

4.3. The Post-Stalin Enterprise: The Contradictions of Soviet Human Relations

From the 1950s through the 1970s, industrial production continued to account for a progressively greater share of total employment and output. Nearly a half-million Soviet citizens migrated each year from the countryside to the cities. The urban work force came to consist of a new generation of highly literate industrial workers and white-collar administrative personnel accustomed to their tasks and routines.[200] During this same period, a new cohort of leaders, with little or no connection to those who had been in the Bolshevik party during the civil war, had to address anew the question of institution-building as they sought to complete Russia's transformation into a technologically advanced urban industrial society but with less reliance on coercive mechanisms. Under these conditions, the door was reopened to some of the issues raised during the debate of the 1920s, especially in relation to the effectiveness and appropriateness of various institutions and practices given the original aims of the Bolshevik Revolution. In the case of the industrial enterprise, this meant that there was a new opportunity to introduce changes in official management ideals and practices that could bring about higher levels of productivity and recapture the work force in the process. As it turns out, however, that opportunity would be squandered.

The three decades following Stalin's death witnessed the emergence of a lasting elite consensus that stressed pragmatism, stability, and a reduction in coercive controls in the place of dogmatism, frenzied campaigns, and overt terror.[201] The preoccupation with stability also limited the scope for fundamental changes to Soviet management practices and blunted the potential impact of new discourses of human relations coming out of the United States and Japan. Although Soviet management specialists did begin to make increasing reference to human aspects of production, as in the United States, this was typically understood to mean that productivity and commitment could be secured *within* the existing system of production by better satisfying workers' needs for physical safety, job security, and material satisfaction. To this end, the regime offered guarantees of full employment, subsidized goods and services, incremental improvements in wages, and tolerance for supplemental earnings through unofficial channels. But, in contrast to postwar Japan where human relations was linked to significant modifications in work organization, the basic assumptions of the scientific organization of labor remained firmly entrenched in Soviet management science and continued to inform official management practices in large-scale firms. The few initiatives that might have constituted a shift in these basic assumptions—such as efforts to introduce more egalitarian wage scales or collective brigade responsibility for a diverse set of tasks—were either rejected or not systematically implemented. Instead, with the regime more interested in industrial peace than ensuring proper implementation of official managerial doctrine, the incongruities between official ideology, formal production processes, and informal shopfloor norms and practices became both wider *and* more apparent than had been the case in the 1920s and 1930s. Under these conditions, Gorbachev's campaign to raise productivity and discipline spurred angry protests, in part because it most closely resembled a return to Stalin's socialist competitions, threatening the informal arrangements that had enabled workers to incrementally improve their material conditions and preserve some measure of autonomy, equality, and flexibility on the shopfloor.

This section discusses, in turn, the nature of the so-called Soviet social contract evident in the new terms of employment established during the 1960s and 1970s; the validity of the regime's claims to have engineered greater wage egalitarianism as part of "developed socialism"; the limited extent to which the language of human relations in Soviet management science affected existing methods of work organization; the gap between the apparent quiescence of the work force and the erosion of commitment to the formal system of production; and the unanticipated consequences of Gorbachev's efforts to revive productivity and discipline.

The Significance of the Post-Stalin Social Contract

Nikita Khrushchev's ascension to power in 1956 marked the emergence of a new consensus that the regime no longer would, or needed to, employ terror to achieve its objectives. The draconian labor laws of the Stalin era were overturned and replaced by a new set of rules and regulations to guide labor-management relations within the framework of "socialist legalism." The new version of the *Rules of Internal Labor Order* (1957) sharply reduced the penalties for workers switching jobs or being late, and it made no demands for "labor discipline" to avoid the Stalinist ring of extreme hierarchical control. Instead, the new rules sought to clearly specify the responsibilities of workers and managers: the latter were obligated to organize labor according to skills, issue proper orders, provide necessary materials, and ensure workplace safety; the former were obliged to work honestly and conscientiously, observe factory rules and safety regulations, care for factory property and equipment, and make modest efforts to marginally overfulfill the more reasonable production targets being set by planners. In addition, a new Commission of Labor Disputes was established to give workers a forum for independently expressing grievances without fear of being arrested or fired.[202]

These measures were a far cry from the kind of autonomy workers had expected to enjoy with the establishment of workers' control commissions and factory committees in the first few months following the revolution. However, neither were these changes insignificant, for they meant that workers now no longer lived every day under the threat of dismissal, execution, and deportation to labor camps. This also meant that, with the threat to their physical security reduced, there was a need for new measures to stave off overt challenges to official authority. In this regard, both Khrushchev and Brezhnev adopted policies and made promises that indicate a broad effort to preempt labor unrest by improving the material welfare of all workers. This commitment was evident in Khrushchev's promotion of new housing construction and his attention to the production of consumer goods. It was also diffusely expressed as a matter of policy at the Twenty-second Congress of the CPSU in 1961 where a new party program incorporated a number of official statements linking the raising of productivity and the national income to dramatic promises about how the standard of living in the USSR would surpass that in the United States by 1980.[203] While the language of the program may not have been specific, it did suggest a new era in Soviet industrial relations whereby the standard of living of the work force, albeit conditional on improved productivity, was recognized as a priority.

Questions still remained, however, as to what concrete measures managers could take to realize this commitment and as to what exactly workers were expected to do in return. Indeed, Khrushchev's own actions a year later made it clear that the 1961 party program did not represent a set of unconditional commitments to specific policies. Responding to reports that productivity levels were falling below planned levels, Khrushchev proceeded to freeze wage increases and raise retail prices for basic goods.[204] This move would prove to be the immediate cause of a massive strike in 1962 at Novocherkassk where thousands of workers gathered to protest the increased food prices and criticize the regime for not honoring its commitment to raising living standards. The strikes represented a major confrontation between workers and the regime, and only ended with a violent crackdown that led to the deaths of several strikers. On the one hand, the fact that Khrushchev raised food prices in response to declining productivity and then cracked down on the ensuing strikes made it clear to workers that there were limits and conditions attached to the new labor codes and the 1961 party program. On the other hand, the fact that such a large, openly confrontational strike could take place in a workers' state suggested to party elites that the 1961 party program needed to be translated into concrete measures to ensure a greater degree of worker satisfaction if the regime was going to improve productivity and check labor unrest without regularly resorting to coercion.[205]

Thus, two years after Khrushchev's ouster, at the Twenty-third Congress of the CPSU (1966), Brezhnev sought to clarify the understandings implied in the 1961 party program, declaring that "the material well-being rises in proportion to the growth of public wealth."[206] In addition, in 1970 the regime officially adopted the Fundamental Principles of Labor Legislation (enacted in 1971) which codified workers' rights to full employment, along with multiple barriers to dismissal even for repeated violations of labor discipline as well as guarantees for new employment for workers released as a result of shifts in technology.[207] The following year, at the Twenty-fourth Party Congress (1971), Kosygin reaffirmed the regime's commitment to rising living standards linked to rising national productivity, declaring that "the distribution of national income is carried out in accordance with the principles of socialism written into our party's Program."[208] Such statements, along with the new party program and labor code, signified a shift in the instruments the regime was now going to rely on to stimulate productivity and maintain industrial peace: repressive labor laws and severe punitive measures against saboteurs and wreckers were no longer to be tolerated, and "the Stakhanov who produces an improbable number of tons of coal a day or the man who calls for impossibly high socialist obligations [was] no longer the hero that he was in the 1930s."[209] In lieu of overtly coercive measures and high-pressure campaigns, the regime now sought to secure the workers' commitment to official productivity goals by making it the condition for guarantees of physical security, full and secure employment, reasonable plan targets, incremental improvements in wage levels and living standards, and cheap access to foodstuffs and other basic necessities.

For the most part, the available evidence indicates that the regime was delivering on its promises and acting upon its various new programs and policies. Between 1960 and 1980, state-sector employment grew by more than 80 percent, far exceeding the growth of the population as a whole. The small number of workers who had been laid off or dismissed, whether for reasons of productivity or discipline, were neither labeled "disorganizers of production" in their labor books nor barred from seeking new employment; in fact, most had little trouble securing new employment thanks to managers' efforts to secure a surplus labor force to guard against unexpected problems or untimely shortages. The minimum wage was revised upward regularly, with average wage increases of 20 percent over each five-year plan period, corresponding to a steady growth in the rate of personal consumption and sales of consumer goods. The per capita consumption of food also rose during this period with bread still being sold in 1980 at 1954 prices and meat at 1962 prices.[210] Finally, although Khrushchev's egalitarian wage schemes had been rejected, the differences in base wages were effectively reduced by raising the earnings of workers in the lowest paid positions and providing all workers with access to living quarters, cheap goods, and various provisions through the enterprise.

These policies and trends have been interpreted by some as evidence of a tacit social contract, a bargain struck between the post-Stalin leadership and the work force that enabled a relatively high degree of industrial peace and political stability from the mid-1960s through the early 1980s.[211] The apparent similarities between this bargain and social pacts negotiated between state, management, and organized labor elsewhere even prompted some to conclude that Brezhnev's "developed socialism" was essentially "a corporatist vision of a consensual society, in which conflict would be managed by an activist state through a series of deals," which, in the case of workers, meant that "steady improvements in the provision of consumer goods were exchanged for political compliance and higher productivity."[212] In fact, many of the features of the so-called Soviet social contract even appeared to bear a strong resemblance to the new social compact reached between moderate unions, business associations, and the state in postwar Japan: in both cases, employment security, benefits distributed through firms, and steady improvements in wages and material conditions were effectively guaranteed as long as overall productivity continued to rise and, in both cases, these guarantees were expected to lead to increased job satisfaction and, subsequently, a more productive, committed work force.[213]

However, despite improvements in job and wage security and overall living standards in the two countries, any similarity between the Soviet social contract and the pacts negotiated in postwar Japan would prove to be superficial. This was not simply because Japanese industry was marked by significantly higher leaps in productivity and living standards compared to the more modest improvements seen in Soviet Russia during the 1960s and 1970s. At least as significant was the disparity in the autonomy and strength of the actors involved. In postwar Japan, the moderate unions and business associations that forged the new social compact retained some degree of autonomy as distinct social actors, and workers, even if coopted or pressured, retained the legal right to challenge employers and contracts. By contrast, the Soviet regime was the only party with the ability to challenge or redefine whatever understanding may have been tacitly negotiated with workers and managers; managerial elites remained constrained by state budgets and directives, and trade unions remained transmission belts for the party-state apparatus, leaving workers with no independent bodies to represent their interests or challenge the terms offered by the regime. The terms of the "contract" were made even more invidious by the fact that it was translated into sharply different terms for different categories of employees: those with connections in high places or working in strategically important "closed" enterprises were offered disproportionate wage increases and a host of privileges and perquisites to improve their living standards, whereas the majority of workers were able to attain only modest improvements in material conditions through official channels, having to rely more on the underground second economy for supplemental goods and earnings.[214]

Thus, the so-called social contract was not so much a negotiated corporatist bargain but a palatable substitute for overt coercion in maintaining stability and spurring incremental gains in productivity. Despite the retreat from Stalin's socialist competitions, the differential terms of the bargain (that is, the supplemental privileges and resources made available to those in key positions and sectors) effectively continued to serve the purposes of coopting those in key positions and preempting collective protest from the fragmented work force. In the absence of independent union bodies and legal opportunities to challenge official policies, workers were powerless to alter the terms of the "contract," and, as the violent crackdown on the Novocherkassk strikes made abundantly clear, there were strict limits on what the regime would tolerate in exchange for its restraint from invoking coercive measures regularly. While these factors may have secured the *compliance* of much of the work force during most of the Brezhnev era, they also contributed to the further decline in the *commitment* of workers to the formal production system as the regime appeared to be permanently accepting the widening gap between officially sanctioned management practice and its socialist rhetoric.

The Struggle for Egalitarianism: Formal and Informal Leveling at the Workplace

One feature of the social contract that did, for a time, appear to represent a narrowing of the gap between workplace realities and the original Bolshevik pronouncements was a renewed public commitment to greater egalitarianism. In marked contrast to Stalin's criticisms of "leftist wage leveling" and "petty bourgeois egalitarianism," both Khrushchev and Brezhnev criticized income stratification and supported greater egalitarianism in wages and enterprise-related benefits. Under Brezhnev, progress toward socioeconomic equality was cited as a key indicator of the arrival of "developed socialism." A closer look at the extent and character of stratification during the 1970s, however, suggests a quite different reality.

Base wages for the lowest-paid jobs were increased, and a host of material benefits were made available to all workers, but output-related bonuses related to individual productivity remained the basis for the official wage scale (once Khrushchev's wage reforms had been turned back). Although managers were able to reduce differentials in earnings within workgroups and shops, this was largely done by ignoring formal wage regulations. In the meantime, a new pattern of stratification emerged as a result of the high rates of bonuses and the special resources and privileges reserved for individuals in favored positions or strategically important sectors. Thus, while the degree of workplace stratification may have declined relative to the Stalin era, the marginal improvement was more a product of ad hoc or informal actions rather than evidence of a change in official wage practices.

Full equality in material conditions was certainly not the objective under socialism; as Lenin had made clear, earnings had to be related to contributions until the higher stage of communism arrived. However, progress toward that higher stage still suggested that differentials in both contributions and earnings would narrow as workers became progressively more literate, skilled, and politically "conscious." Khrushchev's initiatives to reduce stratification and promote wage egalitarianism, had they succeeded, may have meaningfully represented this progress, certainly to a far greater extent than Stalin's socialist competitions had done. A special seven-year plan introduced in 1959 effectively offered the work force a "progressive raise," increasing wages across the board but projecting greater amounts for workers with lower or average levels of pay than for the highest-paid workers.[215] In addition, a new Committee on Labor and Wages was set up by Khrushchev to revise the official wage scales so as to make the base wage a higher proportion of total earnings, with enterprises instructed to decrease the total funds allocated for the "material stimulation fund" (from which output-related bonuses were allocated) while increasing the size of the "social consumption fund" (which was used to provide apartments, utilities, transportation, educational facilities, child care, and other standard benefits unrelated to contributions of labor). Although a part of the total material earnings of workers would still reflect differentials related to skill and output, that portion would now be markedly less than was the case in the Stalin era as overall differentials would begin to narrow significantly.[216]

The very fact that these initiatives were vigorously resisted by officials and managerial elites, many of them the bureaucrats and Red Directors promoted under Stalin, suggests that the reforms did indeed constitute a real effort to transform wage practices. Khrushchev did manage to temporarily gain the Central Committee's approval for the wage-scale revisions, but he had very little success in implementing the changes; and once he was ousted, official Soviet wage policy officially overturned Khrushchev's reforms and reestablished the official wage system inherited from the Stalin era. Whatever the merits of Khrushchev's wider economic reforms, his ouster brought an end to the last serious effort to reduce the incongruities between official wage practices in Soviet industry and the egalitarian ethos associated with "socialist labor" in the minds of most workers.

Under Brezhnev, it is true that there was a significant narrowing in base wage differentials both between workers of different skill-grades and between blue-collar production workers and white-collar technicians and engineers.[217] These trends were proclaimed by Soviet officials, and by some Western scholars, as evidence of the regime's success in realizing the original communist ideals of egalitarianism.[218] However, there are several reasons to question this claim and the significance of the supporting evidence.

First, while the lowest-paid categories of work did see the biggest rise in *base* wages, this had no bearing on officially mandated differentials in earnings resulting from the substantial performance-related bonuses and other perquisites reserved for skilled workers and technical employees. In fact, output-related bonuses accounted for about a third of the total earnings of most workers, magnifying the effects of even small differentials in base wages between different categories of workers and supervisory personnel.[219] Khrushchev's wage reforms, by reducing the significance of bonuses, attempted to address this problem, but the official wage scales retained under Brezhnev did not. As a result, unless managers themselves chose to circumvent regulations concerning bonus payments, the differences in actual earnings far exceeded the differentials in base wages, reproducing income stratification even in the absence of new socialist competitions.

Second, *within* the same category of work, any progress toward more egalitarian income distribution was achieved by managers choosing to ignore or bypass formal regulations for performance-related differentials in favor of unsanctioned efforts to limit sharp differences. Neither the managers seeking to retain a surplus labor force nor the workers who remained with their enterprises for long periods of time had any interest in a system of evaluation that accentuated differences among employees and produced social tensions on the shopfloor. In fact, because the managers who engaged in this sort of unofficial "equality-mongering" *(uravnilovka)* were usually more successful in limiting social tensions at the workplace, the regime tacitly approved of their practices although they contradicted formal regulations.[220] Thus, the main source for whatever leveling of incomes did take place within job categories was the acknowledged gap between the formal rules concerning bonus payments, which were still based on individual norm-fulfillment, and the de facto manipulation of wage and bonus payments so as to engineer more income-leveling in the enterprise.[221]

Third, the few officially sanctioned initiatives to alter incentive structures in particular sectors or firms actually aimed to *increase* the significance of performance-related differentials as a means to stimulate individual productivity. The 1965 Kosygin reforms, for example, included measures to improve the standardization of norm-determination techniques so that managers might make bonus payments more directly proportional to precisely measured differences in individual performance. But this initiative was intended to ensure more systematic implementation of existing incentive schemes rather than to introduce new practices; and, in any case, in the absence of coercive pressures and adequate monitoring, the reform did not actually succeed in checking the widespread discrepancies between formal bonus regulations and actual bonus payments.[222] The same was true of Brezhnev's decree of July 1979, which also called for the more systematic implementation of the official bonus regulations and which also ended up being ignored at the enterprise level without provoking any response from the regime.[223] A more targeted effort to boost performance-related incentives was evident in the case of an experimental policy introduced at the Shchekino Chemical Combine in 1967. The combine was required to trim the work force so as to save the wage and bonus funds for the more productive and skilled, and the factory's reported success turned it into a model for other factories instructed to replicate the "Shchekino method."[224] While a number of factories reported reductions in the labor force and increases in both productivity and average earnings, these turned out to be mostly short-term trends in regions where the method was being showcased and where local officials brought additional pressures and resources to bear to make the experiment appear a success. Most managers were eager to avoid dramatic cuts in the work force in a labor-short economy, while those who did trim the labor force ended up later hiring new workers or rehiring dismissed workers.[225] Thus, these efforts to boost productivity not only failed to achieve their objectives, but served to cast doubt on the regime's diffuse commitment to egalitarianism.

Finally, the regime also paved the way for broader processes of social stratification that effectively undermined the limited progress toward income-leveling in Soviet industry. These processes were largely a result of the higher bonus rates and special privileges and resources reserved for various categories of employees: those possessing special skills in short supply, those with high-level political connections, and those who worked in strategically important production activities and whose loyalty was consequently more valued. The reduced differentials in the base wages for most citizens could not make up for the multiplying effects of unequal access to special bonuses, quality housing, and goods that were imported or in short supply.[226] Moreover, children of employees with jobs demanding greater skills and education tended to disproportionately gain access to those institutions of higher education from which new generations of employees and technicians would be recruited, setting the stage for the reproduction of stratification related to occupational position.[227] In addition, the Brezhnev regime quietly tolerated a growing realm of quasi-legal exchange relationships in the underground second economy as long as these did not undermine the production process in the most important sectors of the economy; this practice, too, only ended up further increasing social inequality among different segments of the citizenry and work force as those with special access to resources and connections were able to more consistently capitalize on this access to further their careers and increase supplemental earnings.[228] Even income-support programs designed to improve living standards for the lowest-paid workers calculated supplementary incomes in terms of *prior* earnings, thus increasing the gap between those earning higher and lower wages among the lower strata of the work force.[229]

In sum, the post-Stalin elite's stated commitment to greater egalitarianism turned out to be little more than part of the wider strategy to maintain stability and forestall labor unrest through less overt forms of control. Reductions in the base wages of different categories of workers enabled the regime to claim it was making progress toward wage egalitarianism in the era of "developed socialism," but the official wage system, in keeping with the Taylorist piece rate system established in the 1920s, continued to place a heavy emphasis on individual material incentives tied to the existing system of job classifications and norm determination. Only where managers chose to ignore formal regulations did income differentials actually narrow among workers in the same shop or factory. Most workers did manage to raise their living standards, helped by quasi-legal exchange relations; but, even so, selected segments of the work force (e.g., those with high-placed connections or employed in "closed" enterprises), like the shock workers and Stakhanovites of the Stalin era, evolved into a new labor aristocracy on the strength of the special rewards, privileges, and perquisites they received.

The Human Side of Soviet Management:
"Old Wine in New Bottles"[230]

During the 1960s and 1970s, the theories and findings of the human relations movement in the United States abroad did draw the attention of
Soviet managerial elites just as Taylorism and Fordism had in the 1920s.
Indeed, the most basic assumption of the human relations school—that
there existed a strong relationship between productivity, work motivation,
and the psychological needs of individuals—dovetailed nicely with the
Soviet elites' belief that productivity could be improved in the post-Stalin
era with less reliance on coercion and more attention to the satisfaction of
workers' needs for physical safety, job security, and improvements in living standards. But, in marked contrast to the substantial modification of
work organization in postwar Japanese firms, the incorporation of human
relations was viewed by Soviet managerial elites as another way to
improve the performance of Taylorist production. For the most part,
"human" aspects of management were emphasized only insofar as they
were consistent with existing socialist ideals or with official practices established as part of NOT, the scientific organization of labor.[231]

In fact, in the post-Stalin era, managerial elites attempted to more systematically and widely implement the basic methods and principles of
NOT after the frenzied productivity campaigns of the Stalin era.
Khrushchev himself, echoing a familiar Bolshevik refrain, asserted: "Why
don't we use that which is rational and economically profitable from what
the capitalists have? In the conditions of a planned economy, all this could
be realized more simply and easily than under conditions of capitalist
competition."[232] Gastev, who had fallen victim to Stalin's purges of Soviet
elites in the late 1930s, was "rehabilitated," officially exonerated of the
crimes he had "confessed" to before his execution. A new Institute of
Labor was set up in 1956 under the State Committee on Labor and Wage
Issues for the purpose of promoting greater standardization in production
norms and product quality. In 1961, a newly established Laboratory for
Problems of Management began to publish a number of new management
texts, including a famous book by Dzherman Gvishani (Premier Alexei
Kosygin's son-in-law) that, following Lenin's approach, offered a token
criticism of capitalist management techniques before proceeding to call for
more explicit application of these same techniques under the conditions of
a socialist economy. In 1963, Gvishani was authorized to create the Scientific Council for Problems of the Scientific Basis of Management to

explicitly promote the principles of NOT and coordinate research and training in Soviet management science.[233]

As in the 1920s, when Kerzhentsev and the Time League had criticized Gastev and the Russian Taylorists, some questioned whether the push to expand NOT adequately took into account the distinctive character of work under revolutionary socialism.[234] After Khrushchev's ouster, however, such criticisms became muted as Soviet premier Kosygin (Brezhnev's near-equal in the politburo through 1969) steadily steered Soviet management closer to Western management science, deemphasizing ideological concerns and calling upon the new generation of managers to "know technology and production techniques to perfection . . . know the economics of production . . . and . . . know the laws of the scientific organization of labor."[235] During this time a collection of Gastev's works was published in 1966, and in the same year, the party central committee formally issued a decree instructing the Academy of Sciences and the Ministry of Higher Education to bring "methods of the scientific organization of labor" to bear in solving the problems being encountered with productivity and economic growth throughout Soviet industry.[236]

As Brezhnev moved to decisively take over the reins of the party toward the end of the 1960s, new questions were again raised about the management institutes and NOT specialists Kosygin had been promoting. Apparently signaling a shift in course, Kerzhentsev's writings were published in 1968, with the editors explicitly lauding the Time League leader for criticizing "those engineers and organizers of NOT who continue to rediscover Taylorism as it exists in America." In early 1969, as Brezhnev consolidated his control over the politburo, he effectively questioned Kosygin's ideological credentials by declaring that managerial problems "are primarily *political* problems, not technical problems."[237] But, as it turns out, such comments were intended mainly to enable the General Secretary to distance himself from Kosygin's broader economic reforms and to call for greater attention to ideologically correct forms of public discourse on economic matters. In fact, Brezhnev, too, proved to be a staunch advocate of the management institutes and the NOT specialists as long as their proposals and texts showed some sensitivity to the language of Marxism-Leninism. Throughout the 1970s, thousands of proposals were circulated by NOT specialists to improve the design of individual workstations based on time-and-motion analyses, and the basic principles of scientific management continued to shape the organization of production in Soviet firms.[238]

In terms of the official structure of workplace authority, "human relations" was loosely invoked to promote a more friendly and collegial relationship between superiors and subordinates (instead of the brute power and detachment Red Directors were urged to demonstrate in the Stalin era) so that managers could develop greater mutual trust and encourage a more concerted effort to improve productivity.[239] However, such exhortations meant little in view of the persistence of the existing system of centralized one-man management. Trade unions continued to act as transmission belts of the party-state apparatus, focusing not on the independent representation of workers' grievances and interests but on the management of pension funds, recreational facilities, and cultural activities for workers. The post-Stalin emphasis on socialist legalism did lead to new laws to prevent managers from dismissing workers without proper cause and trade union consent, but these laws were either ignored or rendered meaningless as factory trade union committees simply rubber-stamped managers' decisions.[240] In any case, new laws—for example, one that made "parasitism" illegal in the workplace—could be readily invoked by directors to throw dissidents out of jobs without objection from trade unions or anyone else. And, despite the guarantee of new employment for dismissed individuals, workers still had to carry their labor books with them, enabling managers to unilaterally enter perceived violations of factory rules, which made it difficult for recalcitrant workers to find *suitable* jobs.[241] Thus, if there was a human dimension to labor relations in the workplace, it was in the form of *informal* networks formed by managerial personnel and their subordinates and not in a transformation of formal authority relations.

Similarly, although *quality control* became an increasingly important part of the vocabulary of Soviet management specialists, the concept was used to refer to standard product quality issues in relation to existing methods and practices. The Tenth Five-Year Plan (1976–80) did incorporate more quality indicators as part of the official targets for shops and factories, with the State Committee for Standards reserving the right to determine which products were ranked in the highest category of quality. However, there was no effort to set up new forums for the regular discussion of quality-control methods, and the production process was kept separate from research and design aspects, with the latter exclusively under the purview of trained white-collar specialists with more ties to research institutes than to other divisions of the firm.[242] Thus, in the end, the Soviet version of quality control devolved into a ritual practice whereby the State Committee for Standards simply rejected, based largely on arbitrary considerations, a few thousand applications from managers seeking to get their products ranked among the highest category of goods.[243]

The human relations movements abroad did prompt Soviet management specialists to pay more attention to the functionality of small groups in satisfying the emotional needs of workers and improving communication within different sectors of the enterprise. According to one typical view, the effective performance of workers and firms depended heavily on "the solidarity of the collective, the degree of confidence of the collective in its leadership, the quality of interpersonal relations, and the attitude *(nastroenie)* of the workers."[244] Such commentaries closely mirrored managerial discourses in postwar Japanese firms; and, had the initiatives they spurred been systematically implemented alongside concomitant changes in the labor process, aspects of Soviet work organization might have come to concretely represent ideals associated with both human relations research and socialist labor as broadly understood by the working masses. However, in the end, the existing system of individualized tasks and norm determination in Soviet enterprises remained firmly entrenched and made it practically impossible to stimulate genuine worker participation or redesign formal production processes to emphasize greater collective responsibility.

Khrushchev, for example, had encouraged teams of factories and work brigades to engage in "creative cooperation" and proceeded to establish "production councils" to promote greater worker participation in discussions of day-to-day aspects of production.[245] But, in the absence of concomitant changes in other aspects of work organization, managers continued to focus on their factory's output targets to secure their bonuses, with little thought to "cooperation" within or among enterprises, while workers cooperated with their colleagues only informally, for the purpose of helping fulfill quotas or exchanging access to special privileges and resources. Moreover, in the absence of a restructuring of one-man management, the rate of participation at production conferences remained low as most workers rightly viewed their suggestions and endorsements as having little impact, if any, on decisions about task assignments, output norms, or the production process.

In the late 1970s and early 1980s, the same fate befell efforts to promote brigade *khozraschet,* joint responsibility for completion of related tasks accompanied by collective remuneration paid to the work brigade as a whole. The idea of collective remuneration had been raised during the first years following the 1917 revolution and was again brought up during

Khrushchev's effort to reform the wage system (discussed above). In 1979, a new policy was introduced to *formally* make members of work brigades collectively responsible for their joint tasks and managing the distribution of tasks and earnings. In the brief period that he was in power, Brezhnev's successor, Yuri Andropov, proved to be a vigorous supporter of the brigade system, even introducing a new "Law on Working Collectives" in 1983 in order to provide a legal basis for the universalization of brigade responsibility.[246] However, despite the attention received by the brigade reforms, and despite reports that some enterprises had successfully introduced the brigade system to increase productivity, work brigades were never systematically incorporated into formal production processes in most sectors.

Once again, the problem was that there had been no concomitant program to link the brigade reforms to a restructuring of task structures, job classifications and norm-determination procedures so that firms might have systematically integrated work brigades into their production processes. The Taylorist organization of production along with the existing system of norm determination remained in place. And official regulations still required managers to maintain detailed records of every individual's performance (following the model of personnel assessments in U.S. firms). As a result, even in enterprises reportedly using the brigade system, managers either reported aggregate figures for the collective work done by a group of individuals performing separate tasks, or claimed to be implementing brigade "reforms" when they were informally relying on workgroup leaders to monitor the completion of a set of tasks and track individual earnings.[247] In none of these circumstances was there any effort to bring about real changes in the system of work organization or in the day-to-day production activities on the shopfloor.[248]

In sum, the organization of work in post-Stalin firms continued to be severely constrained by officially sanctioned management practices that had crystallized in the 1920s and 1930s. For the most part, one-man management, maximal task specialization, individual productivity norms, and significant output-related wage differentials remained the basis for the formal system of production. To the extent that some of the ideas associated with human relations—for example, collective labor organized around work brigades—may have resonated with workers, these ideas also served to reinforce *informal* forms of shopfloor cooperation that, if anything, undermined compliance with formal rules and commitment to official production goals.[249]

Quiescence without Commitment: Workers in Soviet Russia
from the 1960s through 1985

Those who interpret the provisions of the so-called social contract as a version of corporatism have argued that, in return for a more secure environment and incremental improvements in their working and living conditions, the Soviet work force was generally responsive to management and supportive of the regime and its policies.[250] Those who see these provisions as an expression of a distinctive socialist ethic have suggested that workers became genuinely incorporated into the industrial system and came to accept official managerial authority as well as many of the ideals espoused by the regime.[251] Others have dismissed the so-called social contract as an invidious arrangement unilaterally implemented by the regime to divide and "atomize" the work force while selectively rewarding a narrow stratum of loyal "labor aristocrats."[252] On balance, the available evidence on the attitudes and behavior of workers in the post-Stalin era suggests a more nuanced view of Soviet industrial relations: while the new terms of employment, buttressed by informal opportunities to improve material conditions, did produce a relatively *compliant* work force, these did not suffice to provide a *committed* work force. In fact, the 1970s and early 1980s witnessed the further erosion of official managerial authority as evident in a number of trends: although there were only a few major strikes, there were increasing problems with temporary stoppages and slowdowns, high unplanned turnover, reports of unmotivated workers with little job satisfaction, and the proliferation of collusive practices and informal exchange relationships that undermined the formal system of production.

While industrial relations in both postwar Japan and post-Stalin Russia were characterized by a relatively low level of labor unrest, in the latter case, this was more suggestive of the continuing threat of coercive retaliation than an indication of rising worker commitment. Even so, strikes, work stoppages, and production slowdowns did occur from time to time, usually in situations where the managers or the regime failed to fulfill implied promises guaranteeing certain provisions in exchange for orderly production. As noted above, the Novocherkassk strike of 1962, in response to rising food prices, was sufficiently large and well-organized to draw a violent crackdown and later prompt the Brezhnev regime to adopt more explicit policies on full employment and subsidized access to basic necessities. But under Brezhnev, too, large-scale strikes again broke out as in the case of strikes in Dnepropetrovsk and Dneproderzhinsk in 1972 and a massive strike wave that hit several automobile plants in 1980 and 1981 and involved tens of thousands of workers.[253] More frequent than strikes, though less obvious and less threatening to the regime, were work stoppages organized by the factory trade union committee; although trade unions remained transmission belts for the party-state apparatus, new laws about working conditions and worker dismissals did enable them to organize brief stoppages and walkouts where managers proved stubbornly unresponsive to particular grievances. The most widespread form of industrial protest in the Soviet era, however, was also the least provocative: the deliberate slowdown of production by workers on the shopfloor until managers showed a willingness to either fulfill unmet obligations or present grievances to higher-level authorities.[254]

Significantly, none of these forms of labor unrest constituted an organized movement aimed at challenging official managerial practices or elements of the so-called social contract. It was when managers or officials appeared to be reneging on implied promises or encroaching upon informal arrangements at the shopfloor level that workers spontaneously became involved in some sort of protest action.[255] For the most part, however, this proved to be more the exception than the rule as the terms of the social contract and the latent threat of coercion generally served to keep workers compliant until the mid-1980s. As other trends in Soviet industrial relations make clear, however, this compliance did not translate into increasing commitment among the bulk of the work force.

As in the Stalin era, turnover came to represent a common substitute for more overt forms of industrial action. The extremely high rates of labor turnover in the first decade of Bolshevik rule were sharply reduced following the introduction of the draconian labor codes of the late 1930s. With the reduction of coercive controls in the post-Stalin era, however, unplanned turnover once again became a widely acknowledged problem, although the internal passport system (which tied employment, residence, and access to resources to particular locales) and the system of labor books (which contained detailed employment histories for each worker) theoretically made it difficult for workers to freely seek new jobs, especially in different towns or districts. During most of the Brezhnev era, the average annual turnover rate stood at about 20 percent for the work force as a whole; this figure rose to about 25 percent for firms not involved in defense-related production, and to nearly 40 percent among younger workers who had higher levels of education and had been trained more recently.[256] Even in labor markets in advanced capitalist societies, an annual turnover rate of 20 to 25 percent would be usually considered excessive in most sectors; in the context of Soviet industry, this same level of turnover suggested an even more serious problem given that the enterprise served as the provider of the most basic necessities in life, from access to housing and cheap foodstuffs to health care, recreation, and cultural activities.[257] This may well be why Soviet economists and managers themselves constantly called attention to the problems created by unplanned turnover; indeed, the frequent complaints about chronic labor shortages in the Soviet economy actually referred not to the absence of an adequate labor supply to enable completion of planned production tasks but to the difficulties managers had in limiting turnover among key categories of employees and maintaining a surplus labor force to deal with unforeseen problems.[258]

The consistently high rate of unplanned turnover had much to do with the growing dissatisfaction among most workers with the frequently repetitive tasks assigned to them as part of the formal organization of production in the enterprise. The most educated and highly skilled employees did have some opportunity to exercise greater discretion and experience greater job diversity in their positions; they were thus less prone to switch jobs or complain about their tasks. But this was not true of most blue-collar production workers who lacked the credentials to move into more rewarding occupational positions but did have sufficient education and ambition to find their work experiences to be unfulfilling.[259] In the absence of efforts to expand or redefine job boundaries within Soviet firms, these workers, unlike their Japanese counterparts, had no real opportunities to expand their skill-sets and experience greater job diversity unless they switched to a different factory. For them, the work ethic stressed by the regime—which emphasized the intrinsic value of socialist labor and the emotional satisfaction stemming from collective endeavors—bore little resemblance to labor processes organized primarily around individualized norms for repetitive, narrowly defined, elemental tasks. As Soviet industrial sociologists themselves noted, high turnover and problems with work motivation stemmed less from frustration over wages or benefits and more from the "content of labor"—that is, from the absence of adequate opportunities for creative and challenging tasks involving greater discretion and responsibility.[260] Thus, workers increasingly came to view their jobs and factories primarily in instrumental terms, with no belief in labor as "a value in itself."[261]

Another indication of eroding commitment among Soviet workers is evident in the declining rate of participation in production conferences and other officially sponsored activities intended to give workers "the feeling of being master" in the factory. Throughout the post-Stalin era, in the absence of coercive pressures, the rate of participation in production conferences and other activities designed to inspire cooperation and enthusiasm (such as Khrushchev's "movement for communist labor") continued to drop, with most workers progressively more cynical about the purpose of these institutions and more convinced that their suggestions or recommendations had no bearing on factory administration.[262] Even among those workers who regularly participated in production conferences, "pro forma activism" took the place of genuine interest in matters pertaining to the formal organization of production. As one Soviet observer wrote in 1970, workers "shout in the meetings, they write on the wall-newspapers, they condemn the parasites and they calm down until the next campaign."[263] Thus, in marked contrast to early 1918, when large numbers of workers participated widely in workers' control committees and other independent workers' bodies, workers in the post-Stalin era had little interest in what they perceived to be superficial participatory institutions effectively controlled by management.

In addition, informal modes of collusion and cooperation—such as the previously mentioned relations of personal connections *(blat)* and circles of mutual protection *(krugovaia poruka)*—became far more widespread and active. The informal networks and understandings, even though they frequently involved the tacit cooperation or participation of supervisors and enterprise directors, did not work to enhance the formal process of production but rather to subvert it by disabling scrutiny from above and diverting working hours and enterprise resources away from the formal production process. In some of the most blatant cases, enterprises produced nothing except on paper, and workers received salaries mainly to buy their silence regardless of their actual output. More typically, groups of workers negotiated with supervisors to obtain soft output norms or turn a blind eye to the use of regular working hours and factory machinery for the provision of goods and services in the underground economy.[264] Soviet officials appeared to be well aware of these practices as far back as 1970, and some even attempted to openly point to the functionality of informal and quasi-legal collusive practices as a way to improve the production and distribution of goods so as to satisfy those needs the formal economic system failed to meet. One Soviet management text even attempted to make a virtue out of informal networks and understandings by euphemistically noting that "the informal structure gives business relations flexibility."[265] While quasi-legal and collusive exchange relations *did* reflect the reproduction of collectivism and mutual trust, what is significant here is that these were largely in the service of unsanctioned private ends and frequently undermined firms' capacities for maintaining the formal system of production.[266]

Finally, it is worth considering the evidence provided by Soviet officials themselves on declining commitment of workers. Although this problem was only acknowledged, and sometimes exaggerated, so as to place blame for the slowdown of the 1970s on workers rather than the economic system, specific observations about declining workers' productivity, violations of workplace discipline, and alcohol consumption have been corroborated by a variety of sources, including Western studies of the Soviet economy.[267] On the question of productivity, for example, Soviet estimates are consistent with Western estimates (calculated strictly in terms of productivity per man-hour) insofar as both sets of statistics reflect a steady decline in labor productivity for the period from 1961 to 1985.[268] The noted Soviet sociologist Iadov has also shown that violations of labor discipline doubled, while the number of workers who surpassed their quotas (as reported by Soviet managers) fell from nearly two-thirds to less than half.[269] Similarly, the problems of excessive alcohol consumption and alcohol-related workplace disruptions in the post-Stalin era are widely acknowledged; according to one study cited in a highly respected analysis of Soviet state-society relations, per capita average annual consumption of vodka in the Moscow region *quadrupled* between the 1920s and 1960s![270] These indications of declining productivity, poor discipline, and increasing alcoholism—although treated by Soviet managerial elites as a cause rather than symptom of broader problems with official production practices— may be considered further evidence that worker commitment to the formal system of production was declining in the post-Stalin era, especially when considered in conjunction with such factors as the proliferation of collusive practices, low rates of participation in production conferences, high unplanned turnover, and work stoppages and slowdowns.

Gorbachev's Workplace Reforms and the Intensification of Labor Unrest

At the time that Mikhail Gorbachev took over as General Secretary of the CPSU in 1985, the question faced by Stalin's immediate successors still needed to be resolved: What was to be done to boost the discipline, morale, and productivity of the work force without overt reliance on coercive measures? Gorbachev's own official pronouncements, usually associated with his overall project of perestroika (restructuring), incorporated both human relations themes as well as familiar Bolshevik refrains concerning worker participation and a true socialist form of workplace "democracy." As he himself put it, "Of prime importance ... is for the people to be the true master of production, rather than a master only in name. For without it, individual workers or collectives are not interested, nor can they be interested, in the final results of their work."[271] Specifically criticizing his predecessors for ignoring the "human factor" and tolerating the growing "alienation" of the citizenry, he promoted greater autonomy of collective production units and even appeared to embrace the earlier syndicalist postures struck by proponents of workers' control in 1917 and 1918: "A work collective naturally develops a reciprocal desire to have the right to run their enterprise and working process, the results of which determine the collective's incomes and life."[272] Significantly, however, the concrete measures Gorbachev initiated in the name of perestroika turned out to be reminiscent of the productivity campaigns of the 1920s and 1930s: workers were exhorted to be more disciplined, alcoholism was condemned, participatory institutions were intended to promote the ends of elites rather than enable some measure of shopfloor autonomy, and sharper differentials in material rewards were established to spur individual productivity.

During his first year (1985–86), Gorbachev focused on the "acceleration" of production and a crackdown on poor discipline and performance. One of the first and most well-publicized initiatives in this regard was the antialcohol campaign, initially organized by Andropov but also reminiscent of early Bolshevik initiatives to discourage alcohol consumption as counterrevolutionary.[273] Gorbachev placed severe limits on the sale of beer and vodka, ostensibly to cut down on the number of workers showing up drunk at the workplace, but, as in the 1920s, workers reacted angrily to the sudden cutbacks in alcohol sales, and vodka production simply went underground while the government lost a significant source of revenue.[274] Gorbachev finally abandoned the campaign in 1987. Another part of Gorbachev's campaign for acceleration was aimed at improving quality control by expanding the role of the national agency for quality-inspection (Gospriemka) in identifying and penalizing poor quality work. This policy, too, drew angry responses as it appeared to hold workers responsible for shoddy work rather than seek to assess and improve the production process at their factories.[275]

A more proactive effort to activate the human factor is evident in Gorbachev's proposal at the Twenty-seventh Party Congress in 1986 to revise the 1961 party program so as to put in place a more differentiated system of incentives to reward the "effort and merit" of punctual, productive, and efficient workers. The party reaffirmed its commitment to the principle of "social justice," but now redefined it to emphasize the elimination of unearned wages or bonuses handed to "parasitic" workers. This required not only greater adherence to official wage practices, but also expanding the significance of individual performance-related bonuses as a portion of total earnings while reducing the size of the social consumption fund from which firms made generous benefits (education, health care, recreation, etc.) available to workers regardless of effort.[276] This policy stood in marked contrast to both Khrushchev's efforts to formally alter the wage scales to reduce differentials and Brezhnev's readiness to turn a blind eye to unofficial wage-leveling practices intended to maintain labor quiescence. At the same time, while the new wage scheme may have appeared to some Western observers to be a departure from a socialist work ethic in favor of the greater reliance on individual incentives found in market economies, it is necessary to recognize that Gorbachev's approach was rooted in Lenin's own assertions about the relationship between contribution and earnings as part of "socialist equality" and Stalin's subsequent promotion of highly differentiated reward structures in lieu of "petty bourgeois egalitarianism."[277] Although wages and labor productivity initially crept up in 1986 and 1987, productivity fell between 1988 and 1990 while average wages actually continued to increase at a rate of 8 to 10 percent annually, attesting to the fact that neither the new bonus regulations nor the new restrictions on the social consumption fund were being adhered to.[278]

Perhaps the most significant efforts by Gorbachev to boost worker commitment were in the provisions of the new Law on State Enterprises introduced in the summer of 1987 as part of the wider project of economic perestroika. The law was primarily designed to put an end to bailouts of unprofitable firms and promote enterprise self-reliance *(khozraschet)* and self-financing *(samo-finasirovanie)*. It was also intended to make managers cut back on wasteful expenses and redundant labor and be more disciplined in using their budgets to reward more efficient and productive workers (as in the case of the Shchekino experiment).[279] At the same time, the new law introduced two articles that appeared to suggest limitations on managerial control and provisions for greater worker autonomy and participation in enterprise administration: Article 6 of the law required that all members of the enterprise administration, from the director down to the brigade leader, be elected by rank-and-file workers, while Article 7 established the "council of the labor collective" (STK) that would theoretically constitute an autonomous enterprise-level body designed to increase worker participation while bypassing the established trade union committees.

On the surface, these reforms appeared to represent a serious effort to reduce centralized industrial administration, make managers accountable to workers, and create opportunities for genuine worker participation. A closer look at the law, however, suggests that this was simply another manifestation of the familiar strategy, used by both Lenin and Stalin, to utilize forms of mass participation and "control from below" for the purpose of realizing the objectives of the central authorities and weakening resistance from entrenched managers and bureaucrats.[280] The introduction of workplace elections did not lead to significant changes in the actual composition of managerial staff since elections of enterprise directors had to be confirmed by higher-level government officials and those of lower-level administrative personnel by the director. Moreover, the newly established STKs, far from representing the syndicalist aspirations of the first workers' control committees, were charged with monitoring individual workers to ensure that wages and bonuses were commensurate with performance. Moreover, precisely because membership in the STK was open, members of managerial staff, union officials, and senior workers with ties to management were able to quickly coopt the STK in an effort to preserve the status quo.[281]

Not surprisingly, in the end, this law too failed to accomplish its stated purpose. Managers managed to avoid wage cutbacks and layoffs and relied on early retirement and transfers of workers to appear compliant.[282] Workers refrained from regular participation in the STK until 1989 through 1991, when frustrated workers at many factories used the elections and STKs to promote new leaders and coordinate various forms of industrial protest.[283] And, faced with mounting political problems in 1988 and 1989, the government itself ignored the law and ended up bailing out or reorganizing insolvent firms while continuing to subsidize enterprise-related benefits.[284]

In the end, the net effect of Gorbachev's attempts to improve productivity and efficiency was to endanger the fragile understanding that had allowed the previous regime to maintain some degree of labor quiescence even in the absence of high commitment. Gorbachev's workplace reforms suggested that the so-called social contract of the past twenty years was suddenly being redefined in terms that were now even less favorable to workers, intruding on the few perquisites and opportunities the regime had allowed in order to enable them to gradually improve their lot.[285] Moreover, Gorbachev's efforts to implement formal wage scales and increase performance-related bonus differentials proved to be one of the main sources of workers' dissatisfaction as these efforts threatened to further increase social differentiation, disrupting whatever sense of egalitarianism managers had been able to create through informal channels.[286] Finally, the original assumption behind Gorbachev's initiatives—that poor discipline and low worker productivity were responsible for the state of the economy—only further angered workers who saw the main problem to be poor working conditions, unsatisfying job assignments, and the general absence of any correspondence between the regime's ideals and the realities on the shopfloor.[287]

Thus, far from reviving worker commitment, Gorbachev opened the door to increasingly overt challenges that gradually extended beyond specific grievances at the workplace to full-blown criticisms of the regime itself. Initially, workers took advantage of glasnost to complain publicly about working conditions and even initiate labor disputes that would require mediation. By 1988, localized strikes and sporadic collective protests broke out in a number of sectors and regions while a number of informal organizations sprang up to represent the concerns of different groups of workers. Then, in the summer of 1989, a strike broke out in the coal mines of Mezhdurechensk which quickly led to waves of highly confrontational strikes throughout the Kuzbass and Donbass regions, with strike committees formed to coordinate protest activities and monitor safety at the mines.[288] Finally, in the spring of 1991, just months before the coup attempt that would lead to the breakup of the USSR, another major miners' strike broke out, this one even more radical than the 1989 strike in terms of the strikers' rhetoric and demands: workers publicly criticized Soviet political and economic institutions and voiced support for greater "democracy" and "market" reforms as a way to secure greater shopfloor autonomy as well as more control over the production and distribution of goods.[289]

These well-organized and overtly confrontational challenges, along with the growth of independent workers' organizations and public expressions of anger and frustration even among nonstriking workers, suggest that a new threshold had been crossed in Soviet labor relations. Despite the best of intentions, Gorbachev's reforms only served to undermine what he called the "artificial stability" of the Brezhnev years without offering a more legitimate alternative. As a result, an uncommitted work force now became progressively less quiescent as Gorbachev's political troubles mounted, industrial production declined, and the Soviet Union itself headed toward collapse.

4.4. Conclusion: The Contradictions and Legacies of Soviet Institution-Building

In 1959, the authors of a key study based on surveys of Stalin-era émigrés noted that "there is a marked congruence between popular values and the goals the system purports to pursue [but] the failure of the Soviet regime to implement these implied values has been a source of real conflict."[290] Forty years later, another study, this time based on surveys of Russian citizens in the period of post-Soviet transition, pointed out that the erosion of support for official state socialism in the late Soviet era was linked to "the contradiction between the promise of justice contained in Marxism-Leninism and the reality of daily life."[291] The analysis presented in this chapter has essentially borne out these observations within the context of a broader argument about how long-standing communal norms and Soviet institution-building efforts affected the character and legitimacy of official management practices. Below, the arguments developed for the 1917 through 1940 period and the post-Stalin period are reviewed briefly, with figures 11 and 12 providing a summary of key points for each period to facilitate comparison with relevant features of industrial relations in prewar and postwar Japan (see figs. 9 and 10). The chapter then concludes with a brief discussion of worker attitudes and expectations in the course of Russian industrialization, reviewing some of the tentative evidence that renders plausible a key assumption behind this study: that certain portable norms and practices embedded in preexisting communities of work shaped the informal norms and understandings that emerged within the context of Soviet, and now post-Soviet, economic institutions.

The Failure of "Revolutionary Modernity"

To the extent that this chapter offers a negative assessment of Soviet institution-building efforts, it has sought to do so in a nuanced manner, taking into account what Soviet elites were trying to achieve, what average Russian citizens themselves expected their leaders to deliver, and which features of official ideology and organization most sharply contradicted these expectations. Thus, the project of "building socialism" is not being treated as an inherently futile endeavor, and the Soviet experiment is not being dismissed as a grand failure in every respect. While the efforts to simultaneously realize a new revolutionary order and coordinate rapid industrialization posed serious challenges for Soviet institution-builders, these challenges were not insurmountable; and, while the legitimacy of Soviet institutions did decline, Soviet elites managed to transform a largely illiterate rural society into a highly literate, urbanized, industrialized state that attained recognition as a military superpower while also raising the standard of living for most of its citizens. In the particular case of the industrial enterprise, however, the argument has been unequivocal: although core elements of socialist ideology originally resonated with much of the work force and might have provided a basis for building managerial authority, officially sanctioned management practices—formulated by those who were most taken by Western scientific management—increasingly diverged from both the official ideology and long-standing norms embedded in past communities of work.

In the months leading up to and immediately following the Bolshevik Revolution, ideological assertions concerning collective labor, socialist equality, and workers' control, whatever specific meanings Lenin himself attached to these concepts, appeared to strongly resonate with the existing sensibilities and expectations of a work force that still retained ties to the newly resurgent peasant commune. In the course of the civil war, however, the growing interest in productivity-boosting Taylorist methods, most clearly evident in Lenin's sponsorship of Gastev and the movement for the scientific organization of labor (NOT), led to the establishment of narrowly defined individual tasks, strict managerial control over production, and individualized productivity norms tied to an increasingly differentiated piece rate wage scheme. After Lenin's death in 1924, a number of reforms were proposed that represented an alternative strategy for building socialism, one that still aimed to bring about a revolutionary transformation, but through a more incremental process of change involving the cultivation of whatever affinities existed between popular expectations and socialist ideals.

With Stalin's triumph in the succession struggle, however, such alternatives were rejected in favor of a more intensified campaign to uproot traditional institutions, advance proletarian culture, and rapidly expand "socialist industry." As it turns out, however, Stalin's approach ended up merely sequencing, not synthesizing, the "revolutionary" destruction of preexisting institutions and the "modernist" construction of a disciplined industrial work force; that is, once uprooted from the commune, the socially mobilized worker was expected to develop "proletarian consciousness" simply by participating in a timed, disciplined, rationalized process of production in "socialist factories." State ownership of industry, centralized planning, and a new generation of Red Directors certainly suggested that the Soviet economy differed radically from the capitalist economies of the West; but what specifically was socialist about the organization of work and authority *within* the Soviet factory never did become quite clear. Despite Stalin's criticism of the "narrowly managerial" views of the Russian Taylorists, the Stalinist enterprise increasingly subjected the growing industrial work force to draconian labor codes, the concentration of production control under "one-man management," the extension of Taylorist job classification schemes to individualized job responsibilities, and, above all, sharply increased differentials in earnings tied to overfulfillment of individual quotas. As a result, workers, far from becoming "masters of the factories," found themselves quietly attempting to resist management techniques that bore greater resemblance to those in capitalist firms than to the images of the factory suggested by such ideals as workers' control and socialist equality (see fig. 11).

Stalin's successors rejected systematic terror and generally tried to refrain from relying on overt coercion in maintaining discipline in the workplace. Instead, they gravitated toward a stable consensus whereby workers, in exchange for industrial peace and a commitment to productivity, were guaranteed physical safety, full employment, steadily improving living standards tied to enterprise-related benefits, and some narrowing of differentials in base wages. Alongside this so-called social contract, post-Stalin management also evinced a consistent trend toward greater pragmatism and rationalization, along with a new vocabulary emphasizing the human aspects of production. In contrast to the more fundamental shift in industrial relations seen in postwar Japan, however, these trends were not accompanied by a systematic effort to reassess and modify the formal system of production except at the margins. One-man management remained firmly entrenched, trade unions remained transmission belts, and managers retained significant power over workers since negative reports in workers' labor books could still keep them from obtaining preferred jobs. The reliance on minutely spe-

Indications of Problems with Worker Commitment

Despite repression of strikes in 1920 and 1921, rise in number of strikes in mid-1920s; coercive controls under Stalin limit strikes, but rate of unplanned turnover *(tekuchest')* rises in 1930s and is officially acknowledged as a serious problem; increasing reliance on informal work groups functioning as artels (e.g., production communes) to offset pressures of productivity campaigns; formal work organization and wage practices contradicted by de facto administration of tasks and earnings on the basis of collective efforts of work groups; gains in industrial production during first two Five-Year Plans (1929-38) mostly a result of large influx of labor.

Partial Explanation

Absence of congruence between (A) official management practices promoted by scientific organization of work (NOT) and socialist competition campaigns, both emphasizing managerial centralization and piece rate wages based on individual norms and productivity; and both (B) official ideology which was commonly perceived to mean some movement towards greater worker participation and wage egalitarianism, and (C) informal norms inherited from past social institutions, reflecting strong traditions of mutual aid, common land use, and egalitarian distributive norms

A. Formal Management Practices

Official system of production crystallized by mid-1930s under direction of loyal "Red Directors" promoted to replace "bourgeois specialists." Despite shifts in balance of rational planning shaped by scientific management and revolutionary heroism, continuity in terms of increasingly steep managerial hierarchy through one-man management; Taylorist deskilling, individualized norm-determination, piece rate wages, and sharply differentiated rewards tied to competitive individual performance.

B. Official Ideology of Labor

Theoretical discussions of core concepts and specific policy ramifications vary with situation, but public postures struck at time of revolution suggest themes broadly consistent with workers' sensibilities: workers' control suggests less steep managerial hierarchy and more workers' participation in management; principles of collective labor suggest group-based work organization (production collective); and wage egalitarianism (despite relevance of output and skill) suggests some reduction in wage differentials seen in tsarist factory.

C. Norms and Expectations of Workers As Conditioned by Legacies of Past

Despite exposure to industrialization, urbanization, and education, both established skilled workers and new arrivals behave in terms suggesting shared understandings derived from past communities of work, both in countryside *(mir)* and city *(artel)*: general sense of universal "right to labor" for all; emphasis on mutual aid and collective responsibility for common tasks and obligations (e.g., taxes); strong collective identity that serves as a basis for membership in commune and in particularistic networks in cities and factories; egalitarian distributive norms as seen in practice of repartitioning of lands in *mir* and equal distribution of wages in *artel*.

Fig. 11.   Ideology, practice, and managerial authority in Russia, 1917–40

cialized job classification schemes, individual-level assignments and norms, and high output-based bonus differentials, effectively made attempts to institute brigade-level responsibility impractical or superficial at best. Once Khrushchev's wage reforms had been scuttled, the regime continued to privilege certain categories of workers and to emphasize performance-based differentials to stimulate productivity. To the extent that differences in living standards did get narrower, this was the result of higher base wages for the lowest strata of workers and of a widening gap between the formal and informal realms of production and distribution (evident in the tacit acceptance of informal wage-leveling, shopfloor collusion, and a growing second economy). This did not reflect a fundamental reevaluation of Stalinist institution-building, but rather a "neotraditional" variant thereof. The system of work and authority was still framed as a novel revolutionary construction, and still reflected the influence of managerial discourses abroad. And yet, within the context of Soviet history, the post-Stalin leadership continued to rely on past ideological tenets and existing production processes, conflating human relations with the creation of a more stable and comfortable environment that would allow workers to be more consistently productive. While this approach did keep workers *quiescent* for a time, it also undermined prospects for regenerating worker *commitment,* setting the state for openly hostile responses to Gorbachev's reforms (see figure 12).

Russian Communities, Soviet Institutions,
and Post-Soviet Reforms

Although it is now clear that Soviet institution-builders never did manage to create the sort of "new Soviet man" the Bolsheviks had envisioned, how workers' attitudes and behavior may have evolved in the course of Soviet industrialization remains an open question with a significant bearing on the prospects of post-Soviet institutions. Some studies suggest that the pressures of "socialist competition" and an expanding underground economy set the stage for greater individuation and a stronger acquisitive impulse.[292] Others argue that workers became "atomized," or at least partly fragmented, under the weight of highly divisive reward structures, coercive pressures, and steeply hierarchical forms of social control.[293] Still others contend that the work force partially internalized Bolshevik scripts and aspects of official ideology, learning to form relatively egalitarian, inclusive workplace communities in the process.[294]

In the absence of more consistent and definitive empirical studies, any

Indications of Continuing Problems with Commitment

Few instances of protracted labor unrest (limited to strikes of 1962 and 1972), but increase in short-term work stoppages and deliberate slow-downs. High unplanned turnover rate (about 25 percent in nondefense industry) acknowledged as a problem despite dependence of workers on internal passport and enterprise for access to key goods and services. Official reports and surveys document decreasing man-hour productivity, fewer workers meeting production norms, dissatisfaction with content of work, and increasing violations of labor discipline and alcohol consumption. Surveys point to dissatisfaction of workers stemming mostly from organization and content of work. Finally, proliferation of informal norms and exchange relations that directly subvert official production practices. Gorbachev's reforms turn hidden problems with commitment into more overt labor protest, most vividly evident in miners' strikes of 1989 and 1991.

Partial Explanation

Absence of congruence betwen (A) official management practices which revive basic tenets of scientific organization of work (NOT) while reducing emphasis on campaigns and excessive pressures in favor of pragmatism and rationalization; and both (B) official ideology which makes more explicit claims about movement toward egalitarianism and collective labor under "developed socialism"; and (C) informal norms and expectations which continue to reflect patterns of mutual assistance and preference for distributive justice and which are reinforced by official ideology and tacit tolerance for informal wage-leveling on shopfloor.

A. Formal Management Practices

So-called social contract reduces reliance on coercion and mandates full employment, higher minimum wages, and steady improvements in productivity conditional on quiescence and productivity. Greater pragmatism along with discussion of human side of work, but continuity in basic elements of scientific organization of labor (NOT): one-man management negates significance of production conferences; narrow task specialization, individual norms and performance-related bonus differentials negate brigade reforms; special privileges for those in strategically valued sectors negate efforts to reduce stratification.

B. Official Ideology of Labor

Under influence of human relations and rhetoric of developed socialism, more explicit statements in favor of collective forms of labor, reduction of stratification, movement toward equality in material conditions, and worker having feeling of being "master of factory." Ironically, official rhetoric--stripped of past qualifications and cautions against "petty bourgeois" conceptions of equality and democracy-- more closely reflects and reinforces workers' own expectations concerning group-based work organization, shopfloor autonomy, and greater egalitarianism in distribution of rewards and status.

C. Norms and Expectations of Workers Conditioned by Legacies of Past

Everyday practices on shopfloor reflect mutual trust and diffuse reciprocity among networks of workers and supervisors who collude to bypass formal regulations in order to realize values favoring collective responsibility, mutual assistance, paternalistic guardianship, and relatively egalitarian distribution of earnings reflecting members' needs and loyalty as much as performance. Resilience of these values seen in recent surveys pointing to mass support for socialist forms of economic organization and welfare management even among supporters of "democracy."

Fig. 12. Quiescence without commitment in post-Stalin Russia, 1956–85

attempt to characterize Russian workers' attitudes in the Soviet period can only be tentative at best. Nevertheless, by considering the factory apart from the economic system as a whole, and by distinguishing between formal and informal aspects of industrial relations, it is possible to craft a reasonable interpretation here that partly reconciles the competing views suggested above: The typical Russian worker simultaneously became alienated from the *formal* system of production, made independent choices in order to satisfy material needs under the existing constraints, but still continued to favor collectivist ideals, particularistic ties, and egalitarian norms whenever possible, most typically in the *informal* relations they shared in their daily lives.[295]

Certainly, some "labor heroes" took advantage of socialist competitions and favorable production quotas to improve their own lots, while others resisted the pressures of Stalinist industrialization through individual acts such as switching jobs. Much more prevalent, however, was participation in circles of protection and collusive practices to evade scrutiny and deflect the pressures of high targets and socialist competitions. Similarly, while exchange relations based on personal connections *(blat)* represented alternative channels for the satisfaction of material needs and wants—and in this sense, may be considered indicative of a growing acquisitive impulse—it is also significant that such networks formed easily and proliferated rapidly because they were based on preexisting social ties and widely understood norms emphasizing mutual trust and cooperation. In effect, "*blat* networks provided a practical context for the familiar communal virtues of personal reciprocity and loyalty, social settings in which the rules of conduct were understandable and the rewards tangible."[296] Such observations suggest that while some workers may well have become atomized, individuated, or genuinely incorporated into the system, most simply aimed to get by within institutions that failed to satisfy their material and ideal interests by quietly reconstructing more meaningful and stable understandings within the informal realms of production. These informal understandings had more in common with the particularistic forms of cooperation and mutual assistance previously seen in the *mir* and *artel* than with the more universal values trumpeted in official ideology (although unqualified versions of the latter frequently reinforced more familiar notions of collectivism and egalitarianism).

It is also important to recognize that opposition to the regime did not mean opposition to the commonly understood versions of socialism that, though not consistent with some of Lenin's own assertions about the party's vanguard role and the meaning of socialist equality, *appeared* to workers to coincide with their own dispositions toward collective labor and greater wage egalitarianism. Significantly, in the course of the intensifying labor unrest during the Gorbachev era, what workers objected to most vehemently were essentially the same practices they had sought to resist in the Stalin era: the regime's readiness to ignore ideals emphasizing collective labor and social equality in favor of sharply disproportionate material rewards to overambitious or well-connected individuals who sought to get ahead more quickly at the expense of others.[297] Moreover, in the miners' strikes of 1989, as one recent study has demonstrated, the demands of the strikers stemmed not from opposition to the values the regime claimed to embrace, but from frustration over the fact that the regime was neither attempting to realize those ideals nor allowing workers to do so on their own terms. In fact, the strikers framed their complaints in terms that prerevolutionary Russian Marxists or the Workers' Opposition of 1920 and 1921 might have enthusiastically endorsed: "The fruits of their labor were taken from them with only just enough returned so they might continue to work, and . . . much of their labor fed an army of managers and clerks who were not necessary for production."[298] Similarly, during the strikes of 1991, although miners pressed for democratization and market reforms, their objective was not to promote liberal democracy or capitalism but rather to gain more control over shopfloor production and over the distribution of enterprise resources so as to fulfill one of the original promises of the revolution—"all factories to the workers!"[299] Until this could happen, however, most workers could only seek to distance themselves from official campaigns and slogans, while trying to expand shopfloor autonomy and attend to the needs of their families through the informal norms and social relations they continued to share and value.

Looking to the future, a preliminary examination of trends in post-Soviet industrial relations suggests that these *informal* understandings may very well represent the most powerful legacy of the USSR.[300] While there are variations across firms and sectors in the degree to which formal contractual agreements are respected and wage regulations are enforced, this diversity is constrained by the continued strength of norms emphasizing particularistic collective solidarities, egalitarianism in material conditions, and expectations of mutual assistance and enterprise paternalism. As in the Soviet era, these informal norms are reflected in the tendency to ignore formal wage regulations that accentuate differences in individual abilities and earnings in favor of standardized wages based on working hours and a fixed package of nonwage benefits. It is also apparent in the bypassing of formal rules and contractual regulation of labor relations in favor of diffuse reciprocal relations involving customary partners or familiar individuals recruited through preexisting social networks and rewarded for their trust rather than occupational competence.[301] In fact, many work collectives supported the process of "insider privatization" mainly because they viewed this as a means of establishing the independence of their enterprises so that they might preserve existing understandings within the enterprise and negotiate greater autonomy on the shopfloor.[302] Moreover, although post-Soviet law no longer mandated enterprise-provided welfare benefits (with local governments partially assuming this responsibility in theory), expectations of enterprise paternalism have remained deeply ingrained, and labor cooperation has frequently depended on whether managers are able to attend to the most basic needs and welfare requirements of workers and their families.[303] These observations collectively suggest that both workers and managers in contemporary Russian firms continue to view formal contracts, rules, and regulations with some suspicion and to place their trust in the more meaningful and predictable social relations that crystallized in the informal realms of Soviet labor relations.

This characterization of the likely orientations of the post-Soviet work force is also supported by surveys of Russian citizens' attitudes toward post-Soviet reforms. Although some surveys conducted immediately after the breakup of the USSR appeared to suggest mass support for market reforms and democratization,[304] this proved to be mainly an expression of lingering hostility toward the old regime and did not correspond to *specific* attitudes and expectations of Russians in relation to employment and welfare. For example, although most citizens have expressed support for "democracy," they have tended to identify the term more consistently with fairness and the satisfaction of material needs than with competitive elections or freedom to criticize the government.[305] A more recent study comparing attitudes of elites and masses shows that mass attitudes generally reflect an "overall socialist orientation," with a high level of support for state-owned industry and economic autarky, along with growing ambivalence toward liberal democracy and rising alienation from the political system "as a result of the asymmetrical structure of economic opportunity."[306] This finding is supported by a number of other studies that have also reported high levels of support among the Russian masses for social equality and standardized guarantees of welfare and employment, with correspondingly low opinions of private business and of wealthy segments of the population.[307] In the latest draft of a new Russian labor code, unions of all stripes—whatever their other differences—consistently demanded, and received, a clause guaranteeing a minimum wage pegged to the official subsistence level for all employment contracts. If nothing else, these findings at least render plausible the assumption made here that rising cynicism toward official state socialism coexisted with values and attitudes that favored collective survival and distributive justice over individualism and achievement-related differentiation.

This appraisal of values and attitudes in Soviet and Russian society, albeit tentative, might have enormous significance for the long-term prospects of post-Soviet reforms. In opting for what most closely resembles a modernist institution-building strategy, liberal reformers may well have underestimated the strength and significance of long-standing norms and practices that survived within Soviet institutions and ultimately eroded their effectiveness. Even if liberal reformers do manage to consolidate market reforms, it is not clear that they would have any more success than Bolshevik institution-builders did in gaining the commitment of the Russian work force. If post-Soviet institution-builders wish to do better than their Soviet predecessors in securing the commitment of their subordinates, they will have to do more than simply transplant institutional models that appear to have been effective elsewhere; they will have to be creative in modifying official ideologies and organizational practices so that these might cohere with those familiar norms and practices that have pervaded Russian communities of work for a very long time.[308]

Chapter 5

Comparisons and Implications

Those natures which, when they meet, quickly lay hold on and mutually affect one another, we call affined. This affinity is sufficiently striking in the case of alkalis and acids which, though they are mutually antithetical, and perhaps precisely because they are so, most decidedly seek and embrace one another, modify one another, and together form a new substance.

— The Captain (in Johann von Goethe, *Elective Affinities*)

The questions addressed in this book may be framed in terms of how the kind of affinity described by Goethe's character might evolve when it comes to the adoption of institutional models across different historical contexts and cultural milieus. As the studies of late-industrializing Japan and Russia suggest, models of management borrowed from the West and legacies inherited from past communities of work did not automatically "seek and embrace one another, modify one another, and together form a new substance." To the extent that a distinctive, stable hybrid formation eventually emerged in postwar Japan, this was the result of the convergence of a great many historical circumstances that included social conflicts, political accommodations, and conscious choices about how to address inherited legacies in the course of adapting borrowed models. Elsewhere, what we find are not elective affinities but tensions between formal institutional practices influenced by borrowed institutional models, ideologies stressing collectivist themes, and informal norms and expectations on the shopfloor shaped by past communities of work. This concluding chapter briefly reviews the case studies with an eye to highlighting the key historical comparisons from which the argument in this book has emerged.

Japan and Russia were both NWLIs in which institution-builders encountered a number of similar challenges and opportunities; but postwar Japanese managerial elites, attempting to recover from defeat, economic chaos, social dislocation, and moral ambivalence following a devastating war, were eventually able to generate a much higher level of managerial authority than their counterparts in prewar Japan or Soviet

Russia. Certainly, there are a variety of reasons why worker commitment in postwar Japan rose so quickly and why post-Stalin Soviet enterprises had such a difficult time maintaining discipline, motivation, and productivity. Endless volumes have been written on Japanese culture and Soviet totalitarianism, and on the merits of export-oriented capitalism and the inefficiencies of a socialist command economy. However, an equally important, but often ignored, part of the story involves the more immediate contexts of everyday life and work, and it is these immediate contexts that this book has sought to problematize and systematically explore. Hence, the partial explanation for variations in worker commitment across late-industrializing Japan and Soviet Russia focuses on the peculiarities of the interaction between legacies inherited from preexisting communities of work and institutional models adapted from referent societies, and on how these peculiarities are manifested in formal and informal aspects of work and authority in large-scale industrial enterprises.

Without ignoring the existence of regional variations and distinctive local traditions, it is possible and reasonable to compare stylized versions of preindustrial communities in Japan and Russia. The discussions in the first sections of chapters 3 and 4 (sections 3.1 and 4.1) reveal that both the Japanese *mura* and the Russian *mir* were corporate entities that distinguished between insiders and outsiders and had a strong sense of collective identity rooted in the concrete mechanisms of coordination and dense networks of mutual assistance in agricultural work. Both the *mura* and the *mir* were to a large extent traditional status societies with wealthier households wielding more power; both also had well developed traditions of mutual aid to ensure the subsistence of member households; and both emphasized certain standard rights and obligations to signify common membership and shared identity. However, members of the Japanese *mura* typically attached a higher value to harmonious social relations, reinforced by practices designed to diffuse tensions and reinforce a system of mutual obligations related to rank and status; at the same time, the *mura* was characterized by steeper hierarchies and higher levels of stratification, both of which were largely tolerated on the condition that those with higher status and authority fulfilled their obligations to treat those less fortunate with benevolence. The Russian peasant commune, by contrast, was less explicit in its valuation of harmony, less inclined to allow high levels of stratification and more reliant on redistributive norms and practices rather than paternalistic benevolence.

These comparisons are *not* invoked to suggest, as many cultural theories do, that distinctive features of preindustrial culture or social structure paved the way for Japan's success and Soviet Russia's failure. But the similarities and the differences are consequential for the purposes of understanding the responses of workers to certain features of industrial management in late-industrializing Japan and Russia. In prewar Japan and Soviet Russia, economic elites and factory managers became progressively drawn to Taylorism and related aspects of scientific management in the United States. They enthusiastically instituted time-and-motion analysis, new job classifications, and sharply differentiated reward structures to disproportionately reward productive workers and penalize unproductive ones. In doing so, however, they paid little attention to the congruence between borrowed management practices and the dominant symbols and ideals being stressed to inspire cooperation and productivity among newly recruited industrial workers. While the normative orientations the latter brought with them from past communities of work may have enabled many workers to partly identify with official ideology, these same orientations also made them stubbornly resistant to many of the officially sanctioned management practices they encountered on the shopfloor.

In prewar Japan, this tension was in evidence since the 1880s but became most clear during the 1920s and 1930s. During this time, managerial elites touted the idea of the family firm to inspire obedience and loyalty among workers while simultaneously introducing management practices reflecting Taylorist methods of control, remuneration, and work organization. While the ideal of the family may not have captured the realities of the diverse large-scale enterprise, the more diffuse notions of community, collective loyalty, and benevolent paternalism did initially resonate with much of the newly mobilized work force, as even leaders of leftist trade unions pointed out; however, the growing influence of scientific management brought with it an expansion of managerial centralization, a more minutely differentiated system of job classifications, individualized responsibilities, and output-based wages for most production workers. Although a narrow stratum of prized employees, most of them in white-collar positions, did appear to gain membership in the "family firm" through offers of greater employment security and seniority-based wages, this only served to accentuate the absence of "benevolent" treatment and common membership among most blue-collar workers. This juxtaposition of the family firm ideal and Taylorism-inspired management practices represented a traditionalist institution-building strategy insofar as traditional ideals were relied upon to preserve industrial harmony while workers readily adopted newly borrowed practices. However, workers' responses at various points—ranging from petitions and work stoppages to rising rates of turnover and participation in independent unions—suggest that this strategy ultimately failed to produce a committed industrial work force (see fig. 9).

In post-1917 Russia, such ideals as workers' control and equality of labor and pay, whatever meanings leading Bolsheviks may have attached to these terms, did resonate with familiar notions of collective labor and distributive justice embedded in past communities of work in rural and urban Russia. The Bolsheviks' public postures and initial policies even seemed to confirm the impression that the workers' revolution, at a minimum, would bring an end to capitalist speedups, sharply differentiated wage scales, and excessive penalties for minor violations of labor discipline. However, the Bolsheviks' significantly more ambitious project of creating a new industrial work culture and catching up to the West was accompanied by a growing fixation with American efficiency, especially with Taylorism and Fordism. Although there were different formulas available for reconciling the imperatives of industrialization and building revolutionary consciousness, Stalin's triumph by the late 1920s led to the juxtaposition of revolutionary campaigns and exhortations alongside a set of concrete management practices that essentially expanded upon efficiency-oriented Taylorist production techniques. This attempt at producing a synthetic "revolutionary modernity," however, tended to pay scant attention to what precisely made the experience of work in a socialist factory revolutionary beyond the fact that it was owned by the state and part of a command economy. Despite the revolutionary rhetoric accompanying the campaigns for socialist competition, on the shopfloor, workers found themselves operating as individual units of production, facing separate responsibilities and productivity norms, and earning incomes according to sharply differentiated wage scales that disproportionately rewarded a narrow stratum of norm-busters. While the threat of being branded a class enemy kept extreme unrest in check, workers continued to resist what they perceived to be new variants of capitalist speedups by frequently switching jobs, seeking out firms where managers informally assigned collective responsibility for tasks and earnings, and forming collusive understandings and networks to bypass formal regulations concerning tasks, norms, and wages (see fig. 11).

Following World War II, the human relations movement in the United States prompted elites in both countries to reconsider their approaches to industrial management on the basis of the assumption that a materially secure and satisfied worker would be a more productive worker. In both countries, this assumption was viewed as consistent with the Taylorist model and was interpreted to mean that greater employment security, generous welfare benefits, steady improvements in living standards, and even some measure of egalitarianism within and across job categories could improve the performance of this model. Moreover, just as Japanese firms emphasized the affinities between aspects of human relations and discourses emphasizing a distinctively Japanese collectivist ethos, Soviet elites sought to relate human aspects of production to distinctive collectivist ideals associated with revolutionary socialism. Thus, despite the differences between the economic and political systems in which they operated, Japanese firms and Soviet enterprises in the 1960s appeared to be going through similar kinds of transformations driven in part by the influence of new management research coming out of the West.

In post-Stalin Russia, however, the new discourses and employment terms did not signify a shift in institution-building strategy, but rather the adoption of a "neotraditional" variant. Revolutionary rhetoric remained ubiquitous and the modernist impulse to assimilate the latest management techniques from abroad remained strong; but, within the context of Soviet history, the justification of work and authority now took place in terms of references to the past, with inherited ideals and management precepts assumed to constitute an invariable model of "socialist labor." The language of "human relations" was incorporated into Soviet management, but only to the extent that improvements in working conditions were essentially seen as a lever to improve and standardize employee performance within the existing system of production. While the regime no longer relied on overt coercion, informal mechanisms (for example, bypassing official wage regulations to minimize performance-related income differentials) were counted upon to stave off excessive turnover and labor unrest. While the median living standard did improve, special categories of workers remained disproportionately privileged in terms of access to goods and services, and the official system of job classifications, individualized assignments, and sharply differentiated wage scales related to norm-fulfillment in place, with a few reforms in operating procedures confined to particular sectors or factories. Under these conditions, although there were few overt challenges to the regime, commitment to official management principles and goals only dropped further as a result of the widely acknowledged discrepancies between the formal and informal realms of production. Thus, not surprisingly, Gorbachev's efforts to increase performance-related differentials only gave way to more openly hostile reactions from workers, culminating in the miners' strikes of 1989 and 1991 (see fig. 12).

In postwar Japan, by contrast, human relations was taken much more seriously, and the lack of specificity in the original American understanding of the concept allowed for more creative efforts to rethink work organization and employment practices. While the pressure to initiate these efforts came largely from the growing and increasingly militant labor movement in the late 1940s, the syncretist formula that emerged after the mid-1950s included a significant modification of borrowed management practices so that these might meaningfully represent a peculiarly Japanese conception of human relations. The blurring of job boundaries and diffusion of skills, the elevation of collective responsibility and small-group technologies, along with enterprise unionism, lifetime employment security, and seniority-based wage increases (for at least a large portion of the wage package) collectively represented a fundamental shift in official management doctrine, contributing to greater congruence between ideology and practice and between the formal and informal aspects of the firm. While new challenges would appear in Japanese industrial relations, the 1950s through the 1970s were a period of significantly greater worker commitment and managerial authority than found in the prewar era (see fig. 10).

The success of postwar Japanese managerial elites in raising worker commitment and sustaining managerial authority does not suggest that the Japanese firm represents a model for management in other NWLIs; in fact, features of the Japanese firm are no more likely to be successfully emulated than features of Western firms where the norms inherited from past communities of work differ from those evident in the course of Japanese industrialization. At the same time, as NWLIs continue to confront the problems of how to balance intensifying external influences with their historical traditions and distinctive cultural inheritances, there may be an important lesson to be drawn from the comparison of the nature and effects of institution-building approaches pursued at different points in late-industrializing Japan and Russia: where strategies blindly emulating institutional models are put into practice, unless preexisting norms are similar to those in societies where the models originated, it is extremely difficult to sustain the commitment of subordinates, and even superficial forms of cooperation may require the application of costly measures. This outcome was avoided by managerial elites in postwar Japan for over three decades in no small measure because of key choices made by managerial elites on how to rescue a positive and flexible version of their past to support innovative modifications in employment practices and work organization initially influenced by foreign management doctrines.

Figure 13 summarizes the key elements of the diachronic and synchronic comparisons that support the tentative hypothesis advanced in this book concerning the merits of syncretism. The comparisons suggest that, under the conditions prevalent in NWLIs, a proactive syncretist approach is likely to offer the path of least resistance since it enables institution-builders to selectively draw upon familiar ideals and portable templates in making the design and purpose of new modern institutions intelligible and worthy of commitment in the eyes of subordinates recruited from a particular cultural milieu. While modernist and revolutionary institution-builders may succeed in establishing highly productive institutions under particular circumstances, in the long term, all other things being equal, it is the sort of syncretist approach evident in postwar Japan that offers the most viable approach to establishing institutions that are simultaneously able to achieve modern ends and provide their members with a familiar, secure, and meaningful environment in which to carry out their tasks.

Although the very definition of *syncretism* suggests that the content of such an approach will vary across contexts, the strategy itself is replicable across historical contexts and distinguishable from the other ideal-typical approaches in light of their orientations toward inherited legacies and borrowed institutional models. Where cases can be operationalized in terms of the problematique of institution-building articulated above, alternative strategies approximating the various ideal-typical approaches will be identifiable in the competing suggestions offered by institution-builders, and syncretist approaches, the hypothesis suggests, will generally lead to higher levels of authority. If, however, strategies that approximate the modernist or revolutionary ideal-types also produce this outcome regularly, or if syncretist strategies are accompanied by a decline in the authority of institutional elites, there will be reason to qualify or reconsider the hypothesis and perhaps even revisit the interpretations of the cases examined in this book. Thus, the comparative-historical study does point to a hypothesis that is, in principle, both generalizable and falsifiable, although care will have to be taken in each new case when identifying the appropriate inherited legacies and institutional models, as well as in distinguishing alternative institution-building strategies and their outcomes.

If this hypothesis is at all plausible in view of currently available evidence, then it will have extremely important implications for the analysis of institutions in non-Western societies continuing to cope with the dilem-

period: (operative model):	1910s-1940 (U.S. scientific management)	1950s-1980 (human relations concepts added)
JAPAN Legacy of past: *mura* • collective identity tied to concrete work practices of village households • subsistence ethic seen in norms of mutual aid, 'right to benevolence' • steeper hierarchy, seen in concentrated landholding & decision-making power • harmony highly valued	***traditionalist*** *(low managerial authority)* • Ideology: warm 'family firm' (nested in *Kokutai*) • Taylorist work organization • no freedom of association • output-based wages/piecerates • minimal cross-strata contact • selective & exclusionary use of job/wage guarantees	***syncretist*** *(high managerial authority)* • Ideology: company 'human relations' (nested in *Nihonjinron*) • job redesign, partial de-Taylorization • enterprise unions, ritualized bargaining • lifetime employment & seniority wages • white/blue-collar boundary less sharp • inclusive definition of 'regular' worker (in employment terms, social norms)
RUSSIA Legacy of past: *mir, artel* • collective identity tied to concrete work practices of commune households • subsistence ethic seen in norms of mutual aid, 'right to work' on land • more egalitarian, seen in repartitioned land strips & assembly participation • less concern for harmony	***revolutionary modernity*** *(lost managerial authority)* • Ideology: ethic of 'socialist labor' (nested in 'new Soviet man') • hyper-Taylorist work organization • unions as 'transmission belts' • steep 'one-man management' • socialist competition of workers • steeply differentiated piecerates, special rewards to 'labor heroes'	***neotraditionalism*** *(quiescence without authority)* • Ideology: 'human factor' added as an element of 'developed socialism' • no major change in work organization • unions remain 'transmission belts' • more collegial factory administration • job & welfare rights (1971 labor code) • reduced base-wage differentials, with informal leveling of output-based wage

Fig. 13. Summary of case studies and key comparisons

mas of catching up under the intensifying pressures of global economic competition. In fact, the historical comparisons suggest that the present debate over the consequences of globalization, however defined, speaks to quite familiar issues that institution-builders in NWLIs have been facing for more than a century. At a minimum, the hypothesis represents a useful and necessary foil against those who, as in the past, are trumpeting a new era of global homogenization characterized by the inexorable diffusion of supposedly universal ideas, practices, and institutional models across nations and regions. In a more constructive vein, it is hoped that the argument developed here can help spur new lines of thinking about the implications of the ongoing encounters between global forces and local sensibilities, especially from the standpoint of various categories of actors who remain involved in the quest for modernity while seeking to retain some sense of attachment to their distinctive inheritances.

Appendix A

Laying Bare the Foundations

Ontological and
Epistemological Considerations

It should be evident that the approach taken in this book, while focused on the study of institutions, is not clearly identifiable with any one of the prevailing research traditions or conventional methodological approaches in contemporary social science. In fact, the approach is consciously founded on an eclectic set of intermediate positions on familiar ontological, epistemological, and methodological issues that continue to be the subject of contentious disputes among contemporary social scientists.[1] These foundational assumptions may be captured in three related positions that are outlined here and defended elsewhere:[2] (a) a Weberian perspective on social reality that, on the one hand, prohibits the application of universal causal laws in the explanation of particular phenomena and, on the other hand, allows for an "explanatory understanding" of intersubjective aspects of social action without necessarily "recapturing" the experiences of the actors involved; (b) a loosely "structurationist" ontology that, in marked contrast to contemporary rational choice, cultural, and structural (historical institutionalist) approaches, deliberately refrains from asserting definitive epistemological first principles concerning the relative significance of agents vis-à-vis structures, or of the material aspects of social life vis-à-vis the ideal aspects; and (c) a middle-range comparative-historical strategy that steers not only between nomothetic and idiographic analysis but also between historical particularism and macrocausal comparative analysis while attempting to relate the discourses of country- or area-specialists to more general theoretical discourses.

A1. Intersubjectivity and Social Science:
A Weberian Perspective

To begin with, the approach in this book is consciously founded on an ideal-typical center between the philosophical positions adopted by committed positivists and skeptical relativists on the question of whether human beings are capable of discerning an objective social reality that exists apart from the subjective perceptions of this reality by other human beings. This center is identified with Max Weber's pragmatic, if sometimes ambivalent, understanding of the relationship between social reality and sociological categories. Weber frequently asserted that his research was not intended to support analytic laws or provide comprehensive causal explanations. In his famous essay, "'Objectivity' in Social Science and Social Policy," in addition to placing quotation marks around the word *objectivity,* Weber indicated that "ideal-type" constructions were intended not to aid in the application of universal causal laws to specific phenomena, but only to generate a more clear interpretation ("explanatory understanding") of an infinitely complex social reality through the "analytic accentuation" of aspects pertinent to the investigator's particular interests. Since social analysis, for Weber, ultimately rested on the meanings attached by individual actors to their experiences, interpretations of social action and resultant modes of organization were inherently incapable of being anything more than plausible hypotheses.[3]

At the same time, however, Weber was hardly prepared to surrender to the kind of subjectivist or relativist orientation evident among postwar hermeneuticians or contemporary postmodernists for whom any understanding of individual or local experience is limited to practical or evocative insights into immediate contexts.[4] For Weber, an explanatory understanding of meaningful social experiences suggested that it was possible to develop interpretations that were comparable across contexts without fully recapturing experiences from the point of view of the specific actors involved.[5] In fact, in his view of ideal-types, Weber, while acknowledging that sociological concepts could not possibly capture the complexity of actual historical reality, argued: "In all cases, rational or irrational, sociological analysis both abstracts from reality and at the same time helps us to understand it, in that it shows with what degree of approximation a concrete historical phenomenon can be subsumed under one or more of these concepts."[6] Thus, on the one hand, Weber was cautious about inferring comprehensive causal explanations from social patterns or regularities given that these regularities were understood by actors themselves on the basis of subjective interpretation, but on the other hand, he assumed that there were realms of intersubjectivity where investigators could gain insight into the meanings attached by actors to their experiences by using precise theoretical constructs across one or more historical contexts.

This pragmatic ambivalence on the issue of objectivity-subjectivity in social reality reflects a reasonable basis for negotiating the gulf that separates contemporary positivists (whether empiricists or formal theorists) from various kinds of hermeneuticians or postmodernists. Taking the lead from this position, the approach in this book proceeds from the assumption that, while the subjectivism of human experiences makes it difficult to derive objective universal laws concerning social reality, this reality is sufficiently *intersubjective* to permit interpretive understandings of at least certain aspects of the regularities found across social contexts by comparison to stylized constructs (such as ideal-types); that is, social reality is characterized by both complexity and regularity, leaving open the possibility of modest partial explanations or deep interpretations based on observable patterns.

This understanding is also related to a flexible understanding of the relationships between facts, values, and social knowledge. In contrast to the relativist assumption that all claims to knowledge are either influenced by normative bias or intended to reproduce power relations, here facts and values are assumed to be distinguishable *in principle* for the self-conscious investigator although this may be difficult to ensure in practice. Even adherence to particular replicable methods or a commitment to internal logical consistency does not guarantee that the fact-value distinction will be maintained, but the social sciences as a whole stand to benefit from a conscious effort on the part of scholars to be aware and open about which aspects of an investigation aim to produce a causal explanation or interpretive understanding and which are intended as normative prescriptions or ideology-critique. In this process, empirical reality-tests (the evaluation of whether observed phenomena support general conditional statements offered by social scientists), while neither consistently replicable nor a sufficient basis for refuting a theory, can serve an important function in the process of persuading audiences as to the merits of a particular hypothesis, interpretation, or critique.[7] Even in the absence of uniform methods for evaluating research products and competing research traditions, it is possible to translate hypotheses or interpretations to compare them to each other and to empirical observational statements, so as to render a proposition more—or less—plausible in the eyes of a given audience.[8]

These positions are related to one other assumption about the nature of social knowledge: that the entire process of social research is an ongoing *collective* search for whatever common patterns and intersubjective meanings might be present within an infinitely complex, socially constructed reality consisting of many subjectively experienced social phenomena. This notion of a "collective" search suggests that neither individual scholars nor narrowly defined communities organized around particular research traditions are likely to produce anything accepted as "progress" for the social sciences as a whole. In fact, whether or not Kuhn's analysis of scientific paradigms is correct or applicable to the social sciences,[9] the very *idea* of paradigms has raised the stakes of the competition between research traditions, enhancing the status of those contributing to the advancement of one research tradition in the estimation of others also working in that tradition, but marginalizing (even penalizing) eclectic research agendas not founded on the system of concepts, assumptions, methods, or evaluative standards provided by one of the established research traditions.[10] Whatever progress is possible in the social sciences will only be understood as such by the community of social scientists as a whole if they can recognize and appreciate the limited, modest improvements in the analytic and practical utility of concepts and frameworks *across* paradigms and research traditions.[11]

In this spirit, the overarching conceptual framework developed and applied in this book is consciously intended to be eclectic and integrative. It does not offer a grand, unified synthesis, but it does offer a loose framework for capturing the relationships between concepts and assumptions typically identified with competing and distinct research traditions (as evident in the articulation of the problematique). Such a framework will not lead to the uncovering of universal causal laws, but it does enable the investigator to pursue more eclectic combinations of assumptions, concepts, methods, and tools to generate original, plausible "explanatory understandings" of social phenomena whether in the form of partial explanations, novel interpretations, or practical lessons for coping with concrete social problems.[12]

A2. A "Structurationist" View of Agency, Structure, and Culture

The vigorous exchanges among proponents of rational choice, cultural, and structural (or historical institutionalist) approaches, although frequently cast in methodological and substantive terms, derive from differences over a wide range of philosophical issues. In the study of institutions, these differences become clear in the sharply different approaches evident in the various "new institutionalisms" pervading the social sciences; con-

temporary rational choice theorists (new economic institutionalists), culturalists (new sociological institutionalists), and structuralists (new historical institutionalists) all make highly specific and mutually exclusive foundational assumptions about the nature and motivations of individual
actors and the epistemological significance of the collective rules, procedures, norms, and rituals that constitute institutions. Rational choice theorists tend to view institutions as the contexts within which knowledgeable, rational actors make informed decisions on the basis of clearly
ordered preferences and expectations, and they view institutional rules
and norms as the products of bargains struck by self-conscious, instrumental actors operating strategically on the basis of some explicit means-
ends calculus.[13] Contemporary historical institutionalists, by contrast,
tend to emphasize the constraints represented by institutionalized rules
and procedures on actors; they highlight the relevance of the kinds of
resources, opportunities, and status particular categories of actors may
have access to by virtue of their *position* vis-à-vis each other within a given
institutional context.[14] Culturalists, or sociological institutionalists, similarly emphasize the common effects of "structural" factors on the routine
interactions and shared attitudes that characterize groups of actors, but
the structures they most commonly posit tend to be ideal rather than material, highlighting the implications of symbols, rituals, and norms for meaningful or emotionally satisfying relationships that individuals come to
share as members of some collectivity.[15] These are not inconsequential differences, for they suggest that the same set of empirical observations can
be interpreted through sharply distinct languages or lenses: one emphasizing agency, usually with a particular focus on material interests; one
emphasizing the impact of material structures on the preferences of agents
and their opportunities and repertoires for action; and a third focusing on
the ideal characteristics, normative or symbolic, of collective life as these
are transmitted and reproduced in recognizably patterned interactions
among individuals.[16]

Of course, there are times when qualified versions of each of the three
approaches seem quite capable of reaching out to, or perhaps subsuming,
their competitors. Indeed, proponents of each perspective have gestured
toward frameworks capable of relating the microlevel analysis of action to
large-scale historical processes and local cultural understandings.[17] These
seemingly reasonable gestures, however, are frequently little more than
rhetorical statements made for the purpose of emphasizing the breadth
and flexibility of a particular research tradition vis-à-vis its competitors. In

the final analysis, most social scientists are not willing to part with the epistemological primacy they explicitly or implicitly assign to agency, structure, or culture. Thus, even the most reasonable formulation of a rationalist approach to institutions observes that the study of institutions must, in the final analysis, be "grounded in strategic rationality," with the epistemological significance of institutional conventions, norms, and rules limited to the information these transmit to individuals about the likelihood of other actors' responses to their choices.[18] Similarly, even reasonable formulations of the structuralist (historical institutionalist) approach ultimately insists on the centrality of "rules and practices," and claims "a privileged, though not exclusive, ability to bind structure and agency to contingency."[19] And while some culturalists are willing to nominally consider agency and structure to be "same-level phenomena," they still regard social science as essentially a "cultural science," treating culture as an intrinsically collective phenomenon that is transmitted over generations and irreducible to individual dispositions.[20] Thus, despite all the rhetoric about integration and flexibility, it is unclear as to how much of a shift actually takes place in the epistemological principles through which the competing research traditions define and distinguish themselves. Even where sophisticated versions of all three approaches may sometimes converge in their specific accounts of particular historical processes, each of the approaches for the most part operates on the basis of fixed, unverifiable first principles about the relative causal significance of agency and structure, and of material and ideal dimensions of social life.

There are, of course, particular situations or questions where such assumptions can be shown to be reasonable or necessary in light of the manner in which particular questions are posed. Questions that focus on the social sources of the preferences of different categories of actors inherently assume that preference-formation has prior causes that can be found in material and ideal structures; similarly, questions that focus on how institutions or cultural norms emerge in the first place may reasonably privilege the causal significance of strategic interactions among instrumental actors. The problem is that the epistemological postulates found to be illuminating in the analysis of certain kinds of questions are all too often thought to hold in the case of all other types of social analysis. To avoid this problem, it is necessary to adopt an ontology that is characterized by genuine flexibility in terms of the range of theoretical problems and interpretations it enables.

Thus, this book very consciously operates on the basis of an eclectic set of assumptions that do not logically point to any particular epistemological first principles in relation to conceptions of agency, structure, and culture. Such a position is anticipated in Weber's interpretive sociology and is more explicitly laid out in contemporary "structurationist" social theory. Some contemporary methodological individualists have attempted to claim the legacy of Weber on the basis of his statement: "Collectivities must be treated as solely the resultants and modes of organization of the particular acts of individual persons, since these alone can be treated as agents in a course of subjectively understandable action."[21] But this statement, when considered in conjunction with Weber's other statements, his philosophy of science, and his actual comparative studies, points to an approach quite distinct from most contemporary expressions of methodological individualism (such as rational choice analysis). In fact, Weber's statement that "subjectively understandable action" must be understood at the individual level actually reflects a commonsense *ontological* position that would not be challenged by culturalists or historical institutionalists since it does not universally accord *causally* significant importance to rational individual actors at the expense of the common influences they may face as members of a category in a given historical context. This is highly significant since it places serious limits on the epistemological function and causal force of the concept of rationality in comparative studies.

Weber not only views the idea of a "conceptually pure type of rational action" as a heuristic methodological device at best, but he explicitly notes the prevalence of *reflexive* behavior in social life: "in the great majority of cases actual action goes on in a state of inarticulate half-consciousness or actual unconsciousness of its subjective meaning. . . . In most cases his action is governed by impulse or habit."[22] More to the point, Weber is insistent that "exploratory understanding" of social phenomena requires considering how the *context of meanings* lend significance to social action; once the issue becomes one of the meanings actions have for actors, as Eckstein notes, "it is a small step to 'collective consciousness', or to culture, in the minimal sense of *shared meanings,* as a condition of social life or indeed just mutually intelligible social behavior."[23] This suggests that groups of individuals that are identified with different status groups, classes, or value systems would act on the basis of different constellations of material and ideal interests. As Weber himself makes clear: "It is . . . possible for large numbers, though dispersed, to be influenced simultaneously or successively by a source of influence operating similarly on all the individuals."[24] And if the flexible character of Weber's ontology is not evident in his explicit foundational statements, his approach in *The Protes-*

tant Ethic and his broader comparative studies of the relationship between different religious ethics and this-worldly economic activities both suggest that differences in patterns of social action (for example, particular modes of economic organization) can be systematically related to differences across *categories* of individual actors, whether defined in terms of class or cultural orientations.[25] These considerations suggest that Weber's approach, far from being a precursor of rational choice analysis as some have claimed, was based on a highly complex view of how the conscious and reflexive behavior of agents, as identified with particular classes or status groups, relate to material and ideal structures across distinct historical contexts.[26]

Such a view is more explicitly articulated in the approaches of a number of contemporary social theorists—such as Giddens, Bourdieu, Sewell, and others—whose approach may be described as structurationist.[27] What distinguishes this category from even the most sophisticated versions of rationalist, culturalist, and structuralist approaches is the emphasis on an ontology that takes as its starting point the *dialectical* relationships among agency and structure, on the one hand, and the *mutually constitutive* relationship between material and ideal dimensions of social life, on the other. Such an ontology explicitly and deliberately eschews any particular set of epistemological first principles, allowing substantive problems and contexts to dictate the possible causal significance of intentional or reflexive action and the material and ideal structures by which this action may be constrained and rendered meaningful.[28] Structurationist approaches recognize that structures are made, reproduced, and transformed through both conscious and reflexive individual action, the former reflecting rational action motivated by both material and ideal interests, and the latter conditioned over time through shared material environments or shared systems of meaning. Moreover, they emphasize that the scope of action for individuals varies with the material and symbolic resources at their disposal.[29] All of these approaches, as in the case of the institutionalist framework outlined in chapter 1 above (see fig. 1), incorporate some set of concepts that can represent plausible mechanisms through which to consider the interplay of agency and material and ideal structures.[30]

The institutionalist ontology adopted in chapter 1 is founded on structurationist principles insofar as it rejects the a priori reification of structures, but leaves open their epistemological significance vis-à-vis the individuals and actions that generate, maintain, or transform them. When juxtaposed, such dichotomous concepts as role/identity, organization/ideology, and formal/informal aspects of institutional life (fig. 1) combine to represent not only the duality of the material and ideal dimensions of individual interest and collective life, but also the manner in which contending categories of actors, under the influence of different sets of material and ideal structures, make the most out of the material and symbolic resources at their disposal whether to advance their conscious interests or enact reflexively formed dispositions. How and why some agents choose to conform to, or reproduce, while others choose to transform, an existing pattern of interactions, rules, norms, and identities in a given institution is an object of empirical investigation that cannot be answered by fiat as proponents of the rationalist, culturalist, and structuralist research traditions are wont to do. Ideal structures may, in some cases, be reducible to material ones, and both material and ideal structures are generally ontologically reducible to individual social actions; but, unless a question is framed in such a way that it inherently assumes adopting certain epistemological first principles, it makes sense to adopt a foundational posture that allows for the widest range of interpretations concerning the relationships between agents and the material and ideal structures that enmesh them at any given time.

A3. Between Theory and Context: Negotiating the Nomothetic-Idiographic Divide

All social scientists face the challenge of negotiating the vast gulf that separates nomothetically oriented theoretical statements—whether in the form of axiomatic propositions or probabilistic inferences—from thickly descriptive idiographic statements about particular contexts. The organizational equivalent of the divide between the nomothetic and idiographic extremes for negotiating this gulf is evident in the divide separating the area studies and the general theoretical discourses of particular disciplines or research traditions.[31] Some scholars have recently launched different initiatives to bridge these divides by emphasizing the application of uniform methods and logics. One of these initiatives has come from empiricist quantitative researchers seeking to bring more rigor to qualitative and interpretive social analysis, and another has come from deductively oriented formal modelers (mostly rational choice theorists) who are eager to link their work to rich area-based field research. Neither approach, however, actually pays much attention to the diverse objectives of, and distinctive intellectual payoffs from, the wide-ranging forms of social analysis that lie *between* the nomothetic and idiographic poles.

In the first case, scholars such as Gary King and his collaborators have attempted to downplay the difference in levels of complexity between interpretive and statistical analysis in light of the infinitely greater level of complexity in the actual world. This enables them to contend that the quantitative-qualitative or nomothetic-idiographic dichotomies are not so sharp as to preclude uniform standards of evaluation, rules of inference, and norms of replication that statistical research and research in the natural sciences are generally based on.[32] Of course, to the extent that even the most thickly descriptive treatments of social phenomena must follow *some* procedure for selecting and arranging "facts" given the infinite complexity of social processes, there is something to be said for being self-conscious about the implications and limitations of that procedure. In the final analysis, however, this search for methodological uniformity and rigor is predicated on a narrowly empiricist view of science; as such, it neither offers any novel insights for qualitative researchers who share this empiricism (many of whom are conscious of such familiar problems as spurious inferences and selection bias) nor considers the distinctive challenges scholars face as they pursue different kinds of objectives at different stages of research along the continuum between the ideal-typical poles of nomothetic and idiographic analysis.[33]

The second strategy has even more serious intellectual and organizational implications for the social sciences. This approach is evident in the notion of "analytic narratives" or "rational choice narrativism" in political science and sociology.[34] The construction of analytic narratives is viewed by its proponents as representing a novel strategy for overcoming the nomothetic-idiographic divide as well as a new basis for relating the research products of area specialists to the theoretical core of nomothetic disciplines.[35] Such an approach is thought by its proponents to overcome some of the criticisms frequently launched at rational choice models,[36] by combining "thick" context-sensitive idiographic research with "thin" formal lines of (deductive) reasoning that can expose the "logic of the processes that generate the phenomena."[37] This approach, however, has its own limitations for one simple reason: although it ostensibly adopts the position that "the empirical content of the narrative is as important as the logical structure of the model,"[38] the narrative itself is considered to have little intrinsic value in and of itself in the process of identifying the core explanatory principles of the analysis. The main function of the narrative is to provide contextual information so that pre-given theoretical logics can be translated into historically specific explanations. While the contributors of "analytic narratives" may indeed care about their case materials and even rely on fieldwork to generate rich empirical data, the idiographic accounts have no *independent* bearing on the *logic* of the explanation, which is already contained in a deductively generated theoretical framework.[39] Ironically, this is not significantly different from the kind of relationship theorists and area specialists shared during the heyday of modernization theory: in both cases, the epistemological primacy of pre-given theoretical constructs is assured by a "negative heuristic" that protects the core postulates of the research program from alternative interpretations inferred directly from cases and comparisons.[40]

In lieu of hegemonic efforts to establish a uniform set of methodological principles or research strategies to bridge the nomothetic-idiographic divide, it is possible to adopt a view of social science in which formal reasoning, large-*n* statistical research, small-*n* comparative studies, case studies, and context-specific narratives all represent different strategies with different *kinds* of payoffs along the continuum between the ideal-typical nomothetic and the idiographic poles. Without going into a detailed consideration of the specific payoffs and limitations of each of these strategies,[41] it is possible to recognize that within a more inclusively defined community of social scientists, each offers distinctive intellectual gains accompanied by distinctive trade-offs. That is, the social sciences may be collectively characterized in terms of a division of labor not only across disciplines and subfields but across different research strategies, with formal models, large-*n* and small-*n* research, case studies, and interpretive narratives each playing a distinct role, each pursuing different objectives, and each able to capture different aspects of "truth" at different levels of generality.

Within this division of labor, the rich and varied tradition of comparative-historical analysis—identified with the works of Moore, Bendix, Tilly, Skocpol, and others[42]—occupies a fairly wide middle ground, in between formal models and quantitative analysis, on the one hand, and interpretations or thick descriptions, on the other. Despite important differences between nomothetically oriented and idiographically oriented comparativists (which are relevant for the purposes of distinguishing the particular kind of comparative-historical approach followed here), practitioners of comparative-historical approaches generally seek to find some

way to develop a rich but stylized interpretation of a few cases for the purposes of comparison to each other in light of particular theoretical questions and historical configurations. That is, their varying levels of theoretical ambition notwithstanding, comparative-historical approaches all
aspire to examine historical trends or patterns in two or more contexts
(synchronically or diachronically) in a sufficiently detailed manner so as to
provide a plausible historically specific explanation of an outcome in each
case, while also providing a sufficiently stylized account so as to permit
comparisons of theoretically significant data points across contexts. Such
approaches at least allow for *some* possibility for original explanatory logics that are at least partially mediated by the investigation and comparison
of particular historical processes to each other and to theoretical concepts
or ideal-typical constructs.[43]

Certain strands of comparative-historical analysis, most notably the
macrocausal approach identified with Skocpol and others who use what
Tilly has called "big-case comparisons," have been recently criticized for
their overreliance on Mill's canons of induction, for their lack of attention
to the causal mechanisms embedded in historical processes, and for their
willingness to conveniently overlook rival interpretations or multiple historical records.[44] While much of the criticism is well-deserved, this does
not reduce the intellectual significance of these works in terms of their ability to stimulate new questions, new directions of research, and new dia-
logues among area specialists and general theorists. At the same time,
however, there are alternative, more modest, comparative-historical
approaches that are less fixated on Mill's canons of induction and more
attentive to the problems of historiography, to the debates among area
specialists in a region, and to the rich complexities of their cases. These
approaches—evident in Geertz's study of Islam in Morocco and Indonesia, Bendix's study of nation-building processes, and Tilly's studies of state
formation among others—are somewhat further away from the nomothetic pole in that they view their cases, or sometimes even a single case, as
objects of investigation in their own right; at the same time, however, they
do value the insights to be gained from highlighting contrasts in patterns
across time- and space-bound contexts.[45]

As noted in chapter 1, the comparative-historical approach under-
taken here is identified as a middle-range variant, lying somewhere
between the historical particularism of these latter works and the macrocausal approach identified with Mill's methods. This approach is not
defined in terms of precise methodological procedures or injunctions.

Rather, it is defined primarily in terms of its epistemological orientation in relation to nomothetic and idiographic scholarly endeavors. Middle-range comparative history is understood here as an ideal-typical methodological center along the nomothetic-idiographic continuum. The resulting research product needs to be theoretically modest enough so as to avoid the charges leveled against Millean "big-case comparisons"; it also needs to be sufficiently attentive to the complexity of historical processes and the multiplicity of historical records so as to reduce the likelihood of selection bias in the identification of facts; at the same time, the narrative needs to be framed in terms of concepts and variables that are generalized enough so as to permit some modest inferences from the study of processes and configurations across comparable contexts.

In terms of practical implications, this does not point to the need to master several languages or engage in long-term fieldwork, but it does require a much deeper familiarity with, and sensitivity to, the wider contexts within which the configurations and outcomes of interest are being examined. Such familiarity and sensitivity may be acquired, for example, through a period of immersion in the countries being studied, through encounters with native scholars, through an in-depth engagement with the discourses and debates evident in the country-specific literature, and through substantial attention to the wider historical and social processes encompassing the particular phenomena that represent the substantive foci of comparison. Through such strategies middle-range comparative studies can comfortably occupy an ideal-typical center along the nomothetic-idiographic continuum. Such a center, however "eclectic" or "messy" it may be,[46] can play a powerful role in enabling greater communication, not only between area specialists and scholars pursuing nomothetic endeavors characteristic of their disciplines, but also among specialists studying different areas.

None of this is intended to suggest that middle-range comparative history, however explicitly it is defined, is in any way superior to statistical analysis, formal modeling, idiographic narratives, or other forms of small-*n* comparison. In fact, all of these approaches, as well as combinations of some of them (including "analytic narratives"), whatever their limitations, have distinctive comparative advantages and unique intellectual payoffs. A middle-range comparative approach, however, can play an invaluable role in filling some of the void between idiographic and nomothetic forms of research, providing a channel for steering between data-rich narratives and general inferences informed by canons of scientific research. This strategy is likely to foster a much more fruitful and civil intellectual exchange among different kinds of social scientists than efforts that seek to combine nomothetic and idiographic analysis in ways that de facto accord primacy to particular methodological tenets or theoretical axioms.

Taken collectively, this set of ontological and epistemological orientations represents a pragmatic foundation for the kind of theoretical problematique and comparative-historical study presented in this book. This perspective may be best identified with the critical realism or relational realism advocated recently by some historical sociologists. This perspective reflects a healthy skepticism with regard to assumptions about universal causal mechanisms or about the meaningfulness of probabilistic inferences across contexts; but, in contrast to the relativism implied at the idiographic extreme, this view allows for the possibility of historically specific explanations that can incorporate causal configurations or sequences that are, in principle, replicable in other contexts.[47] Such an approach cannot serve as a foundation for the testing of formal models or the generation of probabilistic inferences, nor does it rely on the presentation of original empirical discoveries or the construction of thick narratives. It can, however, serve as a basis for developing stylized interpretations and historically specific partial explanations of particular phenomena, while permitting modest hypotheses about the consequences of particular configurations of structures and actions where certain well-defined conditions are in evidence. In a social science marked by the proliferation of narrowly defined turfs and contentious methodological disputes, this type of approach represents an eclectic strategy for seeking distinctive insights that can complement, and mediate between, different forms of expert knowledge and theoretical interpretation generated by diverse subfields and contending research traditions.

Appendix B

Managing "Modernity" in Japanese and Russian Studies

Contending Perspectives on Continuity and Change

The debates over if, when, and how aspects of "modernity" may have emerged in the course of Japanese and Russian history revolve around substantively different problems. The postwar study of Japan has been largely dominated by debates over the sources and timing of Japan's rise as an economic power, with discussions of labor relations featuring prominently in these debates. The revisionist strand in Japanese studies adopts a critical view of Japanese political economy, focusing on social costs of Japan's achievements and the continued concentration of power in the hands of bureaucrats and business elites at the expense of workers. By contrast, Soviet/Russian studies was originally driven largely by debates over the origins and implications of a totalitarian communist regime, its command economy, and its impact on society, with studies of labor relations used mainly as a lens to capture flaws in the command economy or the peculiar character of social change under totalitarianism. And what counts as revisionist historiography in Russian/Soviet studies is marked by a rejection of the totalitarian school, and by substantially greater attention to the social bases of the regime, particularly to the increasing reciprocity and complexity in relations between the regime and working class.

These substantive differences, along with the additional problem of assessing the "revolutionary" character of Leninism, account for why the following discussions of Japanese and Russian studies are not identical in organization and structure. This should not, however, detract attention from the marked similarities in the axes around which some of the central debates in Japanese and Russian studies have consistently revolved. In fact, both sets of debates evince similar recurrent problems in interpreting the extent and direction of change. These problems are evident in contending perspectives on the extent to which the respective country's historical experiences are comparable to the previous experiences of established modern societies and the extent to which these experiences represent a continuous or punctuated process of transformation. The purpose of this essay is not to provide a comprehensive account of the varied perspectives on these issues, but to juxtapose selected representatives of contending views so as to reveal some essential similarities across the debates in Japanese and Russian studies and, in the process, implicitly suggest how the interpretations in chapters 3 and 4 reflect a common effort to strike a synthetic or intermediate posture in relation to stark oppositions in Japanese and Russian studies.

B1. Continuity, Change, and the Idea of Modernity in Japanese Studies

As a consequence of postwar Japan's remarkable success in becoming the first NWLI to join the ranks of the advanced industrial economies, the field of Japan studies has come to be marked by sharply contentious debates over the nature, origins, and significance of Japan's economic achievements. Discussions over the more recent economic recession notwithstanding, Western and Japanese scholars alike have been preoccupied with questions concerning the reasons behind Japan's economic success, the relationship between economic change and cultural factors, the role of political and economic institutions, key turning points in Japanese history, and, more broadly, the possibility of a Japanese variant of modernity that may or may not be replicable elsewhere. Three recurrent points of contention stand out as particularly divisive in the field of Japanese studies. The first, significant within a comparative context, revolves around the question of whether Japanese society has converged with other modern industrial societies and whether aspects of Japanese political and economic institutions may be replicated in other industrialized or late-industrializing economies. The second, significant within the context of the historiography of Japan, addresses the question of continuity and change since the time of the Meiji Restoration (1868) primarily within the context of debates over the origins of key features of modern Japanese society and political economy. The third, significant from a normative perspective, cuts across the first two axes and is evident in the quite different images suggested by those who glorify the achievements of modern Japan and those who emphasize the social costs of these achievements as evident in the persistence of socioeconomic inequalities, the suppression of individual autonomy within rigid hierarchies, and a subpar quality of life for the working masses. Without canvassing every possible permutation of the various positions on these issues, it is possible to identify several well-established intellectual traditions in the study of Japanese history, society, and political economy, each of which provides a framework for the articulation of competing arguments about particular aspects of industrial management and labor relations in prewar and postwar Japan.

Japan's "Positive" Past: Particularism, Universalism, or Alternative Model?

The majority of works on Japanese society and political economy, whether by Japanese or Western scholars, have tended to project a positive image of Japan as a successful late industrializer that made giant strides toward modernity over the course of the twentieth century (its current economic woes notwithstanding). In these positive treatments of Japanese history, Japanese firms are viewed as highly efficient, labor-management relations are viewed as relatively orderly and cooperative, and workers are viewed as highly committed and productive. But there exist sharp differences on the question of just how distinctive Japan's path to modernity has been when compared to the paths traveled by the advanced industrial societies of the West.

Particularists have tended to treat Japan's recent history as a distinctive route toward a uniquely Japanese variant of modernity. From their perspective, there is nothing fundamentally contradictory between the impressive material and technological gains achieved in postwar Japan and the persistence of a distinctive Japanese cultural ethos consisting of such resilient norms as group loyalty, harmony, and conformity. In fact, the latter, far from being viewed as remnants of the past, are frequently regarded as having paved the way for a uniquely harmonious and homogeneous modern Japanese society, organized around distinctive political and economic institutions that function in a peculiarly Japanese manner.[1] In particularist treatments, Japanese firms are viewed as uniquely cooperative and innovative, Japanese employers are thought to be highly far-sighted and benevolent, and Japanese workers are thought to be especially diligent, loyal, and responsive to paternalistic authority.[2] Thus, such features as lifetime employment and seniority-based wage systems are viewed as extensions or reconstructions of a traditional, distinctively Japanese tendency to seek long-term attachment to groups and value seniority over individual merit.[3] Enterprise unionism is seen as a distinctive variant of labor incorporation that allows for a more genuine and meaningful form of worker participation and labor-management cooperation.[4] Similarly, such aspects of work organization as job enlargement, the diffusion of skills, and quality-control circles are viewed as evidence that Japanese managers have sharply broken away from Western models of scientific management in favor of a distinctive system of work and authority founded on resilient aspects of traditional Japanese social organization.[5] And all of these features are collectively viewed as responsible for contributing to a uniquely harmonious system of industrial relations.

At the other end, universalists emphasize the similarities between Japanese and Western social history, and dismiss particularist narratives as myths invented by conservative cultural elites to minimize the growing pluralism, complexity, and heterogeneity of Japanese society.[6] Some universalist approaches, invoking concepts and assumptions found in modernization theory, treat Japanese industrialization and social change as part of a wider evolutionary process that has made Japan progressively more like other modern industrial societies;[7] others emphasize the long history of foreign borrowing and the steady diffusion of Western ideas and organizational models since the mid–nineteenth century.[8] Many universalists do not doubt that Japanese industrial relations have been marked by greater industrial peace, higher productivity, and higher worker commitment in comparison to the past; they do, however, challenge the notion that this trend is unique to Japan. For some, the Japanese system of industrial relations is viewed as having converged with patterns of industrial relations found in other modern systems of production as a result of growing levels of technology, more complex systems of work organization, the emergence of a more differentiated labor market, and more meritocratic systems of pay and promotion.[9] Thus, while industrial relations in postwar Japan may be viewed as more stable and cooperative than in prewar industry, many scholars note that Japanese industrial relations are neither more cooperative nor characterized by higher levels of worker commitment than one finds in other advanced industrial economies.[10] Others go even further, noting that many of the supposedly distinctive features of Japanese-style management and industrial relations are, in fact, a result of the continuing influence and deliberate adaptation of Western management models and discourses.[11] Even among those universalists who do view Japanese firms as more innovative, efficient, and cooperative than firms in the West, Japanese management is simply viewed as the first to have adapted to *new* technologies and *new* imperatives of lean production through techniques that are being adopted by managers in other post-industrial economies.[12] Despite their different degrees of enthusiasm for Japanese-style management, then, universalists all view the factors contributing to increased stability and productivity in postwar industrial relations as essentially the same factors that contribute to similar outcomes in other societies.

The relatively stark distinctions between the universalist and particularist accounts of postwar Japan's economic success frequently become blurred when it comes to discussions about whether aspects of Japan's strategy of economic development and the Japanese system of industrial relations deserve to be treated as constituent elements of an alternative model for societies and firms elsewhere. For proponents of a Japanese (or East Asian) developmental model, there is a profound ambivalence in comparing Japan's developmental experience to that of the West and that of other NWLIs: on the one hand, if Japan is to replace the West as an alternative model of modernity, then it is necessary to note differences between the functioning of political and economic institutions in Japan and the functioning of equivalent institutions in advanced industrial economies; on the other hand, if these institutions are to serve as a model, then it is necessary to emphasize that their distinguishing features are replicable in diverse historical and cultural contexts.[13]

Within the particular context of Japanese management and industrial relations, this ambivalence has been most famously articulated in Ronald Dore's argument that Japan's organization-oriented system enabled a more orderly, cooperative, and coordinated process of industrial production in the course of late industrialization than would be possible through the market-oriented models adopted in Britain and in other Western industrializers.[14] Although Dore himself would subsequently move away from this view in order to account for the role of cultural factors,[15] the notion of an alternative Japanese model has remained popular in contemporary discussions of shifts in industrial relations where Japanese management techniques are viewed as necessary for a more cooperative and productive system of labor-management relations, especially in developing or postsocialist countries.[16]

Critical Perspectives: The Limits and Price of "Success"

The generally positive images of Japanese political economy shared by the contending perspectives described above have been consistently challenged by a well-established tradition of revisionist historiography that dates back to the prewar era. This critical tradition emphasizes the social costs of both the Meiji-era modernization drive and postwar Japan's economic achievements, rejecting the notion that Japan's "success" makes it a reasonable model for other societies. Moreover, to the extent that aspects of Japanese society and history are considered to be unique, these aspects are thought to have prevented or delayed the emergence of a more equitable society and a higher quality of life among Japan's working masses. Thus, the revisionist tradition in Japanese historiography tends to blur the boundary between universalist and particularist accounts precisely because its critical thrust is simultaneously aimed at all of the scholarly traditions that take for granted the significance of postwar Japan's economic and social achievements.

In prewar Japan, the ambivalence on the question of universalism and particularism is most clearly evident in the perspective of prewar Marxists who critiqued capitalism but also attacked the persistence of feudal traditions that gave Japanese labor relations its distinctive character.[17] In the immediate postwar era, Marxists were joined by "progressive" liberal intellectuals who were frustrated that Occupation-era reforms ultimately failed to prevent the rise of conservative "forces of reaction" in the postwar era, as evident in the resurgence of conservative nationalist ideologies and the resurrection of corporate conglomerates with close ties to the government.[18] Although these critical discourses became somewhat marginalized in the period of high-growth economics and relative social stability during the 1960s and 1970s, they have since resurfaced in the form of arguments emphasizing the need to address the social costs of economic growth, the social frustrations produced by rigid hierarchies and excessive conformity, the hidden mechanisms through which political and economic elites collaborate in controlling and manipulating the working masses, and the continuing inequalities across class, gender, and sectoral lines.[19]

Within the particular context of studies of industrial relations and Japanese management, critical discourses in the 1950s were rooted in the prewar Marxist tradition, interpreting the defining features of postwar industry as simply extensions or refinements of feudal aspects of prewar Japanese labor relations.[20] However, in light of the decline of industrial conflict and the rise in industrial productivity, worker incomes, and new patterns of work organization in the 1960s and 1970s, critics of Japanese industrial relations have had to shift their focus to the more subtle mechanisms through which postwar Japanese managers have refined their control over the labor process. Thus, the emphasis is on the negative consequences of

Japanese-style management and the Japanese system of industrial relations for worker solidarity, shopfloor autonomy, the quality of working life, and the marginalization of the less privileged segments of the labor force (most notably, women, subcontractors, and nonpermanent employees).[21]

Somewhat more nuanced critical approaches acknowledge that Japanese managers did do something differently during the 1960s and 1970s that accounted for a high degree of managerial authority and worker commitment, but they point out that management practices during this period were partly a response to some of the demands of the militant labor movement of the 1940s and 1950s and partly an attempt to offer carrots to the work force in exchange for ceding whatever remained of its shopfloor autonomy to managers in such areas as pay determination and job assignments. The more serious problem is identified in the longer-term impact of this social compact, with worker productivity and commitment being accompanied by longer work hours, mental stress, exhaustion, and a poor quality of working life. Thus, to the extent that these problems may be viewed as mitigable, critics call attention to the social democratic countries of Europe where workers have supposedly made significant gains in terms of workplace participation, reduced working hours, more egalitarian wage structures, and more inclusive systems of labor incorporation.[22]

Continuities and Great Divides: From the Meiji Restoration to Postwar Japan

These contending narratives of Japanese political economy and industrial relations intersect with yet another set of issues having to do with the question of how to characterize the historical processes that accompanied the transformation of Japan since the mid–nineteenth century, with obvious implications for the question of just when and how key aspects of "modern" Japan originated. As with the issue of the distinctiveness of Japanese political economy and society, this issue too is marked by several distinct strands of interpretation, again evident across both positive and critical appraisals of the achievements of postwar Japan. In this context, some emphasize an essential continuity between the Meiji era (1868–1912) and the postwar period, downplaying the social unrest of the Taisho period (1912–26) and the later rise of Japanese militarism as interruptions or historical aberrations. This interpretation is popular among many who emphasize the uniqueness of Japanese culture and the distinctiveness of Japanese modernity,[23] but it is also found among those who see Japan as steadily converging with, or emulating, other modern societies since the time of the Meiji Restoration.[24] Within the context of industrial relations, this perspective on Japanese history points to the continuity between the prewar ideology of familialism and postwar Japanese human relations, viewing many of the supposedly innovative or distinctive aspects of the postwar firm—including lifetime employment and small-group-based work organization—as direct extensions of traditional forms of social organization such as master-apprentice relationships.[25] More universalist variants of this continuity perspective interpret the transformation of management practices either as the result of an evolutionary process driven by increasing levels of technology and differentiation or else as evidence of a continuous process of emulation and adaptation in response to Western models of management.[26]

Interestingly, many critical perspectives also embrace narratives stressing historical continuity, although they reinsert the period of rising militarism (World War II) into Japanese history. Viewing this period as an outgrowth of an earlier period of ultranationalism and etatism, they bemoan the persistence of these trends after the postwar reforms failed to prevent the resurrection of prewar corporate organization and the resurgence of a new tide of cultural nationalism.[27] This critical view of historical continuity is particularly prominent in many treatments that view labor-management relations in postwar firms as direct extensions of prewar feudal characteristics. It is also evident in the view of critics who interpret managerial innovations in the postwar era—most notably, quality-control circles and job and wage security in exchange for reduced worker autonomy and unionization—as merely new mechanisms within a consistent strategy intended to weaken organized labor and extend managerial control in a given institutional and technological environment.[28]

For many scholars, however, narratives emphasizing historical continuity—whether invoked to glorify or critique postwar Japanese society—fail to grasp the enormous changes that have occurred during the postwar era, notably following the period under the Allied Occupation that is viewed as a great divide in Japan's developmental path. In this view, prewar Japanese society and political economy may be subjected to critical treatment, but the reforms initiated by the Allied Occupation authorities and the defeat of the militarists are viewed as a crucial turning point; the impressive social and economic transformations of the postwar period, far from being a product of preexisting historical continuities or cultural traditions, became possible only after prewar institutions and ideologies were discredited, and only after Japan embraced market capitalism, liberal democracy, and a pacifist foreign posture.[29] This great-divide view is compatible with the idea of an emergent Japanese model and with some arguments emphasizing convergence between Japan and the West: among those who view the postwar Japanese political economy as an alternative model, the Occupation-era reforms checked the excessive centralization of the prewar state and allowed for new financial institutions and new forms of industrial coordination within a market environment;[30] and among those who downplay the distinctiveness of the postwar Japanese economy, the Occupation-era reforms remain significant in that they reduced the scope for government intervention, enabling capital and labor markets to function smoothly and driving private firms to become more productive and profitable.[31]

Within the context of industrial relations, the initial period of labor unrest immediately after World War II as well as the subsequent establishment of enterprise unionism are thought to represent a major turning point, paving the way for new, distinctively Japanese forms of enterprise unionism that did not produce a strong organized labor movement but did lead to an unprecedented level of worker participation that makes Japanese industrial relations distinctive.[32] Alternatively, from a universalist perspective, what is significant about the marked difference between prewar and postwar industrial relations is the manner in which enterprise unionism and small-group participation provided a functional equivalent for a new mode of labor incorporation and worker participation that are becoming increasingly popular in an era of post-Fordist lean production.[33]

More recent historiography, however, has cast much doubt on all of these contending perspectives on the question of transwar continuity and change. This historiography, some of it more critical than others, dismisses stark views of historical continuity or a great divide, noting the significance of both broad evolutionary trends as well as important turning points *within* the prewar and postwar periods. Whatever positive gains may have been made by managers and/or workers in the postwar era, these gains are viewed as having emerged gradually, in piecemeal fashion, through complex historical processes involving social and political conflict. For example, the end of the Taisho period (mid-1920s) is often emphasized in both positive and critical treatments of postwar Japan as the period during which key elements of postwar Japanese political economy and industrial relations first emerged albeit in rudimentary form.[34]

Others point to the 1930s and wartime Japan as the critical juncture when a fundamentally distinctive strategy and ideology of development, marked by a distinctive pattern of industrial organization and government-business cooperation, first began to take shape.[35]

Nuanced views on postwar history emphasize the significance of the 1950s when the high levels of labor militancy and industrial disputes began to decline and a long period of industrial peace commenced. More critical interpretations of this period focus on the piecemeal evolution of postwar management practices in response to the pressures brought to bear on management by a militant labor movement; it is this period of intense industrial unrest that is viewed as necessitating more proactive measures among management for coordinating industry, negotiating key social pacts, and standardizing many of the defining features of postwar political economy.[36] A more nuanced positive appraisal of postwar Japanese industrial relations emphasizes the gains made by workers since the 1960s, downplaying historical and cultural factors, but highlighting the steady improvements in employment and wage security, working conditions and hours, worker participation, and industrial peace.[37] Interestingly, while the two views differ on the significance of the gains made by workers in the postwar era, they do converge on several common points in their readings of postwar history: that industrial conflict in the late 1940s and early 1950s necessitated changes in management approaches, that specific adjustments made in the 1950s and 1960s did lead to a mutually beneficial social compact, and that postwar industrial relations subsequently entered a long period of relatively low industrial conflict and high worker commitment that lasted at least through the 1970s.

The characterization of prewar and postwar industrial relations offered in chapter 3 generally takes the nuanced perspectives noted above as the point of departure. The interpretation offered in that chapter discounts both highly effusive and sharply critical views of postwar industrial relations, recognizing the limits and costs of what postwar managers achieved but also appreciating the simultaneous increase in worker commitment and the material well-being of most employees in large-scale firms. This interpretation also respects both the enormity of the changes over the past century as well as aspects of industrial relations that point to the prewar origins of postwar institutions and to the resilience of certain long-standing norms and expectations. The interpretation also recognizes distinctive aspects of Japanese institutions that do not neatly conform to universal models of development or industrial relations, but at the same time it places the experiences of prewar and postwar Japan in a wider comparative context. In the final analysis, however, what sets apart the interpretation in chapter 3 from most of the works discussed above is the framing of the experiences of prewar and postwar managers and workers in terms of the constraints and opportunities facing institution-builders and their subordinates in non-Western late industrializers.

B2. Continuity, Change, and the Idea of Modernity in Russian/Soviet Studies

While many of the first studies of post-Soviet Russia tended to dismiss Soviet-era historiography and political economy as irrelevant or failed enterprises, the difficulties of the postcommunist transition have led to renewed interest in the potential significance of past debates in Russian/Soviet studies in understanding the ebbs and flows of political, economic, and social processes in contemporary Russia.[38] It is for this reason that chapter 4 has sought to consciously address, and partly reconcile, competing intellectual traditions within the vast and varied scholarly research in Russian/Soviet studies while developing an interpretation that can provide a point of departure for theoretically informed and historically grounded analyses of post-Soviet Russia.[39] The following sections review different strands of particularist and universalist perspectives, as well as more complex views that combine features of both with a recognition of the extraordinary aims and organizational culture of Leninism. Cutting across these contending perspectives are different views on the significance of key turning points in Russian/Soviet history as well as different normative positions implied in assessments of the effectiveness and legitimacy of various regimes.

*Particularist Images: Soviet Totalitarianism
and Russian History*

Until the 1970s, the dominant approaches in Soviet/Russian studies were particularist in that they tended to view Soviet Russia as a unique historical entity that cannot be understood through standard categories invoked to interpret historical processes in "normal" modernizing societies. The Soviet regime was characterized as a quintessential totalitarian system that was defined not in terms of its proclaimed ideals or its ability to forcibly industrialize Russia, but by its efforts to perfect its system of control from above at the expense of autonomous social institutions and a viable Russian civil society. Different strands of particularist historiography embrace competing views on the relationship between the Soviet period and the rest of Russian history, as well as on whether the latter might constitute a viable path toward modernity, but they converge upon a strongly negative image of the Soviet regime as an extraordinarily repressive and morally bankrupt system that had its own dynamics and characteristics.[40]

One strand of this particularist historiography stresses the continuity between Soviet and Russian history, treating Soviet totalitarianism as an extension of tsarist autocracy supported by an unchanging Russian political culture. Whatever the stated policies or intentions of different Soviet leaders, the essence of the Soviet regime is thought to be the same kind of steeply hierarchical, highly centralized, and fundamentally repressive political structure that characterized the old tsarist regime for centuries. Such structures, as well as the terror required to keep them intact, may be replicable as the general concept of totalitarianism suggests; but, significantly, this totalitarian rule is viewed as having a particularly strong affinity with a distinctive Russian national character that for centuries emphasized hierarchy, deference to authority, fatalism, and psychological dependence.[41] Thus, the Bolsheviks are viewed as having seized power in "an act of revitalized restoration," proceeding to simply graft Marxist ideology "onto the sturdy stem of Russia's patrimonial heritage" in the process of perfecting the use of hierarchy and terror.[42] While terror and repression may have declined after Stalin's death, the post-Stalin regime is thought to consist of little more than a "totalitarian residue" with different measures invoked to substitute for overt coercion.[43] Following the collapse of the USSR, some have partially appropriated this logic by likening Yeltsin's patriarchal style of leadership to that of Russian tsars and Soviet-era commissars.[44]

While these arguments are explicitly or implicitly critical of political structures and processes across Soviet and Russian history, there are some sympathetic versions of particularist analyses that also stress the continuity between aspects of prerevolutionary Russia and the Soviet experience. This interpretation was evident long ago in Berdyaev's famous argument about a distinctive Russian messianic idea which is thought to share an affinity with Russian Marxism.[45] A more recent treatment suggests that the dilemmas and dynamics evident under various Soviet and post-Soviet leaders are inevitable products of the age-old struggle between the imperatives of modernization and the components of a distinctive "Russian idea" that is egalitarian, collectivist, and generally anti-Western at its core.[46]

In contrast to these views, a different kind of particularist historiography draws a stark distinction between the Soviet period and other periods in Russian history, characterizing the former as a tragic accident that deflected the historical trajectory Russia had been following prior to World War I. But, even within this approach, there are differences over just how distinctive that trajectory might have been absent the Bolshevik coup. One version of this historiography essentially extends the perspectives on Russian history and culture offered by nineteenth-century Slavophiles who emphasized the virtues of Russia's unique traditions of grassroots participation in local public affairs, in combination with the moral authority of the tsar and Orthodox Christian ideals; while some ambitious Slavophiles even went as far as to propose a Panslavic Union, others downplayed the international status of Slavs and opted for a populist rendering focusing on the Russian commune as "the ultimate repository of all the highest moral qualities."[47] Such nostalgic images of prerevolutionary Russia are invoked to suggest that the Soviet regime was the result of a "cancer-like disease" that tragically crippled Russia's distinctive path of development by disavowing its rich spiritual past, ruthlessly attacking the peasant commune, and rejecting Slavic identity as a basis for political community. Looking to the post-Soviet future, a Slavophile perspective would suggest that Russia is once again in a position to realize its own distinctive path to modernity, linked to the revival of Orthodox spirituality and past traditions of local self-governance.[48]

Another particularist treatment of Soviet totalitarianism also seeks to rescue a positive Russian past as a foundation on which to build a post-Soviet social order; but this past itself is viewed in universalist terms, supposedly marked by progress toward liberal democracy and industrial capitalism long before 1917. In one recent treatment of Russian history, the eighteenth century is seen as a period of "enlightened despotism," and the last several decades of tsarist rule are viewed as evincing the same trends that eventually engendered constitutional democracies across Europe *without* the chaos or violence of revolution; Soviet communism is thus treated as an "impossible leap out of real history [that] would . . . lead to a dead-end world."[49] The growth of the Russian economy between the 1890s and beginning of World War I, the growth of the liberal intelligentsia, the emerging democratic orientations among peasants and workers in a nascent civil society, and the establishment of a provisional government under the leadership of the liberal Constitutional Democrats (Kadets) following the tsar's abdication are all viewed as evidence that Russia was in the process of evolving toward a modern society prior to the Bolshevik seizure of power.[50] The Bolsheviks' putsch, however, set the stage for a totalitarian political system that not only suppressed the democratic spirit of the masses, but also retarded Russia's economic development in the long run by rejecting the disciplining force of the market. Thus, the post-Soviet transitions toward market capitalism and liberal democracy, whatever their limitations and problems in the short run, are thought to constitute the only viable and logical path for Russia after years of stagnation brought about by the "abject bankruptcy of Sovietism."[51]

Within the specific context of labor relations, those who proceeded from the assumptions of the totalitarian school viewed the regime—in all its incarnations under successive leaders—as successfully manipulating, repressing, and atomizing the work force to an extent far beyond what one finds in other industrializing societies. More recent approaches generally accept this view although they do find evidence that workers managed to resist the regime in the narrow spaces where they had the opportunity to do so.[52] In the post-Stalin era, the decline of overt coercion does not detract from the neo-Stalinist regime's continuing ability to exert social control over the work force and fragment it by generously rewarding a narrow stratum of loyal employees in key sectors.[53] All these arguments view the relationship between the regime and the workers as an essentially adversarial one, characterized by the domination of the latter by the former within a distinctive totalitarian system that hindered or delayed the appearance of modern labor relations.

Universalist Historiography: Bolshevism and Soviet History as "Ordinary"

Universalist perspectives in Russian studies, whatever their other differences, view the whole of Russian history, including the period of Soviet communism, as constituting a variant of the same historical processes that have given rise to modern societies elsewhere. While earlier universalist interpretations constituted a minority view, challenging the totalitarian school by pointing to the developmental functions performed by the political elites and institutions of the new Soviet state, a more recent revisionist historiography has gained more acceptance in Russian/Soviet studies. This view also offers a relatively benign interpretation of Soviet history, focusing on social processes that are regarded as essentially similar to ordinary modernization processes elsewhere.[54]

In regard to the Bolshevik Revolution, universalist treatments portray the success of Lenin and his followers in 1917 as a legitimate and understandable response to the old regime's failure to cope with the various challenges of delayed modernization in a timely manner. The events of 1917 represent a key turning point not because they interrupted the course of Russian history but because they helped to remove the obstacles to its progress. The elite- or state-centered version of this narrative views the revolution as significant in that it allowed for the emergence of a new elite with a new vision capable of carrying out the necessary tasks of industrialization, state-building, and social transformation; thus, Lenin and the Bolshevik party are viewed as the instruments of history insofar as they enabled Russia to more vigorously pursue the modernizing tasks that the old regime had wavered on.[55] The revisionist social history shifts the focus to the affinity between the Bolshevik vision of change and the desires and interests of a frustrated urban proletariat that saw the tsarist regime and its liberal successor (in February–October 1917) as failing to improve their material conditions; far from being manipulated bystanders as some particularist interpretations suggest, Russian workers are viewed as active and radicalized agents of change, challenging the tsarist regime and later constituting a crucial social base for the Bolsheviks during the last months of 1917.[56] Ironically, this latter view partially contradicts official Soviet historiography, which also stresses the role of the urban proletariat, but emphasizes that the latter's revolutionary consciousness had to be drawn out by a "vanguard" party.[57]

Universalist accounts also tend to view the terror and chaos of the Stalin period not as defining features of the regime but as unfortunate byproducts of the turbulent changes and social processes unfolding in a "quicksand society."[58] State- or elite-centered versions take on the totalitarian model by arguing that the extreme centralization of power under Stalin, and even elements of Stalin's own temperament, were functional for the enormous task of forcibly industrializing Russia and defending the Soviet state from hostile forces.[59] A newer cohort of revisionist social historians do not dispute this interpretation, but distinguish themselves by insisting on greater attention to social processes and to the social bases for the Stalin regime and its programs.[60] Thus, the purges of the Stalin era are attributed not to the systematic consolidation of totalitarian control under an omnipotent dictator, but to chaotic local administration and uncontrollable social processes.[61] Moreover, while the revisionists are ambivalent as to whether Stalinism represents the fulfillment of the revolutionary ideals of 1917, they do view the regime's policies as products of a compromise negotiated with an upwardly mobile stratum of workers and professionals who provided the social support for the regime to implement its policies, eventually acquiring individualistic impulses and middle-class values in the course of industrialization.[62] Revisionist treatments of labor relations have recently extended this argument to suggest that atomization was merely a temporary result of the social mobility of peasants-turned-workers,[63] and that different strata of workers came to form an inclusive community, displacing the old labor aristocracy and learning to speak Bolshevik scripts while participating in the making of a new Stalinist civilization.[64] This newer revisionist cohort also adopts a more discursive approach to the question of *class,* emphasizing the significance of the term in helping to forge a new identity among the diverse social and occupational groups that supported Stalinist industrialization.[65]

In light of the decline of coercion, the rationalization of Soviet planning, and the apparent social stability of the 1960s and 1970s, universalist treatments of the post-Stalin period were more confident in rejecting particularist critiques of the regime and embracing a view of Soviet history that focused on its "ordinary" aspects. In response to evidence of new forms of political participation *within* the Soviet establishment, Jerry Hough explicitly invoked modernization theory and argued that the Soviet Union was basically "a kind of pluralistic society with certain types of restrictions."[66] Others have offered complementary society-centered perspectives, noting how the increasing education, mobility, and sophistication of key segments of Soviet society led to new social pacts with Stalin's successors and, later, propelled Gorbachev's efforts to restructure the Soviet economy to encompass new demands.[67] Such characterizations also form the basis for studies that treat Soviet labor relations as constituting a variant of corporatist labor relations found in other industrial societies; rather than a one-sided system of social control, the relationship between the regime and working class is thought to revolve around a tacit social contract whereby the regime guaranteed job security and access to cheap necessities in exchange for labor passivity, at least until Gorbachev's reforms ended up directly or indirectly disrupting this pact.[68]

Although most of these arguments offer a relatively benign and optimistic view of Soviet state-society relations, it should be noted that universalist logics have also informed a range of studies that offer critical or negative assessments of the Soviet regime. This is true of Marxian perspectives that invoke the "laws of history" to criticize the Bolshevik Revolution, or to fault the new regime's reliance on the same kinds of inequalities, stratification, and techniques of social control found in capitalist societies.[69] This is also true of the functionalist argument that the Soviet regime's utopian programs and political institutions, having jump-started industrialization in Russia at a tremendous human cost, outlived their usefulness and had to give way to more pragmatic economic policies and more rationalized institutional procedures as in other developing societies.[70] More recently, rational choice explanations of the decline of the Soviet Union have argued that command economies and highly centralized institutions cannot survive in the long run since the complex developmental tasks they face eventually destabilize existing "distributional coalitions" and produce intractable collective action problems.[71]

The Leninist Response to Backwardness: Bolshevik Ideology and Organization

In contrast to starkly universalist and particularist views of Soviet history, both of which tend to downplay the stated purposes and organizational features of the Bolshevik party, there exist a number of interesting studies that are referred to here as a *Leninist* perspective in that they focus on the nature of Lenin's leadership, the ideology and organization of his Bolshevik party, and the extent to which these are replicated or transformed by Lenin's successors.[72] These studies are also distinguished by their eclectic position on the question of how comparable the Soviet experience is to the experiences of other societies undergoing socioeconomic change: in contrast to universalist historiography, the focus is on the *extraordinary* dynamics resulting from the convergence of Russia's backwardness with a powerful chiliastic vision that promised to simultaneously create a more just moral order and a strong industrial state; yet, in contrast to the particularists, this quest is viewed as replicable in principle since both the pressures of backwardness and the particular amalgam of moral commitments and organizational strategies identified with Leninism are seen as unrelated to the peculiarities of Russian history. At the same time, this Leninist approach encompasses quite diverse views on the relative significance of ideology and organization in defining Leninism, and on the extent to which either was meaningfully translated into viable institutions and everyday practices over time.

Among those who take seriously the distinctive ideological commitments of the Leninist party, the most important question revolves around the extent to which these commitments were translated into reality once the party actually took power. The most skeptical view in this regard is that of Barrington Moore who appreciates the Bolsheviks' commitment to the goals of freedom and equality, but points to the tragic consequences of their efforts to realize these goals "by means of an organization that denied these same principles"; that is, the very tactics and methods Lenin employed to seize power are thought to have set the precedents for the systematic and regular reliance on terror and totalitarian control over the course of Soviet history.[73] Others also posit a connection between socialist ideals and Leninism, but find genuine, pragmatic efforts to realize these ideals prior to Stalin's rise to power; Lenin's tactics in the revolutionary seizure of power as well as his economic programs during the civil war are seen as justifiable under the circumstances, but Stalin's ruthless consolidation of power, his systematic use of terror even against party members, and his unwarranted and counterproductive push to collectivize agriculture and invoke excessively high plan targets to boost productivity—are all viewed as betraying the ideals of Leninism, ideals that might have been otherwise realized by continuing the New Economic Policy adopted in 1921.[74]

Such views are challenged by others who trace key features of the Stalinist and even post-Stalin regimes back to Marxist roots. One of the strongest arguments along these lines suggests that Stalin's class war and the centralization of power can be understood as legitimate efforts to realize the ideal of "perfect unity" viewed by Marx as a precondition for the construction of communism; while Stalin's particular formula differed from others in the degree of reliance on terror, it can be understood as a logical extension of Lenin's own efforts to achieve unity within the Bolshevik party.[75] Finally, whatever the ideological content of Stalinism, some studies of the post-Stalin era point to the steady reductions in wage differentials and the efforts to maintain full employment as genuine expressions of the original socialist ethic of egalitarianism.[76] All of these perspectives do find something distinctive and salvageable in the original ideals espoused by the Bolsheviks, although they differ sharply over the legitimacy of different leaders' methods for realizing these ideals after 1917.

A somewhat different characterization of Leninism, articulated in the writings of Robert Tucker and Ken Jowitt among others, downplays the significance of the Bolsheviks' ideals, focusing instead on the extraordinary organizational culture that distinguishes Leninism from other efforts at political and economic development. Leninism is understood largely in terms of Lenin's formulas for leadership and organization during the period of the revolution and the civil war (War Communism); thus, the compromises implied in the New Economic Program (as evident in the tolerance of traditional peasant institutions and the partial reliance on markets) are viewed as a temporary respite that could not have been extended indefinitely given the continuing strength of the "bolshevik mores of war communism" among the party's rank and file.[77] This also implies that many of the distinguishing features of Stalinism—attacking the gradualist position of the party's Right Opposition, the assault on the kulak (rich peasant) class, the collectivization of agriculture, and the aggressive pursuit of militarized industrialization—need to be understood not as irrational or costly efforts to realize ordinary developmental ends but as components of a strategy for strengthening the party's precarious position in a largely illiterate peasant society surrounded by hostile capitalist forces.[78]

Within this framework, the main point of contention has to do with interpreting the process through which the original revolutionary momentum of Leninism is perpetuated or dissipated. For Tucker, Stalinism is treated as a new, distinct stage of a dramatic revolutionary transformation begun by Lenin during the civil war years but interrupted by NEP; Stalin's program, however, is characterized as a much larger project of transformation from above, a project that was partly influenced by the action-oriented political culture of Leninism but also included elements of prerevolutionary elite political culture, appeals to Russian nationalism, as well as Stalin's own personality traits.[79] Such a revolution, of course, could not be sustained once one of its key elements, the leader and his personal qualities, was removed from the equation; thus, Stalin's death and Khrushchev's declaration that there existed "many roads to socialism" mark the "deradicalization" of Leninism, leaving behind only an "extreme communist conservatism of strong Russian-nationalist tendency."[80]

Jowitt also sees Stalinism as a new stage in the revolutionary process, but offers a distinctive treatment of the essential and developmental features of Leninism. In Weberian language, Jowitt defines Leninist organization as the amalgam of "charismatic" elements (evident in the vanguard party's claim on the commitment of its members by virtue of its extraordinary insight into the laws of history) and "impersonal" modes of behavior (evident in the emphases on comradeship in lieu of personal ties, and on "science" as the basis for the regime's policy); it is this "charismatic-impersonalism," exemplified by the "correct line" (which is simultaneously scientific and absolute), that sets Leninism apart from other developmental regimes.[81] Extending this analysis, Stalinism is seen not only as a revolution from above but also as the next logical step that must follow any revolutionary seizure of power: the consolidation of that power by transforming, and insulating the regime from, a hostile social environment.[82] In the post-Stalin era, Jowitt finds the regime seeking to address the new task of "inclusion" that revolutionary regimes must address once their position in the wider society has been consolidated: thus, the decline of terror and the expansion of political participation are seen not as deradicalization or the triumph of modernizing processes but as cautious efforts by the party elite to extend membership and voice to previously untrusted social groups. In the absence of a new combat task, however, this process threatened to blur the distinction between the vanguard party and the wider society, and prompted the party apparatchiki to resort to "neotraditionalism" to protect itself; hence, the regime's tolerance of the second economy and personal networks, although intended to satisfy the material needs of the population, unintentionally produced an invidious relationship between a privileged "parasitic party" and a "scavenger society."[83] This process may not have doomed Leninism, but it did prompt fresh efforts by Andropov and Gorbachev to revive the charismatic impersonalism of Leninism, using methods that ultimately undermined the vanguard position of the party, effectively bringing an end to Leninism even before the breakup of the USSR. While labor does not figure directly in this analysis, the implication is clear: once expected to combine heroic feats of labor with the disciplined execution of tasks, workers never did become "included" as partners of the party, and were left instead to "scavenge" on the shopfloor to improve their material conditions without altering the status quo.[84]

Universalists do well to point to the social bases of the Soviet regime and to suggest similarities between changes in Soviet society and patterns of change in other modernizing societies; yet, in doing so, they discount the significance of preexisting historical characteristics and Bolshevik revolutionary visions. Particularists do well to recognize the continued influence of authority patterns that date back to the tsarist regime, and to recognize the sharply reduced scope for autonomous social action under the Stalin regime; at the same time, they also ignore the subtle ways in which various actors supported or challenged the regime, while discounting the revolutionary ambitions of the Bolsheviks and the developmental imperatives they faced. And the insightful works focusing on the features of Leninist ideology and organization, while avoiding these aforementioned pitfalls, have their own limitations in that they pay scant attention to the influence of borrowed technologies and institutional models on the design of Soviet institutions and tend to downplay the effects of the wider social milieu within which these institutions had to function and recruit members. In attempting to overcome the limitations inherent in each of these different strands in Russian/Soviet studies, the interpretation in chapter 4 has been constructed by rejecting both universalist and particularist historiography while bringing together the most compelling elements of both within a more complex narrative that pays attention to prerevolutionary historical legacies, ordinary developmental imperatives and processes, the significance of external influences, as well as the extraordinary commitments and organizational challenges taken on by Lenin and the Bolshevik party. In so doing, the argument offered in chapter 4 eclectically but systematically weaves together a range of observations and assessments noted in different strands of the literature in Russian/Soviet studies, with the intention of developing a complex, original interpretation that can speak to the broader problem of institution-building in NWLIs.

Notes

Preface

1. Francis Fukuyama, *The End of History and the Last Man* (New York: Free Press, 1992).
2. These theories are addressed in chap. 2 (section 2.1) in the discussion of universalist perspectives on institutions and organizational change.
3. E.g., Reinhard Bendix, "Tradition and Modernity Reconsidered," *Comparative Studies in Society and History* 9 (April 1967): 292–346; Robert Nisbet, *Social Change and History* (New York: Oxford University Press, 1967); Charles Tilly, *Big Structures, Large Processes, Huge Comparisons* (New York: Russell Sage, 1984); Theda Skocpol, "Sociology's Historical Imagination," in Theda Skocpol, ed., *Vision and Method in Historical Sociology* (Cambridge: Cambridge University Press, 1984); and Theda Skocpol, "Bringing the State Back In," in Peter Evans, Dietrich Rueschemeyer, and Theda Skocpol, eds., *Bringing the State Back In* (Cambridge: Cambridge University Press, 1985).
4. Fukuyama, *End of History;* Fukuyama, "Confucianism and Democracy," *Journal of Democracy* 6, 3 (April 1995): 20–33; and Lucian Pye, "Political Science and the Crisis of Authoritarianism," *American Political Science Review* 84, 1 (March 1990), esp. 7–11. The term *neomodernist* is borrowed from Edward Tiryakian, "Modernization: Exhumetur in Pace," *International Sociology* 6, 2 (1991).
5. On the convergence in values in postmodern societies, see Ronald Inglehart, *Modernization and Postmodernization: Cultural, Economic, and Political Change in 43 Societies* (Princeton: Princeton University Press, 1997), esp. 3–33. On the homogenizing effects of globalization in various realms, see Martin Albrow, *The Global Age* (Stanford: Stanford University Press, 1997); Philip Cerny, "Globalization and the Changing Logic of Collective Action," *International Organization* 49 (autumn 1995): 595–625; Anthony Giddens, *Runaway World: How Globalization is Reshaping Our Lives* (New York: Routledge, 2000); Kenichi Ohmae, ed., *The Evolving Global Economy* (Boston: Harvard Business Review, 1995); and Ronald Robertson, *Globalization: Social Theory and Global Culture* (London: Sage, 1992).
6. See, e.g., Robert Bates, *Open-Economy Politics: The Political Economy of the World Coffee Trade* (Princeton: Princeton University Press, 1997); Ernst Haas, *Nationalism, Liberalism and Progress,* vol. 1 (Ithaca: Cornell University Press, 1997); Stephan Haggard and Robert Kaufman, *The Political Economy of*

Democratic Transitions (Princeton: Princeton University Press, 1995); Yael Tamir, *Liberal Nationalism* (Princeton: Princeton University Press, 1993); Axel Hadenius, *Democracy and Development* (New York: Cambridge University Press, 1992); and Adam Przeworski, Michael Alvarez, Jose Cheibub, and Fernando Limongi, *Democracy and Development: Political Institutions and Material Well-Being in the World, 1950–1990* (New York: Cambridge University Press, 2000).

7. Benjamin Barber, *Jihad vs. McWorld* (New York: Times Books, 1995). See also James Mittelman, *The Globalization Syndrome: Transformation and Resistance* (Princeton: Princeton University Press, 2000).

8. E.g., Fred Riggs, *Administration in Developing Societies* (Boston: Houghton Mifflin, 1964), and Lloyd Rudolph and Susanne Hoeber Rudolph, *The Modernity of Tradition: Political Development in India* (Chicago: University of Chicago Press, 1967).

9. On this point, see Rudra Sil, "The Questionable Status of Boundaries: The Need for Integration," in Sil and Eileen Doherty, eds., *Beyond Boundaries? Disciplines, Paradigms and Theoretical Integration in International Studies* (Albany: State University of New York Press, 2000). See also the insightful report of the Gulbenkian Commission, published as Immanuel Wallerstein et al., *Open the Social Sciences* (Stanford: Stanford University Press, 1996).

Chapter 1

1. Reinhard Bendix, *Work and Authority in Industry: Ideologies of Management in the Course of Industrialization* (New York: Wiley, 1956), 251. All subsequent references are to the revised edition (Berkeley: University of California Press, 1974).

2. Harry Eckstein, "Congruence Theory Explained," in Eckstein, Frederic Fleron, Erik Hoffman, and William Reisinger, *Can Democracy Take Root in Post-Soviet Russia?* (Lanham, MD: Rowman and Littlefield, 1998), 23.

3. I deliberately sidestep the problem of precisely defining the categories of "tradition" and "modernity" since this book is concerned with what features actors themselves attribute to these concepts across societies and institutional contexts (allowing for the possibility that these actors do not even view the categories as mutually exclusive). By "modern" objectives, I simply mean such commonly sought ends as the application of science and technology to industrial production, along with increases in material goods, military prowess, and international respect.

4. Chapter 2 explores in greater detail the validity and implications of the early/late industrializer and Western/non-Western distinctions in relation to institutions of work.

5. *Late industrializer* is thus a relative category; it depends on the objective fact of relative backwardness as well as the subjective definition by elites that their society is in some respects a follower society that needs to catch up to some referent society. As such, the category can be extended to encompass the position of most countries at some point in time, including the cases studied here: Japan (through the 1970s) and Russia (through the present). On the perceptions of backwardness in follower societies, see Reinhard Bendix, "Relative Backwardness and

Intellectual Mobilization," in Bendix, *Unsettled Affinities,* ed. John Bendix (New Brunswick: Transaction Books, 1993), 85–102.

6. The classic work on this subject, of course, is Alexander Gerschenkron, *Economic Backwardness in Historical Perspective* (Cambridge: Harvard University Press, 1962). The logic of Gerschenkron's analysis is also evident in recent studies of effective institutional mechanisms for resolving the "collective dilemmas" of development; see, e.g., David Waldner, *State Building and Late Development* (Ithaca: Cornell University Press, 1999). See also the discussion in chap. 2, section 2.3.

7. On the positive benefits of borrowed technologies and institutional practices for late-industrializers, see Thorstein Veblen, *Imperial Germany and the Industrial Revolution* (New York: Viking, 1954). A more ambivalent treatment that also considers how "international demonstration effects" shape intellectual orientations, life-styles, and consumption patterns of elites is evident in Bendix, "Relative Backwardness"; and Andrew Janos, "The Politics of Backwardness in Continental Europe, 1780–1945," *World Politics* 41, 3 (April 1989): 325–58.

8. For a view of late-industrializer effects that emphasizes the higher premium often placed on social stability, see Ronald Dore, *British Factory, Japanese Factory: The Origins of National Diversity in Industrial Relations* (Berkeley: University of California Press, 1973). The merits and limitations of Dore's approach are considered in chap. 2, while the attention devoted to stable industrial relations in Japan and Russia is considered in chaps. 3 and 4 respectively.

9. S. N. Eisenstadt, "Modernity and the Construction of Collective Identities," *International Journal of Comparative Sociology* 39, 1 (February 1998): 138–58, 139.

10. Chap. 2 (section 2.2) considers the plausibility of this assumption in the context of addressing the problem of institutional variation in theoretical and historical contexts.

11. Thus, individualism as a social value may be compatible with efforts to generate some sense of identification with organizations, societies, or nation-states as long as members of these units believe their shared individualistic norms to be part of their collective life. Such norms *may* correspond to a greater sense of self-worth or a stronger ego at the level of the individual, but such a correspondence is neither assumed nor necessary for the argument in this book. Similarly, the conception of collectivism as a social value should not be assumed to point to psychological dependence or the absence of broader discourses of self in a society. This understanding of individualism and collectivism as *social values* has been influenced by such works as Robert Bellah, Richard Madsen, William Sullivan, Ann Swidler, and Steven Tipton, *Habits of the Heart: Individualism and Commitment in American Life* (Berkeley: University of California Press, 1985); Michael Carrithers, Steven Collins, and Steven Lukes, eds., *The Category of the Person* (Cambridge: Cambridge University Press, 1985); Louis Dumont, *Essays on Individualism: Modern Ideology in Anthropological Perspective* (Chicago: University of Chicago Press, 1986); Richard Ellis, Michael Thompson, and Aaron Wildavsky, *Cultural Theory* (Boulder: Westview, 1990); Reinhard Bendix, "Definitions of

Community in Western Civilization," in Bendix, *Unsettled Affinities*, 35–84; and Eisenstadt, "Modernity." See also chap. 2, section 2.2.

12. The Western/non-Western distinction thus rests on the acceptance of a qualified version of Max Weber's famous argument in *The Protestant Ethic and the Spirit of Capitalism* (New York: Scribner's, 1958). I interpret the Weber thesis as follows: while some conception of the individual self may be traced back to Roman law and early Christianity, it is the Calvinist doctrine of individual salvation as articulated in Britain that was the catalyst in elevating an individualistic ethos that a nascent middle class could invoke to legitimate the institutions of industrial capitalism among the working masses in the wider society. See also the discussion in chap. 2, section 2.2.

13. The significance of individualism for the adoption and spread of specific managerial ideologies, technologies, and organizational characteristics in the West is noted in Reinhard Bendix, *Work and Authority*, 202–4, 261–77. The many other studies that support this observation include Bellah et al., 43–47; Wilbert Moore, "Attributes of an Industrial Order," in Sigmund Nosow and William Form, eds., *Man, Work, and Society* (New York: Basic Books, 1962), 93–97; Alan Fox, *Beyond Contract: Work, Power, and Trust Relations* (London: Faber and Faber, 1974), 163–70; Robert Cole, *Work, Mobility, and Participation: A Comparative Study of American and Japanese Industry* (Berkeley: University of California Press, 1979), 102–3; Judith Merkle, *Management and Ideology: The Legacy of the International Scientific Management Movement* (Berkeley: University of California Press, 1980), 7–8; and Mauro F. Guillen, *Models of Management: Work, Authority, and Organization in Comparative Perspective* (Chicago: University of Chicago Press, 1994), 30–44.

14. Precursors of this view include Veblen who wrote that late-industrializing Germany could effectively borrow the institutions of advanced powers in order to break down old habits and customs on the route to industrialization; see Veblen, *Imperial Germany*, esp. 39. Deutsch famously defined "social mobilization" as the social, cultural, and psychological transformations that followed from the uprooting of large numbers of people from their preexisting communities and the introduction of "advanced" practices in culture, technology, and economic life on a large scale; see Karl Deutsch, "Social Mobilization and Political Development," *American Political Science Review* (September 1961): 493–511. Within the context of the working classes, this logic informed the popular view that new, modern institutions of work would produce relatively uniform structures, practices, and attitudes everywhere. See Clark Kerr, J. T. Dunlop, F. H. Garbison, and C. A. Myers, *Industrialism and Industrial Man* (Cambridge: Harvard University Press, 1960); and Alex Inkeles and David Smith, *Becoming Modern: Individual Change in Six Countries* (Cambridge: Harvard University Press, 1974).

15. On the emergence of new values alongside new systems of factory authority, see Neil Smelser, *Social Change in the Industrial Revolution* (Chicago: University of Chicago Press, 1959); and Sidney Pollard, *The Genesis of Modern Management: A Study of the Industrial Revolution in Great Britain* (Cambridge: Harvard University Press, 1965). For evidence on the strength of individualistic values even among lower echelons of the work force in the West, see Adriano

Tilgher, "Work Through the Ages," in Nosow and Form; Ely Cinoy, *Automobile Workers and the American Dream* (Boston: Beacon, 1970); Joseph Feagin, "Poverty: We Still Believe That God Helps Those Who Help Themselves," *Psychology Today* (Nov. 1972), esp. 107–8; Kay Lehman Schlozman and Sidney Verba, *Insult to Injury* (Cambridge: Harvard University Press, 1979); Jennifer Hochschild, *What's Fair? American Beliefs about Distributive Justice* (Cambridge: Harvard University Press, 1981); and Adrian Furnham, *The Protestant Work Ethic: The Psychology of Work-Related Beliefs and Behaviours* (New York: Routledge, 1990). See also the discussion in chap. 2, section 2.2.

16. As this book is concerned with *late* industrialization, present debates over whether individualism may *now* be making greater inroads in industrialized non-Western societies (such as Japan) are moot as are more recent contentions positing convergence on postmaterialist values (e.g., Inglehart, *Modernization and Postmodernization*). Chaps. 3 and 4 discuss the plausibility of assuming that individualism remained on the margins in *late-industrializing* Japanese and Russian society.

17. See, e.g., F. R. Kluckhohn and F. L. Strodtbeck, *Variations in Value Orientations* (Evanston, IL: Row Peterson, 1961); Geert Hofstede, *Culture's Consequences: International Differences in Work-Related Values* (Beverly Hills: Sage, 1980), 218–32; Harry Triandis, "Collectivism and Development," in D. Sinha and H. S. R. Kao, eds., *Social Values and Development: Asian Perspectives* (New Delhi: Sage, 1988); Triandis, "Cross-Cultural Studies of Individualism and Collectivism," in J. Berman, ed., *Nebraska Symposium on Motivation 1989* (Lincoln: University of Nebraska Press, 1989); Gunter Bierbrauer, H. Meyer, and U. Wolfradt, "Measurement of Normative and Evaluative Aspects in Individualistic and Collectivistic Orientations," in U. Kim, H. C. Triandis, C. Kagitcibasi, S. Choi, and G. Yoon, eds., *Individualism and Collectivism: Theory, Method, and Applications* (Thousand Oaks: Sage, 1994); and James Kleugel, David Mason, and Bernard Wegener, eds., *Social Justice and Political Change: Public Opinion in Capitalist and Post-Communist States* (New York: Aldine De Gruyter, 1995). Evidence presented by many modernization theorists can also be cited here despite the fact that the latter automatically interpreted the survival of collectivist attitudes as suggestive of an earlier stage of development rather than as a challenge to their evolutionary premises. See, e.g., Inkeles and Smith; and Daniel Lerner, *The Passing of Traditional Society* (New York: Free Press, 1958).

18. As will be evident below, the focus on institutions of work in this book requires limiting the consideration of legacies to the particular norms and practices related to cooperation, distribution, and authority relations in preexisting *communities of work*.

19. Clifford Geertz, *Peddlers and Princes* (Chicago: University of Chicago Press, 1963), esp. 84–85.

20. Peter Evans, "Introduction: Development Strategies across the Public-Private Divide," in Evans, ed., *State-Society Synergy: Government and Social Capital in Development,* Research Series No. 94 (Berkeley: International and Area Studies, 1997), 1. See also Mark Granovetter, "Economic Sociology of Firms and Entrepreneurs," in Alejandro Portres, ed., *The Economic Sociology of Immigra-*

tion: Essays on Networks, Ethnicity, and Entrepreneurship (New York: Russell Sage, 1995).

21. This definition is essentially an adaptation of Weber's definition for an "administrative organization"; Max Weber, *Economy and Society,* 2 vols., ed. G. Roth and C. Wittich (Berkeley: University of California Press, 1978 [1968]), 52. The terms *organization* and *institution* are sometimes used interchangeably in discussions of the literature on firms and organizations in chap. 2, but generally *organization* will be reserved to refer to the manner in which roles and tasks are defined and coordinated within an *institution.*

22. This view of institutions is predicated on a structurationist ontology that emphasizes the duality of material and ideal dimensions of social life while emphasizing the dialectical relationship between agents and the multiple and fluid structures that they produce, reproduce, or transform. Significantly, in contrast to the foundational assumptions of contemporary rational choice, cultural, or historical institutionalist analysis, structurationism does not posit any universal epistemological first principles and places the burden on substantive investigation to determine the relative significance of aspects of social life in a given context. See the discussion in section A2 of appendix A, and for a more extensive discussion, see Rudra Sil, "The Foundations of Eclecticism: The Epistemological Status of Agency, Culture, and Structure in Social Theory," *Journal of Theoretical Politics* 12, 3 (July 2000): 353–87.

23. George Herbert Mead, *Mind, Self and Society* (Chicago: University of Chicago Press, 1962).

24. This understanding of *identity* within institutions is simply adapted from common understandings of the term among anthropologists and sociologists who invoke it to connote "both a persistent sameness within oneself . . . and a persistent sharing of some kind of essential character with others." Anita Jacobson-Widding, "Introduction," in Jacobson-Widding, ed., *Identity: Personal and Socio-Cultural* (Uppsala, Sweden: Uppsala Studies in Cultural Anthropology 5, 1983), 14.

25. On this point, see Ralph Turner, "Role-Taking: Process versus Conformity," in A. Rose, ed., *Human Behavior and Social Process* (Boston: Houghton Mifflin, 1962).

26. The value of this stylized dichotomy has long been established in organization theory; see, e.g., James Krantz, "The Managerial Couple: Superior-Subordinate Relationships as a Unit of Analysis," *Human Resource Management* 28, 2 (summer 1989): 161–75.

27. As Simon has noted, "boundedly rational" subordinates typically require some sense of collective purpose to identify with so that they can fulfill their tasks without continually having to reexamine their decision to remain part of the institution; see Herbert Simon, *Administrative Behavior,* 2d ed. (New York: Macmillan, 1957). The term *organizational ideal* is borrowed from Howard Schwartz to suggest how institutional superordinates seek to create an image of the institution as a "perfect" unified entity with a long tradition of achievement that members can share by playing out their prescribed roles; see Howard Schwartz, "The Psychodynamics of Organizational Totalitarianism," *Journal of General Management* 13, 1 (1987): 41–54.

28. For psychological research that speaks to this assumption, see Larry Hirschorn, *The Workplace Within: Psychodynamics of Organizational Life* (Cambridge: MIT Press, 1988); and Howell Baum, *Organizational Membership: Personal Development in the Workplace* (Albany: SUNY Press, 1990). See also the more extensive discussion in chap. 2 (section 2.4).

29. On this point, see Selznick's famous discussion of how familiar norms brought in from the wider community produce a resilient "organizational gestalt" that survives in new institutional settings. See Philip Selznick, *TVA and Grassroots* (Berkeley: University of California Press, 1949).

30. This dynamic has been articulated in Paul DiMaggio and Walter Powell, "The Iron Cage Revisited: Institutional Isomorphism and Collective Rationality in Organizational Fields," *American Sociological Review* 48 (1983): 147–60. Here, the logic is extended to capture the influence of foreign institutional models on institution-builders in particular societies.

31. This distinction was articulated as far back as the 1930s in the work of Barnard who distinguished "official" and "unofficial" hierarchies and rules in complex organizations in order to highlight the importance of combining material inducements with indoctrination so as to ensure that unofficial groups would direct their reserved energies toward the achievement of organizational goals; see Chester Barnard, *The Functions of the Executive* (Cambridge: Harvard University Press, 1938), esp. 116. A similar distinction is also implied in Selznick's differentiation between "organization" and "institution," where the latter is viewed as encompassing informal attitudes and behavioral features shaped by the wider community from which actors are recruited into organizations; see Philip Selznick, *Leadership in Administration* (New York: Harper and Row, 1957), 16–17.

32. On how subordinates can employ the informal realm to exert some influence of their own, see the classic piece by David Mechanic, "Sources of Power of Lower Participants in Complex Organization," *Administrative Science Quarterly* 7, 4 (December 1962): 349–64. This dynamic is also captured in Burawoy's classic study of a Chicago factory where workers were found to have gained lower-level managers' support in exercising considerable autonomy without having to challenge official hierarchies; see Michael Burawoy, *Manufacturing Consent: Changes in the Labor Process under Monopoly Capitalism* (Chicago: University of Chicago Press, 1979).

33. This definition is merely an adaptation of Weber's ideal-typical treatment of bureaucracy and rational-legal authority; see *Economy and Society,* 217–26, 956–58.

34. The importance of leadership and choice is captured nicely in Selznick's *TVA* and his *Leadership and Administration.* See also the classic essay by John Child, "Organizational Structure, Environment, and Performance: The Role of Strategic Choice," *Sociology* 6 (1972): 1–22; and the more recent discussion in Robert Thomas, *What Machines Can't Do: Politics and Technology in the Industrial Enterprise* (Berkeley: University of California Press, 1994), 16–30.

35. For an excellent study of how institutional models in Western referent societies influenced institution-building in a non-Western late industrializer, see

D. Eleanor Westney, *Imitation and Innovation: The Transfer of Western Organiza-tional Patterns to Meiji Japan* (Cambridge: Harvard University Press, 1987).

36. Note that the idea of a traditionalist approach to introducing modern institutions is not considered a paradox here. Traditionalist strategies see the bor-rowing of technologies and institutional models from abroad as a necessary adap-tation that is consistent with the preservation of preexisting ultimate values and distinctive ideals characteristic of past model communities.

37. E.g., Don Kullick, *Language Shift and Cultural Reproduction: Socializa-tion, Self, and Syncretism in a Papua New Guinean Village* (New York: Cambridge University Press, 1992); Charles Stewart and Rosalind Shaw, *Syncretism/Anti-Syncretism: The Politics of Religious Synthesis* (London: Routledge, 1994); Christopher Balme, *Decolonizing the Stage: Theatrical Syncretism and Post-Colo-nial Drama* (New York: Oxford University Press, 1999).

38. On syncretic political strategies and syncretism in nationalist ideologies, see respectively Guiseppe Di Palma, *Political Syncretism in Italy: Historical Coali-tion Strategies and the Present Crisis* (Berkeley: Institute of International Studies, University of California, 1978); and Haas, *Nationalism,* 51–52.

39. See Eric Hobsbawm and Terence Ranger, eds., *The Invention of Tradi-tion* (New York: Cambridge University Press, 1983). While the notion of "invented traditions" is helpful in its suggestion that all traditions are socially constructed, the concept does not by itself help in differentiating between more or less embed-ded traditional features in a given context, and it does not anticipate the possibil-ity of different strategies for *reinventing* or *adapting* specific traditional features in a given institutional setting.

40. Weberian ideal-types are not universal a priori categories intended to contribute to the "practically impossible" task of classifying all social phenomena and providing exhaustive causal accounts; they do, however, enable the "analyti-cal accentuation of certain elements of reality" that are of particular interest to the investigator. In this case, the four ideal-types are being used to gain comparable approximations of actual institution-building strategies that probably involve combinations of several ideal-types but are likely to reflect the dominant features of one more than the others. Such an approach is valuable for the purpose of gen-erating modest partial explanations and original hypotheses, but not for creating universal typologies or full-blown causal explanations. On Weber's comments on ideal-types, see Max Weber, "'Objectivity' in Social Science and Social Policy," in *The Methodology of the Social Sciences,* trans. and ed. E. A. Shils and H. A. Finch (New York: Free Press, 1949), 50–113.

41. See the further discussion of this point in chap. 2, section 2.4.

42. Weber, *Economy and Society,* 943–46, quote from 946.

43. Weber, *Economy and Society,* 213–14, quote from 53.

44. This definition of industrial enterprises is not intended to draw absolute distinctions between traditional and modern forms of production; it does, how-ever, suggest that industrial production will involve *some* shift in the organization of work along with a sense of timed, mechanized labor, a greater degree of task specialization, and a higher level of coordination. See Craig Littler, "Work in Tra-

ditional and Modern Societies," in Littler, ed., *The Experience of Work* (Aldershot, UK: Gower, 1985), 34–49.

45. This view of the large-scale enterprise is adapted from Chandler's definition of the multiunit "modern business enterprise" in Alfred Chandler, *The Visible Hand: The Managerial Revolution in American Business* (Cambridge: Harvard University Press, 1977), 1–3. The definition I offer is more generalized so as to deemphasize multiple product lines (which Chandler identifies as a distinguishing feature of the modern American business enterprise) and to allow for the experiences of firms in NWLIs, many of which are charged by the state with manufacturing single products while still being administered by professional salaried managers overseeing distinct subdivisions within a large bureaucratic enterprise.

46. The precise number of employees that qualifies a firm as large-scale in a given sector or society may vary depending on the questions asked in particular contexts, but the significant point is that the employees as a whole do not share some prior social bonds as members of the same preindustrial primary communities (e.g., a single family, clan, or village).

47. Dietrich Rueschemeyer, *Power and the Division of Labor* (Stanford: Stanford University Press, 1986), 59.

48. See Bendix, *Work and Authority,* esp. 198–253. The distinction between diffuse, high-trust and specific, low-trust authority relations is from Fox.

49. Joseph Schumpeter, in *Capitalism, Socialism and Democracy* (New York: Harper and Brothers, 1942), 106. On the importance of small businesses in the early economic development of the West, however, see Fox; Rueschemeyer, *Power,* 57–62; Smelser, *Social Change,* 185–95; David Landes, "French Business and the Businessman: A Social and Cultural Analysis, " in Hugh Aitken, ed., *Explorations in Enterprise* (Cambridge: Harvard University Press, 1965); and Jurgen Kocka, "Family and Bureaucracy in German Industrial Management," *Business History Review,* 45 (1971): 133–54.

50. The assumption that there exist theoretically significant differences in national patterns or styles of management and labor relations is taken up again in section 1.3 in the context of discussing the design of the comparative-historical study.

51. "Scientific management" refers to techniques advocated by Frederick Taylor who emphasized maximum specialization so as to minimize job-learning times, optimize efficiency in the production process, enable precise measurements of individual performance, and link these measurements to material rewards and sanctions for individual workers; see Frederick Taylor, "Scientific Management," in *Compiled Writings* (New York: Harper, 1974), originally published as *Shop Management* (New York: Harper and Brothers, 1911). These techniques were incorporated into the system of assembly-line mass production popularized by Henry Ford's Model T plant and eventually came to influence industrial management in Europe and elsewhere. Taylorism and Fordism are discussed in detail in chap. 2.

52. This assumption is clearly evident, for example, in the work of Veblen

who was a major admirer of Frederick Taylor and viewed scientific management as a universal method for maximizing the efficient appropriation of technology. See Thorstein Veblen, *The Theory of the Business Enterprise* (New York: Scribner's, 1904); and Veblen, *The Instinct of Workmanship and the State of the Industrial Arts* (New York: Macmillan, 1914). See also the discussion in chap. 2, section 2.1.

53. Thus, the human relations movement spurred by Elton Mayo and the Hawthorne studies, while challenging Taylor's focus on material incentives and the physical aspects of the work process, relied on universal assumptions about the goals and needs of workers everywhere. As noted in chap. 2, however, it is far from clear just how fundamental a challenge this was to Taylorism and just how much difference it made for management practices in the United States. On the theoretical and empirical basis for the human relations movement, see Elton Mayo, *The Social Problems of an Industrial Civilization* (Boston: Graduate School of Business Administration, Harvard University, 1945); and Burleigh Gardner, *Human Relations in Industry* (Chicago: Richard D. Irwin, 1945).

54. "Flexible" or "lean" production nests concerns for the employee's emotional well-being within the more fundamental observation that efficient production in a post-Fordist age requires more teamwork, more communication among production and design-improvement teams, just-in-time supply networks, the fast turnover of inventories, and production in small batches. However, as noted in chap. 2, the shift to lean production does not unequivocally suggest a universal alternative to Taylorism and may not even break fundamentally with some of the latter's assumptions. On the origins and character of lean or flexible production, see Charles Sabel and Michael Piore, *The Second Industrial Divide: Possibilities for Prosperity* (New York: Basic Books, 1985); "Manufacturing the Right Way," *Fortune* (May 21, 1990); Paul Adler, "Automation and Skill: New Directions," *International Journal of Technology Management* 2 (1987): 761–72; J. Womack, D. Jones, and D. Roos, *The Machine That Changed the World* (New York: Rawson Macmillan, 1990); Martin Kenney and Richard Florida, *Beyond Mass Production: The Japanese System and Its Transfer to the U.S.* (New York: Oxford University Press, 1993); and Harry Katz and Owen Darbishire, *Converging Divergences: Worldwide Changes in Employment Systems* (Ithaca: Cornell University Press, 1999).

55. On this general point, see Rueschemeyer, *Power;* and Thomas among others. On the range of diversity in lean production, see Frederic Deyo, "Introduction," in Deyo, ed., *Social Reconstructions of the World Automobile Industry: Competition, Power, and Industrial Flexibility* (New York: St. Martin's Press, 1996); and Lowell Turner and Peter Auer, "A Diversity of New Work Organization: Human-Centered, Lean and In-Between," in Deyo, ed., *Social Reconstructions.* See also chap. 2, sections 2.2–2.3.

56. The virtue of focusing on legacies inherited from communities of work (as opposed to, say, the legacies inherited from large-scale feudal political organization) in this study are noted in chap. 2, section 2.3.

57. This wording is adapted from the subtitle to James Scott, *Weapons of the Weak: Everyday Forms of Peasant Resistance* (New Haven: Yale University Press, 1985).

58. E.g., the scales for measuring employee commitment employed in Richard Mowday, Lyman Porter, and Richard Steers, *Employee-Organization Linkages: The Psychology of Commitment, Absenteeism, and Turnover* (New York: Academic Press, 1982), 221.

59. In any case, the particular variations examined across the case studies here are not controversial; thus, the main contribution of the comparative study is the construction of a partial explanation for that variation, not a definitive model for measuring it. The adjustments I refer to for different contexts are based on common sense: A turnover rate of 20 percent in prewar Japan or other NWLIs may not be as suggestive as it was for managers in Soviet Russia where enterprises offered a wide range of necessities and benefits (apartments, health care, education, recreation, etc.) to retain a stock of surplus labor. Similarly, the low level of industrial conflict in postwar Japan is more indicative of high managerial authority than the even lower level of industrial conflict in Soviet Russia given the regime's intolerance for overt protest; hence the need to substitute qualitative evidence of covert forms of noncompliance in the latter case. Such considerations and adjustments follow the logic of "contextualized comparison" as outlined in Richard Locke and Kathleen Thelen, "Apples and Oranges Revisited: Contextualized Comparisons and the Study of Comparative Labor Politics," *Politics and Society* 23, 3 (September 1995): 337–67.

60. This understanding is not uncommon among economists and management specialists. For example, George Akerlof suggests that higher levels of worker effort and wages may be viewed as an exchange of gifts between managers and workers. Gary Miller similarly notes that the cooperation of employees is gained not through a convergence of goals but rather through the evolution of norms of reciprocity in long-term employment relationships. See George Akerlof, "Labor Contracts as Partial Gift Exchange," *Quarterly Journal of Economics* 97, 2 (1982): 543–69; and Gary Miller, *Managerial Dilemmas: The Political Economy of Hierarchy* (New York: Cambridge University Press, 1992), esp. 198.

61. See the discussion of modernists and nativists in Bendix, "Relative Backwardness." On the formation of hybrid systems resulting from mixtures of traditional/modern or native/foreign elements, see Riggs; Rudolph and Rudolph; and Sudhir Kakar, "Authority Patterns and Subordinate Behavior in Indian Organizations," *Administrative Science Quarterly* 16 (1971): 298–307.

62. Peter Evans, "Government, Social Capital, and Development: Reviewing the Evidence on Synergy," in Evans, ed., *State-Society Synergy*, 178.

63. Frederic Shaeffer, *Democracy in Translation: Understanding Politics in an Unfamiliar Culture* (Ithaca: Cornell University Press, 1998), 146.

64. James Scott, *Seeing Like a State: How Certain Schemes to Improve the Human Condition Have Failed* (New Haven: Yale University Press, 1998), 1–8.

65. Bertrand Badie, *The Imported State: The Westernization of the Political Order* (Stanford: Stanford University Press, 2000), 234.

66. Harry Eckstein, "A Theory of Stable Democracy," in Eckstein, *Regarding Politics: Essays on Political Theory, Stability, and Change* (Berkeley: University of California Press, 1992), esp. 188–92, 201–7. This essay first appeared as "Appendix B: A Theory of Stable Democracy" in Eckstein, *Division and Cohesion in*

Democracy: A Study of Norway (Princeton: Princeton University Press, 1966). The differences between Eckstein's approach and mine are discussed at the end of chap. 2, section 2.4.

67. The significance of these two dimensions is considered in greater detail in chap. 2, section 2.4. Note especially the discussion accompanying figure 8.

68. This assumption is also adapted from Eckstein, "A Theory of Stable Democracy," 201–7. But, as will be made clear in chap. 2 (section 2.4), Eckstein's formulation is somewhat different from mine. In tracing incongruities across *different* social contexts, Eckstein discounted the possibility of compartmentalization of roles; the assumption made here is more plausible because it is not as restrictive, limiting the focus to dispositions of individuals facing incongruent authority patterns *within* institutions or across *functionally similar* institutions.

69. On the general cognitive dispositions and tendencies deriving from anxiety, see Harry Sullivan, *The Fusion of Psychiatry and Social Science* (New York: W. W. Norton, 1964). On the significance of anxiety and the need for a sense of emotional security in organizational contexts, see Wilfred Bion, *Experiences in Groups* (London: Tavistock, 1961); Chris Argyris, *Integrating the Individual and the Organization* (New York: John Wiley, 1964); Douglas LaBier, "Emotional Disturbances in the Federal Bureaucracy," *Administration and Society* 14, 4 (1983): 403–48; Eric J. Miller, *The 'Leicester' Model: Experiential Study of Group and Organizational Processes,* Occasional Paper No. 10 (London: Tavistock Institute of Human Relations, 1989); and Hirschorn.

70. See, e.g., Hirschorn; and Baum, *Organizational Membership.*

71. On the psychological difficulties created by unfamiliar environments, see Adrian Furnham and Stephen Bochner, *Culture Shock: Psychological Reactions to Unfamiliar Environments* (London: Methuen, 1986).

72. Where revolutionary approaches, for example, happen to advocate ideals that are consistent with preexisting norms, there is congruence even though the new elites may view their ideals as a fundamental break with the past. For example, the Bolsheviks' initial advocacy of wage egalitarianism and collective labor resonated with much of the work force; only when the Bolsheviks departed from these ideals in practice did marked incongruities and frustrations appear in Soviet factories (see chap. 4).

73. For Japan, the period of late industrialization is assumed to hold through the 1970s, corresponding to the period when Japan still lagged significantly behind the United States in per capita income, and most Japanese—both elites and masses—still regarded themselves as relatively economically backward (see chap. 3, section 3.3). In Russia's case, despite the massive gains in production and the attainment of superpower status between the 1930s and 1970s, events of the past two decades clearly justify the treatment of Russia as a continuing late industrializer.

74. Tadashi Anno provides a rich and compelling treatment of antisystemic discourses and movements in Japan and Russia as a particular kind of response to the Western-dominated liberal world order; see Tadashi Anno, *The Liberal World Order and Its Challengers: Nationalism and the Rise of Anti-Systemic Movements in*

Russia and Japan, 1860–1950 (Ph.D. diss., University of California at Berkeley, 1999).

75. Even in Soviet Russia, the path to international proletarian revolution was consistently regarded as contingent on the prior construction of a sound industrial base that could match and surpass *(dognat i peregnat)* the capitalist West in production.

76. The use of Japan and Russia as especially revealing cases of the quest for modernity in NWLIs is not unprecedented. In the early 1970s, Japan and Russia were considered to be two of the most successful cases of modernization in non-Western settings; see, e.g., Cyril Black et al., *The Modernization of Japan and Russia* (New York: Free Press, 1975). More recent comparisons of Japan and Russia, however, emphasize how different modernizing projects yielded quite different results in the attempt to respond to pressures created by encounters with the West; see the two books by Johann Arnason, *The Future That Failed: Origins and Destinies of the Soviet Model* (London: Routledge, 1993) and *Social Theory and the Japanese Experience: The Dual Civilization* (London: Kegan Paul International, 1997).

77. Post-Soviet Russia is not analyzed as a separate case here since no coherent strategy is yet in evidence, but the implications of Soviet-era legacies for contemporary Russian enterprises are briefly considered in the conclusion to chapter 4. A more elaborate discussion is in Rudra Sil, "Privatization, Labor Politics, and the Firm in Post-Soviet Russia: Non-market Norms, Market Institutions, and the Soviet Legacy," in Christopher Candland and Rudra Sil, eds., *The Politics of Labor in a Global Age: Continuity and Change in Late-Industrializing and Post-Socialist Economies* (New York: Oxford University Press, 2001).

78. Chapter 2 discusses at greater length the extent to which evidence of labor turnover, industrial disputes, labor discipline (violations of factory rules), workers' attitudes, and the diversion of time and resources to activities deemed unproductive for the enterprise can be *collectively* employed as reasonable approximations of managerial authority at least for the purposes of establishing large differences. The particular observations about workers' attitudes and behaviors in Japan and Soviet Russia are discussed in greater detail within their respective historical contexts, in chapters 3 and 4.

79. One cross-national study published in 1980, for example, found Japan to be the least individualistic of all the industrialized societies surveyed; see Hofstede, esp. 230–32. Similarly, despite the fall of the USSR, recent surveys point to a marked absence of individualism among the masses; see Judith Kullberg and William Zimmerman, "Liberal Elites, Socialist Masses, and Problems of Russian Democracy," *World Politics* 51 (April 1999): 323–58. Further evidence on the resilience of collectivist orientations in Japan and Russia is incorporated into the discussion in sections 3.1 and 4.1 of chaps. 3 and 4 respectively.

80. My treatment thus differs from recent characterizations of Japanese industrial management as constituting a model for lean production worldwide. Examples of the latter view include Kenney and Florida; Tony Elger and Chris Smith, eds., *Global Japanization? The Transnational Transformation of the Labour Process* (London: Routledge, 1994); Raphael Kaplinsky, "Technique and System:

The Spread of Japanese Management Techniques to Developing Countries,"
World Development 23, 1 (1995): 57–71; and Paul Adler, "'Democratic Taylorism':
The Toyota Production system at NUMMI," in Steve Babson, ed., *Lean Work:
Empowerment and Exploitation in the Global Auto Industry* (Detroit: Wayne State
University Press, 1995).

81. As noted in chap. 4, in their theoretical writings, Bolshevik leaders interpreted "workers' control" to mean not workers' self-management but all workers'
collective control of all factories through a unified system of national administration under the "dictatorship of the proletariat"; and communist equality meant not
absolute equality of material conditions but the abolition of classes and the eventual realization of the principle "from each according to ability, to each according
to need."

82. See the epigraph to chap. 4.

83. Charles Tilly, "Means and Ends of Comparison in Macrosociology,"
Comparative Social Research 16 (1997): 43–53.

84. See Douglass North, "The New Institutional Economics," *Journal of
Theoretical and Institutional Economics,* 142 (1986): 230–37; and North, *Institutions, Institutional Change, and Economic Performance* (New York: Cambridge
University Press, 1990).

85. Despite his criticisms of big case comparisons, Tilly does recognize
specific situations where cross-national comparison is feasible (for example, where
state behavior or state-circumscribed institutions are involved). In fact, his own
coauthored book on work under capitalism makes numerous references to
national-level features of work and managerial behavior that reflect distinctive cultural influences and are shaped by state policies or influences. See Tilly, "Means
and Ends," 46–47; and Chris Tilly and Charles Tilly, *Work Under Capitalism*
(Boulder: Westview, 1998), 99, 204, 241–42.

86. On the developmental state, see Alice Amsden, "The State and Taiwan's
Economic Development," in Evans et al.; Chalmers Johnson, "Political Institutions and Economic Performance: The Government-Business Relationship in
Japan, South Korea, and Taiwan," in Frederic C. Deyo, ed., *The Political Economy of the New Asian Industrialism* (Ithaca: Cornell University Press); Peter Evans,
Embedded Autonomy: States and Industrial Transformation (Princeton: Princeton
University Press, 1995); and Robert Wade, *Governing the Market: Economic Theory and the Role of Government in East Asian Industrialization* (Princeton: Princeton University Press, 1990).

87. In the case of Japan, select universities such as Tokyo University and
Keio University provided much of the top-echelon managerial elites during the
twentieth century; as far back as 1924, 244 of the top 384 business managers in
Japan had college degrees, with 200 graduating from just three institutions: Tokyo
University, Tokyo Higher Commercial School, and Keio Academy. In the case of
Soviet Russia, of course, all universities and training institutes were controlled and
managed by the party-state apparatus, and the most well-known and important
engineers of the Stalin era came out of a handful of institutions (such as the
Moscow Higher Technical School or the Polytechnic Institute in Leningrad) and
formed relatively cohesive managerial networks. See, respectively, Mansel Black-

ford, *The Rise of Modern Business in Great Britain, the United States, and Japan,* 2d ed. (Chapel Hill: University of North Carolina Press, 1998), 120; and Kendall Bailes, *Technology and Society under Lenin and Stalin: Origins of the Soviet Technical Intelligentsia, 1917–1941* (Princeton: Princeton University Press, 1988), 101, 265–70.

88. DiMaggio and Powell.

89. Well-known studies that address typical features of "the Japanese firm" or "the Soviet firm" are cited throughout chapters 3 and 4 respectively. The value of cross-national comparisons of firms and organizations is also evident in Bendix, *Work and Authority;* Cole, *Work, Mobility, and Participation;* C. J. Lammers and D. J. Hickson, eds., *Organizations Alike and Unalike: International and Inter-Institutional Studies in the Sociology of Organizations* (London: Routledge and Kegan Paul, 1979); Craig Littler, *The Development of the Labour Process in Capitalist Societies: A Comparative Study of the Transformation of Work Organization in Britain, Japan, and the U.S.A.* (London: Heinemann, 1982); Bernard Silberman, *Cages of Reason: The Rise of the Rational State in France, Japan, the United States, and Great Britain* (Chicago: University of Chicago Press, 1993); and Sonja A. Sackman, ed., *Cultural Complexity in Organizations: Inherent Contrasts and Contradictions* (Thousand Oaks: Sage, 1997).

90. Most recently, see the study by Tilly and Tilly who use the terms *producers* and *recipients* of the use-value added by work to refer respectively to workers and managers; see Tilly and Tilly, *Work under Capitalism,* 69–93.

91. In fact, evidence from firms dominated by white-collar tasks and skills (banks, for example) is included in the discussion of Japanese and Russian large-scale enterprises as long as the organization of work and authority reflects principles similar to those found in manufacturing enterprises where the majority of tasks correspond to blue-collar work.

92. For those interested in the distinctive experiences of women in Japan and Russia, there already exists an excellent body of scholarly work. On Japan, see, e.g., E. Patricia Tsurumi, *Factory Girls: Women in the Thread Mills of Meiji Japan* (Princeton: Princeton University Press, 1990); Dorine Kondo, *Crafting Selves: Power, Gender, and the Discourses of Identity in a Japanese Workplace* (Chicago: University of Chicago Press, 1990); and Mary Brinton, *Women and the Economic Miracle: Gender and Work in Postwar Japan* (Berkeley: University of California Press, 1993). On Russia, see Gail Lapidus, *Women in Soviet Society: Equality, Development, and Social Change* (Berkeley: University of California Press, 1978); Lapidus, ed., *Women, Work and Family in the Soviet Union* (Armonk, NY: M. E. Sharpe, 1982); and Mary Buckley, *Perestroika and Soviet Women* (New York: Cambridge University Press, 1992).

93. Bruce Bueno de Mesquita, "Toward a Scientific Understanding of International Conflict," *International Studies Quarterly* 29 (1985): 121–36. This view represents a qualified version of the position taken by such philosophers of science as Carl Hempel; see "The Function of General Laws in History," *Journal of Philosophy* 39 (1942).

94. The hypothesis-generating comparative approach is discussed in Arend Lijphart, "Comparative Politics and the Comparative Method," *American Politi-*

cal Science Review 65 (1971): 682–93. As applied here, it also constitutes an extension of Becker's building-block approach insofar as an initial hypothesis emerged from first contrasting prewar and postwar Japan, with a more refined version emerging by extending the comparison to Soviet Russia; see Howard S. Becker, "Social Observation and Case Studies," *International Encyclopedia of the Social Sciences* 11 (1968): 232–38.

95. These uses of small-*n* comparative research correspond respectively to the "macro-causal," "contrast of contexts," and "parallel demonstration" comparative approaches in Theda Skocpol and Margaret Somers, "The Uses of Comparative History in Macrosocial Inquiry," *Comparative Studies in Society and History,* 2, 2 (April 1980): 174–97. See also James Mahoney, "Nominal, Ordinal, and Narrative Appraisal in Macrocausal Analysis," *American Journal of Sociology* 104, 4 (1999): 1154–96. Mill's methods of induction are outlined in John Stuart Mill, *A System of Logic* (New York: Harper and Row, 1888).

96. For a more detailed discussion of the defining characteristics and trade-offs associated with middle-range comparative history and other strategies for theory-building and empirical analysis, see Rudra Sil, "The Division of Labor in Social Science Research: Unified Methodology or 'Organic Solidarity'?" *Polity* 32, 4 (summer 2000): 499–531.

97. On this point, see Ian Lustick, "History, Historiography, and Political Science: Multiple Historical Records and the Problem of Selection Bias," *American Political Science Review* 90, 3 (September 1996): 605–18.

98. Burawoy critiques Skocpol's *States and Social Revolutions* for doing just this, noting that her analysis relies on contradictory commitments: on the one hand, she wishes to have facts speak to theoretical statements, but on the other hand, she "freezes history" in order to highlight the significance of particular factors rather than the processes leading to them. See Michael Burawoy, "Two Methods in Search of Science: Skocpol versus Trotsky," *Theory and Society* 18 (1989): 759–805, esp. 769–73; and Theda Skocpol, *States and Social Revolutions* (New York: Cambridge University Press, 1979).

99. The typical oppositions in both cases revolve around three recurrent and overlapping issues: (a) whether the treatment of political economy and society in Japan or Russia is positive or critical (with revisionist historiography on Japan adopting a more critical stance and revisionist treatments of Russian history offering a more benign treatment of Soviet history); (b) whether the developmental experience of the relevant country is historically unique, or whether it reflects a peculiar variation on more processes found elsewhere (e.g., modernization in the West); and (c) whether particular events in Japanese and Russian history (e.g., the Occupation in Japan and the post-Stalin transition in Russia) represent fundamental divides in Japanese and Russian history.

100. For example, both positive and critical appraisals of postwar Japanese labor relations recognize the increased levels of managerial authority in the 1960s and 1970s when compared to the past. Similarly, both positive and critical views on the stability of industrial relations in the Brezhnev era acknowledge the substitution of informal mechanisms for more coercive measures for checking worker unrest.

101. See Ellen Immergut, "The Theoretical Core of the New Institutional-ism," *Politics and Society* 26, 1 (March 1998): 5–34; and Peter Hall and Rosemary Taylor, "Political Science and the Three New Institutionalisms," *Political Studies* 44 (1996): 936–57.

102. In this respect, I concur with Selznick that too much is made of the dis-tinction between the "old" and "new" institutionalism; the latter's contributions are most useful where its claims are more modest and less dogmatic. See Philip Selznick, "Institutionalism: 'Old' and 'New'," *Administrative Science Quarterly* 41 (1996): 270–77.

103. See the second section of appendix A and the more elaborate discussion of these issues in my "Foundations of Eclecticism."

104. Paul Pierson, "Increasing Returns, Path Dependence, and the Study of Politics," *American Political Science Review* 94, 2 (June 2000): 251–67.

105. The concept of "elective affinity," borrowed from Goethe (see the epi-graph to chap. 5), was invoked by Weber to suggest that particular ideas could be fruitfully "elected" by social groups in promoting particular interests and activi-ties; the absence of such an affinity implied dysfunctional tensions between ideas and interests. Thus, in *The Protestant Ethic* thesis, Calvinism did not "cause" cap-italism or emerge in response to "needs"; but, several of its core ideals proved func-tional for the consolidation of capitalism given its "elective affinity" with the inter-ests and activities of the middle class. On this reading of Weber's thesis, see the discussion at nn. 92–93 in chap. 2.

106. Typical functionalist explanations posit that "the consequences of some behavior or social arrangement are essential elements of that behavior"; Arthur Stinchcombe, *Constructing Social Theories* (New York: Harcourt, Brace and World, 1968), 80. Contemporary functionalists tend to follow the "weak program" of functionalist analysis outlined in Robert Merton, *Social Theory and Social Structure* (New York: Free Press, 1966). Such approaches are supposedly more empirically driven, and acknowledge the importance of unintended consequences of individuals and groups, but they still continue to accept some variant of the logic of "natural selection" in explaining the decline and proliferation of particular ways of life. This is evident, for example, in Ellis et al., 106; and Inglehart, 16. For excellent critiques of mainstream functionalism, see Stinchcombe, *Constructing Social Theories,* 80–85; Alvin Gouldner, *The Coming Crisis of Western Sociology* (New York: Basic Books, 1970), 126; and Jon Elster, *Ulysses and the Sirens: Stud-ies in Rationality and Irrationality* (New York: Cambridge University Press, 1979).

Chapter 2

1. Charles Sabel, *Work and Politics: The Division of Labor in Industry* (Cambridge: Cambridge University Press, 1982), 10.

2. Claus Offe, "Designing Institutions for East European Transitions," in J. Hausner, B. Jessop, and K. Nielson, eds., *Strategic Choice and Path-Dependency in Post-Socialism: Institutional Dynamics in the Transformation Process* (Alder-shot, UK: Gower, 1995), 57.

3. In this chapter, the term *organization* may be used interchangeably with

institution insofar as both refer to bounded entities akin to bureaucratic firms. Elsewhere, however, the term *organization* is reserved for the manner in which roles and tasks are formally differentiated and structured within an *institution.*

4. I define as *universalist* those approaches that are founded on the unquestioned assumption that the common sources and characteristics of political, economic, and social change are epistemologically more significant than historical or contextual factors thought to account for systematic variations or idiosyncratic characteristics.

5. Adam Smith, *An Inquiry into the Nature and Causes of the Wealth of Nations* (New York: Modern Library, 1937), 5.

6. Differentiation is formally defined by Rueschemeyer as "a process whereby one social role or organization . . . differentiates into two or more roles or organizations. . . . The new social units are structurally distinct from each other, but taken together are functionally equivalent to the original unit"; see Rueschemeyer, *Power,* 3.

7. See Herbert Spencer, *Principles of Sociology* (New York: Appleton, 1986); and his *On Social Evolution,* ed. J. D. Y. Peel (Chicago: University of Chicago Press, 1972). Insightful discussions of Spencer's work include Robert G. Perrin, "Herbert Spencer's Four Theories of Social Evolution," *American Journal of Sociology* (May 1976); and Jerzy Szacki, *History of Sociological Thought* (Westport, CT: Greenwood, 1979), 206–29.

8. On this point, see Andrew Janos, *Politics and Paradigms: Changing Theories of Change in Social Science* (Stanford: Stanford University Press, 1982), 20–28.

9. Karl Marx, "Excerpts from *Capital,* Volume Three," in *The Marx-Engels Reader,* ed. Robert Tucker, 2d ed. (New York: W. W. Norton, 1978), esp. 439–41.

10. Karl Marx, "Economic and Philosophic Manuscripts of 1844," in *Marx-Engels Reader,* esp. 72; and Marx, "Selections from *Capital,* Volume One," in *Marx-Engels Reader,* 403–11.

11. Tönnies feared that the "natural" intimate social relations of *Gemeinschaft* would irretrievably give way to more "transitory and superficial" social relations of *Gesellschaft;* see Ferdinand Tönnies, *Community and Society* [*Gemeinschaft und Gesellschaft*], trans. and ed. Charles Loomis (New York: Harper and Row, 1957), esp. 33–40, 76–80.

12. See Emile Durkheim, *The Division of Labor in Society* (New York: Free Press, 1933), esp. chaps. 2 and 3. Note that while Tönnies refers to the "organic" nature of *Gemeinschaft* and the "mechanistic" quality of *Gesellschaft,* Durkheim's opposition of "mechanical" and "organic" solidarity (conceived of in biological terms) is intended to correspond respectively to Tönnies's *Gemeinschaft* and *Gesellschaft.*

13. Emile Durkheim, *Suicide: A Study in Sociology* (Glencoe: Free Press, 1951), esp. 257–58.

14. See Durkheim, *Suicide,* 361–92.

15. In contrast to "traditional" authority, which rested on the acceptance of "the sanctity of immemorial traditions," "rational-legal" authority rested on "a

belief in the 'legality' of patterns of normative rules and the right of those elevated to authority under such rules to issue commands." At the individual level, Weber conceptualized rationality in terms of "value-rational" and "instrumental-rational" action, based respectively on a conscious commitment to a course of action and on consciously determined ideal and material interests; he distinguished these from "affectual" and "traditional" action, based respectively on emotions and habituated practices. The first two categories of social action and the rational-legal type of authority, in conjunction with the appearance of industrial capitalism, may be considered as indicative of Weber's conception of modernity for the purposes of the discussion to follow (Weber, *Economy and Society,* 24–26, 215–41, quotes from 215).

16. Weber, *Economy and Society,* 119.

17. See H. H. Gerth and C. W. Mills, *From Max Weber* (New York: Oxford University Press, 1949), 62–63.

18. See the discussion in this chapter at nn. 92–93.

19. Weber, *Economy and Society,* 1401.

20. Weber, *Economy and Society,* 988–92, quote from 988; the "iron cage" is referred to in Weber, *The Protestant Ethic,* 181–82.

21. This view is most explicit in Weber's discussions of how "domination by virtue of constellation of interests" becomes progressively transformed into "domination by virtue of authority"; see *Economy and Society,* 944–45.

22. Weber, *Economy and Society,* 1402.

23. On the epistemological foundations of Taylorism, see Merkle, esp. 292, n. 25. And, on the influence of the discourses of "systems" among engineers on Taylor's view of firms, see the rich discussion in Yehouda Shenhav, *Manufacturing Rationality: The Engineering Foundations of the Managerial Revolution* (New York: Oxford University Press, 1999), esp. 45–101.

24. See Frederick Taylor, "A Piece-Rate System, Being a Step toward Partial Solution of the Labor Problem," *Transactions, American Society of Mechanical Engineers* 16 (1895): 856–83. See also the discussion in Chandler, *The Visible Hand,* 275–77.

25. These practices are outlined in F. Taylor, "Scientific Management," passim. See also the discussion in Bendix, *Work and Authority,* 277–79; Merkle, 7–8; Guillen, 43–44; and section 2.2 on the implementation of scientific management practices in historical context. For detailed discussions of Taylor and his contributions, see Frank Copley, *Frederick W. Taylor, Father of Scientific Management,* 2 vols. (New York: Harper and Brothers, 1923); Samuel Haber, *Efficiency and Uplift: Scientific Management in the Progressive Era, 1890–1920* (Chicago: University of Chicago Press, 1964); Daniel Nelson, *Frederick W. Taylor and the Rise of Scientific Management* (Madison: University of Wisconsin Press, 1980); and Robert Kanigel, *The One Best Way: Frederick Winslow Taylor and the Enigma of Efficiency* (New York: Viking, 1997).

26. In fact, Taylor even viewed trade unions as unnecessary under scientific management. On this point, see Merkle, 7–8, 290–91.

27. Veblen's image of the firm and the worker are contained, respectively, in *The Theory of the Business Enterprise* and *The Instinct of Workmanship.* On the

critical treatment of conspicuous consumption by the leisure class, see Veblen, *The Theory of the Leisure Class: An Economic Study in the Evolution of Institutions* (New York: Macmillan, 1899). On Veblen's writings and activities, see Haber, chaps. 5–8; E. Layton, "Veblen and the Engineers," *American Quarterly* 14, 1 (spring 1962): 64–72; and Ed Taylor, *Closing the Iron Cage: The Scientific Management of Work and Leisure* (New York: Black Rose Books, 1999), chap. 5. For an excellent critique of the technological determinism underlying Veblen's writings, see Bendix, "Tradition and Modernity."

28. Parsons edited and introduced a major compilation of Weber's writings; see Max Weber, *The Theory of Social and Economic Organization* (New York: Free Press, 1964), ed. Talcott Parsons. Parsons's sympathetic attitude toward Taylor is evident in his "Social Classes and Class Conflict in the Light of Recent Sociological Theory," in Parsons, *Essays in Sociological Theory,* rev. ed. (New York: Free Press, 1964).

29. On modernization theory as a Kuhnian paradigm, see Janos, *Politics and Paradigms.*

30. Parsons, *The Social System* (New York: Free Press, 1951); and his *Societies: Evolutionary and Comparative Perspectives* (Englewood Cliffs: Prentice-Hall, 1966), esp. 28–29. With the shift to the language of systems and functional equilibrium, the concern for agency in Parsons's earlier treatise, *The Structure of Social Action* (New York: Free Press, 1937), essentially disappeared.

31. Talcott Parsons and Edward Shils, *Toward a General Theory of Action* (New York: Harper and Row, 1951), 76–88.

32. These changes were more explicitly traced in Parsons's later works, which emphasized the emergence of several functionally interrelated "evolutionary universals," including social stratification, role differentiation, bureaucratization, the use of money and markets, a universal legal system, and democratic pluralism—all of which combined to enhance "adaptive capacity" and "operative flexibility." See Talcott Parsons, "Evolutionary Universals in Society," *American Sociological Review* 29 (June 1964): 339–57; and Parsons, *Societies.*

33. Parsons himself insisted that Weber's cautions about the utility of his ideal-typical constructs reflected the intellectual environment in which he wrote and masked Weber's more deterministic view of rationalization; however, Weber's warnings are taken much more seriously by others such as Bendix and Giddens who (correctly) interpret Weber's discussions of social change in view of his explicit comments on ontology and epistemology. See Talcott Parsons, "Evaluation and Objectivity in Social Science: An Interpretation of Max Weber's Contribution," *International Social Science Journal* 17, 1 (1965): 46–63; Reinhard Bendix, *Max Weber: An Intellectual Portrait,* rev. ed. (Berkeley: University of California Press, 1977); and Anthony Giddens, *Capitalism and Modern Social Theory* (Cambridge: Cambridge University Press, 1974), 119–84.

34. Key works in different disciplines that reflect this set of core assumptions include Lerner; Gabriel Almond and James Coleman, eds., *The Politics of the Developing Areas* (Princeton: Princeton University Press, 1960); Walt W. Rostow, *The Stages of Economic Growth: A Non-Communist Manifesto* (Cambridge: Cambridge University Press, 1962); Gabriel Almond and Sidney Verba, *The Civic Cul-*

ture: Political Attitudes and Democracy in Five Nations (Princeton: Princeton University Press, 1963); Marion Levy, *Modernization and the Structure of Societies* (Princeton: Princeton University Press, 1966); Cyril Black, "Phases of Modernization," in Jason Finkle and Karl Gable, eds., *Political Development and Social Change* (New York: John Wiley, 1966); and David McClelland, "The Achievement Motive in Economic Growth," in Finkle and Gable. See also the detailed critical discussion of these works in Rudra Sil, *Historical Legacies, Late-Industrialization, and Institution-Building: A Comparative Study of Industrial Enterprises and Worker Commitment in Japan and Russia* (Ph.D. thesis, University of California, Berkeley, 1996), 54–66.

35. See Kerr et al.; and Clark Kerr and Abraham Siegel, "The Inter-Industry Propensity to Strike," in Kerr et al., eds., *Labor and Management in Industrial Society* (Garden City: Anchor, 1964). As evidence of the increasing number of specialized jobs, W. Moore notes that the U.S. Department of Labor listed nearly 30,000 separate occupational titles by 1960!

36. See, e.g., Ferdynand Zweig, *The Worker in an Affluent Society: Family Life and Industry* (London: Heinemann, 1961); and John Goldthorpe and David Lockwood, "Affluence and British Class Structure," *Sociological Review* 11 (July 1963): 133–63.

37. Robert Blauner, *Alienation and Freedom* (Chicago: University of Chicago Press, 1964).

38. Stinchcombe's analysis was based on a study of careers and work roles in steel plants in Argentina, Venezuela, and Chile; see Arthur Stinchcombe, *Creating Efficient Industrial Administration* (New York: Academic, 1974), esp. 29–39.

39. Inkeles and Smith, esp. 154–75.

40. Those who focused on technology-driven explanations of organizational structure include Joan Woodward, *Industrial Organization: Theory and Practice* (London: Oxford University Press, 1965); James Thompson, *Organizations in Action* (New York: McGraw-Hill, 1967); and Harrison White, *Chains of Opportunity: Systems Models of Mobility in Organizations* (Cambridge: Harvard University Press, 1970). On the implications of increases in organizational size, see D. S. Pugh and D. J. Hickson, *Organizational Structure in Its Context: The Aston Programme I* (London: Saxon House, 1976); D. S. Pugh and C. R. Hinings, eds., *Organizational Structure: Extensions and Replications* (Farnborough, UK: Saxon House, 1976); and D. J. Hickson, C. J. McMillan, K. Azumi, and D. Horvath, "Grounds for Comparative Organization Theory: Quicksands or Hard Core?" in Lammers and Hickson.

41. See the insightful discussion of this point in Dietrich Rueschemeyer, "Structural Differentiation, Efficiency, and Power," *American Journal of Sociology* 83, 1 (1977): 1–25.

42. See the discussion of Barnard's influence on different strands of organization theory in Charles Perrow, *Complex Organizations: A Critical Essay* (Glenview: Scott, Foresman, 1972), 83–85.

43. Simon, *Administrative Behavior.*

44. Richard Cyert and James March, *The Behavioral Theory of the Firm* (Englewood Cliffs: Prentice-Hall, 1963).

45. See Simon, *Administrative Behavior;* Simon, *Models of Man, Social and Rational: Mathematical Essays on Rational Human Behavior in a Social Setting* (New York: Wiley, 1957); and James March and Herbert Simon, *Organizations* (New York: Wiley, 1958). On the limited extent to which these theorists broke with Taylorism, see Stephen Waring, *Taylorism Transformed: Scientific Management Theory since 1945* (Chapel Hill: University of North Carolina Press, 1991), 58–63.

46. William H. Whyte, *The Organization Man* (New York: Simon and Schuster, 1956). For a critical theory perspective echoing these same concerns, see Herbert Marcuse, *One-Dimensional Man* (Boston: Beacon, 1964). See also the critique of Simon and his colleagues for adopting the top-down view of managerial personnel in Sheldon Wolin, *Politics and Vision* (Boston: Little, Brown, 1960), esp. 38–81.

47. The classic example here is Harry Braverman, *Labor and Monopoly Capital: The Degradation of Work in the Twentieth Century* (New York: Monthly Review Press, 1974). See also Steven Marglin, "What Do Bosses Do? The Origins and Functions of Hierarchy in Capitalist Production," *Review of Radical Political Economy* 6 (1974): 60–112.

48. On the possibilities for negotiating arenas of autonomy, see, e.g., Richard Edwards, *Contested Terrain: The Transformation of Work in the Twentieth Century* (New York: Basic Books, 1979); and Burawoy, *Manufacturing Consent.* On the significance of government regulation in the labor process, see, e.g., Michael Burawoy, *The Politics of Production* (London: Verson, 1985); and Michel Aglietta, *A Theory of Capitalist Regulation* (London: Verson, 1987).

49. On this point, see also Shenhav, 1–15.

50. Neil Smelser, "Mechanisms of Change and Adjustment to Change," in Bert F. Hoselitz and Wilbert E. Moore, *Industrialization and Social Change* (The Hague: Mouton/UNESCO, 1970).

51. See Henry A. Landsberger, "Parsons' Theory of Organizations," in Max Black, ed., *The Social Theories of Talcott Parsons* (Englewood Cliffs: Prentice-Hall, 1961), 214–49.

52. Mayo, 112, 10.

53. See Gardner; F. J. Roethlisberger and W. J. Dickson, *Management and the Worker* (Cambridge: Harvard University Press, 1946); W. Lloyd Warner and O. J. Low, *The Social System of the Modern Factory* (New Haven: Yale University Press, 1947); William F. Whyte, *Human Relations in the Restaurant Industry* (New York: McGraw-Hill, 1948); and Morris Viteles, *Motivation and Morale in Industry* (New York: Norton, 1953).

54. Viteles, 14.

55. Larry Hirschorn and Carole Barnett, "Introduction," in Hirschorn and Barnett, xiv. The Tavistock approach is evident in Bion; E. J. Miller; E. L. Trist, G. W. Higgin, H. Murray, and A. B. Pollock, *Organizational Choice: Capabilities of Groups at the Coal Face under Changing Technologies* (London: Tavistock Institute, 1963); and Fred Emery, *The Emergence of a New Paradigm of Work* (Canberra: Centre for Continuing Education, Australian National University, 1978). More recent approaches that build on this psychoanalytic perspective are summa-

rized in Larry Hirschorn and Carole Barnett, eds., *The Psychodynamics of Organizations* (Philadelphia: Temple University Press, 1993).

56. Abraham Maslow, *Motivation and Personality* (New York: Harper and Row, 1954).

57. Among the many works in the 1960s and 1970s that reflected this orientation are Argyris; Douglas McGregor, *The Human Side of Enterprise* (New York: McGraw-Hill, 1960); and Rensis Likert, *The Human Organization: Its Management and Value* (New York: McGraw-Hill, 1967).

58. See Womack et al.; Kenney and Florida; and Adler, "'Democratic Taylorism." The treatment of employee productivity in these works is partially adapted from past investigations into what U.S. firms could do to match the productivity and stability of Japanese firms. See, e.g., Peter Drucker, "What We Can Learn from Japanese Management," *Harvard Business Review* 49 (March–April 1971): 110–22; and William Ouchi, *Theory Z: How American Business Can Meet the Japanese Challenge* (Reading: Addison-Wesley, 1981).

59. See Alvin Gouldner, *Patterns of Industrial Bureaucracy* (New York: Free Press, 1954); and Amitai Etzioni, *A Comparative Analysis of Complex Organizations* (New York: Free Press, 1961).

60. Peter Blau, "The Hierarchy of Authority in Organizations," *American Journal of Sociology* 73 (January 1968); and Jerald Hage and Michael Aiken, "Relationship of Centralization to Other Structural Properties," *Administrative Science Quarterly* 12 (1967): 72–92.

61. Perrow criticizes these typologies for making too much out of commonplace issues that are inherent in any complex, bureaucratic organization; Perrow, *Complex Organizations,* esp. 55.

62. See Oliver Williamson, *Markets and Hierarchies* (New York: Free Press, 1975); and Williamson, *The Economic Institutions of Capitalism* (New York: Free Press, 1985). On the extent to which Williamson and other contemporary organization economists break with assumptions of past organization theorists about market coordination and efficiency-maximizing decision making, see also G. Miller, 5.

63. See Ronald Coase, "The Nature of the Firm," *Economica* 4 (1937): 386–405; and Schumpeter.

64. Chandler, *The Visible Hand,* and his *Strategy and Structure: Chapters in the History of the Industrial Enterprise* (Cambridge: MIT Press, 1962).

65. See, e.g., William G. Ouchi, "Markets, Bureaucracies and Clans," *Administrative Science Quarterly* 25, 1 (March 1980): 129–41; and Gary Hamilton and Nicole Biggart, "Market, Culture and Authority: A Comparative Analysis of Management and Organization in the Far East," *American Journal of Sociology* 94 (Supplement 1988): S52–S94.

66. See, e.g., Bendix, *Work and Authority;* Sabel; Rueschemeyer, *Power;* Shenhav; Thomas; and Tilly and Tilly. For a more general treatment of how historical factors have influenced the introduction of particular technologies, see also Wiebe Bijker, Thomas Hughes, and Trevor Pinch, *The Social Construction of Technological Systems: New Directions in the Sociology and History of Technology* (Cambridge: MIT Press, 1987); and Michael Tushman and Lori Rosenkopf,

346 Notes to Pages 76–78

"Organizational Determinants of Technological Change: Towards a Sociology of Technological Evolution," *Research in Organizational Behavior* 14 (1992): 311–47.

67. Pollard, 186–91. In fact, until the 1830s, large segments of the political elite also relied on traditional paternalistic ideals to address the growth of pauperism and other social problems (as famously evident in the Speenhamland Act of 1795); see Karl Polanyi, *The Great Transformation* (Boston: Beacon, 1944), chap. 7.

68. Smelser, *Social Change,* 107. This observation is also found in revisionist accounts of class formation and factory culture in England as evident in Fox; E. P. Thompson, *Making of the English Working Class* (New York: Vintage, 1963); Patrick Joyce, *Work, Society and Politics: The Culture of the Factory in Later Victorian England* (New Brunswick: Rutgers University Press, 1980); and Eric Hobsbawm, *Worlds of Labour: Further Studies in the History of Labour* (London: Weidenfeld and Nicolson, 1984).

69. See Chandler, *The Visible Hand,* 13–78; Herbert Gutman, *Work, Culture and Society in Industrializing America* (New York: Knopf, 1976); and Walter Licht, *Industrializing America: The Nineteenth Century* (Baltimore: Johns Hopkins University Press, 1995), 21–63.

70. Bendix, *Work and Authority,* 58, 198–253; and Pollard, 104, 181.

71. See Licht, 46–63; and Edward Shorter, "The History of Work in the West," in Shorter, ed., *Work and Community in the West* (New York: Harper and Row, 1973), 16–28.

72. In Britain, Smelser points to the protests in the mid–nineteenth century that culminated in the massacre at Peterloo. In the United States, the protests of Luddites, artisans, and crafts shop organizers may be viewed as a parallel phenomenon. See Smelser, *Social Change;* and Licht, 46–63, 166–96.

73. Pollard, 160, 270–72; and Guillen, 205–27.

74. For more extensive discussions of how the Taylor system was incorporated into U.S. industry, see Haber; Kanigel; and Daniel Nelson, *Managers and Workers: Origins of the New Factory System in the United States, 1880–1920* (Madison: University of Wisconsin Press, 1975).

75. The variants of scientific management proposed by Emerson, Gilbreth, Gantt, and Bedaux are outlined in, respectively, Harrington Emerson, *Efficiency as a Basis for Operation and Wages* (New York: Arno Press, 1979 [1911]); Frank B. Gilbreth, *Motion Study: A Method for Increasing the Efficiency of the Workman* (New York: Van Nostrand, 1911); Henry Gantt, *Organizing for Work* (New York: Harcourt, Brace and Howe, 1919); and Charles E. Bedaux, *The Bedaux Efficiency Course for Industrial Application* (Cleveland: Bedaux Industrial Institute, 1921). Also, on tensions between Taylorist managers and efficiency engineers, see Shenhav, 102–33.

76. Chandler, *The Visible Hand,* 276–79.

77. Guillen, 56–57.

78. Daniel Bell, "Work and Its Discontents: The Cult of Efficiency in America," in his book *The End of Ideology* (New York: Free Press, 1965). See also Shenhav, 45–101; and the broader discussion of "rationality" as an organizational belief among managers in James March and Martha Feldman, "Information in

Organizations as Signal and Symbol," *Administrative Science Quarterly* 26 (1981): 171–84.

79. Guillen, 52–57. See also the more detailed treatment in Stephen Meyer III, *The Five Dollar Day: Labor Management and Social Control in the Ford Motor Company, 1908–1921* (Albany: State University of New York Press, 1981); and for a comparative examination of the evolution of Fordist practices in other places, see Littler, *Development of the Labour Process.*

80. Charles Maier, "Between Taylorism and Technocracy: European Ideologies and the Vision of Industrial Productivity in the 1920s," *Journal of Contemporary History* 2 (1970): 27–61, esp. 55–60; and Craig Littler and Graeme Salaman, "The Design of Jobs," in Littler, 85–104.

81. Rich and detailed discussions of this transformation include Chandler, *The Visible Hand,* 81–283; and Neil Fligstein, *The Transformation of Corporate Control* (Cambridge: Harvard University Press, 1990), 1–115. For a more brief overview, see Licht, 133–65.

82. Maier, 32. See also Nelson, *Managers and Workers;* Shenhav, 134–94; and David Montgomery, *The Fall of the House of Labour* (New York: Cambridge University Press, 1987).

83. See Melvyn Dubofsky, *The State and Labor in Modern America* (Chapel Hill: University of North Carolina Press, 1994), 61–76; Guillen, 47–48; Blackford 98–100; and the more elaborate discussion in Nadworny, passim.

84. Guillen, 47–57; Rueschemeyer, *Power,* 79–93. On the functionality of job classifications from the perspective of managers and unions, see also Michael Piore, "Upward Mobility, Job Monotony, and Labor Market Structure," in James O'Toole, ed., *Work and the Quality of Life: Resource Papers for Work in America* (Cambridge: MIT Press, 1974), 73–87; and Katherine Stone, "The Origins of Job Structures in the Steel Industry," *Review of Radical Political Economics* (summer 1974): 113–73.

85. Maier, 55–60; and Shenhav, 205–6.

86. Haber, 120; Guillen, 205–27; Merkle, chap. 7; and E. Taylor, 72–73.

87. Maier, 37–45; Merkle, chaps. 5–6; and Guillen, 91–121. For a more detailed study of the spread of scientific management in 1920s Europe, see Paul Devinat, *Scientific Management in Europe,* ILO Studies and Reports, Series B, no. 17 (Geneva: International Labor Organization, 1927).

88. Maier, 55–60; and E. Taylor, 72–73.

89. In Britain, for example, the Anglo-American Council on Productivity and the British Productivity Center (created with Marshall Plan agencies) collaborated to promote American management techniques and engineer social pacts to gain their acceptance by labor. See Guillen, 220–27.

90. Bellah and his colleagues point to four different kinds of individualism in the United States alone: the biblical, republican, utilitarian, and expressive variants. It is the latter two that become dominant in the course of industrialization, and it is precisely these variants that bear the closest resemblance to the understanding of individualism adopted here for the purposes of defining and distinguishing the categories of Western and non-Western. See Bellah et al., 333–36.

91. See the discussion of collective identity and modernity in Eisenstadt, "Modernity," esp. 139–43.

92. The relevance of the earlier Judeo-Christian tradition for economic activity is suggested by Weber himself in his comparative sociology of religion; see *Economy and Society*, 611–30. The significance of Roman law and the Renaissance and Enlightenment has been suggested by Marcel Mauss, Durkheim's nephew; see Mauss, "A Category of the Human Mind," in Carrithers et al., 12–22.

93. This reading of Weber's argument has been shaped by considering Weber's specific contentions in *The Protestant Ethic* alongside his other writings as well as observations that his critics, such as Luthy and Trevor-Roper, and defenders, such as Troeltsch and Tawney, have since offered. See Weber, *The Protestant Ethic*; and *Economy and Society*, 611–30; Herbert Luthy, "Once Again: Calvinism and Capitalism," *Encounter* 22, 1 (January 1964): 26–68; H. R. Trevor-Roper, *Religion, the Reformation, and Social Change* (London: Macmillan, 1967); Ernst Troeltsch, *Protestantism and Progress* (Boston: Beacon, 1958); and Robert Tawney, *Religion and the Rise of Capitalism* (London: John Murray, 1933). For a more elaborate discussion of the different positions in the debate over the Weber thesis, see Ephraim Fischoff, "The Protestant Ethic and the Spirit of Capitalism: The History of a Controversy," *Social Research*, 99 (1944): 54–77; S. N. Eisenstadt, ed., *The Protestant Ethic and Modernization: A Comparative View* (New York: Basic Books, 1968); and Sil, *Historical Legacies*, 168–75.

94. Tilgher, 18–20.

95. Weber, *The Protestant Ethic*, 79–92, 117–18; Bendix, *Work and Authority*, 258–64; Bendix, "Definitions of Community"; and Guillen, 30–34.

96. Tilgher, 19.

97. Bendix, *Work and Authority*, 261–64; Guillen, 30–34; and Shenhav, 94–96.

98. Pollard, 197.

99. See Bendix, *Work and Authority*, 202–4, 261–77; Guillen, 30–44; and Shenhav, 162–94. On this point, see also the discussion in Bellah et al. about the role of utilitarian-type individualism in supporting the assumptions and methods of American managers in large-scale firms; Bellah et al., 43–47.

100. Bendix, *Work and Authority*, 274–78; and Guillen, 42–44. Taylor's phrases are from F. Taylor, "A Piece-Rate System," as quoted in Guillen.

101. In addition to Bendix, others who have explicitly noted the link between individualism and the assumptions of scientific management include Merkle, 7–8; Moore, 93–97; Cole, *Work, Mobility, and Participation*, 102–3; Arthur Stinchcombe, "Social Structure and Organizations," in James March, ed., *Handbook of Organizations* (Chicago: Rand McNally, 1965), 145ff; and Harry Triandis, "Subjective Culture and Economic Development," *International Journal of Psychology* 8 (1973): 163–80, esp. 166.

102. See Robin Williams, *American Society*, 3d ed. (New York: Knopf, 1970).

103. This is evident in the writings of present-day communitarianism, certain strands of organizational sociology, and certain treatments of political culture. See, e.g., Michael Sandel, *Liberalism and the Limits of Justice* (New York: Cambridge University Press, 1982); Selznick, *The Moral Commonwealth: Social Theory*

and the Promise of Community (Berkeley: University of California Press, 1992); Amitai Etzioni, *The Spirit of Community* (New York: Crown, 1993); and Robert Putnam, "Bowling Alone: America's Declining Social Capital," *Journal of Democracy* 6, 1 (January 1995): 65–78.

104. Anthropological studies, attitude surveys, and comparative studies of firms all confirm the view that the vast majority of American workers, blue-collar and white-collar, essentially accept an individualist work ethic and the economic inequalities that might go with it. See Francis L. K. Hsu, "American Core Values and National Character," in Hsu, ed., *Psychological Anthropology: Approaches to Culture and Personality* (Homewood, IL: Dorsey Press, 1961); D. Nelson and S. Campbell, "Taylorism vs. Welfare Work in American Industry," *Business History Review* 46 (1972): 1–16; Robert Davies and Nan Weiner, "A Cultural Perspective on the Study of Industrial Relations," in Peter J. Frost et al., eds., *Organizational Culture* (Beverly Hills: Sage, 1985); Hsu; Cinoy; Feagin; Sclozman and Verba; Hochschild, Bellah et al., 55–56; and Furnham.

105. See Feagin; Sclozman and Verba; and Hochschild.

106. Bendix, *Nation-Building,* 66–126. For an insightful treatment of the origins and spread of individualism in Britain, see Alan MacFarlane, *The Origins of English Individualism* (Oxford: Basil Blackwell, 1978).

107. See Louis Dumont, "Collective Identities and Universalist Ideology: The Actual Interplay," *Theory, Culture, and Society* 3, 3 (1986): 25–35. For empirical evidence of individualism in postwar (western) Germany, see Bernd Wegener and Stefan Liebig, "Dominant Ideologies and the Variation of Distributive Justice Norms: A Comparison of East and West Germany, and the United States," in Kleugel et al.; and Adam Swift, Gordon Marshall, Carole Burgoyne, and David Routh, "Distributive Justice: Does It Matter What People Think?" in Kleugel et al.

108. On the distinctive routes through which different sorts of individualism emerged in Britain and France, see Bendix, "Definitions of Community."

109. See the survey results reported in Hofstede, 222.

110. See Kluckhohn and Strodtbeck; Hofstede; and Triandis, "Cross-Cultural Studies of Individualism and Collectivism." In Hofstede's "individualism index" based on work-related values, for example, the fifteen most individualistic of the forty countries analyzed were all from North America and Western Europe, while the twenty least individualistic were all non-Western societies (including Japan) with the exceptions of Greece and Portugal; see Hofstede, 222. More recent studies conducted as part of the International Social Justice Project also point to relatively uniform values across the West when compared to postcommunist East European; see Kleugel et al. The contributions by Wegener and Liebig and by Swift et al. in this volume note similarities in attitudes across the United States, Britain, and Germany (despite the relatively stronger ethos of individualism in the United States), while noting marked differences between Western countries and postcommunist Europe in relation to attitudes toward market-based inequalities.

111. Mayo, 111.

112. Hugo Muensterberg, *Psychology and Industrial Efficiency* (Boston:

Houghton Mifflin, 1913). See also the discussion in Guillen 44–45; and E. Taylor, 75.

113. Guillen, 70–80.

114. The distinctive appropriation of human relations in supporting organizational innovation in postwar Japanese industry is considered in chap. 3 (section 3.3). The Soviet version of human relations, while providing greater material security to workers, did not have the same effect on the organization of work; see chap. 4 (section 4.3).

115. Guillen, 66.

116. This point was already anticipated in the 1950s by Bendix although he was writing during the heyday of the human relations revolution and was therefore tentative in challenging its novelty. Subsequent studies emphasize that managers in the United States were being instrumental in using suggestions from the human relations school in conjunction with the promotion of the Taft-Hartley Act (1947) to buttress their authority and undermine the unions. Some treat this approach as contributing to a long period of union decline; others see it as unsuccessful in stripping the influence of unions; and more critical treatments view practitioners of human relations as nothing more than the "maintenance crew for the human machinery" under Taylorist production. See, respectively, Blackford, 179; Dubofsky, 200–215; and Braverman, 87. For the purposes of this book, what counts is the convergence of these three interpretations on the point that managerial elites selectively invoked human relations to buttress their authority rather than reorganize production.

117. C. Wright Mills, "Contributions of Sociology to Studies of Industrial Relations," *Berkeley Journal of Sociology* (1970, reprint from 1948), 22–23. On this point, see also Waring 15; and E. Taylor, 75.

118. In addition to Maslow, see Argyris; Likert; and McGregor.

119. Special Task Force to the Secretary of Health, Education and Welfare [Elliot Richardson], *Work in America* (Cambridge: MIT Press, 1973). See also the accompanying essays in O'Toole, ed.; and the discussion of the report in Waring, 132–59. Other works in a similar vein include Thomas G. Cummings and Edmond Molloy, *Improving Productivity and the Quality of Working Life* (New York: Praeger, 1977); George Strauss, "Is There a Blue-Collar Revolt against Work?" in O'Toole, ed.; G. Palm, *The Flight from Work* (New York: Cambridge University Press, 1977), esp. 100–108; and Harold Wilensky, "Family Cycle, Work and the Quality of Life: Reflections on the Roots of Happiness, Despair and Indifference in Modern Society," in B. Gardell and G. Johansson, eds., *Working Life* (New York: Wiley, 1981).

120. See the excellent discussion of these criticisms in Waring, 149–55.

121. Littler and Salaman, 101–4.

122. See Sabel and Piore; Womack et al.; and Deyo, "Introduction." A concise description of lean production is contained in "Manufacturing the Right Way." For treatments that explicitly trace the features of post-Fordist lean production to Japanese management practices, see Drucker, Ouchi, *Theory Z;* and Kenney and Florida.

123. Adler, "Automation"; Littler and Salaman, "The Design of Jobs,"

90–93; Kenney and Florida; and Womack et al. On the prospects for new forms of firm-centered unionism linked to workplace participation under post-Fordism, see Adler, "Democratic Taylorism"; and Charles Heckscher, *The New Unionism: Employee Involvement in the Changing Corporation* (New York: Basic Books, 1988), chap. 6.

124. For an excellent discussion of competing perspectives on the subject, see Stephen Wood, "The Transformation of Work?" in Wood, ed., *The Transformation of Work?* For perspectives that emphasize the diversity of lean production and challenge technology-driven views of convergence, see Turner and Auer; Kirsten Wever and Lowell Turner, "A Wide-Angle Lens," in Wever and Turner, eds., *The Comparative Political Economy of Industrial Relations* (Madison: Industrial Relations Research Association, 1995); and Richard Locke, Thomas Kochan, and Michael Piore, "Reconceptualizing Comparative Industrial Relations: Lessons from International Research," *International Labour Review* 134, 2 (1995). For the "regulation school" perspective, which relates the turn to lean production to broader shifts in forms of government regulation and changing agendas, see Aglietta; Robert Boyer, *The Regulation School* (New York: Columbia University Press, 1990); and Alain Lipietz, *Toward a New Economic Order: Postfordism, Ecology and Democracy* (Cambridge, UK: Polity Press, 1992). And, for sharply critical treatments that dismiss the novelty of lean production and see its features as extending capitalist networks and managerial control, see James Rinehart, *The Tyranny of Work: Alienation and the Labor Process* (Toronto: Harcourt Brace, 1996); Rinehart, Christopher Huxley, and David Robertson, *Just Another Car Factory? Lean Production and Its Discontents* (Ithaca: ILR Press/Cornell University Press, 1997); and Tony Smith, *Technology and Capital in the Age of Lean Production: A Marxian Critique of the 'New Economy'* (Albany: State University of New York Press, 2000).

125. See Johann-Gottlieb Fichte, "Der geschlossene Handelsstaat" [The closed trading state], in Fichte, *Ausgewahlte Werke* [Selected works], vol. 3 (Darmstadt: Wissenschaftliche Buchgesellschaft, 1964), 417–544; Friedrich List, *The National System of Political Economy,* trans. Sampson S. Lloyed (London: Longmans, 1916); and the discussion of these pieces in Janos, "The Politics of Backwardness," 327, n. 6.

126. Veblen still remained a technological determinist in that he expected imported practices to help break down dysfunctional traditional attitudes and habits; but he also argued that a "backward" society with the right "cultural pedigree" would benefit from being able to more efficiently borrow and utilize the latest technologies, thus able to leapfrog earlier stages of industrialization and catch up more rapidly. See Veblen, *Imperial Germany,* esp. 38–39.

127. See Gerschenkron; Albert Hirschman, *The Strategy of Economic Development* (New Haven: Yale University Press, 1958); and David Apter, "System, Process, and the Politics of Economic Development," in Hoselitz and Moore.

128. On Latin America, see Guillermo O'Donnell, *Modernization and Bureaucratic-Authoritarianism: Studies in South American Politics* (Berkeley: Institute of International Studies, University of California at Berkeley, 1973). On East Asia, see Deyo, ed., *Political Economy;* Johnson, "Political Institutions"; Wade;

and Evans, *Embedded Autonomy*. Even the World Bank grudgingly acknowledged the positive role of governmental intervention in East Asian development; see World Bank, *The East Asian Miracle: Economic Growth and Public Policy* (New York: Oxford University Press, 1993). More recently, see Waldner for a sophisticated treatment of the payoffs and potential costs of coalitions and social bargains orchestrated by late-developing states prior to substantial industrial growth.

129. Bendix, "Relative Backwardness"; and Janos, "The Politics of Backwardness," esp. 325–36, 355–58.

130. Some modernization theorists did acknowledge that social disturbances were inevitable in the course of industrialization, but they still viewed these problems in the context of a universal evolutionary process; that is, they assumed that a more stable pattern of norms and social relations would crystallize by the time modern industrial societies evolved, and they found no fundamental differences between the dynamics of social change in early and late industrializers. This is evident in both Smelser, "Mechanisms of Change," and Samuel Huntington, *Political Order in Changing Societies* (New Haven: Yale University Press, 1967), 32–92.

131. As noted in chaps. 3 and 4, both Japanese and Russian elites in the late nineteenth century were constantly preoccupied with whether and how the problems of social unrest in the West could be avoided in their respective countries.

132. Certainly, even without factoring in levels of industrialization, technical definitions of efficiency vary significantly across industrial cultures. For example, postwar Japanese managers focused on the rate at which materials move through the production process, and Soviet managers focused on improving overall output; see Tilly and Tilly, 99. These differences are significant, but primarily because they reflect different responses to the *common* imperatives and dynamics that affect industrial management in NWLIs. Thus, it is significant that Japanese and Soviet managers, despite differences in their managerial cultures, came to be at least as anxious about the rate of *total* output and about stable employment patterns as about unit production costs and task efficiency.

133. Neither the Bolshevik Revolution in Russia, nor the Meiji Restoration, nor the Occupation period in Japan qualifies as such an event although all three involved dramatic social transformations. The Bolsheviks may have despised Russian traditions, but the ideological emphasis on collectivism (although recast in revolutionary terms) unintentionally reinforced among the average citizens preexisting understandings of collectivism linked to families and communities. Meiji modernizers promoted "Western learning," but did so while explicitly trumpeting collectivist ideals linked to traditional conceptions of the family. The Occupation era in Japan did witness an attempt to wipe out many of the ideologies and symbols of collectivism employed by prewar elites, but the growing threat posed by communism in Asia prompted the Occupation administrators to soften the attack, allowing native Japanese elites to reassess their past in their own terms and to develop a different, less aggressive, image of collectivism as a basis for a new institutional order.

134. To make an obvious point, an individualist work ethic is less likely to resonate where the dominant norms tend to publicly value actions justified as

being in the collective interest of some group or organization. This suggests that an individual-centered system for organizing work and evaluating and rewarding performance, while certainly practicable anywhere, may not be the most effective basis for creating a *valued* system of work and authority.

135. See Dore, *British Factory, Japanese Factory,* esp. chaps. 1, 8–9, and 15.

136. Dore, "Industrial Relations in Japan and Elsewhere," in Albert Craig, ed., *Japan: A Comparative View* (Princeton: Princeton University Press, 1979), 334–66; see also the critique of Dore's *British Factory, Japanese Factory* in Sabel, 28.

137. See, e.g., Ronald Rogowski, *Rational Legitimacy* (Princeton: Princeton University Press, 1974); Elizabeth Colson, *Tradition and Contract: The Problem of Order* (Chicago: Aldine, 1974); and Samuel Popkin, *The Rational Peasant* (Berkeley: University of California Press, 1979).

138. On this point, see Bendix, "Tradition and Modernity"; Dankwart Rustow, *A World of Nations* (Washington, DC: Brookings, 1967), esp. 12; and Samuel Huntington, "The Change to Change," *Comparative Politics* (April 1971): 283–322.

139. Bendix, *Work and Authority,* passim; and his "Industrialization, Ideologies, and Social Structure," *American Sociological Review* 24, 5 (October 1959), 614–20.

140. Studies from different eras that emphasize the effects of distinctive historical processes and cultural milieus on organizations and industrial relations include Michael Crozier, *The Bureaucratic Phenomenon* (Chicago: University of Chicago Press, 1964); Michael Aiken and Samuel Bacharach, "Culture and Organizational Structure and Process: A Study of Local Government Administrative Bureaucracies in the Walloon and Flemish Regions of Belgium," in Lammers and Hickson; Cole, *Work, Mobility, and Participation;* Sabel; Rueschemeyer, *Power;* Guillen; Thomas; Shenhav; and Tilly and Tilly, esp. 99, 139–40.

141. These problems led Bendix to interpret the "iron discipline" and hierarchy in early Soviet factories as mere extensions of "the legacies of Tsarist rule" without considering the organization of work in prerevolutionary communes and work collectives *(arteli),* and without examining whether historical legacies affected managers and workers in the same way; see *Work and Authority,* 250. The more nuanced understanding of legacies adopted here makes possible the quite different interpretation of Soviet management practices in chap. 4.

142. Bronislaw Malinowski, "The Primitive Economics of the Trobriand Islanders," in Littler, ed., 13–22.

143. Burawoy, *Manufacturing Consent,* 212–13.

144. Of course, there are countries where local variations are too significant to permit cross-national comparisons of legacies and management patterns (e.g., where tribal communities with quite different work-related norms and practices happen to coexist within the territorial boundaries of a nation-state). This would not, however, alter the general logic of the argument here as long as necessary adjustments were made to the units of comparison (e.g., by shifting the focus to patterns of management in particular locales). This is not necessary for the purposes of this book given the cases examined. In both Japan and Russia, where the

boundaries of the present-day nation-states appeared long ago, the degree of variation within nations may be plausibly assumed to be less significant in comparison to the more substantial variations across them. Country specialists writing on preindustrial Japan and Russia (discussed in chaps. 3 and 4) have themselves made similar assumptions. This is also true of Victor Magagna's cross-national comparative study of peasant communities, *Communities of Grain: Rural Rebellion in Comparative Perspective* (Ithaca: Cornell University Press, 1991).

145. In this regard, see the discussion of the sources of corruption in developing regions in Huntington, *Political Order,* 59–71; and Robert Price, *Society and Bureaucracy in Contemporary Ghana* (Berkeley: University of California Press, 1975).

146. See Evans, "Introduction: Development Strategies"; and Granovetter, "Economic Sociology of Firms." This view was anticipated in Geertz, *Peddlers and Princes,* 126. See also Cyril Belshaw, "Adaptation of Personnel Policies in Social Context," in Wilbert Moore and Arnold Feldman, eds., *Labor Commitment and Social Change in Developing Areas* (New York: Social Science Research Council, 1960), 106; and Melville Herkovits, "The Organization of Work," in Moore and Feldman, 123–35.

147. See Child, "Organizational Structure"; and Child, "Managerial Strategies, New Technology, and the Labour Process," in D. Knights, H. Willmott, and D. Collinson, eds., *Job Redesign: Critical Perspectives on the Labour Process* (London: Gower, 1985), 107–41.

148. Barnard, 233.

149. Simon, *Administrative Behavior,* esp. 131–8, 198–205, and 228–35.

150. E.g., Child, "Managerial Strategies"; and James March, "Decisions in Organizations and Theories of Choice," in Andrew Van de Ven and William Joyce, eds., *Perspectives on Organization Design and Behavior* (New York: John Wiley, 1981).

151. Selznick, *Leadership in Administration,* passim. See also his *TVA* on the importance of the wider communities from which informal norms and patterns emerge within organizations founded in those communities.

152. Burawoy, *Manufacturing Consent,* 1–5, 81–93, and passim. This approach can be contrasted to the more blunt Marxist critiques of capitalist labor processes as evident, e.g., in Braverman.

153. On this point, see also Rene Bouwen, "Organizational Innovation as a Social Construction: Managing Meaning in Multiple Realities," in Siegward Lindenberg and Hein Schreuder, eds., *Interdisciplinary Perspectives on Organization Studies* (New York: Pergamon, 1993), 133–49.

154. Bendix, *Work and Authority,* xii.

155. The revolutionary type of managerial strategy was attempted in Russia, but is perhaps best approximated in Chinese industry during the 1960s and 1970s, when wage practices reflected both material rewards and *biaoxian* (moral and political rewards) for demonstrating the "correct" attitudes at the workplace. See Andrew Walder, *Communist Neo-Traditionalism: Work and Authority in Chinese Industry* (Berkeley: University of California Press, 1986), chap. 6.

156. This may go against the instincts of some revolutionary leaders, but vir-

tually every revolutionary upheaval in history *has* been followed by competing visions about how to construct a new order, with some attempting to break with the past more radically than others. Following Lenin's death, for example, many Soviet leaders (such as Bukharin), although no less committed to socialism than Stalin, envisioned a more gradual path that would seek to inspire confidence among the masses that the new revolutionary order was essentially consistent with their own sensibilities and desires; thus, ideals of collective labor and wage egalitarianism could be framed as revolutionary extensions of norms found in past communes and workers' collectives. Similarly, Chinese land reform in the 1954–56 period can be considered syncretist in that it established Agricultural Producers' Cooperatives (APCs) that largely coincided with existing village boundaries and built on existing patterns of mutual assistance; this approach was succeeded, however, by the "revolutionary" Great Leap Forward (1958–1961), which promoted gigantic communes and broke more sharply with past forms of village organization.

157. The push for national learning in Meiji Japan, especially during the 1870s, may be viewed as revolutionary in this context given the proactive effort to not only borrow Western institutions but also transform the habits and attitudes of former samurai and old merchants. A traditionalist approach, which is what emerged by the end of the 1880s, emphasized the preservation of preexisting ideals and values (e.g., through the Imperial Rescript for Education) alongside the borrowing of institutions. A modernist strategy, had it emerged, would have been limited to simply borrowing new technologies and institutions, expecting past norms and values to be either irrelevant or evolve into modern orientations.

158. See the discussion in chap. 1, esp. at n. 42.

159. Sabel similarly notes that even contentious behavior framed as a matter of wages or working conditions is frequently a response to "management's violations of workers' expectations of propriety and justice"; Sabel, 15. This view of worker behavior does not reject rational choice theorists' emphasis on agency, but questions their insistence that the material incentive—or more broadly, instrumental rationality—is universally more important than other individual-level dispositions such as the need for familiarity and stability. Moreover, the very notion of a rational response only makes sense given a set of available alternatives and a template for assigning meaning to these alternatives; the factors that define this set and account for the values attached to each alternative are epistemologically no less significant than the choosing of a particular course of action. See appendix A (section A2) and the more elaborate discussion of rationality, culture, and structure in my "Foundations of Eclecticism."

160. Mowday et al., 27; see also Richard M. Steers and Lyman Porter, "Employee Commitment to Organizations," in Steers and Porter, eds., *Motivation and Work Behavior* (New York: McGraw-Hill, 1983).

161. A good discussion of the different meanings and indicators of commitment may be found in Paula Morrow, *The Theory and Measurement of Work Commitment* (Greenwich, CT: JAI Press, 1993).

162. For example, in one of the classic texts that emerged during the human relations movement, Harbison and Myer argued that the motivation and produc-

tivity of workers depended on the creation of "conditions in which the goals of the workers, as seen by the worker, are substantially the same as those of the management" (Frederick Harbison and Charles Myers, *Management in the Industrial World* [New York: McGraw-Hill, 1959], 31). For similar views in studies of the success of Japanese-style management or lean production models, see Adler, "Democratic Taylorism"; Kenney and Florida; and Womack et al. See also the discussion in James Lincoln and Arne Kalleberg, *Culture, Control, and Commitment: A Study of Work Organization and Work Attitudes in the United States and Japan* (Cambridge: Cambridge University Press, 1990), esp. 12.

163. See, e.g., O'Toole, ed; Cummings and Molloy; Wilensky; Adler, "Automation and Skill"; and Womack et al.

164. See, e.g., J. Meyer and N. J. Allen, "The Measurement and Antecedents of Affective, Continuance, and Normative Commitment to the Organization," *Journal of Occupational Psychology* 63 (1990): 1–18.

165. See Howard S. Becker, "Notes on the Concept of Commitment," *American Journal of Sociology* 66 (1960): 32–42; Akerlof, "Labor Contracts"; and G. Miller, esp. 198.

166. This is evident in Edwards; and Burawoy, *Manufacturing Consent.* Similar views are also echoed in contemporary critiques of lean production and Japanese-style management which are viewed as creating a semblance of participation and teamwork while reducing worker autonomy and union power. See, e.g., T. Smith; Rinehart; and Rinehart et al., esp. 158–59.

167. See, e.g., Baum, *Organizational Membership;* and Hirschorn.

168. See, e.g., the "organizational commitment questionnaire" (OCQ) in Mowday et al., 221; see also the survey of different quantitative measurements of work commitment in Morrow.

169. For example, where states intervene directly in labor markets and where enterprises represent distribution points for welfare benefits, even a low rate of industrial conflict and turnover might suggest little worker commitment, while the same rates in an industrialized capitalist economy could be consistent with a high level of commitment.

170. See Albert Hirschman, *Exit, Voice, and Loyalty: Responses to Decline in Firms, Organizations, and Nations* (Cambridge: Harvard University Press, 1970), esp. 78.

171. Arnold Feldman and Wilbert Moore, "Spheres of Commitment," in Moore and Feldman, 4.

172. This is obviously the case in the Soviet Union, but even there, meaningful inferences can be drawn from the few strikes that took place in the Stalin period, and from the increasing number of strikes accompanying the decline in coercion in the post-Stalin era.

173. Hirschman, *Exit, Voice, and Loyalty,* 86.

174. Susan Rhodes and Richard Steers, *Managing Employee Absenteeism* (Reading: Addison-Wesley, 1990), 9.

175. As Mowday et al. note, "almost all organizations need to avoid excessive absenteeism and turnover. When these two indices of non-linkage are high, costs

almost always go up" (Mowday et al., 4). See also Richard Steers and Richard Mowday, "Employee Turnover in Organizations," in Steers and Porter.

176. In fact, as will be evident in chap. 4, the most serious problems in Soviet industry had to do precisely with such subtle forms of noncooperation.

177. On "contextualized comparisons" see Locke and Thelen. See also chap. 1, n. 59.

178. See, respectively, Scott, *Seeing Like a State;* and Evans, "Government, Social Capital, and Development." See also the discussion in chap. 1 at nn. 62–63.

179. Clifford Geertz, "Ritual and Social Change: A Javanese Example," in *The Interpretation of Cultures,* 169.

180. Along the first dimension, it is probably only the compatibility of management ideologies and practices that actually makes a difference; for the most part, informal norms and unofficial shopfloor practices (the two boxes on the second row of fig. 8), because they are spontaneously constructed on the basis of existing understandings among workers, will tend to be mutually supportive. In any case, there is little that managers can do directly about congruence between informal norms and practices.

181. Eckstein, "A Theory of Stable Democracy." In the empirical study that gave rise to this argument, Eckstein argued that the stability of Norwegian democracy was a result not of cross-cutting cleavages but of the "remarkable congruence of structures" across governmental and nongovernmental authority structures, all of which reflected the well-established patterns of authority at the level of the typical Norwegian commune *(samfunn).* See Eckstein, *Division and Cohesion,* esp. 132–76, quotes from 136.

182. Eckstein, "A Theory of Stable Democracy," 201–7.

183. See, e.g., Ronald Rogowski, "Eckstein and the Study of Private Governments: An Appreciation, Critique, and Proposal," *Comparative Political Studies* 31, 4 (August 1998): 444–63.

184. See Sullivan; Bion; LaBier; E. J. Miller; Hirschorn; and Baum, *Organizational Membership.*

185. On the psychological effects of sudden encounters with unfamiliar environments, see Furnham and Bochner.

186. Peter Hammond, "Management in Economic Transition," in Moore and Feldman, 122.

187. Eckstein, "Lessons for the 'Third Wave' from the First: An Essay on Democratization," in Eckstein et al., 264.

188. Eckstein, "Congruence Theory Explained," 23.

Chapter 3

1. From a speech given by the Vice-Minister of Commerce and Agriculture in 1896, quoted in Byron Marshall, *Capitalism and Nationalism in Pre-War Japan: The Ideology of the Business Elite, 1868–1941* (Stanford: Stanford University Press, 1967), 55.

2. From a document published in November 1955 by the Japan Committee of Economic Development *(Keizei Doyukai,* also referred to as the Economic

Friends' Association). Originally cited in Nihon Seisansei Honbu [The Japan Productivity Center], *Seisansei undo 30 nen shi* [A thirty year history of the productivity movement] (Tokyo: Nihon Seisansei Honbu, 1985), 137; as translated and quoted in Bai Gao, *Economic Ideology and Japanese Industrial Policy: Developmentalism from 1931 to 1965* (New York: Cambridge University Press, 1997), 215.

3. See Ruth Benedict, *The Chrysanthemum and the Sword: Patterns of Japanese Culture* (Cambridge: Houghton Mifflin, 1946), 81.

4. References to Japanese authors in this chapter follow the Japanese tradition of family name first only where Japanese-language publications are cited; the standard English system is used where the works in question are in English. Also note that English transcriptions of Japanese words and names do not include diacritical marks often accompanying such transcriptions.

5. Anthropologists, historians, and sociologists studying Japanese preindustrial communities and cultural values—including revisionist treatments emphasizing social conflict—have provided ample precedents for this assumption in their competing efforts to characterize defining features of Tokugawa village life. See, e.g., Thomas Smith, "The Japanese Village in the Seventeenth Century," *Journal of Economic History*, 12 (winter 1952): 1–20; Robert Bellah, *Tokugawa Religion: The Cultural Roots of Modern Japan* (New York: Free Press, 1985 [1957]); Richard Beardsley, John Hall, and Robert Ward, *Village Japan* (Chicago: University of Chicago Press, 1959); Tadashi Fukutake, *Japanese Rural Society*, trans. Ronald Dore (New York: Oxford University Press, 1967); Chie Nakane, *Kinship and Economic Organization in Rural Japan* (New York: Humanities Press, 1967); Anne Walthall, *Social Protest and Popular Culture in Eighteenth-Century Japan* (Tucson: University of Arizona Press, 1986); James White, *Ikki: Social Conflict and Political Protest in Early Modern Japan* (Ithaca: Cornell University Press, 1995); Herman Ooms, *Tokugawa Village Practice: Class, Status, Power, Law* (Berkeley: University of California Press, 1996); and Irwin Scheiner, "The Japanese Village: Imagined, Real, Contested," in Stephen Vlastos, ed., *Mirror of Modernity: Invented Traditions of Modern Japan* (Berkeley: University of California Press, 1998), 67–78. Comparative studies making a similar assumption in analyzing preindustrial communities in both Japan and Russia include Black et al. and Magagna.

6. Of course, competing historiographies offer quite different characterizations of Tokugawa village life. Conventional studies have tended to emphasize only the positive features of orderly group life, sometimes invoking these to directly explain aspects of contemporary Japanese society. More recently, a revisionist historiography has highlighted instances of contentious behavior, but without considering the normative basis for these. To cope with this problem, the characterization offered here draws upon the conventional historiography only in relation to specific observations about the *norms* and *ideals* affecting *attempts* to coordinate common endeavors and justify social hierarchies. This does not imply that social relations in Tokugawa communities were in fact consistently harmonious, or that the norms and structures of traditional rural communities directly shaped the peculiar features of contemporary Japanese society. See the comments at notes 16 and 25 in this chapter, as well as the more general discussion of competing perspectives in Japanese studies in appendix B.

7. Fukutake, 40. See also Chie Nakane, *Japanese Society* (Berkeley: University of California Press, 1973), 60. Nakane's broader argument about how Japanese culture shapes distinctive aspects of contemporary Japanese society is part of a particularist discourse on the uniqueness of Japan, but her own anthropological investigations into Tokugawa culture and social structure are generally regarded as serious scholarly works; this research is most systematically presented in her *Kinship and Economic Organization.*

8. Bellah, 17–18; see also George De Vos, *Social Cohesion and Alienation: Minorities in the United States and Japan* (Boulder: Westview, 1992), 65. In this context, while the Japanese term for individualism, *kojinshugi,* connotes a sort of selfishness and immaturity, the term *kosei,* referring to the individuality of the self, conveys the sense of personal development and the ability to function in society; see Joy Hendry, "Individualism and Individuality: Entry into a Social World," in Roger Goodman and Kirsten Refsing, eds., *Ideology and Practice in Modern Japan* (New York: Routledge, 1992), 56.

9. Nakane emphasizes the importance of distinguishing collective identities based on preexisting attributes and the emphasis in Japanese communities on *ba,* or the concrete, physical frame within which members resided, interacted, and cooperated with one another in the course of everyday work; Nakane, *Japanese Society,* 1–3.

10. Black et al., 50.

11. Thomas Smith, *Native Sources of Japanese Industrialization* (Berkeley: University of California Press, 1988), 203–20; and Fukutake, esp. 31.

12. Thomas Smith, *Nakahara: Family Farming and Population in a Japanese Village, 1717–1830* (Stanford: Stanford University Press, 1977), 114.

13. For example, in contrast to the Chinese Confucian tradition which emphasized propriety *(li)* in performing rituals as an abstract way of fulfilling obligations, Japanese Confucianism focused more on concrete social relations as evident in the tremendous value placed on reciprocal obligations, duty, and loyalty; see Gilbert Rozman, "The East Asian Region in Comparative Perspective," in Rozman, ed., *The East Asian Region: The Confucian Heritage and Its Modern Adaptation* (Princeton: Princeton University Press, 1991), 24.

14. See Benedict, 105–16; and Robert Smith, *Japanese Society: Tradition, Self and the Social Order* (Cambridge: Cambridge University Press, 1983), 47.

15. As Bellah puts it, "Harmony must be maintained in the collectivity because conflicts between the members would not only be disloyal to the head but would disrupt the smooth attainment of collective goals. Thus, harmony, willingness to compromise, unaggressiveness, etc. are highly valued, whereas disputatiousness, contentiousness, overweening ambition or other disruptive behavior is strongly disvalued" (15).

16. It is not necessary to assume that the value placed on harmony necessarily made village life in Japan uniquely harmonious as past historians and anthropologists tended to suggest. In the past two decades, revisionist historiography has increasingly highlighted the competitive aspects and social conflicts in Tokugawa Japan. See, e.g., Tetsuo Najita and Victor Koschmann, eds., *Conflict in Modern Japanese History: The Neglected Tradition* (Princeton: Princeton University Press,

1982); Herbert Bix, *Peasant Protest in Japan, 1590–1884* (New Haven: Yale University Press, 1986); and Stephen Vlastos, *Peasant Protest and Uprisings in Tokugawa Japan* (Berkeley: University of California Press, 1986).

17. Even the study by Ooms, which generally emphasizes the prevalence of conflicts and legal disputes in Tokugawa Japan, notes that most lawsuits were resolved informally through mediation designed to quickly restore order, with an emphasis on apologies rather than a final legal settlement conforming to abstract principles of justice. See Ooms, 8–9.

18. Smith, 40.

19. Thomas Smith, *The Agrarian Origins of Modern Japan* (Stanford: Stanford University Press, 1959), 61.

20. John O. Haley, "Consensual Governance: A Study of Law, Culture, and the Political Economy of Postwar Japan," in Shumpei Kumon and Henry Rosovsky, eds., *The Political Economy of Japan, Volume 3: Cultural and Social Dynamics* (Stanford: Stanford University Press, 1992), 43–44.

21. The significance of these informal conflict-resolution mechanisms in preindustrial Japan can be more easily appreciated when considered in a comparative context. See, e.g., the contrast to Russia in Black et al., 52–53; and Magagna. See also the broader comparisons in Eisenstadt, "Patterns of Conflict and Conflict Resolution in Japan: Some Comparative Indications," in S. N. Eisenstadt and Eyal Ben-Ari, eds., *Japanese Models of Conflict Resolution* (London: Kegan Paul International, 1990), 12–35.

22. De Vos notes that traditional attitudes toward superiors in Japan were psychologically ingrained and resembled the kinds of beliefs directed only toward God in Western religion; see De Vos, 16.

23. Nakane regards the "vertical principle" as the most distinguishing feature of the structure of rural Japanese society and views it as a positive derivative of Confucian ethics; Nakane, *Japanese Society,* x. See also Bellah; and De Vos.

24. See, e.g., Ooms; Bix; Vlastos, *Peasant Protest;* Walthall; White; and Scheiner, "The Japanese Village."

25. Irwin Scheiner, "Benevolent Lords and Honorable Peasants: Rebellion and Peasant Consciousness in Tokugawa Japan," in Tetsuo Najita and Scheiner, eds., *Japanese Thought in the Tokugawa Period* (Chicago: University of Chicago Press, 1978), 46. See also Walthall, xii, 100–101.

26. See Scheiner, "The Japanese Village"; T. Smith, *Agrarian Origins,* 154–57; Walthall; and White, esp. 10–16, 108. For an interpretation of this dynamic in a wider comparative framework, see Magagna, 299.

27. Nakane, *Japanese Society,* 81, 88, 102. Clearly, the absence of role-specificity is not unique to preindustrial Japan, but it is worth noting the fact that rank did not necessarily correspond to a hierarchy of social roles, in marked contrast to India, where rank was intimately associated with a particular role or occupation that was considered invariable; hence, the comparative rigidity and low level of social mobility within the traditional Indian caste system.

28. Fukutake, 67–70, 85–86.

29. See Scheiner, "Benevolent Lords and Honorable Peasants," 43–47.

30. In some cases, the *gumi* consisted of members of the same extended fam-

ily *(dozokudan)* with the neighbors being members of the branch families that had evolved from a single stem family.

31. Smith, "The Japanese Village." See also Bellah, 41; Fukutake, 96–110; and Magagna, 231.

32. Fukutake, 138–45; and Black et al., 50.

33. Haley, 44.

34. See Yasusuke Murakami, "The Japanese Model of Political Economy," in Kozo Yamamura and Yasukichi Yasuba, eds., *The Political Economy of Japan,* vol. 1, *The Domestic Transformation* (Stanford: Stanford University Press, 1987), 35–36.

35. Fukutake, 39.

36. The original *ie* and the branch families maintained some common identity as members of the same *dozokudan* (the more inclusive term for the original stem family and all of the related branch families). Often it was the case that members of a *dozokudan* would occupy neighboring houses, and branch families would often work the same fields and jointly participate in community activities. In the village hierarchy, however, the stem families invariably provided the leadership for the five-family groups and were disproportionately represented in the village assembly. See Fukutake, 65–67.

37. Thus, while elder brothers being groomed to inherit the headship of the household, younger sons were treated as understudies who would be held in reserve should the elder son die prematurely. In addition, the vertical ties binding the members of a household to the head of that household were given far more significance than horizontal ties among persons of equal status (younger siblings, for example). See Fukutake, 47; and Nakane, *Japanese Society,* passim.

38. Thus, it is significant that within the *ie,* individual incomes or individual contributions to the collective farmwork of the household did not directly affect one's position within the household and were not even calculated on a regular basis; see Fukutake, 46, 51.

39. Anthropologists, cultural sociologists, and scholars in the humanities, for example, tend to take for granted the distinctiveness of contemporary Japanese society and relate it to past cultural attributes, while most economists, revisionist historians, and many political scientists tend to downplay the distinctiveness and continuity of Japanese society. See appendix B for a discussion of how universalists and particularists interpret aspects of society, political economy, and industrial relations in Japanese studies.

40. Hiroshi Hazama, *The History of Labor Management in Japan* (New York: St. Martin's Press, 1997), 28–30, 59–65.

41. Sheldon Garon, *The State and Labor in Modern Japan* (Berkeley: University of California Press, 1987), 17; Andrew Gordon, *The Evolution of Labor Relations in Japan, 1853–1955* (Cambridge: Harvard University Press, 1985), 120; and Gordon, "The Invention of Japanese-Style Labor Management," in Vlastos, ed., 36.

42. Thomas Smith, "The Right to Benevolence: Dignity and the Japanese Workers, 1890–1920," in T. Smith, *Native Sources of Japanese Industrialization,* 239.

43. This attitude is evident, for example, in the position of Suzuki Bunji, a key leader in the founding of the largest labor federation in prewar Japan. See Suzuki Bunji, *Nihon no rodomodai* [Labor problems in Japan] (Tokyo: Kaigai shokumin gakko suppanbu, 1919); and the discussion of Suzuki's position in Hazama, *History of Labor Management*, 65–66. On this point, see also Gordon, "The Invention of Japanese-Style Labor Management," 36.

44. See, e.g., the characterization of the postwar Japanese workplace in James Abegglen, *The Japanese Factory* (New York: Free Press, 1958); Nakane, *Japanese Society;* and Ezra Vogel, *Japan as Number One* (New York: Harper and Row, 1979).

45. Robert Marsh and Hiroshi Mannari, *Modernization and the Japanese Factory* (Princeton: Princeton University Press, 1976). The survey they cite is Hayashi Chikiio, Nishira Sigeki, Suzuki Tatsuzo, et al., *Nihonjin No Kokuminsei: A Study of the Japanese National Character* (Tokyo: Idemitsushoten, 1970). This survey has been conducted every five years since 1953, but through the 1970 survey, there was no evidence of a decline in the percentage of workers preferring paternalistic managers. Marsh and Mannari, attempting to reconcile this fact with their project of demonstrating the convergence between Japanese factories and modern factories elsewhere, concluded that this preference for paternalism was only a "marginal" aspect of Japanese industrial relations suggesting that Japanese industry had only undergone "partial modernization" at the time. If we reject the premises of convergence, however, a more compelling interpretation would treat this preference for paternalism as a reflection of a consistently positive orientation toward authority relations in which superiors properly discharge their duties to attend to the welfare of subordinates as part of the network of reciprocal obligations underpinning any community.

46. James Lincoln and Arne Kalleberg, *Culture, Control and Commitment: A Study of Work Organization and Work Attitudes in the United States and Japan* (New York: Cambridge University Press, 1990), 64–65.

47. Andrew Gordon, "Contests for the Workplace," in Gordon, ed., *Postwar Japan as History* (Berkeley: University of California Press, 1993), 379, 385–86; and Makoto Kumazawa, *Portraits of the Japanese Workplace: Labor Movements, Workers, and Managers* (Boulder: Westview, 1996), 49–51.

48. Ikio Kume, *Disparaged Success: Labor Politics in Postwar Japan* (Ithaca: Cornell University Press, 1998), chap. 4; and Eyal Ben-Ari, "Ritual Strikes, Ceremonial Slowdowns: Some Thoughts on the Management of Conflict in Large Japanese Enterprises," in Eisenstadt and Ben-Ari, eds.

49. In fact, more than 80 percent of the cases brought against management under the "Unfair Labor Practice" codes were eventually withdrawn or resolved through mediation and compromise; Yauhiko Matsuda, "Conflict Resolution in Japanese Industrial Relations," in Taishiro Shirai, ed., *Contemporary Industrial Relations in Japan* (Madison: University of Wisconsin Press, 1983), 200. See also Tadashi Hanami, "Conflict and Its Resolution in Industrial Relations and Labor Law," in Ellis Krauss, Thomas Rohlen, and Patricia Steinhoff, eds., *Conflict in Japan* (Honolulu: University of Hawaii Press, 1984).

50. Compare, for example, Ooms's treatment of the Tokugawa village and

Upham's treatment of postwar Japanese society. Both attempt to dispel the notion that Japanese culture is uniquely harmonious and that Japanese communities discourage litigation. Both highlight the use of legal mechanisms to challenge oppressive measures or settle disputes. And yet, both recognize that these disputes, once made public through the initiation of litigation, tend to be resolved quickly and through informal mediation rather than through a decisive legal decision. See Ooms; and Frank Upham, *Law and Social Change in Postwar Japan* (Cambridge: Harvard University Press, 1987).

51. Surveys conducted in 1967 suggest that 55 percent of the Japanese employees (compared to 23 percent in the U.S. sample) expected employers to honor the employment relationship irrespective of individual performance. Only 4 percent (compared to 20 percent in the U.S. sample) believed that unqualified employees should be terminated. In a 1980 survey, only 30 percent of the Japanese sample (as compared with 70 percent in the U.S. sample) felt that managers should make evaluations public and inform each worker of both strengths and weaknesses; 48 percent (as compared with 19 percent in the United States) felt that direct evaluations and individual comparisons should be avoided or kept hidden from workers. See Shin-ichi Takezawa and Arthur Whitehill, *The Other Worker: A Comparative Study of Industrial Relations in the United States and Japan* (Honolulu: East-West Center Press, 1968); and Takezawa and Whitehill, *Work Ways: Japan and America* (Tokyo: Japan Institute of Labor, 1981).

52. Thus, it is now widely recognized that the distinctive features of the postwar wage system in the 1950s through 1970s period, previously thought to be products of a distinctive style of management, reflect partial concessions to the preferences of Japanese workers and unions. See Gordon, "Contests," 386; and Kumazawa, chap. 3. At the same time, it is worth noting the continuity of these preferences over time and their compatibility with norms embedded in past communities of work.

53. The most comprehensive survey is Hayashi et al. This survey, conducted every five years, demonstrates little change in the preference for collectivist values over individualistic ones between the 1950s and 1970s. This finding is also confirmed in E. Hamaguchi, "Nihonteki shudan shugi towa nanika" [What is Japanese collectivism?], in E. Hamaguchi and Shumpei Kumon, eds., *Nihonteki shudan shugi* [Japanese-style collectivism] (Tokyo: Yuhikau, 1982). A more critical treatment that emphasizes the negative consequences of persistent collectivist orientations but nonetheless finds these to be prevalent in postwar Japanese society is H. Araki, *Nihonjin no knoudou youshiki* [Behavioral style of the Japanese] (Tokyo: Kodansha, 1973). For a more recent nuanced discussion that strikes a reasonable balance between positive and negative appraisals of collectivism, see Susumu Yamaguchi, "Collectivism among the Japanese: A Perspective from the Self," in Uichol Kim, Harry C. Triandis, Cigdem Kgitcibasi, Sang-Chin Choi, and Gene Yoon, eds., *Individualism and Collectivism: Theory, Method, and Applications* (Thousand Oaks: Sage, 1994), 175–88.

54. Thomas Rohlen, *For Harmony and Strength: Japanese White-Collar Organization in Anthropological Perspective* (Berkeley: University of California

Press, 1976); and Rohlen, "Order in Japanese Society: Attachment, Authority, and Routine," *Journal of Japanese Studies* 15, 1 (winter 1989): 5–40.

55. See, e.g., Geert Hofstede, *Culture's Consequences: International Differences in Work-Related Values* (Beverly Hills: Sage, 1980), 218–32; and Carmi Schooler, "History, Social Structure, and Individualism: A Cross-Cultural Perspective on Japan," in Masmichi Sasahi, ed., *Values and Attitudes across Nations and Time* (Leiden, the Netherlands: Brill, 1998).

56. Examples of *Nihonjinron* arguments include Takeo Doi, *The Anatomy of Dependence* (Tokyo: Kodansha International, 1973); Michio Morishima, *Why Has Japan 'Succeeded'? Western Technology and the Japanese Ethos* (Cambridge: Cambridge University Press, 1982); Murakami Yasusuke, Kumon Shumpei, and Sato Seizaburo, *Bunmei to shite no ie shakai* [The Ie society as a pattern of civilization] (Tokyo: Chuokoronsha, 1979); Shoichi Watanabe, *The Peasant Soul of Japan* (London: Macmillan, 1989); and Shichihei Yamamoto, *The Spirit of Japanese Capitalism and Selected Essays,* trans. Lynne Riggs and Takechi Manabut (New York: Madison Books, 1992). Western scholars who share this general view of Japanese society include R. Smith; Vogel, *Japan as Number One;* and Edwin O. Reischauer, *The Japanese* (Cambridge: Belknap, 1978).

57. Critics of the substantive claims of the *Nihonjinron* literature include Peter Dale, *The Myth of Japanese Uniqueness* (New York: St. Martin's Press, 1986); Ross Mouer and Yoshio Sugimoto, *Images of Japanese Society* (New York: Kegan Paul International, 1986); and Harumi Befu, "Symbols of Nationalism and *Nihonjinron,*" in Goodman and Refsing. Dale, although a critic of the "Japanese national character" view, notes that between 1946 and 1978 there were at least 700 academic titles published in the *Nihonjinron* tradition along with scores of nonacademic works and nonliterary media that propagated this tradition; Dale, 15. See also the evidence of the popularity of *Nihonjinron* in Tsujimura Akira, *Sengo Nihon no taishu shinri: shinbun, seron, besutosera* [Mass consciousness in postwar Japan: Newspapers, public opinion and best sellers] (Tokyo: Tokyo Daigaku Suppankai, 1981); and the discussion of the popularity of *Nihonjinron* among Japanese business elites and teachers in Kosaku Yoshino, *Cultural Nationalism in Contemporary Japan* (New York: Routledge, 1992).

58. Ronald Dore, "Mobility, Equality and Individuation in Modern Japan," in Dore, ed., *Aspects of Social Change in Modern Japan* (Princeton: Princeton University Press, 1967), 113–50.

59. The notion of learning from foreign powers was not itself an alien conception to Japanese leaders before the Meiji Restoration, as evident in the longstanding notion of "Chinese learning, Japanese spirit" and the period of "Dutch learning" in the late Tokugawa period after the Dutch established a trading post on an island off Nagasaki. After the Meiji Restoration, however, the reference societies came to include the United States, Britain, France, Germany, as well as Austria and Belgium. On foreign borrowing, see Marius Jansen, "On Foreign Borrowing," in Albert Craig, ed., *Japan: A Comparative Perspective* (Princeton: Princeton University Press, 1979), 18–48; and D. Eleanor Westney, *Imitation and Innovation: The Transfer of Western Organizational Patterns to Meiji Japan* (Cambridge: Harvard University Press, 1987), 13.

60. The key figure identified with national learning is Fukuzawa Yukichi, who introduced Western texts and Western educational philosophies in the curriculum at Keio University to promote a new set of attitudes appropriate for the quest for "national wealth and honor." Many of the first political leaders and managerial elites (e.g., the Mitsubishi managers) turned out to be graduates of Keio University. Governmental elites cooperated in this effort as evident in the travel program launched by Ito Hirobumi so that Japanese officials and students could go abroad, partly to learn more about Western laws, institutions, and society, but also partly to distance themselves from the traditional attitudes that supposedly barred Japan's entry into the modern world. See Johannes Hirschmeier, *The Origins of Entrepreneurship in Meiji Japan* (Cambridge: Harvard University Press, 1964), 122–24, 162–64; and Earl Kinmonth, *The Self-Made Man in Meiji Japanese Thought: From Samurai to Salary Man* (Berkeley: University of California Press, 1974), 45–54.

61. See Yasuzo Horie, "Modern Entrepreneurship in Meiji Japan," in William Lockwood, ed., *The State and Economic Enterprise in Japan* (Princeton: Princeton University Press, 1965), 183–208. Many government leaders, themselves being former samurai, were sympathetic to the plight of the samurai and thus took a more active stand in encouraging other ex-samurai to take a leading role in entrepreneurship and industrial production now that their traditional privileges were gone; Hirschmeier, 51–55.

62. Mansel Blackford, *The Rise of Modern Business in Great Britain, the United States, and Japan* (Chapel Hill: University of North Carolina Press, 1998), 41–42.

63. Marshall, 50.

64. The reinterpretation of Smiles's ideal of "self-help" is evident in the highly popular 1871 Japanese translation by Nakamura Keiu, who linked individual achievement explicitly to national security and prosperity; Kinmonth, 20–21. On Shibusawa's role in articulating this linkage, see Hirschmeier, 162–74; and Marshall, 33–41.

65. See Gordon, *Evolution of Labor Relations*, 29–40.

66. The Meiji reorganization of the prefectures and the end to feudalism brought many young male villagers to the cities looking for work to join the girls and young women already working in the textile industry for extremely low wages. The resulting depression of wages contributed to widespread pauperization, but the Meiji government, while urging "mercy and benevolence," placed responsibility for the welfare of the poor squarely on families and local communities rather than on the government. The 1874 Relief Regulation explicitly disavowed governmental responsibility for social welfare and limited assistance to impoverished individuals without any resources or family and community ties. See Dean Kinzley, *Industrial Harmony in Modern Japan* (London: Routledge, 1991), 1–10.

67. Noted in Kinzley, 16–18; and Sidney Crawcour, "The Japanese Employment System," *Journal of Japanese Studies* 4, 2 (summer 1978), 228–29.

68. Garon, 12–19. See Yokoyama Gennosuke, *Nihon no kaso shakai* [The lower strata in Japanese society] (Tokyo: Kyobunkan, 1899) for a firsthand account of living conditions of Japanese workers in the 1880s and 1890s.

69. Marshall, 51–53.

70. This perspective is most clear in the position of Ito Hirobumi who viewed Japan's feudal legacy as providing a foundation for a distinctive kind of superordinate-subordinate relationship in the course of economic development; ironically, some prewar Marxists adopted the same view though with the intention of critiquing Japanese capitalism. See Andrew Barshay, "'Doubly Cruel': Marxism and the Presence of the Past in Japanese Capitalism," in Vlastos, ed. For a general survey of the role of myths and invented traditions in prewar Japan, see Carol Gluck, *Japan's Modern Myths: Ideology in the Late Meiji Period* (Princeton: Princeton University Press, 1985); and the brief but illuminating discussion in Stephen Vlastos, "Tradition: Past/Present Culture and Modern Japanese History," in Vlastos, ed., 1–16.

71. Hozumi Yatsuka, Dean of the Tokyo Imperial University Law Faculty (1889–1912), was the chief proponent of *kokutai*, declaring: "He who represents in the present the spirits of the racial ancestors is the natural sovereign. To make racial sovereignty dependent upon the agreement of equal men is to go against the great principle of ancestry worship. . . . This is why, in the national organization of blood-related group in which the great principle of ancestor worship is a prime moving force, monarchy is taken from the first as the basis of organization" (quoted in Richard Minear, *Japanese Tradition and Western Law: Emperor, State and Law in the Thought of Hozumi Yatsuka* [Cambridge: Harvard University Press, 1970], 70).

72. The call for "moral education" was articulated in the Imperial Rescript on Education (1890). Prime Minister Yamagata is quoted as saying: "The ways of loyalty among the people are the essence of the strength of a country. Unless the people love their country as their parents and are willing to safeguard it with their lives . . . the country cannot exist even for a day. . . . Only education can cultivate and preserve the notion of patriotism in people" (quoted in Gluck, *Japan's Modern Myths,* 118). On the increasing emphasis on Shinto traditions, see Helen Hardacre, *Shinto and the State, 1868–1988* (Princeton: Princeton University Press, 1989), 20–39.

73. Kinzley, 13–16.

74. Gordon, "The Invention of Japanese-Style Labor Management," 19–21; and his *Evolution of Labor Relations,* 68.

75. Shoda Heigoro, quoted in Gordon, "The Invention of Japanese-Style Labor Management," 21.

76. Soeda Juichi, a high-ranking official in the Ministry of Finance, as quoted in Garon, 25.

77. See Garon, 26–38; Marshall, 53–54; and Kinzley, 16–25.

78. Marshall, 52–55.

79. Garon, 28–29; and Gordon, "The Invention of Japanese-Style Management," 22.

80. Marshall, 54; citing *Shibusawa Eiichi denki shiryo* [Biographical materials on Shibusawa Eiichi], 50 vols. (Tokyo: Shibusawa Seien Kinen Zaidan Ryumonsha, 1955–1963), vol. 23, 492.

81. See Edwin Reischauer, *Japan: The Story of a Nation,* 3d ed. (New York: Knopf, 1981), 166–75.

82. A more detailed discussion of economic trends in the Taisho era may be found in George Allen, *A Short Economic History of Modern Japan* (London: Macmillan, 1981), 100–106.

83. See Garon, 12–18, 40–43; Kinzley, 27–32; and Andrew Gordon, *Labor and Imperial Democracy* (Berkeley: University of California Press, 1991), 131–33.

84. Until 1910, the majority of the industrial work force was female, but the steady growth of large-scale factories in heavy industrial sectors (e.g., metals, ship-building) eventually made male workers a majority of the industrial work force during the 1910s; see Blackford, 51.

85. On this point, revisionist historians more or less concur with Thomas Smith's contention that workers in the 1910s were primarily motivated by a desire for "improved treatment" and "status *(chii)* justice" rather than by any commitment to transforming class relations. See T. Smith, "The Right to Benevolence," 239; Gordon, *Evolution of Labor Relations,* 120; and the discussion in this chapter at nn. 41–43.

86. Hazama, *History of Labor Management,* 8.

87. Kinzley, 32–47.

88. To promote these aims, the Cooperation and Harmony Society set up its own workers' training program that began with the principle that "before being workers or capitalists, first we are people." Teachers and trainees shared meals and lodgings, and trainees were continuously reminded of the value of ethical, cooperative behavior on the shop floor. By 1929, 11,000 trainees had passed through the Society's training centers. The Society also ran settlement homes for poor or unemployed workers so as to reach more workers with its message of cooperation and harmony. See Kinzley, 90–99; and Garon, 51–53.

89. See Mark Fruin, "The Japanese Company Controversy: Ideology and Organization in a Historical Perspective," *Journal of Japanese Studies* 4, 2 (summer 1978): 290.

90. Hazama, *History of Labor Management,* 13.

91. On these two interpretations, see, respectively, Hazama, *History of Labor Management;* and Gordon, "The Invention of Japanese-Style Labor Management."

92. Mogi Shichizaemon, director of Kikkoman Company; quoted in Mark Fruin, *Kikkoman: Company, Clan and Community* (Cambridge: Harvard University Press, 1983), 115.

93. Quoted in Marshall, 72.

94. Muto Sanji, from a lecture at Tokyo Imperial University in 1920, quoted in Hazama Hiroshi, "Nihonjin no kachikan to kigyo katsudo—Shudan shugi wo chushin to shite" [Japanese values and entrepreneurship: The problem of collectivism], in Hazama, ed., *Nihon no kigyo to shakai* [Japanese company and society] (Tokyo: Nihon keizai shimbun, 1977), 58. I am grateful to Tadashi Anno for providing the translation.

95. In 1924, 72 percent of the top managerial elites were sons of businessmen or samurai, with more than half of the top 384 business managers holding a college

degree from one of just three institutions of higher education (Tokyo University, Keio University, and Tokyo Higher Commercial School); noted in Blackford, 120.

96. Hazama, *History of Labor Management,* 12–13.

97. Hiroshi Hazama (with Jacqueline Kaminsky), "Japanese Labor-Management Relations and Uno Reimon," *Journal of Japanese Studies* 5, 1 (1979): 75–76.

98. This view was most clearly articulated by then home minister Tokonami Takejiro, and he was backed by business elites (notably in the Japan Industrial Club) as well as members of the Seiyukai-dominated Diet and the Kiyoura cabinet; thus, although some "imperial democrats" in government were urging recognition of compliant workers' demands, managers, business elites, and bureaucrats formed a united front against efforts to legalize independently organized unions. See Gordon, "The Invention of Japanese-Style Management," 24–27; Gordon, *Labor and Imperial Democracy,* 134–35; and T. J. Pempel and Kiichi Tsunekawa, "Corporatism without Labor? The Japanese Anomaly," in Philippe Schmitter and Gerhard Lehmbruch, eds., *Trends toward Corporatist Intermediation* (Beverly Hills: Sage, 1979), 253.

99. As in the case of the 1911 Factory Bill, the laws passed in 1926 were watered-down versions of bills sponsored by more progressive bureaucrats and the Kenseikai party, and the key element of the legislation—designed to protect and legalize independent unions—was decisively defeated. By the late 1920s, independent unions had been pushed out of the major shipyards, machine factories, and steel mills, and in 1931, the trade union bill was even more decisively defeated in the House of Peers as it became evident that neither the state nor the managerial elites could conceive of "cooperation and harmony" outside of the context of "labor-capital verticalism." See Garon, 89–110; Gordon, *Labor and Imperial Democracy,* 136–41; and Stephen Large, *Organized Workers and Socialist Politics in Interwar Japan* (Cambridge: Cambridge University Press, 1981), chap. 4.

100. Gordon, "The Invention of Japanese-Style Management," 24–26.

105. Kinzley, 84–119.

102. The number of industrial disputes in 1922 was 250 and the number of participants was 41,503. These figures represented a modest decline since 1919, but by 1930, the number of industrial disputes had climbed to 906, with 81,329 participants involved. The figures are from a government survey published as Nihon tokei kenkyusho, *Nihon keizai tokeishu* [Economic statistics of Japan] (Tokyo: Nihon hyoron sha, 1958); cited in Hazama, *History of Labor Management,* 48–49.

103. Quoted in Hazama, 67.

104. That college graduates shared in the anxiety of blue-collar workers is not surprising considering that for Tokyo Imperial University, for example, the non-placement rate was 40 percent during the 1922–26 period, and many highly educated and trained people were forced to work on menial tasks. See Kinmonth, 296–307, and Gordon, *Evolution of Labor Relations,* chap. 4.

105. The process through which rudimentary versions of these features of postwar Japanese labor relations originally emerged is discussed in detail in Large, chap. 4; and Gordon, *Evolution of Labor Relations,* chaps. 4–6.

106. Fruin suggests that, from the managers' point of view, the offer of life-

time employment and seniority wages to a select group of employees could still be considered as falling within the *ie* system, which did distinguish between core members who had property rights and other members, often servants, who shared in the identity of the family but were lower-status individuals incorporated into the household but without property rights. It is unlikely, however, that workers ever considered their role within the firm in these simplified terms; and even if they did, they still could not count on superiors tending to their basic material needs in the way that servants within an *ie* might be able to. See Fruin, "The Japanese Company Controversy," 289–90.

107. On the sharp differences in levels of white-collar unionization in the prewar and postwar periods, see Solomon Levine, "Unionization of White-Collar Employees in Japan," in Adolf Sturmthal, ed., *White-Collar Trade Unions* (Urbana: University of Illinois Press, 1966); and Pempel and Tsunekawa, 263–64.

108. Yasukichi Yasuba, "The Evolution of Dualistic Wage Structure," in Hugh Patrick, ed., *Japanese Industrialization and Its Social Consequences* (Berkeley: University of California Press, 1976), 249–98.

109. See T. Smith, "The Right to Benevolence," 245; see also Kinmonth; and Gordon, *Evolution of Labor Relations,* passim. On the low level of white-collar union involvement, see n. 107 above.

110. See Gordon, *Evolution of Labor Relations,* chap. 2.

111. Oka Minoru, a government official involved in promoting new factory legislation, quoted in Hazama, "Nihonjin no kachikan to kigyo katsudo" [Japanese values and entrepreneurship], 57. Translation provided by Tadashi Anno.

112. For example, in the 1922 Yawata steelworkers' strike, workers were not challenging differentials in material rewards but protesting the fact that the workers who were below the "primary status groups"—i.e., anyone not in a management or supervisory position—were subject to qualitatively different employment terms and wage practices; T. Smith, "The Right to Benevolence," 251–52, 260–61. See also Yasuba.

113. A 1932 welfare facilities survey of 2,384 factories indicated that only 24 percent had some provision for illness or injury of workers, but only 9.4 percent extended these provisions to the worker's family; only 11 percent had some sort of profit-sharing scheme, while just 5 percent provided employee housing or bonuses related to attendance or length of service. Noted in Hazama, *History of Labor Management,* 78–79, 83.

114. This pamphlet, published in Japanese as *Mueki no tesu o habuku hiketsu,* was the most noteworthy of several pieces on scientific management penned by Ikeda Toshiro following his tour of the United States; noted in William Tsutsui, *Manufacturing Ideology: Scientific Management in Twentieth Century Japan* (Princeton: Princeton University Press, 1998), 18–19.

115. Tsutsui, 29–31. Tsutsui also notes that officials from Soviet Railways even invited officials from Japan National Railways to advise on shop management procedures!

116. Tsutsui, 20–21. Ueno's influence on Japanese industry may be worth comparing to that of Alexei Gastev, "the Russian Taylor," who led the charge for

incorporating Taylorist techniques into the first Soviet factories. See chap. 4 (section 4.2)

117. Tsutsui, 58–59.

118. Tsutsui, 22.

119. Tsutsui, 65–75.

120. Robert Cole, *Work, Mobility and Participation: A Comparative Study of American and Japanese Industry* (Berkeley: University of California Press, 1979), 108–9; see also Okuda Kenji, "Nihon no noritsu undoshi" [A history of the Japanese movement], *IE Review,* nos. 9–12 (1968–71).

121. Tsutsui, 39–45. This was precisely the claim of trade unionists and the "right opposition" in Soviet Russia as they sought to limit the application of Taylorist methods during the 1918–25 period.

122. Hazama, "Japanese Labor-Management Relations," 89.

123. Tsutsui, 68–69.

124. For example, Cole notes that the idea of competitive performance evaluations could be adapted to simulate competition among work teams and department sections within the framework of the "family firm" (much like "socialist competition" in Soviet factories was initially intended to promote a friendly competition among brigades and shops to overfulfill production quotas). See Cole, *Work, Mobility and Participation,* 110–11; and on socialist competition, see the discussion in chap. 4.

125. Cole, *Work, Mobility and Participation,* 109. On the dualistic employment structure, see Yasuba.

126. A survey of 270 firms in sectors ranging from textiles to shipbuilding, machinery, chemicals, mining, and construction indicated that as early as 1921, over half of the firms calculated wages at least partially on the basis of piece rates. Tokuzo Fukuda, *Shakai undo to rogin seido* [Social movements and wage systems] (Tokyo: Kaizosha, 1922, 283–84; cited in Hazama, *History of Labor Management,* 73.

127. Gordon, *Evolution of Labor Relations,* 254.

128. Many of the old zaibatsus and leading business figures were initially resisting the growing power of the military, but after 1936, any business elites who stood in the way of a concerted policy of economic mobilization and military expansion were forced to resign in the face of corruption charges while others engaged in *tenko* (conversion) and agreed to serve the economic and military objectives defined by the government. See Arthur Tiedemann, "Big Business and Politics in Prewar Japan," in James Morley, ed., *Dilemmas of Growth in Prewar Japan* (Princeton: Princeton University Press, 1974), 267–316.

129. For a detailed description of the Sanpo movement and the "imperial work ethic," see Garon, chap. 6; and Gordon, *Evolution of Labor Relations,* chaps. 7 and 8.

130. Noguchi Yukio, *1940-nen taisei: saraba 'senji keizai'* [The 1940 system: Farewell to a wartime economy], 27fn; and Gordon, *Evolution of Labor Relations,* chap. 7, passim. Noguchi explicitly locates the origins of postwar employment practices in this period of wartime mobilization, while Gordon goes further back (to the 1920s).

131. On the functioning of the workers' councils and right-wing unions under the Sanpo movement, see, respectively, Garon, 208–18; and Gordon, "Invention of Japanese-Style Management," 27–28.

132. Tsutsui, 96–98. The term *translated mimicry* is from Ando Yaichi, an expert on clerical work, critically commenting on the tendency of some efficiency experts of the 1910s and 1920s to rely excessively on foreign management practices; quoted in Tsutsui, 24.

133. It is these Sanpo-led workplace councils (rather than the prewar unions) that Large, Noguchi, and others have pointed to as providing the basis for the rapid spread of postwar enterprise unionism (although Noguchi alone makes the broader claim about the wartime roots of the entire postwar employment system). See Large, 230–31; Noguchi; and Keisuke Nakamura, "Worker Participation: Collective Bargaining and Joint Consultation," in Mari Sako and Hiroki Sato, eds., *Japanese Labour and Management in Transition: Diversity, Flexibility, and Participation* (New York: Routledge, 1997).

134. The across-the-board wage reductions were supported by one of the key labor unions in Sanpo, the Japanist Labor Movement, which had been founded by a right-wing labor leader, Kamino Sini'ichi, who denied the very existence of conflicts of interests between labor and capital in Japan. In the 1934 Tokyo street-car workers' strike, for example, the Japanist Labor Movement accepted a "compromise" 20 percent wage cut and replaced striking workers who had rejected the proposal. In this manner, the "new order" bureaucrats were able to force out even pragmatic unions that had been willing to accept government arbitration of labor disputes, while the Sanpo unions essentially became entrenched as instruments of the state (not unlike the transformation of unions into "transmission belts" under Stalin). See Garon, 192–97, 207–18; and Garon and Mike Mochizuki, "Negotiating Social Contracts," in Gordon, ed., 155–56.

135. On the new efficiency and rationalization campaigns, see Tsutsui, 92; and Sasaki Satoshi, "The Rationalization of Production Management Systems in Japan during World War II," in Sakudo Jun and Shiba Takao, eds., *World War II and the Transformation of Business Systems* (Tokyo: University of Tokyo Press, 1994), 30–54. On wage practices and other aspects of the employment system between the late 1930s and 1945, see Gordon, *Evolution of Labor Relations,* chap. 7; and Noguchi, passim.

136. For a detailed discussion of labor controls in wartime Japan, see Garon, 208–18.

137. On workers' reactions to wartime management practices, see Garon, 219–27; on workers' attitudes toward the rhetoric of Sanpo, see Gordon, *Evolution of Labor Relations,* chap. 8.

138. Aside from a temporary dip in 1922, the level of industrial conflict steadily rose and peaked in 1930 before being sharply brought down through coercive measures during the 1930s. The number of strikes and lockouts rose to 907 in 1930 but came down to 271 by 1940; the number of participants in these disputes peaked at 81,329 before being brought down to 33,000; and the number of working days lost per striking worker rose to 13.39 before falling to just 1.63. Statistics

are adapted from *International Historical Statistics* (New York: New York University Press, 1983).

139. Pempel and Tsunekawa, 253; and Allen, 120–30. Unionized employees still represented only 6.9 percent of the total work force, but a much larger segment of the work force in large industrial firms. However, as Taira notes, the absence of a strong crafts tradition in Japan led to unions formed around workgroups and delayed the emergence of industry-wide and nationwide federations; see Koji Taira, "Characteristics of Japanese Labor Markets," *Economic Development and Cultural Change* 10 (1962): 150–68.

140. See Gordon, *Evolution of Labor Relations,* chap. 4, passim.

141. Garon, 219–27.

142. It should be noted that, as this book is about strategies of institution-building in the case of large enterprises, this section focuses on regular full-time employees in these enterprises even though they account for only a third of the postwar work force.

143. It is only during the 1960s that industrial manufacturing came to account for a majority of factory output and manpower, with industrial output growing at an average annual rate of 16.6 percent during that time. Moreover, the percentage of the work force employed in the tertiary sector in 1970 was still significantly lower than in the advanced industrial West, with the gap only narrowing in 1980 when employment in that sector in Japan finally surpassed the primary and secondary sectors combined. In addition, the process of urbanization— which had been partially reversed during the war as workers fled urban industrial centers for the security of their villages—resumed with the postwar land reforms and continued until 1970 before leveling off. Hence, it is not unreasonable to regard Japan as a late industrializer through the 1970s. The economic figures are from Allen, 192–94, 213, 258, 285; Gary Saxonhouse, "Industrial Restructuring in Japan," *Journal of Japanese Studies* 5, 2 (summer 1979): 273–320; and Ardath Burks, *Japan: A Postindustrial Power,* rev. ed. (Boulder: Westview, 1991), 131–41. The statistics on rural-urban migration are from *Japan Statistical Yearbook, 1993/94* (Tokyo: Bureau of Statistics, Management and Coordination Agency).

144. On the prewar roots of Japan's postwar industrial policy and employment system, see respectively Chalmers Johnson, *MITI and the Japanese Miracle* (Stanford: Stanford University Press, 1982); and Gordon, *Evolution of Labor Relations.* On the significance of wartime practices, see Noguchi; and Gao.

145. This term is from Gary Allinson, *Japanese Urbanism: Industry and Politics in Kariya, 1872–1972* (Berkeley: University of California Press, 1975), chap. 6.

146. Beginning in 1946, the Work Standards Law, the Trade Union Law, and the Labor Relations Arbitration Law went into effect as the basis for postwar industrial democracy. Immediately, the number of independent trade unions skyrocketed to 35,000, and the number of unionized workers rose to 7 million in 1949, with most associated with one of two large federations; during this time, the rate of unionization peaked at 55 percent. See Solomon Levine, "Labor Markets and Collective Bargaining in Japan," in Lockwood, ed., esp. 652–53; and, for a more extensive discussion, John Price, *Japan Works: Power and Paradox in Postwar Industrial Relations* (Ithaca: ILR Press/Cornell University Press, 1997), 37–126.

147. The conservative Yoshida cabinet became more energized in tackling labor unions after 1946 as the Allied Occupation authorities became more concerned with containing communism than protecting union rights. The Japanese Socialist Party briefly took power in 1947–48, and the Katayama cabinet set up new labor councils in which union representatives were to participate. Yoshida, however, regained power in 1949 and set out to quickly implement the Dodge Line which encouraged Japanese firms to cut wage bills to become more competitive in the international market. With U.S. support, he and the more hard-line business federation *(Nikkeiren)* went on the offensive, cracking down on many union activists and weakening the more militant unions. See Garon and Mochizuki, 156–58; and Gordon, "Contests," 380.

148. Gordon, "Contests," 379–81; Garon and Mochizuki, 156–59; and Gao, 30, 215–21.

149. In 1955, the conservative parties united under the banner of the LDP, while the socialists formed a unified minority opposition. See Masumi Junnosuke, "The 1955 System: Origin and Transformation," in Kataoka Tetsuya, ed., *Creating Single Party Democracy: Japan's Postwar Political System* (Stanford: Hoover Institution Press, Stanford University, 1992); and John Dower, "Peace and Democracy in Two Systems: External Policy and Internal Conflict," in Gordon, ed., 3–33.

150. Garon and Mochizuki, 156–59. The Japan Productivity Center was created as part of the Ministry of International Trade and Industry (MITI) and was influenced by the Japan-U.S. Council for Promoting Productivity, an organization modeled after the U.S.-backed productivity councils established throughout Europe after World War II; see Gao, 217–18.

151. A key figure in promoting these principles was Nakayama Ichiro, Vice President of the Japan Productivity Center, who saw the linkage between productivity and job and wage security as the basis for a meaningful common ground. In 1966, the LDP would adopt a "Labor Charter" committing itself to full employment, improved working conditions, and the expansion of social security, and extending these benefits to full-time public sector employees whose wages were revised upward to match the wages of private-sector employees. The Sohyo-backed steelworkers' and metalworkers' unions would subsequently become the national pattern setters in the coordinated and ritualized process of wage bargaining *(shunto)*. See Gao, 215–18; Price, 154; and Garon and Mochizuki, 158–62. On Nakayama's position, see Nakayama Ichiro, "Sensansei kojo undo hihan o hanhihan suru" [A reply to the criticism of the productivity movement], *Chuo koron* (January 1956): 46–52; also noted in Gao, 218.

152. For example, Kume recognizes the relevance of the period of labor militancy from 1945 through the 1950s, but emphasizes that workers subsequently made significant gains and became reasonably well incorporated while restraining from participation in labor conflict. Revisionist historians such as Gordon and Kumazawa adopt a more critical stance in regard to the coercive aspects of the postwar social compact, but they, too, recognize that the 1960s and 1970s were marked by a creative managerial strategy that eventually produced a relatively high level of commitment and managerial authority despite problems with long

hours, exhaustion, and gender inequality. Moreover, in a comparative study designed to challenge the alleged "commitment gap" between Japanese and U.S. employees, Lincoln and Kalleberg acknowledge that those aspects of management that are most strongly correlated with high levels of commitment have been found to be more systematically developed in postwar Japanese firms. See Kume, 1–15; Andrew Gordon, *Wages of Affluence: Labor and Management in Postwar Japan* (Cambridge: Harvard University Press, 1998), chaps. 7–8; Gordon, "Contests," 383–86; Kumazawa, chaps. 1–3; and James Lincoln and Arne Kalleberg, "Commitment, Quits, and Work Organization in Japanese and U.S. Plants," *Industrial and Labor Relations Review* 50, 1 (October 1995): 39–59. For a detailed examination of the rise in worker conformity and commitment in response to changing practices at Toyota's plant in Kariya, see Allinson, *Japanese Urbanism.*

153. In prewar Japan, the number of working days lost per worker had been in the double digits, but the number of working days lost per participant in industrial disputes fell to 5.35 in 1960, and then declined to 2.27 in 1970. The significance of these figures in a comparative context can be gauged by considering that in India, another relatively democratic late industrializer with legalized unions, the number of working days lost per striking worker was 17.78 in 1950, 6.63 in 1960, and 19.16 in 1975. In comparing Japan to advanced industrial countries, between 1978 and 1987, the number of working days lost per worker due to labor disputes in Japan was only 0.14, compared to 1.27 for the United States, 4.73 for Britain, 3.92 for Australia, and 1.53 for Sweden. The comparison of Japan and India is based on statistics on "industrial disputes" for each country in *International Historical Statistics;* on Japan and advanced industrial economies, see International Labor Organization, *ILO Yearbook of Labor Statistics* (Geneva: ILO, 1988), also cited in Kumazawa, 5. See also Gordon, *Wages of Affluence,* 23; and Kume, 7–15.

154. In 1980, there were 4,376 labor disputes recorded, of which 3,038 were strikes lasting less than 4 hours. See Matsuda, 194.

155. Masahiko Aoki, "The Japanese Firm in Transition," in Yamamura and Yasuba, 270–72.

156. See Garon and Mochizuki, 159–60; Gordon, "Contests," 383; and the more detailed discussion in Price, 191–218.

157. Gordon, "Contests," 388–90. Although the government granted the unions' right to strike, the unions lost public support and were eventually crushed as the government went ahead with its plan to privatize the railways without meeting the demand for higher wages.

158. Kumazawa, 6.

159. See Kume, chap. 4; Price, 142–43; and Mari Sako, "Shunto: The Role of Employer and Union Coordination at the Industry and Inter-Sectoral Levels," in Sako and Sato, 236–64. Note that the bureaucracy played a significant role in this process by providing crucial information about the state of the economy, expected growth rates, and cost-of-living increases, all of which were used to signal the range within which appropriate wage agreements were to be negotiated.

160. The growth in industrial production as a whole was partly a result of the growth of the work force and external economic conditions, but man-hour productivity can be invoked as a reliable indicator of employee performance particu-

larly in comparison with rates elsewhere. Thus, while man-hour productivity rose by 97 percent in Japan between 1953 and 1961, the increase in the United States was 24 percent and in the United Kingdom only 22 percent; noted in Martin Bronfenbrenner, "Economic Miracles and Japan's Income-Doubling Plan," in Lockwood, ed., 548. Moreover, while even man-hour productivity increases partly reflect changing technologies and production processes, Patrick notes that nearly half of the growth in labor productivity in the postwar period remains unaccounted for in explanations focusing purely on macroeconomic factors or technological innovation; Patrick, 225. See also L. R. Christensen, Dianne Cummings, and Dale W. Jorgenson, "Economic Growth, 1947–1973: An International Comparison," in J. Kendrick and B. Vaccara, eds., *New Developments in Productivity Measurement, Studies in Income and Wealth,* vol. 41 (New York: National Bureau of Economic Research, 1977); cited in Hugh Patrick, "The Future of the Japanese Economy: Output and Labor Productivity," *Journal of Japanese Studies* 3, 2 (summer 1977): 219–49.

161. Comparisons of the number of vehicles turned out per worker at Japanese and American auto plants also show a dramatic difference: while the average of GM, Ford, and Chrysler remained about 11 vehicles per employee between 1960 and 1975, the number of vehicles per employee at Toyota jumped from 15 to 50 while Nissan reported an increase from 12 to 41 in the same period; see Suzuki Jidosha Kogyo Rodo Kumiai, *Niju go nen shi* [Twenty-five years] (Hamana Gun: Suzuki Kumiai, 1976), 249–50, cited in Price, 230. Another study indicates that the average number of hours required to assemble televisions sets in Japan was less than half that of the United States and Germany, and one-third that of the United Kingdom; see Ira C. Magaziner and Thomas M. Hout, *Japanese Industrial Policy* (Berkeley: Institute of International Studies, 1980), 27. In addition, a Westinghouse project to build identical nuclear power plants in the United States and in Japan was completed in Japan by 2,500 workers on a single shift in four years while twice as many U.S. workers took twice as long to complete the same project; reported in the *New York Herald Tribune* (October 18, 1984), cited in Ronald Dore, *Taking Japan Seriously: A Confucian Perspective on Leading Economic Issues* (Stanford: Stanford University Press, 1987), 87.

162. See, e.g., Abegglen, who relied largely primarily on statements provided by managers and was subsequently discredited in Marsh and Mannari, 328–29.

163. The average separation rates for U.S. firms were 4.3 in 1960, 4.1 in 1970, and 4.0 in 1980, while in Japanese firms, the corresponding figures were: 2.1, 2.3, and 1.4; see Kazutoshi Koshiro, "The Quality of Working Life in Japanese Factories," in Shirai, 67.

164. Cole, *Work, Mobility and Participation,* 64. Turnover rates in Detroit also declined, but the proportion of never-changing employees peaked in 1970 at 36.8 percent, half the rate among workers in comparable jobs in Yokohama. Although Cole uses a relatively small sample and focuses only on two cities, the cities, industries, and job types are sufficiently similar to suggest that the trends evident in Yokohama and Detroit are indicative of wider shifts in turnover rates in Japan and the United States. In any case, the change in turnover rates in Yokohama between 1930 and 1970 is sufficiently large to be taken seriously, especially in

light of the fact that during the 1950s and 1960s, the Japanese economy was experiencing high-speed growth as well as rapid social change, conditions under which employers would seek to retain only the more recently trained employees, and workers would be prone to seeking out new opportunities.

165. In comparing turnover rates and workers' attitudes in an electric firm, a shipbuilding company, and a sake-brewing factory, Marsh and Mannari found that the shipbuilding firm was the outlier in that it had the lowest percentage of workers who had worked only in their present firm (38.6 percent as compared to 76.3 percent in the electric firm). But even here, 71.2 percent of the firm's workers agreed that ideally an individual should aspire to remain in one company while only 28.8 percent agreed that an individual could become more satisfied by continually changing jobs. See Marsh and Mannari, 235–36.

166. Koshiro, 64–65. For the purposes of comparison, it is worth noting that the Swedish firm Volvo, which is noted for having some organizational features similar to (according to many, superior to) those of Japanese firms, reported a sickness rate of 10 percent. Moreover, Volvo ended up having to shut down its Udevalla plant, which had been invoked as a superior model of how to humanize work. See Price, 4.

167. The study was conducted by the Japanese Economic Planning Agency in 1970 and published as *The Japanese and Their Society: Part II of the Report on National Life* (Tokyo: Economic Planning Agency, 1972); cited in Cole, *Work, Mobility and Participation,* 231.

168. Takezawa and Whitehill, *The Other Worker,* 115.

169. In the 1967 version of this survey, two-thirds of the Japanese respondents stated that they viewed their companies as at least as important as their personal lives, as compared to only 23 percent in the United States; in the 1980 version of the same survey, the percentage of respondents giving the same answer *rose* to 73 percent in Japan while dipping slightly to 21 percent in the United States. See Takezawa and Whitehill, *The Other Worker,* 111; and Takezawa and Whitehill, *Work Ways,* 57–62.

170. See Kumazawa, chaps. 4–5; Price, 6–35; and Gordon, *Wages of Affluence,* 171.

171. On improvements in wages and working conditions, see Kume, 7–13. In fact, Kume notes that even by comparison to Western standards, the number of average annual working hours per worker in Japan in 1992 stood at just 1,972, compared to 1,948 in the United States, and 1,953 in the United Kingdom two years before; Kume, 13.

172. Gordon, "Contests," 391. See also Gordon, *Wages of Affluence,* chap. 8; Garon and Mochizuki; and Kumazawa.

173. See Maruyama Masao, "Nationalism in Japan: Its Theoretical Background and Prospects" (trans. David Titus, 1951), in his *Thought and Behavior in Modern Japanese Politics* (New York: Oxford University Press, 1963), esp. 151–54. The argument that Japan needed a cultural revolution resembling the Protestant Reformation was made explicitly by Otsuka Hisao who was influenced by Weber and keen on witnessing in Japan the kind of transformation Weber had described in the context of the rise of capitalism in England; see Otsuka Hisao, *Kindaika no*

ningenteki kiso [The moral basis for modernization] (Tokyo, 1968).

174. This reverse course *(gyaku-koku),* orchestrated under prime minister Yoshida, consisted of banning strikes, enhancing the ability of business elites and the government to crack down on labor militancy, recentralizing government, and retreating from reforms in the education system that had originally been designed to replace the emphasis on Japanese morality and ethics with an American-style curriculum. See John W. Dower, *Japan in War and Peace: Selected Essays* (New York: New Press, 1993), 155–207; and Ivan Morris, *Nationalism and the Right Wing in Japan: A Study of PostWar Trends* (London: Oxford University Press, 1960), 59–63, 105–10.

175. See Carol Gluck, "The Past in the Present," in Gordon, ed.; and her book *Japan's Modern Myths,* 4–5. On the marginalization of the liberal critique of prewar Japan, see Andrew Barshay, "Toward a History of the Social Sciences in Japan," *Positions* 4, 2 (1996): 217–51, esp. 238–42.

176. Some examples of *Nihonjinron* are cited above (n. 56). For surveys and evaluations of this literature, see Dale; Yoshino; Minami Hiroshi, *Nihonjinron no keifu* [A genealogy of *Nihonjinron*] (Tokyo: Kodansha, 1980); and Befu Harumi, *Zoho ideorogi to shite no Nihon bunkaron* [The theory of Japanese culture as an ideology] (Tokyo: Shiso no kagaku, 1987).

177. See, e.g., Mouer and Sugimoto; Dale; and Befu, "Symbols of Nationalism."

178. See Tsujimura for empirical data on the enormous popularity of works emphasizing the positive and functional aspects of Japanese national culture since the early 1950s. See also Dale, 15; and Yoshino, 2–4.

179. The populist historiography, identified with such intellectuals as Irokawa Daikichi and Kano Masanao, emphasized the life-styles and behaviors of ordinary Japanese people, particularly the rural population. Similarly, some postwar communist intellectuals such as Tekeuchi Yoshimi criticized the universalist discourses of the postwar progressive intellectuals and emphasized more particularist themes stressing the link between socialism and the Japanese *Volk.* See Irokawa Daikichi, *Kindai kokka no shuppatsu* [The beginning of a modern state] (Tokyo: Chuo Koronsha, 1967); Kano Masano, ed., *Shin shiso no taido* [The emergence of new currents of thought] (Tokyo: Chikuma Shobo, 1969); and on Takeuchi, see Victor Koschmann, *Revolution and Subjectivity in Post-War Japan* (Chicago: University of Chicago Press, 1996), 203–20.

180. In one study of businessmen and educators, over 90 percent of the businessmen had been exposed to the *Nihonjinron* literature, and 75 percent sought out this literature out of active interest given its implications for management. One of the most important reasons cited by businessmen for their interest in *Nihonjinron* was its value in promoting human relations in the workplace. See Yoshino, 131–39.

181. Tsutsui, 158–59.

182. As noted in chapter 2, while Mayo and his followers recognized the relationship between the worker's mental state and his/her job satisfaction and productivity, it is far from clear what impact the human relations movement actually

had on specific management practices beyond the introduction of personnel departments, suggestion boxes, and morale surveys.

183. Gao, 215–17, quote from 215. See also the second epithet at the beginning of this chapter.

184. Tsutsui, 136, 150; Gordon, "Contests," 380–85.

185. Rodney Clark, *The Japanese Company* (New Haven: Yale University Press, 1969), 197–201; Nakane, *Japanese Society,* 84; and Ernest Van Helvoort, *The Japanese Working Man: What Choice? What Reward?* (Vancouver: University of British Columbia Press, 1979), 64–67.

186. Thomas Rohlen, "The Company Work Group," in Ezra Vogel, ed., *Modern Japanese Organization and Decision-Making* (Berkeley: University of California Press, 1975), 185–209.

187. Clark, 155–66, 197–201. A similar pattern of training and socialization was initiated in the training institutes established by the *Renri* (Ethics) movement founded by Maruyama Toshio. By the end of the 1980s, the Ethics movement was still 100,000 strong and the Ethics School in Tokyo offered workers and managers special seminars dealing with issues of ethics and how to put them into practice in the workplace. See Dorrine Kondo, *Crafting Selves: Power, Gender and the Discourses of Identity in a Japanese Workplace* (Chicago: University of Chicago Press, 1990), 78–80.

188. Allinson, *Japanese Urbanism,* 175–80.

189. Rohlen, *For Harmony and Strength,* 201–2.

190. Rohlen, *For Harmony and Strength,* 55.

191. Clark, 140; emphasis added.

192. Rohlen, *For Harmony and Strength,* 44.

193. Cole, *Work, Mobility and Participation,* 249. On the psychology of dependence in Japanese society, see Doi.

194. See Rohlen, *For Harmony and Strength,* 105–7; Cole, *Japanese Blue Collar,* 142–45; and Clark, 110. On the tendency of most Japanese (90 percent) to identify themselves as middle class and to exhibit remarkably similar consumption habits, see Yasusuke Murakami, "The Reality of the New Middle Class," *Japan Interpretor* 12, 1 (winter 1978), 1–4; and Bernard Eccleston, *State and Society in Post-War Japan* (Cambridge, UK: Polity Press, 1989), 172–73.

195. Fruin, *Kikkoman,* 9.

196. Note that the difference in connotations attached to the "family firm" and human relations is analogous to the different understanding of group membership in the preindustrial *ie* and *mura.* See the discussion at the end of section 3.1 (at nn. 35–38).

197. See Gordon, *Evolution of Labor Relations,* chap. 9.

198. Price, 150–54.

199. Gordon, "Contests," 383.

200. E.g., Nitta Michio, *Nihon no rodosha sanka* [Worker participation in Japan] (Tokyo: Tokyo University Press, 1988); Nakamura, 280–95; and Kazuo Koike, *The Economics of Work in Japan* (Tokyo: Long Term Credit Bank International Library Foundation, 1995).

201. Gordon, "Contests."

202. The joint-consultation machinery (JCM) was introduced in large firms to resolve minor disputes before unions got involved. More than 90 percent of the firms with over 1,000 unionized employees and about 83 percent of all Japanese firms with trade unions have developed JCMs. On the extent to which JCMs create new opportunities for worker participation, see Kazuo Koike, "Human Resource Development and Labor-Management," in Yamamura and Yasuba, esp. 320–21; and Nakamura.

203. Kume, chap. 4; and Sako, "Shunto."

204. See Levine, "Labor Markets," 656; and Pempel and Tsunekawa, 263–64.

205. This point is even noted in critical interpretations of postwar labor politics. See, e.g., Kumazawa, 6, and chap. 3, passim; Gordon, "Contests"; and Garon and Mochizuki, 160. More favorable treatments of the role of enterprise unions may be found in Levine; Pemple and Tsunekawa; Kume, 7–8; and Nitta.

206. The term *coercive consensus* is from Gordon, *Wages of Affluence,* 156. What is significant here is the different *levels* and *forms* of coercion in prewar and postwar Japan. While the prewar factory councils and Sanpo movement were predicated on the assumption that the interests of workers and managers were not fundamentally opposed, postwar enterprise unions at least offered recognition for the separate interests of the workers and left open the possibility of industry-wide coordination of strikes or slowdowns.

207. See Levine, "Unionization of White-Collar Employees," 219–36; and Pempel and Tsunekawa, 263–64.

208. Quotes are from, respectively, Kumazawa, 49; and Gary Allinson, "The Moderation of Organized Labor in Postwar Japan," *Journal of Japanese Studies* 1, 2 (spring 1975), 433.

209. Note that nuanced versions of the critical and positive treatments of postwar industrial relations converge on the point that enterprise unions buttressed the position of the company as the primary source of identity. Compare, e.g., the interpretations in Levine, "Labor Markets," 655–56; Pempel and Tsunekawa; Allinson, "Moderation of Organized Labor"; Kumazawa, chap. 3; and Gordon, *Wages of Affluence,* chap. 8.

210. Garon and Mochizuki, 159–60.

211. Gao, 221, citing Nihon Seisansi Honbu, *Gijutsu kakushin to nihon keizai* [Technological innovation and Japan's economy] (Tokyo: Nihon Seisan Honbu, 1960).

212. E.g., Koji Taira, *Economic Development and the Labor Market in Japan* (New York: Columbia University Press, 1970).

213. See Cole, *Work, Mobility and Participation,* 24.

214. See Kume, 12–13. Kume notes that during the 1980s, a 20 percent decline in production led to only a 7 percent reduction in the work force in Japan. For purposes of comparison, note that, in the United States, a 13.1 percent loss in production output corresponded to a 10.7 percent reduction of the work force, while in West Germany, a 10.9 percent loss of production corresponded to a 11.5 percent reduction in employment.

215. See the more detailed discussion and evidence in Thomas Rohlen, "'Per-

manent Employment' Faces Recession, Slow Growth, and an Aging Work Force," *Journal of Japanese Studies* 5, 2 (summer 1979): 235–72.

216. See Cole, *Work, Mobility, and Participation*, 88; and the earlier discussion of turnover rates (at nn. 162–65).

217. Kumazawa, chap. 3. See also Gordon, *Evolution of Labor Relations*, chaps. 9–10.

218. Gordon, "Contests," 386. For a detailed discussion of the emergence of the postwar wage system, see Gordon, *Evolution of Labor Relations*, chap. 9.

219. See Isao Ohashi, "On the Determinants of Bonuses and Basic Wages in Large Japanese Firms," in Kenichi Imai and Ryutaro Komiya, eds., *The Business Enterprise in Japan* (Cambridge: MIT Press, 1993). On how this new wage system was introduced at Toyota and Suzuki, see respectively Allinson, *Japanese Urbanism*, 175–77; and Price, 164–66. On the distinctiveness of postwar Japan's wage system, see Masahiko Aoki, *Information, Incentives, and Bargaining in the Japanese Economy* (Cambridge: Cambridge University Press, 1988), 11–20.

220. See Ryushi Iwata, "The Japanese Enterprise as a Unified Body of Employees," in Kumon and Rosovsky, 187–88; and Ronald Dore, *British Factory, Japanese Factory* (Berkeley: University of California Press, 1973), chap. 3.

221. Ohashi, 275–77. By contrast, only 11 percent of the 2,384 factories surveyed in 1932 had some sort of profit-sharing scheme; noted in Hazama, *History of Labor Management*, 78–82.

222. See Hiroshi Ishida, Seymour Spilerman, and Kuo-Hsien Su, "Educational Credentials and Promotion Prospects in a Japanese and an American Organization," Working Paper 92 of the Center on Japanese Economy and Business (Columbia University, New York, 1995); and Kenichi Imai and Ryutaro Komiya, "Characteristics of Japanese Firms," in Imai and Komiya, 21–22. The competition among employees to advance more rapidly was also partly offset by the fact that much of the competition was among members who had joined the company in the same year and had developed a high degree of solidarity as members of the same entering class. On the latter point, see Robert Cole, *Japanese Blue-Collar: The Changing Tradition* (Berkeley: University of California Press, 1971), 101–5.

223. Dore, *Taking Japan Seriously*, 99; and Thomas Rohlen, *Japan's High Schools* (Berkeley: University of California Press, 1983), 135–37.

224. Kumazawa, 49–51.

225. Gordon, "Contests," 386.

226. Cole, *Japanese Blue Collar*, 78–79, 86–88.

227. According to some reports, merit-based considerations by the 1980s had once again become a "powerful tool in management's arsenal of incentives"; Price, 170. The evidence invoked to demonstrate this point, however, is too recent and scant to refute conventional treatments of wage practices in large firms during the period of interest in this chapter (1950s–70s). Price's contention is based on a 1988 study of managers' statements about wage practices at Suzuki, which supposedly based 70 percent of the average wage increases for employees on merit-related criteria; see Price, 166 (fn. 16). Gordon *(Wages of Affluence)* also makes the same claim, but his evidence is based on recent trends at a prominent steel company, NKK (Nippon Kokkan). In any case, as both positive and critical interpretations

recognize, the understanding of competence or merit in postwar companies incorporated factors unrelated to individual task performance or output (such as a demonstrated commitment to company goals, quickness in learning new skills, and the ability to work cooperatively with peers, superiors, or subordinates). On this point, note the convergence between Gordon, "Contests," 386; and Cole, *Japanese Blue-Collar*, 101–5.

228. Critical perspectives highlighting the loss of labor autonomy and other social costs of postwar industrial peace include Price, esp. 166–70; Kumazawa, chap. 5; Kunth Dohse, Ulrich Jurgens, and Thomas Malsch, "From 'Fordism' to 'Toyotaism'? The Social Organization of the Labor Process in the Japanese Automobile Industry," *Politics and Society* 14, 2 (1985): 115–46; Totsuka Hideo and Hyodo Tsutomu, *Roshi kankei no tenkan to sentaku* [Transition and choice in industrial relations] (Tokyo: Nihon Hyoron Sha, 1991); and Hideo Totsuka, "The Transformation of Japanese Industrial Relations: A Case Study of the Automobile Industry," in Steve Babson, ed., *Lean Work: Empowerment and Exploitation in the Global Auto Industry* (Detroit: Wayne State University Press, 1995).

229. Keisuke Nakamura and Michio Nitta, "Developments in Industrial Relations and Human Resource Practices in Japan," in Richard Locke, Thomas Kochan, and Michael Piore, eds., *Employment Relations in a Changing World Economy* (Cambridge: MIT Press, 1995), 325–58, quote from 326–27.

230. For more ambivalent or critical treatments that acknowledge this point, see Kumazawa, chap. 3; Gordon, "Contests," 385–91; and Gordon, *Evolution of Labor Relations*, chap. 9.

231. Tsutsui, 197–212; Robert Cole, *Strategies for Learning: Small Group Activities in American, Japanese, and Swedish Industry* (Berkeley: University of California Press, 1989); and Goshi Kohei, "Successful Performance of the Productivity Movement in Japanese Enterprises," in British Institute of Management, *Modern Japanese Management* (London: British Institute of Management, 1970), 123.

232. See Dore, *British Factory, Japanese Factory*, chap. 9; Aoki, *Information, Incentives, and Bargaining*, esp. 11–20; Koike, "Human Resource Development"; and Cole, *Work, Mobility and Participation*, 112. Cole points out that even Marsh and Mannari, who were attempting to demonstrate the convergence between U.S. and Japanese firms, were impressed by the level of job diversification in the shipbuilding factory they analyzed; Marsh and Mannari, 91. Similarly, in his classic study of Uedagin bank, Rohlen notes that there were no formal job descriptions for individual employees and that sets of tasks were communicated to workgroups as a whole; Rohlen, *For Harmony and Strength*, 30. One study of a public corporation did find that individual work assignments were prevalent, but the study also noted that this company was characterized by a higher level of tensions and conflicts among employers and employees (making it more the exception than the rule); see Kenneth Skinner, "Conflict and Command in a Public Corporation in Japan," *Journal of Japanese Studies* 6, 3 (summer 1980): 301–29.

233. Cole, *Work, Mobility and Participation*, 109–19.

234. On this point, see Imai and Komiya, 24.

235. See Cole, *Strategies for Learning;* Koike, "Human Resource Develop-

ment"; Koike, "Learning and Incentive Systems in Japanese Industry," in Masahiko Aoki and Ronald Dore, eds., *The Japanese Firm: The Sources of Competitive Strength* (New York: Oxford University Press, 1994); and Mari Sako, "Training, Productivity, and Quality Control in Japanese Multinational Corporations," in Aoki and Dore. Koike's argument is particularly interesting since it attempts to relate the "white-collarization" of blue-collar employees to increasing workplace motivation.

236. For an extensive discussion of the QC concept and its emergence in Japan, see William Edward Deming, *Statistical Control of Quality in Japan,* Proceedings of the International Conference on Quality Control, 1969 (Tokyo: Union of Japanese Scientists and Engineers, 1970); William Ouchi, *Theory Z: How American Business Can Meet the Japanese Challenge* (Reading: Addison-Wesley, 1981), esp. Appendix II; Cole, *Strategies for Learning;* and Tsutsui, chaps. 5–6. For a detailed (though critical) analysis of this process at Suzuki, see Price, 170–90.

237. See Cole, *Work, Mobility and Participation,* 137; and Koike, "Human Resource Development," 291.

238. Ishikawa notes six specific differences between QC activities in U.S. and Japanese firms: the latter were supposedly characterized by significantly higher levels of participation, an emphasis on greater education and expanded training, the more regular use of statistical methods, the greater variety of QC activities, a system for auditing and rewarding QC achievements, and the nationwide promotion of the QC movement. Others such as Tsutsui and Price question just how sharply the QC movement broke with the scientific management practices borrowed from the United States, but even they acknowledge that the Japanese QC movement could be distinguished from its American counterpart, in marked contrast to the emulation of U.S. scientific management practices during the prewar rationalization movement. See Ishikawa Kaoru, *Nihon teki hinshitsu kanri* [Japanese quality control] (Tokyo: Nikka Giren Shuppan Sha, 1988), also cited in Price, 184; see also Tsutsui, 208–12.

239. Cole, *Work, Mobility and Participation,* 138–41, 201–2; Koike, "Learning and Incentive Systems"; and Arthur Whitehill, *Japanese Management: Tradition and Transition* (New York: Routledge, 1991): 236–37. On similar trends in Japanese firms abroad, see Sako, "Training, Productivity, and Quality Control."

240. In firms with more than 5,000 employees, 83.4 percent of the managers viewed QC circles as successful; Koike, "Human Resource Development," 291.

241. On the decline in working hours and improved working conditions, see Kume, 9–13. As evidence of the positive benefits of QC involvement, Cole points out that QC members regularly attended presentations at companywide and national conventions, and subsequently enjoyed socializing with their peers, engaging in bouts of singing and beer drinking; Cole, *Strategies for Learning,* 290. While this characterization may mask the subtle pressures many workers probably felt to join in these activities, more nuanced critical analyses also recognize a degree of voluntarism in the spread of QC circles, noting that QC members were positioned to offer alternatives to staffing cuts or work speedups in the course of evaluating the quality of products and production processes; Gordon, *Wages of Affluence,* 170.

242. This perspective is explicit in Ishikawa, but is also implicit in Aoki, "The Japanese Firm as a System of Attributes," in Aoki and Dore; and Koiki, *Economics of Work.*

243. See, e.g., Adler, "'Democratic Taylorism'"; Kenney and Florida; and Womack et al.

244. Price, esp. 172; Dohse et al; and Kumazawa, chap. 5. Kumazawa even characterizes the QC circle as a case of "mandatory volunteering."

245. As Cole notes, the distinctiveness and success of postwar Japanese work organization rested on its "ability to integrate hierarchy with the traditional, small-group collective organization"; Cole, *Work, Mobility and Participation,* 208–9.

246. Thus, this interpretation challenges that offered in Tsutsui, 176–235; and Price, 184–90. Both provide evidence to call into question Ishikawa's thesis that Japanese work organization was distinctive and had native roots; they also do well to question the universality of a technology-driven shift to post-Fordist lean production. However, in the absence of any other comparative referent, both are forced to leave unanswered the question of just where the boundaries of Taylorism or scientific management lie. As a result, almost any innovation in postwar Japanese work organization is summarily dismissed as merely an adjustment or refinement of Taylorism. Tsutsui does acknowledge in passing that Taylorism was "revised" to suit Japan's own conditions, leading to a "distinct trajectory of development" (Tsutsui, 11), but the difference between the prewar borrowing of scientific management and the postwar construction of "revised Taylorism" is suppressed to highlight the essential continuity with past scientific management and the continuing influence of U.S. management practices.

Chapter 4

1. From a lecture given at Sverdlov University shortly after Lenin's death, transcribed in J. V. Stalin, *Problems of Leninism,* trans. 8th ed. (Moscow: Foreign Languages Publishing House, 1953), 111.

2. Leon Trotsky, *The Revolution Betrayed: What Is the Soviet Union and Where Is It Going?* rev. ed. (New York: Pathfinder, 1972 [1937]), 112–13.

3. David L. Hoffman, *Peasant Metropolis: Social Identities in Moscow, 1929–1941* (Ithaca: Cornell University Press, 1994), 19; emphasis added. This position was taken by Finance Minister Kankrin as well as Slavophile intellectuals touting the moral qualities of the commune; see Reginald Zelnik, *Labor and Society in Tsarist Russia: The Factory Workers of St. Petersburg, 1855–1970* (Stanford: Stanford University Press, 1971), 24–28, 71–72.

4. Among Western historians, this point was first emphasized in Leopold Haimson, *The Russian Marxists and the Origins of Bolshevism* (Cambridge: Harvard University Press, 1955); see also Zelnik, 6.

5. The term is borrowed from David Shearer, *Industry, State, and Society in Stalin's Russia, 1926–1934* (Ithaca: Cornell University Press, 1996), 158.

6. A succinct version of this statement is in Richard Pipes, "Did the Russian Revolution Have to Happen?" *American Scholar* (spring 1994): 215–38. See also Pipes, *Russia under the Old Regime* (New York: Scribner's, 1974); Nathan

Leites, *A Study of Bolshevism* (Glencoe: Free Press, 1953); Zbigniew Brzezinski, "Soviet Politics: From the Future to the Past?" in Paul Cocks et al., eds., *The Dynamics of Soviet Politics* (Cambridge: Harvard University Press, 1976), esp. 340–42; and Brzezinski and Carl Friedrich, *Totalitarian Dictatorship and Autocracy* (Cambridge: Harvard University Press, 1956).

7. On the patriarchal household, see Moshe Lewin, *Russian Peasants and Soviet Power* (New York: Norton, 1975), esp. 25–26; James Mandel, "Paternalistic Authority in the Russian Countryside, 1856–1906" (Ph.D. diss., Columbia University, 1978); David Ransel, ed., *The Family in Imperial Russia* (Urbana: University of Illinois Press, 1978); and Christine Worobec, *Peasant Russia: Family and Community in the Post-Emancipation Period* (Princeton: Princeton University Press, 1991).

8. Timothy McDaniel, *The Agony of the Russian Idea* (Princeton: Princeton University Press, 1996), 32–51; and Stephen White, *Political Culture and Soviet Politics* (New York: St. Martin's Press, 1979), chap. 2.

9. On the tenor of agrarian life, see Moshe Lewin, *Making of the Soviet System* (New York: Pantheon, 1985), 49–87. On the impact of Russian Orthodoxy, see Paul Miliukov, *Outlines of Russian Culture,* rev. ed. (Philadelphia: University of Pennsylvania Press, 1960); and Nikolai Berdyaev, *The Russian Revolution* (Ann Arbor: University of Michigan Press, 1961), chap. 1. On pre-Muscovite local governance, see Sergei Pushkarev, *Self-Government and Freedom in Russia* (Boulder: Westview, 1988).

10. Lewin, *Making,* 56; and Theodor Shanin, *Russia as a 'Developing Society'* (London: Macmillan, 1985), 73–74.

11. Pipes, *Russia,* 141–42.

12. Pushkarev, 45–46.

13. On Herzen and Chernyshevskii's views on the commune, see Shanin, *Russia,* 78–81.

14. As in the case of rural Japan (see chap. 3, n. 5), area specialists such as anthropologists, historians, sociologists, and students of political culture have themselves provided ample precedents for the assumption made in this chapter concerning the homogeneity of norms, orientations, and practices across prerevolutionary Russia. See, e.g., Edward Keenan, "Muscovite Political Folkways," *Russian Review* 45, 2 (April 1986): 115–81; Lewin, *Making;* Lewin, *Russian Peasants;* Pipes, *Russia;* Shanin, *Russia;* White; and Worobec. The most noted variation, that between the repartitional commune (prevalent across most of European Russia) and the nonrepartitional commune (found primarily in the western and southwestern peripheries of the empire) did not actually correspond to any fundamental differences in the norms and principles governing agrarian work and life in the commune. On this point, see Shanin, *Russia,* 77–78.

15. Lewin, *Making,* 59–60; and Pipes, *Russia,* 161.

16. Keenan, 117–21; see also Shanin, 83–84.

17. These two features of the prerevolutionary inheritance correspond to two of the "four affirmations" at the core of the "Russian idea" articulated by McDaniel (*Agony,* 40–53): the desire for a higher moral community and the shared preference for an equality of outcomes. The other two affirmations, not relevant

for everyday work-related matters, supposedly include a commitment to a unitary set of "ultimate values" and a conception of the good state as a "government of truth" that should embody these values.

18. Given the resilience of local pre-Christian beliefs and rituals, representatives of the latter did not automatically gain the trust of most peasants; but the integration of Christian beliefs and icons was sufficient to produce a powerful, recognizable Slavic Christian *(provoslavnyi)* identity that buttressed community solidarity throughout Russia; see Lewin, *Making,* 60–70.

19. White, 59.

20. Pipes, *Russia,* 159–60; McDaniel, *Agony,* 40–46; Worobec, esp. chap. 7; Magagna, 206–12; and Paul Avrich, *Russian Rebels, 1600–1800* (New York: Schocken Books, 1972). The public display of reverence for tsarist officials to obviate outside intervention in communal affairs is discussed extensively in Daniel Field, *Rebels in the Name of the Tsar* (Boston: Routledge Chapman, 1976).

21. Shanin, *Russia,* 83–84.

22. See Pipes, *Russia,* 141–42; and Lewin, *Making,* 80.

23. On the role of the *mir* during the period of serfdom, see Pipes, *Russia,* 109; Magagna, 195; and Peter Kolchin, *Unfree Labor: American Slavery and Russian Serfdom* (Cambridge: Harvard University Press and Belknap Press, 1987), 203–4. An authoritative Russian text is V. A. Aleksandrov, *Sel'skaia Obshchina v Rossii (XVII–nachala XIX v.)* [The rural commune in Russia (from the seventeenth century to the beginning of the nineteenth century)] (Moscow, 1976).

24. It is estimated that across Russia, peasants received title to only about four-fifths of the land they were previously tilling on average; in some of the more fertile regions, the gentry managed to hold on to as much as 40 percent of the land and closed off forested areas or access to water. See Nicholas Riasanovsky, *A History of Russia,* 4th ed (New York: Oxford University Press, 1984), 414.

25. Riasanovsky, 414, 479. For a more detailed discussion of the functions of the *mir* in post-Emancipation Russia, see Boris Mironov, "The Russian Peasant Commune after the Reforms of the 1860s," *Slavic Review* 44, 3 (fall 1985): 438–67.

26. Burds, 90. See also Lewin, *Making,* 79–80; Shanin, *Russia,* 73–75; and Worobec, 23–24. As Worobec notes, however, while wealthier communal households did absorb the costs of caring for neighbors struck by illness or accidents, "communes could not justify maintaining repeated tax evaders, alcoholics or those believed to be lazy, at the expense of other communal members."

27. Burds, 96–97. One of the best Russian language sources on the communal tradition of *pomoch* is M. M. Gromyko, *Traditsionnye Normy Povedeniia i Formy Obshcheniia Russkikh Krest'ian XIX v* [Traditional norms of behavior and forms of relations among the nineteenth-century Russian peasantry] (Moscow: Nauka, 1986).

28. For example, after the abolition of serfdom, the tsarist state set up the *volost* as a rural assembly that would combine a number of village assemblies and gradually take over the functions of the *mir.* Like the Japanese plan for the amalgamation of *mura* into larger units, however, this effort failed to weaken the authority or solidarity of the *mir.*

29. Pipes, *Russia,* 156–58; and Shanin, *Russia,* 83–84. See Burds, chap. 7, for a discussion of the "culture of denunciation" in post-Emancipation Russia.

30. Lewin, *Making,* 79; and Theodor Shanin, *The Awkward Class: Political Sociology of Peasantry in a Developing Society, Russia, 1910–1925* (Oxford: Clarendon, 1972), 141.

31. Even during the large-scale uprisings led by Stepan Razin and Emile Pugachev in the 1670s and 1770s respectively, the original aim of most peasants was simply to restore a moral status quo that they believed to have been violated. See Pipes, *Russia,* 155–58.

32. On this point, see also McDaniel, *Agony,* 46–51.

33. Efforts to apply class analysis to the Russian peasant commune have been convincingly refuted by Shanin *(Awkward Class)* and Lewin *(Russian Peasants)* among others.

34. On Chernov and the Socialist Revolutionaries, see Oliver Radkey, *The Agrarian Foes of Bolshevism* (New York: Columbia University Press, 1958), 82–87. Their view of the commune is consistent with the "soft line" espoused by the noted agricultural economist Chayanov and others in the Soviet People's Commissariat of Agriculture during the early 1920s (although their position would be emphatically rejected by Stalin in 1928). See A. V. Chayanov, *Theory of the Peasant Economy,* ed. Daniel Thorniley et al. (Madison: University of Wisconsin Press, 1986); and the discussion in Markus Wehner, "The Soft Line on Agriculture: The Case of Narkomzem and Its Specialists, 1921–27," in Judith Pallott, ed., *Transforming Peasants: Society, State and the Peasantry, 1861–1930* (London: Macmillan, 1998).

35. Lewin, *Making,* 76–82. This "right to labor" principle was also extended to conceptions of household membership: individuals adopted into the household, for example, could always claim a share of the common property of the household, while blood relatives who left the commune for an extended period forfeited any claims. In this regard, Russian households were not different from the Japanese *ie.*

36. Shanin, 76–77. See also Worobec, 20; and Dorothy Atkinson, *The End of the Russian Land Commune, 1905–1930* (Stanford: Stanford University Press, 1983), 26–33.

37. This was in marked contrast to the Japanese *ie,* where all of the property of a household was automatically transferred to the eldest son. This also meant that younger sons in Russia were less likely to go to the cities than was the case in Japan where younger sons frequently left the *ie* in order to set up separate branch families or seek new employment. See Cathy Frierson, *"Razdel:* The Peasant Family Divided," *Russian Review* 46 (1987): 35–52; and Worobec, 10.

38. Atkinson, 26–37; Lewin, *Making,* 79–80; Worobec, 20–24; and Magagna, 200.

39. Shanin, *Russia,* 77–78.

40. The relatively small gap in the status and living standards of rich and poor peasants is widely noted in studies of the Russian countryside, even in narratives that seek to emphasize the rising tensions associated with wealthier peasants' access to grain reserves to survive difficult times in the post-Emancipation period. An example of the latter is Burds, 119. On the low level of stratification generally,

see, e.g., Shanin, *Russia,* 94–102; and Worobec, 20–41. Shanin specifically notes that despite the wealthier peasants' wider margin of subsistence, only 4 percent of rural households regularly hired wage-labor in the post-Emancipation period while about 90 percent remained uniformly engaged in subsistence-oriented farming regulated by the commune.

41. Worobec, 41.

42. Keenan, 128. See also Lewin, *Making,* 79–80; and Shanin, *Russia,* 74–75. This point is also noted in one of the first Western accounts of rural Russia; see Howard Kennard, *The Russian Peasant* (London: T. Werner Laurie, 1907), 129–30.

43. White, 58. See also Donald Male, *Russian Peasant Organization before Collectivization: A Study of Commune and Gathering, 1925–1930* (Cambridge: Cambridge University Press, 1971), 72.

44. See nn. 6–7. In industrial relations, Bendix's treatment of the early Soviet factory also attributes its hierarchical features to preexisting hierarchical traditions in tsarist Russia; see *Work and Authority,* 250.

45. Worobec, 20.

46. In any case, within the context of a subsistence economy, both collective ideals and self-interest were served by ensuring that no one family could advance too rapidly lest the rest of the village community suffer sharp declines in its collective fortunes. On this point, see also Pipes, *Russia,* 110.

47. See Atkinson, 29–32; and Riasanovsky, 430–32. Russia's population grew from 74 million in 1858 to 129 million in 1897.

48. Burds, 41. On the various means through which commune elders, local officials, and family members continued to check individual farmholding and preserve preexisting arrangements, see Burds, chap. 3, passim; as well as Atkinson, 71–82, 155–64; and Shanin, *Awkward Class,* 9–62.

49. Worobec, 14.

50. Burds, 115–34; quote from 130. On the role of village ties in urban settlements, see the classic account in Robert E. Johnson, *Peasant and Proletarian: The Working Class of Moscow at the End of the Nineteenth Century* (Camden, NJ: Rutgers University Press, 1979). On similar dynamics in St. Petersburg, see also Evel Economakis, "Patterns of Migration and Settlement in Prerevolutionary Petersburg: Peasants from Iaroslavl and Tver Provinces," *Russian Review* 56, 1 (1997): 8–24.

51. Magagna, 199; Shanin, *Awkward Class,* 29–39; and Worobec, 17. Alexander II's attempt to promote larger-scale administrative units is not unlike the Meiji attempt to create amalgamated village units. In both cases, the larger, amalgamated units proved to be ineffective in subverting the local authority of the village assembly and its head.

52. See Male, 18–19; Lewin, *Making,* 81; Pipes, *Russia,* 19; and Riasanovsky, 430–33. In terms of land held by the commune, Male points to Soviet reports that 222 million hectares were farmed on the basis of repartitional commune holdings and common crop rotations, while individual farmsteads and socialist collective farms accounted for only 10 million hectares.

53. For example, by 1920, Moscow had lost 40 percent of its 1917 popula-

tion due to the out-migration of workers returning to their villages; Hoffman, 20–23. See also Diane Koenker, "Urbanization and Deurbanization in the Russian Revolution and Civil War," *Journal of Modern History* 57 (1985): 424–50.

54. Lewin, *Russian Peasants,* 26, 39fn.; and Shanin, *Awkward Class,* 168.

55. Jowitt makes essentially the same point, but from the Bolshevik party's point of view: the Bolsheviks' emphasis on values such as loyalty and collectivism seemed intelligible to peasants but only because the latter interpreted these within their traditional normative framework and failed to recognize the "charismatic" and "impersonal" aspects of Leninism. See Ken Jowitt, *New World Disorder: The Leninist Extinction* (Berkeley: University of California Press, 1992), 32–38. See, however, the point at n. 57.

56. Hoffman, 26; see also Kuromiya, "Workers' Artels and Soviet Production Relations," in Sheila Fitzpatrick, Alexander Rabinowitch, and Richard Stites, eds., *Russia in the Era of NEP* (Bloomington: Indiana University Press, 1991). Carr and Shanin have estimated that during this time, some 20 million peasant households spontaneously and voluntarily attached themselves to 300,000 to 400,000 communes. See Shanin, *Awkward Class,* 165; and E. H. Carr, *Socialism in One Country, 1924–1926* (London: Macmillan, 1964), 214. See also the discussion of the resurgence of the commune and its norms in Lewin, *Russian Peasants,* 82–90; and Male, 20–22.

57. Shanin, *Awkward Class,* 199.

58. The dramatic confrontations between the traditional peasantry and party officials during the collectivization campaigns are captured vividly in Lewin, *Russian Peasants,* esp. 460–515; and Merle Fainsod's classic study, *Smolensk under Soviet Rule* (Cambridge: Harvard University Press, 1958), esp. chaps. 11–12.

59. This characterization is from Robert Tucker, "Stalinism as Revolution from Above," in Tucker, ed., *Stalinism* (New York: W. W. Norton, 1977).

60. See Stephen Kotkin, *Magnetic Mountain: Stalinism as a Civilization* (Berkeley: University of California Press, 1995), 204–5, 235–36.

61. Thus, the interpretation in this section combines the most persuasive aspects of the revisionist historiography (which emphasizes the social support for the regime among upwardly mobile workers) with perspectives that emphasize how workers sought to resist the Stalinist regime's attempts to control and fragment the work force. On the former, see Sheila Fitzpatrick, *Education and Social Mobility in the Soviet Union, 1921–1934* (Cambridge: Harvard University Press, 1979); Kotkin, *Magnetic Mountain;* and Kenneth Straus, *Factory and Community in Stalin's Russia* (Pittsburgh: University of Pittsburgh Press, 1998). Examples of the latter include Donald Filtzer, *Soviet Workers and Stalinist Industrialization: The Formation of Modern Soviet Production Relations, 1928–1941* (Armonk, NY: M. E. Sharpe, 1986); Sarah Davies, *Popular Opinion in Stalin's Russia: Terror, Propaganda and Dissent, 1934–1941* (New York: Cambridge University Press, 1997); and Jeffrey Rossman, "The Teikovo Cotton Workers' Strike of April 1932: Class, Gender, and Identity Politics in Stalin's Russia," *Russian Review* 56, 1 (January 1997): 44–69. See appendix B for a more detailed comment on competing perspectives on Russian/Soviet history.

62. For a detailed study of peasant-workers' mobility and behavior, see R. Johnson.

63. Russian workers referred to this as *Zubatovism* in reference to Sergei Zubatov, the Moscow chief of police with a reputation for using harsh tactics to preempt labor unrest; see Jeremiah Schneiderman, *Sergei Zubatov and Revolutionary Marxism: The Struggle for the Working Class in Tsarist Russia* (Ithaca: Cornell University Press, 1976).

64. Zelnik, 123–25.

65. See "Industrial Workers in the 1880s: From the Reports of Factory Inspectors," in Thomas Riha, ed., *Readings in Russian Civilization, Volume 2: Imperial Russia, 1700–1917,* rev. ed. (Chicago: University of Chicago Press, 1969), 414–15, adapted from S. Dmitriev, ed., *Khrestomatiia po Istorii SSSR* [Selections from Russian history], vol. 3 (Moscow, 1952).

66. Theodore Von Laue, "Factory Inspection under the Witte System," *American Slavic and East European Review* (October 1960).

67. Timothy McDaniel, *Autocracy, Capitalism, and Revolution in Russia* (Berkeley: University of California Press, 1988), 169.

68. See Zelnik, 16–35; and Charters Wynn, *Workers, Strikes and Pogroms: The Donbass-Dnepr Bend in Late Imperial Russia, 1870–1905* (Princeton: Princeton University Press, 1992), 51–52, 98.

69. Straus, 13.

70. Wynn, 63.

71. See Hoffman, 62; and Victoria Bonnell, "Introduction," to Bonnell, ed., *The Russian Worker: Life and Labor under the Tsarist Regime* (Berkeley: University of California Press, 1983), 8–13.

72. Zelnik, 21. In fact, one of the Shtakel'berg Commission's proposals for reforming labor relations included a (short-lived) plan for new labor laws to be accompanied by the creation of *artel*-like labor associations to collectively fill large orders, sell products from communal stores, and procure raw materials and other necessities; see Zelnik, 137–45.

73. See Bonnell, "Introduction," 14–15; and Wynn, 38, 50.

74. The foreman, viewed as an oppressive figure coopted by management, was particularly vulnerable to retaliatory attacks, for example, through the "wheelbarrow-and-sack" treatment: workers attacked the foreman, covered his head with a dirty sack (which also served to protect the identity of the workers), and carted him around in a wheelbarrow until he expressed repentance. See P. Timofeev, "What the Factory Worker Lives By," in Bonnell, ed., 102–8.

75. In contrast to those who see the urban work force as a genuine revolutionary proletariat, and others who see workers as merely "peasants in the factory," the characterization here returns to Haimson's view that while workers were indeed ready to revolt against the status quo, most were discontented semiproletarian workers, and it is their preexisting social ties (more than their proletarian consciousness) that led to the spread and radicalization of protest after the turn of the century. See Haimson, *Russian Marxists;* and his article "The Problem of Social Stability in Urban Russia, 1905–1917," *Slavic Review* 23 (1964): 619–42, 24 (1965): 1–22. On the view emphasizing workers' growing revolutionary conscious-

ness, see Victoria Bonnell, *Roots of Rebellion: Workers' Politics and Organizations in St. Petersburg and Moscow, 1900–1914* (Berkeley: University of California Press, 1983); and McDaniel, *Autocracy.* The alternative approach, partly echoing the Slavophile characterization of an earlier generation of Russian workers (see n. 3), is evident in Theodore Von Laue, "Russian Peasants in the Factory," *Journal of Economic History* 23 (1961): 61–80. These contending views of the work force are also discussed in Burds, 6–9; and Stephen Kotkin, "'One Hand Clapping': Russian Workers and 1917," *Labor History* 32, 4 (fall 1991): 604–20.

76. See the discussion of workers' memoirs in Koenker, "Urbanization and Deurbanization." On the exodus from the cities during the civil war, see Hoffman, 20–23.

77. Hoffman, 58–63.

78. See Kuromiya, "Workers' Artels"; Lewis Siegelbaum, "Production Collectives and Communes and the 'Imperatives' of Soviet Industrialization, 1929–1931," *Slavic Review* 44 (spring 1986): 65–84. The fate of these collective units under Stalin is discussed below.

79. After the summer of 1917, the Bolsheviks secured majorities in the Moscow and Petrograd workers' soviets and, later, gained a majority of the votes among urban workers during the Constituent Assembly elections of November 1917, although the Socialist Revolutionaries won a plurality (40 percent) of the total vote. See E. H. Carr, *The Bolshevik Revolution, 1917–1923* (Harmondsworth, UK: Penguin, 1950), 103; Sheila Fitzpatrick, *The Russian Revolution,* rev. ed. (New York: Oxford University Press, 1994), 66–67; and, for a detailed analysis, Oliver Radkey, *Russia Goes to the Polls: The Election to the All-Russian Constituent Assembly 1917* (Ithaca: Cornell University Press, 1989). Other studies emphasizing worker support for the revolution include Diane Koenker, *Moscow Workers and the 1917 Revolution* (Princeton: Princeton University Press, 1981); and Steve Smith, *Red Petrograd: Revolution in the Factories, 1917–1918* (New York: Cambridge University Press, 1983).

80. I. Lenin, *What Is to Be Done? Burning Questions of Our Movement,* in *The Lenin Anthology,* ed. Robert Tucker (New York: W. W. Norton, 1975), 12–114, esp. 67–79. This is one of the issues over which the Russian Social-Democratic Party split in 1903, with a more open mass party being advocated by Lenin's opponents (later dubbed the Mensheviks or the "minority," though, in fact, they were the majority).

81. I. Lenin, *The State and Revolution: The Marxist Teaching on the State and the Tasks of the Proletariat in the Revolution,* in *The Lenin Anthology,* 311–98.

82. I. Lenin, "Can the Bolsheviks Retain State Power?" in *The Lenin Anthology,* 399–406.

83. Lenin, *State and Revolution,* esp. 381–82.

84. V. I. Lenin, *Pol'noe Sobranie Sochinenii* [Complete collection of works], vol. 23 (Moscow: Politizdat, 1970), vol. 23, 18–19; also quoted in Mark Beissinger, *Scientific Management, Socialist Discipline, and Soviet Power* (Cambridge: Harvard University Press, 1988), 22–23.

85. Lenin, "The Tasks of the Proletariat in the Present Revolution (April Theses)," in *The Lenin Anthology,* 297–98.

86. Carmen Sirianni, *Workers' Control and Socialist Democracy: The Soviet Experience* (London: New Left Books, 1982), 52–56.

87. On *kollegial'nost'*, see Frederick Kaplan, *Bolshevik Ideology and the Ethics of Soviet Labor, 1917–1920* (New York: Philosophical Library, 1968), 320–32.

88. Lenin, *State and Revolution,* 346; references to "equality of labor and pay" or "equality of labor and wages" appear on 381, 383.

89. Quoted in Robert V. Daniels, *The Conscience of the Revolution: Communist Opposition in Soviet Russia* (Cambridge: Harvard University Press, 1960), 82.

90. Sirianni, 95–98, 109–11; and Margaret Dewar, *Labour Policy in the USSR, 1917–1928* (London: Royal Institute of International Affairs and Oxford University Press, 1956), 18–26, 103–6. Other notable studies of workers' control during and immediately after 1917 include Paul Avrich, "The Bolshevik Revolution and Workers' Control in Russian Industry," *Slavic Review* 27 (1963): 47–63; and Maurice Brinton, "Factory Committees and the Dictatorship of the Proletariat," *Critique* 4 (spring 1975): 78–86. On the point of labor discipline, Bukharin and Preobrazhensky, two of Lenin's favorite Bolshevik theoreticians, explicitly stated that "comradely labor discipline" was something to be managed by workers themselves without monitoring from above; Nikolai Bukharin and Evgenii Preobrazhensky, *The ABC's of Communism* (Harmondsworth, UK: Penguin Books, 1969), 340.

91. Lenin first made this assertion at a speech to the Second All-Union Congress of the Commissars of Labor in 1918; noted in V. I. Gerchikov, "The Human Factor and Industrial Democracy," translation of "Chelovecheskii faktor i proizvodstvennaia demokratiia," *Izvestiia Sibirskogo otdeleniia akademii nauk SSSR* [Report of the Siberian Section of the USSR Academy of Sciences], *Soviet Sociology* 1 (1989): 32–42.

92. The *Subbotnik* movement began on the Moscow-Kazan railway line in May 1919, when workers decided to show up to work on Saturdays on their own to expedite the completion of the railroad. While the subsequent movement was largely orchestrated by party members and managerial elites, the Bolsheviks themselves characterized the movement as spontaneously initiated and praised this spontaneity. See Timothy Luke, *Ideology and Soviet Industrialization* (Westport, CT: Greenwood Press, 1985), 126–30; and Lewis Siegelbaum, "State and Society in the 1920s," in Robert Crummey, ed., *Reform in Russia and the USSR: Past and Prospects* (Urbana: University of Illinois Press, 1989), 129–30.

93. In reality, these limits were probably aimed less at preventing fatigue and more at discouraging turnover among workers who would have otherwise sought to speedily accumulate earnings before quitting and returning to their villages (Kaplan, 337–38).

94. The new scale would have reduced differentials between the highest-paid employees and lowest-paid to a ratio of 1.75 to 1, with exceptions made for "specialists" or foreigners who were essential to managing certain technical aspects of production (Dewar, 63–65; and Sirianni, 223).

95. Laura Phillips, "Message in a Bottle: Working-Class Culture and the

Struggle for Revolutionary Legitimacy, 1900–1929," *Russian Review* 56, 1 (January 1997): 25–43, 33.

96. Siegelbaum, "State and Society," 128–29.

97. V. I. Lenin, *The Immediate Tasks of the Soviet Government,* as reprinted in *The Lenin Anthology,* 438–60, quote from 448. See also Daniels, 83–84; and Beissinger, 31. On Lenin's use of bourgeois specialists, see Kendall Bailes, *Technology and Society under Lenin and Stalin: Origins of the Soviet Technical Intelligentsia, 1917–1941* (Princeton: Princeton University Press), 48–66.

98. Sirianni, 215; citing Lenin, *Collected Works* (London 1964), vol. 28, 139–40. On the restoration of the bourgeois specialists, see also Kaplan, 320–32; and Jeremy Azrael, *Managerial Power and Soviet Politics* (Cambridge: Harvard University Press, 1966), 13–17.

99. Noted in Beissinger, 32.

100. This interpretation was developed by Nikolai Bukharin, one of the most highly regarded theorists among the Bolsheviks; see Kaplan, 311–19. One leader in the trade union movement, Abram Gol'tsman, even took this interpretation a step further in suggesting that the regime train an aristocracy of "technically gifted" workers who could manage production on behalf of all workers; opponents referred to this as the replacement of *kollegial'nost* by *genial'nost.* See Beissinger, 34.

101. For a detailed discussion of economic policies under War Communism and NEP, see Alec Nove, *An Economic History of the USSR,* rev. ed. (Harmondsworth, UK: Penguin Books, 1984), 46–118.

102. For a discussion of the Workers' Opposition, see Daniels, 119–43; quote from 128.

103. For a detailed examination of labor unrest in the transition from War Communism to NEP, see Jonathan Aves, *Workers Against Lenin: Labour Protest and the Bolshevik Dictatorship* (London: I. B. Tauris, 1996), chaps. 3–4; and, on the Kronstadt Rebellion, see Paul Avrich, *Kronstadt 1921* (Princeton: Princeton University Press, 1970).

104. See Lenin, "Draft Resolution on the Syndicalist and Anarchist Deviation in Our Party" (introduced at the Tenth Party Congress, 1921), in *The Lenin Anthology,* 499.

105. Bukharin himself idealized this process as the emergence of "the state form of workers' socialism." See Daniels, 133.

106. Dewar, 86–95; and Lewis Siegelbaum, "Soviet Norm Determination in Theory and Practice, 1917–1941," *Soviet Studies* 36, 1 (January 1984): 47–48.

107. Noted in E. H. Carr, *The Interregnum, 1923–24* (London: Macmillan, 1954), 47. This interpretation about the relationship between the Bolsheviks and the working class during Lenin's time subsumes both revisionist accounts that stress working-class support for the Bolsheviks (e.g., Koenker, *Moscow Workers;* McDaniel, *Autocracy*) and accounts that stress the alienation of workers from the new regime from the very outset (e.g., Aves). See also the discussion in appendix B.

108. There were other efforts to instill new skills and labor discipline in workers—for example, through "factory-workshop schools" (*fabrichno zavodskoe uchilishche,* or FZUs)—but these reached a small segment of the work force and

tended to focus on narrowly technical training rather than the creation of new work habits. See Arvid Brodersen, *The Soviet Worker: Labor and Government in Soviet Society* (New York: Random House, 1966), 84–85.

109. See Kendall Bailes, "The American Connection: Ideology and the Transfer of American Technology to the Soviet Union, 1917–1941," *Comparative Studies in Society and History* 23 (1981): 421–48; and Hans Rogger, *"Amerikanizm* and the Economic Development of Russia," *Comparative Studies in Society and History* 23 (1981): 382–420. For specific comments by Lenin, Trotsky, Bukharin, and Stalin on the need to combine Bolshevism with *Americanizm,* see Rogger, 384–85.

110. Bailes, "The American Connection," 423–25.

111. Lenin, *Pol'noe Sobranie,* vol. 26, 116; also quoted in Bailes, *Technology,* 49.

112. Lenin, *Pol'noe Sobranie,* vol. 24, 371; also quoted in Beissinger, 23. On Soviet Taylorism, see Beissinger, 20–90; Kendall Bailes, "Alexei Gastev and the Soviet Controversy over Taylorism, 1918–24," *Soviet Studies* 29, 3 (July 1977): 373–94; Zenovia A. Sochor, "Soviet Taylorism Revisited," *Soviet Studies* 33, 2 (1981): 246–64; and Rainer Traub, "Lenin and Taylor: The Fate of 'Scientific Management' in the Early Soviet Union," *Telos* 37 (fall 1978).

113. Lenin, "Immediate Tasks," 448–49; portions also quoted (in slightly different translations) in Merkle, 113; and Traub, 82–84.

114. Bailes, "The American Connection," 428–30.

115. Leon Trotsky, *Sochineniia* (Moscow: Gosizdat, 1927), vol. 15, 92–93; portions also quoted (with slightly different translations) in Beissinger, 33; and Merkle, 119.

116. Karl Marx, *Capital,* vol. 1 (New York: International Publishers, 1967), 557; as quoted in Beissinger, 24.

117. Kaplan, 337–38.

118. Daniels, 161; Kaplan, 389–90. For further discussion of opposition to Taylorism in 1920–21, see Beissinger, 24–39; Kaplan, 335–38; and Traub, esp. 85.

119. Beissinger, 38. For the pamphlet presented by Gastev at the first NOT conference, see Alexei Gastev, *Kak Nado Rabotat': Prakticheskoye Vvedenie v Nauku Organizatsii Truda* [How one should work: Practical introduction to the scientific organization of work] (Moscow: Ekonomika, 1966).

120. Luke, 164; Siegelbaum, "Soviet Norm Determination," 48–49. Siegelbaum notes, however, that until the 1930s, in practice, output targets often ended up being determined either by negotiation or by casual observations on the spot; where conflicts occurred, the Rates and Conflicts Commission acted as mediator.

121. See Siegelbaum, "Soviet Norm Determination," 47; Traub, 87–91.

122. This is what Jowitt, drawing upon Weber's typology of authority, refers to as "charismatic impersonalism" to capture the synthetic essence of the Leninist party; Hanson builds on this framework to suggest a Leninist synthesis of charismatic and rational conceptions of time, with the Time League representing the former and the NOT movement the latter. See Jowitt, 1–31; and Stephen Hanson, *Time and Revolution: Marxism and the Design of Soviet Institutions* (Chapel Hill: University of North Carolina Press, 1997), 69–128.

123. Beissinger, 54, quoting from the charter of the Time League.

124. See Luke, 159–61.

125. In comparing Marx and Ford, Gastev emphasized "the thing that completely unexpectedly brings these two gigantic figures together—that is, their views on production, and their analytic approach to that production" (Gastev, 311; also quoted in Hanson, *Time,* 124).

126. Quoted in Beissinger, 55.

127. Thus, while Jowitt and Hanson may be right in characterizing Leninist organization as a synthesis of charismatic and rational features (n. 122), whether this synthesis has a functional equivalent in the concrete organization of everyday industrial production is a different problem. See n. 144 below on differences between Hanson's interpretation and mine on just how effectively the Stalinist factory addressed this problem.

128. Dewar, 124–27.

129. In the course of the debates, Trotsky and the Left held to the position that an international proletarian revolution was imminent and argued that the Soviet Union should thus maintain a state of "permanent revolution," pursuing militarized industrialization financed by "squeezing the peasantry" (even if this meant vigorously borrowing techniques of organization and production from the capitalist West). Bukharin and the Right Opposition, in contrast, implicitly adopted the position that the Soviet Union had to set out to build socialism by itself, which meant a sustainable long-term approach along the lines of NEP (even if this meant a more gradual pace of change and greater attention to whatever affinities existed between preexisting norms and socialist ideals). Stalin essentially adopted the Right's position by setting out to "build socialism in one country," but after ousting Trotsky, made his famous "Left Turn" by pursuing collectivized agriculture and militarized industrialization organized around many of the same principles previously advocated by Trotsky. Competing perspectives in Western Sovietology on the merits of these different positions are considered briefly in appendix B. For a brief overview of the political struggles and debates of the 1920s, see Fitzpatrick, *Russian Revolution,* 98–134. For a more detailed analysis, see Daniels, 236–412; and Alexander Erlich, *The Soviet Industrialization Debates, 1924–1929* (Cambridge: Cambridge University Press, 1967).

130. See Azrael, 87–89; Daniels, 345; Dewar, 134–37; Filtzer, *Soviet Workers and Stalinist Industrialization,* 103–4; and Siegelbaum, "Soviet Norm Determination."

131. Evgenii Preobrazhensky, *From the New Economic Policy to Socialism* (London: New Park Publications, 1973), 62–68; also noted in Filtzer, *Soviet Workers and Stalinist Industrialization,* 103. Preobrazhensky is best known for his theory of "primitive socialist accumulation," which contended that the triumph of socialist revolution prior to industrial maturity required the exploitation of some "backward" category of producers so that the proletariat could complete the tasks of industrialization.

132. The official in question is N. F. Charnovskii, who went on to criticize the NOT movement's excessive enthusiasm for the latest Western technologies and, not surprisingly, would be one of the defendants in the Industrial Party trial

orchestrated in 1930 by Stalin to purge any who might question his particular strategy of industrial organization. See Shearer, *Industry,* 138–39.

133. See Daniels, 355–56; and Sirianni, 361–66. The reference to the "commune state" is from Lenin, *State and Revolution.*

134. During the 1920s, a philosophical controversy between "mechanists" and "dialecticians" ran parallel to the debates of the 1920s; in contrast to the mechanists, the dialecticians emphasized qualitative jumps in development and expected incongruities between different kinds of phenomena. Although the mechanists were initially dominant, the dialecticians eventually won out once Stalin rose to power. See Daniels, 360–61.

135. Stalin, quoted in Sheila Fitzpatrick, "Cultural Revolution as Class War," in Fitzpatrick, ed., *Cultural Revolution in Russia* (Bloomington: Indiana University Press, 1977), 10. Stalin's victory partly reflected the fact that his revolutionary rhetoric, his urgency with regard to industrialization and social transformation, and his assault on "class enemies" probably struck a chord with some in the party who still retained the old Bolshevik mores of the civil war era; see Robert C. Tucker, *Political Culture and Leadership in Soviet Russia* (New York: Norton, 1987), 86. However, some of the support Stalin received also reflected his success in placing loyal supporters within the party's Central Committee (through control of personnel files as head of the Organization Bureau) and out-maneuvering Trotsky, Bukharin, and others who commanded substantial respect in the party; see Daniels, 194.

136. See Azrael, 52–77, 99–104.

137. For an excellent overview of the collectivization drive, see Lewin, *Russian Peasants.*

138. Quoted in Hanson, *Time,* 128.

139. The term *planned heroism* is from Hanson, *Time,* 15. On the dialectical foundations of this position, see Daniels, 360–62.

140. Note that this aspect of Stalinism is considered modernist not because of the incorporation of scientific or rational-legal elements (which may be present in revolutionary institution-building), but because of the orientations toward legacies and borrowed institutional models that define modernist institution-building. See the discussion accompanying figures 2 and 7.

141. See Wehner; see also n. 34, especially in relation to the "soft line" in the People's Commissariat of Agriculture. This line was also supported by Bukharin and Rykov who implied that some form of "agrarian cooperative socialism" could build on certain elements of preexisting communal organization; see Tucker, *Political Culture,* 63–64.

142. Stephen Kotkin, "Coercion and Identity: Workers' Lives in Stalin's Showcase City," in Lewis Siegelbaum and Ronald Suny, eds., *Making Workers Soviet: Power, Class and Identity* (Ithaca: Cornell University Press, 1994), 281. See also Walter D. Connor, *The Accidental Proletariat: Workers, Politics, and Crisis in Gorbachev's Russia* (Princeton: Princeton University Press, 1991), 34.

143. On this "peasantization" of the party and factory following the urban migration, see Sheila Fitzpatrick, "The Great Departure: Rural-Urban Migration in the Soviet Union, 1929–1933," in William Rosenberg and Siegelbaum, eds.,

Social Dimensions of Soviet Industrialization (Bloomington: Indiana University Press, 1993), esp. 22, 34; Hoffman, 58–63; Lewin, *Making,* 56; and Tucker, *Political Culture,* 94–95.

144. Thus, even if Hanson (*Time,* 129–79) is right in arguing that the Five-Year Plans represented the economic institutionalization of a synthesis of "charismatic" and "rational" time-use, the argument here emphasizes the significance of the fact that the substantive ideals suggested by "socialism" were not translated into concrete practices on the shopfloor where pressures to emulate efficiency-oriented Western management techniques led to growing incongruities between ideology and practice.

145. This argument is also evident in Bailes, "American Connection," 444–45; Siegelbaum, "Soviet Norm Determination," 52.

146. Hiroaki Kuromiya, *Stalin's Industrial Revolution: Politics and Workers, 1928–32* (Cambridge: Cambridge University Press, 1988), 62–64. See also Connor, 29; and Dewar, 72–75.

147. See Kuromiya, *Stalin's Industrial Revolution,* 54–55.

148. As a party text on personnel policy noted: "There are no schools and no books that can create an executive; he advances and is tempered in the process of life itself, at work." Quoted in Beissinger, 151.

149. See Jerry Hough, *The Soviet Prefects: The Local Party Organs in Industrial Decision Making* (Cambridge: Harvard University Press, 1969), 80–83; and Hiroaki Kuromiya, "Odinonachalie and the Soviet Industrial Manager, 1928–37," *Soviet Studies* 2 (1984): 185–204. Quote from G. A. Kozlov and S. Pervushin, eds., *Kratkii ekonomicheskii slovar* [Short economic dictionary] (Moscow, 1958), 75; translated and quoted in Hough, *Soviet Prefects,* 80.

150. See Lewin, *Making,* 237, 252; Kaganovich's statement is quoted on 252.

151. Vladimir Andrle, *Workers in Stalin's Russia: Industrialization and Social Change in a Planned Economy* (New York: St. Martin's Press, 1988), 130–31. See also Connor, 29. The reference to Lenin's remarks is at n. 98.

152. Azrael, 104–5.

153. Shearer, *Industry,* 111–38.

154. Beissinger, 107–8.

155. Beissinger, 133–34; Kuromiya, *Stalin's Industrial Revolution,* 220; and Siegelbaum, "Soviet Norm Determination," 59–61. On how foremen made key norming decisions "by the eye"*(na glazok),* see Lewis Siegelbaum, "Masters on the Shop Floor: Foremen and Soviet Industrialization," in Rosenberg and Siegelbaum, 178.

156. Siegelbaum, "Soviet Norm Determination," 52.

157. These remarks were made in a speech given on June 23, 1931, titled "New Conditions, New Tasks"; quoted in Siegelbaum, "Production Collectives," 80.

158. Quoted in Kuromiya, *Stalin's Industrial Revolution,* 307.

159. Andrle, 45; and Nove, *Economic History,* 209.

160. For an excellent study of the Stakhanovite movement, see Lewis Siegelbaum, *Stakhanovism and the Politics of Productivity in the USSR, 1935–41* (Cambridge: Cambridge University Press, 1988).

161. Beissinger, 135; see also Hanson, *Time,* 153, 164.

162. Kotkin, *Magnetic Mountain,* 210. Kotkin notes that in some cases, the rewards were so much higher that some workers were suddenly able to acquire homes and take extended vacations.

163. Kotkin, *Magnetic Mountain,* 204–5; Connor, 179; and Merkle, 129. Kharkhordin has recently argued that such campaigns had the unintended consequence of engendering a greater level of individual self-consciousness, but as the survival of collectivist norms in informal social relations and the reliance on familiar social networks suggests (see below), this observation by no means implies that a shared *ethos* of individualism emerged in Soviet industry at large. See Oleg Kharkhordin, *The Collective and the Individual in Russia: A Study of Practices* (Berkeley: University of California Press, 1999), esp. chap. 6.

164. As a result, the targets established in 1936, while higher than previous levels (on average by about 36.8 percent), were still far below the level sought by leaders in the Stakhanovite movement. See R. W. Davies, "The Management of Soviet Industry, 1928–1941," in Rosenberg and Siegelbaum, 114; Merkle, 132–34; and Siegelbaum, "Soviet Norm Determination," 59–61.

165. See Merkle, 103.

166. Kuromiya, *Stalin's Industrial Revolution,* 220.

167. Even the official Soviet history of the working class, which generally portrays Stakhanovism as successful in raising the quality of the industrial work force, admits: "At times, the urge for records tended to decrease the concern for raising the productivity of labor at the enterprise as a whole. . . . The records set by individual innovators were not matched in all the production processes and naturally bred disproportions" (Y. S. Borisova, L. S. Gaponenko, A. I. Kotelents, and V. S. Lelchuk, *Outline History of the Soviet Working Class* [Moscow: Progress, 1970], 206).

168. Connor, 179. On the significance of the "right" class background and party membership, see Kotkin, *Magnetic Mountain,* 211, 216.

169. Kuromiya, *Stalin's Industrial Revolution,* 103–7; Straus, 156–69.

170. Dunham has referred to this as the "big deal" whereby new groups of upwardly mobile workers and professionals came to form an emerging Soviet middle class as a result of wealth, status, and privilege gained in exchange for their endorsement of the regime's goals. See Vera Dunham, *In Stalin's Time: Middle-Class Values in Soviet Fiction* (Cambridge: Cambridge University Press, 1976), esp. 1–18.

171. See Andrle, 114–15; and Siegelbaum, *Stakhanovism,* passim.

172. On the extent of fragmentation and stratification in the Stalinist factory, see Hoffman, 110; Kotkin, *Magnetic Mountain,* 204; Kuromiya, *Stalin's Industrial Revolution,* 130–32; and Luke, 204.

173. Bailes, *Technology,* 188–215; Fitzpatrick, *Russian Revolution,* 132.

174. Kotkin, *Magnetic Mountain;* and Straus.

175. See Dunham; and Kharkhordin, chap. 6.

176. Aves, chaps. 2–3. The strike referred to occurred at the Tula munitions plant.

177. Brodersen, 34–35.

178. On the migration out of factories through the early 1920s, see Hoffman, 20–23; and Koenker, "Urbanization." On the prosecution of "deserters," see Aves, chap. 2.

179. Phillips, passim; quotes from 33.

180. Leonard Schapiro, *The Communist Party of the Soviet Union* (New York: Vintage, 1964), 388.

181. See the insightful discussion in S. Davies, chap. 1.

182. Rossman, "Teikovo Cotton Workers' Strikes."

183. Siegelbaum, "Masters on the Shop Floor," 178; see also Beissinger, 133.

184. Lewin, *Making,* 255.

185. While the average annual rate of discharge in the mid-1920s was 100 percent, meaning that on average every worker changed jobs about once a year, in the early 1930s, the rate climbed to over 150 percent. See Kuromiya, *Stalin's Industrial Revolution,* 209; Nove, *Economic History,* 198.

186. Bruno Grancelli, *Soviet Management and Labor Relations* (London: Allen and Unwin, 1988), 36; see also Siegelbaum, "Soviet Norm Determination."

187. See Kuromiya, esp. 209, 252.

188. While one recent study (Straus, 105–7) claims that turnover served the regime's purpose of promoting new arrivals and pushing out established "labor aristocrats," this view does not account for the regime's *own* assessment of the complications and chronic labor shortages created by "unplanned" turnover. In official management doctrine, "unplanned" turnover referred to workers whose departure or dismissal interfered with production, while "planned" turnover represented more acceptable "objective" reasons for leaving jobs (education leaves, maternity leaves, retirement, etc.); see Clifford Gaddy, *The Price of the Past: Russia's Struggle with the Legacy of a Militarized Economy* (Washington, DC: Brookings, 1996), 109–13. See also the official Soviet history of the working class which specifically notes that the high rate of turnover "had a negative impact on the work of production collectives and disorganized intrafactory planning" in the 1930s; Borisova et al., 201.

189. See Kuromiya, "Workers' Artels." On the survival of "traditional characteristics of production and social organization" in the Soviet enterprise, see also David Shearer, "Factories Within Factories: Changes in the Structure of Work and Management in Soviet Machine-Building Factories, 1926–1934," in Rosenberg and Siegelbaum, 194.

190. Production communes were informal groups of workers with diverse sets of skills who would divide wages up equally regardless of skill level, often taking family needs and other circumstances into account; production collectives were part of the officially existing organization of work, and the skill grades of workers were taken into account in the distribution of wages. See Siegelbaum, "Production Collectives," 65–75.

191. Siegelbaum, "Production Collectives," 76.

192. In iron and steel factories, for example, 60 to 70 percent of "piecework" was actually paid collectively at the end of 1931; Filtzer, *Soviet Workers and Stalinist Industrialization,* 103–4. See also the insightful discussion in Kuromiya, *Stalin's Industrial Revolution,* 247–48.

193. Joseph Berliner, *Factory and Manager in the USSR* (Cambridge: Harvard University Press, 1957), 182; Grancelli, 50–52; and Filtzer, *Soviet Workers and Stalinist Industrialization,* 236.

194. See Berliner, *Factory and Manager,* 324–25.

195. Andrle, 114–15; Filtzer, *Soviet Workers and Stalinist Industrialization,* 236; and Hoffman, 93–99.

196. Straus, 187–205, 281.

197. Filtzer, *Soviet Workers and Stalinist Industrialization,* 9.

198. S. Davies, 184.

199. See appendix B for further consideration of the competing perspectives on Soviet/Russian political economy and labor history.

200. Connor, 48–51.

201. George Breslauer, *Khrushchev and Brezhnev as Leaders: Building Authority in Soviet Politics* (London: Allen and Unwin, 1982), 269–75; see also Seweryn Bialer, *Stalin's Successors: Leadership, Stability, and Change in the Soviet Union.* (New York: Cambridge University Press, 1980), 145–48. Khrushchev contributed to the formation of the consensus on stability and pragmatism, but all too frequently pursued an agenda of his own that consisted of destabilizing campaigns resisted by other party leaders. Khrushchev's major reform initiatives included his promotion of *aktivs,* advisory bodies of knowledgeable citizens who were not party members, a 1957 decree to decentralize economic planning through regional economic councils, and a 1962 plan to divide the economic bureaucracy into separate industrial and agricultural agencies. These reforms are not relevant here except insofar as they inclined the party-state apparatus to oust Khrushchev in 1964 and subsequently resist fundamental changes to existing institutions and practices.

202. See Breslauer, *Khrushchev and Brezhnev,* 106–7; Donald Filtzer, *Soviet Workers and De-Stalinization: The Consolidation of the Modern System of Production Relations, 1953–64* (Cambridge: Cambridge University Press, 1992), 35–40; Mary McAuley, *Labour Disputes in Soviet Russia, 1957–1965* (Oxford: Clarendon, 1969), chap. 3; and Robert Conquest, *Industrial Workers in the USSR* (New York. Praeger, 1967), 111–13.

203. This was the Third Party Program adopted by the CPSU, replacing the Second Party Program adopted in 1919. See Linda Cook, *The Soviet Social Contract and Why It Failed* (Cambridge: Harvard University Press, 1993), 19.

204. Cook, 22.

205. Cook, 70–71.

206. Quoted in Cook, 22.

207. Blair Ruble, "Full Employment Legislation in the USSR," *Comparative Labor Law* 2 (fall 1977). See also David Granick, *Job Rights in the USSR: Their Consequences* (Cambridge: Cambridge University Press, 1987); and David Lane, *Soviet Labour and the Ethic of Communism: Full Employment and the Labour Process in the USSR* (Boulder: Westview, 1987).

208. See Cook, 22; and Vladimir Shlapentokh, "Standard of Living and Popular Discontent," in M. Ellman and V. Kontorovich, eds., *The Destruction of the Soviet Economic System* (Armonk, NY: M. E. Sharpe, 1998), 31–34.

209. Hough, *The Soviet Prefects,* 278.

210. See Cook, 23–29.

211. See Cook; Bialer, *Stalin's Successors,* 141–82; and Gail Lapidus, "Social Trends," in Robert Byrnes, ed., *After Brezhnev: Sources of Soviet Conduct in the 1980s* (Bloomington: Indiana University Press, 1983). While Dunham characterized the Stalin era in roughly similar terms, the "big deal" she discusses was limited to a small segment of the most upwardly mobile workers and professionals; even if this were an accurate portrayal of Stalinist industrial relations, the post-Stalin "social contract" was supposedly distinguished by the fact that it was tacitly negotiated with, and intended to benefit, a much wider segment of the population.

212. Valerie Bunce, "The Political Economy of the Brezhnev Era: The Rise and Fall of Corporatism," *British Journal of Political Science* 13 (April 1983): 129–58, quote from 134. See also Blair Ruble, *The Applicability of Corporatist Models to the Study of Soviet Politics* (Pittsburgh: Carl Beck Papers in Russian and East European Studies, University of Pittsburgh, 1983).

213. On the Soviet understanding, see Bunce, 140–41. On postwar Japan, see the relevant discussions in chap. 3, section 3.3.

214. On the differentiation resulting from the privileges accorded to "closed" cities and enterprises, see Victor Zaslavsky, *The Neo-Stalinist State: Class, Ethnicity, and Consensus* (Armonk, NY: M. E. Sharpe, 1994), chap. 6. This is one of the reasons why Jowitt (226–28) regards the "social contract" as a case of "parasitic" elites using their privileges to gain support for their own objectives from a "scavenger society" seeking scarce goods. This view also converges with Zaslavsky's assessment that the elements of the "social contract" were actually mechanisms for extending "social control" with less frequent and less overt reliance on coercive measures; see Zaslavsky, *Neo-Stalinist State,* esp. 153–60.

215. See Alfred B. Evans, "Economic Reward and Inequality in the 1986 Program of the Communist Party of the Soviet Union," in Donna Bahry and Joel Moses, eds., *Political Implications of Economic Reform in Communist Systems* (New York: New York University Press, 1990), 167.

216. On the reforms to increase wage egalitarianism, see Evans, 167–69; Filtzer, *Soviet Workers and De-Stalinization,* 96–99; and David Lane and Felicity O'Dell, *The Soviet Industrial Worker: Social Class, Education and Control* (Oxford: Martin Robertson, 1978), 79–80. Khrushchev also initiated a program in 1958 designed to give workers opportunities for part-time study in higher education, giving blue-collar workers an opportunity to learn new skills and raise their base wages; see Connor, 59–61.

217. Whereas the highest-paid 10 percent of the work force earned more than three times what the lowest-paid 10 percent earned in the Stalin era, in the Brezhnev era, the base earnings of the most-skilled and educated blue-collar workers was 30 to 50 percent greater than those of unskilled, less educated workers; and whereas the earnings of white-collar technical employees had been more than 75 percent higher than those of blue-collar production in 1950, the gap had been narrowed to just 10 percent by 1984. See Basile Kerblay, *Modern Soviet Society* (New York: Pantheon, 1977), 227; Lane, *Soviet Labour,* 178; Lane and O'Dell, 80–88; and Murray Yanowitch, *Social and Economic Inequality in the Soviet Union* (White Plains, NY: M. E. Sharpe, 1977), 30.

218. For this view in Western scholarship, see, e.g., Lane, *Soviet Labour.*

219. Joseph Berliner, *Soviet Industry* (Ithaca: Cornell University Press, 1988), 283–85; and Ed Hewett, *Reforming the Soviet Economy: Equality versus Efficiency* (Washington, DC: Brookings, 1987), 137–41.

220. See Beissinger, 218–19; and, for the discussion of *uravnilovka,* see Berliner, *Soviet Industry,* 284–85.

221. Hewett, 209–11.

222. Hewett, 241–44; for a detailed discussion of Kosygin's economic reforms, see 227–45.

223. Hewett, 250–55.

224. See Peter Rutland, "The Shchekino Method and the Struggle to Raise Labor Productivity in Soviet Industry," *Soviet Studies* 3 (1984): 345–65.

225. In fact, between 1967 and 1980, only 6 percent of the work force was actually made redundant at enterprises where the Shchekino method was applied, and most instances of increasing productivity had more to do with additional inputs and local pressures than work force reductions. Beissinger also notes that when the Shchekino experiment was later used as a case study in the training of new managers, most viewed the experiment as unnecessarily risky. See Beissinger, 229–30; Rutland, "The Shchekino Method"; and David Dyker, "Planning and the Worker," in Joseph Godson and Leonard Schapiro, eds., *The Soviet Worker: From Lenin to Andropov,* 2d ed. (London: Macmillan, 1984), 58–59.

226. Connor, 104–5, 117–19; and Zaslavsky, *Neo-Stalinist State,* chap. 6.

227. Lane and O'Dell, 130–31. For a broader discussion of the sources and consequences of social stratification, see Alec Nove, "Is There a Ruling Class in the Soviet Union?" *Soviet Studies* 27, 4 (October 1975).

228. Cook, 53. On the growth of the underground economy, see also Gregory Grossman, "The Second Economy of the USSR," *Problems of Communism* (September–October 1977), 25–40; and James Millar, "The Little Deal: Brezhnev's Contribution to Acquisitive Socialism," in Terry Thompson and Richard Sheldon, eds., *Soviet Society and Culture: Essays in Honor of Vera S. Dunham* (Boulder: Westview, 1988).

229. See Connor, 108–9; and Alistair McAuley, "Welfare and Social Security," in Godson and Schapiro, 206.

230. This characterization is from Berliner, *Soviet Industry,* 277–85.

231. Ironically, Soviet managers behaved like their counterparts in the United States (but not Japan) in that they viewed human relations as an extension of scientific management, simply enabling managers to rely on a diverse set of mechanisms to raise the motivation level of the individual worker. See chap. 2 (section 2.2) on the limited extent to which human relations led to changes in Western firms.

232. Beissinger, 169; quote from N. S. Khrushchev, *Razvitie Ekonomiki SSSR i Partiinogo Rukovodstva Narodnym Khoziaistvom* [The development of the economy of the USSR and party administration of the national economy] (Moscow: Izd-vo Pravdy, 1962), 33.

233. Beissinger, 164–69. See also Dzherman Gvishani, *Sotsiologiia Biznesa: Kriticheskii Ocherk Amerikanskoi Teorii Menedzhmenta* [The sociology of busi-

ness: A critical analysis of the American theory of management] (Moscow: Sot-sial'no-Ekonomicheskaia Literatura, 1962).

234. See Beissinger, 174.

235. Beissinger, 170–78; quote of Kosygin from 175.

236. See Beissinger, 177–81; and Siegelbaum, "Soviet Norm Determination," 64.

237. Quoted in Beissinger, 180–83.

238. Beissinger, 183–88, 232–33.

239. Yanowitch, 144.

240. Kathrine Hendley, *Trying to Make Law Matter: Legal Reform and Labor Law in the Soviet Union* (Ann Arbor: University of Michigan Press, 1996), 85–98.

241. Filtzer, *Soviet Workers and De-Stalinization,* 1–6, 40–49; and Connor, 155–56.

242. See David Granick, *Red Executive: A Study of the Organizational Man in Russian Industry* (London: Macmillan, 1960), 247–48, 259–60.

243. Beissinger, 241.

244. Iu. V. Kolesnikov, "On the Social Functions of a Leader of a Socialist Production Collective," in V. G. Afanas'ev, ed., *Nauchnoe Upravlenie Obshch-estvom* [Scientific management of society] 6 (Moscow, 1972), 108; quoted in Yanowitch, 142.

245. See Brodersen, 149–51; Filtzer, *Soviet Workers and De-Stalinization,* esp. 41–45, 115–17; and McAuley, *Labour Disputes in Soviet Russia,* chap. 3.

246. See Connor, 180–81; and Dyker, 59–61.

247. See Beissinger, 218–19; and Connor, 180–81.

248. Dyker, 59–60.

249. Beissinger, 201–3.

250. Bunce; and Cook, esp. 67–75.

251. See Arcadius Kahan, "Introduction," and Blair Ruble, "Factory Unions and Workers' Rights," in Kahan and Ruble, eds., *Industrial Labor in the USSR* (New York: Pergamon, 1979); and Lane and O'Dell, 51–52.

252. See, e.g., Filtzer, *Soviet Workers and De-Stalinization,* passim; and Zaslavsky, *Neo-Stalinist State,* 44–59. These treatments basically extend Schwartz's analysis of worker atomization under Stalinism.

253. See Cook, 73–74. The miners' strikes of 1989 and 1991 are discussed separately below in assessing the consequences and limits of Gorbachev's workplace reforms.

254. See Grancelli, 184–88; and Alex Pravda, "Spontaneous Workers' Activities in the Soviet Union," in Kahan and Ruble, 348–50.

255. Connor, 221.

256. Kerblay, 190–91; and Gaddy, 111–26.

257. This situation is described as one of "mutual dependence" in Stephen Crowley, *Hot Coal, Cold Steel: Russian and Ukrainian Workers from the End of the Soviet Union to the Post-Communist Transformations* (Ann Arbor: University of Michigan Press, 1997), 15–17.

258. Soviet studies officially acknowledging high turnover to be a problem in

the post-Stalin era include Mikhail Sonin, *Sotsialisticheskaia Disciplina Truda* [Socialist labor discipline] (Moscow: Profizdat, 1986), 77–78; and A. Kotliar and V. Trubin, *Problemy Regulirovaniia Pereraspredeleniia Rabochei Sily* [Problems of regulating the distribution of the work force] (Moscow: Ekonomika, 1978), 41–42. See also Vladimir Shlapentokh, *Public and Private Life of the Soviet People, Changing Values in Post-Stalin Russia* (New York: Oxford University Press, 1989), esp. 54.

259. This trend is noted even by those who tended to view the typical worker as generally "incorporated" into the Soviet enterprise; see, e.g., Lane and Odell, 67–73.

260. A. Iadov, V. Rozhin and A. G. Zdravomyslov, *Man and His Work,* trans. Stephen Dunn (White Plains: International Arts and Sciences Press, 1970), 47–48, 103, 286. Their findings are based on a major study of the attitudes of young workers in Leningrad. See also Pravda, 356; and, for a comparison of U.S. and Soviet employees' rankings of job-appreciation factors, see Kerblay, 192.

261. See the discussion of this evidence in Vladimir Magun, "Labour Culture," in Dmitri Shalin, ed., *Russian Culture at the Crossroads* (Boulder: Westview, 1996), 283; and Elena Shershneva and Jurgen Feldhoff, *The Culture of Labour in the Transformation Process: Empirical Studies in Russian Industrial Enterprises* (New York: Peter Lang, 1998), 22.

262. In one chemical plant in Sverdlovsk in the 1970s, only 3.4 percent of the employees judged participation in the production conferences to be a satisfying experience. In a 1977 study of five enterprises in Murmansk, only 12.2 percent said that they felt they "personally participated" in managing the enterprise (while 65.7 percent said that they did not). A similar survey in Gorky in 1980 found that only 16.4 percent of the workers felt they could "affect decisions on matters concerning the development of their own collectives." See Russell Bova, "On *Perestroyka:* The Role of Workplace Participation," *Problems of Communism* 36 (July–August 1987): 79–81; Connor, 166; and Grancelli, 107–8.

263. Grancelli, 168, quoting from I. M. Shatunovsky, *Trudiascisia Tuneiadets* [Laboring parasites] (Moscow: Sovetskaia Rossia, 1970); see also Grancelli, 152–58.

264. See Berliner, *Soviet Industry,* 34–35; Grossman; and Millar, "The Little Deal," 8–14. On the increase in time theft, see Paul Gregory, "Productivity, Slack and Time Theft in the Soviet Economy," in James Millar, ed., *Politics, Work, and Daily Life in the USSR: A Survey of Former Soviet Citizens* (Cambridge: Cambridge University Press, 1987).

265. Gavril Popov, *Problemy Teorii Upravleniia* [Problems of administrative theory], 2d ed. (Moscow: Ekonomika, 1974), 95; cited in Beissinger, 201. For references to other Soviet sources acknowledging the spread of quasi-legal and informal economic activities, see Grancelli, 96–104, 168–80. On how the acceptance of such activities reflected the neotraditional character of the regime, see Jowitt, 130.

266. Beissinger, 201–3; and Shlapentokh, *Public and Private Life,* 133. For a detailed discussion of how the informal networks developed and survived in the wider economy, see Alena Ledeneva, *Russia's Economy of Favors: Blat, Networking, and Informal Exchange* (New York: Cambridge University Press, 1998).

267. See Pravda, 339; Hewett, 72–73.

268. See, for example, the data from CIA statistics on total factor productivity in Soviet industry; cited in Hewett, 74, table 2.6. See also Gertrude Schroeder, "The Slowdown in Soviet Industry, 1976–1982," *Soviet Economy* 1, 1 (1985): 42–71.

269. These findings were based on surveys of Leningrad workers conducted from 1962 to 1976. See V. A. Iadov, "Motivatsiaa Truda: Problemy i puti razvitiia issledovanii" [Work motivation: Problems and methods for the development of research], in T. Riabushkin and G. Osipov, eds., *Sovietskaia Sotsiologiia* [Soviet sociology] 2 (Moscow: Nauka, 1982), 29–38; and Shlapentokh, *Public and Private Life,* 52–58.

270. Per capita average annual consumption rose from six liters of vodka and samogon (the home brew) in the 1920s to twenty-three liters in the Moscow region by the 1960s; see G. Strumilin and M. Ia. Sonin, "Alkogol'nye poteri i bor'ba snimi" [Alcohol consumption and the fight against it], *Ekonomika i organizatsiia promyshlennogo prizvodstva* [Economics and organization of industrial production] 4 (1974): 37. Zaslavsky (*Neo-Stalinist State,* 53–54) relies on these findings, along with the absence of active measures to reverse the trend, to argue that the growth of alcohol consumption was tolerated by the regime as a means of providing an artificial sense of satisfaction so as to preempt overt conflict.

271. Mikhail S. Gorbachev, *Perestroika: New Thinking for Our Country and the World* (New York: Harper and Row, 1987), 69.

272. Gorbachev, 88.

273. Phillips, passim.

274. For typical reactions of workers to the antialcohol campaign, see Stephen Kotkin, *Steeltown, USSR: Soviet Society in the Gorbachev Era* (Berkeley: University of California Press, 1991), 136–39.

275. Beissinger, 273–80.

276. Evans, 169–73. See also Connor, 143–44; and Hewett, 326–32.

277. See, respectively, the discussions at nn. 83 and 157. Thus, while Gorbachev may have shared Khrushchev's penchant for decentralization in the course of fundamental reforms, his attitude toward wage egalitarianism had more in common with Stalin's than with Khrushchev's.

278. Cook, 110–11.

279. Enterprise *khozraschet* now meant that only half of the planned outputs of enterprises were to be based on "state orders" while the rest of the products were to be sold in a competitive market. Revenues from sales were to be the main basis for the enterprise's budget, and the state would no longer commit to bailing out enterprises operating with losses year after year. Moreover, directors were free to manage enterprise-owned property or to enter into mergers or joint ventures, but only as long as they relied entirely on their own revenues. See Hewett, 326–27.

280. Bova, 84.

281. Bova, 82–83.

282. Cook, 197; see also Rutland, "The Shchekino Method."

283. On workers' lack of participation or interest in the new STKs, see Con-

nor, 167, 180–82. On the transformation of the STKs between 1988 and 1991, see Crowley, 32–33.

284. Cook, 148.

285. For a characterization that treats Gorbachev's workplace reforms as part of a broader effort to renegotiate the post-Stalin social contract, see Peter Hauslohner, "Gorbachev's Social Contract," *Soviet Economy* 3, 1 (1987); and Janine Ludlam, "Reform and the Redefinition of the Social Contract under Gorbachev," *World Politics* 43, 2 (January 1991): 284–312.

286. On rising socioeconomic differentiation as a primary cause of increasing anger toward Gorbachev's reforms, see Crowley, 63–65, 96; Kotkin, *Steeltown,* 28–29, 258–59; and Shlapentokh, "Standard of Living," 39. Kotkin *(Steeltown,* 28) cites the complaints of one worker from the steel-producing town of Magnitagorsk as representative of most production workers' attitudes: "These worker-heroes—it's a lie, a fiction . . . 100 percent artificial. They find such people early on, the ones who 'pull the one blanket toward themselves.' They get apartments earlier, various privileges. Then we read all about how in the West, the bourgeoisie control the workers by creating a worker aristocracy!"

287. Connor, 143–45, 182–83. See also the discussion of steelworkers' reactions to Gorbachev's campaign for order and discipline in Crowley, 63–65, 96.

288. For an overview of increasing labor unrest, see Peter Rutland, "Labor Unrest and Movements in 1989 and 1990," *Soviet Economy* 6, 4 (1990): 345–84. On the 1989 miners' strikes, see Crowley, chap. 2.

289. Crowley, 123–45.

290. Alex Inkeles and Raymond Bauer, *The Soviet Citizen* (Cambridge: Harvard University Press, 1959), 291.

291. Judith Kullberg and William Zimmerman, "Liberal Elites, Socialist Masses, and Problems of Russian Democracy," *World Politics* 51 (April 1999): 323–58, 329.

292. See Dunham, 3–5; Kharkhordin; Millar, "Brezhnev's Little Deal"; and Sheila Fitzpatrick, "Sources of Change in Soviet History: State, Society and the Entrepreneurial Tradition," in S. Bialer and M. Mandelbaum, eds., *Gorbachev's Russia and American Foreign Policy* (Boulder: Westview, 1988).

293. E.g., Schwarz; Filtzer, *Soviet Workers and Stalinist Industrialization;* Conquest, *Industrial Workers,* chap. 2; and Zaslavsky, *Neo-Stalinist State,* passim.

294. E.g., Kotkin, *Magnetic Mountain;* Lane; and Straus.

295. This view is not unlike Clarke's depiction of how officially endorsed ideals such as solidarity, egalitarianism, and justice were reappropriated in more familiar and meaningful terms in the informal relations formed by workers. See Simon Clarke, "Formal and Informal Relations in Soviet Industrial Production," in Clarke, ed., *Management and Industry in Russia: Formal and Informal Relations in the Period of Transition* (Brookfield, VT: Edward Elgar, 1995), esp. 22.

296. Andrle, 55.

297. Crowley, 134–35; and Kotkin, *Steeltown,* 28, 146, 259. See also the discussion at nn. 310–12, and n. 322.

298. Crowley, 41.

299. Crowley, 143. A similar interpretation of the miners' strikes as a syndi-

calist struggle is also offered in Michael Burawoy, "The State and Economic Involution: Russia through a China Lens," *World Development* 24 (June 1996): 1105–17.

300. This view is developed in my "Privatization, Labor Politics, and the Firm."

301. Shershneva and Feldhoff, 25–26; 70–72. On the proliferation of informal networks and exchange relations, see also Michael Burawoy and Pavel Kratov, "The Soviet Transition from Socialism to Capitalism: Worker Control and Economic Bargaining in the Wood Industry," *American Sociological Review* 57 (February 1992); S. G. Klimova and L. V. Dunayevskii, "New Entrepreneurs and Old Culture," *Sociological Studies* [Russ.] 5 (1993): 64–69; Ledeneva; and V. A. Radaev, "On Some Features of Normative Behaviour of Russia's Entrepreneurs," *World Economy and International Relations* [Russ.] 4 (1994): 31–38.

302. Simon Clarke, "Privatisation and the Development of Capitalism in Russia," in Clarke, Peter Fairbrother et al., eds., *What about the Workers? Workers and the Transition to Capitalism in Russia* (London: Verso, 1993), 240. In the case of the privatization of the Zil automobile factory in 1994, for example, the plant's director and other management personnel were buying up most of the stock, and workers supported this transaction because they expected (albeit mistakenly) to thereby retain their jobs and income levels while preserving their personal relationships with superiors; see Victor Zaslavsky, "From Redistribution to Marketization: Social and Attitudinal Change in Post-Soviet Russia," in Gail Lapidus, ed., *The New Russia: Troubled Transformation* (Boulder: Westview, 1995), 126.

303. Petr Bizyukov, "The Mechanisms of Paternalistic Management of the Enterprise," in Clarke, 99–138. Baglione and Clark note that at the giant Tulachermet plant, a familiar understanding has been reached whereby cooperation and industrial peace has brought workers higher job security and access to enterprise-related benefits and resources; see Lisa Baglione and Carol Clark, "A Tale of Two Metallurgical Enterprises: Marketization and the Social Contract in Russian Industry," *Communist and Post-Communist Studies* 30, 2 (June 1997): 153–80. Similarly, based on their case studies, Shershneva and Feldhoff note that even in joint-venture firms, white-collar engineers and blue-collar production workers alike tend to favor diffuse personal relationships in which supervisors demonstrate interest for the personal well-being of the subordinates; Shershneva and Feldhoff, 60–65.

304. See, e.g., several of the contributions to Arthur Miller, William Reisinger, and Vicki Hesli, eds., *Public Opinion and Regime Change: The New Politics of Post-Soviet Societies* (Boulder: Westview, 1993).

305. See James Millar and Sharon Wolchik, "The Social Legacies and the Aftermath of Communism," in Millar and Wolchik, eds., *The Social Legacy of Communism* (Washington, DC, and New York: Woodrow Wilson Center Press and Cambridge University Press, 1994), 8.

306. Kullberg and Zimmerman, 336, quote from 325.

307. See, e.g., Robert Brym, "Reevaluating Mass Support for Political and Economic Change in Russia," *Europe-Asia Studies* 48 (1996): 751–66; and William

Miller, Stephen White, and Paul Heywood, *Values and Political Change in Post-communist Europe* (New York: St. Martin's Press, 1998).

308. This argument has points in common with, but should ultimately be distinguished from, McDaniel's treatment of a historically unique "Russian idea" that is fundamentally incompatible with the logic underlying Western institutions. McDaniel recognizes that the Marxist ideal of social equality and harmony may have allowed for a synthesis between modernization and the Russian idea, but in the end, insists that "fundamental dilemmas . . . , born of the attempt to marry a despotic state, modernization, and the Russian idea were unsolvable." This chapter acknowledges the dilemmas that have faced Russian institution-builders who ignore deeply held popular values in their quest for rapid modernization. However, the Russian idea is viewed as neither unique nor so inflexible as to be incompatible with modernizing tasks and institutions; it is the particular *strategy* followed by Soviet institution-builders that led to the declining legitimacy of Soviet economic institutions. Looking to the future, this chapter shares McDaniel's view that Yeltsin's approach (most closely resembling a "modernist" institution-building strategy) only extended the "nightmare of failed Americanization," and that the task of new leaders will be to forge a new order based on "a pragmatic vision in accord with Russian culture and institutions" (presumably by adopting a syncretist approach instead). See McDaniel, *Agony,* 16, 19, 21.

Appendix A

1. Note, e.g., the exchanges in such recent symposia as "The Qualitative-Quantitative Disputation," *American Political Science Review* 89, 2 (June 1995); "The Replication Debate," *APSA-CP: Newsletter of the APSA Organized Section in Comparative Politics* 7, 1 (winter 1996); *Comparative Social Research* 16 (1997); "Controversy in the Discipline: Area Studies and Comparative Politics," *PS: Political Science and Politics* 30, 2 (June 1997); and "Symposium on Historical Sociology and Rational Choice Theory," *American Journal of Sociology* 104, 3 (November 1998).

2. For a more elaborate discussion and substantiation of these three positions, see, respectively, Sil, "Against Epistemological Absolutism: Towards a 'Pragmatic' Center?" in Sil and Doherty, 145–75; Sil, "The Foundations of Eclecticism"; and Sil, "The Division of Labor."

3. Weber, "'Objectivity' in Social Science"; and *Economy and Society,* esp. 9.

4. Despite differences among scholars identified as postmodern, these scholars do share a clear skepticism of the founding discourses of the social sciences and reject the very idea of meaningfully "representing" the experiences of individuals or communities given the essentially subjective nature of all human experience. Postwar hermeneuticians tend to build on Heidegger's existentialist ontology and thus, in the place of the antirepresentationalism of more extreme relativists, are able to seek context-bound practical insights into the consciousness of particular communities by attempting to decipher repeated social practice through exercises of translation. Even so, neither group of scholars is sufficiently "inter-

408 Notes to Pages 288–90

subjective" in its orientation to social reality to permit interpretations that may be comparable through abstract constructs. See the discussion in Sil, "Against Epistemological Absolutism"; Pauline Rosenau, *Post-Modernism and the Social Sciences* (Princeton: Princeton University Press, 1992), esp. 8–9; and Alex Callenicos, "Postmodernism, Post-Structuralism and Post-Marxism?" in *Theory, Culture and Society* 2, 3 (1985): 85–102. The basic perspective of postwar hermeneuticians is evident in Hans-Georg Gadamer, *Philosophical Hermeneutics* (Berkeley: University of California Press, 1976); Charles Taylor, "Interpretation and the Sciences of Man," *Review of Metaphysics* 25 (1971): 3–34, 45–51; and Paul Ricoeur, "The Model of the Text: Meaningful Action Considered as Text," *Social Research* 38 (1971): 529–55.

5. Weber distinguished between "direct observational understanding," which is a first-order interpretation in direct response to observation (e.g., understanding anger as manifested in facial expressions), and "explanatory understanding," which involves a deeper search into motives of the actors being observed within the distinctive contexts within which these actors subjectively assign meanings to their actions and experiences. For Weber, the latter was more difficult to achieve but was a feasible endeavor even in the absence of directly experiencing a phenomenon from the point of view of the actors (Weber, *Economy and Society*, 5–8).

6. Weber, *Economy and Society*, 20.

7. Even critical theorists who explicitly intend their research to serve the function of ideology-critique or social transformation (what Horkheimer called the "theory-praxis nexus") stand to benefit from modes of argument that relate empirical observations to their critiques of existing ideologies and their call for political action. For example, the Frankfurt School theorists (such as Max Horkheimer, Theodor Adorno, and, to some extent, Jürgen Habermas in his earlier years) frequently relied upon empirical statements to persuade their audiences of their critiques of bourgeois ideology and political economy; see Max Horkheimer and Theodor Adorno, *The Dialectic of Enlightenment*, trans. John Cummings (New York: Seabury Press, 1972 [1944]). For a broader discussion of the Frankfurt School, see Phil Slater, *Origin and Significance of the Frankfurt School: A Marxist Perspective* (London: Routledge and Kegan Paul, 1977).

8. In this context, see the pragmatic discussion of "rational persuasion" and "successful translations" in, respectively, Richard Bernstein, *Beyond Objectivism and Relativism: Science, Hermeneutics, and Praxis* (Philadelphia: University of Pennsylvania Press, 1983); and Margaret Archer, "Resisting the Revival of Relativism," in Martin Albrow and Elizabeth King, eds., *Globalization, Knowledge, and Society* (London: Sage, 1990), 19–33.

9. Thomas Kuhn, *The Structure of Scientific Revolutions* (Chicago: University of Chicago Press, 1962).

10. On this point, see Albert Hirschman, "The Search for Paradigms as a Hindrance to Understanding," *World Politics* 22 (April 1970).

11. Thus, I understand "progress" in the social sciences to mean at most some modest, incremental improvements in the precision and utility of concepts

across paradigms; see Stephen Toulmin, *Human Understanding* (Princeton: Princeton University Press, 1972), esp. 22–166, 224–79.

12. In addition to owing a debt to Weber, this perspective is close in spirit to a realist philosophy of science as articulated in Roy Bhaskar, *The Possibility of Naturalism* (Sussex, UK: Harvester, 1979); Anthony Giddens, *The Constitution of Society: Outlines of a Theory of Structuration* (Cambridge, UK: Polity Press, 1984); and George Steinmetz, "Critical Realism and Historical Sociology," *Comparative Studies in Society and History* 40, 1 (January 1998): 170–86. Some aspects of this realist perspective are also evident in Ernst Haas, "Reason and Change in International Life: Justifying a Hypothesis," *Journal of International Affairs* (spring/summer 1990); and Peter Katzenstein, contribution to "The Role of Theory in Comparative Politics: A Symposium," *World Politics* 48, 1 (October 1995): 10–15.

13. See, e.g., Kenneth Shepsle, "Studying Institutions: Some Lessons from the Rational Choice Approach," *Journal of Theoretical Politics* 1, 2 (1989): 131–47; Jack Knight, *Institutions and Social Conflict* (New York: Cambridge University Press, 1992); and Randall Calvert, "The Rational Choice Theory of Social Institutions," in Jeffrey Banks and Eric Hanushek, eds., *Modern Political Economy* (New York: Cambridge University Press, 1995).

14. E.g., Kathleen Thelen and Sven Steinmo, "Historical Institutionalism in Comparative Politics," in Steinmo, Thelen, and Frank Longstreth, eds., *Structuring Politics: Historical Institutionalism in Comparative Analysis* (Cambridge: Cambridge University Press, 1992); James March and Johan Olsen, *Rediscovering Institutions: The Organizational Basis of Politics* (New York: Free Press, 1989); Ira Katznelson, "The Doleful Dance of Politics and Policy: Can Historical Institutionalism Make a Difference?" *American Political Science Review* 91, 1 (March 1998): 191–97; and Margaret Somers, "'We're No Angels': Realism, Rational Choice, and Relationality in Social Science," *American Journal of Sociology* 104, 3 (November 1998): 722–84.

15. See Paul DiMaggio, "Cultural Aspects of Economic Organization and Behavior," in Roger Friedland and A. F. Robertson, eds., *Beyond the Marketplace: Rethinking Economy and Society* (New York: De Gruyter, 1990); John Meyer and Brian Rowan, "Institutionalized Organizations: Formal Structure as Myth and Ceremony," in Walter Powell and Paul DiMaggio, eds., *The New Institutionalism in Organizational Analysis* (Chicago: University of Chicago Press, 1991); and Lynne Zucker, "The Effects of Institutionalization in Cultural Persistence," in Powell and DiMaggio.

16. There are obviously other differences within each category as well as orientations that cut across the three categories, but the distinction between rationalists, culturalists, and structuralists—or between new economic institutionalists, sociological institutionalists, and historical institutionalists—rests on a well-established set of criteria, particularly in terms of assumptions concerning the relative merits of agency/structure and the material/ideal dimensions of social life. See the more elaborate discussion of the bases for this threefold distinction in my "Foundations of Eclecticism." See also the somewhat different treatments in Hall and Taylor; and Mark Lichbach and Alan Zuckerman, "Research Traditions and Theory in Comparative Politics," in Lichbach and Zuckerman, eds., *Comparative Pol-*

itics: Rationality, Culture, and Structure (New York: Cambridge University Press, 1997).

17. Some rational-choice institutionalists, for example, recognize that "the constraints that institutions impose on individual choices are pervasive" (North, *Institutions,* 5). See also Robert Bates, Avner Greif, Margaret Levi, Jean-Laurent Rosenthal, and Barry Weingast, *Analytic Narratives* (Princeton: Princeton University Press, 1998); Margaret Levi, *Of Rule and Revenue* (Berkeley: University of California Press, 1988), esp. 8; Michael Hechter, "Rational Choice Theory and Historical Sociology," *International Social Science Journal* 133 (August 1992): 369; and Edgar Kiser and Hechter, "The Role of General Theory in Comparative-Historical Sociology," *American Journal of Sociology* 97, 1 (1998): 785–816. Some historical institutionalists similarly characterize institutions as "middle-level mediations between large-scale processes and the microdynamics of agency and action; see Ira Katznelson, "Structure and Configuration in Comparative Politics," in Lichbach and Zuckerman, 84. See also Thelen and Steinmo. Culturalists, for their part, have begun to emphasize a variable and fluid conception of cultural coherence, emphasizing how actors treat culture as a "tool-kit" of world views, symbols, rituals, and narratives from which to draw upon to solve particular problems; Ann Swidler, "Culture in Action: Symbols and Strategies," *American Sociological Review* 51 (April 1986): 273. See also Margaret Archer, *Culture and Agency* (New York: Cambridge University Press, 1988); Jack Goldstone, "Ideology, Cultural Frameworks, and the Process of Revolution," *Theory and Society* 20 (May 1991); and Neil Smelser, "Culture: Coherent or Incoherent?" in Richard Munch and Smelser, eds., *Theory of Culture* (Berkeley: University of California Press, 1992).

18. Knight, 82.

19. Katznelson, "The Doleful Dance of Politics and Policy," 196.

20. Harry Eckstein, "Social Science as Cultural Science, Rational Choice as Metaphysics," in Richard Ellis and Michael Thompson, eds., *Culture Matters* (Boulder: Westview, 1997).

21. Weber, *Economy and Society,* 13. This statement is cited, e.g., by Hechter, "Rational Choice Theory," 370.

22. Weber, *Economy and Society,* 7, 21.

23. Harry Eckstein, "Culture as a Foundation Concept for the Social Sciences," *Journal of Theoretical Politics* 8, 4 (1996): 471–97, 485.

24. Weber, *Economy and Society,* 23.

25. Weber, *The Protestant Ethic;* and *Economy and Society,* 576–633.

26. This interpretation of Weber thus contests the appropriation of Weber by some contemporary scholars who view rational choice theory as a Weberian view of sociology, overemphasizing the causal significance Weber assigned to intentional action in actual historical contexts, while inexplicably dismissing Weber's philosophy of social science, his cautions about the limits of ideal-typical concepts, and his actual comparative studies. See Edgar Kiser and Michael Hechter, "The Debate on Historical Sociology: Rational Choice Theory and Its Critics," *American Journal of Sociology* 104, 3 (November 1998): 785–816, esp. 798–99; and Ronald Rogowski, "Rational Choice as a Weberian View of Culture," *APSA-CP: Newsletter of the Organized Section in Comparative Politics of the*

American Political Science Association 8, 2 (summer 1997): 14–15. The interpretation here follows the more widely accepted treatments of Weber's interpretive sociology as presented in Guenther Roth, "Introduction" to *Economy and Society;* Giddens, *Capitalism and Modern Social Theory;* Bendix, *Max Weber;* Rogers Brubaker, *The Limits of Rationality: An Essay on the Social and Moral Thoughts of Max Weber* (London: Allen and Unwin, 1984); Randall Collins, *Weberian Sociological Theory* (Cambridge: Cambridge University Press, 1986); and John Eldridge, "Work and Authority: Some Weberian Perspectives," in Larry Ray and Michael Reed, *Organizing Modernity: New Weberian Perspectives on Work, Organization, and Society* (London: Routledge, 1994).

27. See Anthony Giddens, *The Constitution of Society;* Pierre Bourdieu, *The Logic of Practice* (Stanford: Stanford University Press, 1990); Bourdieu, *Practical Reason: On the Theory of Action* (Stanford: Stanford University Press, 1998); Alain Touraine, *The Return of the Actor: Social Theory in Postindustrial Society,* trans. M. Godzich (Minneapolis: University of Minnesota Press, 1988); William Sewell, "A Theory of Structure: Duality, Agency and Transformation," *American Journal of Sociology* 98, 1 (July 1992): 1–29; and Alexander Wendt, *Social Theory of International Politics* (New York: Cambridge University Press, 1999).

28. On this point, see also Ira Cohen, "Structuration Theory and Social Praxis," in Anthony Giddens and Jonathan Turner, eds., *Social Theory Today* (Stanford: Stanford University Press, 1987).

29. In Giddens's *(The Constitution of Society)* structurationist ontology, knowledgeable human actors may be acting rationally in many situations, but in their everyday lives, they also engage in social practices and encounters in reflexive or unconscious ways to produce and reproduce structures. The notion of duality of structure essentially suggests a basic recursiveness of social life as constituted in social practices. Patterns of social interaction over time and space are reproduced or transformed depending on the consistency of legal institutions (dominated by normative rules), symbolic orders (dominated by interpretive rules), and through political and economic institutions (dominated by the power of allocative and authoritative resources).

30. Bourdieu's *(Logic of Practice)* famous concept of habitus points to a realm that mediates the relationship between these common influences and meaningful individual action, enabling individuals to carry collective schemata as they interpret a given situation before undertaking a course of action. The habitus is manifested in both the conscious and reflexive dimensions of individual thought and action, and in both cases, it reflects group-specific dispositions that guide individual action whether or not that action is instrumental or gain-maximizing. At the same time, the common influences that produce these group-specific dispositions are not assumed to be fixed, inexorable structures that reproduce distributions of material and symbolic capital ad infinitum.

31. See, e.g., the sharply different postures struck in Robert Bates, "Area Studies and the Discipline: A Useful Controversy?"; Chalmers Johnson, "Preconception vs. Observation, or the Contributions of Rational Choice Theory and Area Studies," and Ian Lustick, "The Disciplines of Political Science: Studying the Cul-

ture of Rational Choice as a Case in Point," all contributions to *PS: Political Science and Politics* 30, 2 (June 1997): 166–79.

32. Gary King, Robert Keohane, and Sidney Verba, *Designing Social Inquiry* (Princeton: Princeton University Press, 1995); King, "Replication, Replication," *Political Science* 28, 3 (September 1995): 444–52; and John Goldthorpe, "Current Issues in Comparative Methodology," *Comparative Social Research* 15 (1996).

33. See, e.g., David Collier, "Translating Quantitative Methods for Qualitative Researchers: The Case of Selection Bias," James Caporaso, "Research Design, Falsification, and the Qualitative-Quantitative Divide," and Ronald Rogowski, "The Role of Theory and Anomaly in Social-Scientific Research," all contributions to "The Qualitative-Quantitative Disputation," *American Political Science Review* 89, 2 (June 1995). See also the more elaborate articulation of this point in my article "The Division of Labor."

34. Bates et al.; and Edgar Kiser: "The Revival of Narrative in Historical Sociology: What Rational Choice Theory Can Contribute," *Politics and Society* (September 1996): 259–71.

35. Bates, "Area Studies and the Discipline."

36. E.g., Donald Green and Ian Shapiro, *Pathologies of Rational Choice Theory* (New Haven: Yale University Press, 1994).

37. Bates et al., 14.

38. Bates et al., 15.

39. For a more elaborate discussion of this problem, see my "Foundations of Eclecticism," 374–76.

40. The concept of "negative heuristic" is, of course, from Lakatos's famous conceptualization of research programs that, in order to survive and experience progress, required hard-core postulates that could not be refuted by single empirical observations; see Imre Lakatos, *The Methodology of Scientific Research Programmes* (Cambridge: Cambridge University Press, 1978); and his *Proofs and Refutations* (Cambridge: Cambridge University Press, 1976). Both modernization theory and contemporary rational choice theory are formulated in a manner that allows empirical evidence to be interpreted in terms that may lead to refinements but not refutations of their respective hard cores. In the case of modernization theory, pre-given axioms concerning the sources, direction, and evolutionary character of social-system change provided the foundations for specific causal or functionalist accounts; the variations that emerged from the rich empirical research into particular countries or regions were usually interpreted not as challenges to the expectations of convergence in modernization theory but as indicators of different stages or sequences of "transition." For an elaborate discussion of this problem, see Janos, *Politics and Paradigms,* 54–60; and Sil, *Historical Legacies,* 60–78.

41. For a detailed discussion, see my "Division of Labor."

42. Barrington Moore, *Social Origins of Dictatorship and Democracy* (Boston: Beacon Press, 1966); Bendix, *Work and Authority* and *Nation-Building;* Skocpol, *States and Social Revolutions;* and Charles Tilly, *Coercion, Capital, and European States, AD 990–1990* (Oxford: Blackwell, 1990).

43. Classic discussions of the aims and types of comparative-historical

research include Reinhard Bendix, "Concepts in Comparative Historical Analysis," in Stein Rokkan, ed., *Comparative Research across Cultures and Nations* (The Hague: Mouton, 1968); Skocpol and Somers; Victoria Bonnell, "The Uses of Theory, Concepts and Comparison in Historical Sociology," *Comparative Studies in Society and History* 2, 2 (April 1980): 156–73; Charles Ragin, *The Comparative Method: Moving beyond Qualitative and Quantitative Strategies* (Berkeley: University of California Press, 1987); and Ragin, *Constructing Social Research: The Unity and Diversity of Method* (Thousand Oaks: Pine Forge Press, 1994). For a recent defense of the original contributions and evolution of the tradition, see David Collier, "Comparative-Historical Analysis: Where Do We Stand?" *APSA-CP: Newsletter of the Organized Section in Comparative Politics of the American Political Science Association* (winter 1998); and "Data, Field Work, and Extracting New Ideas at Close Range," *APSA-CP* (winter 1999).

44. See Tilly, "Means and Ends of Comparison." The problem of rival interpretations is discussed in relation to Skocpol's *States and Social Revolutions* in Burawoy, "Two Methods in Search of Science"; see also the more elaborate discussion of this problem in Lustick, "History, Historiography, and Political Science."

45. See, e.g., Reinhard Bendix, *Nation-Building,* and his *Kings or People: Power and the Mandate to Rule* (Berkeley: University of California Press, 1978); Clifford Geertz, *Islam Observed: Religious Development in Morocco and Indonesia* (Chicago: University of Chicago Press, 1971); and Tilly, *Coercion.* This approach represents what Skocpol and Somers identify as the "contrast of contexts" approach, in contrast to the "macro-causal" or "parallel demonstration" types of small-*n* comparison. What characterizes this approach is not the actual number of cases or the length of the case studies, but the *attitude* of the comparativist toward the historical processes studied in one, two, or several cases vis-à-vis some set of concepts to permit meaningful comparisons.

46. This is a reference to the "eclectic, messy center" discussed in Peter Evans, Contribution to "The Role of Theory in Comparative Politics: A Symposium," *World Politics* 48, 1 (October 1995): 2–3. See also my "Division of Labor," esp. 525–31.

47. See Steinmetz, "Critical Realism"; and Somers, "'We're No Angels'."

Appendix B

1. Works emphasizing the uniqueness of Japanese society include Benedict; Nakane, *Japanese Society;* Doi; Murakami et al.; Vogel, *Japan as Number One;* and R. Smith. On the role of culture in explaining Japanese economic success, in addition to Vogel, *Japan as Number One,* see Murakami, "The Japanese Model of Political Economy"; Dore, *Taking Japan Seriously;* and Michio Morishima, *Why Has Japan 'Succeeded'? Western Technology and the Japanese Ethos* (Cambridge: Cambridge University Press, 1982). For works that modify this view to encompass the significance of a wider East Asian Confucian ethos in economic development, see Peter Berger and Michael Hsiao, eds., *In Search of an East Asian Development*

Model (New Brunswick: Transaction Books, 1988); Ezra Vogel, *The Four Little Dragons* (Cambridge: Harvard University Press, 1991); and Rozman, ed.

2. The classic example of this view is Abegglen, but see also Rohlen, *For Harmony and Strength;* Iwata; Imai and Komiya, eds.; and Aoki and Dore, eds.

3. On the cultural roots of the lifetime or permanent employment system in large firms, see Abegglen; and Cole, *Japanese Blue Collar.* On the distinctive nature of the wage system, see Aoki, *Information, Incentives, and Bargaining.*

4. See Levine, "Labor Markets"; Nitta; and Koike, *Economics of Work.*

5. Aoki, *Information, Incentives and Bargaining;* and Ishikawa.

6. See, e.g., Dale; Mouer and Sugimoto; and Vlastos, "Tradition."

7. E.g., Bellah; Cyril Black et al., *The Modernization of Japan and Russia* (New York: Free Press, 1975); Marion Levy, "Contrasting Factors in the Modernization of China and Japan," *Economic Development and Cultural Change* 2, 3 (1953); Marius Jansen, ed., *Changing Japanese Attitudes toward Modernization* (Princeton: Princeton University Press, 1965); and Donald Shively, ed., *Tradition and Modernization in Japanese Culture* (Princeton: Princeton University Press, 1971).

8. See Jansen, "On Foreign Borrowing"; Westney; and Tsutsui. The role of foreign borrowing in prewar Japan was sufficiently noteworthy to prompt Veblen to suggest that Japan, like Imperial Germany, had the conditions required to successfully adopt Western technologies in the course of rapid late industrialization; see Thorstein Veblen, "The Opportunity of Japan," in *Essays in Our Changing Order,* ed. L. Andzrooni (New York: Viking Press, 1943).

9. The general view of the Japanese factory as converging with factories in the West in the course of modernization may be found in Marsh and Mannari. For the economistic argument that postwar Japan's wage and employment practices were nothing more than practical and rational responses to labor market conditions, see Taira, *Economic Development.*

10. See Lincoln and Kalleberg, *Culture, Control and Commitment;* and Yoshio Sugimoto, "Comparative Analysis of Industrial Conflicts in Australia and Japan," in R. D. Walton, ed., *Sharpening the Focus* (Brisbane: Griffith University Press, 1986).

11. See Tsutsui; and Malcolm Warner, "Japanese Culture, Western Management: Taylorism and Human Resources in Japan," *Organization Studies* 15, 4 (1994): 509–33.

12. See, e.g., Womack, Jones, and Roos; Kenney and Florida; and Nick Oliver and Barry Wilkinson, *The Japanization of British Industry* (Oxford: Blackwell, 1988). For a review of debates spurred by this argument, see Stephen Wood, ed., *The Transformation of Work* (London: Unwin and Hyman, 1989); Tony Elger and Chris Smith, eds., *Global Japanization? The Transnational Transformation of the Labour Process* (London: Routledge, 1994); and Deyo, ed.

13. While cultural traditions or historical inheritances are not taken as seriously as in the case of the particularists, much emphasis is placed on the payoffs of an export-led strategy of industrialization in conjunction with a high level of administrative guidance and close cooperation between business and government. This argument is most evident in Johnson, *MITI,* and Wade, but see also discus-

sions of an East Asian model of development in Chalmers Johnson, "Political Institutions and Economic Performance: The Government-Business Relationship in Japan, South Korea and Taiwan" in Frederic C. Deyo, ed., *The Political Economy of New Asian Industrialism* (Ithaca: Cornell University Press, 1987); Bela Balassa, "The Lessons of East Asian Development: An Overview," *Economic Development and Cultural Change* 36, 3 (April 1988); Paul Kuznets, "An East Asian Model of Economic Development: Japan, Taiwan and South Korea," *Economic Development and Cultural Change* 36, 6 (April Supplement, 1988): S11–S43; and Atul Kohli, "Where Do High Growth Political Economics Come From? The Japanese Lineage of Korea's 'Developmental State'," *World Development* 22, 9 (September 1994): 1269–93.

14. As noted in chapter 2, Dore's approach in *British Factory, Japanese Factory* emphasized the distinctive challenges and dynamics associated with catching up, highlighted the contrast between Japanese and Western (British) firms and management techniques, and proceeded to view the features of the Japanese firm as the components of an alternative model that effectively addressed the imperatives of late industrialization.

15. In a piece published in 1979, six years after the publication of *British Factory, Japanese Factory,* Dore first acknowledged that his notion of a unified model of industrial relations for all late industrializers discounted factors specific to Japan. In a book published another eight years later, Dore was more explicitly discussing the significance of a distinctive Confucian ethos in supporting Japan's flexible patterns of production and industrial organization. See, respectively, Ronald Dore, "Industrial Relations in Japan and Elsewhere," in Craig, ed.; and Dore, *Taking Japan Seriously.*

16. E.g., Raphael Kaplinsky, "Technique and System: The Spread of Japanese Management Techniques to Developing Countries," *World Development* 23, 1: 57–71; and Anita Chan, "Chinese Danwei Reforms: Convergence with the Japanese Model?" in Xiaobo Lu and Elizabeth Perry, eds., *Danwei: The Changing Chinese Workplace in Historical and Comparative Perspective* (Armonk, NY: M. E. Sharpe, 1997).

17. This perspective is evident in the writings of Yamada Moritaro; see the discussion in Barshay, "'Doubly Cruel'."

18. The postwar "progressive" liberal position is perhaps best represented by Maruyama Masao who argued that while traditional nationalist ideals (including the Emperor system and intensely particularistic nationalism of the prewar years) were weakened by defeat, the core elements of prewar particularism—primary groups, along with the values of loyalty and hierarchy—remained untransformed and pervasive at the subnational level and hindered Japan's progress toward a civilized modern society; see Maruyama. See also the discussion in Gluck, "Past in the Present"; and Barshay, "Toward a History."

19. This perspective is suggested in several of the essays in Gordon, ed.; Kumazawa; Price; and Watanabe Osamu, *Gendai Nihon no shihai kozo bunseki: kijuku to shuhen* [An analysis of the ruling structure in contemporary Japan: Its central and marginal elements] (Tokyo: Kadensha, 1988). A critical treatment in a

somewhat different (and more journalistic) vein is evident in Karel Van Wolferen, *The Enigma of Japanese Power* (New York: Vintage 1989).

20. See, e.g., Okochi Kazuo et al., eds., *Nihon no rodosha* [Japan's working class] (Tokyo: Toyo keizai shimpo, 1955); Sumiya Mikio, *Nihon no rodo mondai* [Labor issues in Japan] (Tokyo: University of Tokyo Press, 1965); and Yamada Ichiro, *Nihonteki keiei no hihan* [Critique of Japanese-style management] (Tokyo: Daisan Shuppan, 1976).

21. On the decline of shop-floor autonomy and quality of working life, see Dohse et al.; Price; and Totsuka and Hyodo. On the wage gap across gender and by size and sector of firms, see Price, 145–47; and Yasuba. On the status of women in the Japanese workplace, see Kumazawa, chap. 7; Mary Brinton, *Women and the Economic Miracle: Gender and Work in Postwar Japan* (Berkeley: University of California Press, 1993); and Jeannie Lo, *Office Ladies, Factory Women: Life and Work at a Japanese Factory* (Armonk, NY: M. E. Sharpe, 1990).

22. See Kumazawa; Gordon, "Contests"; Gordon, *Wages of Affluence;* Totsuka Hideo and Tokunaga Shigeyoshi, *Gendai Nihon no rodo mondai: atarashii paradaimu o motomete* [Labor issues in contemporary Japan: In search of a new paradigm] (Tokyo: Minerva Shobo, 1993).

23. See, e.g., the approaches taken in the volume by Lockwood that treat the Meiji and postwar states as reflecting an essential continuity in goals and strategies for national economic development.

24. This convergence perspective is implicit in Black et al., and in many of the essays in Jansen; and Shively. This is also the perspective evident in the "Reischauer line" that many postwar Japanese scholars would embrace; this line treats the Meiji Restoration as a peaceful, pragmatic "revolution from above" that made possible Japan's eventual convergence with the West despite the aberrations of the 1930s and 1940s. See Reischauer, *Japan;* and the discussion in Gluck, "Past in the Present," 80–81.

25. E.g., Abegglen; Ishikawa; and Hazama.

26. The technology-driven evolutionary perspective is evident in Marsh and Mannari; and the borrowing of Western management models is emphasized in Tsutsui.

27. This is true of the "progressive" liberal intellectuals such as Maruyama as well as leftist critics such as Okochi and Watanabe.

28. E.g., Okochi et al; Sumiya; Kumazawa; and Price.

29. See William Chapman, *Inventing Japan: The Making of a Postwar Civilization* (New York: Prentice Hall, 1991); and Kiyoko Takeda, *The Dual Image of the Emperor* (New York: New York University Press, 1988).

30. See, e.g., Richard Samuels, *Business of the Japanese State: Energy Markets in Competitive Perspective* (Ithaca: Cornell University Press, 1987); and the discussions of Japan in John Zysman, *Governments, Markets and Growth* (Ithaca: Cornell University Press, 1983).

31. This view is evident in Koji Taira's critique of the continuity/uniqueness thesis as well as Daniel Okimoto's critique of Johnson's model of the Japanese developmental state, both of which emphasize the role of market forces and economic actors' calculated adjustments to market conditions. See Taira, *Economic*

Development; and Daniel Okimoto, *Between MITI and the Market: Japanese Industrial Policy for High Technology* (Stanford: Stanford University Press, 1989).

32. E.g., Levine, "Labor Markets and Collective Bargaining"; Nitta; and Pempel and Tsunekawa.

33. E.g., Kenney and Florida; and Adler, "'Democratic Taylorism.'" On alternative notions of worker participation in the United States that basically resemble the Japanese pattern as described by Kenney and Florida, see Charles Heckscher, *The New Unionism: Employee Involvement in the Changing Corporation* (New York: Basic Books, 1988).

34. This view is evident in Johnson's treatment of the Japanese developmental state; see Johnson, *MITI,* esp. 29–33. In industrial relations, it is evident in Gordon's view that some of the key features of the post-1950s system of Japanese industrial relations were initiated in rudimentary form in the mid-1920s; see Gordon, *Evolution of Labor Relations,* chaps. 4–6. The significance of the 1920s is also noted in some Japanese treatments of industrialization; see, e.g., Odaka Konosuke, "Nihonteki ro-shi kankei" [Japanese-style labor-capital relations] in Okazaki Tetsuji and Okuno Masahiro, eds., *Gendai Nihon keizai shisutemu no genryu* [The sources of contemporary Japan's economic system] (Tokyo: Nihon keizai shimbun, 1993).

35. E.g., Gao; and Noguchi.

36. Gordon, "Contests"; Gordon, *Wages of Affluence;* Garon and Mochizuki.

37. This nuanced positive appraisal is evident in Cole, *Work, Mobility, and Participation;* Cole, *Strategies for Learning;* Koike, "Human Resource Development"; and Kume. Cole's earlier work *(Japanese Blue-Collar)* tended to emphasize cultural uniqueness, but the more recent work emphasized aspects of industrial relations that are partly distinctive, but also partly indicative of necessary responses to fulfilling standard, universal requirements of work.

38. On the continuing need to consider the Soviet experience in understanding peculiarities of post-Soviet Russia, see Stephen F. Cohen, "Russian Studies without Russia," *Post-Soviet Affairs* 15, 1 (January–March 1999); and Stephen E. Hanson, "Social Theory and the Post-Soviet Crisis: Sovietology and the Problem of Regime Identity," *Communist and Post-Communist Studies* 28, 1 (1995), 119–20. For a sympathetic review of Sovietology as a field, see George Breslauer, "In Defense of Sovietology," *Post-Soviet Affairs* 8, 3 (1992): 197–238; and Alfred Meyer, "Observations on the Travails of Sovietology," *Post-Soviet Affairs* (April–June 1994).

39. For an initial examination of post-Soviet labor relations that builds on aspects of the argument in chapter 4, see my "Privatization, Labor Politics, and the Firm."

40. This view may be substantively similar to the Marxist or Marxian critiques of the Soviet regime in the focus on repression and social control, but the latter view these aspects as no different from the features of the bourgeois state in capitalist settings.

41. See the treatment of the Bolshevik putsch in Pipes, *Russia.* See also

Pipes, *The Russian Revolution* (New York: Vintage, 1990); and Schapiro. On the features of Soviet totalitarianism, see Brzezinski and Friedrich. Keenan, although less interested in criticizing totalitarianism, also documents the more general cultural continuity between 1930s Stalinism and the old court culture of tsarist Russia. Earlier studies of Russian national character may be found in G. Gorer and J. Rickman, *The People of Great Russia* (London: Cresset Press, 1949); and Nathan Leites, *A Study of Bolshevism* (Glencoe: Free Press, 1953).

42. Quotes from Brzezinski, 340; and Pipes, "Did the Russian Revolution Have to Happen?" 227.

43. Brzezinski, 342.

44. E.g., George Breslauer, "Boris Yel'tsin as Patriarch," *Post-Soviet Affairs* 15, 2 (April–June 1999); and Vladimir Brovkin, "The Emperor's New Clothes: Continuity of Soviet Political Culture in Contemporary Russia," *Problems of Post-Communism* (May/June 1995): 21–28.

45. Berdyaev, *Russian Revolution.*

46. McDaniel, *Agony.*

47. On the Slavophile perspective writ large, see Nicholas Riasanovsky, *Russia and the West in the Teaching of the Slavophiles: A Study of Romantic Ideology* (Cambridge: Harvard University Press, 1952). The pan-Slavic view, best represented in Nikolai Danilevskii's *Russia and Europe,* is discussed at length in Michael Petrovich, *The Emergence of Russian Panslavism, 1856–1870* (New York: Columbia University Press, 1956). On Russian populism *(narodnichestvo),* most closely associated with the writings of Nikolai Mikhailovsky, see James Billington, *Mikhailovsky and Russian Populism* (Oxford: Clarendon, 1958).

48. Quote from Aleksandr Solzhenitsyn, "Misconceptions about Russia Are a Threat to America," *Foreign Affairs* 58, 4 (spring 1980): 797–834; see also Solzhenitsyn, *The Russian Question: At the End of the Twentieth Century,* trans. Yermolai Solzhenitsyn (New York: Farrar, Straus and Giroux, 1995). On the significance of pre-Soviet traditions of local self-government and grassroots democracy, see Pushkarev; and Victor Sergeyev and Nikolai Biryukov, *Russia's Road to Democracy: Parliament, Communism, and Traditional Culture* (Brookfield, VT: Elgar, 1993).

49. Martin Malia, *Russia under Western Eyes: From the Bronze Horseman to the Lenin Mausoleum* (Cambridge: Belknap Press of the Harvard University Press, 1999); quote from 314.

50. For the argument that rates of industrial growth in the period from 1890 to 1914 were steady and that the communist revolution was neither necessary nor beneficial for Russia's economic modernization, see Shanin, *Russia,* 111–14; and Alexander Gerschenkron, "Problems and Patterns of Russian Economic Development," in Cyril Black, ed., *The Transformation of Russian Society* (Cambridge: Harvard University Press, 1960). On an evolving pre-Soviet civil society, see Arthur Mendel, "Peasant and Worker on the Eve of the First World War," *Slavic Review* (March 1965); and S. Frederick Starr, "Soviet Union: A Civil Society," *Foreign Policy* 70 (spring 1988): 26–41. On Russia's liberal political tradition—associated with such figures as Peter Struve, Fedor Rodichev, and Kadet party leaders Paul Miliukov and Alexander Kerensky—see Miliukov's own *Russia*

Today and Tomorrow (New York: Macmillan, 1922); and George Fischer, *Russian Liberalism: From Gentry to Intelligentsia* (Cambridge: Harvard University Press, 1958).

51. Martin Malia, "Communist Legacy Foreclosed Choices," *New York Times* (March 27, 1999). On the link between emerging pre-Soviet aspirations for liberal democracy and the post-Soviet democracy, see Starr, "Soviet Union"; and Nikolai Petro, *The Rebirth of Russian Democracy* (Cambridge: Harvard University Press, 1995). On the inherent deficiencies of a socialist economy; see Janos Kornai, *The Socialist System: The Political Economy of Communism* (Princeton: Princeton University Press, 1992).

52. The earlier version of the atomization thesis is evident in the work of Schwartz; see also Conquest, *Industrial Workers.* For recent approaches that acknowledge marginal possibilities for worker resistance, see Aves; S. Davies; and Rossman. Such views are also found in Marxist accounts of control, atomization, and worker resistance in Soviet industry, but, as noted below, Marxists use a universalist language to compare these dynamics to labor relations under industrial capitalism everywhere; see, e.g., Filtzer, *Soviet Workers and Stalinist Industrialization.*

53. See Zaslavsky, *Neo-Stalinist State.*

54. See Jerry Hough, *The Soviet Union and Social Science Theory* (Cambridge: Harvard University Press, 1977); and, for a brief retrospective view, see Francis Fukuyama, "The Modernizing Imperative: The USSR as an Ordinary Country," *National Interest* 32 (1993): 10–19. For a penetrating discussion of the impact of modernization theory in the analysis of communist regimes, see Andrew Janos, "Social Science, Communism and the Dynamics of Political Change," *World Politics* 44, 1 (October 1991): 81–112, esp. 90–91.

55. This view is anticipated in Carr, *Socialism in One Country,* but is most explicitly argued in Theodore Von Laue, *Why Lenin? Why Stalin? Why Gorbachev?* rev. ed. (New York: HarperCollins, 1993), esp. chap. 2.

56. See, e.g., the accounts in Koenker, *Moscow Workers;* and Smith, *Red Petrograd.* A slightly different argument by McDaniel *(Autocracy),* in contrast to his more recent particularist treatment *(Agony),* links these portrayals of a frustrated, radical urban proletariat to an analysis of the inherent contradictions under tsarist "autocratic capitalism" which pursued modernization but resisted labor incorporation in the process.

57. On this point, see Stephen Kotkin, "'One Hand Clapping': Russian Workers and 1917," *Labor History* 32, 4 (fall 1991): 604–20.

58. Lewin, *Making,* 221.

59. See Theodore Von Laue, "Stalin in Focus," *Slavic Review* (fall 1983): 373–89. This view is also anticipated in Carr's treatment of the 1920s debates in his *Socialism in One Country.*

60. For an excellent overview of revisionist treatments of the Stalin era, see Sheila Fitzpatrick, "New Perspectives on Stalinism," *Russian Review* 45, 4 (October 1986): 357–73.

61. On the question of the purges, see especially J. Arch Getty, *Origins of the*

Great Purges: The Soviet Communist Party Reconsidered, 1933–1938 (Cambridge: Cambridge University Press); Gabor Rittersporn, *Stalinist Simplifications and Soviet Complications: Social Tensions and Political Conflicts in the USSR, 1933–1953* (Chur, Switzerland: Harwood, 1991); and Peter Solomon, "Local Power and Soviet Criminal Justice, 1922–1941," *Soviet Studies* 37, 3 (July 1985). These views are criticized for treating Stalinist terror as "humdrum politics" in Peter Kenez, "Stalinism as Humdrum Politics," *Russian Review* 45, 4 (October 1986): 395–400.

62. On the support for Stalinist policies among mobile segments of the population, see Fitzpatrick, *Education and Social Mobility;* Fitzpatrick, "Cultural Revolution"; and Lynne Viola, *The Best Sons of the Fatherland: Workers in the Vanguard of Soviet Collectivization* (New York: Oxford University Press, 1987). On middle-class values and individuation under Stalinism, see Dunham, 3–5; and, more recently, Kharkhordin, *The Collective and the Individual,* chap. 6.

63. Fitzpatrick, "New Perspectives," 365.

64. See, e.g., Kotkin, *Magnetic Mountain;* Kuromiya, *Stalin's Industrial Revolution;* and, most recently, Straus.

65. See Sheila Fitzpatrick, "Ascribing Class: The Construction of Social Identity in Soviet Russia," *Journal of Modern History* 65 (December 1993); Steve Smith, "Russian Workers and the Politics of Social Identity," *Russian Review* 56, 1 (January 1997): 1–7; Shearer, *Industry, State, and Society,* esp. 16–17; and Lewis Siegelbaum and Ronald Suny, "Class Backwards? In Search of the Soviet Working Class," in Siegelbaum and Suny, eds.

66. Hough, *The Soviet Union,* 14; see also Hough, "The Soviet System: Petrification or Pluralism," *Problems of Communism* (March–April 1972). More recently, to cope with the unraveling of the Soviet Union under Gorbachev, an extension of this argument has developed to capture how a "bourgeois" class of officials and technocrats, finding their growing aspirations stifled by the existing system, purposefully allowed the system to collapse, thus engineering the "second Russian revolution" so as to fashion a new order. See Hough, *Democratization and Revolution in the USSR, 1985–1991* (Washington, DC: Brookings, 1997).

67. The rise of a "mature industrial society" is most famously laid out in Lewin, *The Gorbachev Phenomenon.* See also Fitzpatrick, "Sources of Change"; Gail Lapidus, "State and Society: Towards the Emergence of Civil Society in Russia," in Seweryn Bialer, ed., *Politics, Society and Nationality inside Gorbachev's Russia* (Boulder: Westview, 1989); and S. Frederick Starr, "The Changing Nature of Change," in Bialer and Mandelbaum.

68. The language of "corporatism" is used by Bunce; and Blair Ruble, *The Applicability of Corporatist Models to the Study of Soviet Politics* (Pittsburgh: Carl Beck Papers in Russian and East European Studies, University of Pittsburgh, 1983). On the Soviet social contract, see Connor, Cook, Hauslohner, and Millar, "The Little Deal." While Millar's title implies that the deal struck between the regime and the working class can be traced back to the "big deal" struck in the Stalin era (a reference to Dunham), Connor draws a sharp distinction between the repression of the Stalin period and the belated incorporation of labor in the post-Stalin era. Both views are consistent with studies that view the labor unrest of 1989

not as a struggle for democracy but as a frustrated response of workers in those sectors where the regime was perceived to have violated the terms of exchange; see Crowley, 49–70.

69. On critiques of the Bolshevik Revolution, see Rosa Luxemborg, *The Russian Revolution, and Leninism or Marxism* (Ann Arbor: University of Michigan Press, 1927); and Georgi Plekhanov, *Fundamental Problems of Marxism* (Moscow: Progress, 1974 [1929]). On the reliance on inequalities and stratification, see Trotsky, *Revolution Betrayed,* 112–13 (esp. the epithet to chap. 4); and Djilas. On the adaptation of capitalist techniques of labor repression and control in Soviet industry, see Filtzer, *Soviet Workers and Stalinist Industrialization.*

70. See John Kautsky, *The Political Consequences of Modernization* (New York: Wiley, 1972); Richard Lowenthal, "Development vs. Utopia in Communist Policy," in Chalmers Johnson, ed., *Change in Communist Systems* (Stanford: Stanford University Press, 1970); and his "On 'Established' Communist Party Regimes," *Studies in Comparative Communism* 7, 4 (winter 1974). These views differ from Hough's ("The Soviet System") in that the latter finds modernization processes *within* an evolving Soviet political and economic system.

71. See Philip Roeder, *Red Sunset: The Failure of Soviet Politics* (Princeton: Princeton University Press, 1993); and Mancur Olson, "The Logic of Collective Action in Soviet-type Societies," *Journal of Soviet Nationalities* 1, 2 (1990): 8–27.

72. Although the term *Leninism* was employed by Stalin following Lenin's death, one of the first works to popularize the concept in Western Sovietology was Alfred Meyer, *Leninism* (Cambridge: Harvard University Press, 1957).

73. This argument was developed in 1950 by Barrington Moore, *Soviet Politics: The Dilemma of Power,* rev. ed. (New York: Harper Torchbooks, 1965 [1950]); quote from 82.

74. For the view that Stalinist terror cannot be viewed as an extension of Leninism, see Stephen Cohen, "Bolshevism and Stalinism," in Tucker, ed. On the viability of the New Economic Policy and the counterproductive results of Stalinist collectivization and industrialization, see James Millar's position in Millar and Alec Nove, "A Debate on Collectivization: Was Stalin Really Necessary?" *Problems of Communism* (July–August 1976). On the connection between collectivization, terror, and Stalin's political aims, see Robert Conquest, *Harvest of Sorrow: Soviet Collectivization and the Terror-Famine* (New York: Oxford University Press, 1986).

75. Leszek Kolakowski, "The Marxist Roots of Stalinism," in Robert Tucker, ed., *Stalinism* (New York: Norton, 1977), 283–98.

76. Lane, *Soviet Labour.*

77. See Tucker, *Political Culture,* 80–86, quote from 86; and Jowitt, chaps. 1–2. For a detailed history of the party's organizational features during and after the civil war, see Robert Service, *The Bolshevik Party in Revolution: A Study in Organisational Change, 1917–1923* (New York: Macmillan, 1979). These treatments focusing on Leninist leadership and organization were previously anticipated in Meyer, *Leninism;* and Philip Selznick, *The Organizational Weapon: A Study of Bolshevik Strategy and Tactics* (Glencoe: Free Press, 1960).

78. This is also the basis for Nove's position contra Millar in the debate fea-

tured in Millar and Nove. See also his argument for a "feasible" socialist economy in Nove, *The Economics of Feasible Socialism* (London: Allen and Unwin, 1983).

79. Tucker, *Political Culture,* chaps. 3–5.

80. Tucker, "Stalinism," 108.

81. Jowitt, 1–4.

82. Jowitt, chap. 3. Also, as noted in chap. 4, specific aspects of the Stalinist economy, such as the Five-Year Plans and the high-pressure socialist competitions, need to be understood not in terms of economic costs and benefits, but as an effort to translate the "charismatic impersonalism" of Leninist political organization into concrete economic institutions; see Hanson, *Time.* The significance and limits of this interpretation are noted in chap. 4, section 4.2.

83. See Jowitt, 88–158.

84. Jowitt, 220–48.

Bibliography

Note: Following the General Bibliography are works cited specific to Japan (page 444) and to Russia/USSR and Communism (page 454).

General

Adler, Paul. "Automation and Skill: New Directions." *International Journal of Technology Management* 2 (1987): 761–72.

———. "'Democratic Taylorism': The Toyota Production System at NUMMI." In *Lean Work: Empowerment and Exploitation in the Global Auto Industry,* ed. Steve Babson. Detroit: Wayne State University Press, 1995.

Aglietta, Michel. *A Theory of Capitalist Regulation.* London: Verso, 1987.

Aiken, Michael, and Samuel Bacharach. "Culture and Organizational Structure and Process: A Study of Local Government Administrative Bureaucracies in the Walloon and Flemish Regions of Belgium." In Lammers and Hickson.

Akerlof, George. "Labor Contracts as Partial Gift Exchange." *Quarterly Journal of Economics* 97, 2 (1982): 543–69.

Albrow, Martin. *The Global Age.* Stanford: Stanford University Press, 1996.

Almond, Gabriel. "Introduction: A Functional Approach to Comparative Politics." In Almond and Coleman.

Almond, Gabriel, and James Coleman, eds. *The Politics of the Developing Areas.* Princeton: Princeton University Press, 1960.

Almond, Gabriel, and Sidney Verba. *The Civic Culture: Political Attitudes and Democracy in Five Nations.* Princeton: Princeton University Press, 1963.

Amsden, Alice. "The State and Taiwan's Economic Development." In Evans et al.

Anno, Tadashi. "The Liberal World Order and Its Critics: Nationalism and the Rise of Anti-Systemic Movements in Russia and Japan, 1860–1950." Ph.D. Diss. University of California at Berkeley, 1999.

Apter, David. "System, Process and the Politics of Economic Development." In Hoselitz and Moore.

Archer, Margaret. *Culture and Agency.* New York: Cambridge University Press, 1988.

———. "Resisting the Revival of Relativism." In *Globalization, Knowledge, and Society,* ed. Martin Albrow and Elizabeth King. London: Sage, 1990.

Argyris, Chris. *Integrating the Individual and the Organization.* New York: John Wiley, 1964.

Badie, Bertrand. *The Imported State: The Westernization of the Political Order.* Stanford: Stanford University Press, 2000.

Balme, Christopher. *Decolonizing the Stage: Theatrical Syncretism and Post-Colonial Drama.* New York: Oxford University Press, 1999.

Barber, Benjamin. *Jihad vs. McWorld.* New York: Times Books, 1995.

Barnard, Chester. *The Functions of the Executive.* Cambridge: Harvard University Press, 1938.

Bates, Robert. "Area Studies and the Discipline: A Useful Controversy?" *PS: Political Science and Politics* 30, 2 (June 1997): 166–69.

———. *Open-Economy Politics: The Political Economy of the World Coffee Trade.* Princeton: Princeton University Press, 1997.

Bates, Robert, Avner Greif, Margaret Levi, Jean-Laurent Rosenthal, and Barry Weingast. *Analytic Narratives.* Princeton: Princeton University Press, 1998.

Baum, Howell. *Organizational Membership: Personal Development in the Workplace.* Albany: State University of New York Press, 1990.

Becker, Howard. "Notes on the Concept of Commitment." *American Journal of Sociology* 66 (1960): 32–42.

———. "Social Observation and Case Studies." *International Encyclopedia of the Social Sciences* 11 (1968): 232–38.

Bedaux, Charles E. *The Bedaux Efficiency Course for Industrial Application.* Cleveland: Bedaux Industrial Institute, 1921.

Bell, Daniel. "Work and Its Discontents: The Cult of Efficiency in America." In Daniel Bell, *The End of Ideology.* New York: Free Press, 1965.

Bellah, Robert, Richard Madsen, William Sullivan, Ann Swidler, and Steven Tipton. *Habits of the Heart: Individualism and Commitment in American Life.* Berkeley: University of California Press, 1985.

Belshaw, Cyril. "Adaptation of Personnel Policies in Social Context." In Moore and Feldman.

Bendix, Reinhard. "Concepts in Comparative Historical Analysis." In *Comparative Research across Cultures and Nations,* ed. Stein Rokkan. The Hague: Mouton, 1968.

———. "Definitions of Community in Western Civilization." In Bendix, *Unsettled Affinities.*

———. "Industrialization, Ideologies, and Social Structure." *American Sociological Review* 24, 5 (October 1959): 613–23.

———. *Kings or People: Power and the Mandate to Rule.* Berkeley: University of California Press, 1978.

———. *Max Weber: An Intellectual Portrait.* Rev. ed. Berkeley: University of California Press, 1977.

———. *Nation-Building and Citizenship.* New York: John Wiley, 1964.

———. "Relative Backwardness and Intellectual Mobilization." In Bendix, *Unsettled Affinities.*

———. "Tradition and Modernity Reconsidered." *Comparative Studies in Society and History* 9 (April 1967): 292–346.

———. *Unsettled Affinities.* Ed. John Bendix. New Brunswick: Transaction Books, 1993.

————. *Work and Authority in Industry: Ideologies of Management in the Course of Industrialization.* Rev. ed. Berkeley: University of California Press, 1974. First published, New York: John Wiley, 1956.

Bernstein, Richard. *Beyond Objectivism and Relativism: Science, Hermeneutics, and Praxis.* Philadelphia: University of Pennsylvania Press, 1983.

Bhaskar, Roy. *The Possibility of Naturalism.* Sussex, UK: Harvester, 1979.

Bierbrauer, G., H. Meyer, and U. Wolfradt. "Measurement of Normative and Evaluative Aspects in Individualistic and Collectivistic Orientations." In Kim et al.

Bijker, Wiebe, Thomas Hughes, and Trevor Pinch. *The Social Construction of Technological Systems: New Directions in the Sociology and History of Technology.* Cambridge: MIT Press, 1987.

Bion, Wilfred. *Experiences in Groups.* London: Tavistock Institute of Human Relations, 1961.

Black, Cyril. "Phases of Modernization." In Finkle and Gable.

Blackford, Mansel. *The Rise of Modern Business in Great Britain, the United States, and Japan.* 2d ed. Chapel Hill: University of North Carolina Press, 1998.

Blau, Peter. "The Hierarchy of Authority in Organizations." *American Journal of Sociology* 73 (January 1968).

Blauner, Robert. *Alienation and Freedom.* Chicago: University of Chicago Press, 1964.

Bonnell, Victoria. "The Uses of Theory, Concepts and Comparison in Historical Sociology." *Comparative Studies in Society and History* 2, 2 (April 1980): 156–73.

Bourdieu, Pierre. *The Logic of Practice.* Stanford: Stanford University Press, 1990.

————. *Practical Reason: On the Theory of Action.* Stanford: Stanford University Press, 1998.

Bouwen, Rene. "Organizational Innovation as a Social Construction: Managing Meaning in Multiple Realities." In *Interdisciplinary Perspectives on Organization Studies,* ed. Siegward Lindenberg and Hein Schreuder. New York: Pergamon, 1993.

Boyer, Robert. *The Regulation School.* New York: Columbia University Press, 1990.

Braverman, Harry. *Labor and Monopoly Capital: The Degradation of Work in the Twentieth Century.* New York: Monthly Review Press, 1974.

Brubaker, Rogers. *The Limits of Rationality: An Essay on the Social and Moral Thoughts of Max Weber.* London: Allen and Unwin, 1984.

Bueno de Mesquita, Bruce. "Towards a Scientific Understanding of International Conflict." *International Studies Quarterly* 29 (1985): 121–36.

Burawoy, Michael. *Manufacturing Consent: Changes in the Labor Process under Monopoly Capitalism.* Chicago: University of Chicago Press, 1979.

————. *The Politics of Production.* London: Verson, 1985.

————. "Two Methods in Search of Science: Skocpol versus Trotsky." *Theory and Society* 18 (1989).

Callenicos, Alex. "Postmodernism, Post-Structuralism and Post-Marxism?" *Theory, Culture, and Society* 2, 3 (1985): 85–102.

Calvert, Randall. "The Rational Choice Theory of Social Institutions." In *Modern Political Economy,* ed. Jeffrey Banks and Eric Hanushek. New York: Cambridge University Press, 1995.

Caporso, James. "Research Design, Falsification, and Qualitative-Quantitative Divide." *American Political Science Review* 89, 2 (June 1995): 457–60.

Carrithers, Michael, Steven Collins, and Steven Lukes, eds. *The Category of the Person.* Cambridge: Cambridge University Press, 1985.

Cerney, Philip. "Globalization and the Changing Logic of Collective Action." *International Organization* 49 (1995): 595–625.

Chandler, Alfred. *Strategy and Structure: Chapters in the History of the American Industrial Enterprise.* Cambridge: MIT Press, 1962.

———. *The Visible Hand: The Managerial Revolution in American Business.* Cambridge: Belknap Press of the Harvard University Press, 1977.

Child, John. "Managerial Strategies, New Technology, and the Labour Process." In *Job Redesign: Critical Perspectives on the Labour Process,* ed. D. Knights, H. Willmott, and D. Collinson. London: Gower, 1985.

———. "Organizational Structure, Environment and Performance: The Role of Strategic Choice." *Sociology* 6 (1972): 1–22.

Christensen, L. R., Dianne Cummings, and Dale W. Jorgenson. "Economic Growth, 1947–1973: An International Comparison." In *New Developments in Productivity Measurement, Studies in Income and Wealth,* vol. 41, ed. J. Kendrick and B. Vaccara. New York: National Bureau of Economic Research, 1977.

Cinoy, Ely. *Automobile Workers and the American Dream.* Boston: Beacon, 1970.

Coase, Ronald. "The Nature of the Firm." *Economica* 4 (1937): 386–405.

Cohen, Ira. "Structuration Theory and Social Praxis." In *Social Theory Today,* ed. Anthony Giddens and Jonathan Turner. Stanford: Stanford University Press, 1987.

Cole, Robert. *Work, Mobility, and Participation: A Comparative Study of American and Japanese Industry.* Berkeley: University of California Press, 1979.

Collier, David. "Comparative-Historical Analysis: Where Do We Stand?" *APSA-CP: Newsletter of the Organized Section in Comparative Politics of the American Political Science Association.* Winter 1998.

———. "Data, Field Work, and Extracting New Ideas at Close Range." *APSA-CP: Newsletter of the Organized Section in Comparative Politics of the American Political Science Association.* Winter 1999.

———. "Translating Quantitative Methods for Qualitative Researchers: The Case of Selection Bias." *American Political Science Review* 89, 2 (June 1995): 461–66.

Collins, Randall. *Weberian Sociological Theory.* Cambridge: Cambridge University Press, 1986.

Colson, Elizabeth. *Tradition and Contract: The Problem of Order.* Chicago: Aldine, 1974.

Copley, Frank. *Frederick W. Taylor, Father of Scientific Management.* 2 vols. New York: Harper and Brothers, 1923.

Crozier, Michael. *The Bureaucratic Phenomenon.* Chicago: University of Chicago Press, 1964.

Cummings, Thomas G., and Edmond Molloy. *Improving Productivity and the Quality of Work Life.* New York: Praeger, 1977.

Cyert, Richard M., and James G. March. *The Behavioral Theory of the Firm.* Englewood Cliffs: Prentice-Hall, 1963.

Davies, Robert, and Nan Weiner. "A Cultural Perspective on the Study of Industrial Relations." In *Organizational Culture,* ed. Peter J. Frost et al. Beverly Hills: Sage, 1985.

Deutsch, Karl. "Social Mobilization and Political Development." *American Political Science Review* (September 1961): 493–511.

Devinat, Paul. *Scientific Management in Europe.* ILO Studies and Reports, Series B, no. 17. Geneva: International Labor Organization, 1927.

Deyo, Frederic C. "Introduction." In Deyo, ed., *Social Reconstructions.*

———, ed. *The Political Economy of the New Asian Industrialism.* Ithaca: Cornell University Press, 1987.

———, ed. *Social Reconstructions of the World Automobile Industry: Competition, Power, and Industrial Flexibility.* New York: St. Martin's Press, 1996.

DiMaggio, Paul J. "Cultural Aspects of Economic Organization and Behavior." In *Beyond the Marketplace: Rethinking Economy and Society,* ed. Roger Friedland and A. F. Robertson. New York: De Gruyter, 1990.

DiMaggio, Paul J., and Walter W. Powell. "The Iron Cage Revisited: Institutional Isomorphism and Collective Rationality in Organizational Fields." *American Sociological Review* 48 (1983): 147–60.

Di Palma, Guiseppe. *Political Syncretism in Italy: Historical Coalition Strategies and the Present Crisis.* Berkeley: Institute of International Studies, University of California, 1978.

Dore, Ronald. *British Factory, Japanese Factory: The Origins of National Diversity in Industrial Relations.* Berkeley: University of California Press, 1973.

———. "Industrial Relations in Japan and Elsewhere." In *Japan: A Comparative View,* ed. Albert Craig. Princeton: Princeton University Press, 1979.

Drucker, Peter. "What We Can Learn from Japanese Management." *Harvard Business Review* 49 (March–April 1971): 110–22.

Dubofsky, Melvyn. *The State and Labor in Modern America.* Chapel Hill: University of North Carolina Press, 1994.

Dumont, Louis. "Collective Identities and Universalist Ideology: The Actual Interplay." *Theory, Culture, and Society* 3, 3 (1986): 25–35.

———. *Essays on Individualism: Modern Ideology in Anthropological Perspective.* Chicago: University of Chicago Press, 1986.

Durkheim, Emile. *The Division of Labor in Society.* New York: Free Press, 1933.

———. *Suicide: A Study in Sociology.* Glencoe: Free Press, 1951.

Eckstein, Harry. "Congruence Theory Explained." In Eckstein et al.

———. "Culture as a Foundation Concept for the Social Sciences." *Journal of Theoretical Politics* 8, 4 (1996).

————. *Division and Cohesion in Democracy: A Study of Norway.* Princeton: Princeton University Press, 1966.

————. "Lessons for the 'Third Wave' from the First: An Essay on Democratization." In Eckstein et al.

————. "Social Science as Cultural Science, Rational Choice as Metaphysics." In *Culture Matters,* ed. Richard Ellis and Michael Thompson. Boulder: Westview, 1997.

————. "A Theory of Stable Democracy." In Eckstein, *Regarding Politics: Essays on Political Theory, Stability, and Change.* Berkeley: University of California Press, 1992. First published as "Appendix B: A Theory of Stable Democracy." In Eckstein, *Division and Cohesion in Democracy.*

Eckstein, Harry, Frederic Fleron, Erik Hoffman, and William Reisinger. *Can Democracy Take Root in Post-Soviet Russia? Explorations in State-Society Relations.* Lanham, MD: Rowman and Littlefield, 1998.

Edwards, Richard. *Contested Terrain: The Transformation of Work in the Twentieth Century.* New York: Basic Books, 1979.

Eisenstadt, S. N. "Modernity and the Construction of Collective Identities." *International Journal of Comparative Sociology* 39, 1 (February 1998): 138–58.

————, ed. *The Protestant Ethic and Modernization: A Comparative View.* New York: Basic Books, 1968.

Eldridge, John. "Work and Authority: Some Weberian Perspectives." In *Organizing Modernity: New Weberian Perspectives on Work, Organization, and Society,* ed. Larry Ray and Michael Reed. London: Routledge, 1994.

Elger, Tony, and Chris Smith, eds. *Global Japanization? The Transnational Transformation of the Labour Process.* London: Routledge, 1994.

Ellis, Richard, Michael Thompson, and Aaron Wildavsky. *Cultural Theory.* Boulder: Westview, 1990.

Elster, Jon. *Ulysses and the Sirens: Studies in Rationality and Irrationality.* New York: Cambridge University Press, 1979.

Emerson, Harrington. *Efficiency as a Basis for Operation and Wages.* New York: Arno Press, 1979 [1911].

Emery, Fred. *The Emergence of a New Paradigm of Work.* Canberra: Centre for Continuing Education, Australian National University, 1978.

Etzioni, Amitai. *A Comparative Analysis of Complex Organizations.* New York: Free Press, 1961.

————. *The Spirit of Community.* New York: Crown, 1993.

Evans, Peter. *Embedded Autonomy: States and Industrial Transformation.* Princeton: Princeton University Press, 1995.

————. "Government, Social Capital, and Development: Reviewing the Evidence on Synergy." In Evans.

————. "Introduction: Development Strategies across the Public-Private Divide." In Evans.

————. "The Role of Theory in Comparative Politics: A Symposium." Contribution. *World Politics* 48, 1 (October 1995).

————, ed. *State-Society Synergy: Government and Social Capital in Development.*

Research Series, No. 94. Berkeley: International and Areas Studies, University of California at Berkeley, 1997.

Evans, Peter, Dietrich Rueschemeyer, and Theda Skocpol, eds. *Bringing the State Back In.* Cambridge: Cambridge University Press, 1985.

Feagin, Joseph. "Poverty: We Still Believe That God Helps Those Who Help Themselves." *Psychology Today* (November 1972).

Fichte, Johann-Gottlieb. "Der geschlossene Handelsstaat" [The closed trading state]. In *Ausgewahlte Werke* [Selected works]. Vol. 3. Darmstadt: Wissenschaftliche Buchgesellschaft, 1964.

Finkle, Jason, and Richard Gable, eds. *Political Development and Social Change.* New York: John Wiley and Sons, 1966.

Fischoff, Ephraim. "The Protestant Ethic and the Spirit of Capitalism: The History of a Controversy." *Social Research* 99 (1944): 54–77.

Fligstein, Neil. *The Transformation of Corporate Control.* Cambridge: Harvard University Press, 1990.

Fox, Alan. *Beyond Contract: Work, Power, and Trust Relations.* London: Faber, 1974.

Fukuyama, Francis. "Confucianism and Democracy." *Journal of Democracy* 6, 3 (1995): 20–33.

———. *The End of History and the Last Man.* New York: Free Press, 1992.

Furnham, Adrian. *The Protestant Work Ethic: The Psychology of Work-Related Beliefs and Behaviours.* New York: Routledge, 1990.

Furnham, Adrian, and Stephen Bochner. *Culture Shock: Psychological Reactions to Unfamiliar Environments.* London: Methuen, 1986.

Gadamer, Hans-Georg. *Philosophical Hermeneutics.* Berkeley: University of California Press, 1976.

Gantt, Henry. *Organizing for Work.* New York: Harcourt, Brace and Howe, 1919.

Gardner, Burleigh. *Human Relations in Industry.* Chicago: Richard D. Irwin, 1945.

Geertz, Clifford. *The Interpretation of Cultures.* New York: Basic Books, 1973.

———. *Islam Observed: Religious Development in Morocco and Indonesia.* Chicago: University of Chicago Press, 1971.

———. *Peddlers and Princes.* Chicago: University of Chicago Press, 1963.

———. "Ritual and Social Change: A Javanese Example." In Geertz, *The Interpretation of Cultures.*

Gerschenkron, Alexander. *Economic Backwardness in Historical Perspective.* Cambridge: Harvard University Press, 1962.

Giddens, Anthony. *Capitalism and Modern Social Theory.* New York: Cambridge University Press, 1971.

———. *The Constitution of Society: Outlines of a Theory of Structuration.* Cambridge, UK: Polity Press, 1984.

———. *Runaway World: How Globalization Is Reshaping Our Lives.* New York: Routledge, 2000.

Gilbreth, Frank B. *Motion Study: A Method for Increasing the Efficiency of the Workman.* New York: Van Nostrand, 1911.

Goethe, Johann Wolfgang von. *Elective Affinities.* Harmondsworth, UK: Penguin, 1971 [1809].

Goldstone, Jack. "Ideology, Cultural Frameworks, and the Process of Revolution." *Theory and Society* 20 (May 1991).

Goldthorpe, John. "Current Issues in Comparative Methodology." *Comparative Social Research* 15 (1996).

Goldthorpe, John, and David Lockwood. "Affluence and British Class Structure." *Sociological Review* 11 (July 1963): 133–63.

Gouldner, Alvin. *The Coming Crisis of Western Sociology.* New York: Basic Books, 1970.

———. *Patterns of Industrial Bureaucracy.* New York: Free Press, 1954.

Granovetter, Mark. "Economic Sociology of Firms and Entrepreneurs." In *The Economic Sociology of Immigration: Essays on Networks, Ethnicity, and Entrepreneurship,* ed. Alejandro Portres. New York: Russell Sage, 1995.

Green, Donald, and Ian Shapiro. *Pathologies of Rational Choice Theory.* New Haven: Yale University Press, 1994.

Guillen, Mauro F. *Models of Management: Work, Authority, and Organization in Comparative Perspective.* Chicago: University of Chicago Press, 1994.

Gutman, Herbert. *Work, Culture and Society in Industrializing America.* New York: Knopf, 1976.

Haas, Ernst. *Nationalism, Liberalism and Progress: The Rise and Decline of Nationalism,* vol. 1. Ithaca: Cornell University Press, 1997.

———. "Reason and Change in International Life: Justifying a Hypothesis." *Journal of International Affairs* (spring/summer 1990).

Haber, Samuel. *Efficiency and Uplift: Scientific Management in the Progressive Era, 1890–1920.* Chicago: University of Chicago Press, 1964.

Hadenius, Axel. *Democracy and Development.* New York: Cambridge University Press, 1992.

Hage, Jerald, and Michael Aiken. "Relationship of Centralization to Other Structural Properties." *Administrative Science Quarterly* 12 (1967): 72–92.

Haggard, Stephen, and Robert R. Kaufman. *The Political Economy of Democratic Transitions.* Princeton: Princeton University Press, 1995.

Hall, Peter, and Rosemary Taylor. "Political Science and the Three New Institutionalisms." *Political Studies* 44 (1996): 936–57.

Hamilton, Gary, and Nicole Biggart. "Market, Culture and Authority: A Comparative Analysis of Management and Organization in the Far East." *American Journal of Sociology* 94 (Supplement 1988): S52–S94.

Hammond, Peter. "Management in Economic Transition." In Moore and Feldman.

Harbison, Frederick, and Charles Myers. *Management in the Industrial World.* New York: McGraw-Hill, 1959.

Hechter, Michael. "Rational Choice Theory and Historical Sociology." *International Social Science Journal* 133 (August 1992): 367–74.

Heckscher, Charles. *The New Unionism: Employee Involvement in the Changing Corporation.* New York: Basic Books, 1988.

Hempel, Carl. "The Function of General Laws in History." *Journal of Philosophy* 39 (1942).

Herkovits, Melville. "The Organization of Work." In Moore and Feldman.

Hickson, D. J., C. J. McMillan, K. Azumi, and D. Horvath. "Grounds for Comparative Organization Theory: Quicksands or Hard Core?" In Lammers and Hickson.

Hirschorn, Larry. *The Workplace Within: Psychodynamics of Organizational Life.* Cambridge: MIT Press, 1988.

Hirschorn, Larry, and Carole Barnett. "Introduction." In Hirschhorn and Barnett.

Hirschorn, Larry, and Carole Barnett, eds. *The Psychodynamics of Organizations.* Philadelphia: Temple University Press, 1993.

Hirschman, Albert. *Exit, Voice and Loyalty: Responses to Decline in Firms, Organizations and States.* Cambridge: Harvard University Press, 1970.

———. "The Search for Paradigms as a Hindrance to Understanding." *World Politics* 22 (April 1970).

———. *The Strategy of Economic Development.* New Haven: Yale University Press, 1958.

Hobsbawm, Eric. *Worlds of Labour: Further Studies in the History of Labour.* London: Weidenfeld and Nicolson, 1984.

Hobsbawm, Eric, and Terence Ranger, eds. *The Invention of Tradition.* New York: Cambridge University Press, 1983.

Hochschild, Jennifer. *What's Fair: American Beliefs about Distributive Justice.* Cambridge: Harvard University Press, 1981.

Hofstede, Geert. *Culture's Consequences: International Differences in Work-Related Values.* Beverly Hills: Sage, 1980.

Horkheimer, Max, and Theodor Adorno. *The Dialectic of Enlightenment.* Trans. John Cummings. New York: Seabury Press, 1972 [1944].

Hoselitz, Bert, and Wilbert Moore, eds. *Industrialization and Social Change.* Rev. ed. The Hague, Netherlands: Mouton/UNESCO, 1970. First published, The Hague: Mouton, 1963.

Hsu, Francis L. K. "American Core Values and National Character." In *Psychological Anthropology: Approaches to Culture and Personality,* ed. Francis Hsu. Homewood, IL: Doresy Press, 1961.

Huntington, Samuel. "The Change to Change." *Comparative Politics* (April 1971): 283–322.

———. *Political Order in Changing Societies.* New Haven: Yale University Press, 1967.

Immergut, Ellen. "The Theoretical Core of the New Institutionalism." *Politics and Society* 26, 1 (March 1998): 5–34.

Inglehart, Ronald. *Modernization and Postmodernization: Cultural, Economic, and Political Change in 43 Societies.* Princeton: Princeton University Press, 1997.

Inkeles, Alex, and David Smith. *Becoming Modern: Individual Change in Six Countries.* Cambridge: Harvard University Press, 1974.

International Historical Statistics. New York: New York University Press, 1983.

International Labor Organization. *ILO Yearbook of Labor Statistics.* Geneva: ILO, 1988.

Jacobson-Widding, Anita, ed. *Identity: Personal and Socio-Cultural.* Uppsala, Sweden: Uppsala Studies in Cultural Anthropology 5, 1983.

Janos, Andrew. *Politics and Paradigms: Changing Theories of Change in Social Science.* Stanford: Stanford University Press, 1982.

———. "The Politics of Backwardness in Continental Europe." *World Politics* 41, 3 (April 1989): 325–58.

Johnson, Chalmers. "Political Institutions and Economic Performance: The Government-Business Relationship in Japan, South Korea and Taiwan." In Deyo, *Political Economy.*

———. "Preconception vs. Observation, or the Contributions of Rational Choice Theory and Area Studies." *PS: Political Science and Politics* 30, 2 (June 1997): 170–74.

Joyce, Patrick. *Work, Society and Politics: The Culture of the Factory in Later Victorian England.* New Brunswick: Rutgers University Press, 1980.

Kakar, Sudhir. "Authority Patterns and Subordinate Behavior in Indian Organizations." *Administrative Science Quarterly* 16 (1971): 298–307.

Kanigel, Robert. *The One Best Way: Frederick Winslow Taylor and the Enigma of Efficiency.* New York: Viking, 1997.

Kaplinsky, Raphael. "Technique and System: The Spread of Japanese Management Techniques to Developing Countries." *World Development* 23, 1 (1995): 57–71.

Katz, Harry, and Owen Darbishire. *Converging Divergences: Worldwide Changes in Employment Systems.* Ithaca: Cornell University Press, 1999.

Katzenstein, Peter. Contribution to "The Role of Theory in Comparative Politics: A Symposium." *World Politics* 48, 1 (October 1995): 10–15.

Katznelson, Ira. "The Doleful Dance of Politics and Policy: Can Historical Institutionalism Make a Difference?" *American Political Science Review* 91, 1 (March 1998).

———. "Structure and Configuration in Comparative Politics." In Lichbach and Zuckerman.

Kenney, Martin, and Richard Florida. *Beyond Mass Production: The Japanese System and Its Transfer to the U.S.* New York: Oxford University Press, 1993.

Kerr, Clark, J. T. Dunlop, F. H. Garbison, and C. A. Myers. *Industrialism and Industrial Man.* Cambridge: Harvard University Press, 1960.

Kerr, Clark, and Abraham Siegel. "The Inter-Industry Propensity to Strike." In *Labor and Management in Industrial Society,* ed. Clark Kerr et al. Garden City: Anchor, 1964.

Kim, U., H. C. Triandis, C. Kagitcibasi, S. Choi, and G. Yoon, eds. *Individualism and Collectivism: Theory, Method, and Applications.* Thousand Oaks, CA: Sage, 1994.

King, Gary. "Replication, Replication." *PS: Political Science and Politics* 28, 3 (September 1995): 444–52.

King, Gary, Robert Keohane, and Sidney Verba. *Designing Social Inquiry: Scientific Inference in Qualitative Research.* Princeton: Princeton University Press, 1994.

Kiser, Edgar. "The Revival of Narrative in Historical Sociology: What Rational Choice Theory Can Contribute." *Politics and Society* (September 1996): 259–71.

Kiser, Edgar, and Michael Hechter. "The Debate on Historical Sociology: Rational Choice Theory and Its Critics." *American Journal of Sociology* 104, 3
(November 1998).

———. "The Role of General Theory in Comparative-Historical Sociology."
American Journal of Sociology 97, 1 (1998): 785–816.

Kleugel, James, David Mason, and Bernard Wegener, eds. *Social Justice and Political Change: Public Opinion in Capitalist and Post-Communist States.* New
York: Aldine De Gruyter, 1995.

Kluckhohn, F. R., and F. L. Strodtbeck. *Variations in Value Orientations.*
Evanston, IL: Row Peterson, 1961.

Knight, Jack. *Institutions and Social Conflict.* New York: Cambridge University
Press, 1992.

Kocka, Jurgen. "Family and Bureaucracy in German Industrial Management."
Business History Review 45 (1971): 133–54.

Kondo, Dorrine. *Crafting Selves: Power, Gender and Discourses of Identity in a
Japanese Workplace.* Chicago: University of Chicago Press, 1990.

Krantz, James. "The Managerial Couple: Superior-Subordinate Relationships as a
Unit of Analysis." *Human Resource Management* 28, 2 (summer 1989):
161–75.

Kuhn, Thomas. *The Structure of Scientific Revolutions.* Chicago: University of
Chicago Press, 1962.

Kullick, Don. *Language Shift and Cultural Reproduction: Socialization, Self, and
Syncretism in a Papua New Guinean Village.* New York: Cambridge University Press, 1992.

LaBier, Douglas. "Emotional Disturbances in the Federal Bureaucracy." *Administration and Society* 14, 4 (1983): 403–48.

Lakatos, Imre. *The Methodology of Scientific Research Programmes.* Cambridge:
Cambridge University Press, 1978.

———. Proofs and Refutations. Cambridge: Cambridge University Press, 1976.

Lammers, C. J., and D. J. Hickson, eds. *Organizations Alike and Unlike: International and Inter-Institutional Studies in the Sociology of Organizations.* London: Routledge and Kegan Paul, 1979.

Landes, David. "French Business and the Businessman: A Social and Cultural
Analysis." In *Explorations in Enterprise,* ed. Hugh Aitken. Cambridge: Harvard University Press, 1965.

Landsberger, Henry. "Parsons' Theory of Organizations." In *The Social Theories
of Talcott Parsons,* ed. Max Black. Englewood Cliffs: Prentice-Hall, 1961.

Layton, E. "Veblen and the Engineers." *American Quarterly* 14, 1 (spring 1962):
64–72.

Lerner, Daniel. *The Passing of Traditional Society.* New York: Free Press, 1958.

Levi, Margaret. *Of Rule and Revenue.* Berkeley: University of California Press,
1988.

Levy, Marion. *Modernization and the Structure of Societies.* Princeton: Princeton
University Press, 1966.

Lichbach, Mark, and Alan Zuckerman, eds. *Comparative Politics: Rationality,
Culture, and Structure.* New York: Cambridge University Press, 1997.

————. "Research Traditions and Theory in Comparative Politics." In Lichbach and Zuckerman.

Licht, Walter. *Industrializing America: The Nineteenth Century.* Baltimore: Johns Hopkins University Press, 1995.

Lijphart, Arend. "Comparative Politics and the Comparative Method." *American Political Science Review* 65 (September 1971).

Likert, Rensis. *The Human Organization: Its Management and Value.* New York: McGraw-Hill, 1967.

Lincoln, James, and Arne Kalleberg. *Culture, Control and Commitment: A Study of Work Organization and Work Attitudes in the United States and Japan.* Cambridge: Cambridge University Press, 1990.

Lipietz, Alain. *Toward a New Economic Order: Postfordism, Ecology and Democracy.* Cambridge, UK: Polity Press, 1992.

List, Friedrich. *The National System of Political Economy.* Trans. Sampson S. Lloyd. London: Longmans, 1916.

Littler, Craig. *The Development of the Labour Process in Capitalist Societies: A Comparative Study of the Transformation of Work Organization in Britain, Japan, and the U.S.A.* London: Heinemann, 1982.

————. "Work in Traditional and Modern Societies." In Littler.

————, ed. *The Experience of Work.* Aldershot, UK: Gower, 1985.

Littler, Craig, and Graeme Salaman. "The Design of Jobs." In Littler.

Locke, Richard, Thomas Kochan, and Michael Piore. "Reconceptualizing Comparative Industrial Relations: Lessons from International Research." *International Labour Review* 134, 2 (1995).

Locke, Richard, and Kathleen Thelen. "Apples and Oranges Revisited: Contextualized Comparisons and the Study of Comparative Labor Politics." *Politics and Society* 23: 3 (September 1995): 337–67.

Lustick, Ian. "The Disciplines of Political Science: Studying the Culture of Rational Choice as a Case in Point." *PS: Political Science and Politics* 30, 2 (June 1997): 175–79.

————. "History, Historiography, and Political Science: Multiple Historical Records and the Problem of Selection Bias." *American Political Science Review* 90, 3 (September 1996): 605–18.

Luthy, Herbert. "Once Again: Calvinism and Capitalism." *Encounter* 22, 1 (1964): 26–68.

MacFarlane, Alan. *The Origins of English Individualism.* Oxford: Basil Blackwell, 1978.

Magagna, Victor. *Communities of Grain: Rural Rebellion in Comparative Perspective.* Ithaca: Cornell University Press, 1991.

Mahoney, James. "Nominal, Ordinal, and Narrative Appraisal in Macrocausal Analysis." *American Journal of Sociology* 104, 4 (1999): 1154–96.

Maier, Charles. "Between Taylorism and Technocracy: European Ideologies and the Vision of Industrial Productivity in the 1920s." *Journal of Contemporary History* 2 (1970): 27–61.

Malinowski, Bronislaw. "The Primitive Economics of the Trobriand Islanders." In Littler.

"Manufacturing the Right Way." *Fortune.* May 21, 1990.

March, James. "Decisions in Organizations and Theories of Choice." In *Perspectives on Organization Design and Behavior,* ed. Andrew Van de Ven and William Joyce. New York: John Wiley, 1981.

March, James, and Martha Feldman. "Information in Organizations as Signal and Symbol." *Administrative Science Quarterly* 26 (1981): 171–84.

March, James, and Johann Olsen. *Rediscovering Institutions.* New York: Free Press, 1989.

March, James, and Herbert Simon. *Organizations.* New York: Wiley, 1958.

Marcuse, Herbert. *One-Dimensional Man.* Boston: Beacon, 1964.

Marglin, Steven. "What Do Bosses Do? The Origins and Functions of Hierarchy in Capitalist Production." *Review of Radical Political Economy* 6 (1974): 60–112.

Marx, Karl. *The Marx-Engels Reader.* Ed. Robert Tucker. 2d ed. New York: Norton, 1978.

Maslow, Abraham. *Motivation and Personality.* New York: Harper and Row, 1954.

Mauss, Marcell. "A Category of the Human Mind: The Notion of Person, the Notion of Self." In Carrithers, Collins, and Lukes. Trans. W. D. Halls.

Mayo, Elton. *The Social Problems of an Industrial Civilization.* Cambridge: Graduate School of Business Administration, Harvard University, 1945.

McClelland, David. "The Achievement Motive in Economic Growth." In Finkle and Gable.

McGregor, Douglas. *The Human Side of Enterprise.* New York: McGraw-Hill, 1960.

Mead, George Herbert. *Mind, Self and Society.* Chicago: University of Chicago Press, 1962.

Mechanic, David. "Sources of Power of Lower Participants in Complex Organization." *Administrative Science Quarterly* 7, 4 (December 1962): 349–64.

Merkle, Judith A. *Management and Ideology: The Legacy of the International Scientific Management Movement.* Berkeley: University of California Press, 1980.

Merton, Robert K. *Social Theory and Social Structure.* New York: Free Press, 1966.

Meyer, J., and B. Rowan. "Institutionalized Organizations: Formal Structure as Myth and Ceremony." In Powell and DiMaggio.

Meyer, J. P., and N. J. Allen. "The Measurement and Antecedents of Affective, Continuance, and Normative Commitment to the Organization." *Journal of Occupational Psychology* 63 (1990): 1–18.

Meyer, Stephen, III. *The Five Dollar Day: Labor Management and Social Control in the Ford Motor Company, 1908–1921.* Albany: State University of New York Press, 1981.

Mill, John Stuart. *A System of Logic.* New York: Harper and Row, 1888.

Miller, Eric J. *The 'Leicester' Model: Experiential Study of Group and Organizational Processes.* Occasional Paper No. 10. London: Tavistock Institute of Human Relations, 1989.

Miller, Gary. *Managerial Dilemmas: The Political Economy of Hierarchy.* Cambridge: Cambridge University Press, 1992.

Mills, C. Wright. "Contributions of Sociology to Studies of Industrial Relations." *Berkeley Journal of Sociology* (1970). Reprint from 1948.

Mittelman, James. *The Globalization Syndrome: Transformation and Resistance.* Princeton: Princeton University Press, 2000.

Moore, Barrington. *Social Origins of Dictatorship and Democracy.* Boston: Beacon Press, 1966.

Moore, Wilbert. "Attributes of an Industrial Order." In Nosow and Form.

Moore, Wilbert, and Arnold Feldman, eds. *Labor Commitment and Social Change in Developing Areas.* New York: Social Science Research Council, 1960.

Morrow, Paula. *The Theory and Measurement of Work Commitment.* Greenwich: JAI Press, 1993.

Mowday, Richard, Lyman Porter, and Richard Steers. *Employee-Organization Linkages: The Psychology of Commitment, Absenteeism and Turnover.* New York: Academic Press, 1982.

Muensterberg, Hugo. *Psychology and Industrial Efficiency.* Boston: Houghton Mifflin, 1913.

Nadworny, Milton. *Scientific Management and the Unions.* Cambridge: Harvard University Press, 1955.

Nelson, Daniel. *Frederick W. Taylor and the Rise of Scientific Management.* Madison: University of Wisconsin Press, 1980.

———. *Managers and Workers: Origins of the New Factory System in the United States, 1880–1920.* Madison: University of Wisconsin Press, 1975.

Nelson, Daniel, and S. Campbell. "Taylorism vs. Welfare Work in American Industry." *Business History Review* 46 (1972): 1–16.

Nisbet, Robert. *Social Change and History.* New York: Oxford University Press, 1967.

North, Douglass. *Institutions, Institutional Change, and Economic Performance.* New York: Cambridge University Press, 1990.

———. "The New Institutional Economics." *Journal of Theoretical and Institutional Economics* 142 (1986): 230–37.

Nosow, Sigmund, and William Form, eds. *Man, Work and Society.* New York: Basic Books, 1962.

O'Donnell, Guillermo. *Modernization and Bureaucratic-Authoritarianism: Studies in South American Politics.* Berkeley: Institute of International Studies, University of California at Berkeley, 1973.

Offe, Claus. "Designing Institutions for East European Transitions." In *Strategic Choice and Path-Dependency in Post-Socialism: Institutional Dynamics in the Transformation Process,* ed. J. Hausner, B. Jessop, and K. Nielson. Aldershot, UK: Gower, 1995.

Ohmae, Kenichi, ed. *The Evolving Global Economy.* Boston: Harvard Business Review, 1995.

Oliver, Nick, and Barry Wilkinson. *The Japanization of British Industry.* Oxford: Blackwell, 1988.

O'Toole, James, ed. *Work and the Quality of Life: Resource Papers for* Work in America. Cambridge: MIT Press, 1974.

Ouchi, William. "Markets, Bureaucracies and Clans." *Administrative Science Quarterly* 25, 1 (March 1980): 129–41.

———. *Theory Z: How American Business Can Meet the Japanese Challenge.* Reading: Addison-Wesley, 1981.

Palm, G. *The Flight from Work.* New York: Cambridge University Press, 1977.

Parsons, Talcott. "Evaluation and Objectivity in Social Science: An Interpretation of Max Weber's Contribution." *International Social Science Journal* 17, 1 (1965): 46–63.

———. "Evolutionary Universals in Society." *American Sociological Review* 29 (June 1964): 339–57.

———. "Social Classes and Class Conflict in the Light of Recent Sociological Theory." In Parsons, *Essays in Sociological Theory.* Rev. ed. New York: Free Press, 1964.

———. *The Social System.* New York: Free Press, 1951.

———. *Societies: Evolutionary and Comparative Perspectives.* Englewood Cliffs: Prentice-Hall, 1966.

———. *The Structure of Social Action.* New York: Free Press, 1937.

Parsons, Talcott, and Edward Shils. *Toward a General Theory of Action.* New York: Harper and Row, 1951.

Perrin, Robert G. "Herbert Spencer's Four Theories of Social Evolution." *American Journal of Sociology* (May 1976).

Perrow, Charles. *Complex Organizations: A Critical Essay.* Glenview: Scott, Foresman, 1972.

Pierson, Paul. "Increasing Returns, Path Dependence, and the Study of Politics." *American Political Science Review* 94, 2 (June 2000): 251–67.

Piore, Michael. "Upward Mobility, Job Monotony, and Labor Market Structure." In O'Toole.

Polanyi, Karl. *The Great Transformation.* Boston: Beacon, 1944.

Pollard, Sidney. *The Genesis of Modern Management: A Study of the Industrial Revolution in Great Britain.* Cambridge: Harvard University Press, 1965.

Popkin, Samuel. *The Rational Peasant.* Berkeley: University of California Press, 1974.

Powell, Walter W., and Paul J. DiMaggio, eds. *The New Institutionalism in Organizational Analysis.* Chicago: University of Chicago Press, 1991.

Price, Robert. *Society and Bureaucracy in Contemporary Ghana.* Berkeley: University of California Press, 1975.

Przeworski, Adam, Michael Alvarez, Jose Cheibub, and Fernando Limongi. *Democracy and Development: Political Institutions and Material Well-Being in the World, 1950–1990.* New York: Cambridge University Press, 2000.

Pugh, D. S., and D. J. Hickson. *Organizational Structure in Its Context: The Aston Programme I.* London: Saxon House, 1976.

Pugh, D. S., and C. R. Hinings, eds. *Organizational Structure: Extensions and Replications, The Aston Programme II.* Farnborough, UK: Saxon House, 1976.

Putnam, Robert. "Bowling Alone: America's Declining Social Capital." *Journal of Democracy* 6, 1 (January 1995): 65–78.

Pye, Lucian. "Political Science and the Crisis of Authoritarianism." *American Political Science Review* 84, 1 (1990): 3–19.

Ragin, Charles. *The Comparative Method: Moving beyond Qualitative and Quantitative Strategies.* Berkeley: University of California Press, 1987.

———. *Constructing Social Research: The Unity and Diversity of Method.* Thousand Oaks: Pine Forge Press, 1994.

Rhodes, Susan, and Richard Steers. *Managing Employee Absenteeism.* Reading: Addison-Wesley, 1990.

Ricoeur, Paul. "The Model of the Text: Meaningful Action Considered as Text." *Social Research* 38 (1971): 529–55.

Riggs, Fred. *Administration in Developing Societies.* Boston: Houghton Mifflin, 1964.

Rinehart, James. *The Tyranny of Work: Alienation and the Labor Process.* Toronto: Harcourt Brace, 1996.

Rinehart, James, Christopher Huxley, and David Robertson. *Just Another Car Factory? Lean Production and Its Discontents.* Ithaca: ILR Press/Cornell University Press, 1997.

Robertson, Ronald. *Globalization: Social Theory and Global Culture.* London: Sage, 1992.

Roethlisberger, F. J., and W. J. Dickson. *Management and the Worker.* Cambridge: Harvard University Press, 1946.

Rogowski, Ronald. "Eckstein and the Study of Private Governments: An Appreciation, Critique, and Proposal." *Comparative Political Studies* 31, 4 (August 1998): 444–63.

———. "Rational Choice as a Weberian View of Culture." *APSA-CP: Newsletter of the APSA Organized Section in Comparative Politics* 8, 2 (summer 1997): 14–15.

———. *Rational Legitimacy.* Princeton: Princeton University Press, 1974.

———. "The Role of Theory and Anomaly in Social-Scientific Research." *American Political Science Review* 89, 2 (June 1995): 467–70.

Rosenau, Pauline. *Post-Modernism and the Social Sciences.* Princeton: Princeton University Press, 1992.

Rostow, Walt W. *The Stages of Economic Growth: A Non-Communist Manifesto.* Cambridge: Cambridge University Press, 1962.

Roth, Guenther. "Introduction." In Weber, *Economy and Society.*

Rudolph, Lloyd, and Susan Rudolph. *The Modernity of Tradition: Political Development in India.* Chicago: University of Chicago Press, 1967.

Rueschemeyer, Dietrich. *Power and the Division of Labor.* Stanford: Stanford University Press, 1986.

———. "Structural Differentiation, Efficiency and Power." *American Journal of Sociology* 83 (1977): 1–25.

Rustow, Dankwart. *A World of Nations.* Washington: Brookings, 1967.

Sabel, Charles. *Work and Politics: The Division of Labor in Industry.* Cambridge: Cambridge University Press, 1982.

Sabel, Charles, and Michael Piore. *The Second Industrial Divide: Possibilities for Prosperity.* New York: Basic Books, 1985.

Sackman, Sonja A., ed. *Cultural Complexity in Organizations: Inherent Contrasts and Contradictions.* Thousand Oaks: Sage, 1997.

Sandel, Michael. *Liberalism and the Limits of Justice.* New York: Cambridge University Press, 1982.

Shaeffer, Frederic. *Democracy in Translation: Understanding Politics in an Unfamiliar Culture.* Ithaca: Cornell University Press, 1998.

Schumpeter, Joseph. *Capitalism, Socialism and Democracy.* New York: Harper and Brothers, 1942.

Schwartz, Howard. "The Psychodynamics of Organizational Totalitarianism." *Journal of General Management* 13, 1 (1987): 41–54.

Sclozman, Kay Lehman, and Sidney Verba. *Insult to Injury.* Cambridge: Harvard University Press, 1979.

Scott, James. *Seeing Like a State: How Certain Schemes to Improve the Human Condition Have Failed.* New Haven: Yale University Press, 1998.

———. *Weapons of the Weak: Everyday Forms of Peasant Resistance.* New Haven: Yale University Press, 1985.

Selznick, Philip. "Institutionalism 'Old' and 'New.'" *Administrative Science Quarterly* 41 (1996): 270–77.

———. *Leadership in Administration.* New York: Harper and Row, 1957.

———. *The Moral Commonwealth: Social Theory and the Promise of Community.* Berkeley: University of California Press, 1992.

———. *TVA and Grassroots.* Berkeley: University of California Press, 1949.

Sewell, William. "A Theory of Structure: Duality, Agency and Transformation." *American Journal of Sociology* 98, 1 (July 1992).

Shenhav, Yehouda. *Manufacturing Rationality: The Engineering Foundations of the Managerial Revolution.* New York: Oxford University Press, 1999.

Shepsle, Kenneth. "Studying Institutions: Some Lessons from the Rational Choice Approach." *Journal of Theoretical Politics* 1, 2 (1989): 131–47.

Shorter, Edward. "The History of Work in the West." In *Work and Community in the West,* ed. Shorter. New York: Harper and Row, 1973.

Sil, Rudra. "Against Epistemological Absolutism: Towards a 'Pragmatic' Center?" In Sil and Doherty, 145–75.

———. "The Division of Labor in Social Science Research: Unified Methodology or 'Organic Solidarity'?" *Polity* 32, 4 (summer 2000): 499–531.

———."The Foundations of Eclecticism: The Epistemological Status of Agency, Culture, and Structure in Social Theory." *Journal of Theoretical Politics* 12, 3 (July 2000): 353–87.

———. *Historical Legacies, Late-Industrialization and Institution Building: A Comparative Study of Industrial Enterprises and Worker Commitment in Japan and Russia.* Ph.D. Diss. University of California, Berkeley, 1996.

———. "The Questionable Status of Boundaries: The Need for Integration." In Sil and Doherty, 1–27.

Sil, Rudra, and Eileen Doherty, eds. *Beyond Boundaries? Disciplines, Paradigms, and Theoretical Integration in International Studies.* Albany: State University of New York Press, 2000.

Silberman, Bernard. *Cages of Reason: The Rise of the Rational State in France, Japan, the United States, and Great Britain.* Chicago: University of Chicago Press, 1993.

Simon, Herbert. *Administrative Behavior.* Rev. ed. New York: Macmillan, 1957. First published in 1945.

———. *Models of Man, Social and Rational: Mathematical Essays on Rational Human Behavior in a Social Setting.* New York: Wiley, 1957.

Skocpol, Theda. "Bringing the State Back In: Current Research." In Evans et al.

———. "Sociology's Historical Imagination." In *Vision and Method in Historical Sociology,* ed. Theda Skocpol. Cambridge: Cambridge University Press, 1984.

———. *States and Social Revolutions.* New York: Cambridge University Press, 1979.

Skocpol, Theda, and Margaret Somers. "The Uses of Comparative History in Macrosocial Inquiry." *Comparative Studies in Society and History* 12, 2 (1980): 174–97.

Slater, Phil. *Origin and Significance of the Frankfurt School: A Marxist Perspective.* London: Routledge and Kegan Paul, 1977.

Smelser, Neil. "Culture: Coherent or Incoherent?" In *Theory of Culture,* ed. Richard Munch and Neil Smelser. Berkeley: University of California Press, 1992.

———. "Mechanisms of Change and Adjustment to Change." In Hoselitz and Moore.

———. *Social Change in the Industrial Revolution.* Chicago: University of Chicago Press, 1959.

Smith, Adam. *An Inquiry into the Nature and Causes of the Wealth of Nations.* New York: Modern Library, 1937.

———. *The Theory of Moral Sentiments.* London: Henry Bohn, 1853.

Smith, Tony. *Technology and Capital in the Age of Lean Production: A Marxian Critique of the 'New Economy.'* Albany: State University of New York Press, 2000.

Somers, Margaret. "'We're No Angels': Realism, Rational Choice, and Relationality in Social Science." *American Journal of Sociology* 104, 3 (November 1998): 722–84.

Special Task Force to the Secretary of Health, Education and Welfare [Elliot Richardson], *Work in America.* Cambridge: MIT Press, 1973.

Spencer, Herbert. *On Social Evolution.* Ed. J. D. Y. Peel. Chicago: University of Chicago Press, 1972.

———. *The Principles of Sociology.* New York: Appleton, 1896.

Steers, Richard M., and Lyman Porter, eds. *Motivation and Work Behavior.* New York: McGraw-Hill, 1983.

Steinmetz, George. "Critical Realism and Historical Sociology." *Comparative Studies in Society and History* 40, 1 (January 1998): 170–86.

Steinmo, Sven, Kathleen Thelen, and Frank Longstreth, eds. *Structuring Politics:*

Historical Institutionalism in Comparative Analysis. New York: Cambridge University Press, 1992.

Stewart, Charles, and Rosalind Shaw. *Syncretism/Anti-Syncretism: The Politics of Religious Synthesis.* London: Routledge, 1994.

Stinchcombe, Arthur. *Constructing Social Theories.* New York: Harcourt, Brace and World, 1968.

———. *Creating Efficient Industrial Administration.* New York: Academic, 1974.

———. "Social Structure and Organizations." In *Handbook of Organizations,* ed. James March. Chicago: Rand McNally, 1965.

Stone, Katherine. "The Origins of Job Structures in the Steel Industry." *Review of Radical Political Economics* (summer 1974): 113–73.

Strauss, George. "Is There a Blue-Collar Revolt against Work?" In O'Toole.

Sullivan, Harry. *The Fusion of Psychiatry and Social Science.* New York: W. W. Norton, 1964.

Swidler, Ann. "Culture in Action: Symbols and Strategies." *American Sociological Review* 51 (April 1986).

Swift, Adam, Gordon Marshall, Carole Burgoyne, and David Routh. "Distributive Justice: Does It Matter What People Think?" In Kleugel et al.

"Symposium on Historical Sociology and Rational Choice Theory." *American Journal of Sociology* 104, 3 (November 1998).

Szacki, Jerzy. *History of Sociological Thought.* Westport, CT: Greenwood, 1979.

Tamir, Yael. *Liberal Nationalism.* Princeton: Princeton University Press, 1993.

Tawney, Robert. *Religion and the Rise of Capitalism.* London: John Murray, 1933.

Taylor, Charles. "Interpretation and the Sciences of Man." *Review of Metaphysics* 25 (1971).

Taylor, Ed. *Closing the Iron Cage: The Scientific Management of Work and Leisure.* New York: Black Rose Books, 1999.

Taylor, Frederick. "A Piece-Rate System, Being a Step toward Partial Solution of the Labor Problem." *Transactions, American Society of Mechanical Engineers,* 16 (1895): 856–83.

———. "Scientific Management." In *Compiled Writings.* New York: Harper, 1974. First published as *Shop Management.* New York: Harper and Brothers, 1911.

Thelen, Kathleen, and Sven Steinmo. "Historical Institutionalism in Comparative Politics." In Steinmo et al.

Thomas, Robert. *What Machines Can't Do: Politics and Technology in the Industrial Enterprise.* Berkeley: University of California Press, 1994.

Thompson, E. P. *The Making of the English Working Class.* New York: Vintage, 1963.

Thompson, James. *Organizations in Action.* New York: McGraw-Hill, 1967.

Tilgher, Adriano. "Work through the Ages." In Nosow and Form.

Tilly, Charles. *Big Structures, Large Processes, Huge Comparisons.* New York: Sage, 1984.

———. *Coercion, Capital, and European States, AD 990–1990.* Oxford: Blackwell, 1990.

————. "Means and Ends of Comparison in Macrosociology." *Comparative Social Research* 16 (1997): 43–53.

Tilly, Chris, and Charles Tilly. *Work under Capitalism.* Boulder: Westview, 1998.

Tiryakian, Edward. "Modernization: Exhumetur in Pace." *International Sociology* 6, 2 (1991).

Tönnies, Ferdinand. *Community and Society [Gemeinschaft und Gesellschaft].* Trans. and ed. Charles P. Loomis. New York: Harper and Row, 1957.

Toulmin, Stephen. *Human Understanding.* Princeton: Princeton University Press, 1972.

Touraine, Alan. *The Return of the Actor: Social Theory in Post-Industrial Society.* Minneapolis: University of Minnesota Press, 1988.

Trevor-Roper, H. R. *Religion, the Reformation and Social Change.* London: Macmillan, 1967.

Triandis, Harry. "Collectivism and Development." In *Social Values and Development: Asian Perspectives,* ed. D. Sinha and H. S. R. Kao. New Delhi: Sage, 1988.

————. "Cross-Cultural Studies of Individualism and Collectivism." In *Nebraska Symposium on Motivation 1989,* ed. J. Berman. Lincoln: University of Nebraska Press, 1989.

————. "Subjective Culture and Economic Development." *International Journal of Psychology* 8 (1973): 163–80.

Trist, E. L., G. W. Higgin, H. Murray, and A. B. Pollock. *Organizational Choice: Capabilities of Groups at the Coal Face under Changing Technologies.* London: Tavistock Institute of Human Relations, 1963.

Troeltsch, Ernst. *Protestantism and Progress.* Boston: Beacon, 1958.

Turner, Lowell, and Peter Auer. "A Diversity of New Work Organization: Human-Centered, Lean and In-Between." In Deyo, ed., *Social Reconstructions.*

Turner, Ralph. "Role-Taking: Process versus Conformity." In *Human Behavior and Social Process,* ed. A. Rose. Boston: Houghton Mifflin, 1962.

Tushman, Michael, and Lori Rosenkopf. "Organizational Determinants of Technological Change: Towards a Sociology of Technological Evolution." *Research in Organizational Behavior* 14 (1992): 311–47.

Veblen, Thorstein. *Imperial Germany and the Industrial Revolution.* New York: Viking, 1954. First published in 1915.

————. *The Instinct of Workmanship and the State of the Industrial Arts.* New York: Macmillan, 1914.

————. *The Theory of the Business Enterprise.* New York: Scribner's, 1904.

————. *The Theory of the Leisure Class: An Economic Study in the Evolution of Institutions.* New York: Macmillan, 1899.

Viteles, Morris. *Motivation and Morale in Industry.* New York: Norton, 1953.

Wade, Robert. *Governing the Market: Economic Theory and the Role of Government in East Asian Industrialization.* Princeton: Princeton University Press, 1990.

Walder, Andrew. *Communist Neo-Traditionalism: Work and Authority in Chinese Industry.* Berkeley: University of California Press, 1986.

Waldner, David. *State Building and Late Development.* Ithaca: Cornell University Press, 1999.

Wallerstein, Imanuelle. *Open the Social Sciences.* Stanford: Stanford University Press, 1996.

Waring, Stephen. *Taylorism Transformed: Scientific Management Theory since 1945.* Chapel Hill: University of North Carolina Press, 1991.

Warner, W. Lloyd, and O. J. Low. *The Social System of the Modern Factory.* New Haven: Yale University Press, 1947.

Weber, Max. *Economy and Society.* 2 vols. Ed. Guenther Roth and Claus Wittich. Berkeley: University of California Press, 1978.

―――. *From Max Weber.* Ed. H. H. Gerth and C. W. Mills. New York: Oxford University Press, 1949.

―――. "'Objectivity' in Social Science and Social Policy." In *The Methodology of the Social Sciences,* ed. E. A. Shils and H. A. Finch. New York: Free Press, 1949.

―――. *The Protestant Ethic and the Spirit of Capitalism.* New York: Scribner's, 1958.

―――. *The Theory of Social and Economic Organization.* Ed. Talcott Parsons. New York: Free Press, 1964.

Wegener, Bernd, and Stefan Liebig. "Dominant Ideologies and the Variation of Distributive Justice Norms: A Comparison of East and West Germany, and the United States." In Kleugel et al.

Wendt, Alexander. *Social Theory of International Politics.* New York: Cambridge University Press, 1999.

Westney, D. Eleanor. *Imitation and Innovation: The Transfer of Western Organizational Patterns to Meiji Japan.* Cambridge: Harvard University Press, 1987.

Wever, Kirsten, and Lowell Turner. "A Wide-Angle Lens." In *The Comparative Political Economy of Industrial Relations,* ed. Wever and Turner. Madison: Industrial Relations Research Association, 1995.

White, Harrison. *Chains of Opportunity: Systems Models of Mobility in Organizations.* Cambridge: Harvard University Press, 1970.

Whyte, William F. *Human Relations in the Restaurant Industry.* New York: McGraw Hill, 1948.

Whyte, William H. *The Organization Man.* New York: Simon and Schuster, 1956.

Wilensky, Harold. "Family Cycle, Work and the Quality of Life: Reflections on the Roots of Happiness, Despair and Indifference in Modern Society." In *Working Life,* ed. B. Gardell and G. Johansson. New York: Wiley, 1981.

Williams, Robin. *American Society.* 3d ed. New York: Knopf, 1970.

Williamson, Oliver. *The Economic Institutions of Capitalism.* New York: Free Press, 1985.

―――. *Markets and Hierarchies.* New York: Free Press, 1975.

Wolin, Sheldon. *Politics and Vision.* Boston: Little, Brown, 1960.

Womack, J., D. Jones, and D. Roos. *The Machine That Changed the World.* New York: Rawson Macmillan, 1990.

Wood, Stephen. "The Transformation of Work?" In *The Transformation of Work?*

Skill, Flexibility and the Labor Process. Ed. Stephen Wood. London: Unwin and Hyman, 1989.

Woodward, Joan. *Industrial Organization: Theory and Practice.* London: Oxford University Press, 1965.

World Bank. *The East Asian Miracle: Economic Growth and Public Policy.* New York: Oxford University Press, 1993.

Zucker, Lynne. "The Role of Institutionalization in Cultural Persistence." In Powell and DiMaggio.

Zweig, Ferdynand. *The Worker in an Affluent Society: Family Life and Industry.* London: Heinemann, 1961.

Zysman, John. *Governments, Markets and Growth.* Ithaca: Cornell University Press, 1983.

On Japan

Abegglen, James. *The Japanese Factory.* New York: Free Press, 1958.

Allen, George. *A Short Economic History of Modern Japan.* London: Macmillan, 1981.

Allinson, Gary. *Japanese Urbanism: Industry and Politics in Kariya, 1872–1972.* Berkeley: University of California Press, 1975.

———. "The Moderation of Organized Labor in Postwar Japan." *Journal of Japanese Studies* 1, 2 (spring 1975).

Aoki, Masahiko. *Information, Incentives, and Bargaining in the Japanese Economy.* Cambridge: Cambridge University Press, 1988.

———. "The Japanese Firm as a System of Attributes." In Aoki and Dore.

———. "The Japanese Firm in Transition." In Yamamura and Yasuba.

Aoki, Masahiko, and Ronald Dore, eds. *The Japanese Firm: The Sources of Competitive Strength.* New York: Oxford University Press, 1994.

Araki, H. *Nihonjin no knoudou youshiki* [Behavioral style of the Japanese]. Tokyo: Kodansha, 1973.

Balassa, Bela. "The Lessons of East Asian Development: An Overview." *Economic Development and Cultural Change* 36, 3 (April 1988).

Barshay, Andrew. "'Doubly Cruel': Marxism and the Presence of the Past in Japanese Capitalism." In Vlastos, ed.

———. "Toward a History of the Social Sciences in Japan." *Positions* 4, 2 (1996): 217–51.

Beardsley, Richard, John Hall, and Robert Ward. *Village Japan.* Chicago: University of Chicago Press, 1959.

Befu, Harumi. "Symbols of Nationalism and *Nihonjinron.*" In Goodman and Refsing.

———. *Zoho ideorogi to shite no Nihon bunkaron* [The theory of Japanese culture as an ideology]. Tokyo: Shiso no kagaku, 1987.

Bellah, Robert. *Tokugawa Religion: The Cultural Roots of Modern Japan.* New York: Free Press, 1985 [1957].

Ben-Ari, Eyal. "Ritual Strikes, Ceremonial Slowdowns: Some Thoughts on the Management of Conflict in Large Japanese Enterprises." In Eisenstadt and Ben-Ari.

Benedict, Ruth. *The Chrysanthemum and the Sword: Patterns of Japanese Culture.* Cambridge: Houghton Mifflin, 1946.

Berger, Peter, and Michael Hsiao, eds. *In Search of an East Asian Development Model.* New Brunswick: Transaction Books, 1988.

Bix, Herbert. *Peasant Protest in Japan, 1590–1884.* New Haven: Yale University Press, 1986.

Black, Cyril, et al. *The Modernization of Japan and Russia.* New York: Free Press, 1975.

Blackford, Mansel. *The Rise of Modern Business in Great Britain, the United States, and Japan.* Chapel Hill: University of North Carolina Press, 1998.

Brinton, Mary. *Women and the Economic Miracle: Gender and Work in Postwar Japan.* Berkeley: University of California Press, 1993.

Bronfenbrenner, Martin. "Economic Miracles and Japan's Income-Doubling Plan." In Lockwood.

Burks, Ardath. *Japan: A Postindustrial Power.* Rev. ed. Boulder: Westview, 1991.

Chan, Anita. "Chinese Danwei Reforms: Convergence with the Japanese Model?" In *Danwei: The Changing Chinese Workplace in Historical and Comparative Perspective,* ed. Xiaobo Lu and Elizabeth Perry. Armonk, NY: M. E. Sharpe, 1997.

Chapman, William. *Inventing Japan: The Making of a Postwar Civilization.* New York: Prentice-Hall, 1991.

Clark, Rodney. *The Japanese Company.* New Haven: Yale University Press, 1969.

Cole, Robert. *Japanese Blue Collar: The Changing Tradition.* Berkeley: University of California Press, 1971.

———. *Strategies for Learning: Small Group Activities in American, Japanese, and Swedish Industry.* Berkeley: University of California Press, 1989.

———. *Work, Mobility and Participation: A Comparative Study of American and Japanese Industry.* Berkeley: University of California Press, 1979.

Craig, Albert, ed. *Japan: A Comparative Perspective.* Princeton: Princeton University Press, 1979.

Crawcour, Sidney. "The Japanese Employment System." *Journal of Japanese Studies* 4, 2 (summer 1978).

Dale, Peter. *The Myth of Japanese Uniqueness.* New York: St. Martin's Press, 1986.

Deming, William Edward. *Statistical Control of Quality in Japan.* Proceedings of the International Conference on Quality Control, 1969. Tokyo: Union of Japanese Scientists and Engineers, 1970.

De Vos, George. *Social Cohesion and Alienation: Minorities in the United States and Japan.* Boulder: Westview, 1992.

Dohse, Kunth, Ulrich Jurgens, and Thomas Malsch. "From 'Fordism' to 'Toyotaism'? The Social Organization of the Labor Process in the Japanese Automobile Industry." *Politics and Society* 14, 2 (1985): 115–46.

Doi, Takeo. *The Anatomy of Dependence.* Tokyo: Kodansha International, 1973.

Dore, Ronald. *British Factory, Japanese Factory.* Berkeley: University of California Press, 1973.

———. "Industrial Relations in Japan and Elsewhere." In Craig.

———. "Mobility, Equality and Individuation in Modern Japan." In *Aspects of Social Change in Modern Japan,* ed. Dore. Princeton: Princeton University Press, 1967.

———. *Taking Japan Seriously: A Confucian Perspective on Leading Economic Issues.* Stanford: Stanford University Press, 1987.

Dower, John. *Japan in War and Peace: Selected Essays.* New York: New Press, 1993.

———. "Peace and Democracy in Two Systems: External Policy and Internal Conflict." In Gordon, ed.

Eccleston, Bernard. *State and Society in Post-War Japan.* Cambridge, UK: Polity Press, 1989.

Eisenstadt, S. N. "Patterns of Conflict and Conflict Resolution in Japan: Some Comparative Indications." In Eisenstadt and Ben-Ari.

Eisenstadt, S. N., and Eyal Ben-Ari, eds. *Japanese Models of Conflict Resolution.* London: Kegan Paul International, 1990.

Elger, Tony, and Chris Smith, eds. *Global Japanization? The Transnational Transformation of the Labour Process.* London: Routledge, 1994.

Fruin, Mark. "The Japanese Company Controversy: Ideology and Organization in a Historical Perspective." *Journal of Japanese Studies* 4, 2 (summer 1978).

———. *Kikkoman: Company, Clan and Community.* Cambridge: Harvard University Press, 1983.

Fukutake, Tadashi. *Japanese Rural Society.* Trans. Ronald Dore. New York: Oxford University Press, 1967.

Gao, Bai. *Economic Ideology and Japanese Industrial Policy: Developmentalism from 1931 to 1965.* New York: Cambridge University Press, 1997.

Garon, Sheldon. *The State and Labor in Modern Japan.* Berkeley: University of California Press, 1987.

Garon, Sheldon, and Mike Mochizuki. "Negotiating Social Contracts." In Gordon, ed.

Gluck, Carol. *Japan's Modern Myths: Ideology in the Late Meiji Period.* Princeton: Princeton University Press, 1985.

———. "The Past in the Present." In Gordon, ed.

Goodman, Roger, and Kirsten Refsing, eds. *Ideology and Practice in Modern Japan.* New York: Routledge, 1992.

Gordon, Andrew. "Contests for the Workplace." In Gordon, ed.

———. *The Evolution of Labor Relations in Japan, 1853–1955.* Cambridge: Harvard University Press, 1985.

———. "The Invention of Japanese-Style Labor Management." In Vlastos, ed.

———. *Labor and Imperial Democracy.* Berkeley: University of California Press, 1991.

———. *Wages of Affluence: Labor and Management in Postwar Japan.* Cambridge: Harvard University Press, 1998.

————, ed. *Postwar Japan as History.* Berkeley: University of California Press, 1993.

Haley, John O. "Consensual Governance: A Study of Law, Culture, and the Political Economy of Postwar Japan." In Kumon and Rosovsky.

Hamaguchi, E. "Nihonteki shudan shugi towa nanika?" [What is Japanese Collectivism?]. In *Nihonteki shudan shugi* [Japanese-style collectivism], ed. E. Hamaguchi and Shumpei Kumon. Tokyo: Yuhikau, 1982.

Hanami, Tadashi. "Conflict and Its Resolution in Industrial Relations and Labor Law." In *Conflict in Japan,* ed. Ellis Krauss, Thomas Rohlen, and Patricia Steinhoff. Honolulu: University of Hawaii Press, 1984.

Hardacre, Helen. *Shinto and the State, 1868–1988.* Princeton: Princeton University Press, 1989.

Hayashi, Chikiio, Nishira Sigeki, and Suzuki Tatsuzo, et al. *Nihonjin No Kokuminsei: A Study of the Japanese National Character,* vol. 4. Tokyo: Idemitsushoten, 1982.

Hazama, Hiroshi. *The History of Labor Management in Japan.* New York: St. Martin's Press, 1997.

————. "Nihonjin no kachikan to kigyo katsudo—Shudan shugi wo chushin to shite" [Japanese values and entrepreneurship: The problem of collectivism]. In *Nihon no kigyo to shakai* [Japanese company and society], ed. Hazama. Tokyo: Nihon keizai shimbun, 1977.

Hazama, Hiroshi, with Jacqueline Kaminsky. "Japanese Labor-Management Relations and Uno Reimon." *Journal of Japanese Studies* 5, 1 (1979).

Hendry, Joy. "Individualism and Individuality: Entry into a Social World." In Goodman and Refsing.

Hirschmeier, Johannes. *The Origins of Entrepreneurship in Meiji Japan.* Cambridge: Harvard University Press, 1964.

Horie, Yasuzo. "Modern Entrepreneurship in Meiji Japan." In Lockwood.

Imai, Kenichi, and Ryutaro Komiya. "Characteristics of Japanese Firms." In Imai and Komiya, eds.

————, eds. *The Business Enterprise in Japan.* Cambridge: MIT Press, 1993.

Irokawa, Daikichi. *Kindai kokka no shuppatsu* [The beginning of a modern state]. Tokyo: Chuo Koronsha, 1967.

Ishida, Hiroshi, Seymour Spilerman, and Kuo-Hsien Su. "Educational Credentials and Promotion Prospects in a Japanese and an American Organization." Working Paper 92 of the Center on Japanese Economy and Business. Columbia University, New York, 1995.

Ishikawa, Kaoru. *Nihon teki hinshitsu kanri* [Japanese quality control]. Tokyo: Nikka Giren Shuppan Sha, 1988.

Iwata, Ryushi. "The Japanese Enterprise as a Unified Body of Employees." In Kumon and Rosovsky.

Jansen, Marius. "On Foreign Borrowing." In Craig.

————, ed. *Changing Japanese Attitudes toward Modernization.* Princeton: Princeton University Press, 1965.

Japan Statistical Yearbook, 1993/94. Tokyo: Bureau of Statistics, Management and Coordination Agency.

Japanese Economic Planning Agency. *The Japanese and Their Society. Part II of the Report on National Life.* Tokyo: Economic Planning Agency, 1972.

Johnson, Chalmers. *MITI and the Japanese Miracle.* Stanford: Stanford University Press, 1982.

———. "Political Institutions and Economic Performance: The Government-Business Relationship in Japan, South Korea and Taiwan." In *The Political Economy of New Asian Industrialism,* ed. Frederic C. Deyo. Ithaca: Cornell University Press, 1987.

Junnosuke, Masumi. "The 1955 System: Origin and Transformation." In *Creating Single Party Democracy: Japan's Postwar Political System,* ed. Kataoka Tetsuya. Stanford: Hoover Institution Press, Stanford University, 1992.

Kano, Masano, ed. *Shin shiso no taido* [The emergence of new currents of thought]. Tokyo: Chikuma Shobo, 1969.

Kaplinsky, Raphael. "Technique and System: The Spread of Japanese Management Techniques to Developing Countries." *World Development* 23, 1: 57–71.

Kenney, Martin, and Richard Florida. *Beyond Mass Production: The Japanese System and Its Transfer to the U.S.* New York: Oxford University Press, 1993.

Kinmonth, Earl. *The Self-Made Man in Meiji Japanese Thought: From Samurai to Salary Man.* Berkeley: University of California Press, 1974.

Kinzley, Dean. *Industrial Harmony in Modern Japan.* London: Routledge, 1991.

Kohei, Goshi. "Successful Performance of the Productivity Movement in Japanese Enterprises." In British Institute of Management, *Modern Japanese Management.* London: British Institute of Management, 1970.

Kohli, Atul. "Where Do High Growth Political Economics Come From? The Japanese Lineage of Korea's 'Developmental State.'" *World Development* 22, 9 (September 1994): 1269–93.

Koike, Kazuo. *The Economics of Work in Japan.* Tokyo: Long Term Credit Bank International Library Foundation, 1995.

———. "Human Resource Development and Labor-Management." In Yamamura and Yasuba.

———. "Learning and Incentive Systems in Japanese Industry." In Aoki and Dore.

Kondo, Dorrine. *Crafting Selves: Power, Gender and the Discourses of Identity in a Japanese Workplace.* Chicago: University of Chicago Press, 1990.

Koschmann, Victor. *Revolution and Subjectivity in Post-War Japan.* Chicago: University of Chicago Press, 1996.

Koshiro, Kazutoshi. "The Quality of Working Life in Japanese Factories." In Shirai.

Kumazawa, Makoto. *Portraits of the Japanese Workplace: Labor Movements, Workers, and Managers.* Boulder: Westview, 1996.

Kume, Ikio. *Disparaged Success: Labor Politics in Postwar Japan.* Ithaca: Cornell University Press, 1998.

Kumon, Shumpei, and Henry Rosovsky, eds. *The Political Economy of Japan, Volume 3: Cultural and Social Dynamics.* Stanford: Stanford University Press, 1992.

Kuznets, Paul. "An East Asian Model of Economic Development: Japan, Taiwan and South Korea." *Economic Development and Cultural Change* 36, 6 (April Supplement, 1988): S11–S43.

Large, Stephen. *Organized Workers and Socialist Politics in Interwar Japan.* Cambridge: Cambridge University Press, 1981.

Levine, Solomon. "Labor Markets and Collective Bargaining in Japan." In Lockwood.

———. "Unionization of White-Collar Employees in Japan." In *White-Collar Trade Unions,* ed. Adolf Sturmthal. Urbana: University of Illinois Press, 1966.

Levy, Marion. "Contrasting Factors in the Modernization of China and Japan." *Economic Development and Cultural Change* 2, 3 (1953).

Lincoln, James, and Arne Kalleberg. "Commitment, Quits, and Work Organization in Japanese and U.S. Plants." *Industrial and Labor Relations Review* 50, 1 (October 1995): 39–59.

———. *Culture, Control and Commitment: A Study of Work Organization and Work Attitudes in the United States and Japan.* New York: Cambridge University Press, 1990.

Lo, Jeannie. *Office Ladies, Factory Women: Life and Work at a Japanese Factory.* Armonk: M. E. Sharpe, 1990.

Lockwood, William, ed. *The State and Economic Enterprise in Japan.* Princeton: Princeton University Press, 1965.

Magagna, Victor. *Communities of Grain: Rural Rebellion in Comparative Perspective.* Ithaca: Cornell University Press, 1991.

Magaziner, Ira C., and Thomas M. Hout. *Japanese Industrial Policy.* Berkeley: Institute of International Studies, 1980.

Marsh, Robert, and Hiroshi Mannari. *Modernization and the Japanese Factory.* Princeton: Princeton University Press, 1976.

Marshall, Byron. *Capitalism and Nationalism in Pre-War Japan: The Ideology of the Business Elite, 1868–1941.* Stanford: Stanford University Press, 1967.

Masao, Maruyama. "Nationalism in Japan: Its Theoretical Background and Prospects." Trans. David Titus, 1951. In Masao, *Thought and Behavior in Modern Japanese Politics.* New York: Oxford University Press, 1963.

Matsuda, Yauhiko. "Conflict Resolution in Japanese Industrial Relations." In Shirai.

Minami, Hiroshi. *Nihonjinron no keifu* [A genealogy of Nihonjinron]. Tokyo: Kodansha, 1980.

Minear, Richard. *Japanese Tradition and Western Law: Emperor, State and Law in the Thought of Hozumi Yatsuka.* Cambridge: Harvard University Press, 1970.

Morishima, Michio. *Why Has Japan 'Succeeded'? Western Technology and the Japanese Ethos.* Cambridge: Cambridge University Press, 1982.

Morris, Ivan. *Nationalism and the Right Wing in Japan: A Study of Postwar Trends.* London: Oxford University Press, 1960.

Mouer, Ross, and Yoshio Sugimoto. *Images of Japanese Society.* New York: Kegan Paul International, 1986.

Murakami, Yasusuke. "The Japanese Model of Political Economy." In Yamamura and Yasuba.

————. "The Reality of the New Middle Class." *Japan Interpretor* 12, 1 (winter 1978).

Murakami, Yasusuke, Kumon Shumpei, and Sato Seizaburo. *Bunmei to shite no ie shakai* [The Ie society as a pattern of civilization]. Tokyo: Chuokoronsha, 1979.

Najita, Tetsuo, and Victor Koschmann, eds. *Conflict in Modern Japanese History: The Neglected Tradition.* Princeton: Princeton University Press, 1982.

Nakamura, Keisuke. "Worker Participation: Collective Bargaining and Joint Consultation." In Sako and Sato.

Nakamura, Keisuke, and Michio Nitta. "Developments in Industrial Relations and Human Resource Practices in Japan." In *Employment Relations in a Changing World Economy,* ed. Richard Locke, Thomas Kochan, and Michael Piore. Cambridge: MIT Press, 1995.

Nakane, Chie. *Japanese Society.* Berkeley: University of California Press, 1973.

————. *Kinship and Economic Organization in Rural Japan.* New York: Humanities Press, 1967.

Nakayama, Ichiro. "Sensansei kojo undo hihan o hanhihan suru" [A reply to the criticism of the productivity movement]. *Chuo koron* (January 1956): 46–52.

Nihon seisansei honbu [The Japan Productivity Center]. *Gijutsu kakushin to nihon keizai* [Technological innovation and Japan's economy]. Tokyo: Nihon seisansei honbu, 1960.

————. *Seisansei undo 30 nen shi* [A thirty-year history of the productivity movement]. Tokyo: Nihon Seisansei Honbu, 1985.

Nihon tokei kenkyusho. *Nihon keizai tokeishu* [Economic statistics of Japan]. Tokyo: Nihon hyoron sha, 1958.

Nitta, Michio. *Nihon no rodosha sanka* [Worker participation in Japan]. Tokyo: Tokyo University Press, 1988.

Noguchi, Yukio. *1940-nen taisei: saraba 'senji keizai'* [The 1940 system: Farewell to a wartime economy]. Tokyo: Toyo keizai shimpo, 1995.

Odaka, Konosuke. "Nihonteki ro-shi kankei" [Japanese-style labor-capital relations]. In *Gendai Nihon keizai shisutemu no genryu* [The sources of contemporary Japan's economic system], ed. Okazaki Tetsuji and Okuno Masahiro. Tokyo: Nihon keizai shimbun, 1993.

Ohashi, Isao. "On the Determinants of Bonuses and Basic Wages in Large Japanese Firms." In Imai and Komiya.

Okimoto, Daniel. *Between MITI and the Market: Japanese Industrial Policy for High Technology.* Stanford: Stanford University Press, 1989.

Okochi, Kazuo, et al., eds. *Nihon no rodosha* [Japan's working class]. Tokyo: Toyo keizai shimpo, 1955.

Okuda, Kenji. "Nihon no noritsu undoshi" [A history of the Japanese movement]. *IE Review,* nos. 9–12 (1968–71).

Oliver, Nick, and Barry Wilkinson. *The Japanization of British Industry.* Oxford: Blackwell, 1988.

Ooms, Herman. *Tokugawa Village Practice: Class, Status, Power, Law.* Berkeley: University of California Press, 1996.

Otsuka, Hisao. *Kindaika no ningenteki kiso* [The moral basis for modernization]. Tokyo: Jwanami Shoten, 1968.

Ouchi, William. *Theory Z: How American Business Can Meet the Japanese Challenge.* Reading: Addison-Wesley, 1981.

Patrick, Hugh. "The Future of the Japanese Economy: Output and Labor Productivity." *Journal of Japanese Studies* 3, 2 (summer 1977): 219–49.

Pempel, J., and Kiichi Tsunekawa. "Corporatism without Labor? The Japanese Anomaly." In *Trends toward Corporatist Intermediation,* ed. Philippe Schmitter and Gerhard Lehmbruch. Beverly Hills: Sage, 1979.

Price, John. *Japan Works: Power and Paradox in Postwar Industrial Relations.* Ithaca: ILR Press/Cornell University Press, 1997.

Reischauer, Edwin O. *Japan: The Story of a Nation.* 3d ed. New York: Knopf, 1981.

———. *The Japanese.* Cambridge: Belknap, 1978.

Rohlen, Thomas. "The Company Work Group." In *Modern Japanese Organization and Decision-Making,* ed. Ezra Vogel. Berkeley: University of California Press, 1975.

———. *For Harmony and Strength: Japanese White-Collar Organization in Anthropological Perspective.* Berkeley: University of California Press, 1976.

———. *Japan's High Schools.* Berkeley: University of California Press, 1983.

———. "Order in Japanese Society: Attachment, Authority, and Routine." *Journal of Japanese Studies* 15, 1 (winter 1989): 5–40.

———. "'Permanent Employment' Faces Recession, Slow Growth, and an Aging Work Force." *Journal of Japanese Studies* 5, 2 (summer 1979): 235–72.

Rozman, Gilbert. "The East Asian Region in Comparative Perspective." In Rozman, ed.

———, ed. *The East Asian Region: The Confucian Heritage and Its Modern Adaptation.* Princeton: Princeton University Press, 1991.

Sako, Mari. "Shunto: The Role of Employer and Union Coordination at the Industry and Inter-Sectoral Levels." In Sako and Sato.

———. "Training, Productivity, and Quality Control in Japanese Multinational Corporations." In Aoki and Dore.

Sako, Mari, and Hiroki Sato, eds. *Japanese Labour and Management in Transition: Diversity, Flexibility, and Participation.* New York: Routledge, 1997.

Samuels, Richard. *Business of the Japanese State: Energy Markets in Competitive Perspective.* Ithaca: Cornell University Press, 1987.

Satoshi, Sasaki. "The Rationalization of Production Management Systems in Japan during World War II." In *World War II and the Transformation of Business Systems,* ed. Sakudo Jun and Shiba Takao. Tokyo: University of Tokyo Press, 1994.

Saxonhouse, Gary. "Industrial Restructuring in Japan." *Journal of Japanese Studies* 5, 2 (summer 1979): 273–320.

Scheiner, Irwin. "Benevolent Lords and Honorable Peasants: Rebellion and Peasant Consciousness in Tokugawa Japan." In *Japanese Thought in the Tokugawa Period,* ed. Tetsuo Najita and Irwin Scheiner. Chicago: University of Chicago Press, 1978.

———. "The Japanese Village: Imagined, Real, Contested." In Vlastos, ed.

Schooler, Carmi. "History, Social Structure, and Individualism: A Cross-Cultural Perspective on Japan." In *Values and Attitudes across Nations and Time,* ed. Masmichi Sasahi. Leiden, the Netherlands: Brill, 1998.

Shibusawa Eiichi denki shiryo [Biographical materials on Shibusawa Eiichi]. 50 vols. Tokyo: Shibusawa Seien Kinen Zaidan Ryumonsha, 1955–1963.

Shirai, Taishiro, ed. *Contemporary Industrial Relations in Japan.* Madison: University of Wisconsin Press, 1983.

Shively, Donald, ed. *Tradition and Modernization in Japanese Culture.* Princeton: Princeton University Press, 1971.

Skinner, Kenneth. "Conflict and Command in a Public Corporation in Japan." *Journal of Japanese Studies* 6, 3 (summer 1980): 301–29.

Smith, Robert. *Japanese Society: Tradition, Self and the Social Order.* Cambridge: Cambridge University Press, 1983.

Smith, Thomas. *The Agrarian Origins of Modern Japan.* Stanford: Stanford University Press, 1959.

———. "The Japanese Village in the Seventeenth Century." *Journal of Economic History* 12 (winter 1952): 1–20.

———. *Nakahara: Family Farming and Population in a Japanese Village, 1717–1830.* Stanford: Stanford University Press, 1977.

———. *Native Sources of Japanese Industrialization.* Berkeley: University of California Press, 1988.

———. "The Right to Benevolence: Dignity and the Japanese Workers, 1890–1920." In Smith, *Native Sources.*

Sugimoto, Yoshio. "Comparative Analysis of Industrial Conflicts in Australia and Japan." In *Sharpening the Focus,* ed. R. D. Walton. Brisbane: Griffith University Press, 1986.

Sumiya, Mikio. *Nihon no rodo mondai* [Labor issues in Japan]. Tokyo: University of Tokyo Press, 1965.

Suzuki, Bunji. *Nihon no rodomodai* [Labor problems in Japan]. Tokyo: Kaigai shokumin gakko suppanbu, 1919.

Suzuki, Jidosha Kogyo Rodo Kumiai. *Niju go nen shi* [Twenty-five years]. Hamana Gun: Suzuki Kumiai, 1976.

Taira, Koji. "Characteristics of Japanese Labor Markets." *Economic Development and Cultural Change* 10 (1962): 150–68.

———. *Economic Development and the Labor Market in Japan.* New York: Columbia University Press, 1970.

Takeda, Kiyoko. *The Dual Image of the Emperor.* New York: New York University Press, 1988.

Takezawa, Shin-ichi, and Arthur Whitehill. *The Other Worker: A Comparative Study of Industrial Relations in the United States and Japan.* Honolulu: East-West Center Press, 1968.

———. *Work Ways: Japan and America.* Tokyo: Japan Institute of Labor, 1981.

Tiedemann, Arthur. "Big Business and Politics in Prewar Japan." In *Dilemmas of Growth in Prewar Japan,* ed. James Morley. Princeton: Princeton University Press, 1974.

Tokuzo, Fukuda. *Shakai undo to rogin seido* [Social movements and wage systems]. Tokyo: Kaizosha, 1922.

Totsuka, Hideo. "The Transformation of Japanese Industrial Relations: A Case Study of the Automobile Industry." In *Lean Work: Empowerment and Exploitation in the Global Auto Industry,* ed. Steve Babson. Detroit: Wayne State University Press, 1995.

Totsuka, Hideo, and Hyodo Tsutomu. *Roshi kankei no tenkan to sentaku* [Transition and choice in industrial relations]. Tokyo: Nihon Hyoron Sha, 1991.

Totsuka, Hideo, and Tokunaga Shigeyoshi. *Gendai Nihon no rodo mondai: atarashii paradaimu o motomete* [Labor issues in contemporary Japan: In search of a new paradigm]. Tokyo: Minerva Shobo, 1993.

Tsujimura, Akira. *Sengo Nihon no taishu shinri: shinbun, seron, besutosera* [Mass consciousness in postwar Japan: Newspapers, public opinion, and best-sellers]. Tokyo: Tokyo Daigaku Suppankai, 1981.

Tsutsui, William. *Manufacturing Ideology: Scientific Management in Twentieth Century Japan.* Princeton: Princeton University Press, 1998.

Upham, Frank. *Law and Social Change in Postwar Japan.* Cambridge: Harvard University Press, 1987.

Van Helvoort, Ernest. *The Japanese Working Man: What Choice? What Reward?* Vancouver: University of British Columbia Press, 1979.

Van Wolferen, Karel. *The Enigma of Japanese Power.* New York: Vintage, 1989.

Veblen, Thorstein. "The Opportunity of Japan." In *Essays in Our Changing Order,* ed. L. Andzrooni. New York: Viking, 1943.

Vlastos, Stephen. *Peasant Protest and Uprisings in Tokugawa Japan.* Berkeley: University of California Press, 1986.

———. "Tradition: Past/Present Culture and Modern Japanese History." In Vlastos, ed.

———, ed. *Mirror of Modernity: Invented Traditions of Modern Japan.* Berkeley: University of California Press, 1998.

Vogel, Ezra. *The Four Little Dragons.* Cambridge: Harvard University Press, 1991.

———. *Japan as Number One.* New York: Harper and Row, 1979.

Walthall, Anne. *Social Protest and Popular Culture in Eighteenth-Century Japan.* Tucson: University of Arizona Press, 1986.

Warner, Malcolm. "Japanese Culture, Western Management: Taylorism and Human Resources in Japan." *Organization Studies* 15, 4 (1994): 509–33.

Watanabe, Osamu. *Gendai Nihon no shihai kozo bunseki: kijuku to shuhen* [An analysis of the ruling structure in contemporary Japan: Its central and marginal elements]. Tokyo: Kadensha, 1988.

Watanabe, Shoichi. *The Peasant Soul of Japan.* London: Macmillan, 1989.

Westney, D. Eleanor. *Imitation and Innovation: The Transfer of Western Organizational Patterns to Meiji Japan.* Cambridge: Harvard University Press, 1987.

White, James. *Ikki: Social Conflict and Political Protest in Early Modern Japan.* Ithaca: Cornell University Press, 1995.

Whitehill, Arthur. *Japanese Management: Tradition and Transition.* New York: Routledge, 1991.

Womack, J. P., D. T. Jones, and D. Roos. *The Machine That Changed the World.* New York: Macmillan, 1990.

Wood, Stephen, ed. *The Transformation of Work.* London: Unwin and Hyman, 1989.

Yamada, Ichiro. *Nihonteki keiei no hihan* [Critique of Japanese-style management]. Tokyo: Daisan Shuppan, 1976.

Yamaguchi, Susumu. "Collectivism among the Japanese: A Perspective from the Self." In *Individualism and Collectivism: Theory, Method, and Applications,* ed. Uichol Kim, Harry C. Triandis, Cigdem Kgitcibasi, Sang-Chin Choi, and Gene Yoon. Thousand Oaks: Sage, 1994.

Yamamoto, Shichihei. *The Spirit of Japanese Capitalism and Selected Essays.* Trans. Lynne Riggs and Takechi Manabut. New York: Madison Books, 1992.

Yamamura, Kozo, and Yasukichi Yasuba, eds. *The Political Economy of Japan,* vol. 1, *The Domestic Transformation.* Stanford: Stanford University Press, 1987.

Yasuba, Yasukichi. "The Evolution of Dualistic Wage Structure." In *Japanese Industrialization and Its Social Consequences,* ed. Hugh Patrick. Berkeley: University of California Press, 1976.

Yokoyama, Gennosuke. *Nihon no kaso shakai* [The lower strata in Japanese society]. Tokyo: Kyobunkan, 1899.

Yoshino, Kosaku. *Cultural Nationalism in Contemporary Japan.* New York: Routledge, 1992.

On Russia/USSR and Communism

Aleksandrov, V. A. *Sel'skaia Obshchina v Rossii (XVII - nachala XIX v.)* [The rural commune in Russia (from the seventeenth century to the beginning of the nineteenth century)]. Moscow: Nauka, 1976.

Andrle, Vladimir. *Workers in Stalin's Russia: Industrialization and Social Change in a Planned Economy.* New York: St. Martin's Press, 1988.

Anno, Tadashi. "The Liberal World Order and Its Critics: Nationalism and the Rise of Anti-Systemic Movements in Russia and Japan, 1860–1950." Ph.D. Diss. University of California at Berkeley, 1999.

Arnason, Johann. *The Future That Failed: Origins and Destinies of the Soviet Model.* London: Routledge, 1993.

Atkinson, Dorothy. *The End of the Russian Land Commune, 1905–1930.* Stanford: Stanford University Press, 1983.

Aves, Jonathan. *Workers Against Lenin: Labour Protest and the Bolshevik Dictatorship.* International Library of Historical Studies, vol. 6. London: I. B. Tauris, 1996.

Avrich, Paul. "The Bolshevik Revolution and Workers' Control in Russian Industry." *Slavic Review* 27 (1963): 47–63.

———. *Kronstadt 1921.* Princeton: Princeton University Press, 1970.

———. *Russian Rebels, 1600–1800.* New York: Schocken Books, 1972.

Azrael, Jeremy. *Managerial Power and Soviet Politics.* Cambridge: Harvard University Press, 1966.

Baglione, Lisa, and Carol Clark. "A Tale of Two Metallurgical Enterprises: Marketization and the Social Contract in Russian Industry." *Communist and Post-Communist Studies* 30, 2 (June 1997): 153–80.

Bailes, Kendall. "Alexei Gastev and the Soviet Controversy over Taylorism, 1918–24." *Soviet Studies* 29, 3 (July 1977): 373–94.

———. "The American Connection: Ideology and the Transfer of American Technology to the Soviet Union, 1917–1941," *Comparative Studies in Society and History* 23 (July 1981): 421–48.

———. *Technology and Society under Lenin and Stalin: Origins of the Soviet Technical Intelligentsia, 1917–1941.* Princeton: Princeton University Press, 1978.

Beissinger, Mark. *Scientific Management, Socialist Discipline, and Soviet Power.* Cambridge: Harvard University Press, 1988.

Berdyaev, Nikolai. *The Russian Revolution.* Ann Arbor: University of Michigan Press, 1961.

Berliner, Joseph. *Factory and Manager in the USSR.* Cambridge: Harvard University Press, 1957.

———. *Soviet Industry.* Ithaca: Cornell University Press, 1988.

Bialer, Seweryn. *Stalin's Successors: Leadership, Stability, and Change in the Soviet Union.* New York: Cambridge University Press, 1980.

Bialer, Seweryn, and Michael Mandelbaum, eds. *Gorbachev's Russia and American Foreign Policy.* Boulder: Westview, 1988.

Billington, James. *Mikhailovsky and Russian Populism.* Oxford: Clarendon, 1958.

Bizyukov, Petr. "The Mechanisms of Paternalistic Management of the Enterprise." In Clarke, ed.

Black, Cyril, et al. *The Modernization of Japan and Russia.* New York: Free Press, 1975.

Bonnell, Victoria. *Roots of Rebellion: Workers' Politics and Organizations in St. Petersburg and Moscow, 1900–1914.* Berkeley: University of California Press, 1983.

———, ed. *The Russian Worker: Life and Labor under the Tsarist Regime.* Berkeley: University of California Press, 1983.

Borisova, Y. S., L. S. Gaponenko, A. I. Kotelents, and V. S. Lelchuk. *Outline History of the Soviet Working Class.* Moscow: Progress, 1973.

Bova, Russell. "On *Perestroyka:* The Role of Workplace Participation." *Problems of Communism* 36 (July–August 1987): 76–86.

Breslauer, George. "Boris Yel'tsin as Patriarch." *Post-Soviet Affairs* 15, 2 (April–June, 1999).

———. "In Defense of Sovietology." *Post-Soviet Affairs* 8, 3 (1992): 197–238.

———. *Khrushchev and Brezhnev as Leaders: Building Authority in Soviet Politics.* London: Allen and Unwin, 1982.

Brinton, Maurice. "Factory Committees and the Dictatorship of the Proletariat." *Critique* 4 (spring 1975): 78–86.

Brodersen, Arvid. *The Soviet Worker: Labor and Government in Soviet Society.* New York: Random House, 1966.

Brovkin, Vladimir. "The Emperor's New Clothes: Continuity of Soviet Political Culture in Contemporary Russia." *Problems of Post-Communism* (May/June, 1995): 21–28.

Brym, Robert. "Reevaluating Mass Support for Political and Economic Change in Russia." *Europe-Asia Studies* 48 (1996): 751–66.

Brzezinski, Zbigniew. "Soviet Politics: From the Future to the Past?" In *The Dynamics of Soviet Politics,* ed. Paul Cocks et al. Cambridge: Harvard University Press, 1976.

Brzezinski, Zbigniew, and Carl Friedrich. *Totalitarian Dictatorship and Autocracy.* Cambridge: Harvard University Press, 1956.

Buckley, Mary. *Perestroika and Soviet Women.* New York: Cambridge University Press, 1992.

Bukharin, N. I., and E. Preobrazhensky. *The ABC's of Communism.* Harmondsworth, UK: Penguin, 1969.

Bunce, Valerie. "The Political Economy of the Brezhnev Era: The Rise and Fall of Corporatism." *British Journal of Political Science* 13 (April 1983): 129–58.

Burawoy, Michael. "The End of Sovietology and the Renaissance of Modernization Theory." *Contemporary Sociology* 21 (November 1992).

———. "The State and Economic Involution: Russia through a China Lens." *World Development* 24 (June 1996): 1105–17.

Burawoy, Michael, and Pavel Kratov. "The Soviet Transition from Socialism to Capitalism: Worker Control and Economic Bargaining in the Wood Industry." *American Sociological Review* 57 (February 1992).

Carr, E. H. *The Bolshevik Revolution, 1917–23.* Harmondsworth, UK: Penguin, 1966.

———. *The Interregnum, 1923–24.* London. Macmillan, 1954.

———. *Socialism in One Country, 1924–26.* London. Macmillan, 1964.

Chayanov, A. V. *The Theory of Peasant Economy.* Ed. Daniel Thorniley et al. Madison: University of Wisconsin Press, 1996.

Clarke, Simon. "Formal and Informal Relations in Soviet Industrial Production." In Clarke, ed.

———. "Privatisation and the Development of Capitalism in Russia." In Simon Clarke, Peter Fairbrother, et al., eds., *What about the Workers? Workers and the Transition to Capitalism in Russia.* London: Verso, 1993.

———, ed. *Management and Industry in Russia: Formal and Informal Relations in the Period of Transition.* Brookfield, VT: Edward Elgar, 1995.

Cohen, Stephen. "Bolshevism and Stalinism." In Tucker, ed.

———. "Russian Studies without Russia." *Post-Soviet Affairs* 15, 1 (January–March 1999).

Connor, Walter D. *The Accidental Proletariat: Workers, Politics, and Crisis in Gorbachev's Russia.* Princeton: Princeton University Press, 1991.

Conquest, Robert. *Harvest of Sorrow: Soviet Collectivization and the Terror–Famine.* New York: Oxford University Press, 1986.

———. *Industrial Workers in the USSR.* New York: Praeger, 1967.

Cook, Linda. *The Soviet Social Contract and Why It Failed.* Cambridge: Harvard University Press, 1993.

Crowley, Stephen. *Hot Coal, Cold Steel: Russian and Ukrainian Workers from the End of the Soviet Union to the Post-Communist Transformations.* Ann Arbor: University of Michigan Press, 1997.

Daniels, Robert V. *The Conscience of the Revolution: Communist Opposition in Soviet Russia.* Cambridge: Harvard University Press, 1960.

Davies, R. W. 1993. "The Management of Soviet Industry, 1928–1941." In Rosenberg and Siegelbaum.

Davies, Sarah. *Popular Opinion in Stalin's Russia: Terror, Propaganda and Dissent, 1934–1941.* New York: Cambridge University Press, 1997.

Dewar, Margaret. *Labour Policy in the USSR, 1917–1928.* London: Royal Institute of Internal Affairs and Oxford University Press, 1956.

Dunham, Vera. *In Stalin's Time: Middle-Class Values in Soviet Fiction.* Cambridge: Cambridge University Press, 1976.

Dyker, David. "Planning and the Worker." In Godson and Schapiro.

Economakis, Evel. "Patterns of Migration and Settlement in Prerevolutionary Petersburg: Peasants from Iaroslavl and Tver Provinces." *Russian Review* 56, 1 (1997): 8–24.

Erlich, Alexander. *The Soviet Industrialization Debates, 1924–1928.* Cambridge: Harvard University Press, 1960.

Evans, Alfred B. "Economic Reward and Inequality in the 1986 Program of the Communist Party of the Soviet Union." In *Political Implications of Economic Reform in Communist Systems,* ed. Donna Bahry and Joel Moses. New York: New York University Press, 1990.

Fainsod, Merle. *Smolensk under Soviet Rule.* Cambridge: Harvard University Press, 1958.

Field, Daniel. *Rebels in the Name of the Tsar.* Boston: Routledge Chapman, 1976.

Filtzer, Donald. *Soviet Workers and De-Stalinization: The Consolidation of the Modern System of Soviet Production Relations, 1953–64.* Cambridge: Cambridge University Press, 1992.

———. *Soviet Workers and Stalinist Industrialization: The Formation of Modern Soviet Production Relations, 1928–41.* Armonk, NY: M. E. Sharpe, 1986.

Fischer, George. *Russian Liberalism: From Gentry to Intelligentsia.* Cambridge: Harvard University Press, 1958.

Fitzpatrick, Sheila. "Ascribing Class: The Construction of Social Identity in Soviet Russia." *Journal of Modern History* 65 (December 1993).

———. "Cultural Revolution as Class War." In Fitzpatrick, ed., *Cultural Revolution in Russia.* Bloomington: Indiana University Press, 1977.

———. *Education and Social Mobility in the Soviet Union, 1921–1934.* Cambridge: Harvard University Press, 1979.

———. "The Great Departure: Rural-Urban Migration in the Soviet Union, 1929–33." In Rosenberg and Siegelbaum, eds., 15–40.

———. "New Perspectives on Stalinism." *Russian Review* 45, 4 (October 1986): 357–73.

———. *The Russian Revolution.* Rev. ed. Oxford: Oxford University Press, 1994.

———. "Sources of Change in Soviet History: State, Society and the Entrepreneurial Tradition." In Bialer and Mandelbaum, eds.

Frierson, Cathy. *"Razdel:* The Peasant Family Divided." *Russian Review* 46 (1987): 35–52.

Fukuyama, Francis. "The Modernizing Imperative: The USSR as an Ordinary Country." *National Interest* 32 (1993): 10–19.

Gaddy, Clifford. *The Price of the Past: Russia's Struggle with the Legacy of a Militarized Economy.* Washington, DC: Brookings, 1996.

Gaman, O. V. "Problemy postindustrial'noi modernizatsii Rossii: Rol' traditsii" [Problems of postindustrial modernization in Russia: The role of tradition]. In Evgenii S. Troitskii, ed., *Russkaia Natsiia: Istoricheskoe proshloe i problemy vozrozhdeniia* [Russian nation: Historical past and problems of revival]. Moscow, 1994.

Gastev, Alexei. *Kak Nado Rabotat': Prakticheskoye Vvedenie v Nauku Organizatsii Truda* [How one should work: Practical introduction to the scientific organization of work]. Moscow: Ekonomika, 1966.

Gerchikov, V. I. "The Human Factor and Industrial Democracy." *Soviet Sociology* 1 (1989): 32–42. Translation of "Chelovecheskii faktor i proizvodstvennaia demokratiia," Izvestiia Sibirskogo otdeleniia akademii nauk SSSR [Report of the Siberian Section of the USSR Academy of Sciences].

Gerschenkron, Alexander. "Problems and Patterns of Russian Economic Development." In *The Transformation of Russian Society,* ed. Cyril Black. Cambridge: Harvard University Press, 1960.

Getty, J. Arch. *Origins of the Great Purges: The Soviet Communist Party Reconsidered, 1933–1938.* Cambridge: Cambridge University Press, 1985.

Godson, Joseph, and Leonard Schapiro, eds. *The Soviet Worker: From Lenin to Andropov.* 2d ed. London: Macmillan, 1984.

Gorbachev, Mikhail S. *Perestroika: New Thinking for Our Country and the World.* New York: Harper and Row, 1987.

Gorer, G., and J. Rickman. *The People of Great Russia.* London: Cresset Press, 1949.

Grancelli, Bruno. *Soviet Management and Labor Relations.* London: Allen and Unwin, 1988.

Granick, David. *Job Rights in the USSR: Their Consequences.* Cambridge: Cambridge University Press, 1987.

———. *Red Executive: A Study of the Organizational Man in Russian Industry.* London: Macmillan, 1960.

Gregory, Paul. "Productivity, Slack and Time Theft in the Soviet Economy." In *Politics, Work, and Daily Life in the USSR: A Survey of Former Soviet Citizens,* ed. James Millar. Cambridge: Cambridge University Press, 1987.

Gromyko, M. M. *Traditsionnye Normy Povedeniia I Formy Obshcheniia Russkikh Krest'ian XIX v* [Traditional norms of behavior and forms of relations among the nineteenth-century Russian peasantry]. Moscow: Nauka, 1986.

Grossman, Gregory. "The Second Economy of the USSR." *Problems of Communism* 26 (September–October 1977): 25–40.

Gvishani, Dzerman. *Sotsiologiia Biznesa: Kriticheskii Ocherk Amerkanskoi Teorii Menedzhmenta* [The sociology of business: A critical analysis of the American theory of management]. Moscow: Sotsial'no-Ekonomicheskaia Literatura, 1962.

Haimson, Leopold. "The Problem of Social Stability in Urban Russia, 1905–1917." *Slavic Review* 23 (1964): 619–42; 24 (1965): 1–22.

———. *The Russian Marxists and the Origins of Bolshevism.* Cambridge: Harvard University Press, 1955.

Hanson, Stephen. "Social Theory and the Post-Soviet Crisis: Sovietology and the Problem of Regime Identity." *Communist and Post-Communist Studies* 28, 1 (1995).

———. *Time and Revolution: Marxism and the Design of Soviet Institutions.* Chapel Hill: University of North Carolina Press, 1997.

Hauslohner, Peter. "Gorbachev's Social Contract." *Soviet Economy* 3, 1 (1987).

Hewett, Ed. *Reforming the Soviet Economy: Equality versus Efficiency.* Washington, DC: Brookings, 1987.

Hoffman, David L. *Peasant Metropolis: Social Identities in Moscow, 1929–1941.* Ithaca: Cornell University Press, 1994.

Hough, Jerry. *Democratization and Revolution in the USSR, 1985–1991.* Washington, DC: Brookings, 1997.

———. *The Soviet Prefects: The Local Party Organs in Industrial Decision Making.* Cambridge: Harvard University Press, 1969.

———. "The Soviet System: Petrification or Pluralism?" *Problems of Communism* (March–April 1972).

———. *The Soviet Union and Social Science Theory.* Cambridge: Harvard University Press, 1977.

Iadov, V. A. "Motivatsiaa Truda: Problemy i puti razvitiia issledovanii" [Work motivation: Problems and methods for the development of research]. In *Sovietskaia Sotsiologiia* [Soviet sociology], vol. 2, ed. T. Riabushkin and G. Osipov. Moscow: Nauka, 1982.

Iadov, V. A., V. P. Rozhin, and A. G. Zdravomyslov. *Man and His Work.* Trans. Stephen P. Dunn. White Plains, NY: International Arts and Sciences Press, 1970. First published in Russian as *Chelovek i evo rabota.* Moscow: Mysl, 1967.

"Industrial Workers in the 1880s: From the Reports of Factory Inspectors." In *Readings in Russian Civilization, Volume 2: Imperial Russia, 1700–1917,* ed. Thomas Riha. Chicago: University of Chicago Press, 1969. Adapted from S. Dmitriev, ed. *Khrestomatiia po Istorii SSSR* [Selections from Russian history], vol. 3. Moscow, 1952.

Inkeles, Alex, and Raymond Bauer. *The Soviet Citizen.* Cambridge: Harvard University Press, 1959.

Janos, Andrew. "Social Science, Communism and the Dynamics of Political Change." *World Politics* 44, 1 (1991): 81–112.

Johnson, Robert E. *Peasant and Proletarian: The Working Class of Moscow at the End of the Nineteenth Century.* Camden, NJ: Rutgers University Press, 1979.

Jowitt, Ken. *New World Disorder: The Leninist Extinction.* Berkeley: University of California Press, 1992.

Kahan, Arcadius, and Blair Ruble, eds. *Industrial Labor in the USSR.* New York: Pergamon, 1979.

Kaplan, Frederick I. *Bolshevik Ideology and the Ethics of Soviet Labor (1917–1920).* New York: Philosophical Library, 1968.

Kautsky, John. *The Political Consequences of Modernization.* New York: Wiley, 1972.

Keenan, Edward. "Muscovite Political Folkways." *Russian Review* 45, 2 (April 1986): 115–81.

Kenez, Peter. "Stalinism as Humdrum Politics." *Russian Review* 45, 4 (October 1986): 395–400.

Kennard, Howard. *The Russian Peasant.* London: T. Werner Laurie, 1907.

Kerblay, Basile. *Modern Soviet Society.* New York: Pantheon Books, 1977.

Kharkhordin, Oleg. *The Collective and the Individual in Russia: A Study of Practices.* Berkeley: University of California Press, 1999.

Khrushchev, N. S. *Razvitie Ekonomiki SSSR I Partinogo Rukovodstva Naordnym Kohziaistvom* [The development of the economy of the USSR and party administration of the national economy]. Moscow: Izd-vo Pravdy, 1962.

Klimova, S. G., and L. V. Dunayevskii. "New Entrepreneurs and Old Culture." *Sociological Studies* [Russ.] 5 (1993): 64–69.

Koenker, Diane. *Moscow Workers and the 1917 Revolution.* Princeton: Princeton University Press, 1981.

———. "Urbanization and Deurbanization in the Russian Revolution and Civil War." *Journal of Modern History* 57 (1985): 424–50.

Kolakowski, Leszek. "The Marxist Roots of Stalinism." In Tucker, ed.

Kolchin, Peter. *Unfree Labor: American Slavery and Russian Serfdom.* Cambridge: Harvard University Press and Belknap Press, 1987.

Kolesnikov, Iu. V. "On the Social Functions of a Leader of a Socialist Production Collective." In *Nauchnoe Upravlenie Obshchestvom* [Scientific management of society] 6, ed. V. G. Afanas'ev. Moscow, 1972.

Kornai, Janos. *The Socialist System: The Political Economy of Communism.* Princeton: Princeton University Press, 1992.

Kotkin, Stephen. "Coercion and Identity: Workers' Lives in Stalin's Showcase City." In Siegelbaum and Suny.

———. *Magnetic Mountain: Stalinism as a Civilization.* Berkeley: University of California Press, 1995.

———. "'One Hand Clapping': Russian Workers and 1917." *Labor History* 32, 4 (fall 1991): 604–20.

———. *Steeltown, USSR: Soviet Society in the Gorbachev Era.* Berkeley: University of California Press, 1991.

Kotliar, A., and V. Trubin. *Problemy Regulirovaniia Pereraspredeleniia Rabochei sily* [Problems of regulating the redistribution of the work force]. Moscow: Ekonomika, 1978.

Kullberg, Judith, and William Zimmerman. "Liberal Elites, Socialist Masses, and Problems of Russian Democracy." *World Politics* 51 (April 1999): 323–58.

Kuromiya, Hiroaki. "Odinonachalie and the Soviet Industrial Manager, 1928–38." *Soviet Studies* 2 (1984): 185–204.

————. *Stalin's Industrial Revolution: Politics and Workers, 1928–1932.* Cambridge: Cambridge University Press, 1988.

————. "Workers' Artels and Soviet Production Relations." In *Russia in the Era of NEP,* ed. Sheila Fitzpatrick, Alexander Rabinowitch, and Richard Stites. Bloomington: Indiana University Press, 1991.

Lane, David. *Soviet Labour and the Ethic of Communism: Full Employment and the Labour Process in the USSR.* Boulder: Westview, 1987.

Lane, David, and Felicity O'Dell. 1978. *The Soviet Industrial Worker: Social Class, Education and Control.* Oxford: Martin Robertson.

Lapidus, Gail. "Social Trends." In *After Brezhnev: Sources of Soviet Conduct in the 1980s,* ed. Robert Byrnes. Bloomington: Indiana University Press, 1983.

————. "State and Society: Toward the Emergence of Civil Society in Russia." In *Politics, Society and Nationality inside Gorbachev's Russia,* ed. Seweryn Bialer. Boulder: Westview, 1989.

————. *Women in Soviet Society: Equality, Development, and Social Change.* Berkeley: University of California Press, 1978.

————, ed. *Women, Work and Family in the Soviet Union.* Armonk, NY: M. E. Sharpe, 1982.

Ledeneva, Alena. *Russia's Economy of Favors: Blat, Networking, and Informal Exchange.* New York: Cambridge University Press, 1998.

Leites, Nathan. *A Study of Bolshevism.* Glencoe: Free Press, 1953.

Lenin, V. I. *The Lenin Anthology.* Ed. Robert C. Tucker. New York: Norton, 1975.

————. *Pol'noe Sobranie Sochinenii* [Complete collection of works]. 5th ed. Vols. 1–55. Moscow: Gosudarstvennoe Izdatelstvo Politicheskoi Literatur, 1967–1970.

Lewin, Moshe. *The Gorbachev Phenomenon.* Berkeley: University of California Press, 1988.

————. *Making of the Soviet System.* New York: Pantheon, 1985.

————. *Russian Peasants and Soviet Power.* New York: Norton, 1975.

Lowenthal, Richard. "Development vs. Utopia in Communist Policy." In *Change in Communist Systems,* ed. Chalmers Johnson. Stanford: Stanford University Press, 1970.

Ludlam, Janine. "Reform and the Redefinition of the Social Contract under Gorbachev." *World Politics* 43, 2 (January 1991): 284–312.

Luke, Timothy. *Ideology and Soviet Industrialization.* Westport, CT: Greenwood Press, 1985.

Luxemborg, Rosa. *The Russian Revolution, and Leninism or Marxism.* Ann Arbor: University of Michigan Press, 1927.

Magagna, Victor. *Communities of Grain: Rural Rebellion in Comparative Perspective.* Ithaca: Cornell University Press, 1991.

Magun, Vladimir. "Labour Culture." In *Russian Culture at the Crossroads,* ed. Dmitri Shalin. Boulder: Westview, 1996.

Male, Donald. *Russian Peasant Organization before Collectivization: A Study of Commune and Gathering, 1925–1930.* Cambridge: Cambridge University Press, 1971.

Malia, Martin. "Communist Legacy Foreclosed Choices." *New York Times.* March 27, 1999.

———. *Russia under Western Eyes: From the Bronze Horseman to the Lenin Mausoleum.* Cambridge: Belknap Press of the Harvard University Press, 1999.

Mandel, James I. "Paternalistic Authority in the Russian Countryside, 1856–1906." Ph.D. diss., Columbia University, 1978.

Marx, Karl. *Capital.* Vol. 1. New York: International Publishers, 1967.

McAuley, Alistair. "Welfare and Social Security." In Godson and Schapiro.

McAuley, Mary. *Labour Disputes in Soviet Russia, 1957–65.* Oxford: Clarendon, 1969.

McDaniel, Timothy. *The Agony of the Russian Idea.* Princeton: Princeton University Press, 1996.

———. *Autocracy, Capitalism and Revolution in Russia.* Berkeley: University of California Press, 1988.

Mendel, Arthur. "Peasant and Worker on the Eve of the First World War." *Slavic Review* (March 1965).

Meyer, Alfred. *Leninism.* Cambridge: Harvard University Press, 1957.

———. "Observations on the Travails of Sovietology." *Post-Soviet Affairs* (April–June 1994).

Miliukov, Paul. *Russia Today and Tomorrow.* New York: Macmillan, 1922.

Millar, James. "The Little Deal: Brezhnev's Contribution to Acquisitive Socialism." In *Soviet Society and Culture: Essays in Honor of Vera S. Dunham,* ed. Terry Thompson and Richard Sheldon. Boulder: Westview, 1988.

Millar, James, and Sharon Wolchik. 1994. "The Social Legacies and the Aftermath of Communism." In *The Social Legacy of Communism,* ed. Millar and Wolchik. Washington, DC, and New York: Woodrow Wilson Center and Cambridge University Press.

Miller, Arthur, William Reisinger, and Vicki Hesli, eds. *Public Opinion and Regime Change: The New Politics of Post-Soviet Societies.* Boulder: Westview, 1993.

Miller, William, Stephen White, and Paul Heywood. *Values and Political Change in Postcommunist Europe.* New York: St. Martin's Press, 1998.

Mironov, Boris. "The Russian Peasant Commune after the Reforms of the 1860s." *Slavic Review* 44, 3 (fall 1985): 438–67.

Moore, Barrington. *Soviet Politics: The Dilemma of Power.* New York: Harper Torchbooks, 1965. First published, Cambridge: Harvard University Press, 1950.

Moore, Barrington, and James Millar. "A Debate on Collectivization: Was Stalin Really Necessary?" *Problems of Communism* (July–August 1976).

Nove, Alec. *An Economic History of the USSR.* Rev. ed. Harmondsworth, UK: Penguin, 1984.

———. *The Economics of Feasible Socialism.* London: Allen and Unwin, 1983.

———. "Is There a Ruling Class in the Soviet Union?" *Soviet Studies* 27, 4 (October 1975).

Olson, Mancur. "The Logic of Collective Action in Soviet-type Societies." *Journal of Soviet Nationalities* 1, 2 (1990): 8–27.

Petro, Nikolai. *The Rebirth of Russian Democracy: An Interpretation of Political Culture.* Cambridge: Harvard University Press, 1995.

Petrovich, Michael. *The Emergence of Russian Panslavism, 1856–1870.* New York: Columbia University Press, 1956.

Phillips, Laura. "Message in a Bottle: Working-Class Culture and the Struggle for Revolutionary Legitimacy, 1900–1929." *Russian Review* 56, 1 (January 1997): 25–43.

Pipes, Richard. "Did the Russian Revolution Have to Happen?" *American Scholar* (spring 1994): 215–38.

———. *Russia under the Old Regime.* New York. Scribner's and Sons, 1974.

———. *The Russian Revolution.* New York: Vintage, 1990.

Plekhanov, Georgi. *Fundamental Problems of Marxism.* Moscow: Progress, 1974 [1929].

Popov, Gavril. *Problemy Teorii Upravleniia* [Problems of administrative theory]. 2d ed. Moscow: Ekonomika, 1974.

Pravda, Alex. "Spontaneous Workers' Activities in the Soviet Union." In Kahan and Ruble.

Preobrazhensky, Evgenii. *From the New Economic Policy to Socialism.* Trans. B. Pearce. London: New Park, 1973.

Pushkarev, Sergei. *Self-Government and Freedom in Russia.* Boulder: Westview, 1988.

Radaev, V. A. "On Some Features of Normative Behaviour of Russia's Entrepreneurs." *World Economy and International Relations* [Russ.] 4 (1994): 31–38.

Radkey, Oliver. *The Agrarian Foes of Bolshevism.* New York: Columbia University Press, 1958.

———. *Russia Goes to the Polls: The Election to the All-Russian Constituent Assembly 1917.* Ithaca: Cornell University Press, 1989.

Ransel, David, ed. *The Family in Imperial Russia.* Urbana: University of Illinois Press, 1978.

Riasanovsky, Nicholas. *A History of Russia.* 4th ed. New York: Oxford University Press, 1984.

———. *Russia and the West in the Teaching of the Slavophiles: A Study of Romantic Ideology.* Cambridge: Harvard University Press, 1952.

Rittersporn, Gabor. *Stalinist Simplifications and Soviet Complications: Social Tensions and Political Conflicts in the USSR, 1933–1953.* Chur, Switzerland: Harwood, 1991.

Roeder, Philip. 1993. *Red Sunset: The Failure of Soviet Politics.* Princeton: Princeton University Press.

Rogger, Hans. "*Amerikanizm* and the Economic Development of Russia." *Comparative Studies in Society and History* 23 (July 1981): 382–420.

Rosenberg, William G., and Lewis H. Siegelbaum, eds. *Social Dimensions of Soviet Industrialization.* Bloomington: Indiana University Press, 1993.

Rossman, Jeffrey. "The Teikovo Cotton Workers' Strike of April 1932, Class, Gender, and Identity Politics in Stalin's Russia." *Russian Review* 56, 1 (January 1997): 44–69.

Ruble, Blair. *The Applicability of Corporatist Models to the Study of Soviet Politics.* Pittsburgh: Carl Beck Papers in Russian and East European Studies, University of Pittsburgh, 1983.

―――. "Factory Unions and Workers' Rights." In Kahan and Ruble.

―――. "Full Employment Legislation in the USSR." *Comparative Labor Law* 2 (fall 1977).

Rutland, Peter. "Labor Unrest and Movements in 1989 and 1990." *Soviet Economy* 6, 4 (1990): 345–84.

―――. "The Shchekino Method and the Struggle to Raise Labor Productivity in Soviet Industry." *Soviet Studies* 3 (1984): 345–65.

Schapiro, Leonard. *The Communist Party of the Soviet Union.* New York: Vintage, 1964.

Schneiderman, Jeremiah. *Sergei Zubatov and Revolutionary Marxism: The Struggle for the Working Class in Tsarist Russia.* Ithaca: Cornell University Press, 1976.

Schroeder, Gertrude. "The Slowdown in Soviet Industry, 1976–1982." *Soviet Economy* 1, 1 (1985): 42–71.

Schwartz, Solomon. *Labor in the Soviet Union.* New York: Praeger, 1952.

Selznick, Philip. *The Organizational Weapon: A Study of Bolshevik Strategy and Tactics.* Glencoe: Free Press, 1960.

Sergeyev, Victor, and Nikolai Biryukov. *Russia's Road to Democracy: Parliament, Communism, and Traditional Culture.* Brookfield, VT: Elgar, 1993.

Service, Robert. *The Bolshevik Party in Revolution: A Study in Organisational Change, 1917–1923.* New York: Macmillan, 1979.

Shanin, Theodor. *The Awkward Class: Political Sociology of Peasantry in a Developing Society, Russia, 1910–1925.* Oxford: Clarendon, 1972.

―――. *Russia as a 'Developing Society.'* London: Macmillan, 1985.

Shatunovsky, I. M. *Trudiascisia tuneiadets* [Laboring parasites]. Moscow: Sovetskaia Rossia, 1970.

Shearer, David. "Factories within Factories: Changes in the Structure of Work and Management in Soviet Machine-Building Factories, 1926–1934." In Rosenberg and Siegelbaum.

―――. *Industry, State, and Society in Stalin's Russia, 1926–1934.* Ithaca: Cornell University Press, 1996.

Shershneva, Elena, and Jurgen Feldhoff. *The Culture of Labour in the Transformation Process: Empirical Studies in Russian Industrial Enterprises.* New York: Peter Lang, 1998.

Shlapentokh, Vladimir. *Public and Private Life of the Soviet People: Changing Values in Post-Stalin Russia.* New York: Oxford University Press, 1989.

―――. "Standard of Living and Popular Discontent." In *The Destruction of the Soviet Economic System,* ed. M. Ellman and V. Kontorovich. Armonk, NY: M. E. Sharpe, 1998.

Siegelbaum, Lewis. "Masters on the Shop Floor: Foremen and Soviet Industrialization." In Rosenberg and Siegelbaum, eds., 166–92.

―――. "Production Collectives and Communes and the 'Imperatives' of Soviet Industrialization, 1929–1931." *Slavic Review* 44 (spring 1986): 65–84.

————. "Soviet Norm-Determination in Theory and Practice, 1917–1941." *Soviet Studies* 36, 1 (January 1984): 45–68.

————. *Stakhanovism and the Politics of Productivity in the USSR, 1935–41.* Cambridge: Cambridge University Press, 1988.

————. "State and Society in the 1920s." In *Reform in Russia and the U.S.S.R.: Past and Prospects.* Ed. Robert O. Crummey. Urbana: University of Illinois Press, 1989.

Siegelbaum, Lewis, and Ronald Suny. "Class Backwards? In Search of the Soviet Working Class." In Siegelbaum and Suny, eds.

Siegelbaum, Lewis, and Ronald Suny, eds. *Making Workers Soviet: Power, Class and Identity.* Ithaca: Cornell University Press, 1994.

Sil, Rudra. "Privatization, Labor Politics, and the Firm in Post-Soviet Russia: Non-Market Norms, Market Institutions and the Soviet Legacy." In *The Politics of Labor in a Global Age: Continuity and Change in Late-Industrializing and Post-Socialist Economies,* ed. Christopher Candland and Rudra Sil. New York: Oxford University Press, 2001.

Sirianni, Carmen. *Workers' Control and Socialist Democracy: The Soviet Experience.* London: New Left Books, 1982.

Smith, Steve. *Red Petrograd: Revolution in the Factories, 1917–1918.* New York: Cambridge University Press, 1983.

————. "Russian Workers and the Politics of Social Identity." *Russian Review* 56, 1 (January 1997): 1–7.

Sochor, Zenovia A. "Soviet Taylorism Revisited." *Soviet Studies* 33, 2 (1981): 246–64.

Solomon, Peter. "Local Power and Soviet Criminal Justice, 1922–1941." *Soviet Studies* 37, 3 (July 1985).

Solzhenitsyn, Aleksandr. "Misconceptions about Russia Are a Threat to America." *Foreign Affairs* 58, 4 (1980): 797–834.

————. *The Russian Question: At the End of the Twentieth Century.* Trans. Yermolai Solzhenitsyn. New York: Farrar, Straus and Giroux, 1995.

Sonin, Mikhail. *Sotsialisticheskaia Disciplina Truda* [Socialist labor discipline]. Moscow: Profizdat, 1986.

Stalin, J. V. *Problems of Leninism.* Trans. 8th ed. Moscow: Foreign Languages Publishing House, 1953.

Starr, S. Frederick. "The Changing Nature of Change." In Bialer and Mandelbaum.

————. "Soviet Union: A Civil Society." *Foreign Policy* 70 (1988): 26–41.

Straus, Kenneth. *Factory and Community in Stalin's Russia.* Pittsburgh: University of Pittsburgh Press, 1997.

Timofeev, P. "What the Factory Worker Lives By." In Bonnell.

Traub, Rainer. "Lenin and Taylor: The Fate of 'Scientific Management' in the Early Soviet Union." *Telos* 37 (1978): 82–92. First published in *Kursbuch* 43 (1976). Trans. Judy Joseph.

Trotsky, Leon. *The Revolution Betrayed: What Is the Soviet Union and Where Is It Going?* Rev. ed. New York: Pathfinder, 1972 [1937].

————. *Sochineniia* [Works], vol. 15. Moscow: Gosizdat, 1927.

Tucker, Robert C. *Political Culture and Leadership in Soviet Russia.* New York: Norton, 1987.

————. "Stalinism as Revolution from Above." In Tucker, ed.

————, ed. *Stalinism.* New York: Norton, 1977.

Von Laue, Theodore. "Factory Inspection under the Witte System." *American Slavic and East European Review* (October 1960).

————. "The Russian Peasant in the Factory." *Journal of Economic History* 23 (1961): 61–80.

————. "Stalin in Focus." *Slavic Review* (fall 1983): 373–89.

————. *Why Lenin? Why Stalin? Why Gorbachev?* Rev. ed. New York: Harper-Collins, 1993.

White, Stephen. *Political Culture and Soviet Politics.* New York: St. Martin's Press, 1979.

Worobec, Christine. *Peasant Russia: Family and Community in the Post-Emancipation Period.* Princeton: Princeton University Press, 1991.

Wynn, Charters. *Workers, Strikes and Pogroms: The Donbass-Dnepr Bend in Late Imperial Russia, 1870–1905.* Princeton: Princeton University Press, 1992.

Yanowitch, Murray. *Social and Economic Inequality in the Soviet Union.* White Plains, NY: M. E. Sharpe, 1977.

Zaslavsky, Victor. "From Redistribution to Marketization: Social and Attitudinal Change in Post-Soviet Russia." In *The New Russia: Troubled Transformation,* ed. Gail Lapidus. Boulder: Westview, 1995.

————. *The Neo-Stalinist State: Class, Ethnicity and Consensus in Soviet Society.* Rev. ed. Armonk, NY: M. E. Sharpe, 1994.

Zelnik, Reginald. *Labor and Society in Tsarist Russia: The Factory Workers of St. Petersburg, 1855–1870.* Stanford: Stanford University Press, 1971.

Index

Note: Authors of cited works are not included unless mentioned in the text or noted as the subject of a substantive comment in the notes. Page references to figures are italicized.